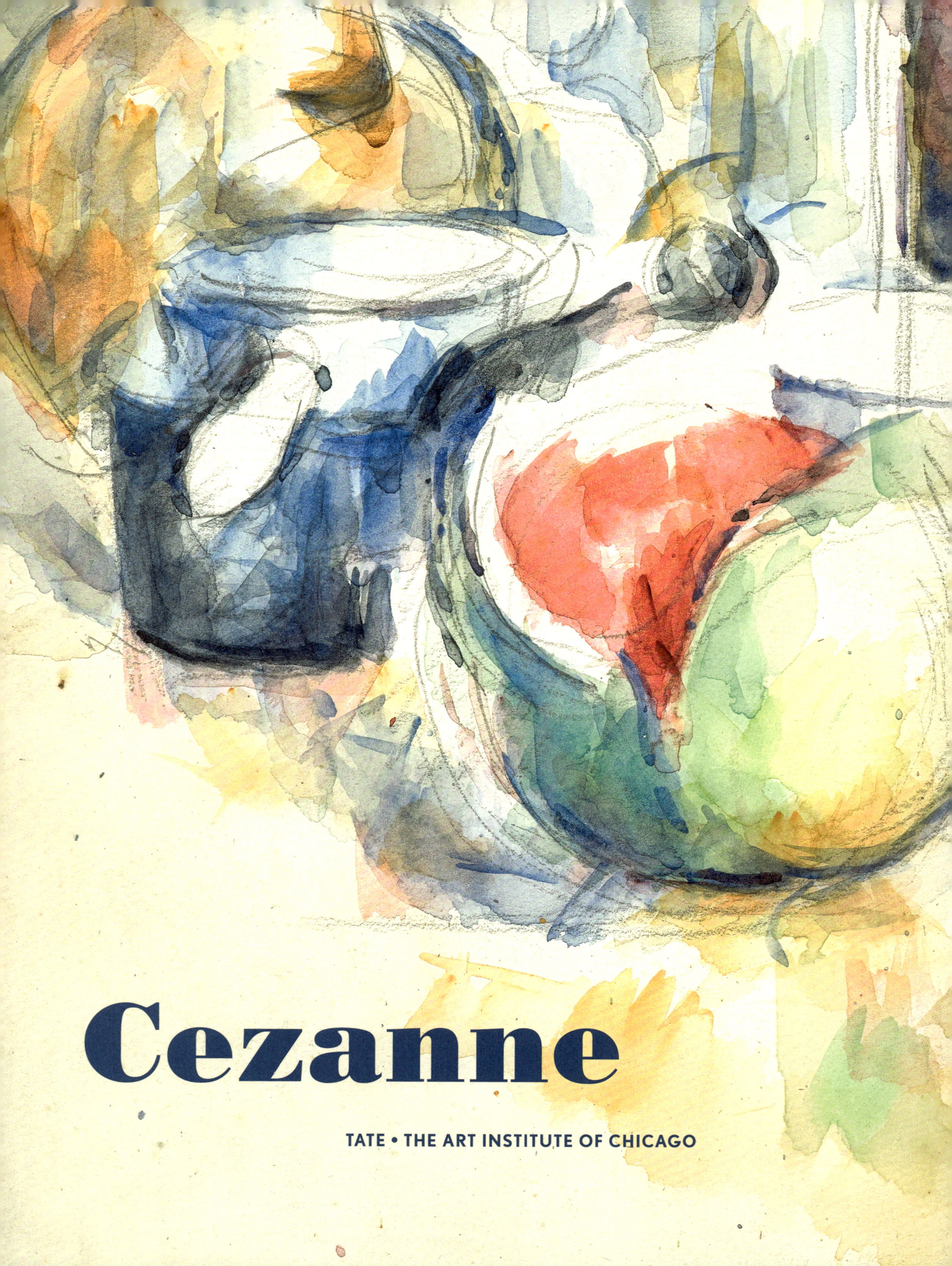
Cezanne
TATE • THE ART INSTITUTE OF CHICAGO

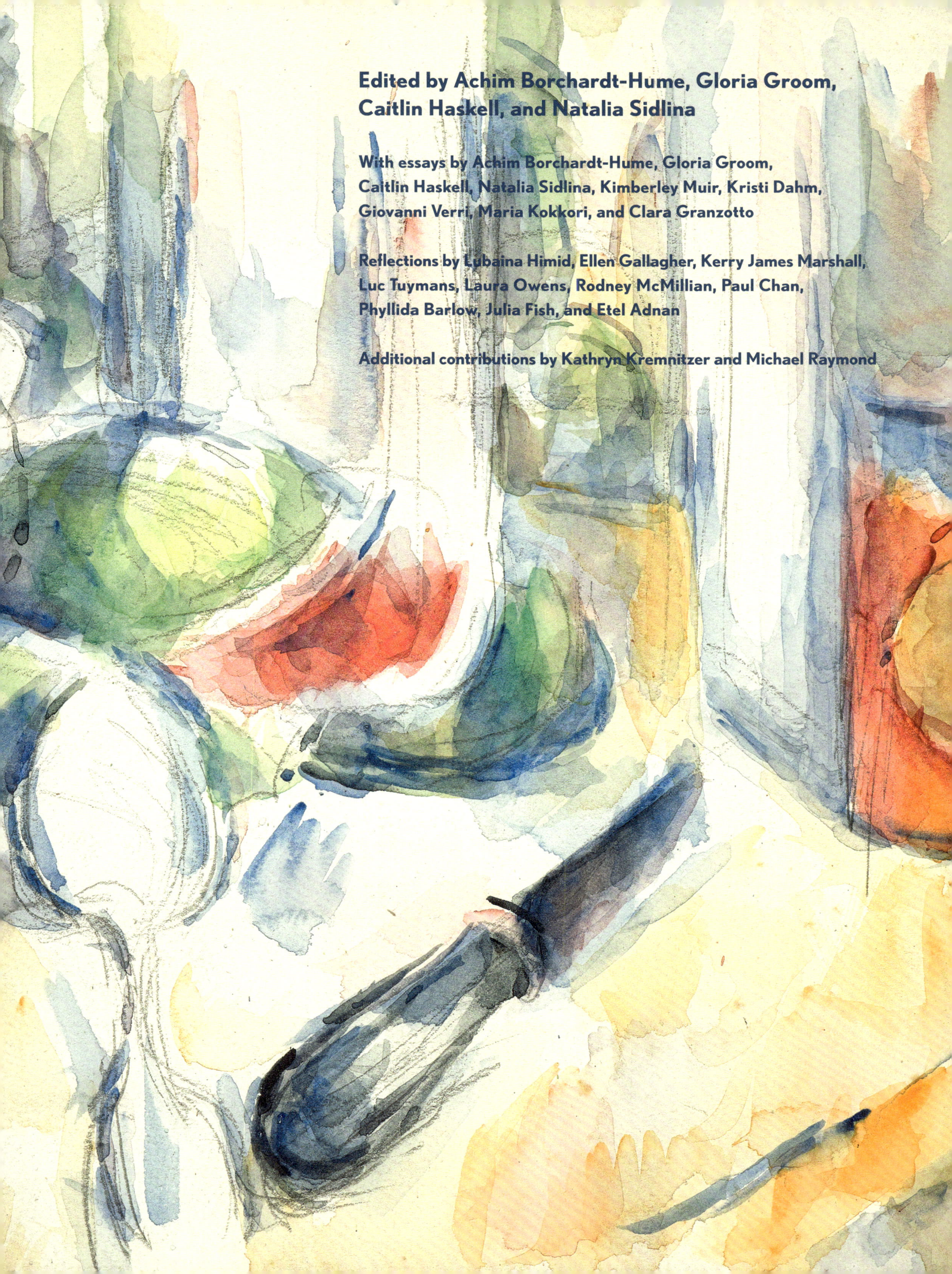

Edited by Achim Borchardt-Hume, Gloria Groom, Caitlin Haskell, and Natalia Sidlina

With essays by Achim Borchardt-Hume, Gloria Groom, Caitlin Haskell, Natalia Sidlina, Kimberley Muir, Kristi Dahm, Giovanni Verri, Maria Kokkori, and Clara Granzotto

Reflections by Lubaina Himid, Ellen Gallagher, Kerry James Marshall, Luc Tuymans, Laura Owens, Rodney McMillian, Paul Chan, Phyllida Barlow, Julia Fish, and Etel Adnan

Additional contributions by Kathryn Kremnitzer and Michael Raymond

This book is dedicated to our co-curator,
Achim Borchardt-Hume
(1965–2021)

FIRST EDITION
Printed in Italy
ISBN: 978-1-84976-828-3 (hardback)
ISBN: 978-1-84976-805-4 (paperback)
A catalogue record for this book is available from
the British Library

PUBLISHED BY
The Art Institute of Chicago
111 South Michigan Avenue
Chicago, IL 60603–6404
artic.edu

Contents

Publishing, the Art Institute of Chicago
Greg Nosan, Associate Vice President, Publishing and
    Interpretation
Lisa Meyerowitz, Editorial Director
Joseph Mohan, Director of Production

Edited by A. Robin Hoffman
Production by Lauren Makholm and Ben Bertin
Photography research by Pauline Lopez, Kylie
    Escudero, Lauren Makholm, and Joseph Mohan
Proofreading by Sarah Robinson
Indexing by Lee Gable

Imaging, the Art Institute of Chicago
Bonnie Rosenberg, Director of Imaging
Aidan Fitzpatrick, Associate Director of Photography
Elyse Allen, Assistant Director of Production
Photography by Robert Lifson, Craig Stillwell, Jonathan
    Mathias, and Bob Hashimoto
Postproduction by Owen Conway

Design and typesetting by Roy Brooks, Fold Four, Inc.
Maps by Scott Reinhard
Separations by Professional Graphics, Rockford, IL
Printing and binding by Conti Tipocolor, Florence, Italy

SUPPORTER'S FOREWORD

EY is honoured to present *The EY Exhibition: Cezanne.* A giant of art history, Paul Cezanne made fundamental contributions to twentieth-century art. His still lifes, landscapes and paintings of bathers gave generations of artists licence to break the mould.

This landmark show marks the tenth exhibition in the EY Tate Arts Partnership. Since 2013, EY has supported major exhibitions at Tate that have shed new light on some of the world's most pioneering modern artists; innovators and trendsetters who markedly inspired their contemporaries and shaped the future of creativity and culture. *Cezanne* is undoubtedly a significant contribution to this series.

At EY, we recognise that the arts are a driving force of creativity and innovation, two essential pillars of the United Kingdom's economic growth and societal wellbeing. Underpinned by the EY ambition of building a better working world, our long-standing commitment to the UK cultural sector remains steadfast.

Michel Driessen
Sponsoring Partner of EY Arts and Senior Partner, UK&I Strategy and Transactions

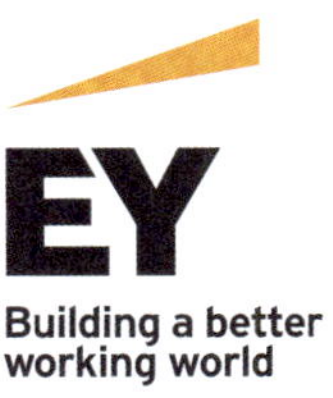

DIRECTORS' FOREWORD

Paul Cezanne (French, 1839–1906) is renowned for the paintings and drawings that resulted from his complex, lifelong endeavor to create pictures one sensation at a time. His approach set him apart from other artists within the Impressionist circle and indeed modern art as a whole. Due to the novelty of his practice, fellow artists were the first to recognize the value of his iconic and, at the time, seemingly unsophisticated approach to color, technique, and materials, which called attention to the painter's mark as well as the ways that a painting was at once a kind of pictorial illusion and an inescapably, even wonderfully, physical object.

Cezanne's work was first shown at the Art Institute of Chicago in 1913, and he has been a cornerstone of the collection since 1926, when *The Basket of Apples* (c. 1893; cat. 56) was acquired. Having achieved the distinction of being one of the first places in the United States where audiences could see his oeuvre firsthand, the museum has consistently displayed the artist's canvases in the permanent collection galleries, and many of the several dozen iconic paintings and drawings now in its holdings are part of this exhibition. Cezanne's work was seen in London during the artist's lifetime when, in January 1905, the Grafton Galleries showcased the French Impressionists. In 1924 the renowned collector Samuel Courtauld established a fund to bring their work and that of the Post-Impressionists into the national collection, and that year Tate, then known as The National Gallery of British Art and Modern Foreign Art, became the first public museum in the United Kingdom to acquire Cezanne's paintings. The artist assumed a key position within their holdings, and when Tate Modern opened its doors in 2000, his *Still Life with Water Jug* (c. 1892–93; cat. 59) was one of the earliest modernist works that visitors encountered.

Cezanne is the first comprehensive exhibition of the painter's work in North America in more than twenty-five years, and the first monographic display focused on him at the Art Institute of Chicago since 1952. Tate Gallery last dedicated a show to the artist in 1996 as part of a retrospective tour commemorating the centenary of his first monographic exhibition. This once-in-a-generation occasion is the result of careful planning and collaboration, as the two museums have brought together approximately ninety oil paintings, forty drawings and watercolors, and two complete sketchbooks from public and private collections in North and South America, Europe, and Asia in order to consider Cezanne's pivotal role in the trajectory of modern art. In this presentation, we pay special attention to the acclaim he has enjoyed as an "artist's artist" from the nineteenth century to the present day. Among other features, the volume is enormously enriched by reflections from ten accomplished artists who bring their own perspectives to bear on particular works in the exhibition: Phyllida Barlow, Paul Chan, Julia Fish, Ellen Gallagher, Lubaina Himid, Kerry James Marshall, Rodney McMillian, Laura Owens, Luc Tuymans, and the late Etel Adnan.

Our goal is to revisit and revitalize Cezanne's legacy by drawing upon the multiple strengths of the organizing institutions. The project weaves together the complementary perspectives of art historians and conservators as well as practicing artists as we reframe his work for our own time. Over the seven decades since the last major Cezanne exhibition at the Art Institute (organized with the Metropolitan Museum of Art, New York), conservation scientists at the museum have developed the tools and knowledge to undertake state-of-the-art technical analysis on all of the oil paintings and the most significant watercolors in the collection, deepening our understanding of how Cezanne conceived and developed his famously deliberate and nonlinear process of constructing an image with color. The insights of this research complement the scholarship of the co-curators, who began crafting the checklist for this exhibition in 2018 and have given us new insights as well as helpful ways to unsettle some of the earlier myths and clichés that have obscured this painter's work. We thank Kimberley Muir, Kristi Dahm, Giovanni Verri, Maria Kokkori, and Clara Granzotto for presenting their findings in the company of essays by Gloria Groom and Caitlin Haskell, from the Art Institute, and Natalia Sidlina and the late Achim Borchardt-Hume, from Tate Modern. We congratulate the curatorial team for their resourcefulness, resilience, and consummate collaboration in assembling the exhibition and co-editing the catalogue. Building upon the scholarship of numerous exhibitions in the last twenty-five years that have divided the artist's oeuvre into discrete chapters, themes, or media, *Cezanne* explores the artist's full career in a comparative manner that underscores commonalities within and among these bodies of work as well as their evolution across themes and through time. The presentation encourages thoughtful comparisons across media and genre in the ways that only a retrospective can allow.

The effort to assemble this group of artworks called upon the commitment of more than seventy lenders, whom we thank for enabling the opportunity to experience Cezanne's work in such a rich context. This extraordinary occasion has also been made possible by our sponsors. At the Art Institute, lead support for *Cezanne* is generously provided by John D. and Alexandra C. Nichols. Major funding is contributed by an anonymous donor, The Marlene and Spencer Hays Foundation, the Butler Family Foundation, Richard F. and Christine F. Karger, the Shure Charitable Trust, Constance and David Coolidge, Amy and Paul Carbone, and Patricia and Ronald Taylor. Special support is provided by Dora and John Aalbregtse, Julie and Roger Baskes, Ethel and Bill Gofen, Natasha Henner and Bala Ragothaman, Barbara and Marc Posner, Margot Levin Schiff and the Harold Schiff Foundation, and Linda and Michael Welsh. Additional funding is provided by the Jack and Peggy Crowe Fund, the Suzanne and Wesley M. Dixon Exhibition Fund, and The Regenstein Foundation Fund. Members of the Luminary Trust provide annual leadership support for the museum's operations, including exhibition development, conservation and collection care, and educational programming. The Luminary Trust includes an anonymous donor, Neil Bluhm and the Bluhm Family Charitable Foundation, Karen Gray-Krehbiel and John Krehbiel, Jr., Kenneth C. Griffin, the Harris Family Foundation in memory of Bette and Neison Harris, Josef and Margot Lakonishok, Robert M. and Diane v.S. Levy, Ann and Samuel M. Mencoff, Sylvia Neil and Dan Fischel, Anne and Chris Reyes, Cari and Michael J. Sacks, and the Earl and Brenda Shapiro Foundation. The corporate sponsor is Bank of America. This exhibition is supported by an indemnity from the Federal Council on the Arts and the Humanities. On behalf of Tate Modern, we extend our deep gratitude to EY for their long-term commitment and generosity as major supporters of the exhibition. This is the tenth exhibition supported by EY through The EY Tate Arts Partnership, which ensures that such visionary and ambitious exhibitions are possible. We would also thank the Huo Family Foundation (UK) Limited, the Cezanne Exhibition Supporters Circle including Eykyn Maclean, and also Tate Patrons and Tate Members for generously supporting this exhibition at Tate Modern.

This project is an undertaking of the highest significance for both the Art Institute and Tate Modern. It represents the collaborative and cross-disciplinary work that we believe makes our organizations uniquely capable of creating exhibitions for future generations. In keeping with the character of this endeavor—at once historic in scale and also invested in the smallest visible detail—*Cezanne* is the first exhibition to present the artist's name the way he signed it, without an accent on the first "e." We have omitted this mark to accord with the artist's preference and that of his family today. The adjustment serves as a humble but potent reminder of the ways in which twenty-first-century viewers can still see this foundational figure of modern art anew. By looking more closely at Cezanne, we can reciprocate and appreciate his focused attention as well as his continuing power to shape the future of painting.

Frances Morris
Director, Tate Modern

James Rondeau
President and Eloise W. Martin Director, The Art Institute of Chicago

ACKNOWLEDGMENTS

The partnership between the Art Institute of Chicago and Tate Modern began five years ago with conversations between James Rondeau, President and Eloise W. Martin Director, The Art Institute of Chicago, and Frances Morris, Director, Tate Modern, to whom we are immensely grateful for their extraordinary enthusiasm, confidence, and support. Since then we have worked together on every aspect of *Cezanne*, which takes a multifaceted look at the artist's work in all media.

We are particularly grateful to the other authors of this catalogue for sharing their unique perspectives on Cezanne, especially those who provided curatorial assistance as well: at Tate Modern, Michael Raymond, and at the Art Institute (and beyond), Kathryn Kremnitzer. In Conservation and Science at the Art Institute, we are indebted to Kimberley Muir, Giovanni Verri, Kristi Dahm, Maria Kokkori, and Clara Granzotto. Early in the planning stages, informal consultation with painters in the Chicago area convinced us that the oft-cited image of Paul Cezanne as an "artist's artist" was more than a platitude: it was an essential consideration that led us to connect with contemporary artists who contributed their insights on particular works in the exhibition. Our sincere thanks to those who have shared with us their thoughts on this profoundly influential maker: the late Etel Adnan, Phyllida Barlow, Paul Chan, Julia Fish, Ellen Gallagher, Lubaina Himid, Kerry James Marshall, Rodney McMillian, Laura Owens, and Luc Tuymans.

This ambitious project would not have been possible without the digital catalogue raisonné by Walter Feilchenfeldt, David Nash, and Jayne Warman, first launched in 2017 (for the paintings) and expanded with the works on paper in 2019. The authors of this extraordinary tool—the result of decades of research and careful looking—have continued to update information including dates, exhibitions, provenance, and especially locations, which was essential in shaping our exhibition. Particularly during a time of limited travel and reduced access to libraries, their comprehensive resource allowed us to continue our work with colleagues around the globe. Likewise, their documentation of the ownership of paintings, drawings, and watercolors throughout the artist's life and beyond enabled us to pursue our ambition to understand Cezanne as the consummate artist's artist historically as well as in the present.

From across the world, more than seventy museums, foundations, and private collectors graciously agreed to make their works accessible for our research and available for display under uncommonly challenging circumstances. These important works on canvas and paper were especially chosen to reinforce our vision of seeing the artist afresh. For generously sharing them both with us and with the public, we wish to thank the following institutions: Amgueddfa Cymru–National Museum of Wales, Cardiff; Art Gallery of Ontario, Toronto; The Baltimore Museum of Art; Cincinnati Art Museum; The Cleveland Museum of Art; The Courtauld Gallery, London; Dallas Museum of Art; Detroit Institute of Arts; Fine Arts Museums of San Francisco; The Fitzwilliam Museum and King's College, University of Cambridge, UK; Finnish National Gallery, Ateneum Art Museum, Helsinki; Fondation Beyeler, Riehen, Switzerland; Göteborgs Konstmuseum, Sweden; Hammer Museum, Los Angeles; The J. Paul Getty Museum, Los Angeles; Kimbell Art Museum, Fort Worth, TX; Kunsthalle Mannheim, Germany; Kunsthaus Zürich; Kunstmuseum Basel; Kunstmuseum Solothurn, Switzerland; Los Angeles County Museum of Art; The Metropolitan Museum of Art, New York; Minneapolis Institute of Arts; The Morgan Library & Museum, New York; Musée d'Art et d'Histoire, Geneva; Musée de l'Orangerie, Paris; Musée d'Orsay, Paris; Musée Granet, Aix-en-Provence, France; Musée Picasso, Paris; Museo Nacional Thyssen-Bornemisza, Madrid; Museu de Arte de São Paulo Assis Chateaubriand; Museum of Fine Arts, Boston; Museum of Fine Arts, Budapest; Museum of Modern Art, New York; Nasjonalmuseet, Oslo; The National Gallery, London; The National Gallery of Art, Washington, DC; National Gallery of Australia, Canberra; National Gallery of Scotland, Edinburgh; The National Museum of Modern Art, Tokyo; Nationalmuseum, Stockholm; Ny Carlsberg Glyptotek, Copenhagen; Henry and Rose Pearlman Foundation, New York; Petit Palais, Musée de Beaux-Arts des la Ville de Paris; Philadelphia Museum of Art; The Phillips Collection, Washington, DC; Saint Louis Art Museum; Princeton University Art Museum, Princeton, NJ; Solomon R. Guggenheim Museum, New York; Städel Museum, Frankfurt; Toledo Museum of Art; Von der Heydt Museum, Wuppertal, Germany; Walker Art Gallery, National Museums, Liverpool, UK; The Whitworth, The University of Manchester, UK; and Yoshino Gypsum Co., Tokyo. We also thank the numerous private collectors who supported the exhibition with key loans, including Jasper Johns, Sharon, CT, and Ruthie and Jay Pack, Dallas, as well as those who prefer to remain anonymous.

We acknowledge here those individuals who made contributions to our display that went beyond professional courtesy, including Maureen Pskowski, Jasper Johns Studio; Peter Bell, Cincinnati Art Museum; Nicole Myers, Dallas Museum of Art; Susan Stein, The Metropolitan Museum of Art; Jodi Hauptman and Samantha Friedman, Museum of Modern Art; Isolde Pludermacher, Musée d'Orsay; Daniel Edelman, Henry and Rose Pearlman Foundation; Gabriele Finaldi, The National Gallery, London; and Mélanie Bernuz, Bruno Ely, and Pamela Grimaud, Musée Granet. In particular, we are grateful to those who made works or technical findings available for our research: Barbara Buckley and Anya Shutov, Barnes Foundation, Philadelphia; Elisabeth

Reissner, Courtauld Institute of Art; Markus Gross and Friederike Steckling, Fondation Beyeler; Devi Ormond, J. Paul Getty Museum; Charlotte Hale, The Metropolitan Museum of Art, New York; Laura Neufeld, Museum of Modern Art, New York; John Griswold and Emily Talbot, Norton Simon Museum, Pasadena, CA; and Kateryna Kostiuchenko, Von der Heydt Museum, Wuppertal, Germany.

This exhibition and catalogue benefited enormously from the collaborative efforts of collectors and scholars around the world, as these colleagues helped us to locate artworks and served as liaisons. For their generous assistance, we recognize Alexander Adler; Erin Bakunas; Frances Beatty; Maxwell Carter, Christie's; Cyanne Chuthow, Christie's New York; Lara Daly, Alan Hobart, and Rachel Owens, Pyms Gallery; Jean Edmonson and Michael Findlay, Acquavella Gallery; Alexander Eiling and Fabienne Ruppen, Städel Museum, Frankfurt; Keith Gill, Christie's London; Claudine Godts, Wildenstein; Tracy Hamilton; Diana Howard; Alma Luxembourg and Daniella Luxembourg, Luxembourg & Dayan; Suzanne McCullagh; Mary Morton, National Gallery of Art, Washington, DC; Kristofer Nõges; Susan Pattock; Kelly Pecore; Lionel and Sandrine Pissarro; Maureen Pskowski; Nora Riccio; Laurie Stein; Abigail Teller; Nancy Whyte; and Yasuko Yamada, Nukaga Gallery.

We are acutely aware of the debt we owe to scholars who have contributed their expertise and time to our project— the list of works cited cannot fully acknowledge the influences that have shaped our thinking. In addition to the catalogue raisonné authors mentioned previously and their precursors, Lionel Venturi and John Rewald, we are grateful to more recent scholars: Nina Athanassoglou-Kallmyer, T. J. Clark, Denis Coutagne, André Dombrowski, Dorothy Price, Fabienne Ruppen, Richard Shiff, Paul Smith, and Mary

Tompkins Lewis. All of them joined us in conversation and shared important texts and bibliographic references. We also thank artists Julia Fish, Richard Deutsch, and Richard Rezac, who shared with us the insights they had gleaned from decades of looking at paintings by Cezanne in the Art Institute's collection. We extend our sincere appreciation to Barbara Buckley and Nancy Ireson at the Barnes Foundation for inviting us to a study day devoted to Cezanne's *Large Bathers* and hosting us along with other art historians, curators, conservators, and scientists. We are equally grateful to the US State Department for endorsing our application for federal indemnity and immunity from seizure, without which no major international loan exhibition in this country would be feasible, and we are indebted to the colleagues who generously lent their expertise during the preparation of these applications: David Nash and Jill Newhouse, and at the National Endowment for the Arts, indemnity administrators Daniel Hoffman and Patricia Loiko. At Tate Modern the exhibition has been made possible by the provision of insurance through the UK Government Indemnity Scheme; we would like to thank HM Government for providing this and the Department for Digital, Culture, Media and Sport and Arts Council England for arranging the indemnity.

The project would not have been possible without support from our sponsors. At the Art Institute of Chicago, lead support for *Cezanne* is generously provided by John D. and Alexandra C. Nichols. Major funding is contributed by an anonymous donor, The Marlene and Spencer Hays Foundation, the Butler Family Foundation, Richard F. and Christine F. Karger, the Shure Charitable Trust, Constance and David Coolidge, Amy and Paul Carbone, and Patricia and Ronald Taylor. Special support is provided by Dora and John Aalbregtse, Julie and Roger Baskes, Ethel and Bill Gofen, Natasha Henner and Bala

Ragothaman, Barbara and Marc Posner, Margot Levin Schiff and the Harold Schiff Foundation, and Linda and Michael Welsh. Additional funding is provided by the Jack and Peggy Crowe Fund, the Suzanne and Wesley M. Dixon Exhibition Fund, and The Regenstein Foundation Fund. Members of the Luminary Trust provide annual leadership support for the museum's operations, including exhibition development, conservation and collection care, and educational programming. The Luminary Trust includes an anonymous donor, Neil Bluhm and the Bluhm Family Charitable Foundation, Karen Gray-Krehbiel and John Krehbiel, Jr., Kenneth C. Griffin, the Harris Family Foundation in memory of Bette and Neison Harris, Josef and Margot Lakonishok, Robert M. and Diane v.S. Levy, Ann and Samuel M. Mencoff, Sylvia Neil and Dan Fischel, Anne and Chris Reyes, Cari and Michael J. Sacks, and the Earl and Brenda Shapiro Foundation. The corporate sponsor is Bank of America. This exhibition is supported by an indemnity from the Federal Council on the Arts and the Humanities. On behalf of Tate, we extend our deep gratitude to EY for their long-term commitment and generosity. This is the tenth exhibition supported by EY through The EY Tate Arts Partnership, which ensures that visionary and ambitious exhibitions such as this are possible. We would also thank the Huo Family Foundation (UK) Limited, the Cezanne Exhibition Supporters Circle including Eykyn Maclean, and also Tate Patrons and Tate Members for generously supporting this exhibition at Tate Modern.

We gratefully recognize the following colleagues for their critical support from the project's conception and throughout its development. At the Art Institute, the exhibition has benefited from the whole-hearted guidance of Sarah Guernsey, Deputy Director of Curatorial Affairs, together with Amanda Block, Claire Burdulis, Jennifer Cohen, Alexander Jen, Maureen Ryan, and Kate

14

Tierney Powell. We are deeply indebted to Ann Goldstein, Deputy Director and Chair and Curator of Modern and Contemporary Art. In Exhibitions, we owe special appreciation to Megan Rader, Executive Director of Exhibitions, and her extraordinary colleague Megan Kosinski, who has been indefatigable in her efforts to keep all of us on track with good grace and compassion. In Collections and Loans, Cayetana Castillo and her team, including Tim Campos and Sara Patrello as well as Maria Paula Armelin, have handled the complicated institutional logistics with ease. The art handlers and specialists were ably led by Leslie Carlson. In the department of Painting and Sculpture of Europe, Gloria thanks current and former colleagues for their tireless effort and flexibility: Zahra Bahia, Geraldine Banik, Emerson Bowyer, Robert Burnier, Jena Carvana, Jacquelyn Coutré, Rufino Jimenez, David Langkamp, Drew Lash, Rebecca Long, and Devon Lee Pyle-Vowles. Gloria and Caitlin extend special appreciation to Kathryn Kremnitzer for her contributions as a catalogue author and for sharing research and insights throughout the catalogue preparation. In the department of Modern and Contemporary Art, Caitlin would like to extend her deepest personal appreciation to Ann Goldstein as well as current and former colleagues Joanna Abijaoude, Jordan Carter, Jennifer Cohen, Mary Coyne, Robyn Farrell, Hendrik Folkerts, and Brian Leahy. At Tate Modern the exhibition could not have occurred without the guidance and backing of Rachel Kent, Head of Programme; and Neil Casey, Head of Business and Operations. The logistics were expertly handled by Travis Miles, Senior Exhibitions Registrar, while Genevieve Barton, as Exhibitions Assistant, provided crucial support to the team.

We are grateful to the dedicated staff at both institutions for their enthusiasm and generosity over the course of years of preparation. The catalogue has benefited in particular from the ongoing contributions of colleagues working in conservation. At the Art Institute, these include the authors of the essay in the present volume on Cezanne's methodology, who worked closely with other members of the department of Conservation and Science led by Francesca Casadio—in Scientific Research, Ken Sutherland; in Paintings and Frames, Allison Langley, Chris Brooks, Milan Bobysud, Kelly Keegan, Julie Simek, and Kirk Vuillemot; in Paper and Books, Mary Broadway, Christine Fabian, and Chris Coniff-O'Shea; and in Objects and Textiles, Emily Heye, all backed by Jann Trujillo. The team is grateful in turn for the collaboration of Annette Suleika Ortiz Miranda, Marc Vermuelen, and Mark Walton at the Northwestern University Center for Scientific Studies in the Arts; to Hirox USA and Keyence Corporation of America, who lent digital microscopes; and to Claire Potter, University of Chicago, who undertook important archival research. As this exhibition looks closely at the relationship between paintings and works on paper, we received invaluable help from our colleagues in Prints and Drawings, led by Kevin Salatino and including Jay Clarke, Mark Pascale, and Emily Vokt-Ziemba. In the Ryerson and Burnham Research Center led by Jill Bugajski, we acknowledge with gratitude Autumn Mather, Nathan Parks, and Bart Rykbosch for keeping the project alive despite the closure of many libraries.

The book was beautifully and intelligently designed by Roy Brooks of Fold Four, Inc., who showed remarkable creativity, patience, and sensitivity during the demanding process. He rose to the challenge of bringing many types of information together into a clear and engaging format. The effectiveness of the presentation is in large part the work of the color specialists at Prographics in Rockford, Illinois, overseen by Pat Goley. The Publishing department, led by Greg Nosan, worked to ensure the catalogue's quality and accessibility, and we are grateful to Lauren Makholm and Joseph Mohan, who worked closely with the curatorial team to shape its contents. Lisa Meyerowitz, Ben Bertin, Alissa Chanin Kolaj, and Kylie Escudero expertly and reliably stewarded the catalogue production at all stages. We also acknowledge Emily Fry, Kit Shields, Ginia Sweeney, and Loren Wright for helping us write didactics as well as sensitively editing wall texts, labels, and videos, all of which helped us to reinterpret Cezanne's art and his legacy for new generations. And last but definitely not least we offer our special thanks to A. Robin Hoffman for leading the extensive editorial enterprise with great intelligence, equanimity, and grace. In Imaging, Bonnie Rosenberg, Elyse Allen, Owen Conway, Aidan Fitzpatrick, Robert Lifson, Jonathan Mathias, and Craig Stillwell produced new photography of the Art Institute's Cezanne paintings and works on paper, including the lush details at one-to-one scale that bring us closer to the artist's inimitable technique. The preparation of this ambitious publication could not have been accomplished without the advocacy of Tom Avery and Emma Poulter in Tate Publishing, who worked tirelessly alongside colleagues in Chicago.

The department of Experience Design, led by Michael Neault and including Gina Giambalvo and Kirill Mazor together with Josh Andrews, Sarah Bump, Bronwyn Gallagher Kuehler, Andrew Meriwether, Kristine Scott Schultz, and Chris Wood produced videos, audio tours, interactives, and immersive projections about Cezanne's techniques for use in the exhibition and on the website. They were assisted by Pilcrow Studio and lead animators Scott North and Jay Noir along with producer Caitlin Cronin at Midnight Snack FX. In the department of Learning and Public Engagement led by Veronica Stein, we thank Sarah Alvarez and Robin Schnur, who worked with Interpretation colleagues to ensure that the display could be accessible for a broad and diverse audience. An optimal experience, however, requires a thoughtful design, and at the Art Institute, this was supplied by Leticia Pardo and the exhibition's architect, Richard Ferrer. Kristin Best created the elegant visual language and signage with Kari McCluskey. In Chicago, our vision was realized by Tom Ryan and Joe Vatinno along with their talented team members, both in-house and from Able Engineering, led by Thomas Smith. We are also grateful to Laticia Annison-Romano and Buildings and Grounds as well as Corey Burrage and all of the staff members in Protection Services for ensuring visitors' safety and comfort.

In Chicago we acknowledge as well current and former colleagues across the museum who contributed to the success of the exhibition. The following creative talents spread the message of *Cezanne* in banners and posters, in print and online: in Public Affairs, Kati Murphy and her colleagues Robyn Day, Vera Mandilovitch, and Amy Tsegai; in Marketing and Communications, Lauren Schultz with Shannon Burke and Katie Rahn as well as Elizabeth Dudgeon, Nora Gainer, Paul Jones, Katy Rose O'Brien, and Nadine Schneller; in External Affairs, led by Christina Pulawksi, Amy Allen Radick, George Martin, and Jonathan Kinkley; Heather Reinholtz and the museum shop staff; in Digital Marketing, Bridget Horgan, Calley Oresick, Elliot Pence, and Robert Sexton; and Robert Hudson and his team in Visitor Services.

At Tate Modern thanks are due to the following people who went to extraordinary lengths to realize the exhibition in London: in Conservation, Anna Cooper, Charity Fox, Annette King, Judith Lee, Bronwyn Ormsby, and Joyce Townsend; in Development, Nia Aronoffsky, Claire Gylphe, Jon Howe, Celeste Ricci, and Adrian Riches; in Corporate Partnerships, Matilda Hartley, Catherine March, Amber Marshall, and Charlotte Reeves; and in Membership, Monica Thomas. The exhibition graphics were beautifully designed by Mark Crowley. We extend warm gratitude to Gillian

Wilson and Elliott Higgs, with whom we worked very closely on the exhibition interpretation, as well as to La Kingsbeer in Marketing, our indefatigable Press Officers Kitty Malton and Joanna Sandler, and dedicated Visitor Experience colleagues David Hingley, Beatrice Limbert, and Sandra Maclean. In the Digital department we were bolstered by the creative talents of Zoe Smith and Scott Morris. We also appreciate the commitment and professionalism of Alessandra Serri, in Intellectual Property, and, in Retail and Merchandise, Tyrone Joseph and Charlotte Yates. Tate Library and Archive proved to be a treasure trove for this project, and we thank Katie Blackford, Adrian Glew, and Victoria Jenkins there for their help and support during a very challenging period. We are most grateful for the advice of our curatorial colleagues at Tate Modern: Osei Bonsu, Carine Harmand, and Portia Malatjie, who very generously shared their research and experience. The London presentation was beautifully designed by Phil Monk and installed thanks to the skill and precision of Richard Install, Adam Wozniak, Carl Richardson, and the team of art handlers.

Our last and greatest thanks go to the late Achim Borchardt-Hume, to whom this exhibition and catalogue are dedicated, for launching us and being a steady guiding presence on this journey into the artist's heart and hand, from his reception in his time to our own.

Gloria Groom
Chair of European Painting and Sculpture and the David and Mary Winton Green Curator, The Art Institute of Chicago

Caitlin Haskell
Gary C. and Frances Comer Curator of Modern and Contemporary Art, The Art Institute of Chicago

Natalia Sidlina
Curator, International Art, Tate Modern

NOTE TO THE READER

The abbreviation *FWN* prefaces identification numbers used in *The Paintings, Watercolors and Drawings of Paul Cezanne: An Online Catalogue Raisonné*, edited by Walter Feilchenfeldt, Jayne Warman, and David Nash (http://cezannecatalogue.com). It reflects the most up-to-date object and ownership information.

English-language titles have been preferred in references to artworks; alternate titles for those by Paul Cezanne can be found in the associated catalogue raisonné entry.

Where dimensions are listed, height precedes width precedes depth.

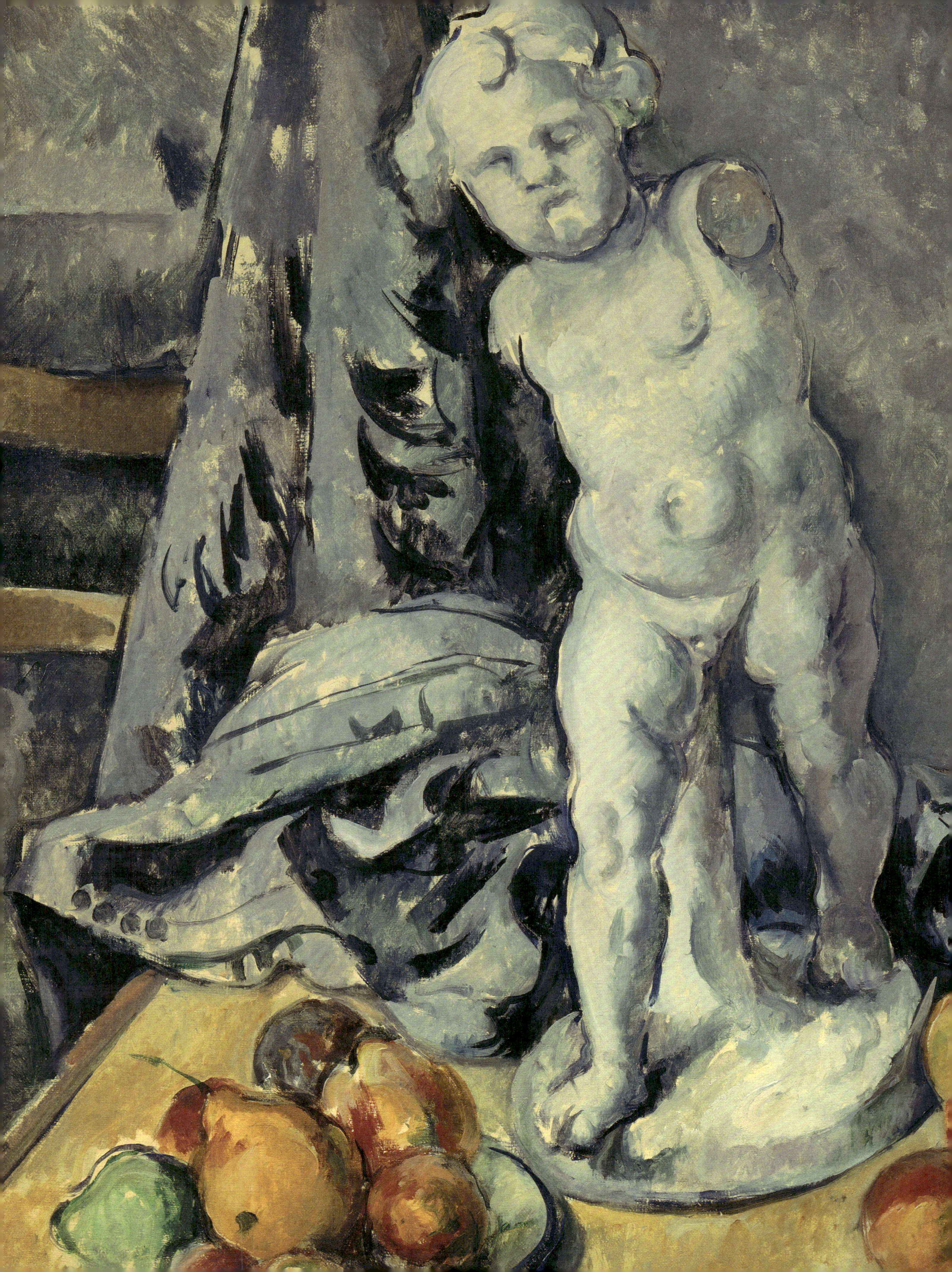

Organized Chaos

LOOKING AT CEZANNE[1]

**Achim Borchardt-Hume, Gloria Groom,
Caitlin Haskell, and Natalia Sidlina**

In October 1907, one year after Paul Cezanne's death, the Salon d'Automne presented a memorial exhibition of the artist's work featuring more than fifty paintings and watercolors.[2] This survey has rightly come to be seen as a watershed moment in the history of modern art. "How I should love to go to Paris for a week. Fifty-six Cezannes are on exhibit there now," the German painter Paula Modersohn-Becker wrote to her mother, having previously described him to her friend Clara Rilke-Westhoff as "one of the three or four powerful artists who have affected me like a thunderstorm, like some great event."[3]

Modersohn-Becker was far from alone in experiencing Cezanne's work as the bedrock of a radically new approach to the ways in which observation translated into representation. Pablo Picasso, often haunted by a wish to outdo those who came before, gladly acknowledged that Cezanne was like a "father," going so far as to buy an actual piece of Montagne Sainte-Victoire, the site that became synonymous with Cezanne's view of Provence (see cats. 120–27), in order to be closer to his spiritual ancestor.[4] Many of Cezanne's peers displayed a similar enthusiasm— some predictable, like his friend Camille Pissarro, with whom he spent many a day painting side by side in the 1870s (see figs. 1–2), and others more surprising, such as Claude Monet, who over the years accumulated the largest group of Cezanne's works by any artist-collector. "Cezanne, he's the greatest of us all," he is reported to have humbly acknowledged.[5]

When one painter identifies another as "the greatest of us all," the intended demographic for this comparison is precisely artists themselves, most often from their own milieu. In other words, the comparison takes place within a particular philosophical construct—if not a worldview, then certainly a view of their world. What may be particularly surprising in hindsight, given the historical context of rapid modernization at the threshold of a new century, is that artists from both sides of the 1900 divide speak in parallel terms about Cezanne's accomplishments. His oeuvre spans from the proto-Impressionist to the proto-Cubist, and for many an artist that came after, it has served as a point of reference, a license to break with conventions of beauty and idealism, and a commandment to make every mark matter. Beyond questions of subject and style, Cezanne's work articulated an ethics of painting—how to practice one's art, how to make and read a painting, how to represent and relate to the world— establishing key tenets for becoming a modern painter. At the same time, his work was appreciated by those artists who did not want to lose connection with the traditions and conventions of European painting, and whose

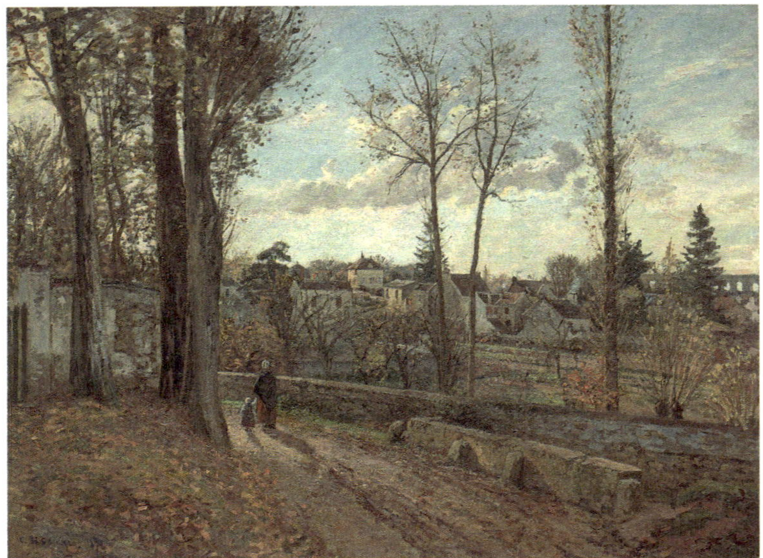

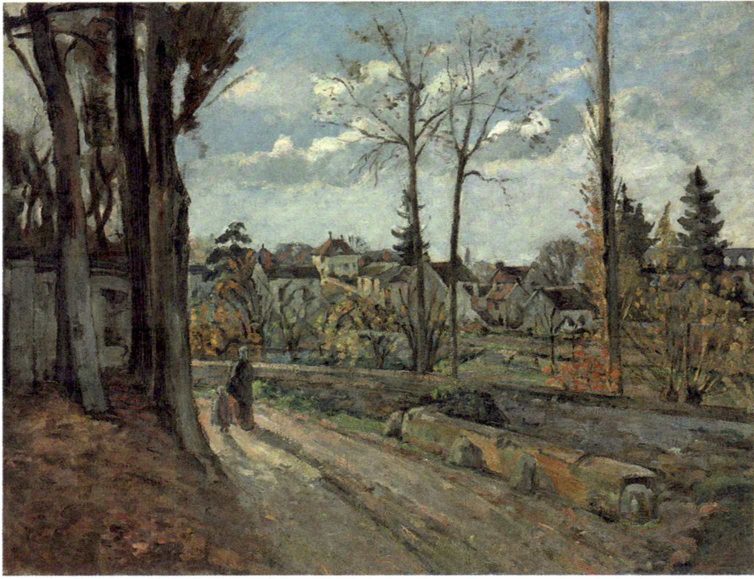

Fig. 1

Camille Pissarro (French, 1830–1903).
Louveciennes, 1871. Oil on canvas;
90 × 116.5 cm (35 7/16 × 45 7/8 in.).
Private collection.

Fig. 2

Paul Cezanne (French, 1839–1906).
Louveciennes, c. 1872. Oil on canvas;
73 × 92 cm (28 11/16 × 36 1/16 in.).
Private collection. (FWN 63)

modernity was moderated by an unwillingness to provoke a clean break between what came before Cezanne, and what came after.

Cezanne's revolution lay not so much in what he painted, but in how he painted, by which we mean not just a process of applying medium to substrate, or formalist invention, but the way he transcribed his experience of looking at the world for others to share. From the Renaissance onward, easel painting has played an instrumental role in cementing the act of looking as the primary sense of registering the world in Western societies. That act as practiced in front of a painting—which, not by chance, for a long period was compared to looking through an open window onto a world unfolding in front of the viewer—is constructed as a way of taking possession of the world: the artist looking at the world, looking at the artist's work, us looking at the world through the artist's work. This daisy chain entails a transmission of ownership that crosses the canyons of time and geography, that divides the world into those who look and those who are there to be looked at, and which therefore is imbued with the trappings of a particular universalism as far as the position of either an artist or a viewer is concerned. In contrast, Cezanne heightened the sense of subjectivity in each of these actions, not least his own, and brought into consciousness both the act of image construction and that of image perception. The viewer he anticipated is the individual—the human being self-aware and isolated in their specificity—who remains at the center of the modernist project. In other words, Cezanne's anticipated viewer is his own mirror image as a subject in all of their unique complexity.

Superlatives such as "the greatest of us all" or "the master of us all" can justly cause unease when read with an awareness of their implied exclusions, as it is hard not to interpret this "us" as predominantly white, male, and European. The question then is, how can we look at Cezanne's work now, not as that of the so-called Master of Aix, best revered from a respectful distance, but as that of a fellow human being who reached extraordinary heights of achievement?[6] How can we continue exploring his legacy today while acknowledging that he was, like all of us, shaped by a network of relationships and conventions that were themselves embedded within specific social and historic circumstances?

One possibility may be, to borrow from the title of Dipesh Chakrabarty's foundational contribution to postcolonial studies, to "provincialize" Cezanne.[7] In suggesting this we do not mean to diminish his contribution—far from it—but rather to pay close attention to his work's particularities, including the regional traditions within which he chose to place himself; the peer conversations he sought out; and the push-and-pull between his affection for his native Provence and the deep conviction that, to become modern, he had to be in Paris. Cezanne's trajectory prompts pertinent questions about the local and the regional in relation to metropolitan culture. We may consider, for instance, the rapport between historic events and artistic evolution. As the Prussians occupied Paris in 1871, Cezanne hid from his military draft to paint the coastline at L'Estaque; the next year, he avoided witnessing the Paris Commune, one of the greatest civil uprisings in modern history with estimated fatalities ranging from 7,000 to 20,000. The right to artistic autonomy and self-determination may also override other social mandates. The latter may be private—like those associated with the nuclear family—or public, such as historical or political commentary. As Émile Zola's *J'Accuse* demasked the systemic anti-Semitism in French society of the time, Cezanne stayed silent in the virulent debates around the infamous Dreyfus affair yet publicly acknowledged his friendship with the Jewish Camille Pissarro. The tension Cezanne created between seemingly dispassionate observation and a painterly self-consciousness for all to see would ultimately have a profound impact on how both subsequent and preceding painting was experienced by the modern viewer.

In a typical modernist paradox, Cezanne's trajectory was imbued with a drive to disrupt even as he consciously held onto tradition. The artist was an avid visitor to the collections of the Louvre as well as the Musée Granet, where he first took drawing lessons in his hometown of Aix. At both sites he showed a predilection for artists from the South of France, including the Baroque painter and sculptor Pierre Puget and the little-known Joseph Léon Roland de Lestang-Parade, whose *Death of Camoens* (fig. 3) reverberates in Cezanne's surprising depiction of a male Black model (cat. 25) commonly referred to as Scipio. The resulting dialogue in Cezanne's work between form and content, looking both forward and backward, invites new readings and interpretations with every successive generation—the present endeavor therefore being but one stop along a well-trodden road with no end in sight.

Among the many milestones of this journey was the landmark retrospective of 1995–96 jointly organized by the Philadelphia Museum of Art, the Réunion des Musées Nationaux/Musée d'Orsay, Paris, and the Tate Gallery, London. It followed several impactful exhibitions looking at particular periods of Cezanne's career and sought, for the first time, to shine a holistic light on his life and work, laying both wide open for further consideration. Since the mid-1990s, a number of exhibitions have also focused on specific genres, media, places, and subjects, providing close readings of a range of aspects. A similar set of categories organizes the digital catalogue

raisonné of the artist's paintings and works on paper, which was published in 2018 after years of intense research.[8] Freely available online, this resource's value to anybody interested in Cezanne's work can hardly be overestimated, for it allows us to see his project in an unprecedented totality. As this bird's-eye view confirms the impossibility of comprehensively summing up that lifelong endeavor, it has provided us with even more encouragement to develop a number of narrative lenses that were all guided by a key question: What motivates our continued engagement with Cezanne? We challenged ourselves to define what spurs this engagement beyond the affirmative—simply validating Cezanne's status once again—and moves it into the realm of the inquisitive by asking questions of the work that take account of both the context within which it emerged and our own experiences of the work today. With this in mind, rather than seeking to resolve ambiguities, we decided to present them as being at the very heart of Cezanne's creative enterprise.

Addressing his work from the 1860s through the end of his life, this exhibition shows how Cezanne laid a foundation for artistic innovations emergent in the early twentieth century. At the same time, it asks us to "un-know" certain long-held beliefs about him. Specifically, it proposes that we set aside the conventional wisdom that Cezanne's paintings should be understood primarily through the lens of Impressionism and that his greatest contributions were within the field of landscape painting,

Fig. 3

Léon Roland de Lestang-Parade (French, 1810–1871). *Death of Camoens,* 1835. Oil on canvas; 196 × 228 cm (77 ³⁄₁₆ × 89 ³⁄₄ in.). Musée Granet, Aix-en-Provence, France, inv. no. 835.8.1.

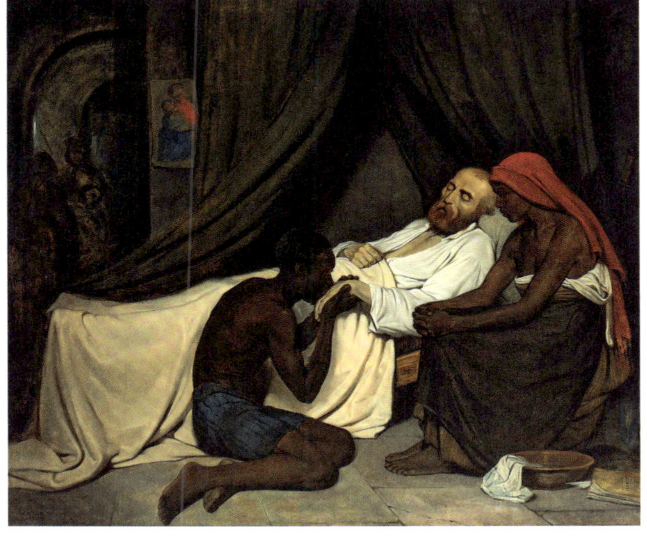

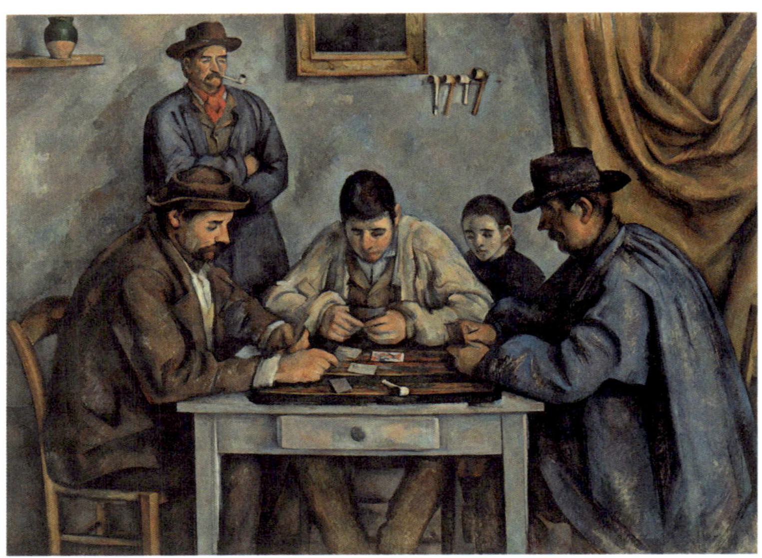

Paul Cezanne. *The Card Players*, 1890–92. Oil on canvas, 135.3 × 181.9 cm (53¼ × 71⅝ in.). Barnes Foundation, Philadelphia, BF564. (FWN 681)

whether from observation (as in his series depicting Montagne Sainte-Victoire) or from imagination (as in his many scenes of bathers; see cats. 92–108). To this end, the exhibition reintegrates bodies of work often considered less central to Cezanne's oeuvre—for example, his still lifes from several moments of his career (see cats. 1 and 4) and allegorical pictures (see, for example, cat. 15)—in order to better understand the pioneering trail he blazed for his own and successive generations of artists. Simultaneously, it asks us not to read Cezanne's work in hindsight, by persistently stressing its proto-modernist aspects, but in its own present tense and process of becoming, by focusing on Cezanne rather than the "Cezanne effect."

An ongoing tension between the emotional attachment to tradition and the intellectual pleasures of rule-breaking, between the "old" and the "new," reverberates throughout much of the modernist project and transnational art histories. Even though Cezanne was, from an early age, determined to be modern, his subject matter, especially through the second and more pathbreaking part of his life, not only remained remarkably traditional—still lifes, landscapes, portraits, nudes in a pastoral scene—but had an almost defiant air of nostalgia (see fig. 4). In his work he celebrated the non-modern authenticity of the South that to this day accounts for much of its allure, not least to his collectors: handmade pottery, locally grown

produce, a "timeless" unchanging landscape, though Cezanne was fascinated by the geological gash the quarry at Bibémus had hewn into his beloved Mont Sainte-Victoire (see cat. 120) as well as the men who worked the garden and land to which he felt so deeply connected (see cat. 136). The ethos of his work is shaped by an appreciation not so much of modern production but of making—of working as an act of perseverance and endurance. This integrity continues to inspire many artists today, especially as postindustrial societies struggle ever more with alienation of the hand from the mind, the maker from the consumer, and the (merely) looking from the (actively) living.

By critically examining the mixture of observed and imagined reality in Cezanne's paintings, this volume, like the exhibition, reopens inquiry into the artist's evolution in relation to his personal and historical context, his adventurous approaches to composition and technique, and his radical representation of a personal reality. Following this introduction, Gloria Groom discusses the extensive intellectual and artistic network that set the artist en route to becoming Cezanne. Caitlin Haskell recounts a parallel story of Cezanne's ethos of resistance and his development of a type of painting that was itself a critical pursuit. Kristi Dahm, Clara Granzotto, Maria Kokkori, Kimberley Muir, and Giovanni Verri examine Cezanne's material engagement with the process of painting, paying special attention to his innovative conception of the relationships between oil painting and watercolor, between density and void, to probe more deeply the artist's experimental approach to picture making and the way he drew upon the reality that was (ostensibly) right in front of him in order to construct a new image on canvas or on paper. Finally, Natalia Sidlina addresses questions of identity and public presentation of the self in Cezanne's work and its paradoxical global appeal, given the artist's profound sense of being rooted locally—in the "province"—during and after negotiating the economic and critical infrastructure of Paris in order to build a successful career. A revealing chronology of time and place compiled by Kathryn Kremnitzer shows how much this purportedly rooted artist was actually on the move throughout most of his life, walking in the mountains or taking the train from Aix or Marseille to Paris and vice versa, while Michael Raymond's complementary contextualization presents a wider view of geopolitical and cultural events and the changing world order of that moment.

We began by recalling that from early on, Cezanne has been described as an "artist's artist," based on the affinities and benchmarking innovations this label implies. We equally acknowledged how what is intended as a badge of honor can become a corset if these affinities are characterized by too narrow a comparison of form or medium. It was with this in mind that we invited ten artists—at various stages in their lives, working in different media, and with diverse experiences of migration, historic circumstance, and gender, racial, and sexual identities—to share with us their thoughts on Cezanne. Their voices amplify the effect of artworks in the display owned not only by Cezanne's generational peers, such as Edgar Degas, Paul Gauguin, Monet, Pissarro, and Pierre-Auguste Renoir, but also by influential twentieth-century artists such as Henri Matisse, Henry Moore, and Picasso, as well as (on the other side of the Atlantic) Jasper Johns, a lender to the exhibition.[9] Some responded to works we proposed based on their interests, access to the original, or past conversations; others eschewed our suggestions for surprising choices of their own. As a result, this catalogue contains highly original contributions by Etel Adnan, Phyllida Barlow, Paul Chan, Julia Fish, Ellen Gallagher, Lubaina Himid, Kerry James Marshall, Rodney McMillian, Laura Owens, and Luc Tuymans. Their gazes are profoundly unlike that of the universalist "artist" still so often implied in the use of the term. They bring Cezanne's uniqueness back to life and help to situate his work within the context of the world as we experience it in our varied ways today. Whether it is Adnan reflecting on Cezanne's late portrait of the gardener Vallier (as in the passage that supplies our epigraph), Himid taking a humorous look at an early canvas with the paint piled high, Gallagher reflecting on the complex history of racial representation, Fish verbalizing the act of looking, or Tuymans speculating on the morality of representation—to name but some—their contributions and the conversations along the way had a profound impact on us, testing our own conventions of looking and seeking to see afresh.

Cezanne was a fastidious observer, tireless in his attention to the very processes of observation. His art is likewise a call to attention. It demands that we be on guard for the gaps that our minds, forever chasing visual resolution, surreptitiously fill in, even more so now in our age of constant image proliferation. The tension between the empty ground and the physicality of the paint, between luminescence and solidity, creates constant suspense: possibility and unpredictability resist optical consumption. As Western modernity set out to become enthralled by disembodied knowledge and accelerated technocratic progress, Cezanne slowed painting down. Time and again, he returned to the same subject and spent his days in the intimate observation of what was familiar yet continually to be discovered anew. With most of his work undated, and several canvases sustaining his attention simultaneously and over prolonged periods, precise chronology eludes us, defying linear progression. If Cezanne's sense of slowing down seemed timely at the turn of the twentieth century, it does so even more now.

Notes

1. We gratefully acknowledge Etel Adnan (1925–2021) as we quote her text in this book (p. 205) in the title of our introduction.
2. See Bettina Kaufmann and Lothar Schirmer, eds., *Paul Cezanne: The Works of His 1907 Exhibition in Paris* (Munich: Schirmer/Mosel Verlag, 2018).
3. Paula Modersohn-Becker to her mother, Oct. 22, 1907; and idem to Clara Rilke-Westhoff, Oct. 21, 1907, in *Paula Modersohn-Becker: The Letters and Journals*, edited by Günter Busch and Liselotte von Reinken; edited and translated by Arthur S. Wensinger and Carole Clew Hoy (Evanston, IL: Northwestern University Press, 1990), 425.
4. "He was the father of us all. He was the one who protected us." Pablo Picasso quoted in Brassaï, *Conversations with Picasso*, translated by Jane Marie Todd (Chicago: University of Chicago Press, 1999), 107.

In 1958 Picasso acquired the Château of Vauvenargues, situated on the north slopes of Mont Sainte-Victoire. He is buried on the grounds of the estate.
5. In 1872, Pissarro wrote a letter to a fellow artist and declared of Cezanne, "Yes, he is the greatest of us all"; cited in Murray Bail, "A Painters' Painter: Introduction," in *Classic Cézanne*, edited by Terence Maloon, exh. cat. (Sydney: Art Gallery of New South Wales, 1998), 167. In a recorded exchange that must have occurred years after Cézanne's death, Monet is quoted saying to Georges Clemenceau, "Yes, Cézanne, he's the greatest of us all"; cited in translation in John Rewald, *The Paintings of Paul Cézanne: A Catalogue Raisonné*, vol. 1 (New York: Abrams, 1996), 424, from the reminiscences of Michel Georges-Michel, *Peintres et sculpteurs que j'ai connus: 1900–1942* (New York: Brentano, 1942), 34–35.
6. Louis Vauxcelles, the art critic of the Parisian literary magazine *Gil Blas*, described in his review of Charles Morice's "Enquête sur les tendences actuelles des artes plastique" the "continuous admiration and enthusiasm the Old Master of Aix-en-Provençe inspired" in him; Louis Vauxcelles, "La vie artistique," *Gil Blas* (Sept. 28, 1905): 1.
7. Dipesh Chakrabarty, *Provincializing Europe: Postcolonial Thought and Historical Difference* (Princeton, NJ: Princeton University Press, 2000).
8. See Walter Feilchenfeldt, Jayne Warman, and David Nash, eds., *The Paintings, Watercolors and Drawings of Paul Cezanne: An Online Catalogue Raisonné* (2018–present), http://cezannecatalogue.com. We salute the editors and their team for having created this extraordinary resource and for generously making it widely available.
9. For a list of works owned by Cezanne's peers that extends beyond this exhibition's checklist, see Appendix 1, compiled by Kathryn Kremnitzer (pp. 226–27).

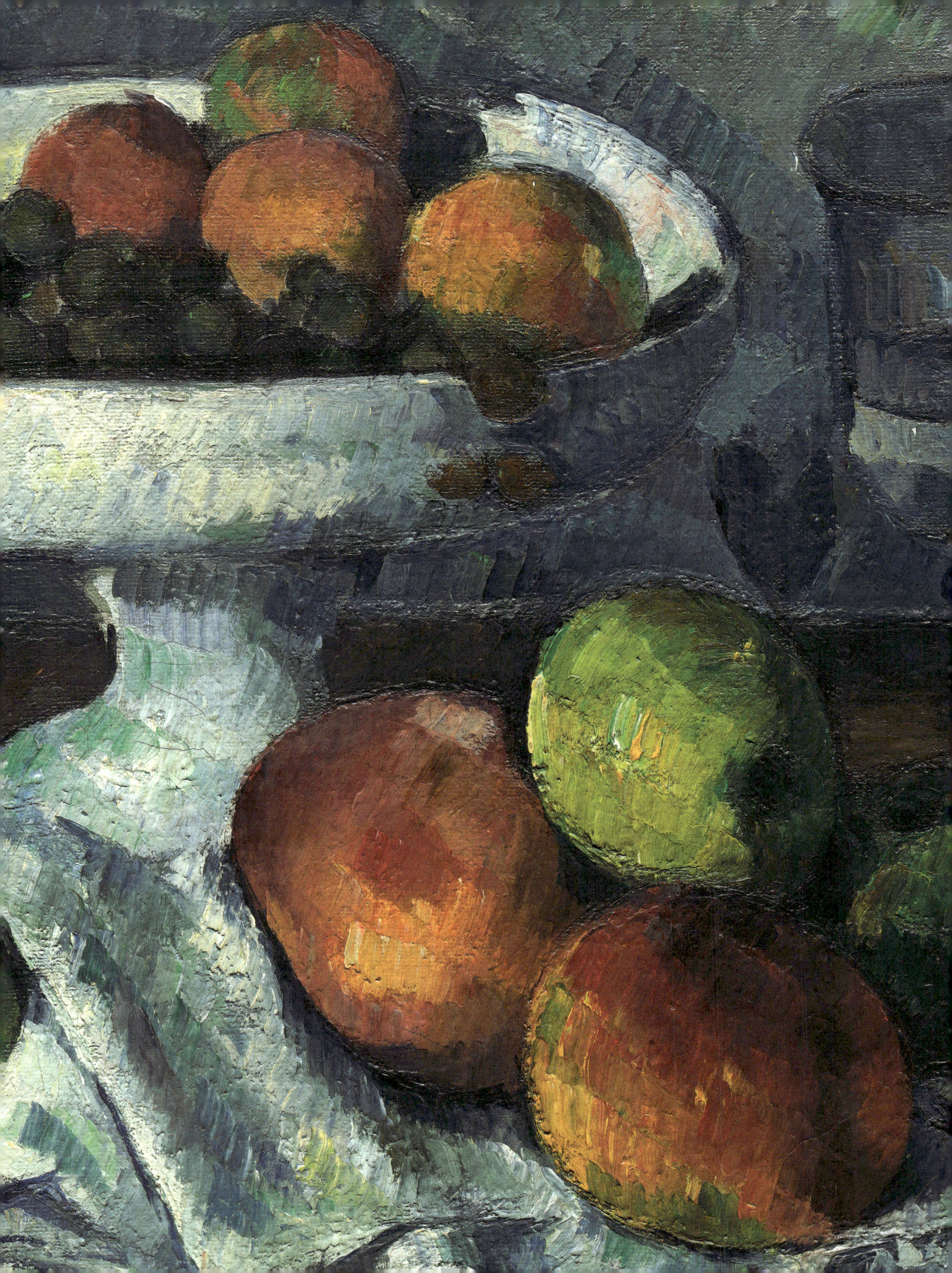

"At Once Unknown and Famous"

CEZANNE IN PARIS[1]

Gloria Groom

Although Paul Cezanne was, and often still is, characterized as the artist "who assimilated nothing of the Parisian," he was far from the mythic recluse revered by a younger generation of artists in the 1890s.[2] He socialized with progressive artists, musicians, journalists, and writers throughout the 1860s and 1870s, and he was famously considered an artist's artist in his own lifetime. Indeed, his importance to the subsequent progression of modern art, a subject thoroughly explored in scholarship and exhibitions that look back to Cezanne from the twentieth century and beyond, has overshadowed the significance of who owned works by him—and which ones—leading up to and immediately following his breakthrough exhibition in 1895 at Ambroise Vollard's gallery in Paris.

The Cezanne most often quoted today by scholars, artists, and art lovers alike is the Cezanne of the decade or so before his death in 1906, when he received visits and corresponded with younger artists including Maurice Denis, Émile Bernard, and Paul Signac, who clung to his every word and then published recollections of their conversations in books and articles. As far as we know, these are not opinions or theories he had fully articulated or shared with his contemporaries, including the Impressionists, with whom he had been in contact since he first came to Paris in 1861. Aside from remarks in his youthful correspondence with Émile Zola, a childhood friend whose career as a novelist bloomed before his own as a painter, there is little insight from Cezanne himself on his approach to art making in the early decades of his career. Most importantly, we do not know why his Impressionist contemporaries felt so strongly that he "was the greatest of us all," as Camille Pissarro and Claude Monet claimed.[3] That they believed this is apparent in their treatment of his work, however. This essay aims to develop a fuller understanding of Cezanne's development and subsequent impact by looking at his trajectory through the Parisian avant-garde. We trace his relationship to writers in the circle of Zola and his interactions with artists associated with the Impressionists and Post-Impressionists who became his most fervent collectors. Their literal investment in his work, especially that of the 1870s and early 1880s, crucially facilitated his subsequent achievements and recognition.

Zola's Literary Orbit

Throughout the first decades of Cezanne's career, the juried Paris Salons refused to accept his paintings. He routinely responded by making increasingly energetic efforts

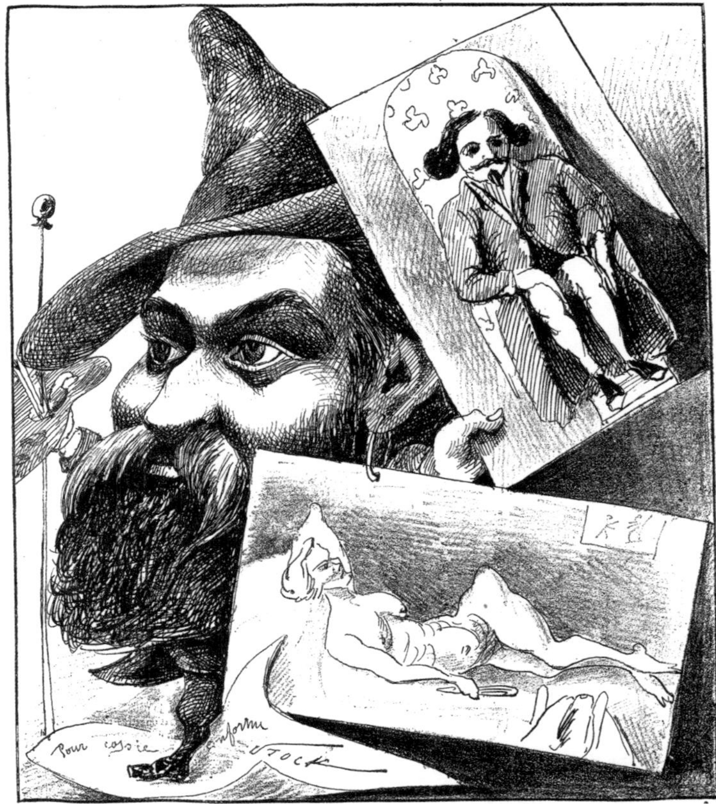

Fig. 1

Henri-Charles Stock (French, 1826–1885). "Le Salon par Stock," in *Stock-Album*, no. 2 (1870).

to provoke them, considering it a virtue to submit works that he knew would shock and repulse. One Salon jury member described his style as "peinture, au pistolet," deriding his heavy brushwork for looking as if it had been shot out of a gun.[4] Cezanne's close friend, artist Antoine Guillemet, concluded that "The less it looks like [a painting], the closer one is to genius. . . . Rejection at the Salon. Homeric struggle."[5]

Although the obstinate and outspoken Cezanne saw limited reward from this fight—despite casting it in epic terms—writers including Paul Alexis, Louis Edmond Duranty, Marius Roux, and others from Zola's group saw the dramatic potential and channeled his personality and antics into their stories.[6] On May 30, 1870, art critic

Théodore Duret wrote to Zola, who was already a successful author living in Paris, asking for an address and a letter of introduction to the "completely eccentric" artist from Aix "whose paintings have been rejected by the [Salon] jury."[7] Duret's inquiry reflects Cezanne's status as simultaneously obscure and notorious, and may have been prompted by a recent caricature (fig. 1) that shows the artist defiantly holding the two paintings that made him "this year's reject" from the state-sponsored Salon: a portrait of his friend Achille Empéraire (FWN 423) and a large (now unlocated and probably destroyed) painting of a nude (FWN 595-TA).[8] The caricature was accompanied by an interview—Cezanne's first in a Parisian journal—in which he resolutely stated what distinguished his art from that of his peers: "I have very strong sensations."[9] This assertion would later be identified by younger, adulating artists as the through line for his art and the basis of his quest for truth, an art without artifice. Before they framed their idol in those terms, though, the phrase was picked up and interpreted variously by writers—especially Zola—for whom Cezanne served as a fictional avatar.[10]

The fact that Duret sought help from the novelist shows how well known their friendship was during Cezanne's first years in Paris. Zola's response to Duret—that Cezanne was not yet ready to show his work—was consistent with his role as Cezanne's promoter–protector.[11] In Paris, however, at least at first, their relationship was more symbiotic than one-sided, resting upon their shared ambition and common spirit of self-preservation.[12] Both felt themselves outsiders in "la ville fiévreuse de Paris" (the feverish city of Paris).[13] Both were also passionate about wanting to outdo their literary and artistic inspirations and competitors (Honoré de Balzac and Édouard Manet, respectively). Cezanne introduced Zola to artists whom the latter defended in his art reviews, and Zola would often glean information from the lives of artist friends to use in his novels.[14] The defiance that Cezanne displayed to the Salon jury in the 1870s—and described throughout correspondence with family and friends—was also part of a cultivated persona. Five years earlier, Zola had dedicated his first novel, *La Confession de Claude* (1865), about a young artist from the provinces, to Cezanne and their Aixois friend, Jean-Baptiste Baille. Zola also asked Marius Roux, another mutual friend from Aix, to review the novel and refer specifically to Cezanne, who was then taking drawing classes at the Académie Suisse.[15] Roux did so, singling him out as fitting the novel's description: a dogged, risk-taking, and modest artist on the rise, but one whose work was never finished. Zola reiterated this description in his reviews of Cezanne's works in the 1870s as well as in his fictional artist-characters.[16]

Zola's circle had ample opportunity to observe the artist firsthand, too, since the friends continued to circulate together in Paris. Cezanne was a habitué of Zola's *jeudis* (social gatherings) in his first decade in Paris and was invited, through Zola, to the bohemian events hosted by Nina de Villard, an eccentric divorcée celebrated in Manet's *Lady with Fans* (1874; Musée d'Orsay, Paris), who demanded that her guests not be bourgeois, acclaimed by the academy, or officially recognized.[17] At any one of her Wednesday or Sunday salons, musicians, poets, journalists, and artists were among the attendees, including Alexis, Ernest Cabaner (an impoverished composer), Edmond de Goncourt, Stéphane Mallarmé, Manet, and Paul Verlaine, as well as Paul Gachet, a doctor; Cezanne's old friend Paul Alexis described the raucous atmosphere of Nina's salon in his novel *Madame Meuriot,* published in 1890.[18] On the opposite end of the spectrum were the salons of the haute-bourgeois Georges and Marguerite Charpentier, who were important publishers of the Goncourt brothers, Gustave Flaubert, and Zola. Cezanne attended with Zola and Pierre-Auguste Renoir; the latter was practically the family painter following the success of his portrait of Marguerite Charpentier and the couple's two children (1878; Metropolitan Museum of Art, New York), while the Impressionists in general were in the minority at these gatherings.[19]

But all this mixing with journalists and novelists generally did not translate into exhibitions or sales for Cezanne. One of the notable exceptions was a purchase by Duret, who sought out the artist in 1870; the author's collection sale in 1894 included three paintings by him.[20] It was Cezanne's mingling with a broader circle of artists that ultimately brought more material returns. Between 1877 and 1878, he lived in the Batignolles neighborhood, near the cafés most frequented by Manet and the younger generation of artists with whom Cezanne would later be associated, and where he encountered more writers. According to one, Georges Rivière, Manet would immediately make a place for Cezanne at the Café de la Nouvelle Athènes, and Manet's biographer, Adolphe Tabarant, recorded that on Friday nights ("really important occasions") at the Café Guerbois, in addition to writers, the artists Henri Fantin-Latour, Renoir, Edgar Degas, and "more seldom" (but still!) Monet and Cezanne, would turn up.[21] On one such occasion, as Monet recalled, Cezanne refused to shake Manet's hand and instead tipped his hat, saying "I won't offer you my hand, Monsieur Manet. I haven't washed in eight days."[22] By serving up anecdotes like this, Cezanne confirmed and perpetuated his image, rooted in Zola's original framing and then circulated in amplified or even caricatural form, as a rough and shaggy Provençal, the combative outsider who would have had no trouble recognizing himself in Zola's Claude or comparable artist characters who challenged aesthetic conventions.

In 1874, nearly ten years after Roux had voiced his faith in Cezanne's future, the struggling artist joined his peers in the first Impressionist exhibition, which was organized outside of the official Salon.[23] Having failed to have even one work accepted at the state-sponsored venue, Cezanne recognized the benefits of attaching himself to this new avant-garde group.[24] His modest showing included two landscapes painted alongside Pissarro, which feature light colors and thickly applied, broken brushstrokes that suggest the older artist's influence. One of these, *The House of the Hanged Man* (c. 1873; FWN 81), was Cezanne's first sale to a collector, Count Armand Doria.[25] But his genre painting *A Modern Olympia* (fig. 2), designed as an *esquisse*, or sketch, garnered more critical attention.[26] The picture was an obvious parody of Manet's *Olympia* (1863; Musée d'Orsay, Paris), the scandal of the 1865 Salon; it was also an experiment, taking Manet's familiar characters and pushing the definition of "finish" even further. In Cezanne's much smaller and less polished confection of eroticism and theatricality, the red drapes part to reveal a woman being unveiled by a Black attendant, with a male admirer (perhaps a self-portrait of the balding artist) seen from behind. It is difficult to deduce Cezanne's intentions in showing this self-proclaimed sketch alongside his Pissarro-esque productions. Was he

Fig. 2

Paul Cezanne (French, 1839–1906). *A Modern Olympia*, 1873–74. Oil on canvas; 46 × 55 cm (18 1/8 × 21 5/8 in.). Musée d'Orsay, Paris, RF 1951-31. (FWN 628)

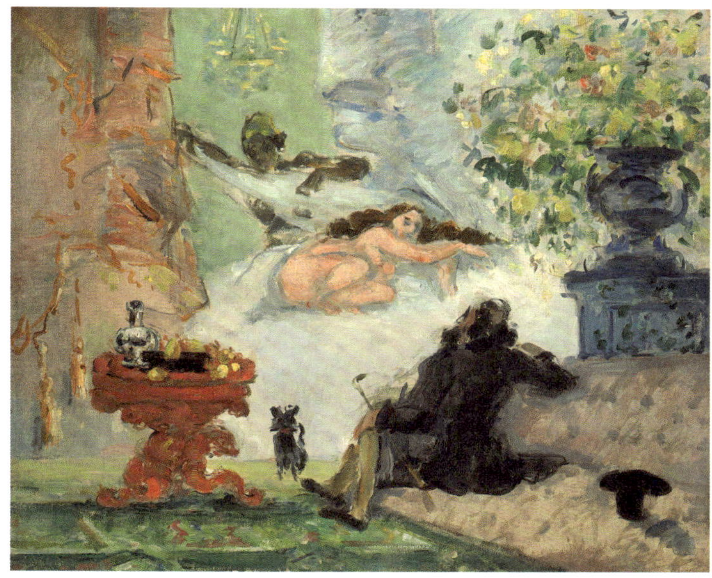

challenging Manet, the unsurpassed painter of modern life? Or was this his way of avoiding being reduced to an Impressionist *pleinairiste*? Whatever his reasoning, not even the disclaimer of "sketch" could soften the critics' aversion to *A Modern Olympia*, which they saw as too bright, disjointed, and superficial.[27]

Despite the negative press his works received at the Impressionists' 1874 exhibition, when planning began for the third group display in April 1877, Cezanne was willing to participate.[28] He was also delighted to learn that his inclusion was hotly contested by Degas and Degas's friends, painters Giuseppe de Nittis and Ludovic Napoléon Lepic, but successfully defended by Monet and Gustave Caillebotte.[29] The latter had taken full control of the 1877 exhibition, both logistically and curatorially, by arranging the entries to achieve maximum coherence and filling in gaps with works from his own collection.[30] As part of this orchestration, Caillebotte asked that all works be signed in red, probably to signal that the group was showing finished works (not mere "impressions"). Cezanne, a habitual nonsigner, conceded to the request but also titled more than half of his seventeen entries as "études."[31] In a letter from July 1876, Pissarro had also stressed the importance of the group showing only fully realized works, to which Cezanne responded with a promise "to show the best I have" with the Impressionists and

something "neutral with the others," presumably referring to artists outside the group.[32] Cezanne's use of the term "neutral" without specific referents leaves its meaning mysterious: conventional? more finished? or lesser in some other way? His choice to label seven works as études had a specific meaning, though, derived from nineteenth-century academic teaching, which framed these studies as "the most sincere expression of the artist, seeing, observing in complete honesty and naïveté with correct and precise means, the reality that one finds in front of oneself and the impressions or sensations that it makes one feel."[33] That Cezanne saw these works as études is consistent with his refusal to measure any work in terms of finish, as Caitlin Haskell discusses in this volume, since the sensations that he was seeking to realize (*réaliser*, a verb he often used later in life to describe his aims) remained by definition unattainable.

Learning, no doubt, from the reaction to *A Modern Olympia*, Cezanne honored his pledge to Pissarro and exhibited "his best" with the Impressionists in 1877: landscapes, figures, and still lifes, many of which, being "d'après nature," aligned more closely with the group's aesthetics. As Caillebotte had hoped, the display clearly represented the group's identity, and Cezanne individually benefited from its success, as it planted the seeds for future appreciations as well as future works. The provisionary title of *Étude, projet de tableau* (now known as *Bathers at Rest*, fig. 3) implies that a follow-up painting was planned; it never materialized, but the artist recycled these figural types and groupings in other paintings and watercolors (FWN 924; FWN 915) as part of a career-long engagement with the subject of bathers. He impulsively gave the work to Cabaner shortly after the exhibition, but Caillebotte eventually acquired it, the first of five by Cezanne that he ultimately owned.[34] Degas, who otherwise was not an advocate for Cezanne, apparently was also taken with this painting and copied the central figure in a large sketchbook, concentrating particularly on the body's unusual bent position.[35]

Following this comparatively fruitful outing, Cezanne continued to expand his social circle, improving prospects for sales. Pissarro became worried that he would pivot like Renoir, who was pushed by Zola and followed the Charpentiers' counsel to submit works to the Salon of 1878, which would prohibit him from showing with the Impressionists at their exhibition that same year.[36] Although Cezanne ultimately returned to Aix and did not contribute to either the Salon of 1878 or the Fourth Impressionist Exhibition (postponed to 1879), he initially allayed Pissarro's misgivings by asking Zola to lend *The Black Clock* (fig. 4), a dark and heavy still life that he had painted in the writer's home and then given to him.[37] Featuring velvety blacks, this still life astutely

Fig. 3

Paul Cezanne. *Bathers at Rest*, c. 1876–77. Oil on canvas; 82.2 × 101.2 cm (32 3/8 × 39 13/16 in.). Barnes Foundation, Philadelphia, BF906. (FWN 926)

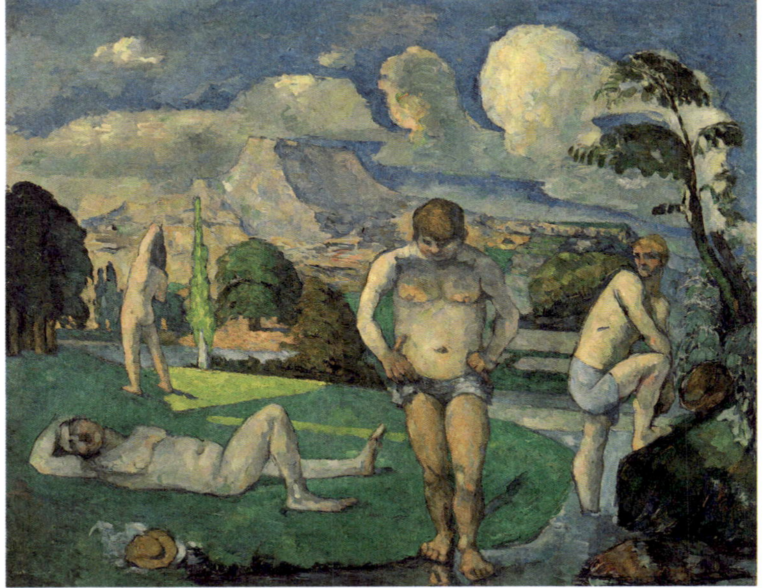

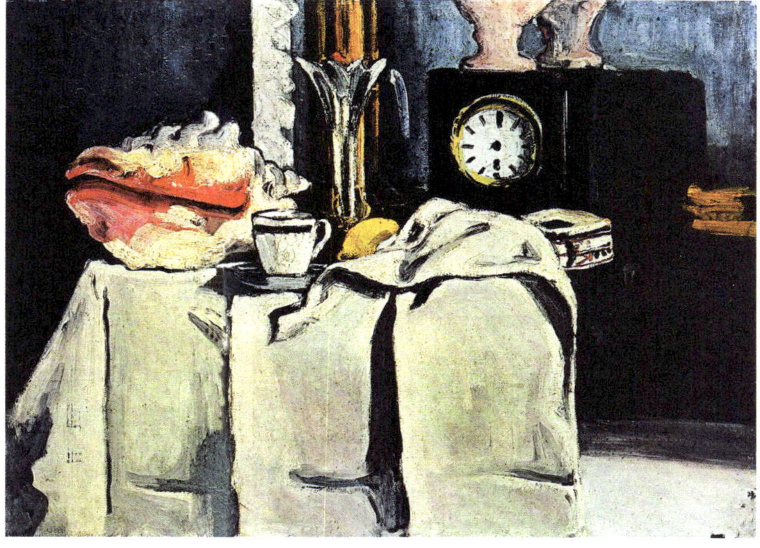

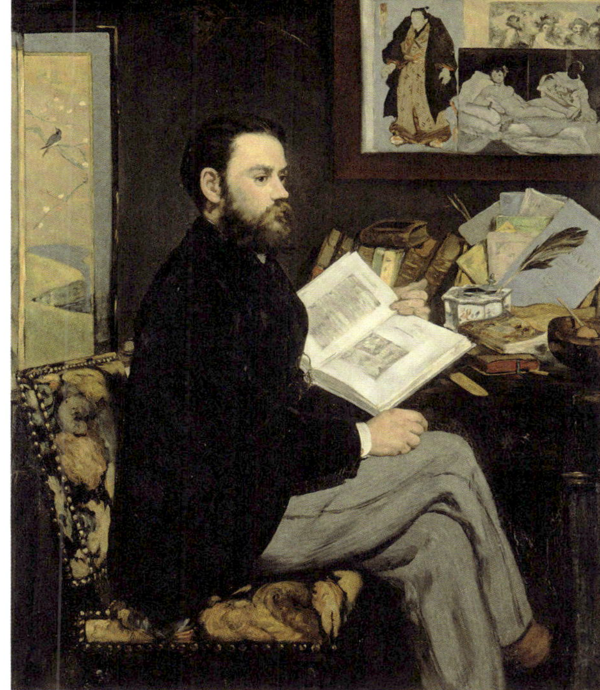

recalled Manet's Salon-exhibited portrait of Zola (fig. 5), complete with the writer's inkwell. By planning to show earlier compositions rather than the landscapes more closely aligned with the aims of his Impressionist colleagues, the artist was recalling not just his works but also his social priorities from the 1860s, when he was closely engaged with a more literary set.[38] Cezanne never showed with the Impressionists again and was finally accepted at the Salon of 1882 with a brooding portrait of his father reading *L'Événement* (1866; cat. 2), the newspaper in which Zola had first endorsed the Impressionists, in front of a small still life (cat. 1) that Cezanne had, like *The Black Clock*, painted in the late 1860s and gifted to the novelist. Not coincidentally, he left Paris shortly thereafter.

Cezanne's Impressionist Collectors

Although Cezanne was more closely entangled with Zola's creative circles than his fellow Impressionists were (with the exception of Manet and Degas), the literati themselves were more interested in observing his complex character—which fit so easily into the earlier literary tradition of the bohemian radical—than in supporting his artistic ambitions. By the 1870s, Zola himself was no longer endorsing Cezanne, whom he felt had taken a wrong turn. He saw in his friend's works a lack of cohesion between compositional elements and facture, perceiving them as in-progress rather than resolved. The writer repeatedly noted his misgivings in reviews of Cezanne's public showings throughout the 1860s and 1870s, concluding rather dismissively in 1880 that "M. Paul Cezanne has the temperament of a great painter who still struggles with problems of technique."[39] Cezanne, on the other hand, as Zola's intimate, was charged on at least two instances to ask the famous novelist to write on his Impressionist colleagues' behalf.[40]

Instead it was Degas, Renoir, Monet, Caillebotte, and Pissarro, as well as others peripherally associated with

Fig. 6

Paul Gauguin (French, 1848–1903).
Woman in Front of a Still Life by Cezanne,
1890. Oil on linen canvas; 65.3 ×
54.9 cm (25 11/16 × 21 5/8 in.).
The Art Institute of Chicago, Joseph
Winterbotham Collection, 1925.753.

the Impressionists, who purchased work by Cezanne during the crucial period around his initial association with the group and especially on the heels of his "breakout" solo exhibition in November 1895; the latter group included figures such as painter and lithographer Armand Guillaumin; pastry chef, author, and self-taught painter Eugène Murer; and even the society painter and printmaker Paul Helleu. With the exception of his Aixois friends and Pissarro, Cezanne had few real artist allies, even among the Impressionists. But his relationship with Pissarro extended over two decades, and he was close to some at certain times. Monet, for example, invited Cezanne to visit him at Argenteuil in the early 1870s and made a special trip to see him in Aix in 1882. Cezanne never gave him artwork (as he did his Académie Suisse colleagues Guillaumin, Pissarro, and Francisco Oller, and possibly Caillebotte, as well as nonartist friends such as Zola and Cabaner). But Monet was one of the few to collect Cezanne's art early on, purchasing a small pastoral fantasy now known as *Picnic on a Riverbank* (1873–74; FWN 626) in the 1870s. This acquisition was followed by three paintings in 1895–96 (FWN 154; FWN 422; FWN 495). Monet continued to augment his holdings (at increasingly high prices) to a total of fourteen paintings and one watercolor, ultimately acquiring more works by Cezanne than by any other artist in a collection that featured Manet, Renoir, and Pissarro, among others. These works were, moreover, representative of the different periods in Cezanne's career and varied in subject and technique.[41]

Through Pissarro, Cezanne met Paul Gauguin, who, while still connected with the Paris *bourse* (stock market), was both buying work by Cezanne for himself and acting as something of an art dealer for his friends. Between 1877 and 1883, he acquired a few works by Manet and the Impressionists and at least six paintings by Cezanne, though the majority of the works in his collection were by Pissarro and Guillaumin.[42] Like Pissarro and Monet, Gauguin prized his Cezannes, refusing to sell *Still Life with Fruit Dish* (1879–80; cat. 53) "except in a case of direst necessity."[43] According to Vollard, in 1893 this painting was given a prominent place in Gauguin's rue Vercingétorix studio, where he would show it to the young painters who frequented his neighborhood restaurant and explain Cezanne to them.[44] This pedagogical discussion was limited by Gauguin's own narrow understanding of the artist's credo, the importance of sensation. In 1890 Gauguin painted a portrait (fig. 6) that included a larger-than-life fragment of *Still Life with Fruit Dish* as part of the background, but his attempt to emulate Cezanne's strokes on an exaggerated scale resulted in marks that, while recognizable, are flatter and airless. In his essay "Racontars de Rapin" (published in

1902 and recently translated into English as "Ramblings of a Wannabe Painter"), Gauguin termed Cezanne "polychromatic or even polyphonic," perhaps a cryptic reference to the artist's efforts to synthesize multiple viewpoints within a single image.[45] Other than this opaque description and another in the memoir–manifesto *Avant et Après* (1903), of the still life that he once owned, Gauguin, like all of the revered painter's collectors from the Impressionists' circle, wrote little about the "why" of Cezanne and the common ground, if any, that guided his own collecting choices.[46] Possession was its own explanation.

The full truth of this became apparent in 1895, when Pissarro, along with Monet, Renoir, and Guillaumin, persuaded Vollard to arrange a show of Cezanne's artworks. They were all gobsmacked by the public display of paintings and watercolors, spanning the artist's output up to that point, that were too strong, too raw, to be readily understood. Pissarro, who pulled out of lending his collection at the last minute, dared to ask aloud the question that he and his fellow artists grappled with in their response:

> I thought of Cézanne's show in which there were exquisite things, still lifes of irreproachable perfection, others *much worked on* and yet unfinished, of even greater beauty, landscapes, nudes and heads that are unfinished but yet grandiose, and so *painted*, so supple. . . . But my enthusiasm was nothing compared to Renoir's. Degas himself is seduced by the charm of this refined savage, Monet, all of us. . . . Are we mistaken? I don't think so. The only ones who are not subject to the charm of Cézanne are precisely those artists or collectors who have shown by their errors that their sensibilities are defective. They properly point out the faults we all see, which leap to the eye, but the charm—that they do not see.[47]

Despite Pissarro's initial confusion, all of the core Impressionists mentioned above (as well as Mary Cassatt) acquired works by Cezanne through Vollard, by purchase or exchange, at or soon after the exhibition. Although their acquisitions ranged widely in subject, scale, and technique, with the exception of Monet's, these did not include either older, more narrative scenes of the perils of modern life or quite recent works, but rather ones conceived in the 1870s and early 1880s.[48]

What was the secret of these "unfinished, but yet grandiose" works? As Pissarro's testimony of the exhibition's stunning effect on him and others suggests, these artists saw something in Cezanne's painting that no theoretical discussion or academic training could fully explain. After the show closed, Pissarro swiftly acquired several of the displayed pictures.[49] Pissarro's collection of works by Cezanne was the largest assembled in Cezanne's lifetime by a fellow artist, with nineteen paintings, twelve drawings, and three watercolors—the majority of which were completed during the years when they commonly worked alongside each other, from 1872 to 1882, and were likely gifts, not purchases. But he was hardly alone in his admiration. Monet reported feeling stymied in his own work when confronted by Cezanne's, and yet he nonetheless felt compelled to own it.[50] Although Monet's collection ultimately included paintings by Caillebotte (three), Manet (three), Berthe Morisot (four), Renoir (ten), and Pissarro (two), most of these were gifts rather than purchases, unlike his many Cezanne acquisitions—which, as he complained later on, were increasingly expensive.[51]

Similarly, Renoir approached Cezanne from multiple, possibly conflicting angles. They had worked alongside each other on occasion, and Renoir owned three landscapes that Cezanne had painted while visiting him at Auvers (1872), Pontoise (1881), and L'Estaque (fig. 7); Renoir also purchased *The Battle of Love* (c. 1880; FWN 657) from the 1895 exhibition. He famously asked, "How does [Cezanne] do it? He can't put two strokes [*touches*] of color on a canvas without it [already] being very good."[52] Renoir had vied with Degas to obtain from Vollard *Three Pears* (c. 1888–90; FWN 1944), one of three works the latter acquired during the run of the exhibition (FWN 760; FWN 913).[53] Between November 1895 and June 1897, Degas made "an orgy of purchases," including two more still lifes (FWN 760; FWN 779), a scene of Venus with Cupid (FWN 652), and a portrait of the collector Victor Chocquet (FWN 438).[54]

Cezanne himself had copied and learned from the Impressionists and was seemingly generous in giving his work to friends—including Zola and Cabaner as well as fellow artists—but he was "notoriously unacquisitive."[55] Although he included the works of his peers in a few of his early paintings—for example, *Still Life with Soup Tureen* (FWN 726)—and made a copy of Renoir's portrait of him (FWN 461) (which became part of Pissarro's collection, probably as a gift from its creator), the artist does not seem to have felt the need to reciprocate their investment in him. If he was given works by his colleagues, there is no evidence that these were ever on view in his many residences, including, later in life, at Les Lauves when he was financially stable.[56] When he painted alongside others—such as Pissarro (in 1872–82), Gauguin (1881), or Renoir (1882, 1888, and 1891)—their work bent to his and not vice versa (see, for example, fig. 7), and the current flowed in the same direction for their more material exchanges.

Fig. 7

Pierre-Auguste Renoir (French, 1841–1919). *Rocky Crags at L'Estaque*, 1882. Oil on canvas; 66.4 × 81 cm (26 ⅛ × 31 ⅞ in.). Museum of Fine Arts, Boston, Juliana Cheney Edwards Collection, 39.678.

Fig. 8

Maurice Denis (French, 1870–1943). *Homage to Cezanne*, 1900. Oil on canvas; 180 × 240 cm (70 ⅞ × 94 ½ in.). Musée d'Orsay, Paris, RF 1977 137, LUX 48.

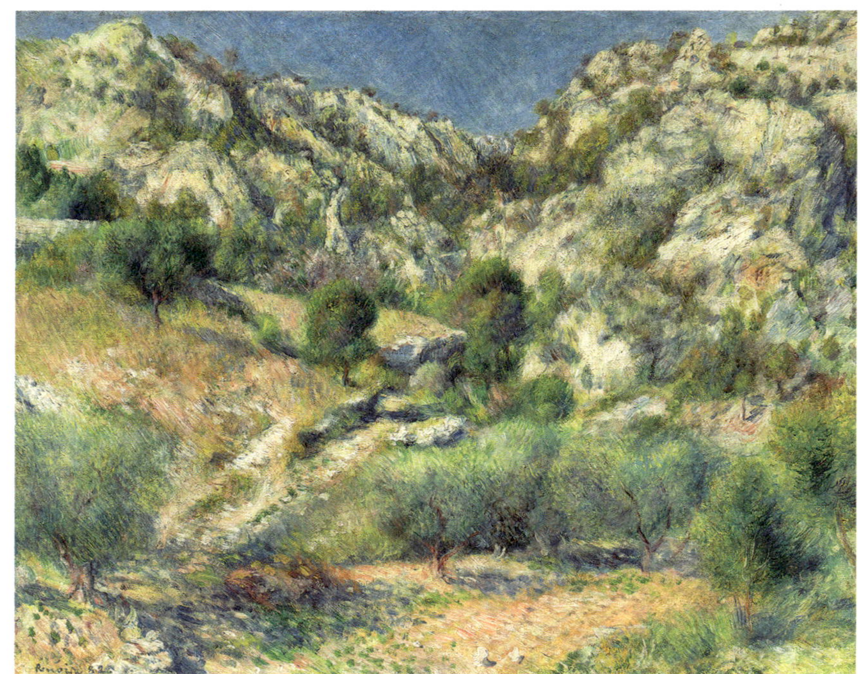

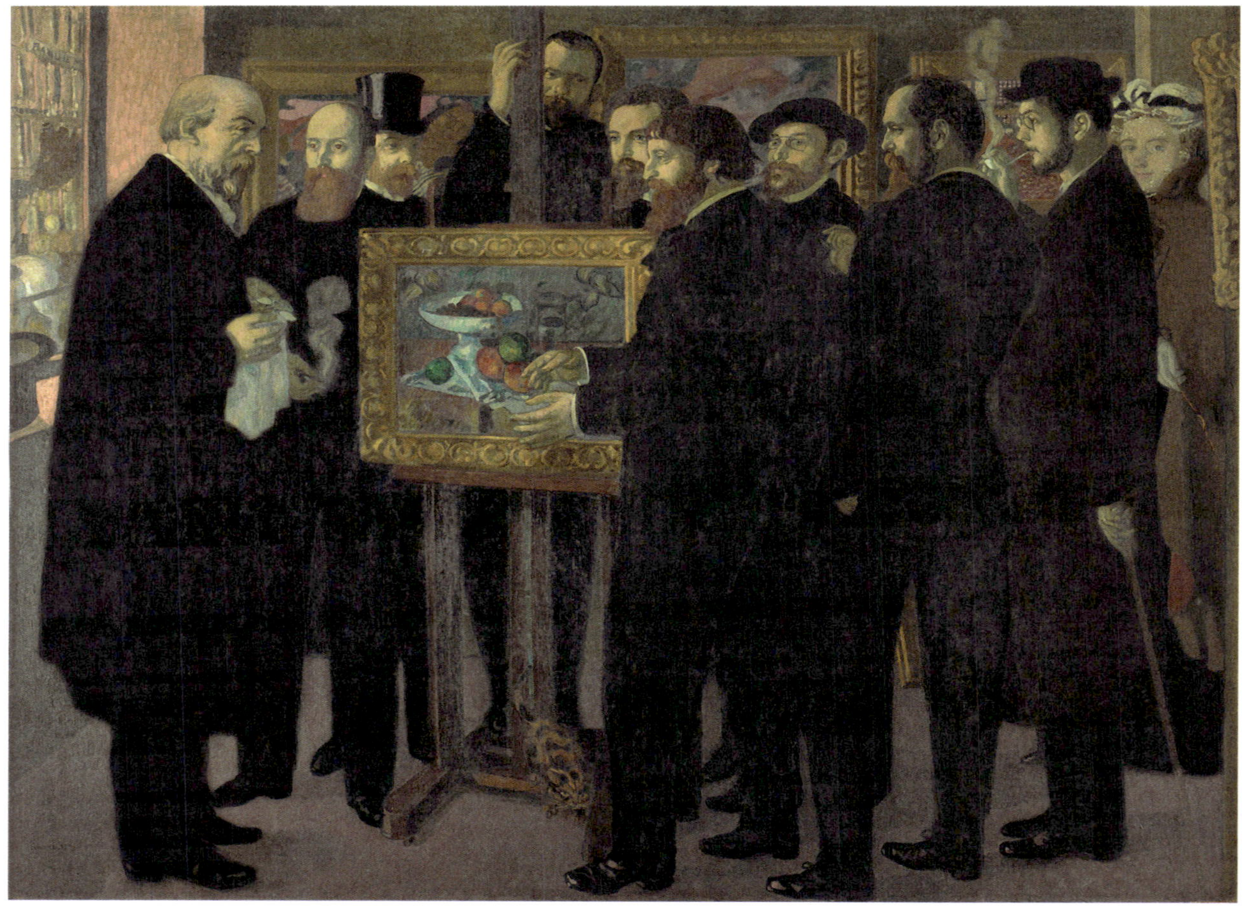

Coda: Cezanne's Multigenerational Appeal

On the occasion of the Salon de la Société Nationale des Beaux-Arts in 1901, Maurice Denis exhibited his billboard-scale painting *Homage to Cezanne* (fig. 8). Denis was the youngest member of the Nabis, the group of artists whose name reflected their "prophetic" ambitions, and he wrote to Cezanne that he hoped his painting would show "how important you are to us."[57] He had yet to meet the older artist, who is represented in *Homage* by the painting on the easel, *Still Life with Fruit Dish*, which Gauguin had recently sold.[58] Like Duret, who had asked Zola for an address in 1870, Denis later recalled that "it was hard to locate Cezanne in 1890" and that he had wondered "whether this invisible painter was not a myth."[59]

By then a broad range of collectors in Europe and abroad considered the Impressionists reliably investible, and they were shown regularly at the Parisian galleries of Paul Durand-Ruel and Georges Petit. Cezanne was a relative newcomer to the market despite strong buying interest among the Impressionists themselves.[60] But Denis pointed to Cezanne's pivotal position between generations by including Odilon Redon in his *Homage*; the older artist was close to the younger group on a personal level and shared many of their collectors.[61] In 1901 Denis's *Homage* was acquired by his friend André Gide, who was fast becoming prominent among France's most esteemed novelists, essayists, and journalists; the acquisition repositioned Cezanne, symbolically at least, in relation to the next generation of literary giants—recalling his earliest years among writers, but with his artistic accomplishments, rather than his reputation, finally predominating. Four years later the writer Charles Morice sent an *enquête*, or survey, to fifty-seven artists with the question "How do you feel about Cezanne?" Several of these emerging and established artists, including Denis, already owned or later collected work by Cezanne.[52] The resulting publication extended the debate about his significance to the future of art.[63]

Cezanne came to occupy a prominent place within broader discussions of art and artists in the early years of the twentieth century because, as suggested at the outset, younger artists like Émile Bernard and Denis, who visited Cezanne in his studio at Les Lauves, published conversations they recalled having with him on the subjects of art, nature, and painting. These fragments are still touchstones for practicing artists. Although they derived at least in part from Cezanne himself, they fail to capture precisely how he achieved his particular way of looking, of perceiving, of realizing his elusive sensations. That remained his secret sauce, which was why, as Denis observed in 1907, the art into which he poured his personality and passion could not be copied or appropriated, since only Cezanne could make a Cezanne.[64]

Notes

1. Gustave Geffroy, 1894, quoted in Richard Shiff, "Introduction," in *Conversations with Cézanne*, edited by Michael Doran and translated by Julie Lawrence Cochran (Berkeley: University of California Press, 2001), xx.

2. Théodore Duret quoted in Shiff, "Introduction," xxiv; originally published in "Biographie," in Octave Mirbeau, *Cézanne* (Paris: Bernheim-Jeune, 1914), 23.

3. Camille Pissarro to Armand Guillaumin, Sept. 3, 1872, in Janine Bailly-Herzberg, ed., *Correspondance de Camille Pissarro: Tome 1, 1865–1885* (Paris: Presses universitaires de France, 1980), 76–77, no. 18. For Monet in a recorded conversation, see Michel Georges-Michel, *Peintres et sculpteurs que j'ai connus: 1900–1942* (New York: Brentano, 1942), 34–35.

4. Ambroise Vollard, *Paul Cézanne: Huit phototypies d'après Cézanne* (Paris: G. Crés et Cie, 1924), 29. For "peinture au pistolet" see John Rewald, *The Paintings of Paul Cézanne: A Catalogue Raisonné* (New York: Abrams, 1996), 107n35.

5. "Connaissance au café Guerbois, de Manet, et coetera Bref, l'école de Batignolles. [Edmund] Duranty, très intime, puis Zola, Césanne [*sic*], les terribles. Inauguration de la peinture, au pistolet. Quid est? Charger un pistolet de tubes et le faire partir sur une toile. Moins cela ressemble à quelque chose, plus on est proche du génie.—Refus au Salon. Lutte homérique"; Antoine Guillemet quoted in Félicien Champsaur, *Masques modernes* (Paris: Dentu, 1889), 27; see also Paul Smith, "Introduction," in Marius Roux, *The Substance and the Shadow*, edited by Paul Smith (University Park, PA: Penn State University Press, 2007), 17n18. Ironically it was Guillemet who arranged for Cezanne's portrait of his father (cat. 2) to be accepted by the Salon jury in 1882.

6. For example, see Paul Alexis, *Émile Zola: Notes d'un ami* (Paris: G. Charpentier, 1882); Edmond Duranty, "Le Peintre Louis Martin," in idem, *Le Pays des arts* (Paris: G. Charpentier, 1881), 313–50; and Marius Roux, *La Proie et l'ombre* (Paris: Dentu, 1878).

7. Théodore Duret to Émile Zola, May 30, 1870, cited in Alex Danchev, *Cézanne: A Life* (New York: Pantheon Books, 2012), 123.

8. For Karl Madsen's description of the large nude shown in 1870 and its possible identification as *La femme du Vidangeur*, which was first owned by Gauguin, see Karl Madsen, "Kunst: Impressionisterne i Kunstforeningen, II," *Politiken*, Nov. 10, 1889. On works by Cezanne owned by Paul Gauguin, see Merete Bodelsen, "Gauguin's Cézannes," *The Burlington Magazine* 104, no. 710 (May 1962): 204, 206–9, and 211.

9. "I have the honor to introduce to you your new master: M. Cezanne. Cezanne comes to us from Aix-en-Provence. He is a realist painter and what is more, a convinced one. Listen to him tell me, in his pronounced Provençal accent: 'Yes, my dear Monsieur Stock, I paint as I see, as I feel—and I have very strong sensations. The others, too, see and feel like me, but they do not dare. They produce salon paintings. Me, I dare, Monsieur Stock, I dare. I have the courage of my convictions—and he who laughs last laughs longest.'" Henri-Charles Stock, "Le Salon par Stock," in *Stock-Album*, translated in Danchev, *Cézanne: A Life*, 120.

10. Examples of such characters include Claude Lantier, the protagonist of Émile Zola's *L'Oeuvre* (1886), and Germaine Rambert, the main character of Marius Roux's 1887 novel *La Proie et l'ombre* (*The Substance and the Shadow*). For Cezanne's significance to Roux's book, see Paul Smith, "Introduction," xi–xlv.

11. For Zola's response to Duret, see Zola's letter of May 30, 1870, in his *Correspondance: Les lettres et les arts* (Paris: Bibliothèque-Charpentier, 1908), 1:72. Duret eventually met Cezanne three years later through Pissarro. See Danchev, *Cézanne: A Life*, 125.

12. See Paul Cezanne to Joris-Karl Huysmans, April 1881, and Paul Cezanne to Émile Zola, June 1881, both translated in Alex Danchev, ed. and trans., *The Letters of Paul Cézanne* (Los Angeles: J. Paul Getty Museum, 2013), 210, letter 102, and 218, letter 108.

13. See Émile Zola to Anthony Valabrègue, May 29, 1867, comparing his Parisian experience to deadening Provence in Zola, *Correspondance*, 1:49.

14. According to art historian Paul Tucker, other than Zola, no references link Monet to writers until Gustave Geffroy in the 1880s and Octave Mirbeau in the 1890s (email to the author, Feb. 21, 2021).

15. Together with Cezanne and Zola, Baille was one of the "trois inséparables," a trio of friends formed during the 1850s when they attended the same school in Aix. See also Alexis, *Émile Zola*, 60. Zola's dedication for *La Confession de Claude*—"À mes amis P. Cézanne et J.-B. Baille"—suggests that he wrote the novel with their generation in mind. See Émile Zola, *La Confession de Claude* (Paris: A. Lacroix, Verboeckhoven and Cie, 1866).

16. Roux's description stressed Cezanne's modernity rather than his rebellious temperament, calling the twenty-seven-year-old artist "one of the good students that our school in Aix provided in Paris," an "intrepid worker," and a "conscientious student" whose modesty "refuses to let him believe that what he has done is enough. . . . I'll wait for him to showcase his work. That day, I will not be the only one speaking"; quoted in Smith, "Introduction," xviin20. Right after the publication of *La Confession de Claude*, Zola made further efforts to support his artist friends in a series of articles, including an important essay on Manet; they were collected and published in 1886 as *Mon Salon*. Although Cezanne is not featured, his lengthy introduction to the book is dedicated to him and their shared idyllic boyhood; see Émile Zola, *Mon Salon* (Paris: Librairie Centrale, 1866). In *La Proie et l'ombre* Roux immortalized these encounters and recast his artist friend as the obstinate and outspoken Provençal painter Germain Rambert; see Smith, "Introduction," xi.

17. Marie Boisvert, "La bohème au salon: les représentations du salon de Nina de Villard," in *Bohème sans frontière*, edited by Pascal Brissette and Anthony Glinoer (Rennes, France: Presses universitaires, 2010), 174.

18. See Paul Alexis, *Madame Meuriot: moeurs parisiens* (Paris: G. Charpentier, 1890), 311–12; this reference is discussed in Paul Smith, "Cézanne's Primitive Self and Related Fictions," in *The Life and the Work: Art and Biography*, edited by Charles G. Salas (Los Angeles: Getty Publications, 2007), 54.

19. Colin Bailey, *Renoir's Portraits: Impressions of an Age* (New Haven, CT: Yale University Press, 1998), 161 and 296n2.

20. Merete Bodelsen, "Early Impressionist Sales 1874–94 in the Light of Some Unpublished 'Procès verbaux,'" *The Burlington Magazine* 110, no. 783 (June 1968): 344–45.

21. Georges Rivière, *Le Maître Paul Cézanne* (Paris: Librairie Floury, 1923), 34–35; and Adolphe Tabarant, *Manet et ses oeuvres*, 3rd ed. (Paris: Gallimard, 1947), 117. I am grateful to Sam Rodary for the Rivière reference.

22. "Je ne vous donne pas la maing, monsieur Manet, je ne me suis pas lavé depuis huit jours." See Marc Elder, *À Giverny, chez Claude Monet* (Giverny, France: Bernheim-Jeune, 1924), 48–49.

23. The First Impressionist Exhibition was held at the studio of photographer Gaspard-Félix Tournachon, known as Nadar, at 35, boulevard des Capucines in Paris from April 15–May 15, 1874.

24. Among his closest colleagues—Monet, Pissarro, Renoir, and Alfred Sisley—Cezanne was the only one who did not have a work accepted at the Salon of 1868.

25. The other was *House of Père Lacroix, Auvers-sur-Oise* (FWN 77). Doria exchanged *The House of the Hanged Man* for another painting by Cezanne, *Melting Snow at Fontainebleau* (FWN 145), with Victor Chocquet, Cezanne's most important non-artist collector, with whom the painting remained until 1899.

26. At Dr. Gachet's, Pissarro and Guillaumin painted the surrounding hills and also tried their hand at etching in the ad hoc printing studio in his attic. See also a related watercolor that is closer to Manet's (cat. 8). According to Wayne Andersen, Renoir's brother Edmond was in charge of the catalogue and titles and sometimes made them up; see his *Cézanne and the Eternal Feminine* (Cambridge, UK: Cambridge University Press, 2005), 7. But the title could easily have come from Cezanne himself, who admired and resented Manet for his courage and the charming personality that had lured away Zola; Andersen, *Cézanne and the Eternal Feminine*, 33.

27. Jules-Antoine Castagnary, "Exposition du boulevard des Capucines: Les

Impressionnistes," *Le Siècle*, April 29, 1874, 3; Marc de Montifaud, "Exposition du Boulevard des Capucines," *L'Artiste*, May 1, 1874, 310.

28. He even persuaded Pissarro, who was thinking of joining another exhibition cooperative, to remain loyal, since "our own affairs must come first"; Paul Cezanne to Camille Pissarro, July 2, 1876, in Danchev, *Letters*, 158, letter 57.

29. Paul Cezanne to his parents, Sept. 9, 1876, in Danchev, *Letters*, 161–62, letter 58. See also Galina Olmsted, "Caillebotte: Making and Exhibiting Modernism: Gustave Caillebotte in Paris, New York, and Brussels," PhD diss. (University of Delaware, 2019), 92–94.

30. In catalogue, as "appartient à M.C."

31. See *Catalogue de la 3e Exposition de peinture*, exh. cat. (Paris: 1877) for exhibited works by Cezanne; FWN 634 was hors catalogue, lent by Chocquet.

32. Paul Cezanne to Camille Pissarro, July 2, 1876, in Danchev, *Letters*, 156–60, letter 57.

33. See "étude" in Pierre Larousse, *Grand dictionnaire universel du XIXe siècle* (Paris: Larousse, 1866–77), 1082–85.

34. For a list of works by Cezanne owned by Caillebotte, see Appendix 1 (p. 226).

35. Richard Kendall, "Degas and Cézanne: Savagery and Refinement," in *The Private Collection of Edgar Degas*, edited by Ann Dumas, exh. cat. (New York: Metropolitan Museum of Art, 1997), 207.

36. Camille Pissarro to Gustave Caillebotte, March 1878, in Bailly-Herzberg, *Correspondance*, 109–10, letter 53. See also Bailey, *Renoir's Portraits*, 161 and 296n2.

37. Paul Cezanne to Émile Zola, March 28 [1878], in Danchev, *Letters*, 166–67, letter 64.

38. The theatrical lighting and sense of foreboding in *The Black Clock* also relates it to a group of dark and difficult paintings that Cezanne had produced while finding his footing in Zola's circle, notably *The Murder* (cat. 23), *The Strangled Woman* (FWN 636), *The Autopsy* (cat. 22), and *The Abduction* (FWN 590). The last was one of several gifted to Zola that attest to their shared fascination with *faits divers* (contemporary newspaper reports detailing everything from everyday banalities to sensational events such as murder, theft, accidents, and kidnappings), which informed Zola's stark realism as much as Cezanne's imagined scenes.

39. Émile Zola quoted in Denis Coutagne, *Cezanne and Paris* (Paris: Musée du Luxembourg, 2011), 200; originally published in "Le Naturalisme au Salon II," *Le Voltaire* (June 19, 1880).

40. Coutagne, *Cezanne and Paris*, 40–41 and 200n27.

41. See Marianne Mathieu, *Monet the Collector* (Paris: Editions Hazan, 2017), 26–69 and 164–81.

42. Whereas Gauguin purchased paintings directly from his friends Guillaumin and Pissarro, he apparently bought (or exchanged for) Cezanne paintings through a seller of artist supplies, Julien-François "Père" Tanguy; see Merete Bodelsen,

"Gauguin, the Collector," *The Burlington Magazine*, 112, no. 810 (Sept. 1970): 590–616, especially catalogue, 604–16. See also FWN 124, FWN 130, FWN 149, FWN 651, FWN 780, and the *Wife of the Sewage Drainer* (FWN 595-TA), tentatively identified as one of the two rejected paintings from the Salon of 1870 (Bodelsen, "Gauguin the Collector," 605, cat. 4).

43. See Paul Gauguin to Claude Émile Schuffenecker, early June 1888, in Victor Merlhès, ed., *Correspondance de Paul Gauguin: Documents; Témoignages, 1873–88* (Paris: Fondation Singer-Polignac, 1984), 182, no. 147.

44. See Merete Bodelsen, "Gauguin, The Collector," 606.

45. Paul Gauguin, *Ramblings of a Wannabe Painter,* edited and translated by Donatien Grau (New York: David Zwirner Gallery, 2016), 23.

46. Paul Gauguin, *Avant et après* (Paris: Les Éditions G. Crès et Cie., 1923), 48–49. For a checklist of the six works by Cezanne owned by Gauguin, see also Richard Brettell and Anne-Birgitte Fonsmark, *Gauguin and Impressionism*, exh. cat. (New Haven, CT: Yale University Press, 2005), 346, nos. 4–9.

47. Camille Pissarro in *Pissarro: Letters to His Son Lucien*, edited by John Rewald (Mamaroneck, NY: P. P. Appel, 1972), 274–76.

48. Cezanne's only public showing in Paris after 1877 was in 1882, when a portrait of his father from 1866 (cat. 2) was accepted by the Salon jury.

49. For a list of works by Cezanne owned by Pissarro, see Appendix 1 (p. 226).

50. See Shiff, "Introduction," xxii; he cites Paul Gsell, "Interview d'Octave Mirbeau par Paul Gsell," in Octave Mirbeau, *Combats esthétiques*, edited by Pierre Michel and Jean-François Nivet (Paris: Nouvelles Éditions Séguier, 1993), 2:420. Ross King has also recently recounted Monet's claim that "whenever his work was not going well, he was forced to drape his Cezannes, unable to work in the presence of such genius. 'I felt a pygmy at the foot of a giant,' he once explained"; see his *Mad Enchantment: Claude Monet and the Painting of Water Lilies* (New York: Bloomsbury Press, 2016), 49 and 207n32.

51. See Mathieu, *Monet the Collector*, 37–38.

52. Recorded by Maurice Denis, *Théories* (Paris: L. Rouart, 1920), 252.

53. See Julie Manet, *Growing Up with the Impressionists: The Diary of Julie Manet* (London: Sotheby's Publications, 1987), 76.

54. Kendall, "Degas and Cézanne," 198.

55. Kendall, "Degas and Cézanne," 215.

56. As visitors to his various residences have mentioned, Cezanne was thoroughly engaged in the process of making art but less in the finished product and seems to have had little interest in inserting his or anyone else's work into neatly arranged domestic settings. See Émile Bernard, "Memories of Paul Cézanne," in Doran, *Conversations*, 50–79, especially "Life Together in the Studio and at Home," 61–66; and Joaquin Gasquet, "Excerpt from *Cézanne*," in Doran, *Conversations*, 108–60, especially "The Studio," 149–60.

57. For a reference to Cezanne's "multi-generational appeal," see Thadée Natanson, "Paul Cézanne [exhibition review]," *La Revue Blanche* (Dec. 1895): 500. For "how important you are to us," see Maurice Denis to Paul Cezanne, June 13, 1901, in *Paul Cézanne: Correspondance*, edited by John Rewald (Paris: Bernard Grasset, 1978), 275; and in *Classic Cézanne*, edited by Terence Maloon, exh. cat. (Sydney: Art Gallery of New South Wales, 1998), 173.

58. In 1896 Gauguin wrote from Tahiti to his Paris dealer Georges Chaudet, instructing him to sell the painting so that he could pay his mounting medical bills; see Douglas Druick, "Vollard and Gauguin: Fictions and Facts," in *From Cézanne to Picasso: Ambroise Vollard and the Avant-Garde*, edited by Rebecca A. Rabinow, exh. cat. (New York: Metropolitan Museum of Art, 2008), 66–68.

59. Maurice Denis quoted in Shiff, "Introduction," xx; originally published in "L'aventure posthume de Cezanne," *Prométhée* 6 (July 1939): 194.

60. During Cezanne's lifetime, Durand-Ruel did not show the artist's work in any of his Paris, New York, or London galleries, which were important sites of discovery for the American collectors who made up much of the Impressionist market beginning in the late 1880s.

61. Redon himself had bought from Vollard an ambitious portrait by Cezanne of an unknown man in an interior (cat. 118); he wrote in 1901 that "You also know prices have risen for paintings by Cezanne and Renoir. In sum everything that's beautiful ultimately makes a place for itself"; Odilon Redon to Andries Bonger, April 19, 1901, cited in Gloria Groom, "Vollard, The Nabis, and Odillon Redon," in Rabinow, *From Cézanne to Picasso*, 98n48.

62. Among the artists surveyed, those that owned work by Cezanne included Maurice Denis, Charles Guérin, Georges Rouault, Claude Émile Schuffenecker, Paul Sérusier, and Paul Signac.

63. Charles Morice's article was published in three parts: "Enquête," *Mercure de France*, Aug. 1, 1905, 346–59; Aug. 15, 1905, 538–55; and Sept. 1, 1905, 61–85. Selections were translated into English; see Françoise Cachin et al., *Cézanne*, exh. cat. (Philadelphia: Philadelphia Museum of Art, 1996), 42–43.

64. Denis wrote, "the appropriator takes a little of the best away with him but lacks the personality and passion to make the marks"; quoted in Richard Shiff, "Sensation, Movement, Cézanne," in Maloon, *Classic Cézanne*, 26; originally published in "Cézanne," *L'Occident*, no. 70 (Sept. 1907): 133. See also George Lecomte's observation in 1910 that it was "estimated that current Paris exhibitions contained at least 200 painters trying to pastiche Cezanne, slavishly, tediously"; quoted in Shiff, "Sensation, Movement, Cézanne," 26; originally published "La crise de la peinture française," *L'Art et les artistes* 12 (Oct. 1910): 27–28.

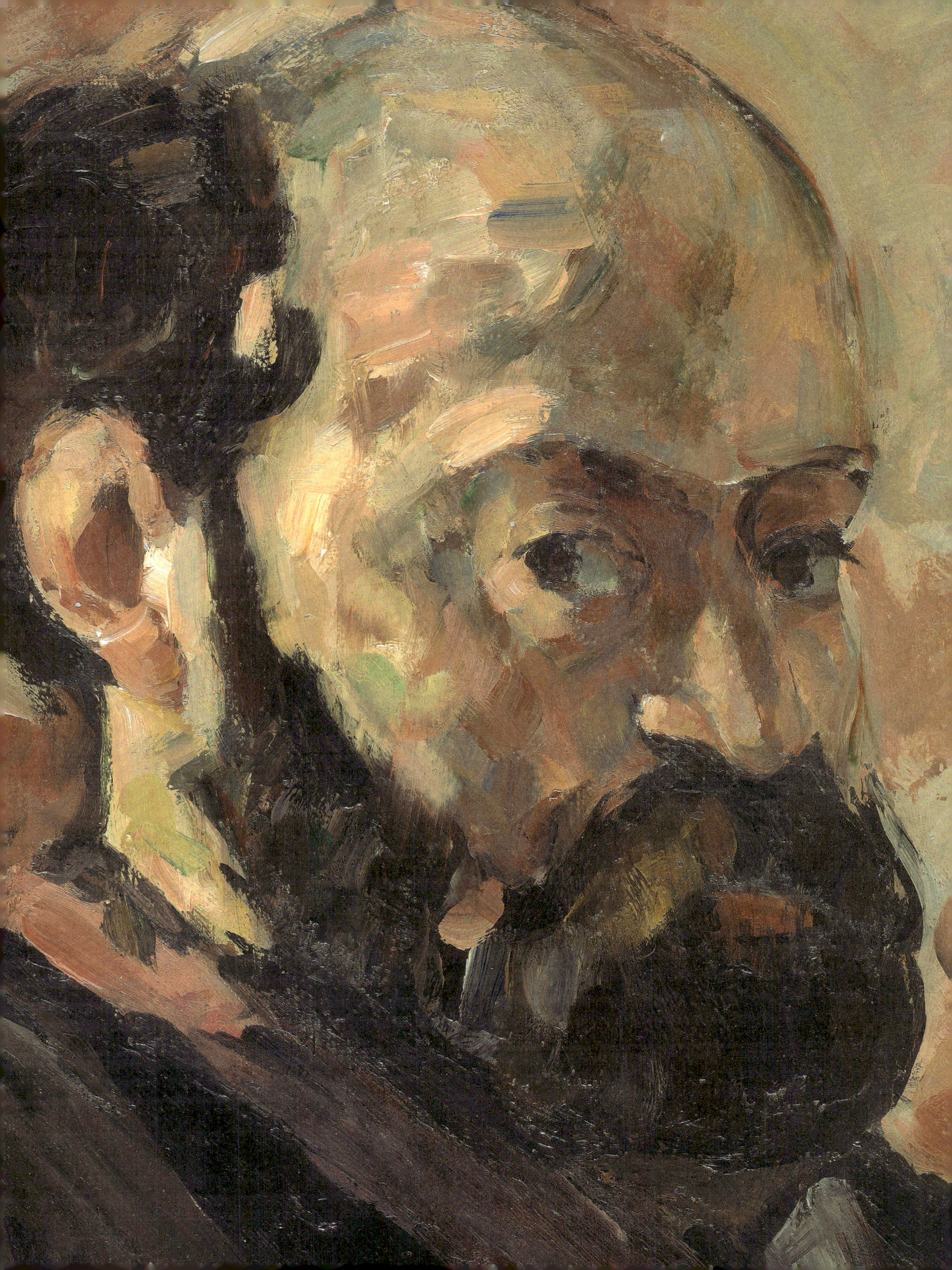

Cezanne's Refusal

Caitlin Haskell

Fourteen times in John Rewald's foundational volume *The History of Impressionism*, we read of Paul Cezanne's "refusal," in the sense of his paintings' exclusion from the annual Salon in Paris.[1] For the artist, this amounted to receiving a rejection roughly twice every three years between the ages of twenty-five and forty-seven, when he finally stopped submitting works for consideration in official exhibitions. Yet this more-or-less continuous dismissal by academic juries was just one of several factors that helped establish Cezanne's standing as one of his era's most rigorously committed nonconformists.

Refusés such as Cezanne and his generational peers, including Édouard Manet and Camille Pissarro, produced artworks that, at their core, sought to foster a type of subject-centered experience for both maker and viewer that state-sponsored channels of culture were reluctant to support. Reasserting the primacy of feeling and personal agency in their paintings, as opposed to rote adherence to an agreed-upon set of conventions, these artists helped develop a mode of modern painting that was itself a critical tool applied to the medium. They interrogated and laid open fundamental aspects of picture making—color, facture, finish, resolution, subject matter, cropping, compositional structure, and still others—to a degree that painting itself became a critical pursuit

simultaneous with its creative and aesthetic ends. Of course, critics continued writing, too. But "making a painting" became a questioning and analytical activity to such an unprecedented extent that it changed key aspects of creating and consuming art. Indeed, the notion of "refusal," meaning an artist registering a principled dissent from the status quo of their discipline, can be understood as a chosen stance during the formative years of Cezanne's career in the 1860s, '70s, and after, rather than merely an assigned position. In this sense, refusal might be regarded as a late nineteenth-century artistic development as notable as concurrent breakthroughs in the realms of technique, palette, and socially engaged content so hard-won by artists remembered today for being among "the refused."

My inclination to approach Cezanne's paintings by way of a negative definition admittedly is not new. In fact, the desire to codify his artistry and his radicalness as the products of some essential negation has been apparent for a more than a century, at least since the time of Cezanne's first posthumous retrospective in Paris in the fall of 1907, an exhibition of about fifty oil paintings and seven watercolors dating from the 1860s to 1906.[2] As the painter and critic Maurice Denis wrote then: "Cezanne's is precisely this essential art which is so difficult for the critic to define and whose realization seems impossible. . . . His efforts are negative, if you will, but they bear witness to an unheard-of instinct for painting."[3]

The aspects of Cezanne's art that most readily supported Denis's assertion of impossibility or indefinability—aspects most profitably discussed in terms of what Cezanne did *not* do—include factors with which art historians still struggle today. For example, among both the oil paintings and the watercolors in the 1907 exhibition, there was an astonishing range in the levels of finish, including seemingly incomplete works, unlike those typically presented in an exhibition, then or now. Collectively they imparted a sense of seeing a composition in an artist's studio or personal storage, where a work is still coming into being or perhaps halted in the creative process, as in the cases of *Large Bathers* (fig. 1) and *Montagne Saint-Victoire (The Arc Valley)* (c. 1885; cat. 111) respectively, both of which were included in the show.[4] The 1907 exhibition also featured a broad range of styles, reflecting forty years of testing varying technical approaches on equally diverse subjects: indoor and outdoor, imagined and observed, based on daily life and drawn from the painter's self-directed study of art. The checklist reveals an artist comfortable with inconsistency, at home with difficulty, and determined to both challenge and participate in long traditions of art (i.e., his engagement with biblical scenes and mythological subjects) as well as the visual culture of his own time—Impressionist, Symbolist, photographic, and popular.

Denis nonetheless identified through lines: for one, Cezanne's resolve to work, regardless of external recognition, as well as his commitment to questioning the norms of painting to the point that his works were considered "bad"—that is, technically inept or unrewarding in their difficulty for viewers.[5] Denis also conveyed Cezanne's immense appeal to fellow artists young and old, including some of those exhibiting at the Salon d'Automne of 1907, such as Georges Braque, Émilie Charmy, Robert Delaunay, Henri Matisse, and Gabriele Münter, to name just a few, who would go on to become committed advocates for Cezanne's achievements and the potential they held for a new generation of painters.[6] In making this point about Cezanne as an artist more consistent in the norms he questioned than in what he adhered to as a painter, Denis confided to his reader the private reaction of another artist, who had been observing Cezanne's work for more than thirty years and whose collectors had begun acquiring Cezannes too: "One day Renoir said to me, 'How does he do it?'"[7] The answer would seem to be a matter of conferring agency where it is due and recentering the material sites where Cezanne's critical engagement with painting occurred. Depending on your position, his activities on the levels of surface facture, subject selection,

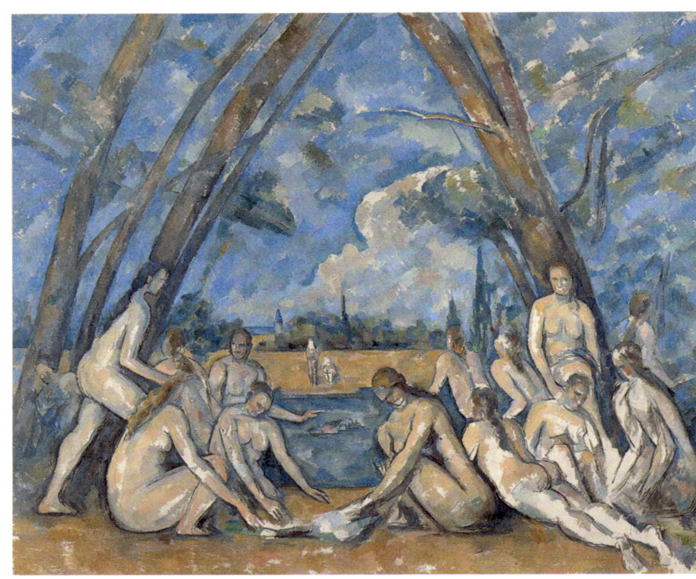

Fig. 1

Paul Cezanne (French, 1839–1906). *Large Bathers* (Grandes baigneuses), 1906. Oil on canvas; 210.5 × 250.8 cm (82 ⅞ × 98 ¾ in.). Philadelphia Museum of Art, purchased with the W. P. Wilach Fund, 1937, W1937-1-1. (FWN 981)

and compositional construction advanced one mistake at a time—or, if you prefer, one refusal after another.

Constructive Criticism

Reviews and commentaries on Cezanne's work published throughout his lifetime and into the early decades of the twentieth century show that his critique of painting via painting could appear wise—insightful and potentially generative on a broader scale—or could be perceived as unknowing and clumsy—in the parlance of the time, "naïve." In his writings on Cezanne over the past fifteen years, art historian Richard Shiff has drawn analogies between the reception of Cezanne's works and those of an earlier generation of landscape painters who were similarly lauded for what they did wrong in the eyes of more sophisticated (or more fully indoctrinated) audiences. A backhanded compliment of the time, "their incapacity is not without a strange seductiveness," in fact confirmed that these awkwardly composed works held the promise of a new way forward for painting via a purge of tradition.[8] By addressing with greater precision the conventions and niceties of art making that these artists stripped from their works, we shift the diminishment of artifice into positive terms and transfer authority from critical beholder to the painting's differently critical author.

In the case of Cezanne, it is particularly instructive to identify where his refusals lie and to attempt to concretize those qualities that most fully transgressed the stated and implicit expectations of artworks in his time. My emphasis in this essay will be on three areas in particular, two of them having to do with composition and motif, and the third concerning mark making, or the novelty of Cezanne's technique vis-à-vis representation. Cezanne's ruptures with tradition in these areas, whether deliberate or apparently unintentional, occurred in daily acts of painting and drawing that continue to attract and hold our attention with their brazenness, ingenuity, and even humor, as the artist moved within and across different modes of signification.[9] The cumulative effect of such statements may be the impression that Cezanne made his refusals in all directions. While these aspects of Cezanne's work are rarely considered together, each has been central to writing and exhibitions on the artist over the past decade and will structure my observations in the paragraphs that follow. With reference to composition, construction, and orientation, the findings by Fabienne Ruppen and by the team assembled by Jodi Hauptman and Samantha Friedman to produce *Cézanne Drawing* (2021) have offered new insights into the artist's deeply unconventional approach to making images in a composite manner. In the realm of composition, recent observations by T. J. Clark and Shiff have shifted our understanding of *what* Cezanne was painting (the nominal subject of the work) and helped to differentiate it from what he was painting *after* (the object of representation), where preexisting pictures regularly serve this role. Finally, remarks by Walter Feilchenfeldt, making use of the early criticism of German historian Julius Meier-Graefe, shed light on Cezanne's refusals having to do with mark making and pictorial resolution. Each of these topics touches on patterns visible across Cezanne's career. At the same time, they suggest that some of Cezanne's most revolutionary gestures need not have been especially public events. Some of his most profound dismissals of convention seem first to have been directed at an audience of one.

Internal Contradictions

A page in one of Cezanne's sketchbooks from the early 1880s (fig. 2) stands out, due to its simultaneous horizontal and vertical orientation, as a clear, if relatively innocuous, example of nonconformism. Here is an artist being resourceful—perhaps simply repurposing an untouched area of the sheet to make a second drawing. Blending and reversing "portrait" and "landscape" formats, however, it demonstrates Cezanne's confidence that viewers of this drawing, perhaps only himself at first, could hold in mind several discordant ideas while looking at the picture, with multiple systems generating what we might colloquially call "internal contradictions." Orientation and genre as well as scale work concurrently, yet independently, within the unifying frame of the single page. Although we can choose to read them separately, to willfully resist their mutual interference, the two subjects also share certain lines in common, with the edge of an arm or the contour of a cheek doubling as delineations in the landscape.[10]

If we are unbothered by the palimpsest-like quality of a sketchbook page, its explanation takes on special urgency when we observe the same mode of compositional reorientation and overlap operating in Cezanne's paintings, such as the deeply ambiguous *Nude Woman*

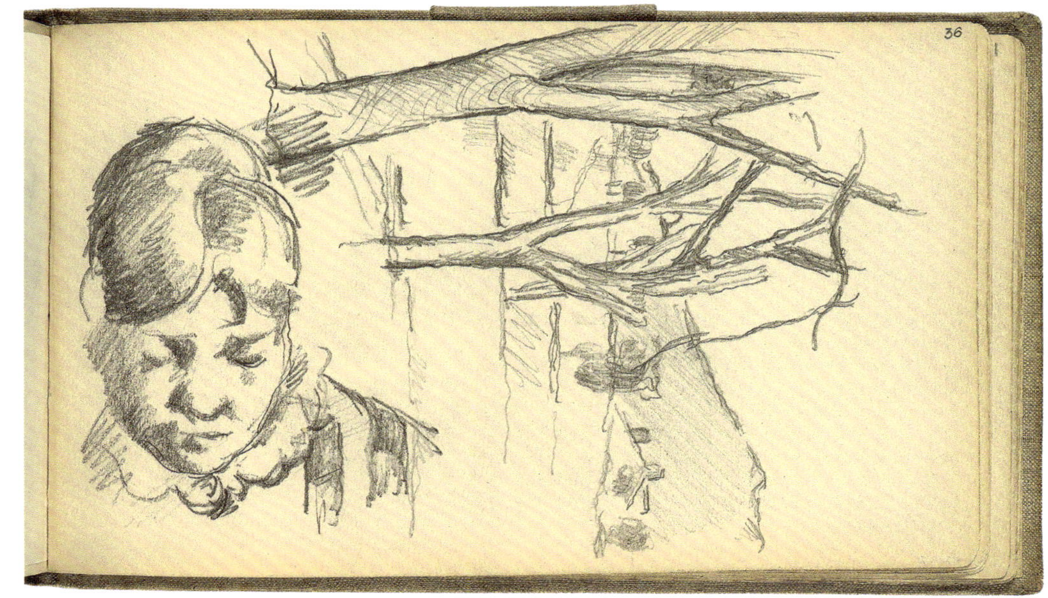

Fig. 2

Paul Cezanne. *Landscape with Bare Trees; Portrait of Madame Cezanne* (p. 36 from *Sketchbook New York*), 1880–85. Graphite on wove paper; 12.6 × 21.7 cm (4 15/16 × 8 9/16 in.). The Morgan Library & Museum, New York, given in honor of the 75th anniversary of the Morgan Library and the 50th anniversary of the Association of Fellows, 1999.9. (FWN 3009-36a; see cat. 42)

(Leda?) (1885–87; cat. 54). Here a nude female figure (likely based on a pictorial source) and a fragment of a still life (potentially rendered from life) confront each other on the canvas as inverted vignettes. Their proximity within a single pictorial field asserts Cezanne's confidence that viewers (again, perhaps only himself at first) could contend with markedly different levels of finish and with disjuncture in scale—between a piece of fruit and a human body or between a tablecloth and a room-sized curtain—when they are both part of one picture. X-radiographs show that the still-life fragment and the larger figural portion were once physically separated from each other with cuts at precise 90-degree angles and were later reunited to reestablish the original compositional relationship (see fig. 3). As the excision seems to have been made after Cezanne stopped working on the canvas, it may be evidence of an overturning of convention too strong for some viewers.[11] Through the recent work of Kiko Aebi and Ruppen, respectively, we are also now able to envision canvases and sheets of watercolor paper as Cezanne saw them—physically contiguous but with discontinuous scenes and subjects—including *Still Life with Apples* alongside *Glass and Apples* (fig. 4) or the watercolors *La Montagne Sainte-Victoire* (1885–87; FWN 1167) and *Provençal Countryside (Near Gardanne?)* (c. 1885; FWN 1155).[12]

The subject and posture of the figure in *Nude Woman (Leda?)* also bring to mind the composition of Cezanne's *The Eternal Feminine*, which exists in two similar versions, both painted roughly a decade earlier (cats. 12 and 13). This image has not been physically rotated in either version; nonetheless, it presents a deeply heterogeneous scene, collapsing and expanding spatiotemporal realms. Alluding to art and artists of the past self-referentially—with a rendering of a painter, possibly Eugène Delacroix, at an easel, and a central spectator resembling himself, seen from behind—the work quite literally posits Cezanne as both painter and observer.[13] In future works the artist did not go so far as to include himself pictorially, but he did continue to cast himself as a spectator of his works as well as a maker—an experienced viewer of paintings who joins us in observing his picture coming into view. Even on the level of brushwork, Cezanne perceived and relied upon his viewers' ability to understand that constituent parts of a painting can share an identity in certain aspects (such as hue) but depart from each other and retain specificity and distinction in others (where hue may signify the local color and/or the optical effect of objects at several locations that jointly hold the same area of canvas—see, for examples, cats. 110 and 111). Conversely, adjacent areas of canvas may refer to aspects of objects not indicated in neighboring ones, as in the highly descriptive textures of oranges (but not apples) in *The*

Basket of Apples (c. 1893; cat. 56) or the rippling waves in selected passages of *Bay of Marseille, Seen from L'Estaque* (c. 1885; cat. 79). These collage-like tendencies—which operate on the level of both iconic and indexical signs—are revelatory with regard to how Cezanne approached representation, where discrete components of pictures had the potential to (and often do) assert themselves on at least two registers. At the same time, we as viewers recognize this as abnormal primarily because it *only* signifies on one or two levels simultaneously (for example, color and direction) and not on more, failing in the kind of painterly illusionism where a single stroke communicates even more varieties of information, but with optical smoothness and on a smaller scale that does not draw attention to itself as a sign.

This treatment of the brushstroke as a discrete, constituent mark was among the factors that led Pissarro to comment in 1873 that Cezanne's studies were "seen in a unique way."[14] As in life, multiple elements in a painting by Cezanne signified multiply, and they did so across frames of reference that earlier styles of painting had elided into a single entity. Forgoing written theories or reliable first-person statements, Cezanne used his compositions to articulate his position as an artist observing in patchwork—color here, texture there, volume described in a third area—and bringing these elements back together in an insistently composite image.

Open Source

Given the characterization of Cezanne as a resolutely solitary and original thinker and seer, it may come as something of a surprise when we encounter evidence that he worked after preexisting images. Over the past decade several scholars have drawn attention to aspects of Cezanne's work that frame him as an appropriative artist—a painter content to adopt a given structure and innovate in relation to it. As alert while looking at pictures as he was while making them, Cezanne regarded these activities in tandem, somewhat like the artist showing us his back in *The Eternal Feminine*. Additionally, he regularly used images from diverse sources—from Caravaggio, El Greco, and Peter Paul Rubens to popular imagery, photographs, and Impressionist paintings—to jumpstart his picture making. Cezanne's own works were equally subject to quotation and repetition, such as the early still-life painting with a sugar bowl (cat. 1) that appears in the background of Cezanne's portrait of his father (cat. 2). The notion of the artist as a type of appropriator, using images that were already part of visual culture, may seem to run against the prevailing reputation he has enjoyed as an innovator, but his self-education working after

Fig. 3

Annotated image of Paul Cezanne's *Nude Woman (Leda?)*, 1885–87 (cat. 54; FWN 661), showing the area that had been cut out of the still life.

Fig. 4

Composite image from *Cezanne Drawing* (New York: Museum of Modern Art, 2021), 199, fig. C.
Left: Cezanne's *Glass and Apples,* 1879–80. Oil on canvas; 31.5 × 40 cm (12 ⅜ × 15 ¹¹⁄₁₆ in.). Rudolf Staechelin, Basel, Switzerland. (FWN 779)
Right: Cezanne's *Still Life with Apples* (rotated 180 degrees), c. 1878. Oil on canvas; 19 × 26.7 cm (7 ½ × 10 ½ in.). Currently on long term loan from King's College, University of Cambridge, UK, to The Syndics of the Fitzwilliam Museum, University of Cambridge. (cat. 3; FWN 760)

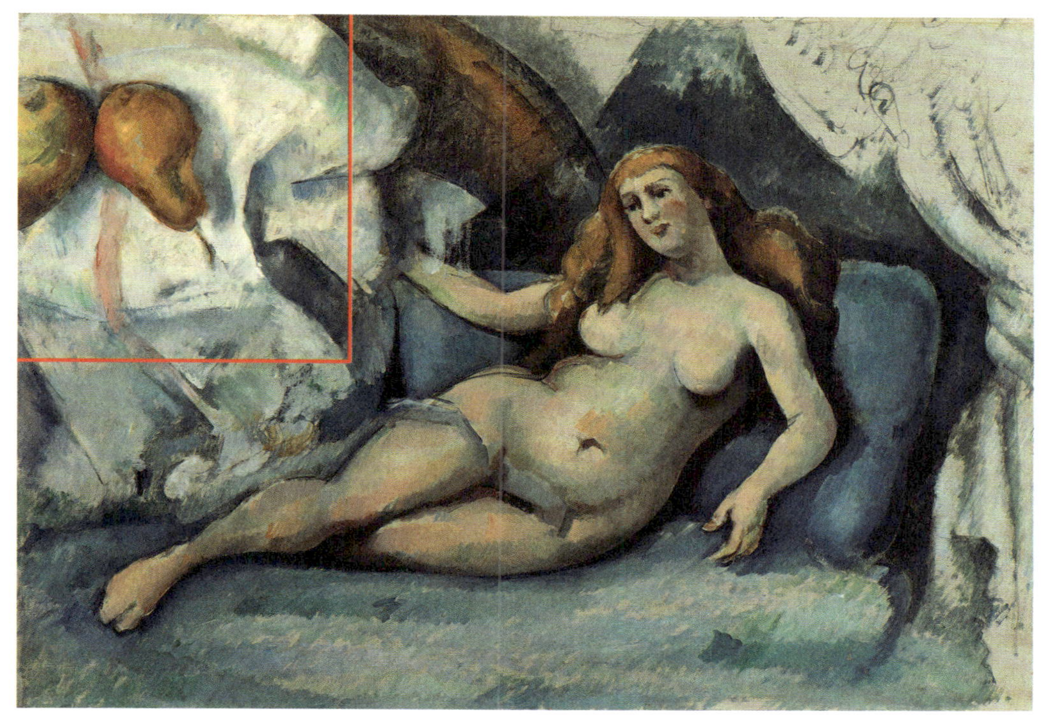

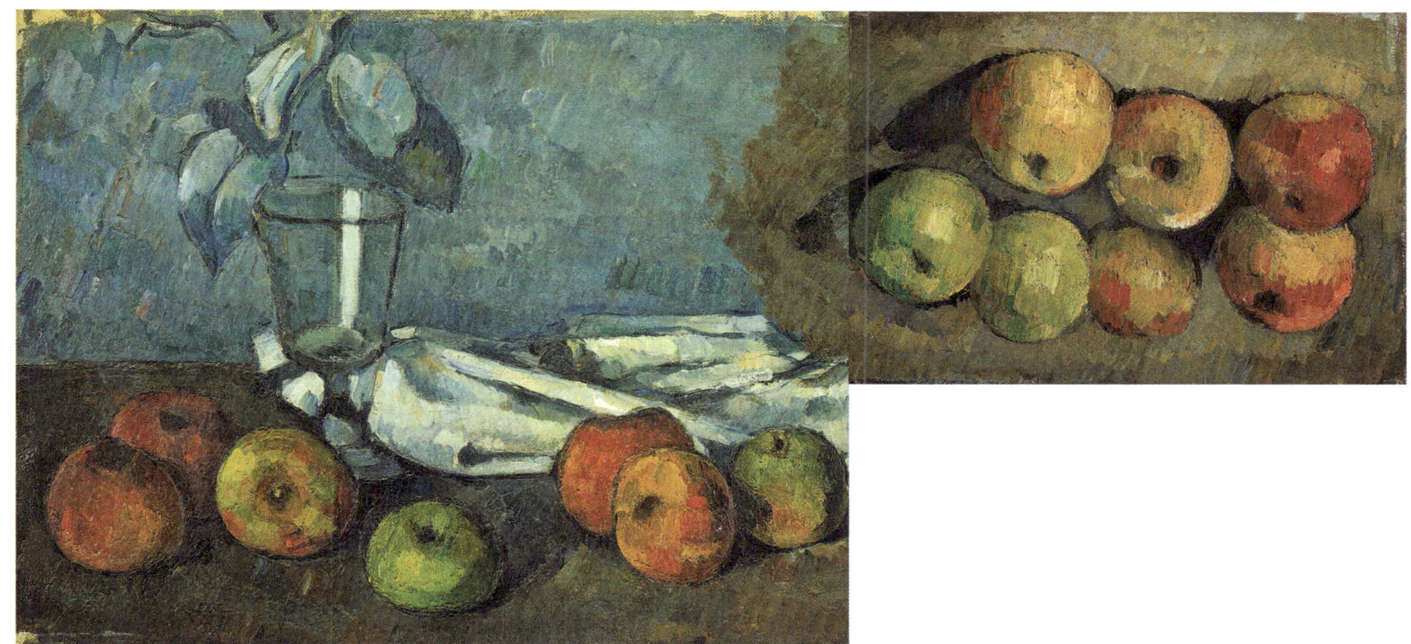

pictures allowed him to develop a type of painting practice that was equally about looking and about making, as coordinated activities. At the same time, it offers us a sense of Cezanne's conception of what a painter could offer on the register of the new.

While recounting the artists' trips to the countryside in the Île-de-France in the early 1870s, T. J. Clark memorably described Cezanne as "Pissarro's best viewer" and also his "strange apprentice."[15] Clark's accounts, which are based on recollections by Pissarro's son Lucien, bring to mind Honoré Daumier's caricature "Les Paysagistes" (fig. 5). This image is doubly useful for our investigation of Cezanne's means. First, it offers a reminder that over the course of his lifetime and his posthumous history, Cezanne has sat in both the first and second easel positions, copying other artists and in turn being copied (strictly and loosely) by followers from Paul Gauguin to Marsden Hartley.[16] Second, the image also reflects the practical reality of the plein-air painter, who relies on existing landscape images to shape their conception of "landscape" composition as much as they use the light and atmospheric conditions of a day spent outdoors as the immediate object of representation.[17] By allowing another artist to select what was depicted, including the subject and arrangement of the composition, Cezanne could then focus a critical eye on *how* it was painted, rendering the scene in a manner that accommodated the forcefulness of his sensations.

Looking closely at Cezanne's paintings based on a range of pictorial models allows us to see what a singularly insightful viewer and, at the same time, what a strange copyist he was. Such comparisons reveal what the artist selected from others and chose to retain in his compositions (copying properly, as it were), and also where he performed "poorly" as a copyist, intentionally breaking down and teasing apart signifying aspects of the visual codes of the original and inventing something distinctly his own. Indeed, in a given picture we may be able to put our finger on the element that Cezanne chose to emphasize or elaborate in an outsized way, although the precise feature can vary drastically from painting to painting, passage to passage. Clark, for example, drew attention to Pissarro's and Cezanne's respective landscapes of Louveciennes (p. 18, figs. 1–2), suggesting that Cezanne was eliminating nuance from Impressionism as he was learning the basics of an indexical mark as well as shifting toward a brighter palette. As is well known, Impressionists such as Pissarro produced works with new optical immediacy by depending on hue and reducing the roles played by light and dark values to model forms in their landscapes. But Cezanne went further still, using larger strokes to cover with one mark passages that Pissarro depicted with several. The lower left corner of

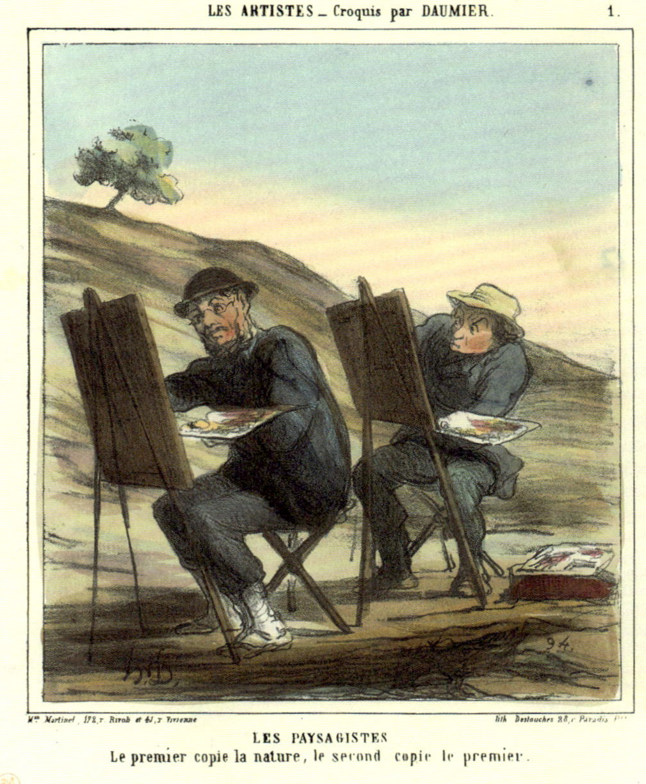

Fig. 5

Honoré-Victorin Daumier (French, 1808–1878). "Les Paysagistes: Le premier copie la nature," 1865.

Cezanne's composition shows the extent to which he was willing to both generalize and condense visual information, essentializing Pissarro's already compact marks into fewer, larger data points to impart color and direction as forcefully as possible—the painterly equivalent of writing prose as a series of one-word sentences with every letter capitalized.

These same emphases, especially the heaviness of mark, come through as well in Cezanne's work after Armand Guillaumin (fig. 7) in which the reflection of a ship's mast on the water appears nearly as solid and reified as the mast itself, and the blunt transition of color in the clouds does not allow for any sense of depth but rather pushes the cloud bank forward, imparting the character of a solid object rather than a transparent optical phenomenon. Unlike Guillaumin's glimpse of the sky above the Seine (see fig. 6), which delights with softly rendered passages that might permit a suspension of disbelief, there is no mistaking Cezanne's sky for anything other than a painted picture. Its truth is that of a made thing, built up by hand, in coordination with the visual sensations Cezanne experienced while viewing Guillaumin's picture, also built up by hand. Put another way, the difference between the two paintings results from Cezanne's attention to the material fact rather than the optical fiction.

Making a landscape after a landscape expanded the ways in which Cezanne could create work as an Impressionist, refusing aspects of its site-specific novelty and making it resemble an indoor pursuit. Several scholars have noted that a painting by Cezanne after a painting by Cezanne—made in the same medium—will have a more even facture, as in the two nearly compositionally identical versions of Madame Cezanne wearing a red dress (figs. 8–9).[18] The smoothness and even transitions of the sitter's face in the Chicago composition (fig. 9), as well as the more continuous depiction of upholstery, lead scholars to believe that it may have been "worked on entirely in the studio, without the presence of the model."[19] "Model," in this sense, however, is used as a synonym for "sitter," when Cezanne's model was by all accounts the Beyeler painting (fig. 8), a source he depended upon perhaps to the point of tracing its contours onto the second composition.[20] The refusal worth noting is not his substitution of a picture for a person while making her portrait (a convention as old as portraiture itself), but rather Cezanne's decision to retain signs that communicate a mixture of immediacy, uncertainty, confidence, and hesitancy while creating a copy with a fixed source.

When Cezanne was working across media, the visual effects of temporal priority tend to be less easily articulated. Late large-scale watercolors such as *The Three Skulls* (1902–6; cat. 141) were developed as works with dimensions and compositions nearly identical to those of their related oil paintings, such as *Three Skulls on a Patterned Carpet* (1904; cat. 140). Despite one being rendered in thick impasto and the other in luminous transparent washes, the sequencing within this pairing has been nearly impossible to determine.[21] However, a possible exception can be found in the watercolor and oil versions of *Man Wearing a Straw Hat* (1905–6), where a surprising repetition suggests a possible relationship between the two images. In the branches behind the seated man's left shoulder in the oil painting (cat. 135), a patch of brilliant blue appears, brighter than the surrounding green foliage. Although Cezanne cropped the

Fig. 6

Armand Guillaumin (French, 1841–1927). *The Seine at Bercy*, 1867–68. Oil on canvas; 56.1 × 72.4 cm (22 1/16 × 28 1/2 in.). Hamburger Kunsthalle, acquired with funds from the Campe'schen Historischen Kunststiftung, 1983, inv. nr. HK-5321.

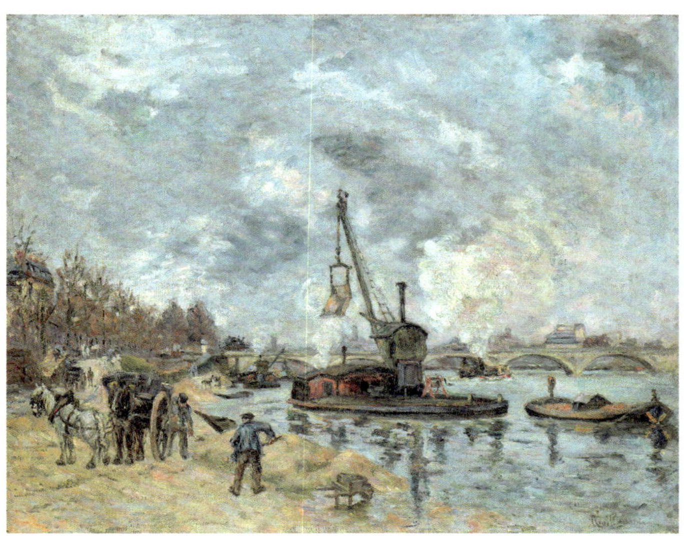

Fig. 7

Paul Cezanne. *The Seine at the Bay of Austerlitz, After Guillaumin*, 1876–78. Oil on canvas; 59 × 72 cm (23 3/16 × 28 5/16 in.). Hamburger Kunsthalle, acquired 1924, inv. nr. HK-2374. (FWN 104)

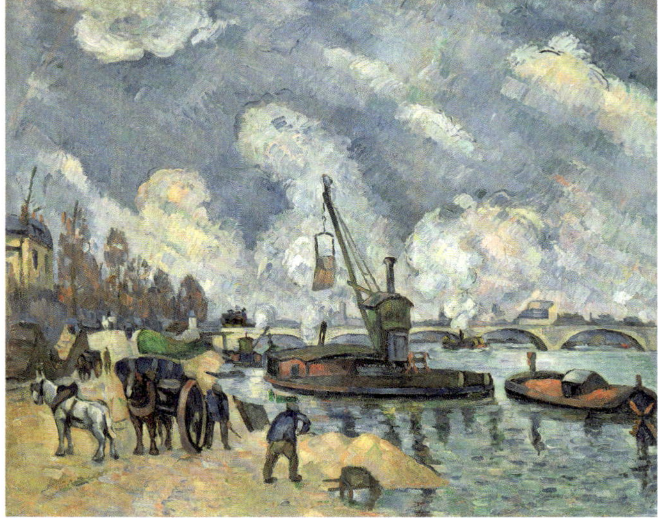

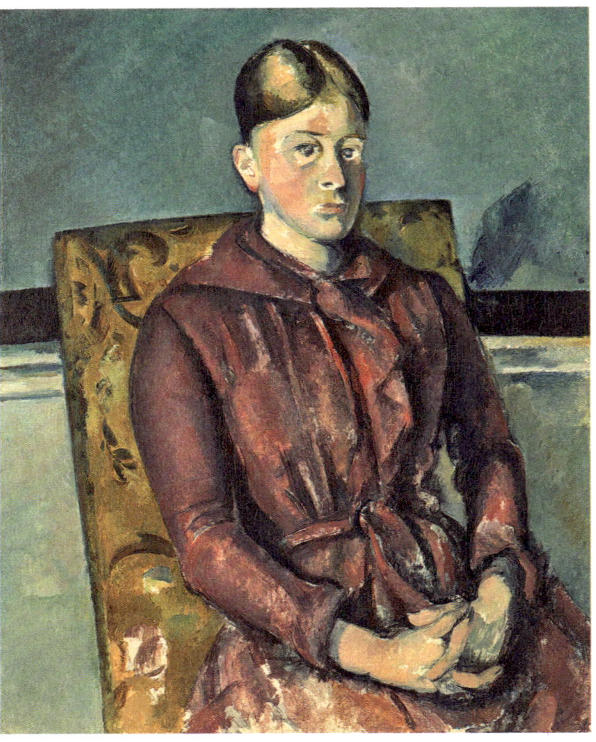

Fig. 8

Paul Cezanne. *Madame Cezanne in a Red Dress*, 1888–90. Oil on canvas; 81 × 65 cm (31⅞ × 25 ⅝ in.). Fondation Beyeler, Riehen/Basel, Sammlung Beyeler, inv. 97.11. (FWN 490)

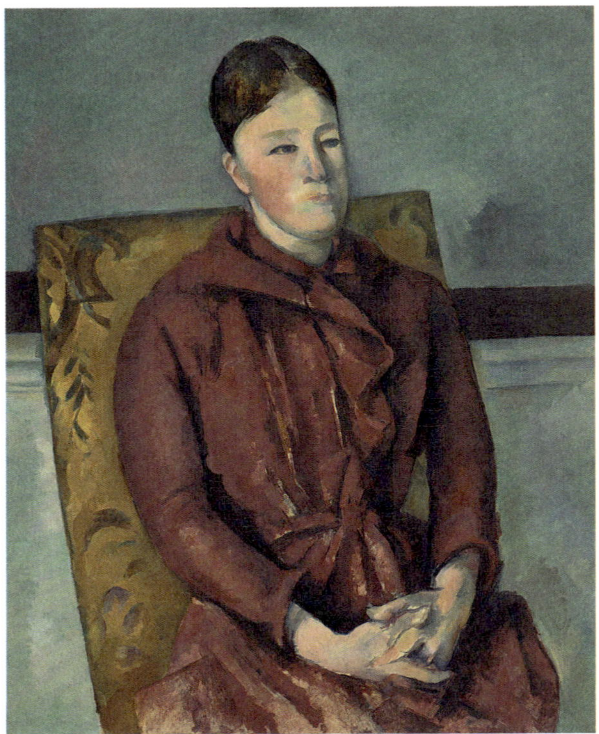

Fig. 9

Paul Cezanne. *Madame Cezanne in a Yellow Chair*, 1888–90. Oil on canvas; 80.9 × 64.9 cm (31⅞ × 25 ⁹⁄₁₆ in.). The Art Institute of Chicago, Wilson L. Mead Fund, 1948.54. (cat. 36; FWN 492)

composition of this sitter differently in the watercolor (cat. 134), this circular passage, which potentially reads as an inadvertent artifact of its making, maintains the same circular structure and position relative to the branch in the oil painting. Close observation of the watercolor shows that strokes in blue and green preserve the circular form, which appears as a reserve of the unpainted sheet.[22] Despite the prevailing uncertain priority of oil and watercolor compositions in similar pairings that Cezanne also made in his final years in his studio at Les Lauves, these two-part examples inform our understanding of him as an artist who continued to teach himself about the properties of pictures by working compositions through different media and observing their specificities and differences as images.

Understanding this tendency in his practice helps us grasp as well why Cezanne may have been attracted to working after photographs.[23] In practical terms the photographic source, functioning much like a painting by Pissarro or Guillaumin, provided an armature, an expedient structure, to which Cezanne applied his sensation. Mechanical and indexical, like the photograph, but enlivened with color, the painting retains the photograph's internal sense of scale but acquires his subjective treatment of hue and facture. Cezanne's works after photographs, such as the winter landscape acquired by Claude Monet in 1899 (see figs. 10 and 11), show that he was open to accepting a compositional structure or pictorial element if it would allow for increased experimentation with regard to his means of execution or technique. These and similar instances show that, for Cezanne, a picture was a thing in the world and could—like a sitter, a skull, or a mountain—function as a model too, perhaps even more effectively than the original object.

Strengths and Weaknesses

Cezanne's resistance to the refinements of painting and his related inability to practice modes of painting "of which he was not the [sole] creator," to paraphrase Denis, took place above all in the processes of making and remain most evident in his technique.[24] This personal language of resistance, developed over decades, is especially evident in late paintings, such as *Mont Sainte-Victoire Seen from Les Lauves* (1904–6; cat. 124). The surface of the picture reads as a coordinated sequence of oversized touches, yet its germs are apparent in the artist's very earliest Impressionist works, such as *Auvers, Panoramic View* (1873–75; cat. 27). Although the marks are smaller here than in the Basel painting and the resolution somewhat tighter than is typical of his later works, the operative principles are in place. Indeed, it was only a few years after 1870—the moment when the name Cezanne became associated with strong sensations—that his works began to manifest a pronounced connection between eye and hand, visual perception and touch, as well as a tacit invitation for viewers to think along with the artist about how a given painting would come together as an image: on the canvas, as in the process of viewing.[25]

As often happens in periods of rapid and radical discovery, Cezanne's material innovation moved faster than intellectual explanation, leading to situations where even admiring critics were at a loss to describe precisely what they were seeing in his work. Writing of Cezanne's paintings in 1905, Julius Meier-Graefe voiced the still-resonant observation that "[t]here is an enlargement and we cannot rightly say what is enlarged."[26] This "enlargement" seems to have applied to each painting in its totality, but it had to do, as well, with the size and clarity of Cezanne's brushstrokes. Counterintuitively, perhaps, the artist's desire to strip away what was not essential in painting led him to develop a stroke that was markedly oversized for the canvases on which he worked.[27] His tandem, and seemingly contradictory, desires to distill and magnify, essentialize and then expand, led to a paradoxical experience for the viewer, which had been building in painting since the 1860s, when artists made a deliberate shift toward painting scenes with a lesser degree of optical resolution. Even if the motivation for the perceived enlargement or the choice of which element to magnify was not immediately apparent to him, the disorienting effect had already been noticed by the critic Charles Blanc, who observed in the wake of the 1866 Salon, "The artist who paints with broad strokes within a small format contradicts himself dramatically because even as the small scale of the frame invites me to come near, the largeness of the execution holds me at a distance."[28]

Although Meier-Graefe surely had Cezanne's marks in mind when he referred to "enlargement," his

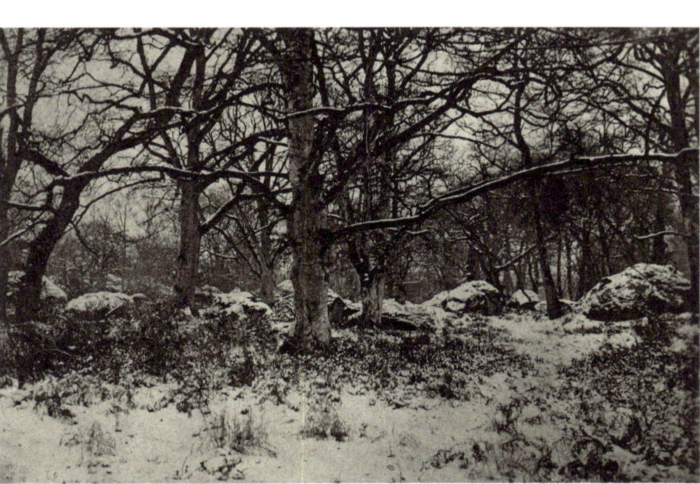

Fig. 10

Possibly Eugène Cuvelier (French, 1837–1900). Untitled [forest at Fontainebleau], c. 1860–75. Photograph; 12.2 x 17.4 cm (4 13/16 x 6 7/8 in.). John Rewald Archive, Department of Image Collections, National Gallery of Art, Washington, DC. This photograph was found by John Rewald among Cezanne's papers.

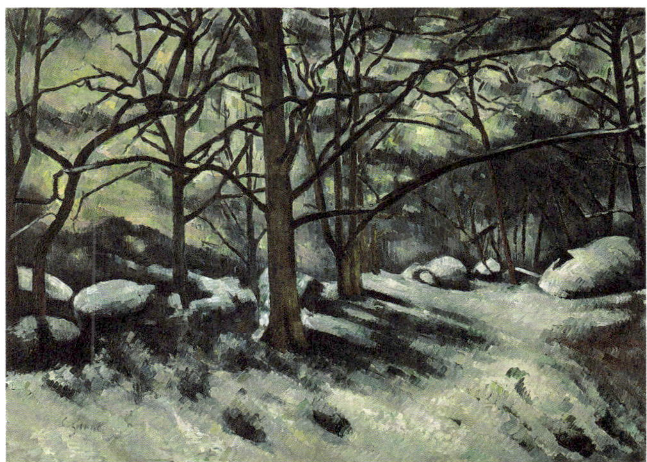

Fig. 11

Paul Cezanne. *Melting Snow at Fontainebleau*, 1879–80. Oil on canvas; 73.7 × 100.7 cm (29 × 39 5/8 in.). The Museum of Modern Art, New York, gift of Mr. and Mrs. André Meyer, 373.61. (FWN 145)

observation holds on another level as well. As the artist placed excessive demands on each patch of color, asking it to signify in multiple ways, he confused and blended codes of signification by forcing them to converge simultaneously on a reduced number of discrete blocks of paint. To put it another way, Cezanne induced a single block of pigment to operate with extreme semantic promiscuity. He could use something that was a sign for depth (primarily) and make it a sign for a different type of description (local color, direction, texture) as well. Potential indications of haptic modeling became optical pattern too, while signs for optical sensation became haptic themselves through their relief, a literal insistence on the volumetric reality of the picture's surface (see, for instance, *The Plate of Apples* [c. 1877; cat. 33]). Cracking open time-honored traditions of Western art such as smoothly graduated chiaroscuro, Cezanne's regularized mark left no room for the rhetorical eloquence of paint handling before his time. Bigger strokes as well as nonblended strokes (also a hallmark of his watercolors) helped to carry this out. Indeed, as if removing a lens that brought the painted image into focus, Cezanne's low-resolution pictures allow for a surplus of paint, which overtly directs attention to itself. One might recall here Pissarro's claim that critics of Cezanne's works "properly point out the faults we all see, which leap to the eye," already suggesting that it was not so much observers who detected these features of the paintings but the artist himself who forced them to be seen.[29] The perceptual tension of these large strokes, each independently a sign, could be read as a type of internal contradiction— one not resolved by severing the image or rotating a sketchbook but nonetheless open to modification or clarification by adjusting one's eyes or squinting. What we see in these exaggerations and overemphases—places in which a single brushstroke carries the load of signifying local and atmospheric color, light and shadow, distance, direction, shape—are all of the ways that Cezanne said "no." No to continuity, no to illusionistic constructions, no to historical precedent submerging sensation.

The contrarian position we recognize in the work today echoes Théodore Duret's assessment of Cezanne in 1906: "This man whose art has seemed to resemble that of a Communard or an anarchist, whose work has instilled terror in directors of the [École des] Beaux-Arts . . . never suspected he might be seen as an insurgent."[30] Cezanne, the student and strange apprentice of historical art as well as Impressionism, surely perceived the artificiality of paintings but couldn't go along with working in a way where the agreed-upon language began to dictate how the experience felt. This refusal to accept the artificial that had always come along with art was integral to Cezanne's development of his technique. Artificiality, what we might call a language of art, must by its nature be predictable and repeatable. The possibility that you could keep this predictability in your mind's eye, and then depart from it, selectively (strangely) was one of the greatest threats his work posed to the École. To see the rules and break from them, visually and explicitly on the canvas, was a direct expression of subjective freedom, even for an audience of one. With the passage of time, Cezanne's demonstration of this ability began to teach other viewers—both artists and ordinary observers—how paintings signify, by opening up and working with the codes and communicative means of pictures themselves. The critical potential of this bold insight would be picked up to an even greater degree by the generation that followed, painting after Cezanne's easel and extending his refusals for all of us to see.

Notes

I wish to thank Kirk Nickel, for helping to improve this essay at several stages, and Richard Shiff, for profoundly informing my thinking on Cezanne and generously reviewing a draft of this text.

1. John Rewald, *The History of Impressionism*, 4th rev. ed. (New York: Museum of Modern Art, 1973; first ed. 1946), n.p, and the tables presented on 592–607. These rejections occurred in 1864, 1866–69, 1876, 1878–79, and 1884, with probable rejections in 1880–81, 1883, and 1885–86.

2. See *Catalogue des ouvrages de Peinture, Sculpture, Dessin, Gravure, Architecture, et Art decoratif* (Paris: Compagnie Française des Papier-Monnaie, 1907), 248–50; and Walter Feilchenfeldt, Jayne Warman, and David Nash, "Exhibition: 1907a Paris," in idem, *The Paintings, Watercolors and Drawings of Paul Cezanne: An Online Catalogue Raisonné* (2018–present), http:// cezannecatalogue.com/exhibitions/entry .php?id=21 (accessed on July 11, 2021). Nine works from the 1907 retrospective are included in the present one.

3. Maurice Denis, "Cézanne," reprinted in *Conversations with Cézanne*, edited by Michael Doran and translated by Julie Lawrence Cochran (Berkeley: University of California Press, 2001), 171. Previously published in Maurice Denis, *Théories* (Paris: L. Rouart, 1920).

4. On this subject see Felix Baumann, et al., eds., *Cézanne: Finished – Unfinished*, exh. cat. (Ostfildern Ruit, Germany: Hatje Cantz, 2000).

5. As Denis presented the case, Cezanne's painting was "bad" to the degree it departed from current norms. "Gauguin said when thinking about Cezanne: Nothing resembles a bad painting more than a masterpiece. Bad painting or masterpiece, we can only understand him in comparison to the mediocrity of modern painting" (Denis in Doran, *Conversations*, 167). See also Gloria Groom's discussion of Antoine Guillemet's comment that "the less it looks like [a painting], the closer one is to genius" (p. 24).

6. On Cezanne's appeal to artists during his lifetime to the exclusion of other publics, consider Charles Morice: "The paintings of Paul Cezanne frighten the public and delight artists—the public as a whole, not all artists"; Charles Morice, "Le Salon d'Automne," *Mercure de France*, Dec. 1, 1905, 390.

7. Recorded by Maurice Denis, *Théories*, 252.

8. Richard Shiff, "Risible Cezanne," in *The Repeating Image*, edited by Eik Kahng (Baltimore: Walters Museum, 2007), 130.

9. With regard to the humor in Cezanne's art, see Shiff, "Risible Cezanne."

10. On sketchbook pages and the creation of compositions through unlike scenes, see Samantha Friedman, "Condensation: Cézanne's Study Sheets," in *Cézanne Drawing*, edited by Jodi Hauptman and Samantha Friedman, exh. cat. (New York: Museum of Modern Art, 2021), 20–45.

11. See Kiko Aebi, "From Study Sheet to Composite Canvas," in Hauptman and Friedman, *Cézanne Drawing*, 182–83; curatorial and conservation documentation and imaging, Kateryna Kostiuchenko, Researcher, Von der Heydt Museum, Wuppertal, Germany, personal communication shared with the author, July 9, 2021. On Ambroise Vollard's role in cutting Cezanne's canvases for purposes of sale see Robert Jensen, "Vollard and Cézanne: An Anatomy of a Relationship," in *Cézanne to Picasso: Ambroise Vollard, Patron of the Avant-Garde*, edited by Rebecca A. Rabinow, exh. cat. (New York: Metropolitan Museum of Art, 2006), 29–47.

12. See Aebi, "From Study Sheet," 182–83. Ruppen argues that, in contradistinction to *Nude Woman (Leda?)*, the examples on paper were severed by Cezanne; see her essay "Tackling Cezanne's Paper: On the Reconstruction of Loose Sheets," in Fabienne Ruppen, Walter Feilchenfeldt, and Yuval Etgar, *Reconstructing Cezanne: Sequence and Process in Paul Cezanne's Works on Paper*, exh. cat. (London: Ridinghouse in collaboration with Luxembourg and Dayan, 2019), 16–44, esp. 17–21.

13. For analysis of *The Eternal Feminine* as Cezanne's comment on the contested space of the artist's studio, see Henri Loyrette, "Cat. 42. *The Eternal Feminine*," in Françoise Cachin, et al., *Cézanne*, exh. cat. (Philadelphia: Philadelphia Museum of Art, 1996), 160–62. See also Steven Platzman, *Cézanne: The Self-Portraits* (London: Thames and Hudson, 2001), 102–3, and 129–37, ill.; and Wayne Andersen, *Cézanne and the Eternal Feminine* (Cambridge, UK: Cambridge University Press, 2005), especially figs. 1, 6–8, and cover ill.

14. Camille Pissarro, Dec. 8, 1873, quoted in Isabelle Cahn, "Chronology," in Cachin, et al., *Cézanne*, 539.

15. T. J. Clark, "Strange Apprentice," *London Review of Books* 42, no. 19 (Oct. 8, 2020), https://www.lrb.co.uk/the-paper/v42 /n19/t.j.-clark/strange-apprentice.

16. On Hartley working after Cezanne, consider paintings such as Hartley's polychromatic *Mont Sainte-Victoire, 1927* (1927) in the collection of the Des Moines Art Center, among others; see Joseph J. Rishel, "Cezanne and Hartley on Sacred Ground," in *Cézanne and Beyond*, edited by Joseph J. Rishel and Katherine Sachs, exh. cat. (Philadelphia: Philadelphia Museum of Art, 2009), 159–83.

17. On this topic in traditions of landscape see Michael Charlesworth, *Landscape and Vision in Nineteenth-Century Britain and France* (Aldershot, England: Ashgate, 2008).

18. On the qualities of Cezanne's paintings when working after two-dimensional pictures in contrast to three-dimensional models, see Richard Shiff, "Cézanne Photographic," *Nonsite*, no. 26 (Nov. 11, 2018), nonsite.org/cezanne-photographic.

19. John Elderfield, *Cézanne: Portraits* (Princeton, NJ: Princeton University Press, 2017), 136.

20. Elderfield, *Cézanne: Portraits*, 136. Elderfield argues "Both these works are on standard canvas size with external contours of dress and chair, and internal contours of dress, almost identical in both, suggesting that the second may have been traced from the first."

21. See the essay by Kimberley Muir, Kristi Dahm, Giovanni Verri, Maria Kokkori, and Clara Granzotto in this volume, p. 49.

22. Kristi Dahm, email to the author, April 16, 2021.

23. Shiff, "Cézanne Photographic."

24. Maurice Denis quoted in Shiff, "Risible Cezanne," 127; originally published in "L'impressionnisme et la France" (1917), in *Nouvelles théories: Sur l'art modern, sur l'art sacré* (Paris: Rouart et Watelin, 1922), 66–67.

25. On Cezanne's mark making, see especially Richard Shiff, *Cézanne and the End of Impressionism* (Chicago: University of Chicago, 1984); and idem, "Mark, Motif, Materiality: The Cezanne Effect in the 20th Century," in Baumann et al., *Cézanne: Finished – Unfinished*, 99–123.

26. Julius Meier-Graefe, *Modern Art: Being a Contribution to a New System of Aesthetics*, translated by Florence Simmonds and George W. Chrystal (New York: G. P. Putnam's Sons, 1908), 1:267. Walter Feilchenfeldt has recently pointed to Meier-Graefe's observation to underline the trouble that early audiences, especially French ones, had in coming to terms with Cezanne's difficult pictures; see his "Introductory Remarks on the Cézanne Research," in *Cézanne: Metamorphoses*, edited by Alexander Eiling, exh. cat. (New York: Prestel, 2017), 12–13.

27. On the topic of stripping away conventional aspects of painting, see Richard Wollheim, *Painting as an Art* (Princeton, NJ: Princeton University Press, 1987), 28–29; he uses *Auvers, Panoramic View* (cat. 27) as a key example.

28. Charles Blanc, quoted in Shiff, "Cezanne Photographic," n15; originally published in "Salon de 1866," *Gazette des beaux-arts* 21 (July 1866): 38.

29. Camille Pissarro in *Pissarro: Letters to His Son Lucien*, edited by John Rewald (Mamaroneck. NY: P. P. Appel, 1972), 274–76. See also Gloria Groom's discussion of this quotation (p. 29).

30. Théodore Duret, quoted in Françoise Cachin, "A Century of Cézanne Criticism: I. From 1865 to 1906," in Cachin, et al., *Cézanne*, 43; originally published in *Histoire des peintres impressionnistes: Pissarro, Claude Monet, Sisley, Renoir, Berthe Morisot, Cézanne, Guillamin* (Paris: 1906), 195.

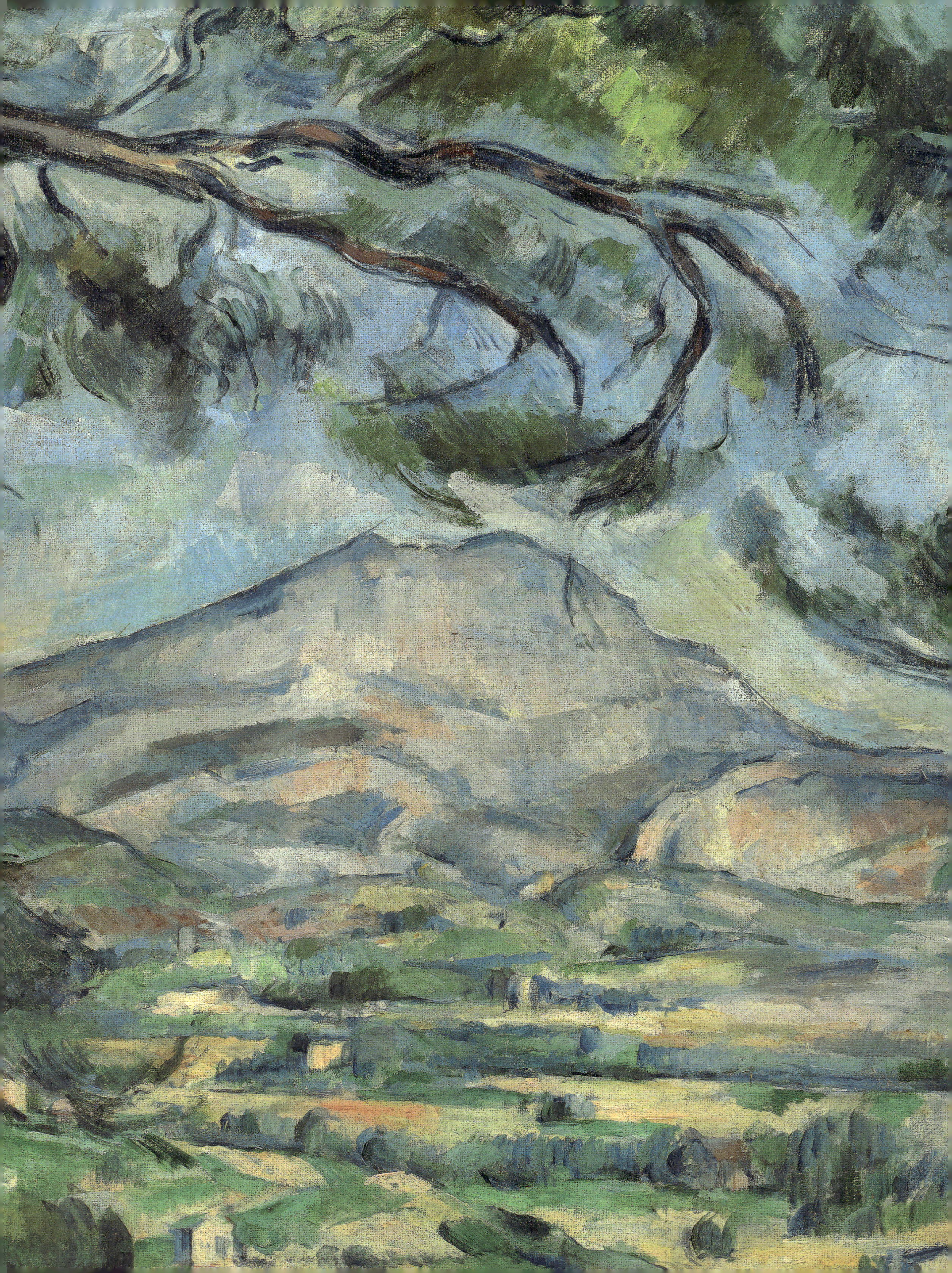

"A Harmony Parallel to Nature"

COLOR, FORM, AND SPACE IN CEZANNE'S WATERCOLORS AND OIL PAINTINGS

Kimberley Muir, Kristi Dahm, Giovanni Verri, Maria Kokkori, and Clara Granzotto

Paul Cezanne flouted many of the conventions of traditional picture making by using a unique and highly personal visual language, one that challenges the viewer to make sense of his complex compositions and to experience the medium and the image simultaneously, yet distinctly from one another. Some of the most intriguing effects of Cezanne's mature works stem from his use of color to model forms and create idiosyncratic spaces within his compositions. Moreover, he challenged traditional notions about what constitutes a finished work of art. He used the term *réalisation* to express his search for pictorial resolution—something that was more about the process and deciding at which point in this process he had achieved his aim than about a preconceived idea for a finished image.[1] This was an elusive, lifelong pursuit and a new proposition with each picture. Thus, Cezanne left compositions in various states of completion: some clearly unfinished and many in which passages were left blank or only sketched in and that cannot be clearly categorized.[2] While close looking reveals much about the artist's methods, scientific investigation of a selection of his watercolors and oil paintings has enhanced our understanding of how he developed color, form, and space in ways not fully visible on the surfaces of his works.[3] Focusing on five still lifes from the Art Institute of Chicago and a private collection (with select reference to other works), this essay unpacks the nonlinear character of Cezanne's working method and shows how he created his singular images by manipulating the relationships between line and color, form and space, in unique and deeply influential ways. In particular, we explore his incremental process in these works, his meticulous approach to developing a sense of space and atmosphere, and the remarkable ways in which he deployed the color blue.

The painter gives concrete expression to his sensations, his perceptions, by means of line and color.
—Paul Cezanne to Émile Bernard, 1904[4]

Cezanne's process was exploratory. It was guided by intense observation of his subjects, but he improvised as he went along, seeing new possibilities for his compositions in the physical act of laying down paint, graphite, and watercolor rather than adhering to a predetermined course.[5] In the works we studied, Cezanne's handling of watercolor can be distinguished from that of oil paint even though he manipulated both to vary their fluidity and opacity.[6] He left regions of the supports unpainted, exploiting the color and reflective properties of his white papers and light-toned canvas primings.[7] Notably, his work in both media shows a distinctive approach to the construction of a composition, one that is characterized by incrementally building up forms through line and color. Cezanne once declared, "I am pursuing success through work," and, in contrast to the polished surfaces of the more academic painters of his time, he allowed different stages of the creative process—of his "work"—to be seen in the final image.[8] Among the watercolors we studied, we found that the artist's technique did not involve subtractive methods; he did not erase graphite lines or scrape, blot, or wipe watercolor washes in order to lighten passages of paint or create highlights, or to make adjustments to forms.[9] In the oils we found no evidence that he had scraped or wiped away unwanted paint layers.[10] As his work progressed, Cezanne continually adjusted and reassessed the overall effect of his composition, but he added on top of what he had already laid down and did not conceal traces of this process. In one particularly striking example of this, *The Vase of Tulips* (1890; cat. 65), an orange that Cezanne painted over at the lower left edge of the vase remains partially visible through his open brushwork.[11]

Cezanne's specific approach to various media is perhaps most clearly illustrated with respect to his watercolors and oils of the same subject. Because many of the still-life watercolors from the last decades of his life are on a large scale and show a high level of finish, scholars interpret them as independent works of art rather than as sketches or studies in the service of the oil paintings.[12] Cezanne frequently painted the same subject in both watercolor and oil as a means of examining his subjects through the unique properties of each: to explore his own sensitivity to perception or to discover variations in tone, atmosphere, or psychological effect resulting from the different mediums. To this end, the strong and convincing effects of light that are possible with watercolor often stand in contrast to the more solid and opaque qualities of oil paint that convey material substance.[13] For instance, when we compare the watercolor *The Three Skulls* (1902–6; cat. 141) and the related oil painting *Three Skulls on a Patterned Carpet* (1904; cat. 140), we find that Cezanne explored the motif in very different ways in the different media. The works are close in size and present the subject from a similar vantage point. In the oil, the artist covered the entire surface with paint and apparently reworked it several times.[14] The dark, rich tones lend the composition a heavy atmosphere and gravity more befitting a traditional *vanitas* image, particularly in the rendering of the skulls, where the range of deep beige colors conveys the hue of aged bone. In the watercolor, by contrast, he left the ivory paper liberally exposed through and between thin veils of vivid watercolor,

imparting an unexpected lightness and ephemeral quality to the somber subject.

In the majority of his watercolors, Cezanne left the graphite drawing visible to some extent instead of concealing it with subsequent layers. In fact, and in contrast to the work of most of his peers, the drawing plays an integral role in Cezanne's final images, doing more than providing an initial guide for placing washes. His watercolors feature a characteristic interplay of line and color that prompts us to continually shift our attention back and forth between the paper, paint, and pencil marks in order to understand how a given subject sits in space. In *The Three Skulls* (see fig. 1), for instance, the drawing, layered watercolor washes, and bright paper support contribute actively and dynamically to the overall image. Cezanne established the major design elements—the skulls, undulating carpet, foliage in the textile pattern, table edges beneath the cloth, and horizontal chair rail—with repeated graphite lines that are more evident in the reflected infrared (IR) image of the work (fig. 2).[15] His pencil handling here was loose and free. To help define forms—particularly contour and shading within the skulls—he left parts of his sketch visible beneath transparent washes and in paper reserves. Indeed, the visual and physical characteristics of the ivory wove paper that the artist chose to use for this work played a key role in the outcome and reflect his larger concern with materials. The relatively smooth surface allowed Cezanne to sketch rapidly and to control the flow of dilute washes in even areas of color. The support also effectively reflects light through the transparent watercolor and from unpainted areas, allowing him to achieve the brilliance described above. In his rendering of the skulls, graphite drawing and watercolor washes often function autonomously, conveying different optical and tactile information in addition to being superimposed. As curator Matthew Simms has put it, the mediums "state the same information twice in two different visual languages."[16] Here, the artist used loose graphite lines to establish the skulls' curvature as well as interior contours and quick zigzag marks to indicate the shadows but relied heavily on pale washes and brilliant white reserved paper to convey the surface of the bone (see fig. 1).[17] He concentrated his watercolor applications in the recesses and spaces around the skulls, where they convey volume and shadow. Cezanne used watercolor and graphite similarly in his treatment of figures as well. In *Man Wearing a Straw Hat* (1905–6; cat. 134), line and color commingle but also function independently within the image. Patches of watercolor and blank paper, which evoke the play of light and shadow on the sitter's face, are not tied to the boundaries of the pencil drawing demarcating the man's facial features (see fig. 3).

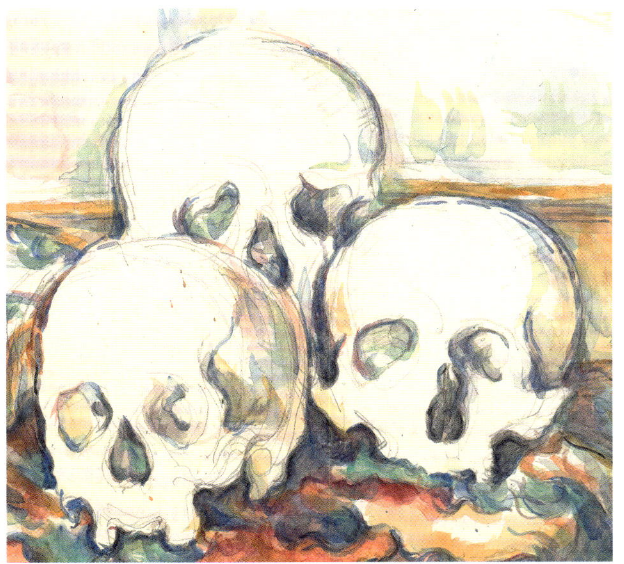

Fig. 1

Detail of the skulls in *The Three Skulls* (cat. 141), showing the interplay of graphite drawing, layered watercolor washes, and reserved paper.

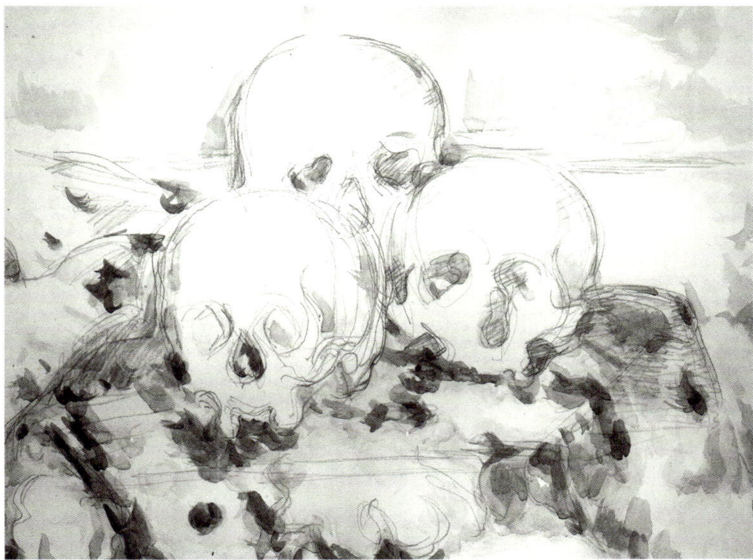

Fig. 2

Detail of a reflected IR image of *The Three Skulls* highlighting Cezanne's graphite drawing.

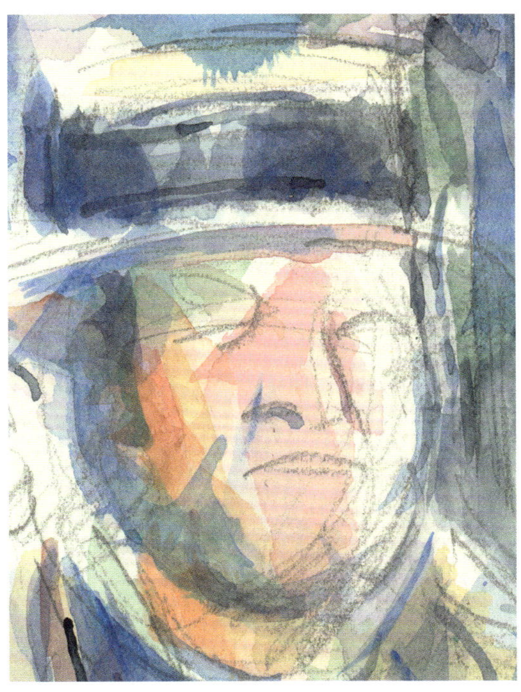

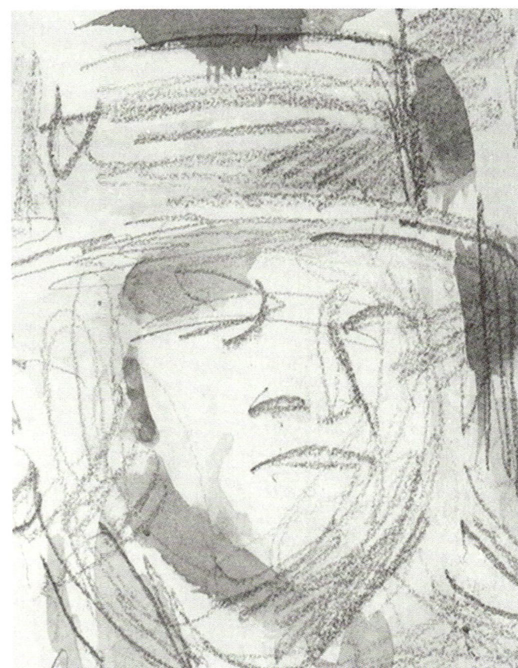

Fig. 3

Left: Detail of the sitter's face in *Man Wearing a Straw Hat* (cat. 134), showing how both drawing and watercolor contribute to the image. **Right**: Reflected IR detail of the sitter's face, highlighting Cezanne's pencil drawing.

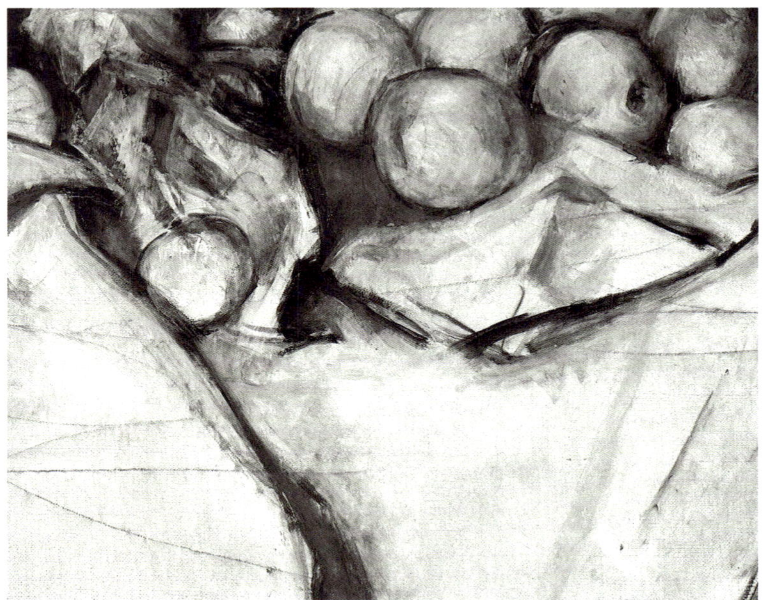

Fig. 4

IR reflectograph detail of *The Basket of Apples* (cat. 56), showing the underdrawing that Cezanne used to sketch in the table and the white cloth.

Among the oil paintings that we studied, the presence and extent of underdrawing vary; more to the point, although it is sometimes visible on the surface, this element is not an integral part of the image, as it is in many of Cezanne's watercolors.[18] It provided a general plan for the composition rather than a rigid framework to be followed as he applied his paint. As the artist's ideas evolved, he adjusted or veered from the drawn composition to suit his painting. This is most apparent in *The Basket of Apples* (c. 1893; cat. 56). The IR reflectograph of this work (fig. 4) reveals that Cezanne executed a fairly detailed underdrawing in a dry carbon-based material (possibly charcoal), roughly mapping out the major elements of the composition.[19] From the outset he had planned some of the aspects that contribute to the finished piece's slightly off-kilter perspective, including the disjunct parts of the front table edge and the tilted position of the bottle (though both were modified in the painting stage). Cezanne further developed areas of the composition with a black "painted underdrawing" applied by brush in long, fluid strokes.[20] With the aid of IR, we see this mainly among the apples, the folds of the white cloth, and the biscuits. While the artist did not introduce major changes to his dry underdrawing at this stage, he did make numerous small adjustments to the placement and

edges of the forms, and also emphasized contours. Both the dry and painted underdrawing are mostly concealed by paint in the finished image, but Cezanne added linear brushstrokes at different stages of painting to reinstate the edges of forms or to separate objects that overlap one another—for example, along the contours of the fruit.

I proceed very slowly. Nature presents itself to me with great complexity, and improvements to make are endless.
—Cezanne to Bernard, 1904[21]

In the works we analyzed, Cezanne's method of building volume and space through patches and strokes of color was distinctively methodical and cumulative. He densely layered watercolor to gradually develop color and form, allowing layers to dry before superimposing more paint. This patient approach was integral to his process; due to the transparency of the medium and the tendency for colors to dull when mixed or layered in certain combinations, he did not have the freedom to repeatedly revisit and rework the watercolor surfaces to the extent that he did in his oil paintings. To return to an illustrative example: Cezanne recorded the rich colors and pattern of the ornate textile in *The Three Skulls* (cat. 141) by applying more opaque watercolor over densely layered transparent washes (see fig. 5). He juxtaposed and manipulated inherently transparent and opaque pigments of the same color group and varied the dilution of individual hues to

Fig. 5

Detail of the textile in *The Three Skulls* showing Cezanne's dense layering of opaque and transparent watercolor applications.

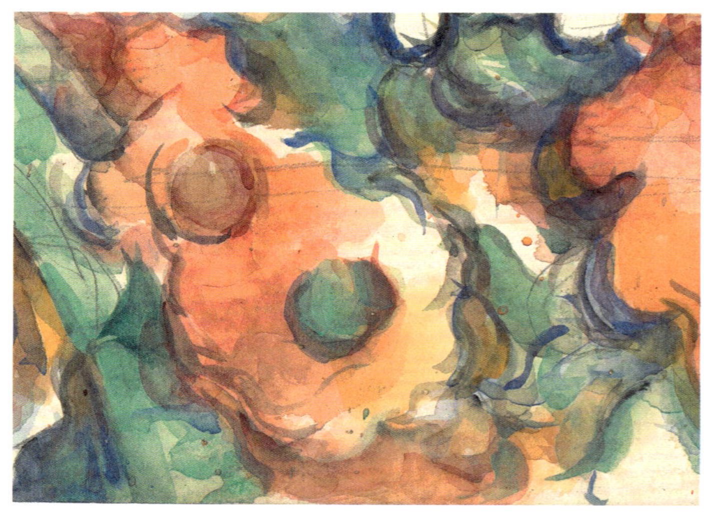

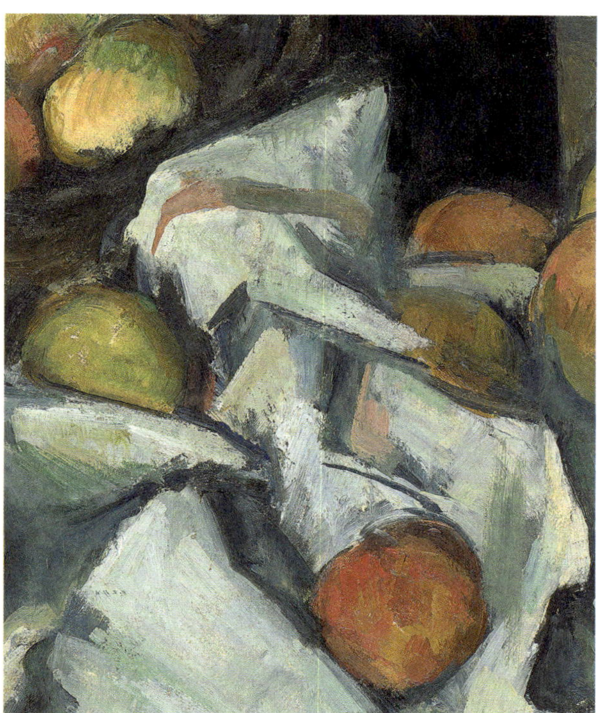

Fig. 6

Detail of the white cloth and fruit in *The Basket of Apples* showing how Cezanne built form by superimposing strokes of color.

generate optical brilliance. For the red floral forms, for instance, the artist layered vivid strokes of a transparent red lake of animal origin, likely cochineal, with patches of opaque orange-red vermillion. He rendered the foliage patterns in emerald green, diluting it to achieve a range of green hues across the design. In contrast to the deep, transparent strokes of indigo applied along the contours and in the recesses of the skulls and in intermittent touches throughout the textile, Cezanne employed cobalt blue, one of the most opaque blue watercolor pigments available to him, to delineate the pattern in short, broken strokes. He layered it on top of other colors without precise adherence to contours. The densest strokes of cobalt blue and emerald green are matte and conceal the paper surface, adding a subtle textural contrast.[22]

Cezanne incorporated textiles into many of his still-life compositions, interwoven with the other objects as important structural features, giving them sustained attention as he constructed their forms through superimposed strokes of paint.[23] In *The Basket of Apples*, the jagged folds of the white cloth appear more like facets of a solid mass than like tented fabric (see fig. 6). The artist

provisionally indicated these folds and creases in the underdrawing and then modified the design with his painted lines before shifting yet again while painting. He suggested the planes of fabric almost exclusively through subtle chromatic shifts rather than tonal modeling, a process he referred to as "modulation."[24] The cloth is actually not white at all but a range of pale pink, yellow, blue, green, and gray hues, carefully calibrated using mixtures of pigments including lead white, emerald green, viridian, Prussian blue, and ultramarine blue. The red vermillion border, which was added in the final stages of painting, often diverges from the edge that it nominally follows; at the peak of the cloth, the red band continues independently, relatively uninterrupted even though the fabric is crumpled. Cezanne indicated only a slight shadow or depression through a subtle contrast of complementary hues, applying a thin stroke of green on top of the vermillion near the center of the red band.[25]

The artist deliberated over the relationship between the cloth and the fruit, working back and forth between them. He first painted the two apples (or oranges?) near the base of the bottle in an arrangement similar to the overlapping pair immediately to the right. After the surface had dried, he added two prominent strokes of light greenish-gray to suggest that additional sections of cloth partially obscure both pieces of fruit. These late-stage brushstrokes imply rather than portray the fabric, compelling the viewer to read them first as paint and then, within the context of the painting, as part of the cloth. The ragged edges of the brush marks register the action of Cezanne's hand as he dragged the paint over the earlier layers, preventing a purely representational reading of the strokes. As Elisabeth Reissner has pointed out, Cezanne's interest was not in copying or imitating what he observed "but, rather, representing, interpreting or finding material equivalents for his sensory experiences."[26] Other final touches confound our ability to distinguish which objects are in front of which. For instance, the artist added some of the dark blue-gray strokes that emphasize shadowed folds last; as a result, even though they should visually recede behind the surface planes of the fabric, they are physically on top of them. These dark contour strokes are often near, but not exactly at, the fabric's edges and make discrete passages challenging to decipher (see fig. 6). Although we can speculate, we cannot know whether particular pictorial effects are expressions of the complexities of visual perception, incidental consequences of Cezanne working on discrete passages in isolation, or intentional responses, the result of choices he made as he reviewed the marks he had already laid down and developed the overall work in progress.[27]

Areas left blank or unresolved, even in Cezanne's more finished works, can introduce ambiguity into the

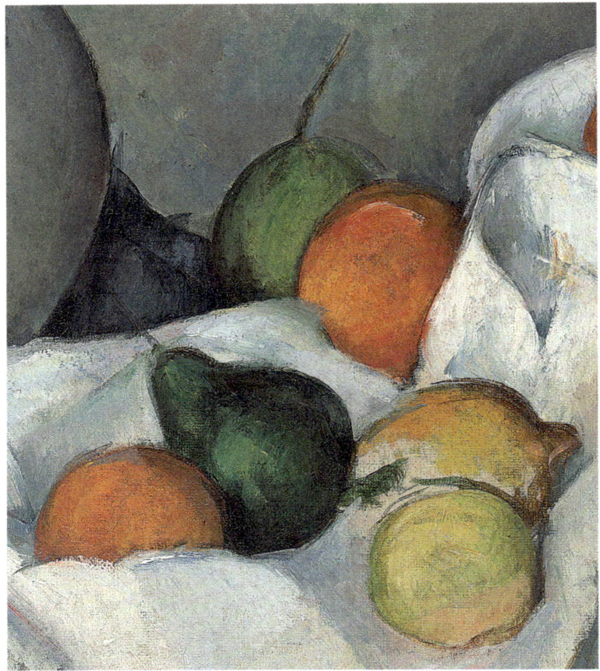

Fig. 7

Detail of the white cloth and fruit in
Curtain, Pitcher, and a Fruit Bowl (cat. 60),
showing an unresolved area of the
composition.

overall effect of his compositions, especially with respect to how objects relate to each other in space. *Curtain, Pitcher, and a Fruit Bowl* (1893–94; cat. 60) offers a compelling example of how this operates with respect to an apparently deliberately unfinished passage: a few disconnected brushstrokes of green paint near the center of the composition are partial indications of a form that Cezanne never fleshed out (see fig. 7). We cannot be certain whether these marks were the beginning of a piece of fruit, the original placement of the green pear to the left, or something else entirely. What is clear is that the artist purposefully preserved these marks in the composition by reserving the area around them and leaving the adjacent lemon only partially realized. By contrast, he built up other areas of the painting such as the stack of fruit at upper right (see cat. 60). Here he completely covered the ground layer with successive strokes of overlapping color; even the spaces between the fruit are built up just as densely as the apples and oranges. The edge of the fruit that emerges from behind the stack on the lower right side of the plate sits entirely in shadow, but examination under the microscope revealed that it was originally painted in a vivid reddish-orange hue, similar to the fruit that sits in front of it. This dark-green layer of paint

establishes a crucial balance in the composition by grounding the pile, which otherwise appears to float, along with the white plate, just above and beyond the table surface.

We observed similar undeveloped passages in Cezanne's watercolors as well. In *The Three Skulls*, the artist did not elaborate the edge of the picture frame on the right side or the border of the textile at the lower edge of the composition, nor did he fully describe the background wall with watercolor washes; he did flesh out these elements in the oil painting of this subject (cat. 140). In another watercolor, *Montagne Saint-Victoire (The Arc Valley)* (c. 1885; cat. 111) Cezanne left the trees in the foreground and at the lower left base of the mountain unfinished, rendered mostly in graphite with minimal wash. He painted these areas more fully in an oil painting that closely relates to the watercolor composition *Mont Sainte-Victoire* (1886–87; cat. 110).[28] Comparison suggests that the leafless tree trunks in the watercolor—which may be read as regions of reflected light—were simply not painted. Viewers may also see some ambiguous drawn marks which Cezanne left unpainted, such as those at the lower left base of the mountain and above the yellow house; these areas were not developed in the oil either.

Light through the overall play of reflections is the enveloping atmosphere.
— Cezanne to Bernard, 1905[29]

Our investigation of how Cezanne painted backgrounds and the interfaces between objects and optical planes shows that he aimed to capture his subjects' interactions with their environment as well as the skulls, apples, flowers, and so on themselves.[30] Imaging techniques proved particularly useful in visualizing the artist's treatment of the spaces behind and around objects, revealing aspects of his technique that are not apparent to the naked eye. In this study, we deployed macro-X-ray fluorescence (XRF) scanning, which records the distribution of individual chemical elements across the surface of the painting (commonly called elemental maps), and hyperspectral imaging, which provides data on the reflective properties of pigments.[31] Together, these imaging techniques revealed the delicate relationships that Cezanne built between objects and their background. They also shed light on how he relied on subtle tonal variation to portray his sensations. These variations are holistically perceived by the viewer but are often too subtle to be easily distinguished without the aid of scientific visualizations.

The Plate of Apples (c. 1877; cat. 33) offers a clear demonstration of this phenomenon and its wider implications. Behind the still-life arrangement in this

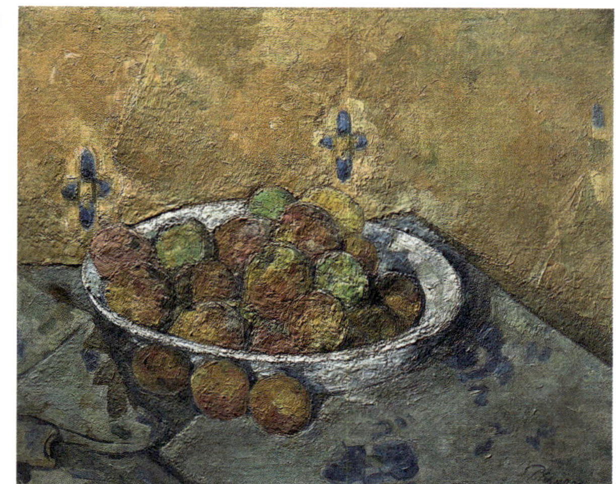

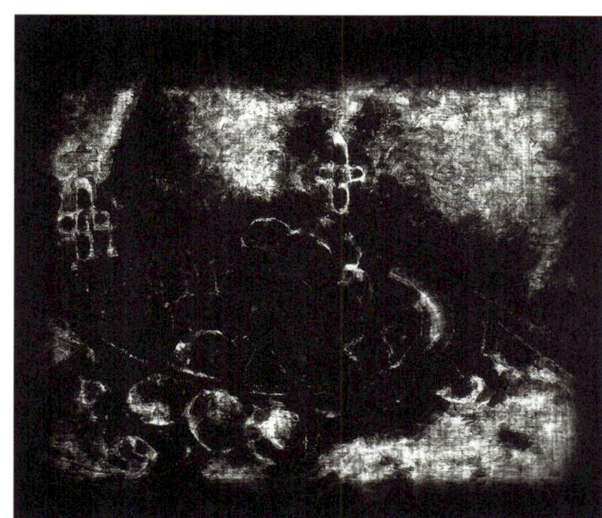

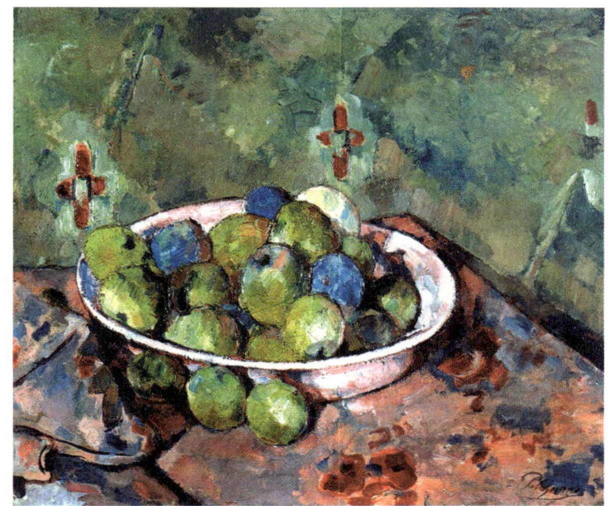

Fig. 8

(a) Raking-light image of *The Plate of Apples* (cat. 33), showing the morphology of the paint application.

(b) Transmitted-IR image showing the density of the paint application: the darker the image, the more dense the paint.

(c) IR false-color image, which provides a visual representation of both IR radiation and visible light, making otherwise-difficult-to-perceive differences among pigments more obvious.

painting, Cezanne depicted the distinctive wallpaper—yellow with blue lozenges—from his rue de l'Ouest apartment in Paris that features in several other still lifes from the 1870s and 1880s (see, for example, *Still Life: Flask, Glass, and Jug* [c. 1877; cat. 34] and *Madame Cezanne in a Red Armchair* [c. 1877; cat. 35]). Here, the artist simplified the design to three blue crosses on a variegated yellow background. IR examination shows that indications of its linear diamond pattern appear in his underdrawing, but in paint, Cezanne only suggested the pattern on the surface with varying shades of yellow. He applied the paint with remarkable thickness in some passages, paying considerable attention to the areas where forms interact. This is apparent in the raking-light (fig. 8a) and transmitted-IR (fig. 8b) images, which give an indication of surface topography and paint density, respectively. The former shows areas where the thick yellow paint from the wallpaper actually protrudes over the tablecloth and the fruit dish.

The IR false-color image of this work registers subtle or otherwise imperceptible aspects of Cezanne's painting technique, specifically the complexity of his paint manipulation and layering.[32] Pigments that have a similar color in visible light but behave differently in the presence of IR radiation display different false colors, allowing us to capture a unique visualization of the artist's admixtures and applications (see fig. 8c). To create the apparent "yellow" background of the wallpaper, the artist mixed an array of pigments—yellow ochre, chrome yellow, emerald green, ultramarine blue, vermillion, bone black, and lead- and zinc-based whites—in varying combinations and proportions.[33] It should also be noted that his use of equally intense color in the foreground and background areas of the painting compresses the pictorial space and more generally affects the viewer's perception of depth: the blue lozenges were painted with an ultramarine blue that is just as intense as the floral motifs on the tablecloth, so they appear to advance in front of the yellow background and optically float on the same plane as the tablecloth.

We find a similarly impactful use of modulated color in *The Vase of Tulips* (c. 1890; cat. 65). The background ostensibly represents a uniform, monochromatic wall, yet the artist enlivened this surface with tonal variations. In this case as well, the IR false-color image enhances these variations, making Cezanne's subtle manipulations more legible. Observations under the microscope revealed that the cyan shades of the background were created by varying mixtures of pigment.[34] These include ultramarine blue, emerald green, viridian, and vermillion mixed with lead- and zinc-based whites (see fig. 9).[35] The IR false-color image together with macro-XRF scanning maps allowed us to study this complex mixing and application in greater detail. They revealed that Cezanne used different mixtures to achieve visually

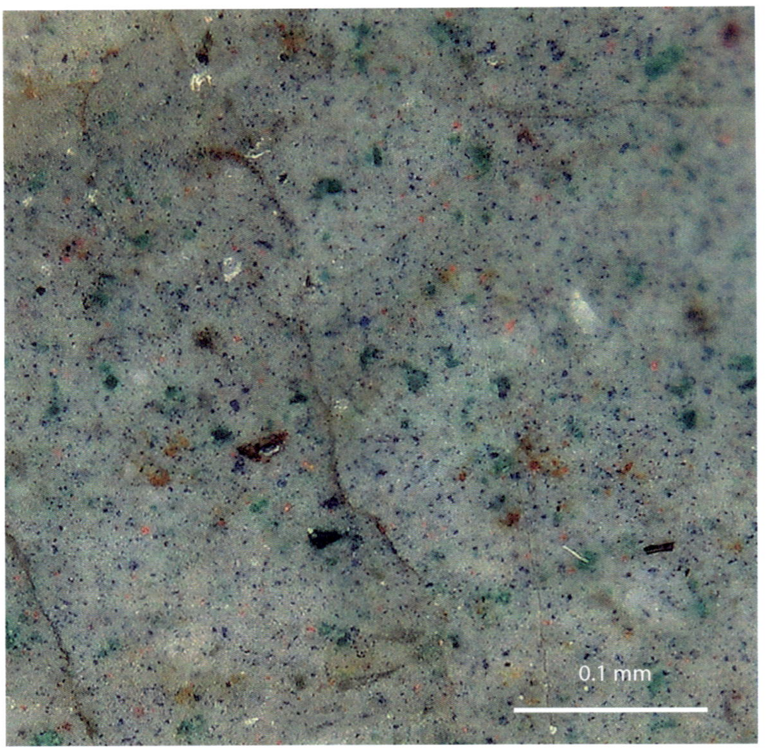

similar hues; this is indicated by the presence of both blue and pink areas in the background in the IR false-color image (fig. 10). He added vermillion in different concentrations to impart a more purple hue in some regions and distributed the lead- and zinc-based whites unevenly as well; use of the latter was concentrated along the right side of the background, but the reasons for this are difficult to infer.[36]

Imaging techniques also show that Cezanne reworked the background in *The Vase of Tulips*, making fine adjustments to local tonal relationships in distinct stages. He revisited the area to the left of the vase, working just up to the edges of preexisting forms (see fig. 11). His deliberate brush marks and the way in which the background color intensifies as it closes in around the apple pulls this part of the wall forward onto the same plane as the flowers, the table, and the fruit. These subtle modulations create an active and pulsating space around the still-life arrangement where foreground and background converge.

Such attention to the nominal background is not unusual for Cezanne. A conversation reported by the French poet and art critic Joachim Gasquet—perhaps with

Fig. 9

Photomicrograph of *The Vase of Tulips* (cat. 65), showing a detail of the cyan background. Magnification reveals that the cyan color is composed of a complex mixture of blue, green, red, and white pigments.

Fig. 10

Left: IR false-color image of *The Vase of Tulips* showing the use of pigments with different reflective properties in the IR range that appear similar to the naked eye.
Right: Elemental maps showing the distribution of the following:
(**a**) cobalt blue (cobalt)
(**b**) viridian and lead chromate (chromium)
(**c**) emerald green (arsenic)
(**d**) emerald green (copper)
(**e**) vermillion (mercury)
(**f**) zinc-based white (zinc)
(**g**) lead-based pigments (lead)
(**h**) likely a barium-based extender (barium).

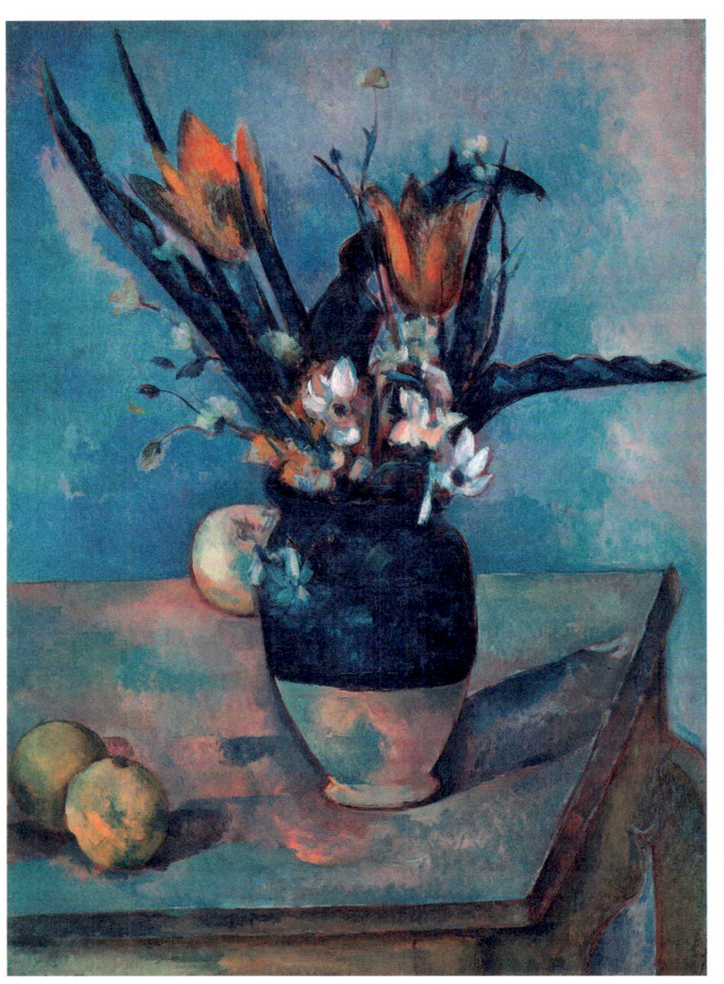

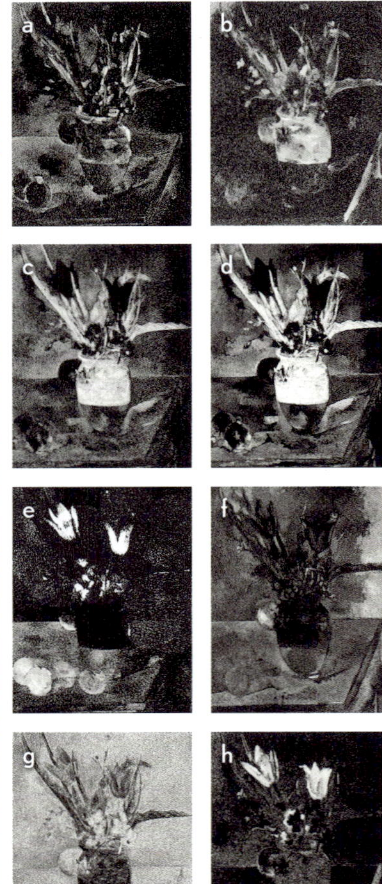

lyrical embellishment—seems to capture the nuanced and very particular way in which the artist perceived the atmosphere that envelops things. Responding to Gasquet's observation that "Provence is often gray," Cezanne replied "Never. Maybe silver. Blue, bluish . . . Never gray, not so much gray as glaring, yellow, flashy, like confetti that confuses all these observers who see nothing."[37] The multitude of colors and the impressionistic brushwork that Cezanne used in the background of *Curtain, Pitcher, and a Fruit Bowl* (see fig. 12a) come together in an overall hue that would be difficult to describe with a single name. "Gray" certainly seems inadequate. The palette he used in this painting is consistent with the pigments we identified in the other still lifes we studied, but here he amplified the intensity of the background colors and applied his paint with more emphatic brushstrokes (see fig. 12b). The ultraviolet-induced luminescence image (fig. 12c) shows the distribution of a red lake pigment of plant origin, likely madder, that appears brilliant orange under this type of lighting.[38] The artist applied the red lake in quick, zigzagging and linear strokes that animate the space around the apples and subtly direct the viewer's eye to disparate regions of the composition.

Fig. 11

Detail of the background of *The Vase of Tulips* showing an area that Cezanne reworked around the existing flowers as he fine-tuned his color relationships.

Fig. 12

(**a**) Detail of *Curtain, Pitcher, and a Fruit Bowl* in visible light.
(**b**) IR false-color image providing a more visually enhanced view of Cezanne's use of pigments in the background.
(**c**) Ultraviolet-induced luminescence image showing the use of madder lake as glowing orange brushstrokes.

a
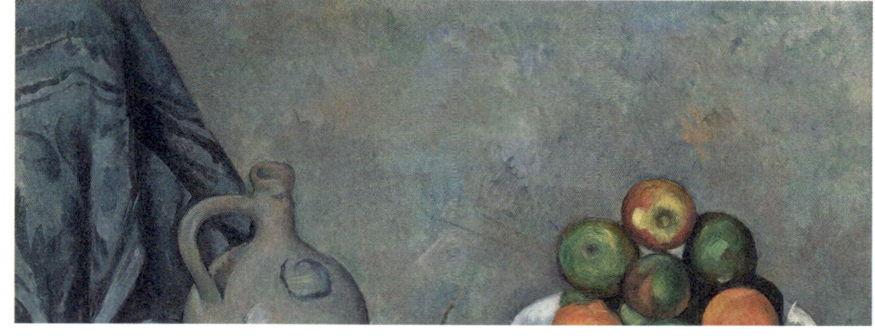

b
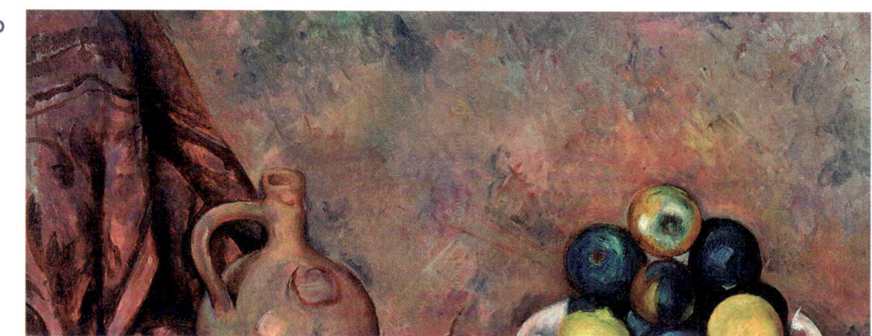

c
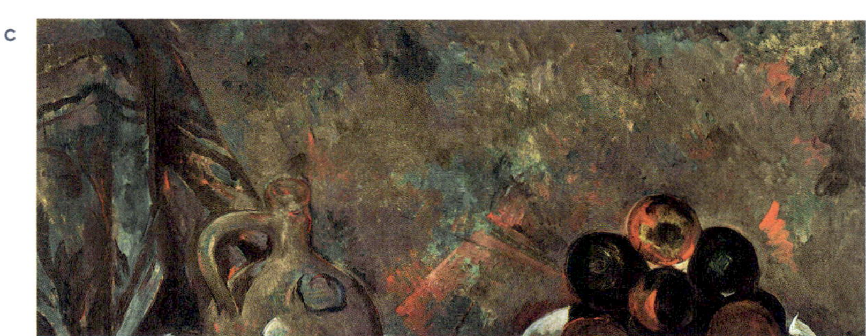

Cezanne paid particular attention to subject–background spatial relationships and the junctures of forms in his late watercolor still lifes as well. In *The Three Skulls*, he defined the plane of the background wall with overlapping transparent washes below the chair rail and reserved paper above. Loading his brush with dilute wash, the artist painted a few vertical brushstrokes side by side, allowing the wash to flow laterally and merge seamlessly on the sheet into amorphous patches of transparent color. Once those were dry, he applied adjacent and overlapping patches using the same method; building up a sense of solidity in this way, Cezanne retained purity and clarity of color in some areas while also creating new colors through optical mixing in areas where colors overlap. Additionally, Cezanne left a large portion of the top of the sheet in reserve; the wall is merely implied, with sparse patches of carefully placed wash concentrated above the chair rail and in the space behind the uppermost skull.

Nature exists for us humans more in depth than in the surface. Therefore, into our vibrations of light, represented by reds and yellows, we need to introduce sufficient blues to make one feel the air.
– Cezanne to Bernard, 1904[39]

While Cezanne clearly pondered the relationships between his still-life objects and their surroundings, he extended this intensity to portraying space without walls, often by deploying the color blue. Indeed, previous researchers have noted his distinctive use of this color along the edges of forms and in the interstitial spaces, which prompted us to examine it in more detail.[40] He called upon blue as color, line, and shadow, and also to evoke space and atmosphere—possibly to represent the air between objects or even, as art historian Yve-Alain Bois has suggested, to allow his works to "breathe."[41] So by way of conclusion, we will take a closer look at the ways in which Cezanne handled blue in several particular works—characteristically taking materials and a color available to everyone and, through his handling of it at every level (the pigment, the brushstroke, the reiteration), making it recognizably and incontrovertibly his own.

The flexibility of blue is particularly apparent in Cezanne's watercolor *Pistachio Tree at Château Noir* (c. 1900; cat. 132). Over his pencil rendering of branches, the artist added a network of short, narrow strokes of cobalt blue, along with yellow ochre, to convey the volume of the limbs.[42] He placed them primarily on the underside of the branches, where blue connotes shadows, while the yellow was placed on their upper surfaces to indicate reflected light. Complementing this more focused use of the color, dilute cobalt blue washes suggest dappled patches of sky between the branches. Cezanne also applied similar blue washes over portions of the thick tree trunk, varying the intensity of the hue. As these patches expand beyond the pencil lines tentatively marking the trunk's boundaries, the function of blue shifts to evoke the air surrounding the more substantial elements of the landscape.

In *Man Wearing a Straw Hat*, the artist developed yet another way to deploy blue, using shimmering and dynamic marks to render sensations of light and air. He added short, intermittent strokes of bright cobalt and Prussian blue, indigo, and mixed purple.[43] These mark the borders of forms in an imprecise, almost agitated manner that is particularly evident through the center of the figure. Cezanne avoided precisely placed outlines and instead suggested definition with linear fragments that hover above and around elements such as the hands, legs, and coat lapels (see fig. 13), conveying energy and vibrancy as well as form.

In other watercolors, though, Cezanne calibrated the effect of his blues both by diluting the intensity of the hue and layering it with strokes and patches of

Fig. 13

Detail of the man's torso from *Man Wearing a Straw Hat* showing Cezanne's use of short, linear strokes of blue watercolor that hover near the edges of the hands, leg, and jacket lapels.

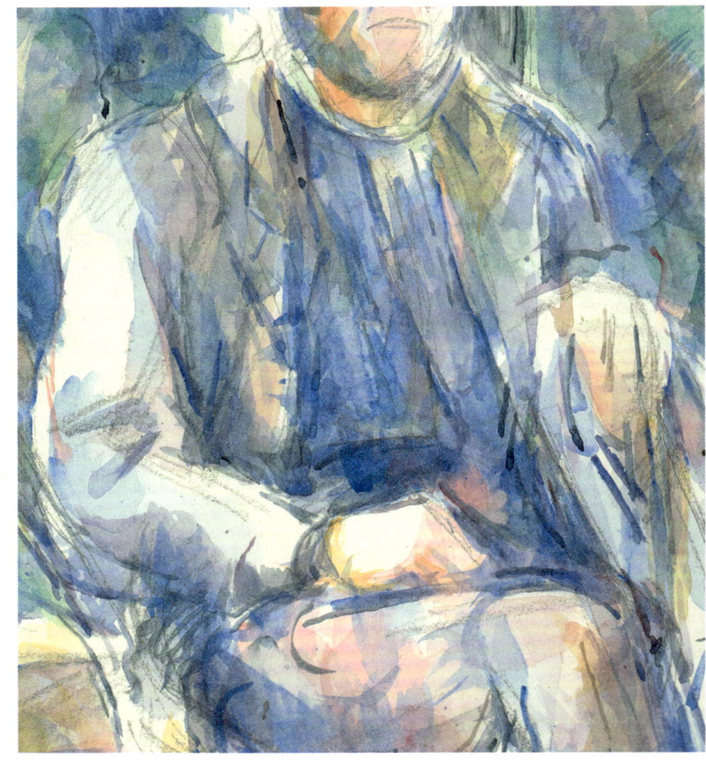

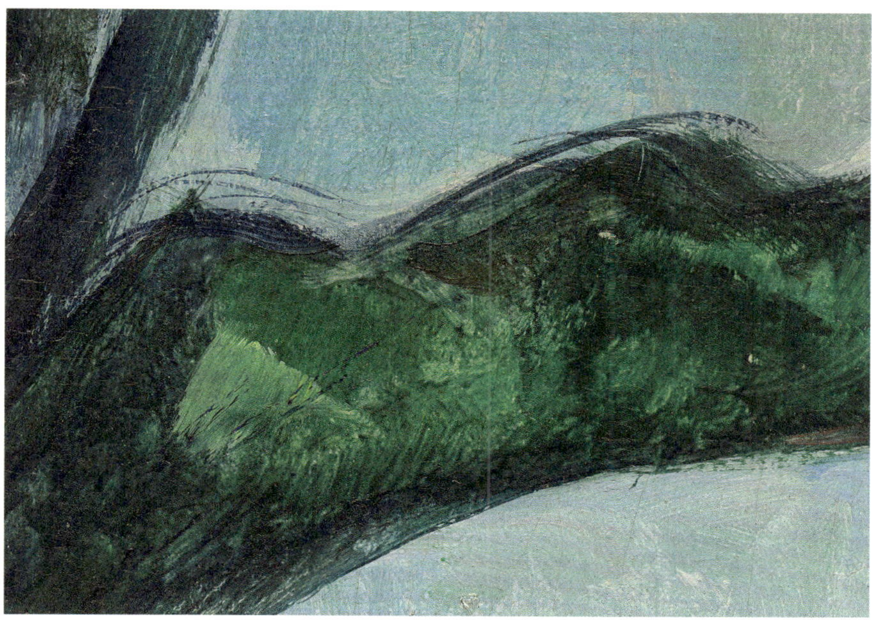

Fig. 14

Detail of a leaf from *The Vase of Tulips* showing the delicate blue lines that float along the upper edge.

other colors. In *The Three Skulls*, he used indigo for the darkest marks, where it appears almost—but not quite—black, as seen in the brushstrokes marking the contours of the skulls and shading their recessed cavities (see fig. 1). Upon close inspection, the "dark blue" areas between the skulls are actually densely overlapping strokes of red and blue watercolor, a variegated surface of rich, saturated color that activates the otherwise empty space.

In the oils studied, Cezanne's "blue" is rarely a consistent color across a work, often ranging from blue to purple to blackish. He adjusted his blue paint mixtures in order to create a range of nuanced hues, combining it with other pigments and modifying the fluidity of his brushstrokes with solvents and mediums, which allowed him to vary the opacity and hue. Although these intricacies become less perceptible with increased viewing distance, the variations in color and transparency imbue the work with a dynamic, vibrating rhythm, especially where repeated lines vacillate along the edges of painted forms, such as the undulating leaf edge in *The Vase of Tulips* (see fig. 14).

Cezanne's unconventional use of blue to convey the fullness of the space around objects epitomizes the way in which his complexly layered surfaces and sometimes puzzling arrangements constitute new ways of representing form and space and, with close looking, draw the viewer's attention to the process of painting. Cezanne used his materials to translate observations and sensations that were filtered through his own subjective experiences, creating enduring images that capture not nature itself but, as he put it, "a harmony parallel to nature."[44]

Notes

1. Cezanne's pursuit of *réalisation* in his art, and his struggles to achieve it, is a persistent theme in his late correspondence. See, for example, Paul Cezanne to various recipients in Alex Danchev, ed. and trans., *The Letters of Paul Cézanne* (Los Angeles: J. Paul Getty Museum, 2013), 332, letter 231; 333, letter 232; 346, letter 242; and 373, letter 269.

2. For discussion of the issue of finish in Cezanne's work, see Evelyn Benesch, "From the Incomplete to the Unfinished: *Réalisation* in the Work of Paul Cézanne," in *Cézanne: Finished - Unfinished,* edited by Felix Baumann et al. (Ostfildern Ruit, Germany: Hatje Cantz, 2000), 41–61; and Elisabeth Reissner, "Ways of Making: Practice and Innovation in Cezanne's Paintings in the National Gallery," *National Gallery Technical Bulletin* 29 (2008): 20–23.

3. The works discussed in this essay were studied using binocular and digital microscopy; X-radiography; reflected- and transmitted-infrared, ultraviolet-induced luminescence, and hyperspectral (HSI) imaging; and X-ray fluorescence spectroscopy (XRF), in some cases supplemented by macro-XRF scanning and Fourier-transform infrared reflectance spectroscopy (FTIR). The current research was supplemented by previous pigment analysis using polarized-light dispersion microscopy (PLM) carried out by Inge Fiedler, former Conservation Microscopist at the Art Institute of Chicago, on *The Plate of Apples* (cat. 33).

4. Paul Cezanne to Émile Bernard, June 27, 1904, in Danchev, *Letters,* 339, letter 235.

5. This work builds on a growing body of technical studies of Cezanne's work. See Marigene H. Butler, "An Investigation of the Materials and Technique Used by Paul Cézanne," in *AIC Preprints, American Institute for Conservation 12th Annual Meeting, Los Angeles, 1984* (Washington, DC: American Institute for Conservation, 1984), 20–33; Charlotte Hale, "A Template for Experimentation: Cezanne's Process and the Paintings of Hortense Fiquet," in Dita Amory et al., *Madame Cézanne,* exh. cat. (New York: Metropolitan Museum of Art, 2014), 45–71; Laura Neufeld, "Belle Formule: Materials and Methods in Cézanne's Watercolors," in *Cézanne Drawing,* edited by Jodi Hauptman and Samantha Friedman, exh. cat. (New York: Museum of Modern Art, 2021), 200–205; Elisabeth Reissner, "Transparency of Means: 'Drawing' and Colour in Cézanne's Watercolours and Oil Paintings in The Courtauld Gallery," in *The Courtauld Cézannes,* edited by Stephanie Buck et al, exh. cat. (London: Courtauld Gallery in association with Paul Holberton, 2008), 49–71; Reissner, "Ways of Making," 4–30; Marjorie Shelley, "Cézanne as Draftsman. Sketchbooks and Graphite Drawings," in Amory et al., *Madame Cézanne,* 107–45; Fabienne Ruppen, "Tackling Cezanne's Paper: On the Reconstruction of Loose Sheets," in Fabienne Ruppen, Walter Feilchenfeldt, and Yuval Etgar, *Reconstructing Cezanne: Sequence and Process in Paul Cezanne's Works on Paper,* exh. cat. (London: Ridinghouse in collaboration with Luxembourg and Dayan, 2019), 16–44; Anya Shutova and Barbara Buckley, "Materials and Techniques: A Study of Cézanne's Paintings in The Barnes Foundation," in *Cézanne in the Barnes Foundation,* edited by André Dombrowski, Nancy Ireson, and Sylvie Patry (New York: Rizzoli Electa, 2021), 31–57; and Faith Zieske, "Paul Cézanne's Watercolors: His Choice of Pigments and Papers," in *The Broad Spectrum,* edited by Harriet Stratis and Brit Salvesen (London: Archetype, 2002), 89–101.

6. Visual examination suggests that Cezanne manipulated his oils with mediums and thinners to achieve a range of consistencies, but, even when thinly applied, the oil paint retained a level of opacity and body that distinguishes it from the more fluid, transparent watercolor. Cezanne rarely used transparent glazes in his oil paintings; for examples, see Reissner, "Ways of Making," 22–23; and Hale, "Template for Experimentation," 58.

7. For discussion of Cezanne's interest in the formal possibilities of blank paper and unresolved areas, see Jodi Hauptman, "Cézanne's Drawings: A Graphology," in Hauptman and Friedman, *Cézanne Drawing,* 17–18; and Hale, "Template for Experimentation," 67.

8. Paul Cezanne to Joachim Gasquet, July 8, 1902, in Danchev, *Letters,* 322. letter 218.

9. Shelley discusses the conspicuous absence of reductive techniques, such as erasing and stumping, in Cezanne's drawings ("Cézanne as Draftsman," 117–18); and Neufeld reports that in the drawings and watercolors she studied, Cezanne did not erase his graphite drawing and incorporated corrections into his images ("Belle Formule," 202).

10. Recent research on the Barnes Foundation's significant collection of Cezanne's oil paintings has revealed evidence that the artist scraped, wiped, and abraded paint layers to achieve various effects in a significant number of works. See Shutova and Buckley, "Materials and Techniques," 45 and 49. Until now, few examples had been reported: Anthea Callen described instances of scraping in Cezanne's early knife paintings; see her *The Work of Art: Plein-air Painting and Artistic Identity in Nineteenth-Century France* (London: Reaktion Books, 2015), 109; and Hale discusses an example of Cezanne scraping earlier paint layers on a repurposed canvas ("Template for Experimentation," 60). Reissner found no evidence that Cezanne had scraped away unwanted layers in her study of his paintings at the National Gallery, London ("Ways of Making," 15). Technical examination of more of Cezanne's works will no doubt enhance our understanding of the artist's working process.

11. Technical imaging revealed that Cezanne originally painted a different arrangement of at least four pieces of fruit in the lower left corner of this painting; the other pieces of fruit are more obscured by the subsequent paint layers. Due to Cezanne's use of vermillion (mercuric sulfide) to paint the earlier pieces of fruit, they are more clearly visible in the macro-XRF elemental map of mercury (see fig. 10).

12. See Carol Armstrong, *Cézanne in the Studio: Still Life in Watercolor* (Los Angeles: J. Paul Getty Trust, 2004), esp. 75–92; and Reissner, "Ways of Making," 11. Neufeld notes that Cezanne's early watercolors, by contrast, were often studies for his oils ("Belle Formule," 203). Three of the Art Institute's watercolors—*The Three Skulls* (cat. 141), *Montagne Saint-Victoire (The Arc Valley)* (cat. 111), and *Man Wearing a Straw Hat* (cat. 134)—have cognates painted in oil. By contrast, only *Study for the Card Players* (cat. 114) is properly a figure study for an oil painting.

13. Although Cezanne's work in both media has been characterized as slow and methodical, a watercolor could typically be completed much more quickly than an oil painting. Cezanne's more ambitious watercolors were likely carried out over multiple working sessions; see Neufeld, "Belle Formule," 204 and 205n19. Several references in his letters describe him working months or even years on his oil paintings. The different speeds of execution may therefore have impacted his choice of one medium over another. See also Caitlin Haskell's discussion in this volume of the relationship between works of the same subject in different media (pp. 41–42).

14. See Paul Smith, "Cézanne's Colour Lab: (not-so-) still life," in *The World Is an Apple: The Still Lifes of Paul Cézanne,* edited by Benedict Leca, exh. cat. (Hamilton, Ontario: Art Gallery of Hamilton in association with D Giles Limited, 2014), 115 and 123; and Birgit Schwarz, "Cat. 56: *Three Skulls on a Patterned Carpet*" in Baumann et al., *Cézanne: Finished - Unfinished,* 240.

15. The reflected-IR image was captured with a Sinarback eVolution 86H digital back equipped with optical filters (850–1000 nm). For more information on camera filtering systems, see Giovanni Verri and David Saunders, "Xenon Flash for Reflectance and Luminescence (Multispectral) Imaging in Cultural Heritage Applications," *The British Museum Technical Bulletin* 8 (2014): 83–92.

16. Matthew Simms, "Painting on Drawing: Cézanne's Watercolors," in *Cézanne in Focus: Watercolors from The Henry and Rose Pearlman Collection,* edited by Laura M. Giles and Carol Armstrong, exh. cat. (Princeton, NJ: Princeton University Art Museum, 2002), 19.

17. Examination under ultraviolet radiation suggests that some portions of the sheet that appear unpainted may be covered with very pale washes that have faded, including areas of the lower left skull and of the textile in the lower left quadrant. Alterations to the original materials may significantly affect color relationships and the reading of space within Cezanne's works. The original

appearance of all of the watercolors that we studied has changed to some extent due to light exposure causing pigments to fade or the discoloration of paper supports.

18. Visible underdrawing has a significant presence in some of Cezanne's oil paintings; see, for example, *Still Life with Plaster Cupid* (c. 1894; FWN 692). The underdrawing of the apples is visible through thin paint layers in a few places and Cezanne even purportedly drew on top of the paint in one area; see Courtauld Institute Galleries, *Impressionist and Post-Impressionist Masterpieces: The Courtauld Collection* (New Haven, CT: Yale University Press, 1987), n.p., cat. 28; see also Reissner, "Transparency of Means," 54.

19. The IR reflectograph was captured with a Goodrich/Sensors Unlimited SU640SDV-1.7RT with J filter (1500–1700 nm).

20. The term "painted underdrawing" is often used with reference to Cezanne's painting technique to describe a specific aspect of compositional planning. It consists of linear brushstrokes used to essentially "draw in paint" the outlines of his subjects and is distinct from both dry-medium underdrawing and more broadly-applied passages of dilute paint that provide initial washes of color. See Reissner, "Ways of Making," 14.

21. Paul Cezanne to Émile Bernard, May 12, 1904, in *Conversations with Cézanne*, edited by Michael Doran and translated by Julie Lawrence Cochran (Berkeley: University of California Press, 2001), 30, letter 2.

22. The pigments listed were inferred using the techniques indicated in parentheses: anthraquinone of animal (likely cochineal) origin (HSI), emerald green (XRF, HSI), cobalt blue (HSI, XRF), vermillion (HSI, XRF), and indigo (HSI). Among the watercolors and oil paintings analyzed, the detection of copper and arsenic in the green paint, along with the bright-green pigment particles observed under microscope examination of the artwork, suggested the presence of emerald green rather than the less commonly used Scheele's green, another copper-arsenic-based green pigment also available at the time. Analysis was performed using a Bruker ArTAX micro-XRF spectrometer (Röntec AG, XS-3, Mo, 50kV, 200s acquisition time). Hyperspectral imaging was undertaken using a Resonon Pika II pushbroom in the 400–1000 nm range, calibrated using a 99% Spectralon reflectance standard; see Marc Vermeulen, Kate Smith, Katherine Eremin, Georgina Rayner, and Marc Walton, "Application of Uniform Manifold Approximation and Projection (UMAP) in Spectral Imaging of Artworks," *Spectrochimica Acta. Part A: Molecular and Biomolecular Spectroscopy* 252 (2021): 119547, https://doi.org/10.1016/j.saa.2021.119547.

23. Changes in the forms and positioning of the textiles are also indicated in *Curtain, Pitcher, and a Fruit Bowl* (cat. 60) and *Still Life with Apples* (cat. 64). We are grateful to Devi Ormond, Associate Paintings Conservator at the J. Paul Getty Museum, Los Angeles, for capturing an IR reflectograph of *Still Life with Apples*.

24. Émile Bernard, "Paul Cézanne," in Doran, *Conversations*, 39; originally published in *L'Occident* (July 1904).

25. The pigments listed were inferred using the techniques indicated in parentheses: lead white (FTIR, XRF), emerald green (XRF, HSI), viridian (HSI, XRF), Prussian blue (FTIR), vermillion (XRF, HSI), and ultramarine blue (HSI). FTIR analysis was performed using a Bruker ALPHA FTIR spectrometer equipped with a noncontact reflectance module.

26. Reissner, "Ways of Making," 50.

27. For further discussion, see, for example, Maurice Merleau-Ponty, "Cezanne's Doubt," in *Sense and Non-Sense*, edited and translated by Hubert L. Dreyfus and Patricia Allen Dreyfus (Evanston, IL: Northwestern University Press, 1964), 9–25; Richard Shiff, "Cezanne's Physicality: The Politics of Touch," in *The Language of Art History*, edited by Salim Kemal and Ivan Gaskell (Cambridge, UK: Cambridge University Press, 1991), 138; and Paul Smith, "Cezanne's 'Primitive' Perspective or the 'View from Everywhere,'" *Art Bulletin* 95, no. 1 (March 2013): 102–19. Regarding the ways in which Cezanne's process may account for both deliberate and unintentional distortion in his works, see, in particular Reissner, "Ways of Making," 27–28; and Armstrong, *Cézanne in the Studio*, 129–30.

28. For further discussion of these works in relation to an oil painting in the Courtauld Gallery that also has unresolved passages, see John House, "Cat. 4: *La Montagne Sainte-Victoire au grand pin*," in Buck et al., *The Courtauld Cézannes*, 84–87.

29. Paul Cezanne to Émile Bernard, 1905, in Danchev, *Letters*, 353, letter 253.

30. Smith also discusses the crucial color relationships Cezanne establishes in his backgrounds ("Cezanne's Color Lab," 128).

31. A custom-designed macro-XRF system developed by Northwestern University was employed in this study. See Emeline Pouyet, Nicholas Barbi, Henry Chopp, Owen Healy, Aggelos Katsaggelos, Sophia Moak, Rick Mott, Marc Vermeulen, and Marc Walton, "Development of a Highly Mobile and Versatile Large MA-XRF Scanner for in Situ Analyses of Painted Work of Arts." *X-Ray Spectrometry* 50, no. 4 (2020): 1–9, https://doi.org/10.1002/xrs.3173. The authors are grateful to Marc Walton, Marc Vermeulen, and Annette Suleika Ortiz Miranda for capturing this data.

32. An IR false-color image is created by digitally editing visible and IR images of the painting. Reflected IR radiation is visualized as red, red light as green, and green light as blue. See A. Aldrovandi, E. Buzzegoli, A. Keller, and D. Kunzelman, "Investigation of Painted Surfaces with a Reflected UV False Color Technique," in *Proceedings of Art '05: 8th International Conference on Non-Destructive Investigations and Microanalysis for the Diagnostics and Conservation of the Cultural and Environmental Heritage, 15–19 May, Lecce, Italy, 2005*, edited by C. Parisi, G. Buzzanca and A. Paradisi (Lecce, Italy: Italian Society of Non-Destructive Testing Monitoring Diagnostics, 2005).

33. The pigments listed were inferred using the techniques in parentheses: lead white (PLM, XRF), zinc-based white (XRF), ultramarine blue (HSI, PLM), emerald green (XRF, PLM), chrome yellow (PLM, XRF), yellow ochre (HSI, XRF, PLM), vermillion (XRF, HSI, PLM), and bone black (PLM). A Zeiss Universal PLM microscope was used.

34. A Keyence VHX-7020 digital microscope equipped with a VH-ZST Dual-Objective zoom lens (20-2000x) was used to examine this painting. The authors are grateful to Keyence for lending their equipment.

35. The pigments listed were inferred using the techniques in parentheses: lead white (XRF), zinc-based white (XRF), ultramarine blue (HSI), emerald green (XRF), viridian (HSI, XRF), and vermillion (XRF, HSI).

36. The elemental maps (see fig. 10) show that barium is not associated with zinc, excluding the use of lithopone, a barium- and zinc-based white pigment. Barium is therefore more likely present as an extender—that is, a colorless compound added by paint manufacturers to bulk up a pigment.

37. In Doran, *Conversations*, 118.

38. The presence of an anthraquinone of vegetable origin (likely madder) was inferred using HSI and ultraviolet-induced luminesence. The presence of other pigments was inferred using the techniques in parentheses: lead white (XRF), zinc white (XRF), cobalt blue (XRF, HSI), ultramarine blue (HSI), Prussian blue (XRF, HSI), emerald green (XRF, HSI), Naples yellow (XRF), yellow ochre (XRF, HSI), and vermillion (XRF, HSI).

39. Paul Cezanne to Émile Bernard, April 15, 1904, in Doran, *Conversations*, 29, letter 1.

40. See, for example, Reissner, "Ways of Making," 17–18; Hale, "Template for Experimentation," 57; Smith, "Cezanne's Color Lab," 123–28; and Armstrong, *Cézanne in the Studio*, esp. 130.

41. Yve-Alain Bois, "Cézanne: Words and Deeds," translated by Rosalind Krauss, *October* 84 (Spring 1998): 39.

42. The pigments listed were inferred using the techniques in parentheses: cobalt blue (HSI, XRF) and yellow ochre (HSI, XRF).

43. The pigments listed were inferred using the techniques in parentheses: cobalt blue (HSI, XRF), Prussian blue (FTIR), and indigo (HSI).

44. "Art is a harmony parallel to nature—what can those imbeciles be thinking who say that the artist always falls short of nature?": Paul Cezanne to Joachim Gasquet, Sept. 26, 1897, in Danchev, *Letters*, 287, letter 181.

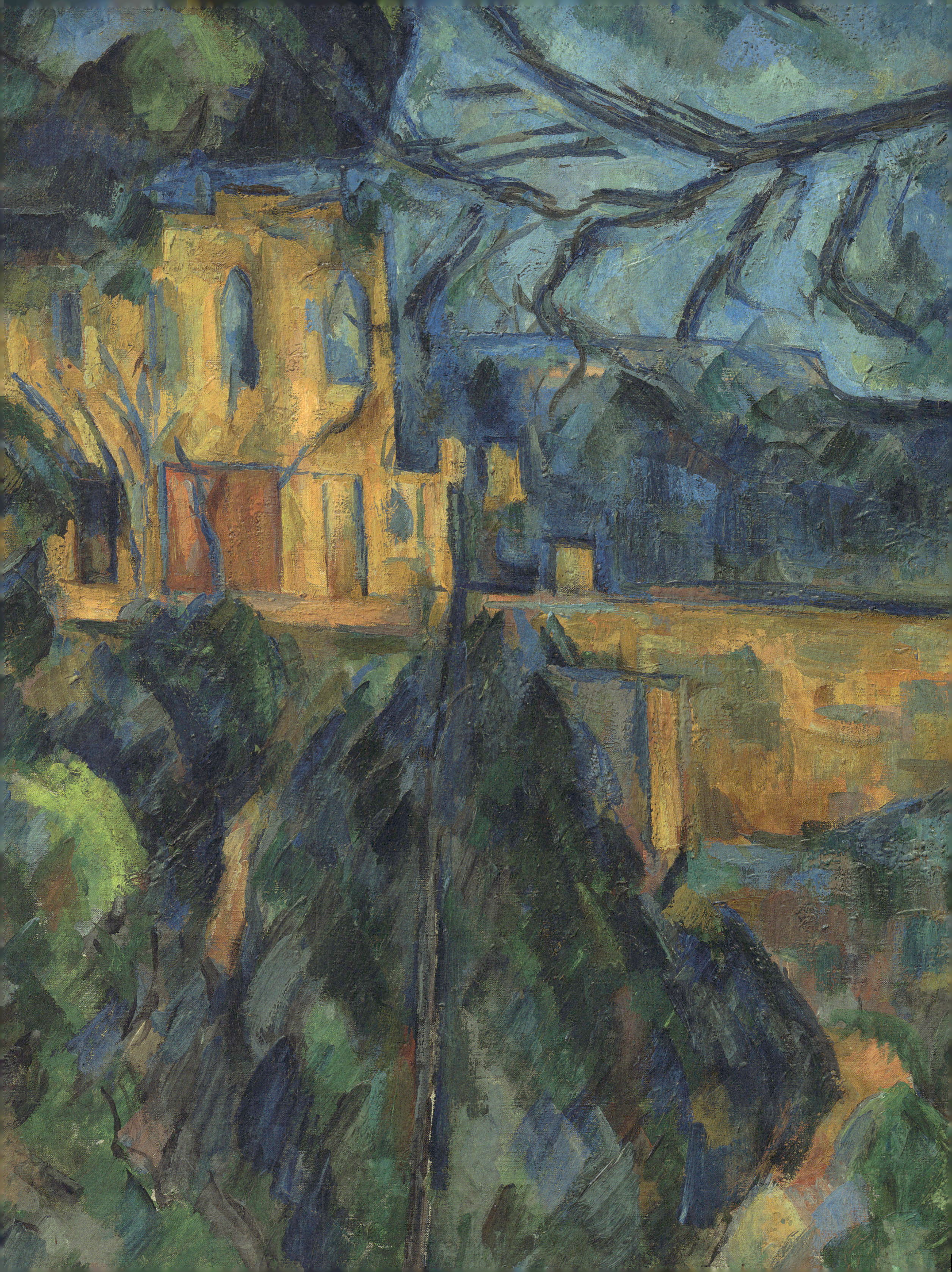

Cezanne's Slow Homecoming

Natalia Sidlina

I work tenaciously, I glimpse the Promised Land. Will I be like the great leader of the Hebrews, or will I be able to enter?
—Paul Cezanne to Ambroise Vollard, 1903[1]

Believe they have that water too and blue when you see blue, is all blue precious too, is all that that is precious too is all that and they meant to absolve you. In this way Cézanne nearly did nearly in this way Cézanne nearly did nearly did and nearly did. And was I surprised. Was I very surprised.
—Gertrude Stein, 1923[2]

In "Mes Confidences"—a questionnaire Paul Cezanne completed at the end of the nineteenth century (see fig. 1)—he stated that Provence and Paris (in this order) were his preferred places to live.[3] The artist spent most of his adult life in seasonal migration from Île-de-France in the North to Provence in the South, taking full advantage of the growing network of French railways.[4] Nonetheless, his biographers and art historians early on attempted to "settle" him in one place at a time: Roger Fry states that Cezanne had "definitively settled in Paris" in 1863 while the artist's dealer, Ambroise Vollard, entitled a concluding chapter of the 1919 edition of his biographical memoir

"Final Return to Aix (1899)," as if toing and froing between the center and the *pays* was unsettling behavior.[5] Quite the contrary—this was a sign of a shift in his center of gravity. And perhaps more to the point, it was in his hometown that the artist had embarked on both his first great project, in the Grand Salon of the family estate, the Jas de Bouffan, and his last: three compositions known individually and collectively as *The Large Bathers* and a programmatic group of paintings featuring the views of the local landmark, Montagne Sainte-Victoire, seen from the hills of Les Lauves just above his studio.

Torn between the pull of the urban center and nostalgia for Provence—a struggle he shared with his childhood friends and fellow intellectuals Émile Zola and Jean-Baptiste Baille—Cezanne strived to achieve fame, respect among his peers, and success on the Paris art market before quietly withdrawing from the capital. Following his father's death in 1886, Cezanne spent most of his time in Aix-en-Provence. He ceased the constant travel between Aix and Paris in 1899, and remained almost constantly in Provence until his death in 1906. Yet his apocryphal boast, "I will astonish Paris with an apple," was recorded by art critic Gustave Geffroy, who met the painter as late as the 1890s.[6] Cezanne's habit of assuming the guise of a provincial rustic while making his appearances in Paris is well

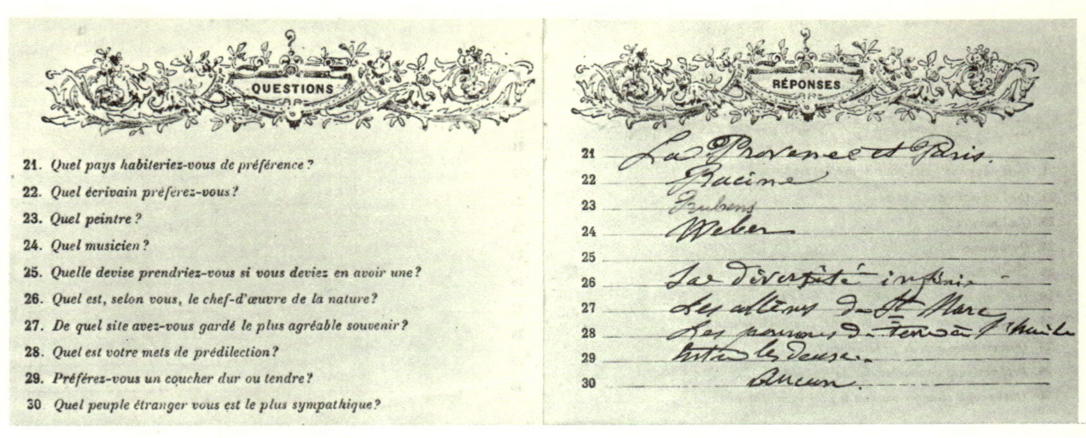

Fig. 1

A spread from "Mes Confidences" with Cezanne's answers. Reproduced in Adrien Chappuis, *The Drawings of Paul Cézanne: A Catalogue Raisonné* (London: Thames and Hudson, 1973), 1:51.

documented; in 1894 he made such an impression on the American painter Matilda Lewis, who thought the artist looked like a quintessential man of the Mediterranean land, of the type described in the popular novels of Alphonse Daudet.[7] Cezanne further testified to his continuous and profound attachment to his homeland by striving to retain his Provençal identity and by expressing his sympathy with the regionalist movement sparked by the Félibrige, a society aiming to support and revive the local way of life.[8] Their efforts to preserve the regional language, culture, and traditions were catalyzed by economic and political changes in France in the second half of the nineteenth century. Cezanne lived during a period of economic upsurge, modernization, and social reorganization, and also bore witness as these processes brought about the disintegration of traditional societal structures. His shifting perception of geopolitical circumstances was mirrored in his landscapes. Those of the 1860s through the 1880s reveal first an explorative eye registering changes in his familiar environment (such as factories' chimneys around picturesque L'Estaque [see cat. 77]) and then consistent adherence to the Impressionist program of capturing the transitory effects of viewing nature in situ (as in *Avenue* [cat. 18]). Finally, the artist's late oeuvre signaled a profound change linked to resentment over Provence's slide to the margins of economic and cultural influence in France: he carefully omitted visible transitory changes to the terrain, instead concentrating on capturing an enduring worldview.

Cezanne's bond with the land that, as he put it, "offers such possibilities for my painting," vividly manifested itself in his renderings of local landmarks: the peak of Montagne Sainte-Victoire and the neo-Gothic manor house Château Noir.[9] This essay focuses on his depictions of these sites precisely because it was here that Cezanne approached the culmination of his project for rendering personal sensory experience (*sensation*) as a phenomenon of universal dimension. In the early nineteenth century, his Provençale predecessors François-Marius Granet and Émile Loubon had focused on history painting, but he focused on spatiality and geography. Cezanne's awareness of landscape as both the visible and conceptual shape of a place came forth in his comment on peasants of Provence who "had never seen, in the cerebral, holistic way we've seen it," the mountain as a landscape—for them, it was simply part of the environment.[10] Sainte-Victoire remained a concrete setting for local culture, while for Cezanne it concerned the process of sense making and understanding his surroundings in an actively responsive way. He perceived the local and concrete on the scale of the universal and even the spiritual, as evidenced by the way his artwork resonated with the creative intellectuals of his own and next generations.

The Moment of Eternity

Cezanne's relationship with Provence—extending from its role as his own center of gravity to his engagement with the geology of the region—became a subject of focused art historical study only recently, with the first monograph published in 2003 and themed exhibitions staged in 2006 and 2017.[11] Scholars working on these projects drew attention to the fact that the artist was situated within the Mediterranean region of France during an economic boom that transformed Marseille into the second-largest city in the country, a center of international trade and immigration. They positioned the artist, the canonical "father" for those pursuing the transcultural modernist project, within the frame of the regional and culturally specific.[12] His approach to landscape in his late oeuvre revealed a very personal investigation into perception of the visible world through the series of works focused on landmarks rich with symbolism for him.

Vollard gives exact, if anecdotal, timing for Cezanne's return to Aix: the day after the artist had finished the dealer's portrait, at the end of 1899. At this time, the artist was aware of his growing renown and legacy, claiming it as his "suitable rank in the history of art."[13] Still, he preferred the relative obscurity and condescension of fellow Aixois.[14] The year 1899 was also a watershed in Cezanne's life, marked by irreversible change: following his mother's death in 1897, the family house was sold.[15] Later that year he sold the contents of his Paris studio to Vollard and, as a capstone to this period of change, set a bonfire in which he destroyed many of his early works held at the Jas de Bouffan.[16] This busy farm on the outskirts of Aix had been his home since 1859, his first studio, and his favorite motif as witnessed by nearly forty extant oil paintings and numerous works on paper executed in the 1860s through mid-1890s. By the end of 1899, though, Cezanne had no property and was looking for a new home. He turned his attention to an unusual building in the environs of Aix, a local "Devil's castle," the Château Noir, situated en route from Aix to the hilled village of Le Tholonet. The artist and his friends had explored the grounds of the unfinished house in their youth; later, Cezanne rented rooms there to store his plein-air equipment, possibly from as early as 1887.[17] In 1899 he tried to acquire the property, but his offer was rejected.[18] A group of views of the château he wanted to make his home—five known paintings executed between 1904 and 1906—are among the darkest and most emotionally charged works of his late career.[19]

Judging by a letter he sent to his friend Joachim Gasquet, a young poet and fellow Aixois, Cezanne found the surrounding landscape of Haute-Savoy—which he toured in summer 1896—to be picture-perfect but insubstantial.[20] Not much could compare with the views offered by his native Provence: "the lake is very good with the big hills all around . . . not much to our country, though truth to tell it's fine. But when you're born down there [in Provence], that's it, there is nothing more to be said."[21] One of the paintings reflecting these sentiments, *Montagne Saint-Victoire and the Château Noir* (fig. 2), was created during his last years and was illustrated in 1921 in the first edition of memoirs that Gasquet published at the end of his life as a statement on his association with the reclusive older painter.[22] Staged rather theatrically, the foreground view appears through an opening framed by overgrown branches of the ancient Aleppo pines. The intense ochre hues of the edifice, which was built from the stones of the nearby Bibémus quarries,

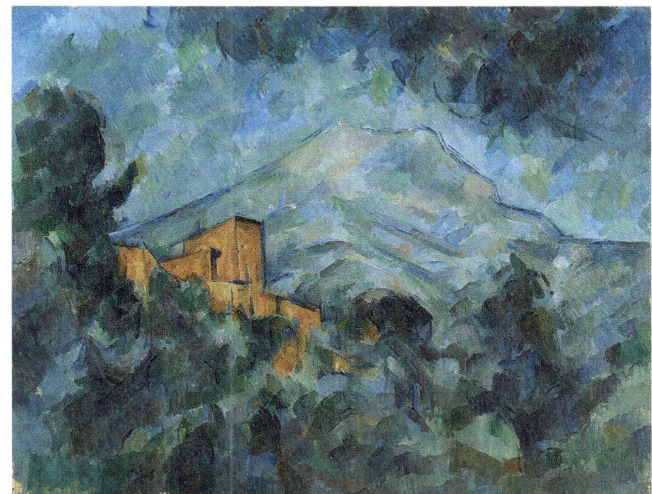

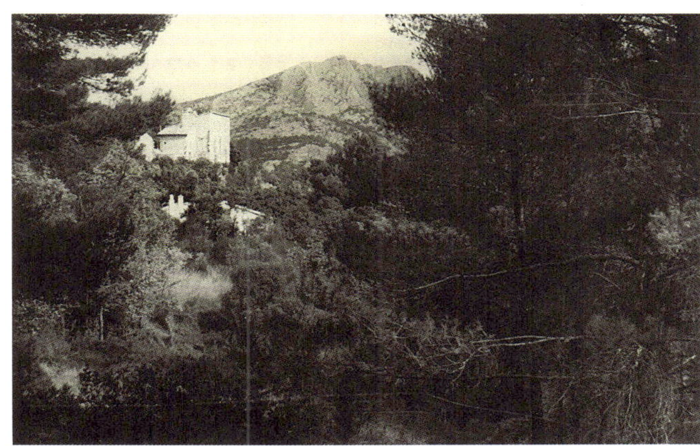

Fig. 2

Paul Cezanne (French, 1839–1906). *Montagne Sainte-Victoire and the Château Noir*, 1904–6. Oil on canvas; 65.6 × 81 cm (25 13/16 × 31 7/8 in.). Artizon Museum, Tokyo. (FWN 362)

Fig. 3

Château Noir seen through the trees, c. 1935. Photograph by John Rewald. John Rewald Archive, Department of Image Collections, National Gallery of Art Library, Washington, DC.

is a construction of geometric cubic forms emphasized with dark outlines against the complex and subtle palette of blues, greens, grays, and browns of the slopes and the mountain peak. Cezanne's fluid handling of semitransparent paints (akin to that in his watercolors) left the weave of the canvas exposed. The majestic manmade landmark is silhouetted against the regal mountain. The composition, revealing the castle as if nestled in the foothills of Saint-Victoire, was painted from the turn of the road now called Route Cézanne, from a vantage point identified by art historian John Rewald in 1935 (see fig. 3).

Despite—or perhaps because of—its highly personal treatment, Cezanne's investment in the subject found a wider appeal among international intellectuals than among those who were complicit in the marginalization of his beloved Provence, as evidenced by the work's afterlife. Mushanokōji Saneatsu, the Japanese writer and intellectual, offered in 1912 that Cezanne's character "allows him to be the most faithful renderer of nature, and yet he is at the same time the best of the mystic."[23] Indeed, his paintings resonated strongly with Japanese creative intellectuals of the early twentieth century, who could relate to the idea that the creative process itself, rather than completion of the work, could be the realization of artistic personality; this aspect of his approach found high praise among the public in Japan, as did *Montagne Saint-Victoire and the Château Noir*.[24] (At around the same time, in France, the US-born writer Gertrude Stein, to whom we will return, also identified this "finished or unfinished" quality in Cezanne's work.[25]) In 1922 the canvas was earmarked for the Shirakaba Museum project—an unrealized initiative of the Shirakaba (White Birch) literary group committed to transnational forms of cultural expression. It was ultimately acquired by a wealthy intellectual, Hara Zen'ichirō, and shipped from Europe to Japan the next summer. The rendering of Montagne Saint-Victoire now in Tokyo is a rare work that positions the house against the mountain peak and treats both with

the same deference. Compared with another view of a mountainous landscape with a castle—*Lake Annecy* (fig. 4)—the Tokyo canvas dispensed with the dreamy romanticism and picturesque qualities of Cezanne's earlier effort in order to convey to the viewer "the spectacle that the *Pater Omnipotents Aeterne Deus* spreads before us."[26]

From 1904 until Cezanne's death in 1906, the Château Noir became a focus of the artist's methodical studies of individual moments—that is, of repeated motif observation rather than a subject of seriality. On the opposite side of the spectrum from the Tokyo canvas created around the same time is *Château Noir*, at the National Gallery of Art, Washington, DC (1900–1904; cat. 131). It is a deeply confounding and dark landscape, often compared to works from the same period that also deal with mortality, such as *Three Skulls on a Patterned Carpet* (1904; cat. 140).[27] The composition is built around the château, rendered in red tones as a medieval ruin; its gaping Gothic windows graced the very rooms Cezanne was renting at the time. To the left the view is overshadowed by the trunks, branches, and rippled foliage of the pines, which rise as barriers on both sides of the path leading to the house. Strangely angular branches form a cross at the top of the pine in the foreground. From the right the house is contained in its isolated spot by the blues and grays of Le Cengle ridge and the menacing claws of dry, protruding tree branches. In contrast with the loose brushwork of *Montagne Saint-Victoire and the Château Noir*, this rendering was worked and reworked over a period of years, as evidenced by its thick impasto built up with overlapping brushstrokes as well as by lumps of dried oil paint protruding from underlying layers. Cezanne had grappled with the composition in a more physical way as well. After starting with a standard-sized, pre-primed canvas (92 × 73 cm [36 ¼ × 28 ¾ in.]), he added two thin canvas strips to the left and right edges to stretch this particular view of the motif (see fig. 5).[28] Moreover, in this oil, akin to his grand project *The Large Bathers*, now at the Barnes Foundation (fig. 6), he did not hide the strips, as thin as they are, as he strived to get the proportions right. Just a few weeks before dying, the artist wrote to his son, "As a painter I'm becoming more clear-sighted in front of nature, but realization of my sensations is still very labored. I can't achieve the intensity that builds in my senses, I don't have the magnificent richness of color that enlivens nature."[29]

The Last Lesson of Sainte-Victoire

Affected by the loss of the Jas de Bouffan and unable to secure the purchase of the Château Noir, Cezanne moved to a small apartment on rue Boulegon within Aix's old

Fig. 4

Paul Cezanne. *Lake Annecy*, 1896. Oil on canvas; 65 × 81 cm (25 ⅝ × 31 ⅞ in.). The Courtauld Gallery, London, The Samuel Courtauld Trust, Courtauld Gift 1932 (P.1932.SC.60). (FWN 311)

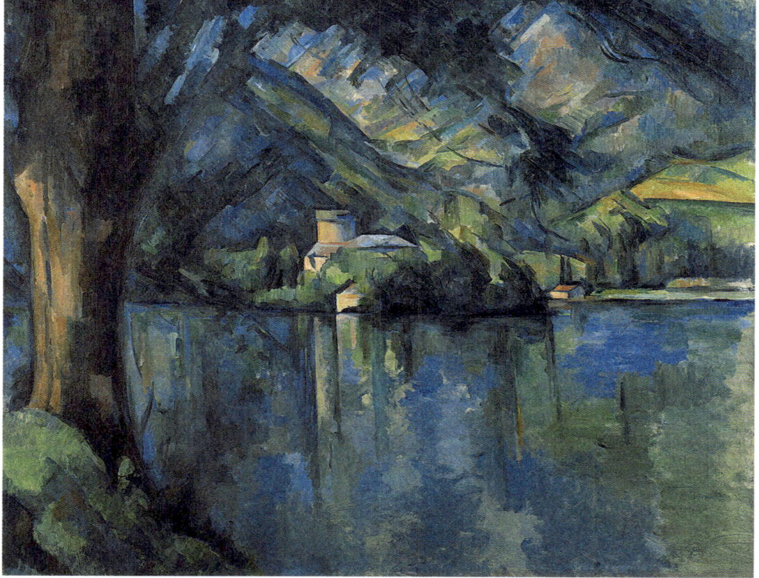

town walls and acquired land just outside the town, in the hills of Les Lauves, to build his first professional studio in the city. He continued to work at the château until the completion of the studio in 1902. Here Cezanne created one of the most famous groups of landscapes of the 1900s: Montagne Sainte-Victoire as seen from Les Lauves.

Cezanne chose every site for his plein-air sessions with the utmost care, mapping the land on his walks in accord with his conviction that a fine view doesn't quite make a motif.[30] His sensory experiences guided him toward identifying these locations. He positioned his easel on a natural terrace on the slopes of Les Marguerites, a site that offered an uninterrupted view of the horizon and the peak of Sainte-Victoire across the open fields of the Arc River Valley. From this vantage point, the artist executed eleven oil paintings in which the mountain assumed an epic scale.[31] All of them are traditionally dated from 1904 to 1906 and range from a heavily reworked, elongated composition with four added strips of canvas, now at the Metropolitan Museum of Art, New York (FWN 356), to one in a private collection, in which Cezanne outlined the tilted, mirage-like shape of the mountain with a few precise brushstrokes on the white plane of primed canvas (cat. 128). For a long time, it was assumed that the last canvas in the sequence—the one with the claim to be most "realized"—was the landscape in the collection of the State Pushkin Museum of Fine Art in Moscow (FWN 368).[32] The museum's own catalogue dates the work as finished about a year earlier than the New York canvas (1904–5); additionally, a recent publication revealed that Cezanne donated the painting to the sale of the Atelier Eugène Carrière at Hôtel Drouot, Paris, in June 1906.[33] That makes it an unlikely candidate for the final canvas, as others from the group remained in the studio and were among those that he continued to work on until his death. These include *Mont Sainte-Victoire Seen from Les Lauves* (cat. 124), now in the collection of the Kunstmuseum Basel. This, the most probable candidate for the final work of the sequence, offers the quintessence of the artist's investigation of the motif with its construction, ominously deep palette, and echoes of classical landscape.

The composition of the Basel oil presents a dramatic view of the plateau and the mountain seen through a luminous clearing framed by the green-blue of foliage and atmosphere. The mountain materializes on the horizon line, curling gently up and south, its peak modeled with white and pale-blue touches lightened up from the west. Its southern side drops down steeply and spreads, outlined by a few streaks of dark blue above and below. This triangular shape dominates the valley, which is defined with dark-green woods and earthy yellow and red touches—the fields, clearings, groves, roofs, and walls

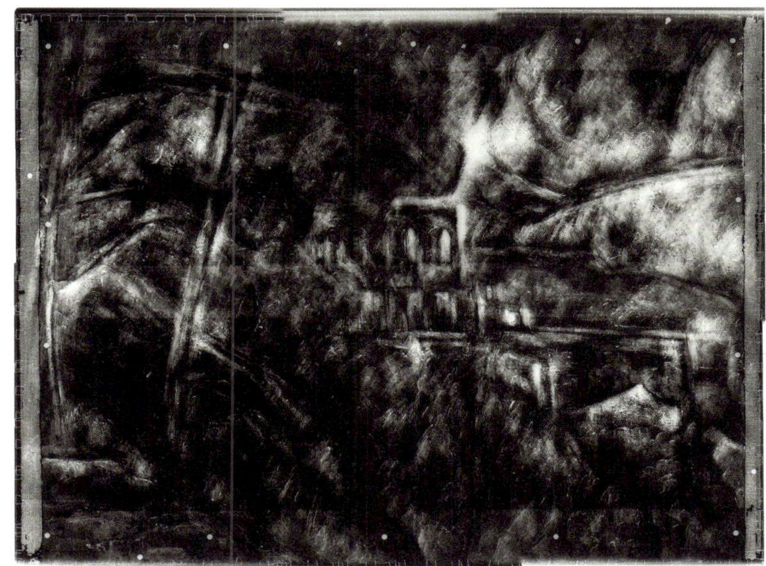

Fig. 5

X-radiograph image of Cezanne's *Château Noir*, 1900–1904 (cat. 131; FWN 359), revealing the addition of strips of canvas to the left and right edges of the painting; they appear as narrow white bands.

Fig. 6

Paul Cezanne. *The Large Bathers* (Les grandes baigneuses), c. 1894–1906. Oil on canvas; 132.5 × 219 cm (52 3/16 × 86 1/4 in.). Barnes Foundation, Philadelphia, BF934. (FWN 980)
The painting has been annotated to indicate the seams of the canvas additions along the right side (B, C, D, E) and at the lower edge (F, G, H) as well as the extended upper tacking edge. From Barbara Buckley, Anya Shutova, and Jennifer Mass "A Technical Study of The Large Bathers," p. 312, fig. 3.

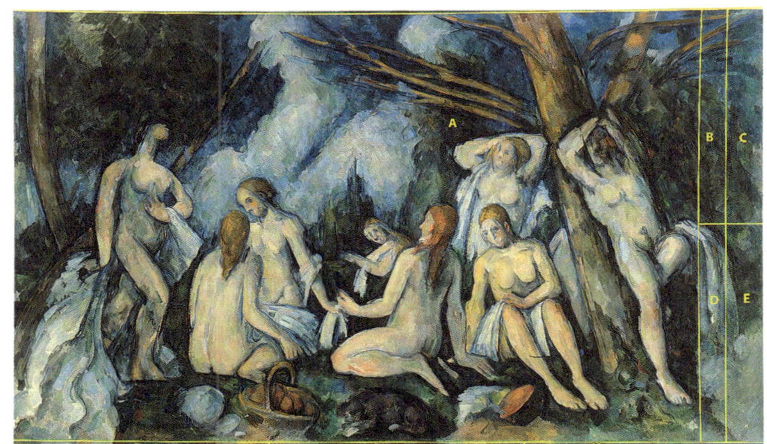

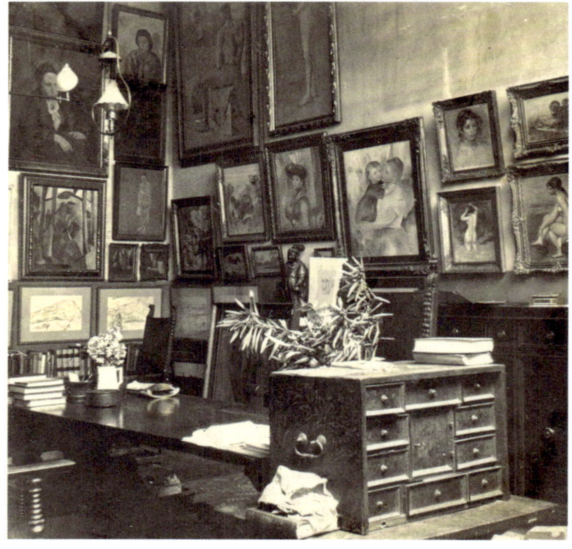

Fig. 7

Photograph of the atelier of Leo and Gertrude
Stein, 27, rue Fleurus, Paris, with two
watercolors of Mont Sainte-Victoire (c. 1900)
at lower left, c. 1910. From the Annette
Rosenshine Papers, The Bancroft Library,
University of California, Berkeley.

of buildings are constructed with fluid and thick, but precise, flat brushwork. The picture is strongly unified by the overall dark palette, which is dominated by the green of the woods and sky, while luminous qualities are reserved for the cool blues of the mountaintop and the warm yellows and reds of the clearing in the foreground. Cezanne remained faithful all his life to Impressionist tenets he learned working *en plein air* at Camille Pissarro's side—but now "how far away it all seems already and yet how near."[34] All the elements so clearly defined in the other landscapes of the motif are there—the woods, the fields, the roofs, and the mountain peak itself—but here Cezanne brought them to the very limit of recognizability. Instead of capturing a fleeting moment, the artist strived to convey a geological embodiment of timelessness.

His intensely personal engagement with the act of representation (both of a site and of a region) impressed Gertrude Stein, who was fascinated by Cezanne's ability to disentangle his realized sensory experience from the visual memory of a subject; she owned a number of his late Sainte-Victoire compositions (see fig. 7). In an interview with Robert Bartlett Haas (a longtime editor of her work) in the early 1960s, Stein summarized the painter's accomplishment: "Up to that time composition had consisted of a central idea, to which everything else was an accompaniment and separate but was not an end in itself, and

Cézanne conceived the idea that in composition one thing was as important as another thing. Each part is as important as the whole, and that impressed me enormously."[35] As one of the most influential modernist authors of the twentieth century, she carried his vision forward both in time and into adjacent fields of creative expression.

Long live our native land, our common mother and land of hope.
—Cezanne to Charles Camoin, 1902[36]

As witnessed by Ambroise Vollard and other contemporaries, Cezanne's artistic achievements left his fellow Aixois unmoved; he wasn't appreciated even by some of the local connoisseurs. Reportedly, in the 1920s Monsieur Pontier, then curator at the Musée Granet, the primary art museum in Aix-en-Provence, declared that there would be no Cezannes in the museum's collection.[37] Almost a century later, in 2019, the Musée Granet organized an exhibition titled *Sainte(s)-Victoire(s)* that traced artists' portrayals of Provence's iconic mountain throughout the nineteenth and twentieth centuries. The highlight was a gallery with Cezanne's Sainte-Victoire oils, including *La Montagne Sainte-Victoire* (1897; FWN 314), from the so-called Gurlitt Trove of art looted during World War II and now owned by the Kunstmuseum Bern.[38] An agreement was struck with Cezanne's heirs in 2018 that it would be regularly displayed at the Granet. That makes Aix's museum only the second public collection in France to display Cezanne's most famous landscape motif.[39] All eleven of the views from Les Lauves are held by private and public collections internationally. The motif's drama and urgency as well as the primordial quality of its color composition and emotional expressiveness manifestly appealed strongly to viewers and collectors from other cultural milieux; perhaps paradoxically, Cezanne's struggle to reclaim his regional identity through meticulous depictions of local historical and geographical landmarks resonated globally. Just as he compared himself to Moses, who returned to the Promised Land to attain his prophetic status, Cezanne's realization of his own project was fulfilled upon his *retour au pays*. The painter himself described this process of reconciliation with eloquent pragmatism: "I believe in the logical development of what we see and feel through the study of nature. . . . Techniques are merely the means of making the public feel what we ourselves feel, and making us acceptable."[40] His powerful and very personal engagement with the local while striving to develop a classical canon for the new era—"something solid and enduring like the art of museums"—ultimately felt relevant and urgent in the world bound for centripetal motion, that of the next modernist era.[41]

Notes

1. Paul Cezanne to Ambroise Vollard, Jan. 3, 1903, in *The Letters of Paul Cézanne*, edited and translated by Alex Danchev (Los Angeles: J. Paul Getty Museum, 2013), 325, letter 222.

2. Gertrude Stein, "Cézanne," in *Portraits and Prayers* (New York: Random House 1934), 11.

3. Paul Cezanne, "My Confidences," in *Conversations with Cézanne*, edited by Michael Doran and translated by Julie Lawrence Cochran (Berkeley: University of California Press, 2001), 102. For the album's provenance, see Adrien Chappuis, *The Drawings of Paul Cézanne: A Catalogue Raisonné* (London: Thames and Hudson, 1973), 1:49. For the arguments regarding the document's dating, see Jean-Claude Lebensztejn, *Les couilles de Cézanne, suivi de Persistance de la mémoire* (Paris: Nouvelles Editions Séguier, 1995).

4. See in this volume "Mapping Cezanne," pp. 213–23.

5. Roger Fry, *Cezanne. A Study of His Development* (London: L. and V. Woolf, 1927), 5; Ambroise Vollard, *Paul Cézanne* (Paris: Galerie A. Vollard, 1919), 147–57. In the first edition (1914) the last chapter is entitled "Les dernières années."

6. Paul Cezanne, quoted by Gustave Geffroy in Doran, *Conversations*, 6; originally published as "Avec une pomme, je veux étonner Paris!" in *Claude Monet, sa vie, son temps, son œuvre* (Paris: Éditions Crès et Cie, 1922), 336.

7. For more discussion of the ways in which Cezanne cultivated a reputation as an unsophisticated outsider, see Gloria Groom's essay in this volume, pp. 23–33. See also Marc Elder, *À Giverny, chez Claude Monet* (Giverny, France: Bernheim-Jeune, 1924), 48, quoted in Isabelle Cahn, "Chronology," in Françoise Cachin et al., *Cézanne*, exh. cat. (Philadelphia: Philadelphia Museum of Art, 1996), 534. Lewis's encounter with Cezanne took place at Monet's house in Giverny; see Matilda Lewis quoted in Alex Danchev, *Cézanne: A Life* (New York: Pantheon Books, 2012), 395n67.

8. Nina Maria Athanassoglou-Kallmyer, *Cézanne and Provence: The Painter in His Culture* (Chicago: University of Chicago Press, 2003), 15–52.

9. Paul Cezanne [draft] letter to his parents [Paris, c. 1874], in Danchev, *Letters*, 155, letter 55.

10. Joachim Gasquet, *Cézanne* (Giverny, France: Les Éditions Bernheim-Jeune, 1921), 88.

11. See Athanassoglou-Kallmyer, *Cézanne and Provence*; Philip Conisbee and Denis Coutagne, eds., *Cézanne in Provence*, exh. cat. (Washington, DC: National Gallery of Art; New Haven, CT: Yale University Press, 2006); and Daniel Marchesseau, ed., *Paul Cezanne: Le Chant de la Terre*, exh. cat. (Martigny, Switzerland: Foundation Pierre Gianadda, 2017). The most recent exhibition in this vein focuses primarily on the geology and landscape of Provence in Cezanne's oeuvre: John Elderfield, *Cézanne: The Rock and Quarry Paintings*, exh. cat. (Princeton, NJ: Princeton University Art Museum, 2020).

12. Pablo Picasso reportedly characterized him as such to the Hungarian–French artist Brassaï, November 1943: "He was the father of us all. He was the one who protected us." Pablo Picasso quoted in Brassaï, *Conversations with Picasso*, translated by Jane Marie Todd (Chicago: University of Chicago Press, 1999), 107.

13. Paul Cezanne to Roger Marx, Jan. 23, 1905, in Danchev, *Letters*, 350, letter 248.

14. The tense relationship between Cezanne and his compatriots didn't escape Vollard's attention. They were described in a quite unsympathetic light in chapter VII, "Aix et les Aixois," in Vollard, *Paul Cézanne*, 109–19.

15. The latest research on Cezanne's family estate was the subject of a conference organized by La Société Paul Cezanne, and held in Aix-En-Provence, Sept. 21–22, 2019; for the proceedings, see Denis Coutagne and François Chédeville, *Cézanne, Jas De Bouffan: Art et Histoire* (Lyon, France: Fage Éditions, 2019).

16. Cezanne's neighbor gave an account of the canvas burning that is supported by that of the artist's housekeeper, charged at the same time with destroying his works on paper; see Danchev, *Cezanne: A Life*, 37 and 387n1.

17. Conisbee and Coutagne, *Cézanne in Provence*, 198.

18. See Cahn, "Chronology," 558.

19. See FWN 358–FWN 362 and a number of related works on paper. Other features of the Château Noir oils and watercolors—those focused on *sous-bois*, with their rocky formations and the detailed studies of its stone walls—are discussed in Elderfield, *The Rock and Quarry Paintings*, 129–49.

20. Paul Cezanne to Joachim Gasquet, July 21, 1896, in Danchev, *Letters*, 276, letter 169.

21. Paul Cezanne to Philippe Solari, July 23, 1896, in Danchev, *Letters*, 277, letter 170.

22. Gasquet, *Cézanne*, 64, pl. 62.

23. Quoted in Shigemi Inaga, "Between Revolutionary and Oriental Sage: Paul Cézanne in Japan," *Japan Review*, no. 28 (2015): 139; originally published in Mushanokōji Saneatsu, "Kōinshōha ni tsuite," *Shirakaba*, Jan. 1912, 15.

24. Inaga, "Between Revolutionary and Oriental Sage," 151.

25. "Finished or unfinished it always was what it looked like the very essence of an oil painting because everything was always there, really there"; Gertrude Stein, "Pictures," in *Poets and Painters: Essays on the Art of Painting by Twentieth-Century Poets*, edited by J. D. McClatchy (Berkeley: University of California Press, 1988), 96.

26. Paul Cezanne to Émile Bernard, Jan. 29, 1904, in Danchev, *Letters*, 373.

27. On Cezanne's preoccupation with death see Paul Smith, "Cézanne's Late Landscapes, or the Prospect of Death," in Conisbee and Coutagne, *Cézanne in Provence*, 59–74.

28. On Cezanne's use of standard-size canvases see Elisabeth Reissner, "Ways of Making: Practice and Innovation in Cezanne's Paintings in the National Gallery," *National Gallery Technical Bulletin* 29 (2008): 5–6.

29. Paul Cezanne to Paul Cezanne *fils*, Sept. 8, 1906, in Danchev, *Letters*, 370, letter 267.

30. Paul Cezanne to Émile Zola, May 24, 1883, in Danchev, *Letters*, 228, letter 121.

31. See FWN 351–56 and FWN 364–68.

32. Joseph J. Rishel, "*Mont Sainte-Victoire Seen from Les Lauves*," in Cachin et al., *Cézanne*, 474, cat. 206.

33. Anne Baldassari, ed., *Icons of Modern Art: The Shchukin Collection*, exh. cat. (Paris: Fondation Louis Vuitton and Gallimard, 2016), 438. The work was acquired by Sergei Shchukin in November 1906 and sent to Moscow. The State Pushkin Museum dates it to 1904–5. It was recorded that the work had a label reading "Exposition 1905" on the stretcher; see Anna Barskaya and Yevgenia Georgievskaya, *Paul Cézanne: 1839–1906* (New York: Parkstone International, 2004), 144. For the related watercolor in Tate's collection, see cat. 126.

34. Paul Cezanne to Paul Cezanne *fils*, July [20] 1906, in Danchev, *Letters*, 360, letter 259.

35. Quoted in Georgina Nugent-Folan, "Personal Apperception: Samuel Beckett, Gertrude Stein, and Paul Cézanne's 'La Montagne Sainte-Victoire.'" *Samuel Beckett Today /Aujourd'hui* 27 (2015): 90; originally published in Robert Bartlett Haas, *Gertrude Stein: A Primer for the Gradual Understanding of Gertrude Stein* (Los Angeles: Black Sparrow, 1971), 15–16.

36. Paul Cezanne to Charles Camoin, Jan. 28, 1902, in Danchev, *Letters*, 313, letter 206.

37. Denis Coutagne, *The Musee Granet, Aix-en-Provence* (Paris: Réunion des musées nationaux in association with Fondation BNP Paribas; Aix-en-Provence: Musée Granet, 2007), 97. The author also explains why the city's art museum is not named after its most internationally renowned artist.

38. On the Gurlitt case see Meike Hoffmann and Nicola Kuhn, *Hitlers Kunsthändler: Hildebrand Gurlitt, 1895–1956: Die Biographie* (Munich: C. H. Beck, 2016). The object record for *La Montagne Sainte-Victoire* (1897; FWN 314) may be consulted at lootedart.com/web_images /pdf2016/Cezanne_ORE_532974.pdf

39. The first had been the Musée d'Orsay, which showed *Montagne Saint-Victoire* (1890; cat. 113); the work entered the collection in 1969 as part of a gift from the granddaughter of collector Auguste Pellerin.

40. Paul Cezanne to Émile Bernard, Sept. 21, 1906, in Danchev, *Letters*, 373, letter 269.

41. Paul Cezanne to Camille Pissarro, March 15, 1865, in Danchev, *Letters*, 119, letter 34.

Catalogue

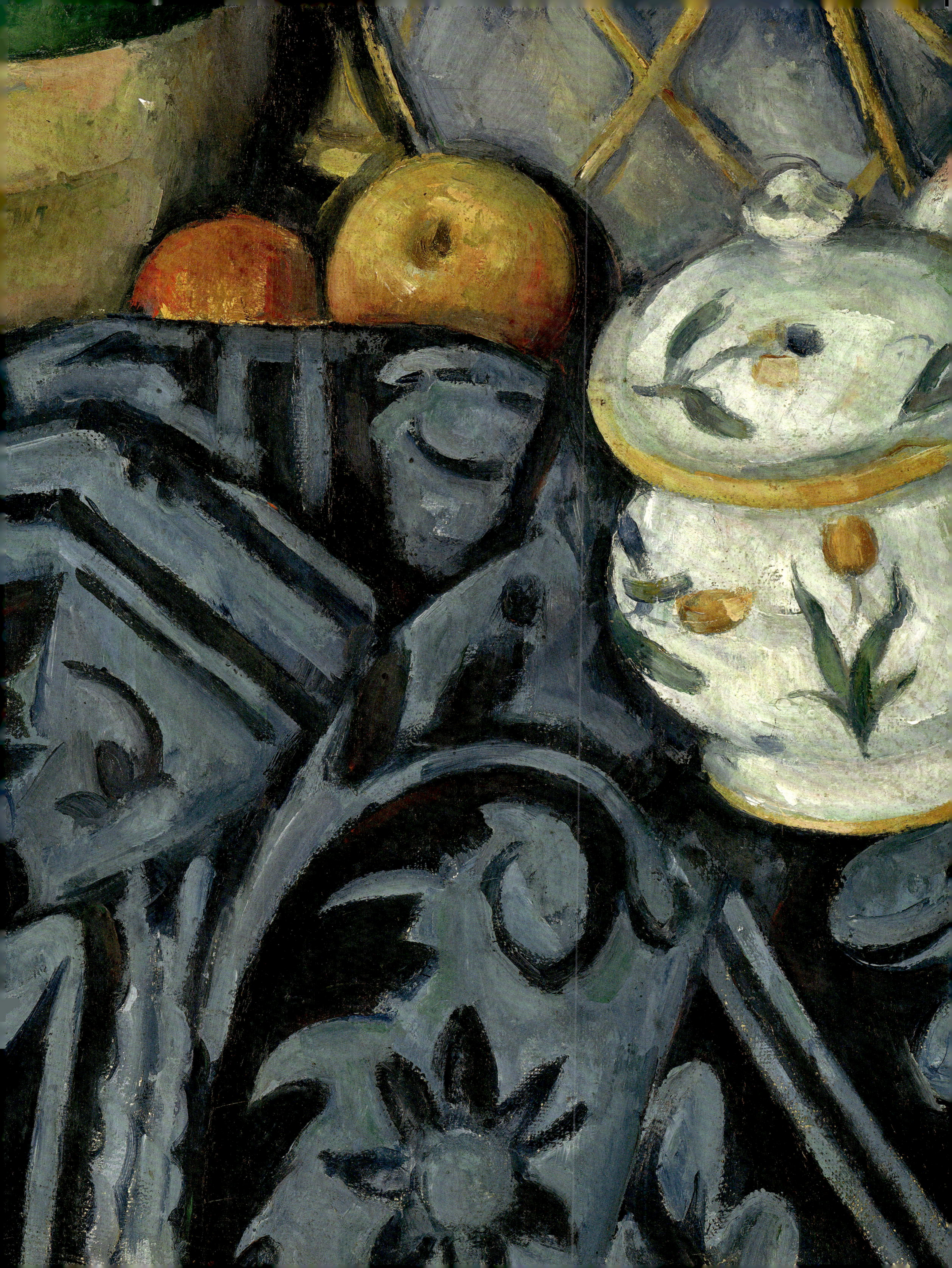

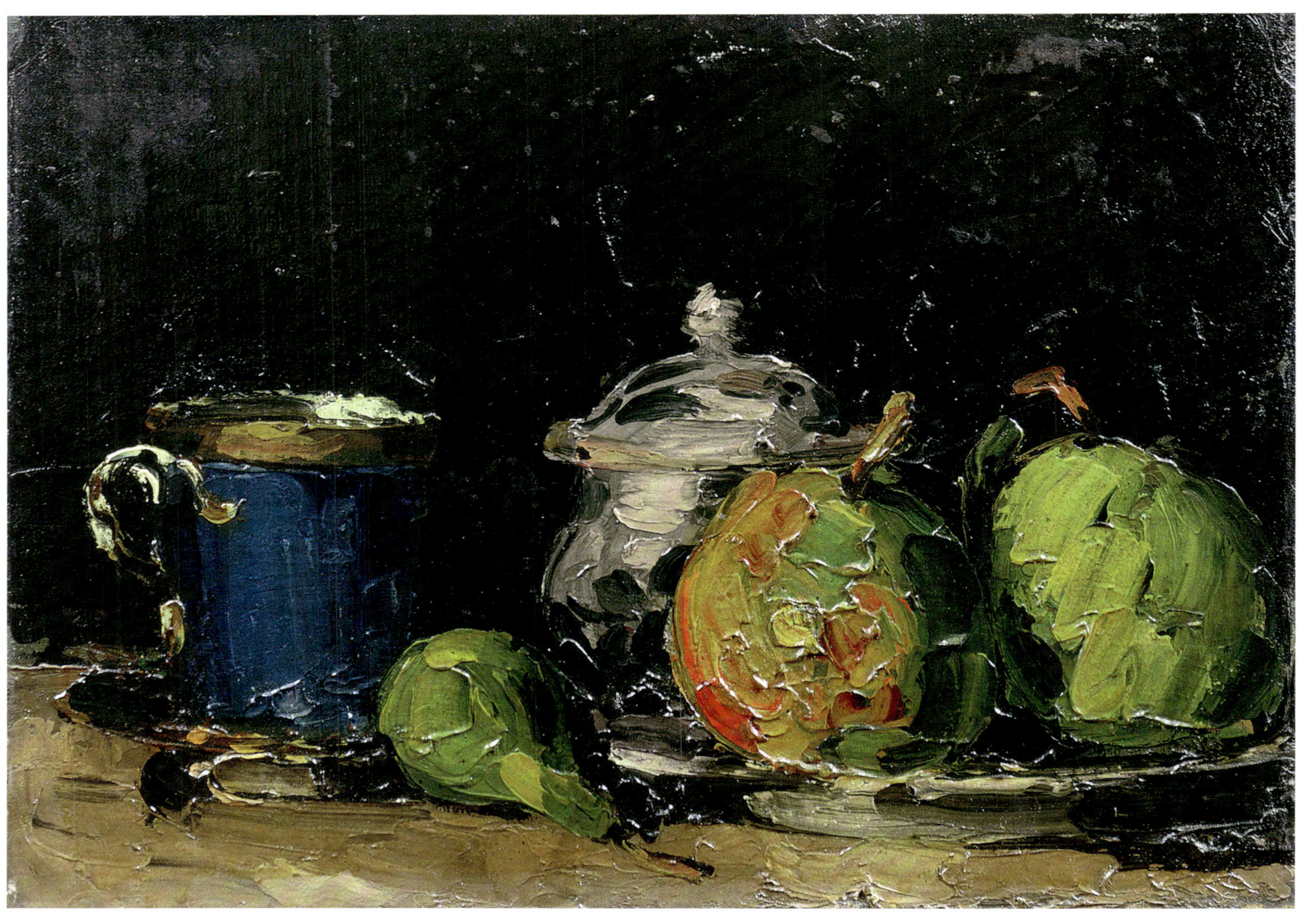

Cat. 1

Sugar Bowl, Pears, and Blue Cup
1865–70
Oil on canvas
30 × 41 cm (11 ¹³⁄₁₆ × 16 ⅛ in.)
Musée d'Orsay, Paris, on deposit to Musée
Granet, Aix-en-Provence, acquis par dation, 1982,
RF 1982-44
FWN 706

Cat. 2

The Artist's Father, Reading "L'Événement"
1866
Oil on canvas
198.5 × 119.3 cm (78 ⅛ × 46 ¹⁵⁄₁₅ in.)
National Gallery of Art, Washington, DC, Collection
of Mr. and Mrs. Paul Mellon, 1970.5.1
FWN 402
Chicago only

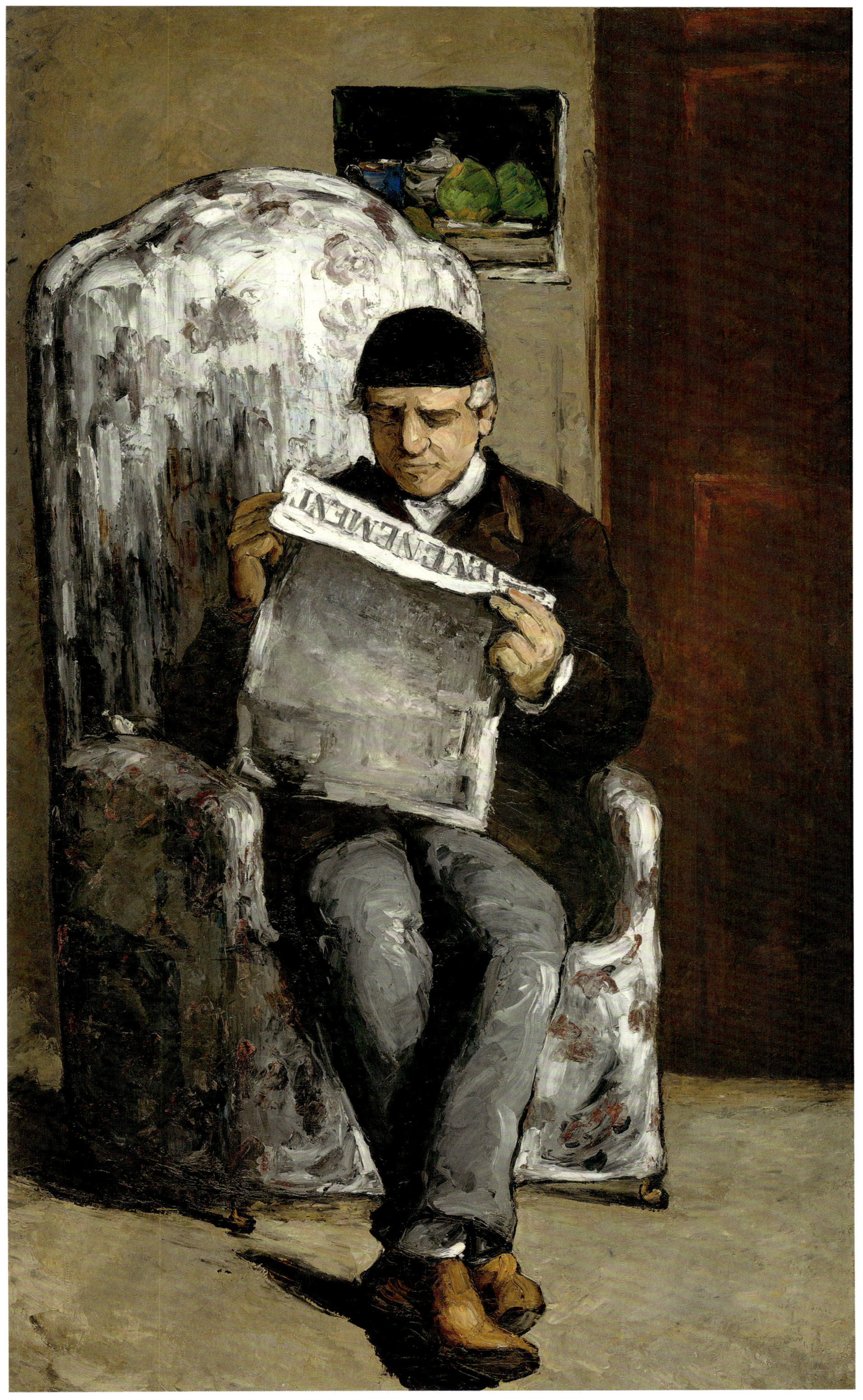

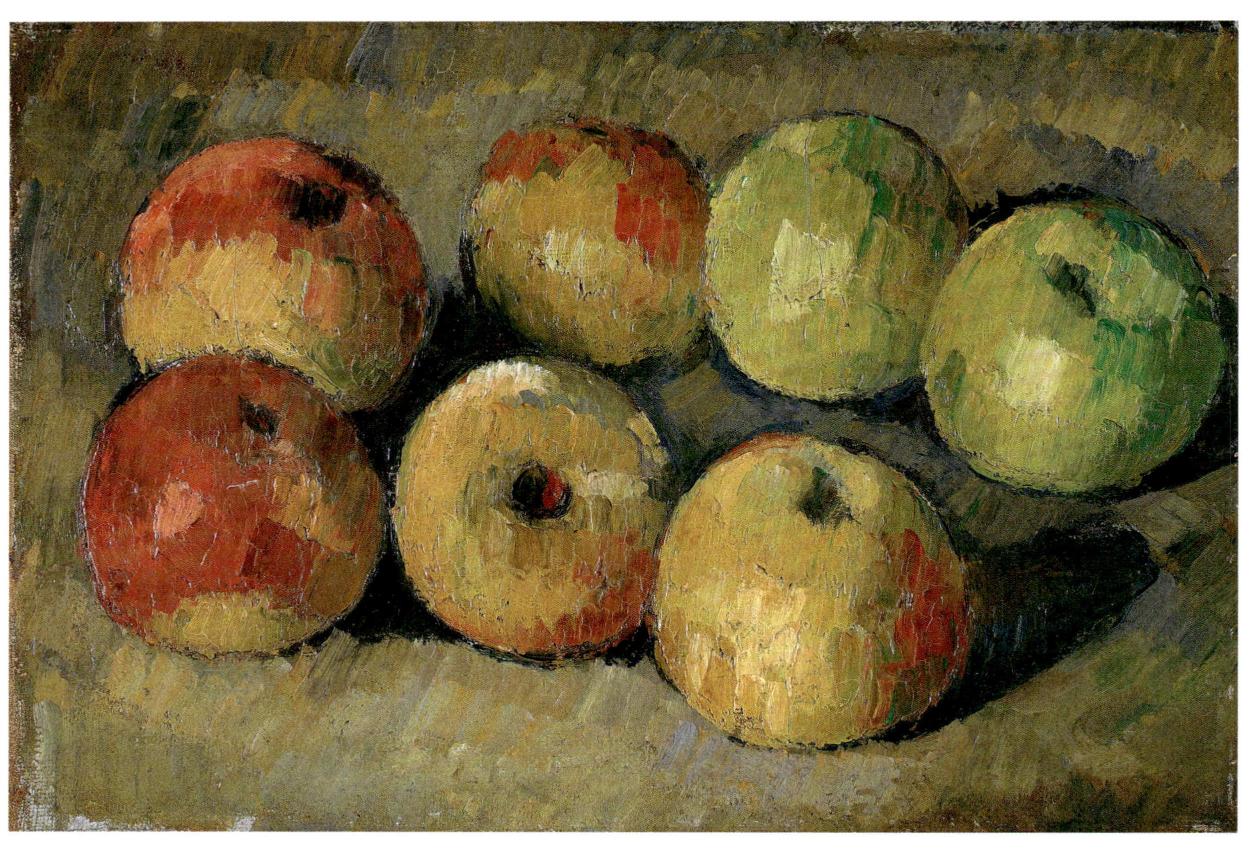

Cat. 3

Still Life with Apples
c. 1878
Oil on canvas
19 × 26.7 cm (7 ½ × 10 ½ in.)
Currently on long term loan from King's College,
University of Cambridge, UK, to The Syndics of
the Fitzwilliam Museum, University of Cambridge,
PDL.3065-006
FWN 760
Chicago only

Cat. 4

Bread and Leg of Lamb
c. 1866
Oil on canvas
27 × 35.5 cm (10 ⅝ × 14 in.)
Kunsthaus Zürich, 1938, 2440
FWN 705
Chicago only

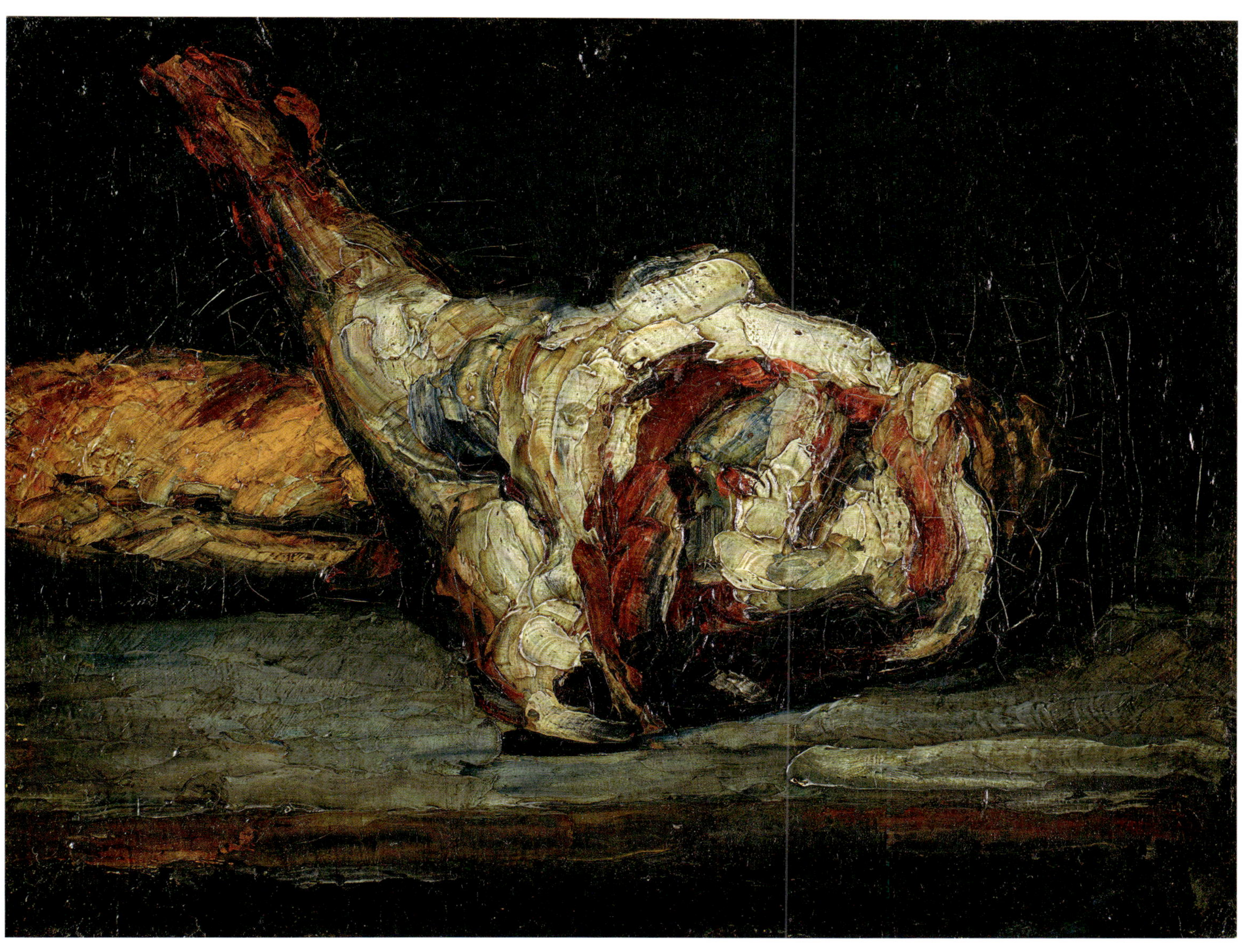

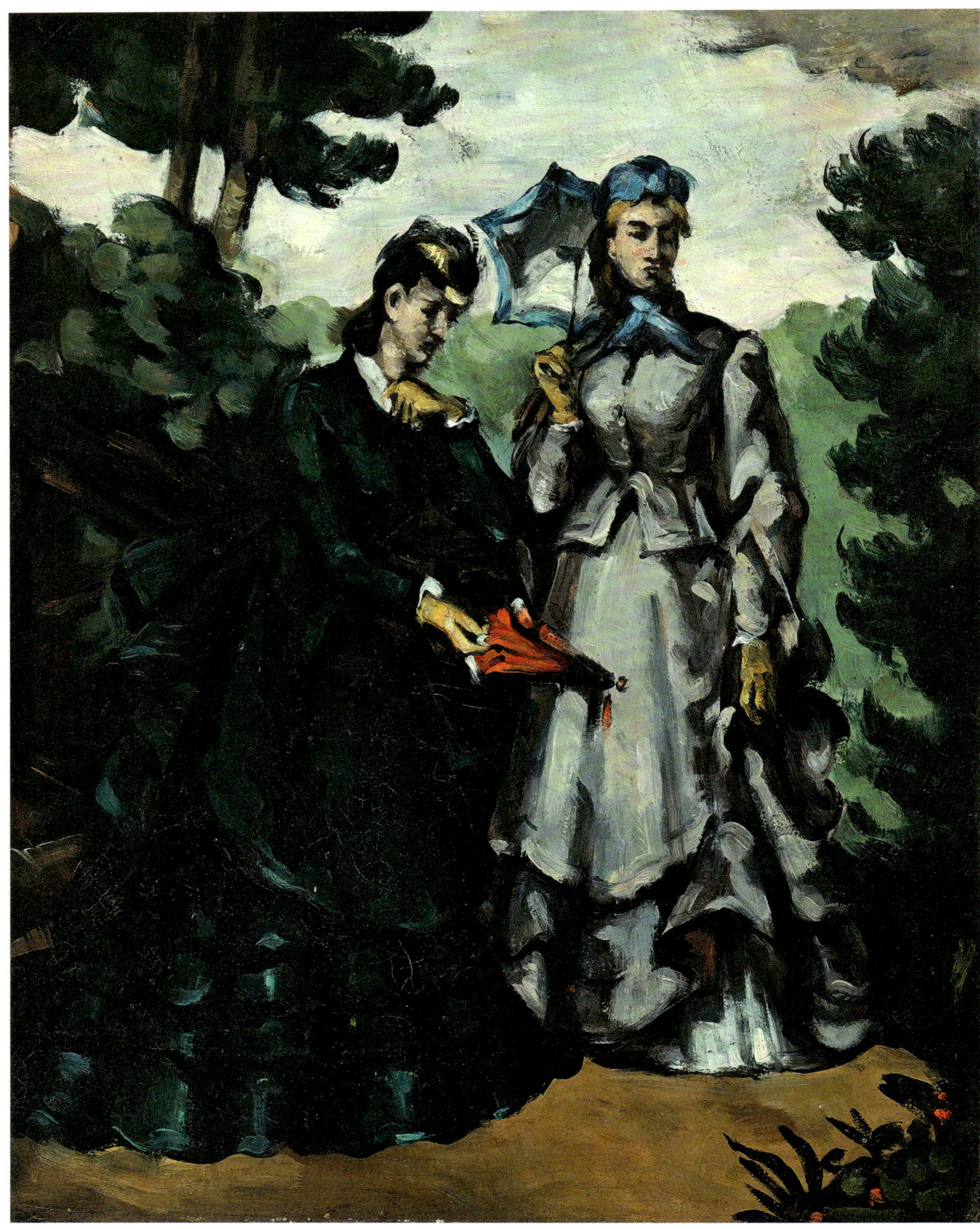

Cat. 5

The Promenade
1871
Oil on canvas
56.5 × 47 cm (22 ¼ × 18 ½ in.)
Private collection
FWN 608
Chicago only

Cat. 6

The Conversation
1870–71
Oil on canvas
92 × 73 cm (36 ³⁄₁₆ × 28 ¹¹⁄₁₆ in.)
Private collection
FWN 607
Chicago only

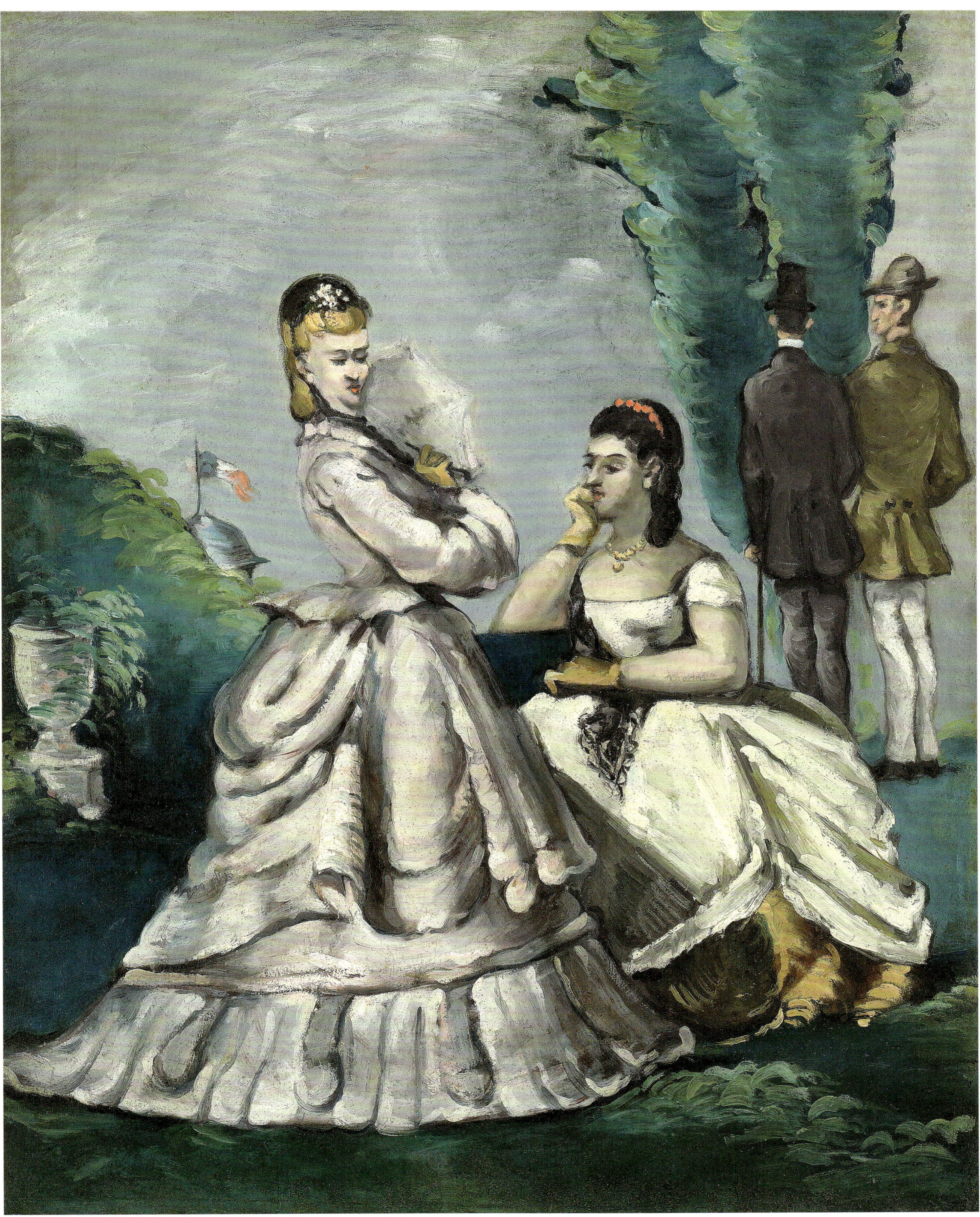

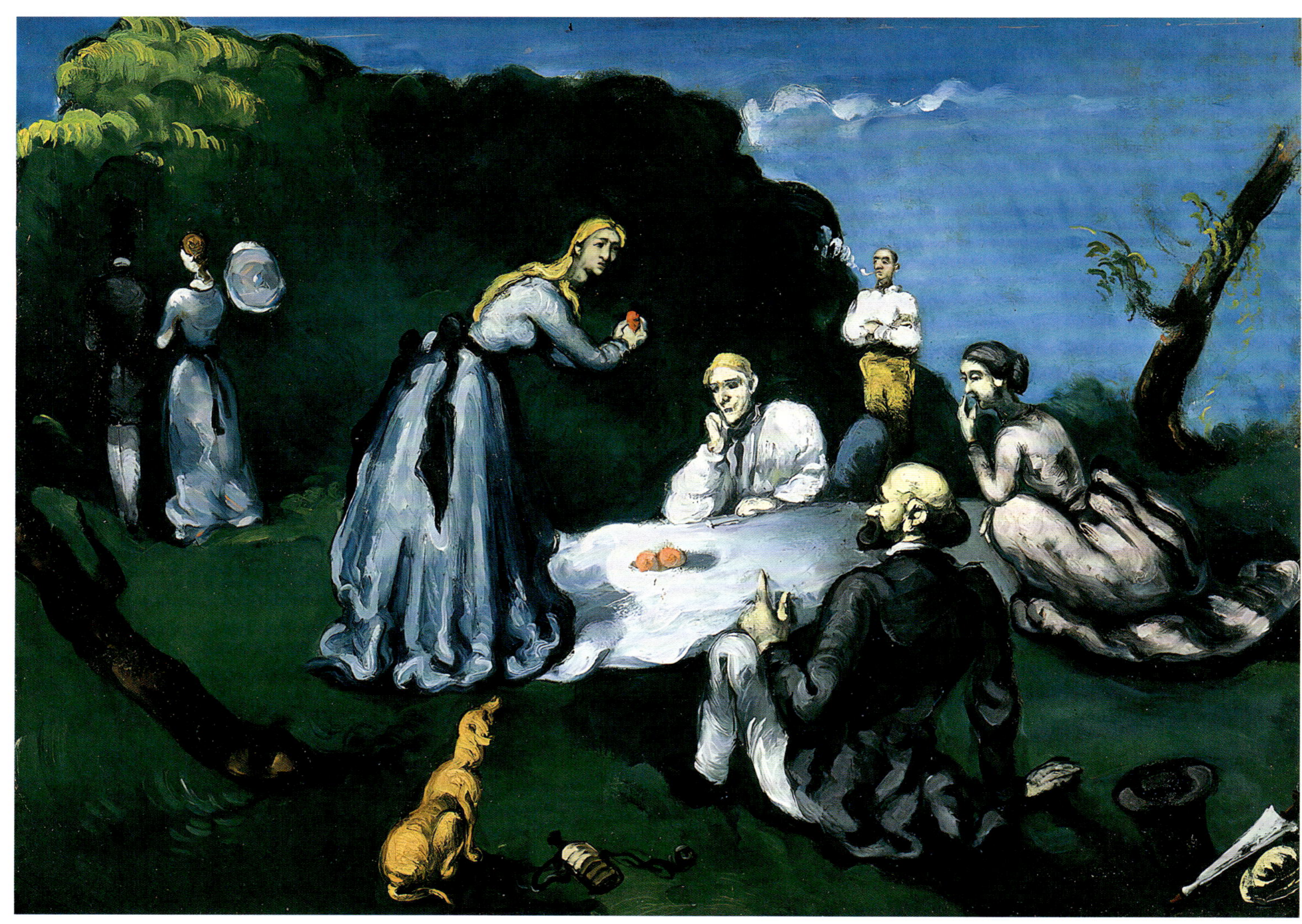

Cat. 7

Luncheon on the Grass
(*Le Déjeuner sur l'herbe*)
c. 1870
Oil on canvas
60 × 81 cm (23 ⅝ × 31 ⅞ in.)
Private collection, New York
FWN 610
Not in exhibition

Lubaina Himid

This painting seems to pull and stretch reality, as if it was painted from a peculiar angle. The paint seems to be still wet and the scene feels as if it could be altered.

Seven people and three oranges is not a good ratio for harmony.

Two have already gone or will soon sweep off into the dark, thick wood to indulge in a little light kissing until the food (hopefully) arrives.

Thank goodness I ate before we came. The man vigorously smoking the pipe fed me little slices of duck and tiny slithers of pork from a beautiful porcelain dish in the kitchen before we came out; it was good. He is kinder than he looks.

I'm worried; the water bottle is empty.

The reason we don't have any food here with us, except for those rather sweet-looking little oranges, is that all of these people are fretting or thinking in a rather single-minded fashion about their complicated relationships with each other.

I feel it might rain; I wish I understood what those clouds mean.

Instead of making a plan and preparing the food themselves or asking our cook, Celeste, to assemble one of her delicious and extravagant baskets, they worried in advance about how to behave when they arrived here. Clearly none of them felt hungry enough to request their favorite early morning deliciousness.

My anxious master hopes he and my mistress will stay together forever but you can tell that her friend is trying her best not to look at either one of them. She knows that I saw them kissing this morning. Of course, women kiss each other all the time when they are not kissing babies, cats, and especially adorable dogs like me. This, however, was a serious moment of tenderness.

I'm seated next to the man who is the least aware of what is going on; he is pontificating as usual about some philosophical theory he has just fallen in love with. He thinks that the three oranges signify something deep and meaningful in relation to numbers and orangeness rather than a distracted lover's mistake. Here we have a man utterly convinced of his own importance. He remembered to bring his tall hat but never thought to offer to carry the food or worry about why everyone is looking anxious and blushing more than usual.

Pipe-Smoker and I have agreed to go back for some warm loaves, pungent soft cheeses and tangy hard ones, homemade sausages, unsalted butter, newly laid eggs (hard-boiled), tomatoes from the greenhouses, wild rocket from the walled garden, and some radishes for color and bite. I think we will bring some more water and perhaps my generous friend will pick up some absinthe for himself and some treats for me.

Why is that tree talking to me about wind and wild weather?

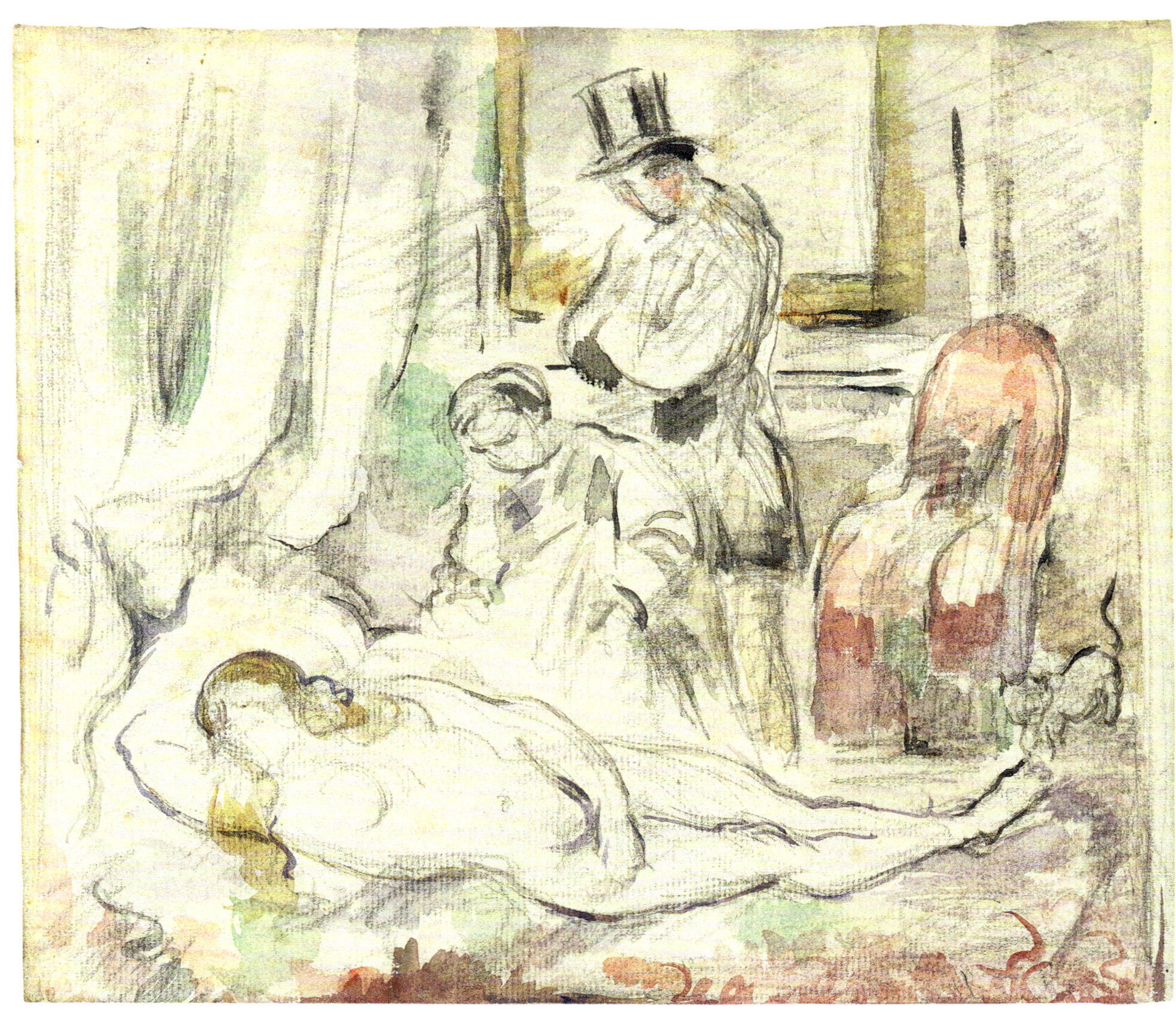

Cat. 8

Olympia
c. 1877
Watercolor and graphite on laid paper
24.1 × 27 cm (9 ½ × 10 ⅝ inches)
Philadelphia Museum of Art: The Louis E. Stern
Collection, 1963, 1963-181-123
FWN 1860
Chicago only

Cat. 9

Afternoon in Naples
1876–77
Oil on canvas
30 × 40 cm (11 ¹³⁄₁₆ × 15 ¹¹⁄₁₆ in.)
Private collection
FWN 646

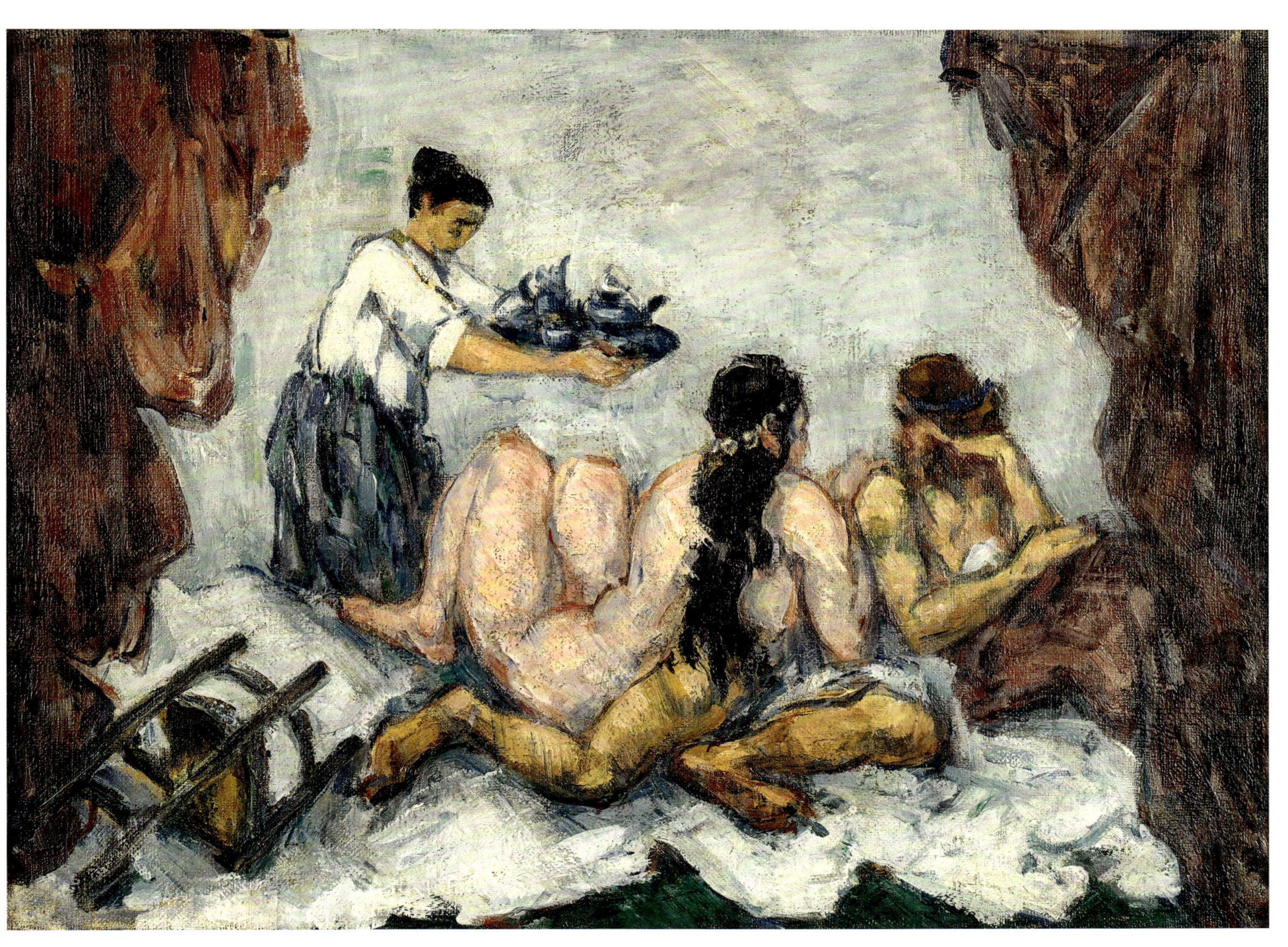

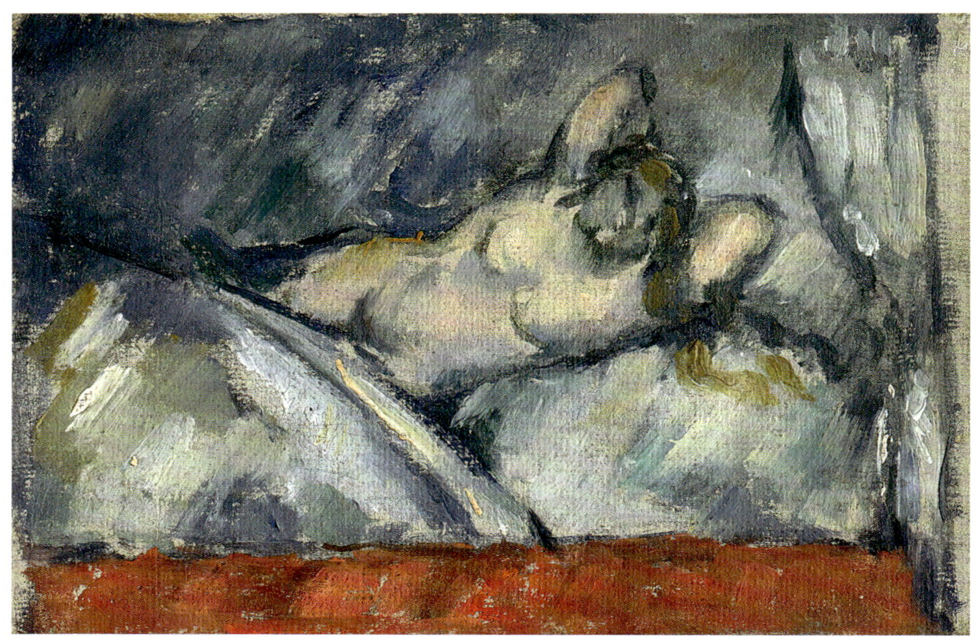

Cat. 10

Nude Woman Lying Down
1875–77
Oil on canvas
8.5 × 13 cm (3 5/16 × 5 1/8 in.)
Collection of Jasper Johns
FWN 635
Chicago only

Cat. 11

Afternoon in Naples
1876–77
Oil on canvas
37 × 45 cm (14 5/8 × 17 11/16 in.)
National Gallery of Australia, Canberra,
purchased 1985, NGA 85.460
FWN 647
Chicago only

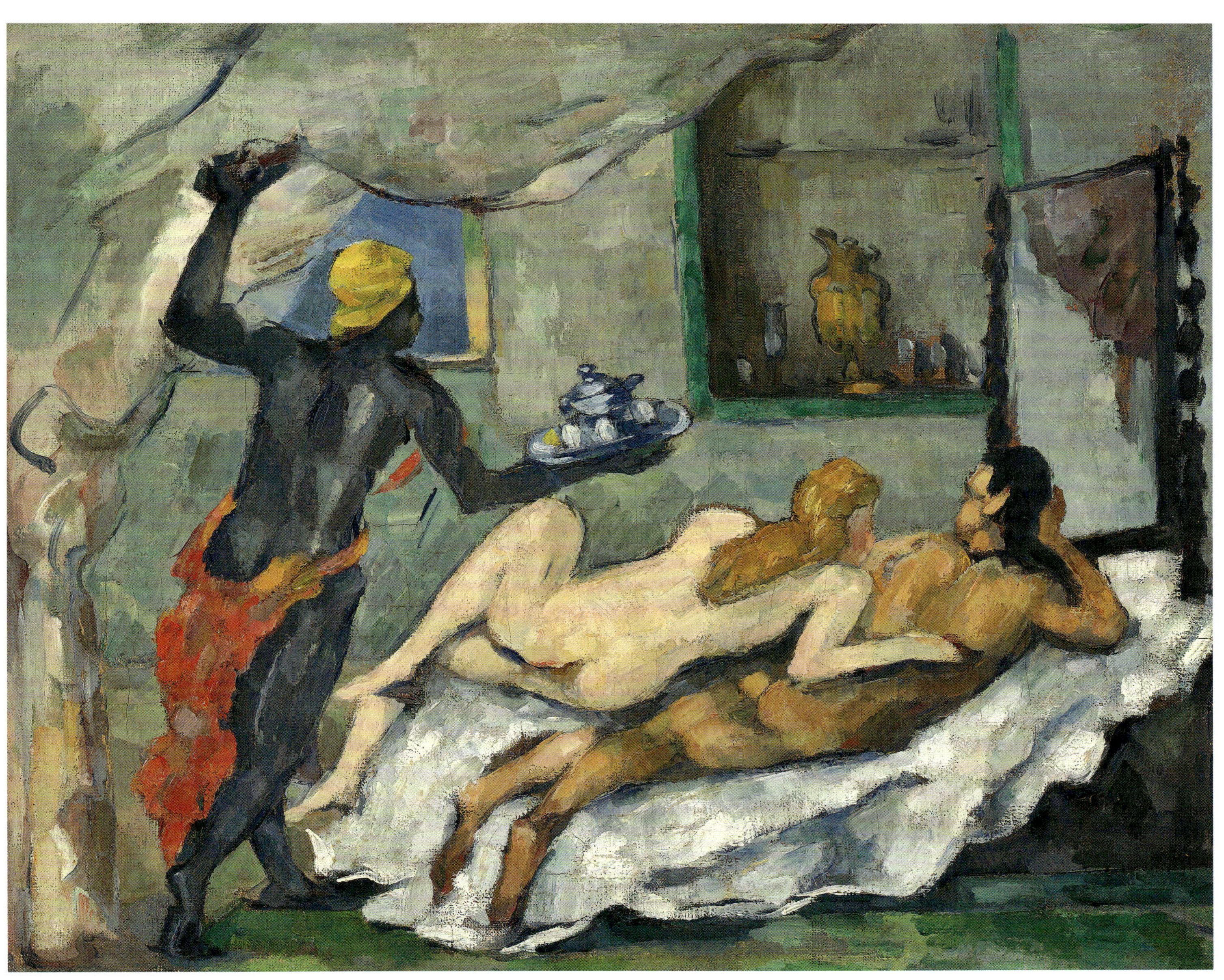

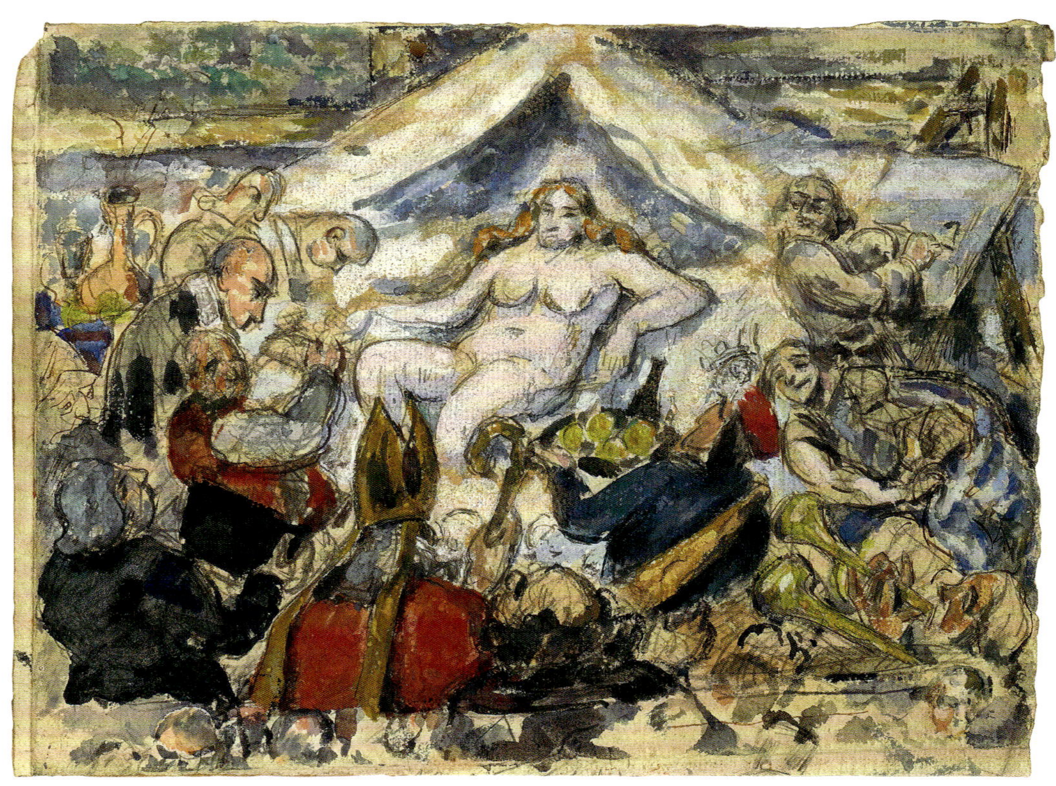

Cat. 12

The Eternal Feminine
c. 1877
Graphite, watercolor, and gouache on laid paper
17.4 × 22.8 cm (6 ⅞ × 8 in.)
Collection of Jasper Johns
FWN 1861

Cat. 13

The Eternal Feminine
c. 1877
Oil on canvas
43.5 × 53.3 cm (17 ⅛ × 21 in.)
The J. Paul Getty Museum, Los Angeles, 87.PA.79
FWN 649

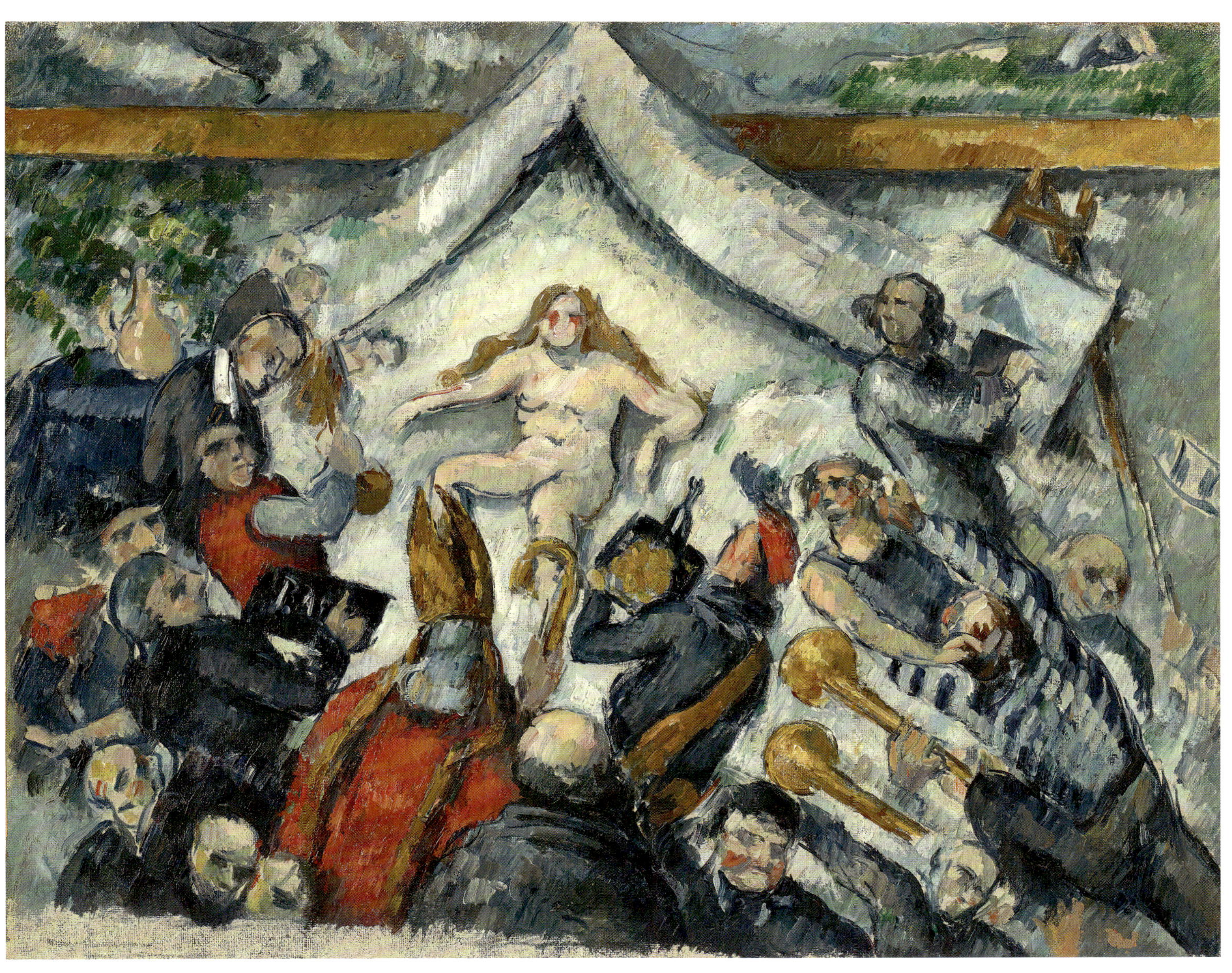

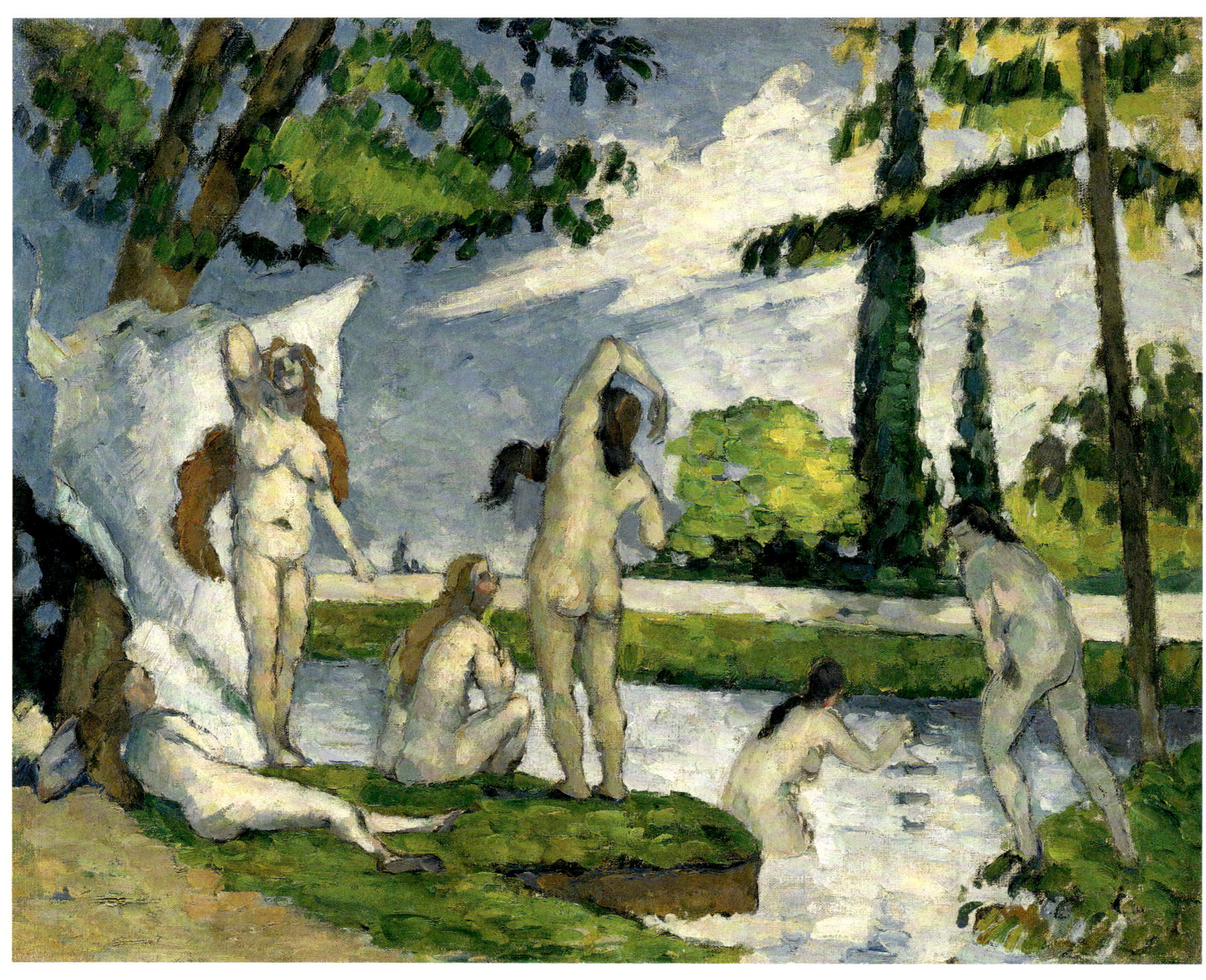

Cat. 14

Bathers
1874–75
Oil on canvas
38.1 × 46 cm (15 × 18 ⅛ in.)
The Metropolitan Museum of Art, New York,
Bequest of Joan Whitney Payson, 1975, 1976.201.12
FWN 916

Cat. 15

The Battle of Love
1879–80
Oil on canvas
42 × 55 cm (16 ½ × 21 ⅝ in.)
Private collection, United States
FWN 656

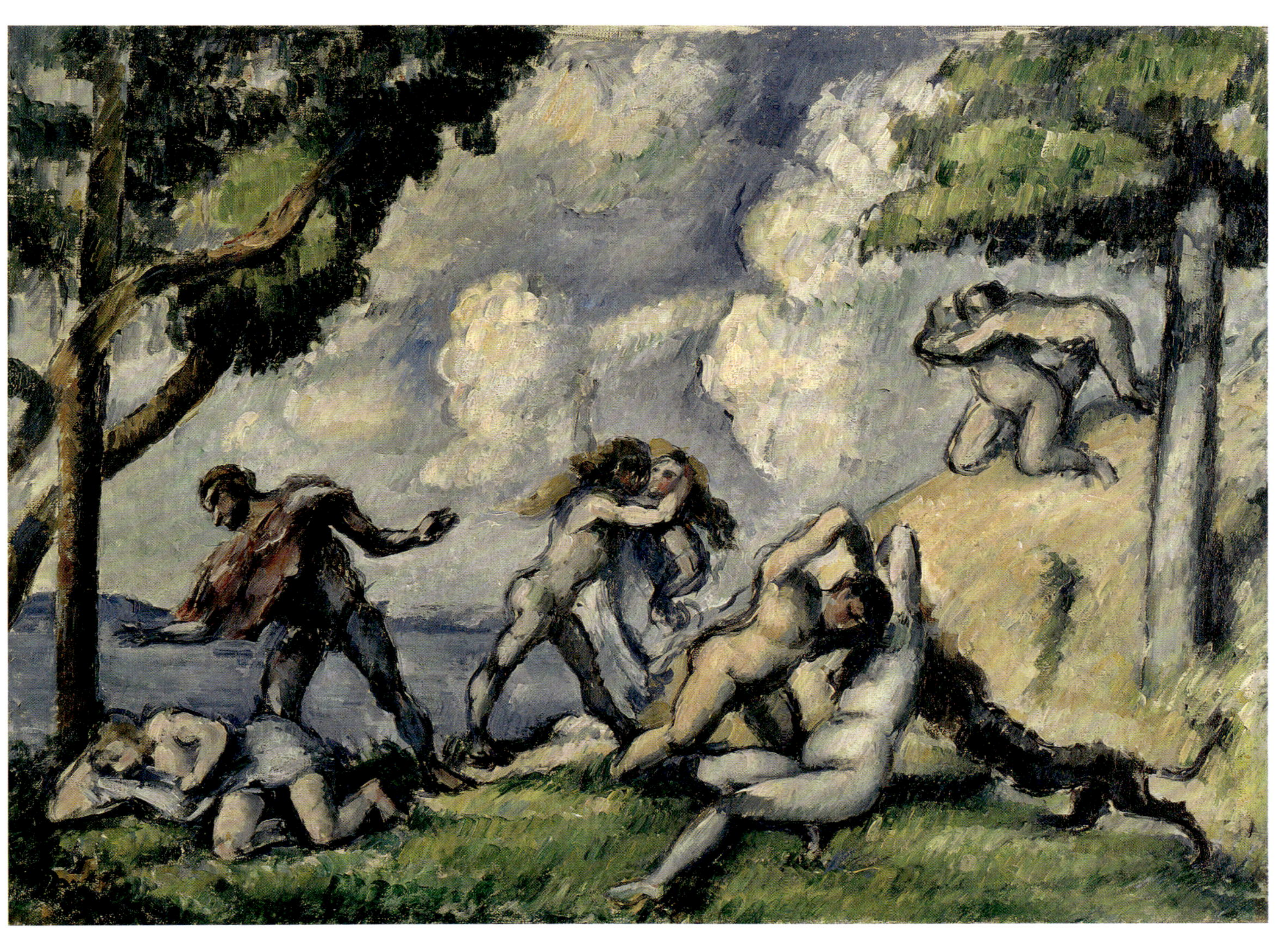

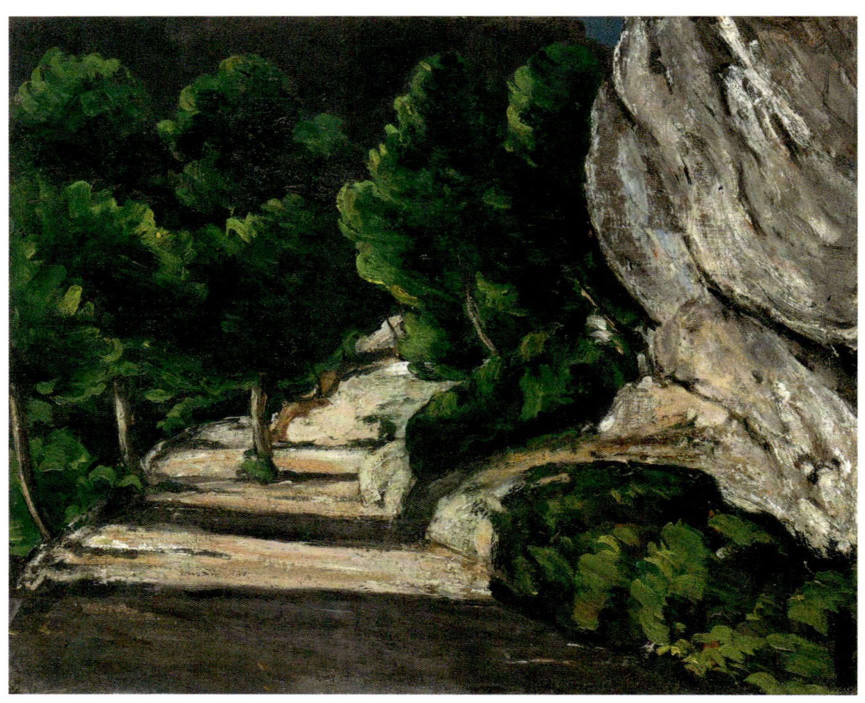

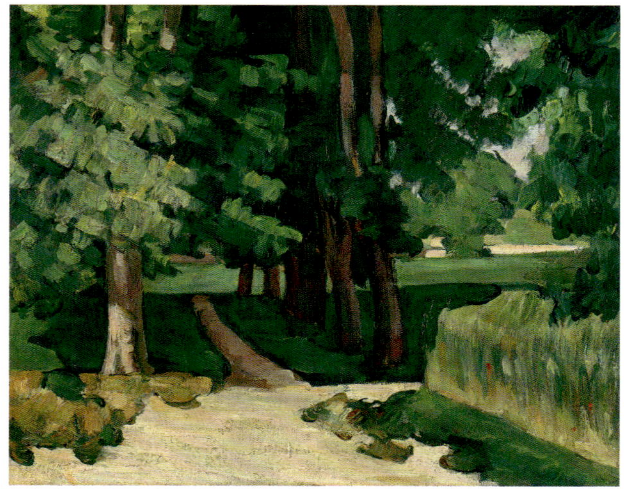

Cat. 16

Landscape: Road with Trees in Rocky Mountains
1870–71
Oil on canvas
54 × 65.2 cm (21¼ × 25 ¹¹⁄₁₆ in.)
Städel Museum, Frankfurt am Main, Germany,
SG 458
FWN 56

Cat. 17

The Avenue at the Jas de Bouffan
c. 1874–75
Oil on canvas
38.1 × 46 cm (15 × 18 ⅛ in.)
Tate London, Bequeathed by the Hon. Mrs A. E.
Pleydell-Bouverie through the Friends of the Tate
Gallery 1968, T01074
FWN 55

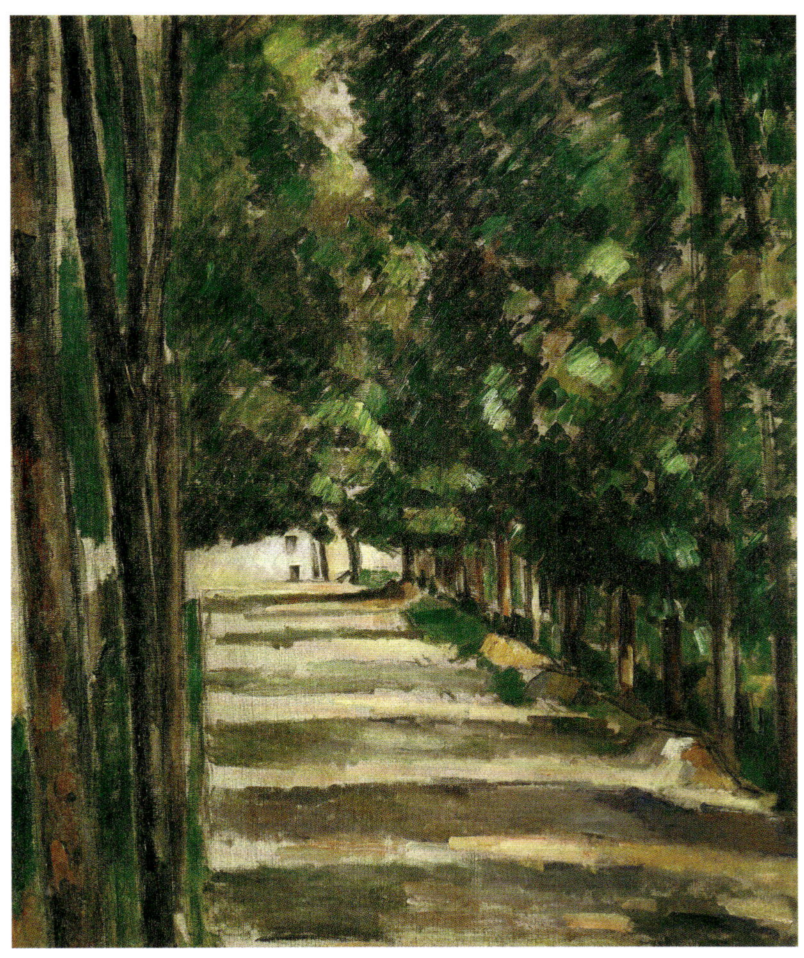

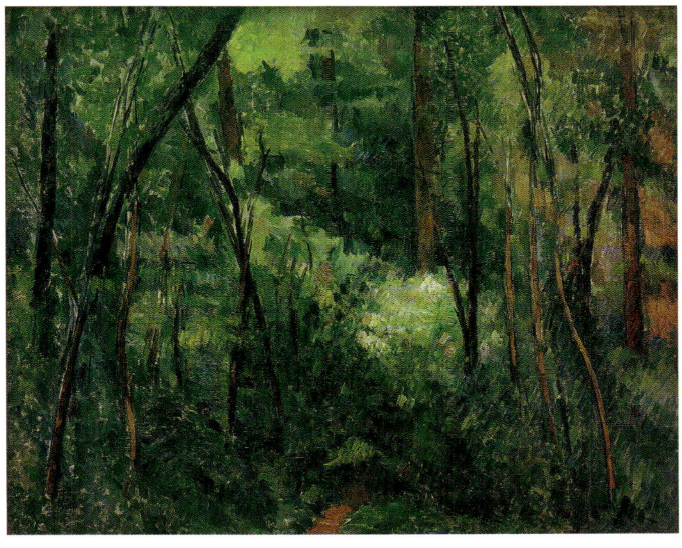

Cat. 18

Avenue
c. 1880–82
Oil on canvas
73.5 × 60.5 cm (28 ⅞ × 23 ¹³⁄₁₆ in.)
Göteborgs Konstmuseum, Sweden,
gift of Gustaf Werner, 1931, GKM 0946
FWN 130

Cat. 19

Interior of a Forest
c. 1885
Oil on canvas
46.4 × 56.1 cm (18 ¼ × 22 ¹⁄₁₆ in.)
Art Gallery of Ontario, Given in loving memory of
Saidye Rosner Bronfman by her family, 1996, 96/321
FWN 209
Chicago only

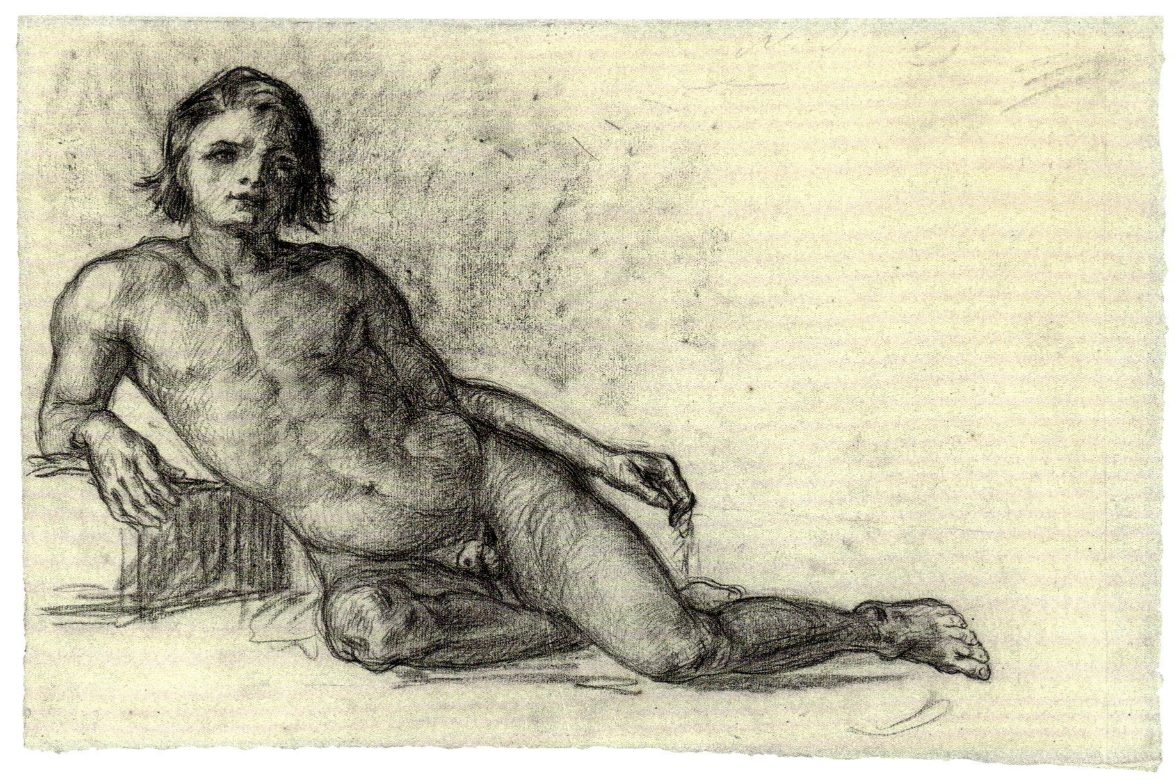

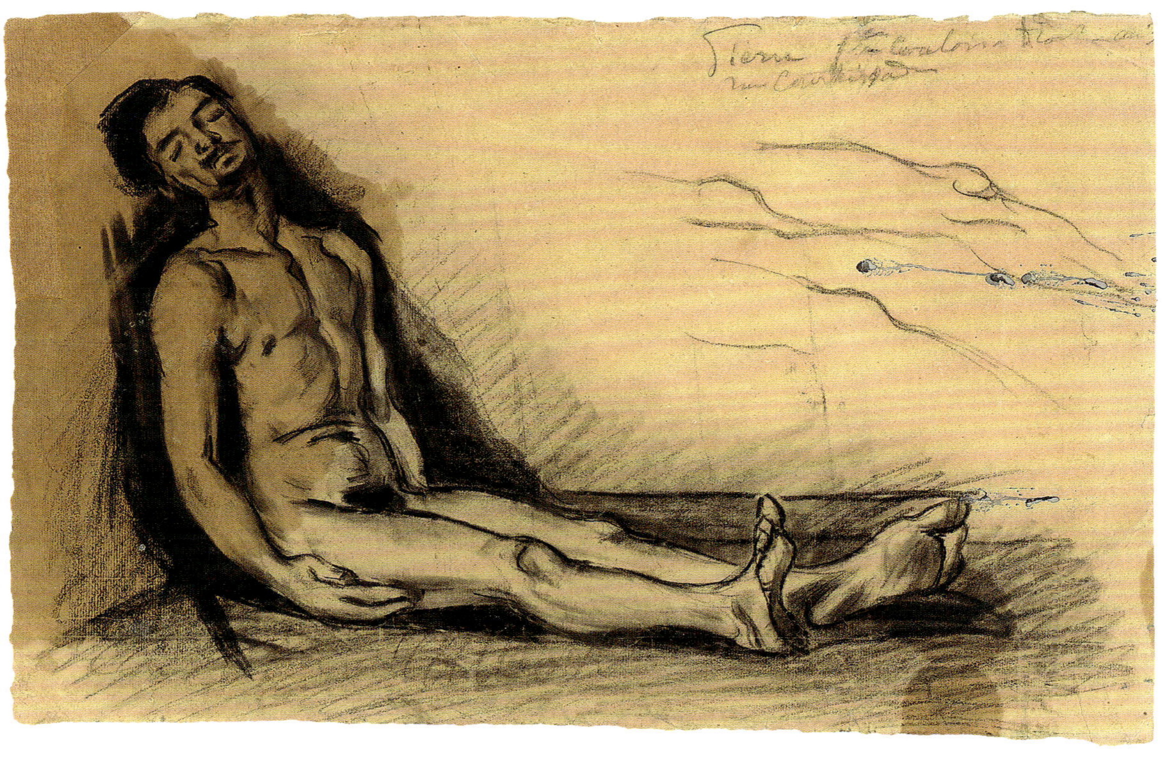

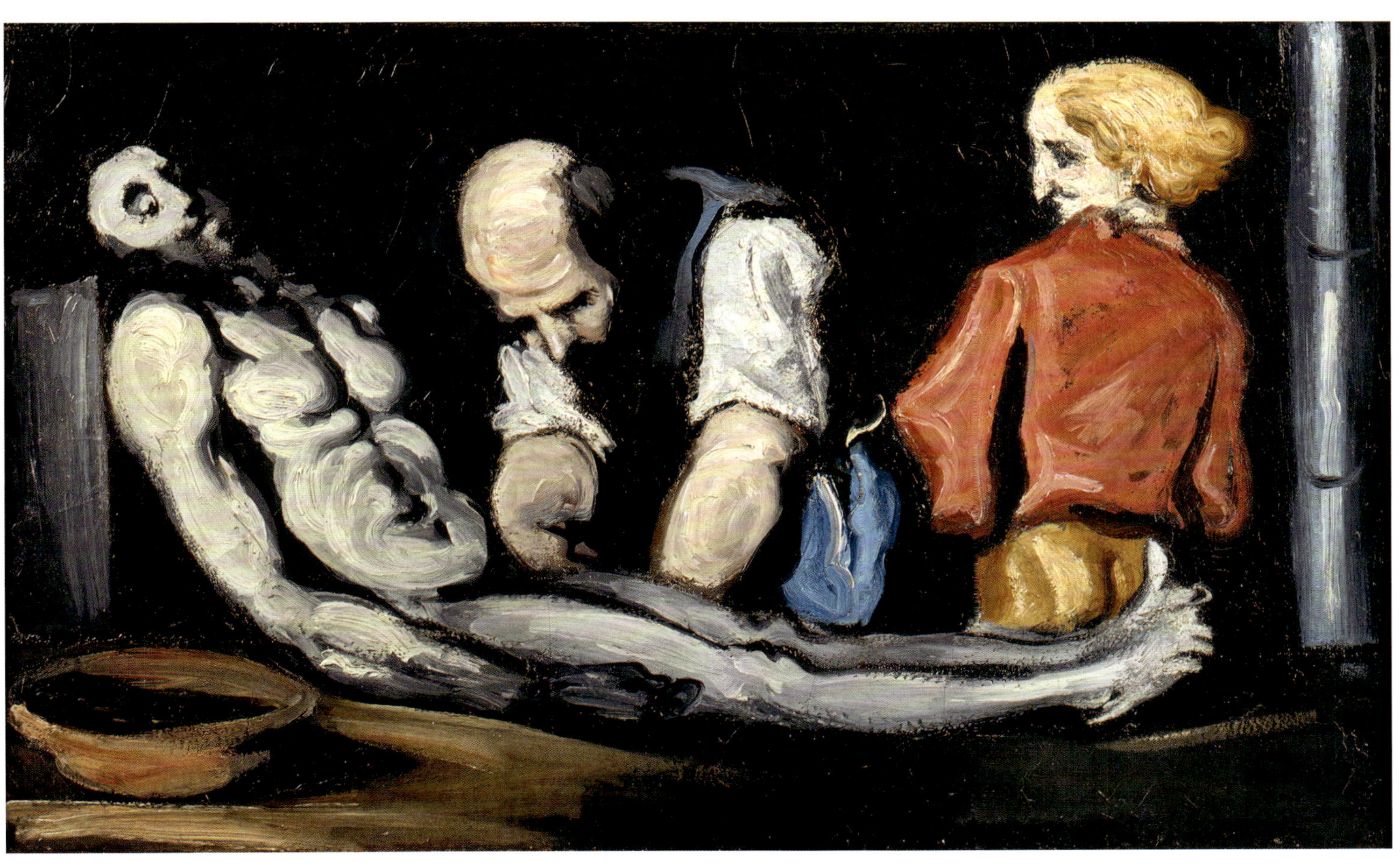

Cat. 20

Male Nude
1863–66
Black chalk, with touches of stumping, on mottled
blue-gray laid paper, altered to a light-gray tone
31.4 × 46.1 cm (12 ⅜ × 18 ⅛ in.)
The Art Institute of Chicago, gift of Dorothy Braude
Edinburg to the Harry B. and Bessie K. Braude
Memorial Collection, 2013.911
FWN 2086
Chicago only

Cat. 21

Study for "The Autopsy"
1867–69
Black chalk with stumping on tan laid paper
32 × 48.7 cm (12 ⅝ × 19 ³⁄₁₆ in.)
The Art Institute of Chicago, gift of Tiffany ard
Margaret Blake, 1947.36
FWN 2111
Chicago only

Cat. 22

The Autopsy
1869
Oil on canvas
49 × 80 cm (19 ⁵⁄₁₆ × 31½ in.)
Private collection; courtesy of Pyms Gallery, London
FWN 597
Not in exhibition

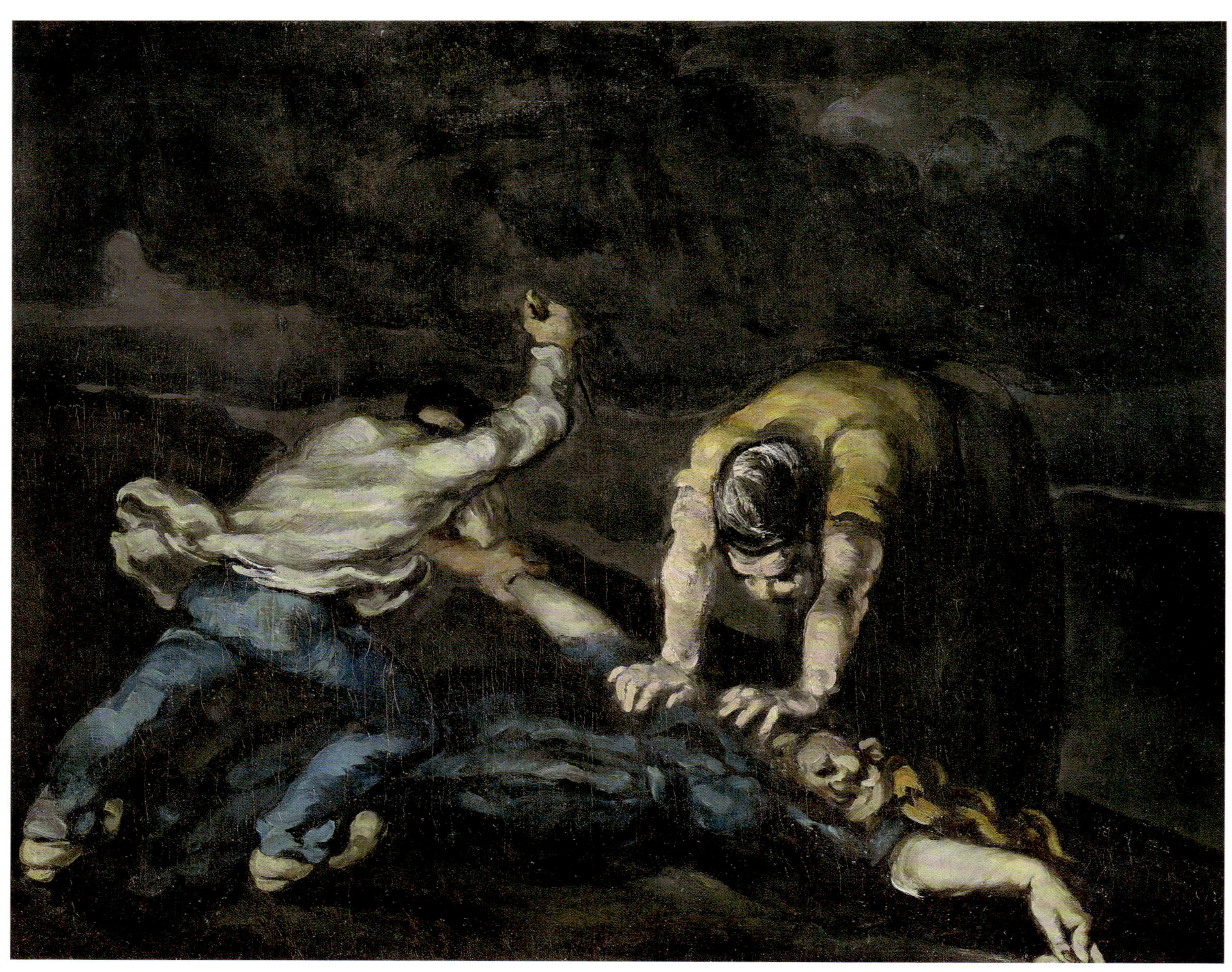

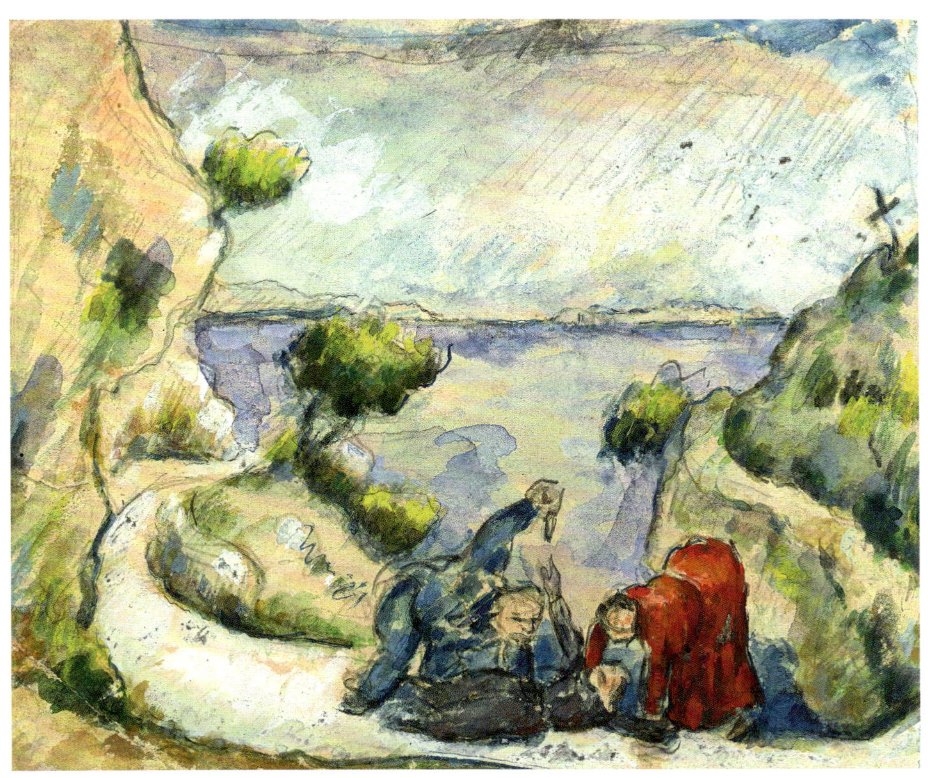

Cat. 23

The Murder
1867–70
Oil on canvas
64 × 81 cm (25 3/16 × 31 7/8 in.)
National Museums Liverpool, Walker Art Gallery,
Purchased by the Walker Art Gallery with the
assistance of Art Fund in 1964, WAG 6242
FWN 613

Cat. 24

The Murder
1874–75
Graphite, watercolor, and gouache on paper
14.6 × 17.5 cm (5 3/4 × 6 7/8 in.)
Keith D. Stoltz, Greenville, Delaware
FWN 1848
Not in exhibition

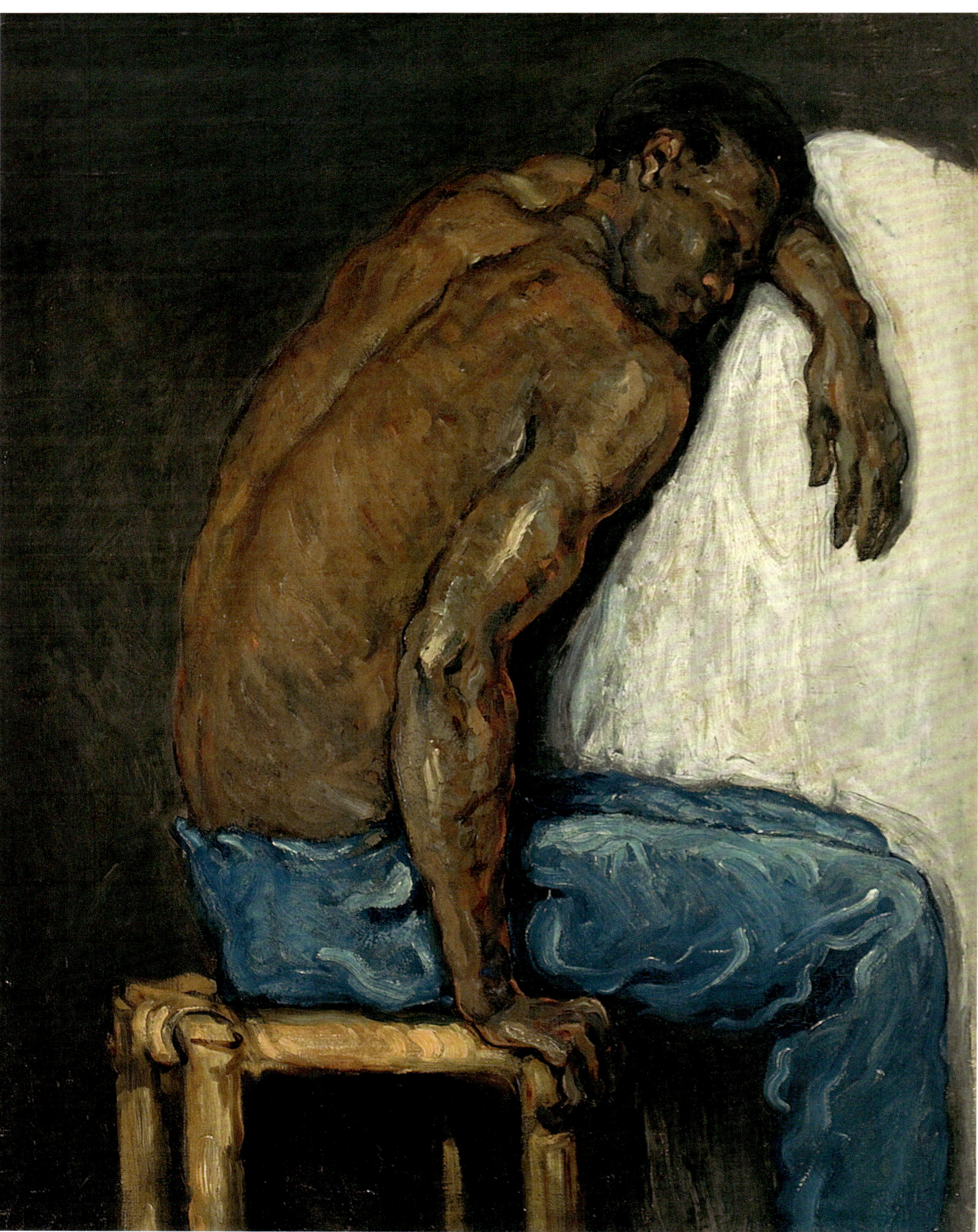

When Is a Place

Ellen Gallagher

Among the newspaper clippings and postcards of painting reproductions that I keep pinned to my studio wall, there is a photographic image. A portrait of an enslaved man named Gordon, broadly circulated within abolitionist networks, the image is a three-quarter view of the man's back, criss-crossed with keloid scar tissue—irrefutable proof of a horrific whipping. Originally reproduced as a carte de visite, on a stiff, light paper support that allowed for distribution via post, the image was reprinted from Boston to London and was also used to make an etched illustration that was prominently featured in an article titled "A Typical Negro" published in *Harper's Weekly* in 1863 (fig. 1).

In the hands of former slaves, reproduction technologies became quicksilver. Both Sojourner Truth and Frederick Douglass used the power of photographic verisimilitude to counter the relentless, violent caricature of their likenesses disseminated through racist mainstream media. Photography's uneasy alliance with sorrow has been addressed in the contemporary by Susan Sontag.[1] But what happens to ethical form when it shifts milieu and begins to evanesce? And what of the art historical legacy of antebellum technologies developed by former slaves?

The instability between what can be seen and what can be felt hovers within the portrait of Paul Cezanne (fig. 2) painted by his close friend Francisco Oller, an Impressionist painter who was born in San Juan, Puerto Rico.[2] It is a small canvas that captures Cezanne painting outdoors under a white umbrella. Following his return to the Americas, Oller would go on to develop as an abolitionist and painter known for his depictions of decayed sugar plantations and New World class struggles. What did they discuss that afternoon of 1864, in the French countryside? The recent move by the newly formed Confederate States of America to cut off England's supply of cotton in 1861? The burgeoning labor wars in France (and elsewhere), as they sat together *en plein air . . .*

By 1867 the political ramifications of King Cotton were evident and would

Fig. 1

"A Typical Negro," *Harper's Weekly*, July 4, 1863.

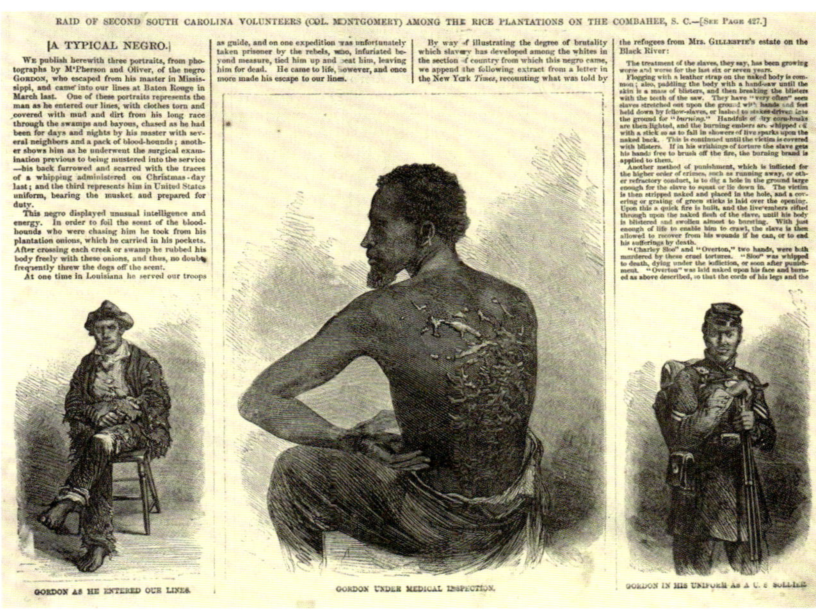

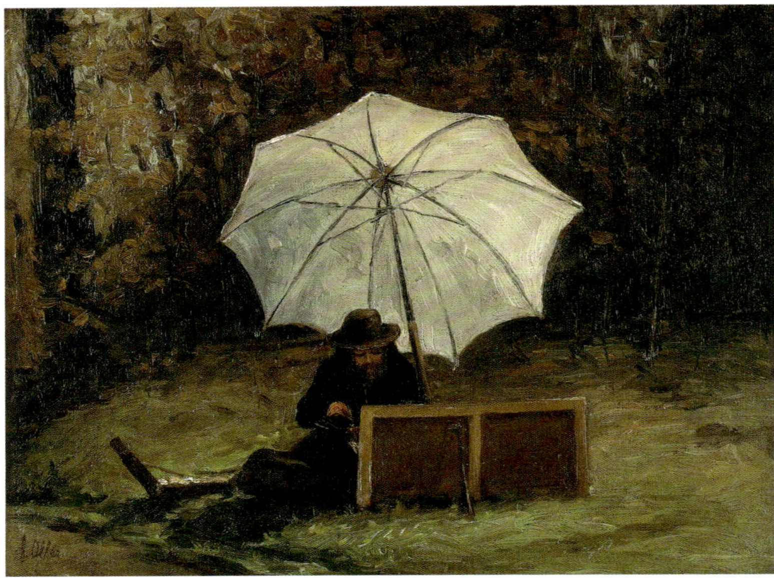

Fig. 2

Francisco Oller (Puerto Rican, 1833–1917). *Paul Cézanne Painting Out of Doors*, c. 1864. Collection of Dr. Luis R. de Corral and Dr. Lorraine Vázquez, Puerto Rico.

have surfaced during the Paris World Fair of that same year alongside the carte de visite showing Gordon's scourged back to drum up support for the abolitionist cause. Given that the Thirteenth Amendment had been ratified in the United States only two years earlier, the horrific image of Gordon would strike a chord in the country that had already emancipated their slaves, not once, but twice! Furthermore, it was during this year that Cezanne painted Negro Scipio. At the very least the nascent alchemies in the photograph would have stirred the painter. More than most, Cezanne would have registered the implications of this new technology and been moved to respond. Faced with the immediacy and transport of the photographic image, the young painter must have been fighting for the epistemological life of painting.

Scipio and Gordon are both wearing thick cotton indigo work pants (denim), slave-produced on cotton plantations throughout the Americas. Unhindered by

the limits of black-and-white photography, Cezanne's blue radiates from the canvas and signals Europe's rampant move into the tropical regions of the Americas following the Indian Indigo Revolt of 1859. Cezanne even shifted the figure from the photographic isolation of manifest evidence to depicting the formerly enslaved Gordon as Scipio leaning on a cotton bale, in grief. There is something discreetly operatic in the gesture. Cezanne wanted nothing less than to move us in time. He has used the language of painting to bring us before the keloid. Not only figuring the scarred back as evidence, Cezanne has brought us temporally before the scar. Creating a disturbance in the plain, what Sun Ra later conceptualized as "Alter Destiny," Cezanne's liquidity transports us through a bifurcation in time: we are now before the open wound. The back of Negro Scipio, layered in thick black and umber slabs of paint with the faint presence of red that seeped from the edge of the

brush, is more liquid, more unfixed than the keloid.

In 1867 the widely disseminated photographic evidence of Gordon's disfiguring mutilation inspired the painter to conceive an unfixed body that could occupy multiple positions in time: the oozing liquidity of an open wound and the sediment of the keloid. Channeling the energy of oppositional imaginaries, Cezanne's black strata is not abstract, but neither is it merely a picture of an object or a person. This liquid response to the call of Gordon's granular photographic alchemy became a springboard for the abstraction put forward by the early theorists of abstract painting: the idea of picturing beyond the object. In Russian, беспредметность is the state of being without object. Cezanne's blacks, applied in thick layers and often with a palette knife, contain vectors that chart a topography both submarine and mineral. When we peer into the black strata of Cezanne's paintings we are aware of the exchange contained within the etch: the blood that still oozes from the wound that is not yet keloidal; and the burial of the keloid into the mineral ground of Mont Sainte-Victoire. An etched immensity both corporeal and geologic that introduced buried time into Western painting. This is the pictorial technique Cezanne would further develop as a catalyst for abstract painting of the twentieth century: the liquid plain of painting hinged to a corporeal past that is not past. It is no wonder Claude Monet kept this canvas and never let it go.

1. See Susan Sontag, *On Photography* (London: Penguin, 1977), and *Regarding the Pain of Others* (London: Penguin, 2003).
2. This painting is identified as *Paul Cezanne Painting Out of Doors* (c. 1864) in Edward Sullivan, *From San Juan to Paris and Back: Francisco Oller and Caribbean Art in the Era of Impressionism* (New Haven, CT: Yale University Press, 2014), 51–52.

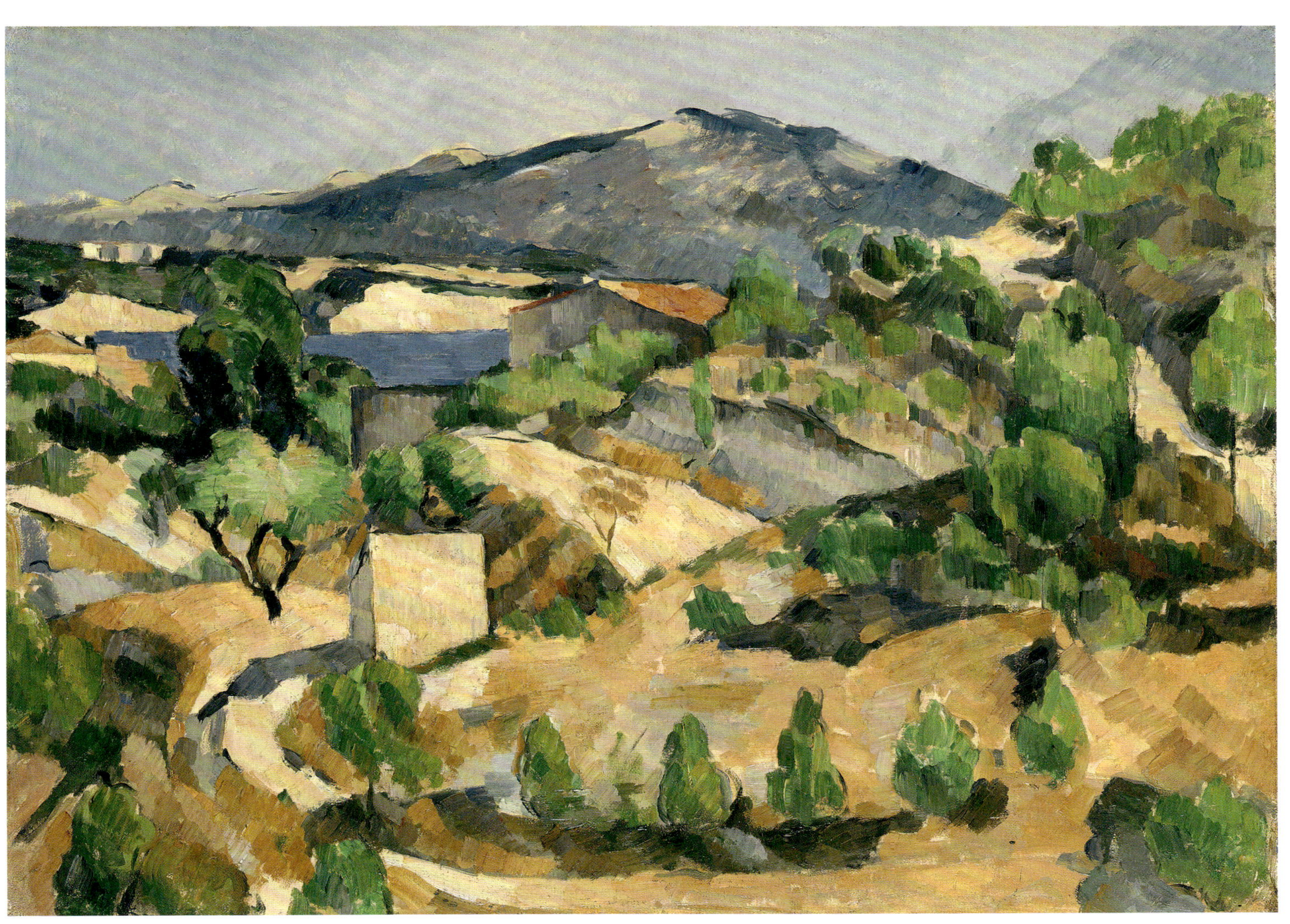

Cat. 26

The François Zola Dam
1877–78
Oil on canvas
53.5 × 72.4 cm (21 1/16 × 28 1/2 in.)
Amgueddfa Cymru – National Museum Wales,
Cardiff, UK, Bequeathed by Gwendoline Davies,
1951, NMW A 2439
FWN 124
London only

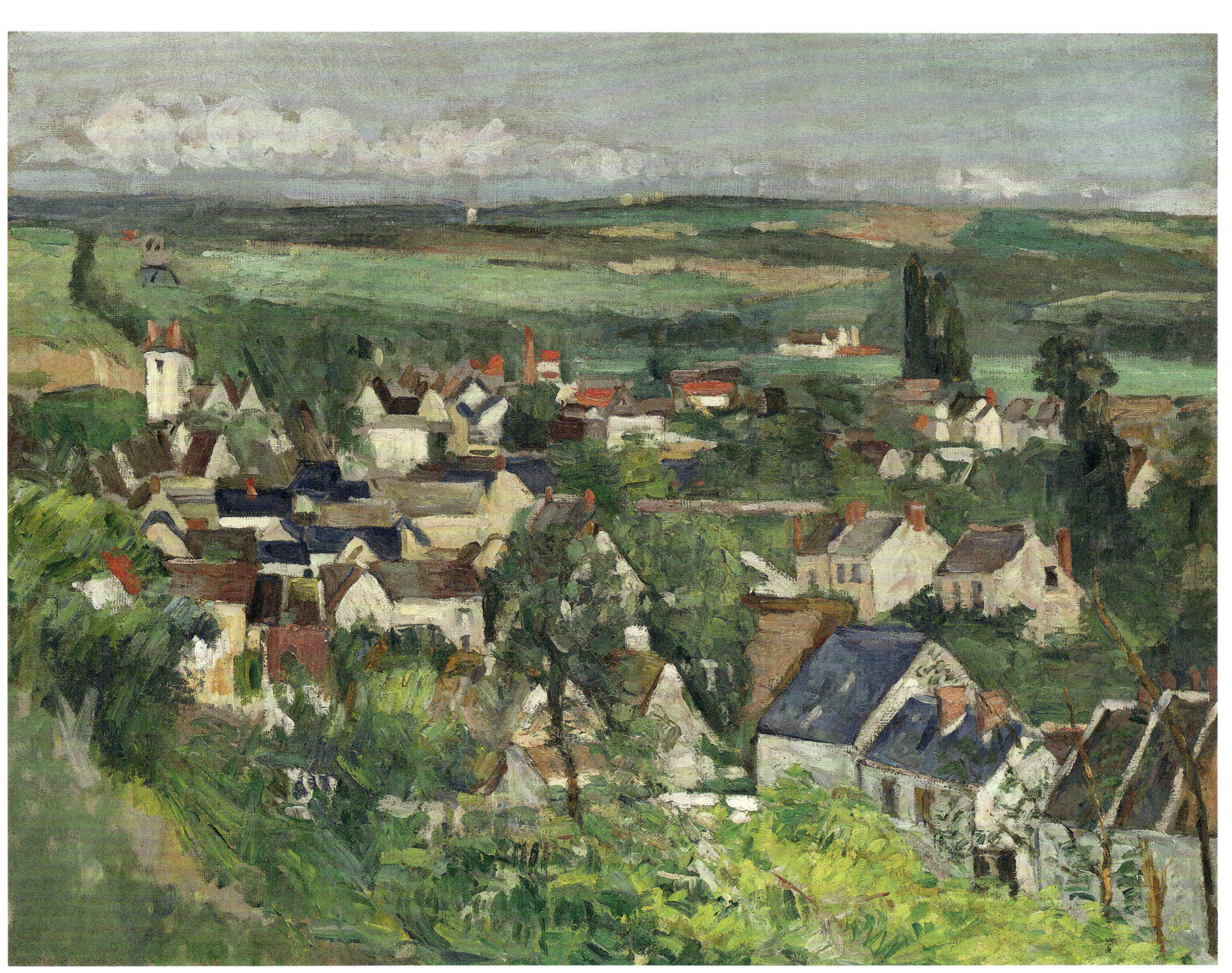

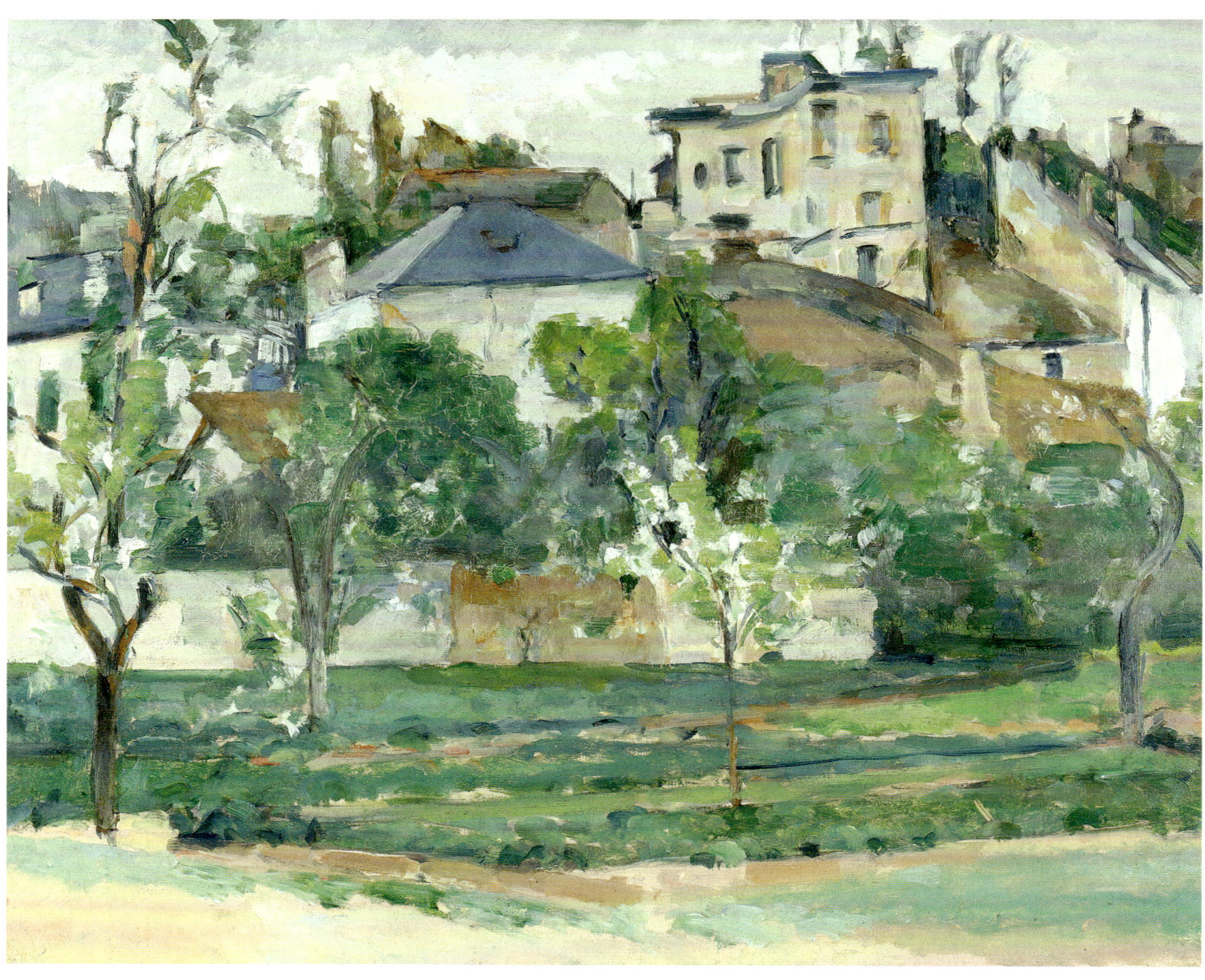

Cat. 28

The Garden at Maubuisson, Pontoise
1877
Oil on canvas
50 × 61 cm (19 ¹¹⁄₁₆ × 24 in.)
Ruthie and Jay Pack, Dallas, Texas
FWN 109
Chicago only

Cat. 29

Turn in the Road
c. 1881
Oil on canvas
60.6 × 73.3 cm (23 ⅞ × 28 ⅞ in.)
Museum of Fine Arts, Boston, Bequest of
John T. Spaulding, 48.525
FWN 163

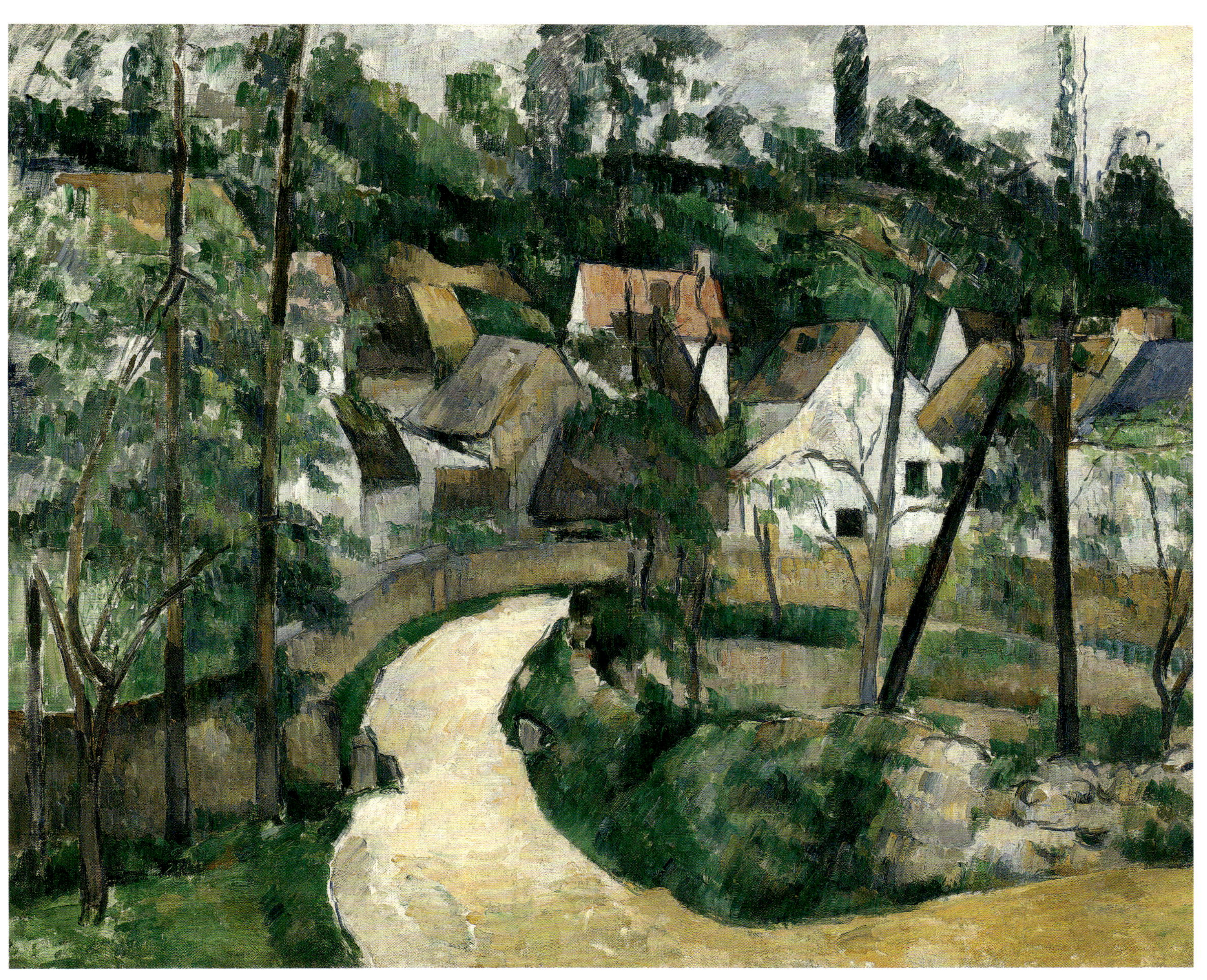

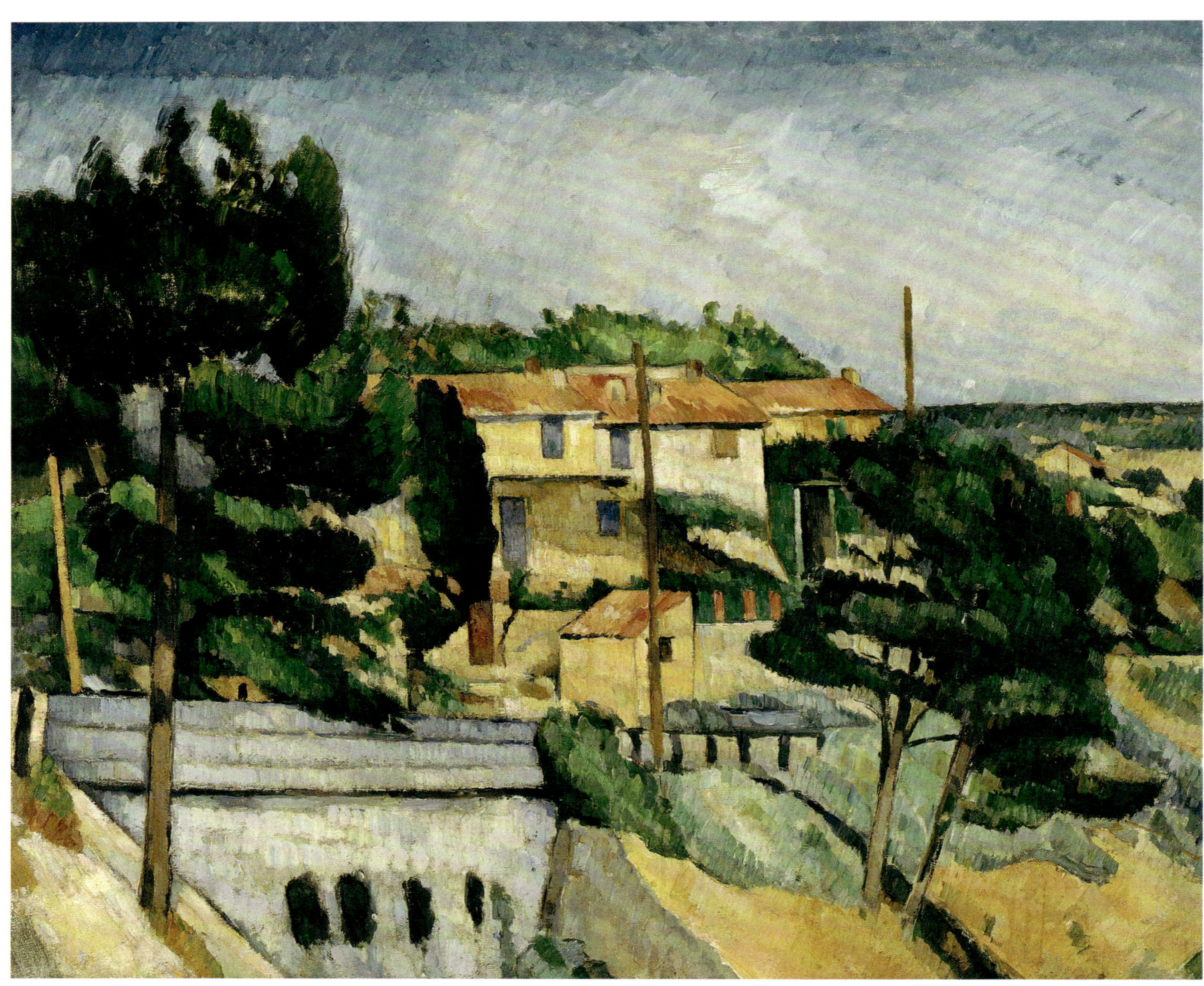

Cat. 30

The Viaduct at L'Estaque
1879–82
Oil on canvas
56 × 65.5 cm (22 1/16 × 25 13/16 in.)
Finnish National Gallery, Ateneum Art Museum,
Helsinki, Antell collections
FWN 151
London only

Cat. 31

Paris Rooftops
c. 1882
Oil on canvas
59.7 × 73 cm (23 1/2 × 28 3/4 in.)
Private collection
FWN 178

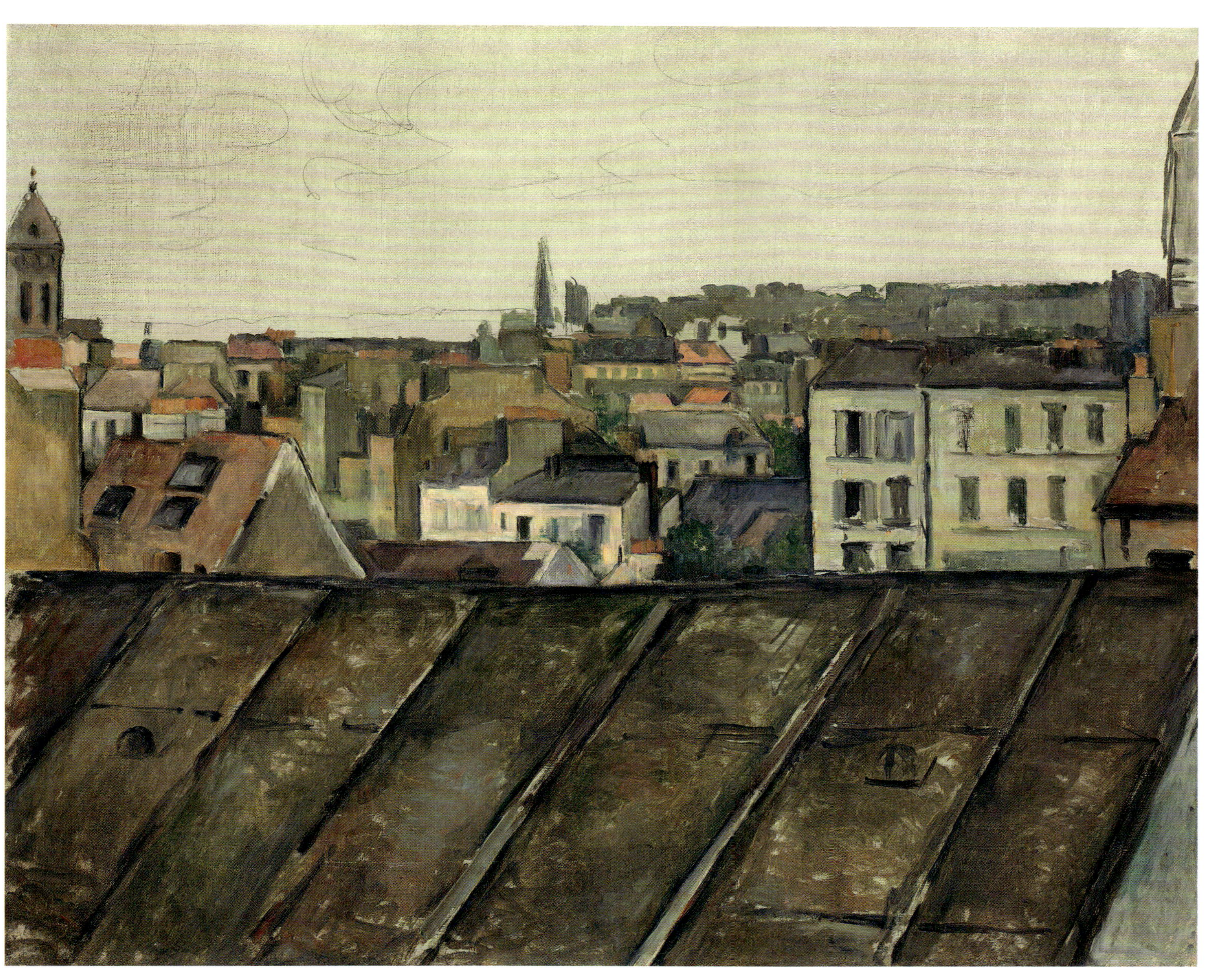

Cat. 32

Portrait of the Artist with Pink Background
c. 1875
Oil on canvas
66 × 55 cm (26 × 21⅝ in.)
Musée d'Orsay, Paris, donation of M. Philippe Meyer,
2000, RF 2000-14
FWN 436

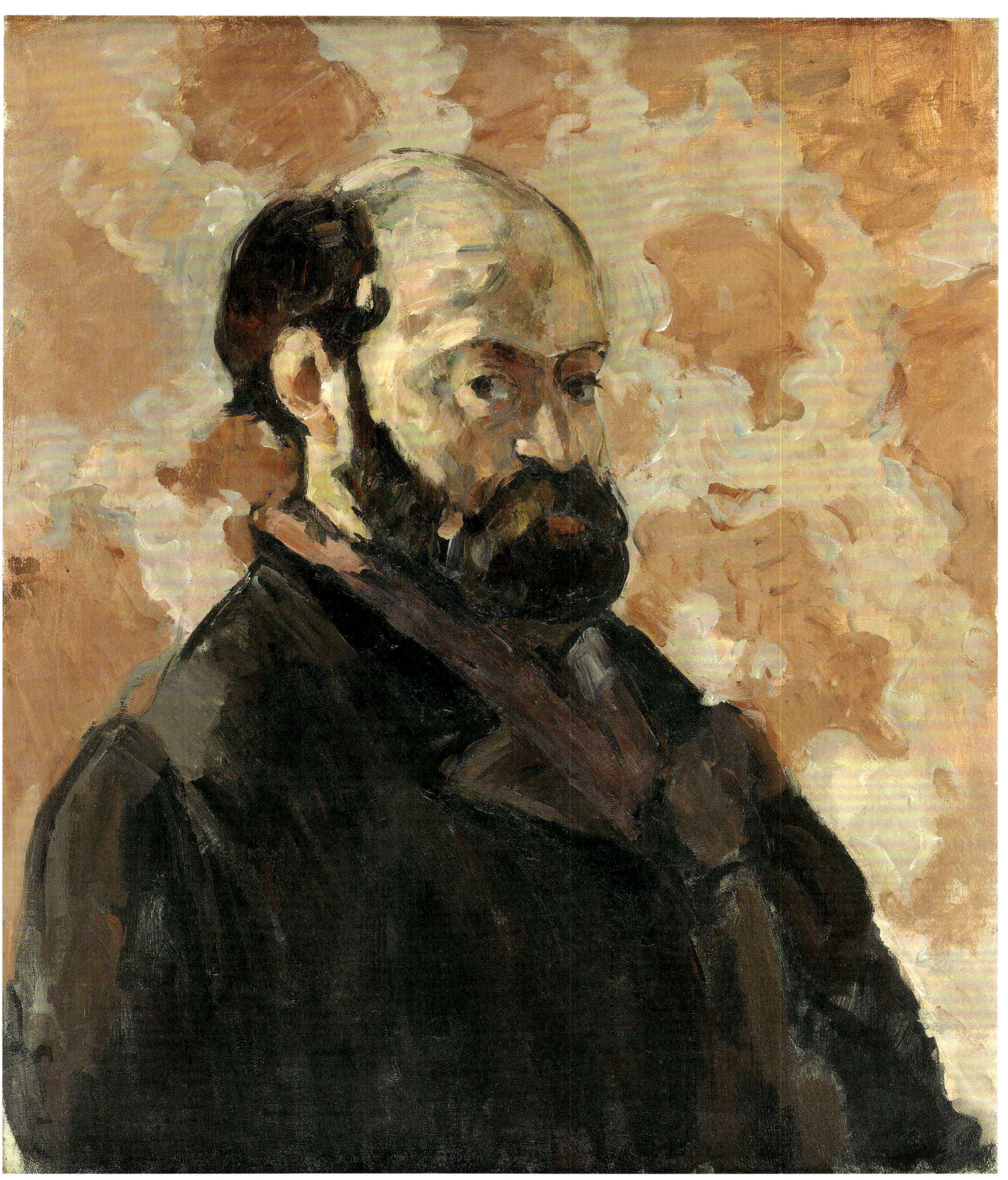

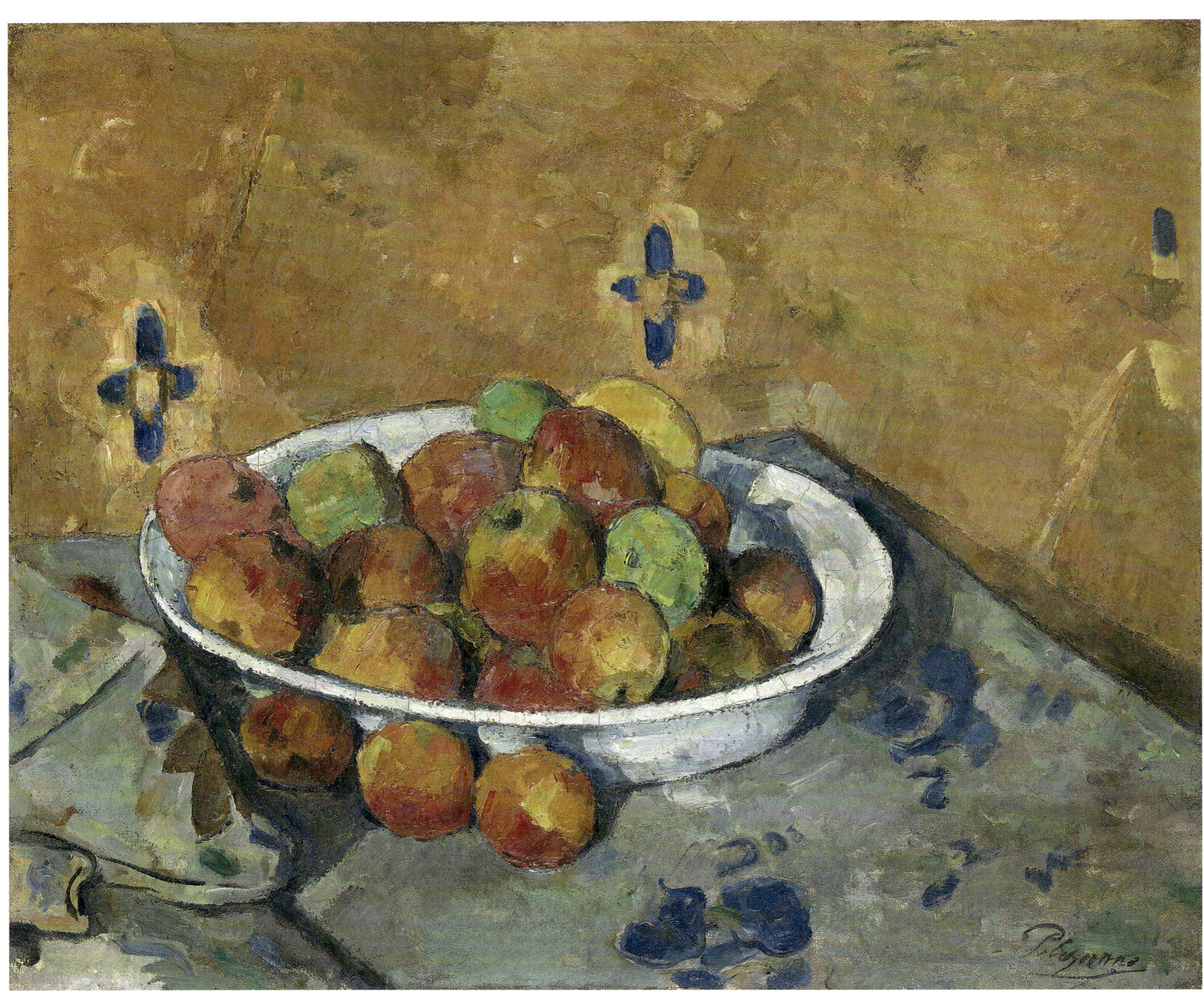

Cat. 33

The Plate of Apples
c. 1877
Oil on canvas
45.8 × 54.7 cm (18 ⅛ × 21 ½ in.)
The Art Institute of Chicago, gift of Kate L. Brewster,
1949.512
FWN 740

Cat. 34

Still Life: Flask, Glass, and Jug
c. 1877
Oil on canvas
46.2 × 55.2 cm (18 ³⁄₁₆ × 21 ¾ in.)
Solomon R. Guggenheim Museum, New York,
Thannhauser Collection, Gift, Justin K. Thannhauser,
78.2514.3
FWN 738
Chicago only

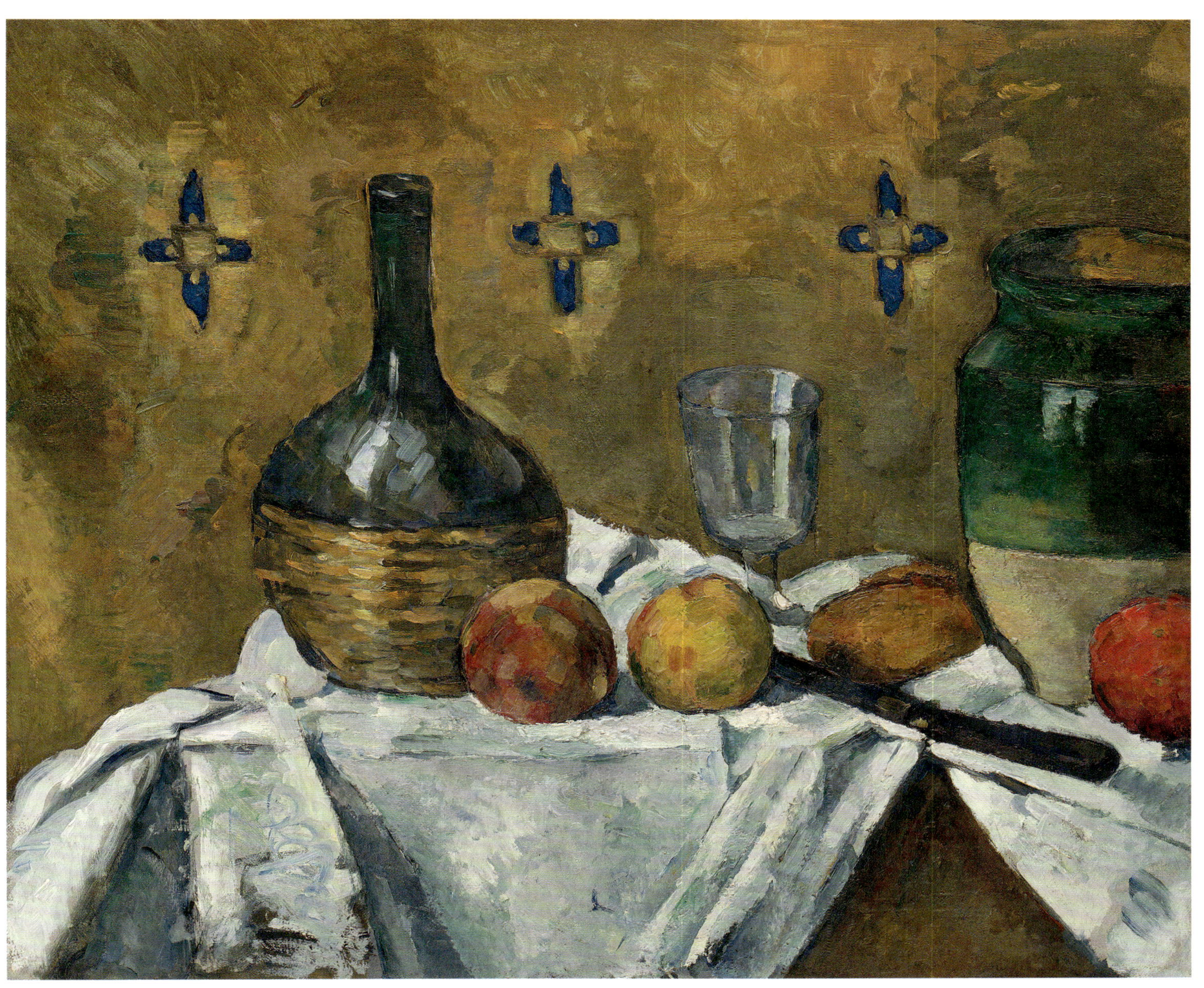

Cat. 35

Madame Cezanne in a Red Armchair
c. 1877
Oil on canvas
72.4 × 55.9 cm (28 ½ × 22 in.)
Museum of Fine Arts, Boston, Bequest of
Robert Treat Paine, 2nd, 44.776
FWN 443

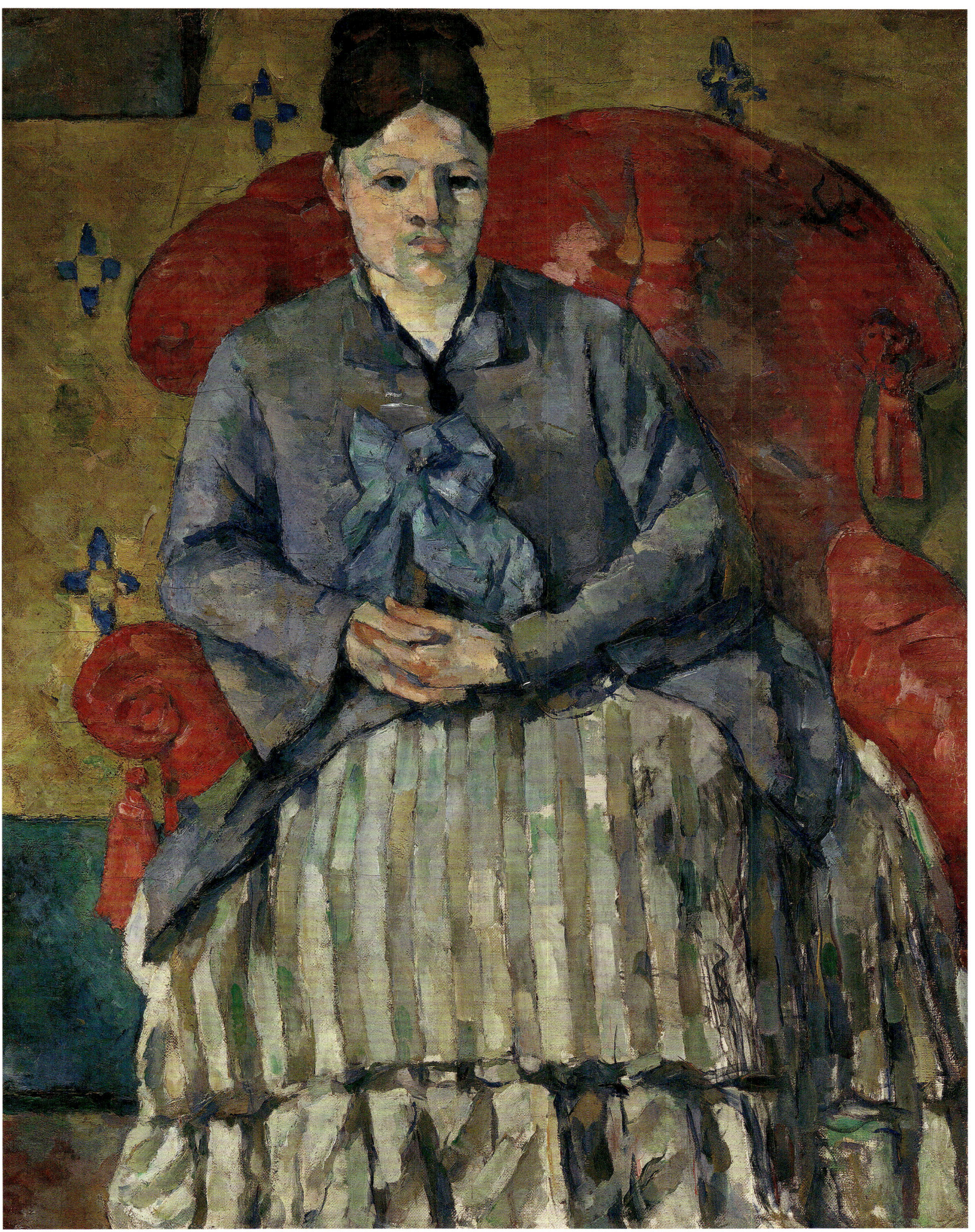

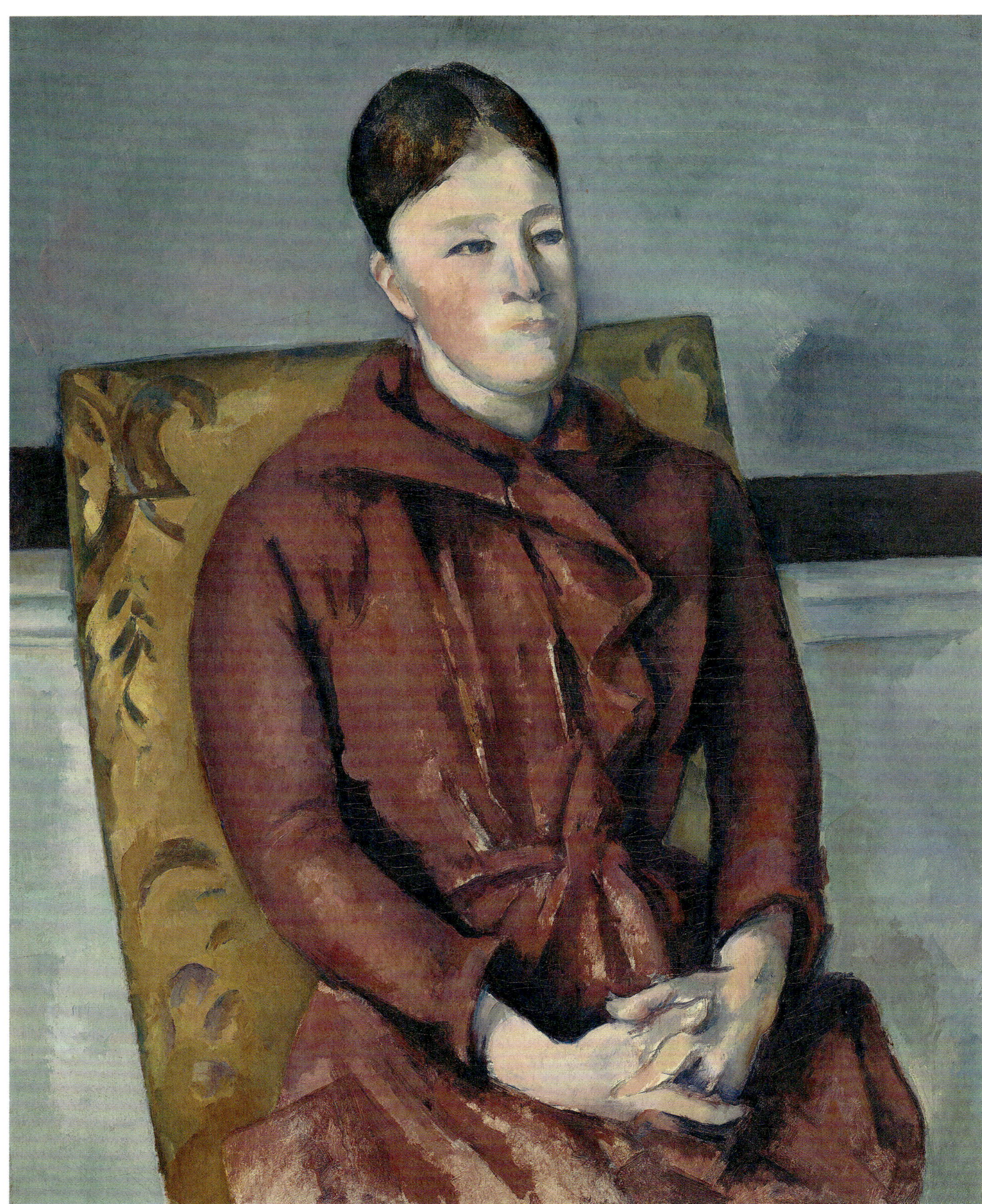

Cat. 36

Madame Cezanne in a Yellow Chair
1888–90
Oil on canvas
80.9 × 64.9 cm (31¹³⁄₁₆ × 25⁹⁄₁₆ in.)
The Art Institute of Chicago, Wilson L. Mead Fund,
1948.54
FWN 492

I PAINT PICTURES TOO!

Kerry James Marshall

I paint pictures too! I am driven by some of the same ambitions Cezanne expressed when he exclaimed his desire to "make of Impressionism an art that is solid and durable, like the art of the museums."[1] Nowadays, there are very few museums that don't have at least one Cezanne painting in their collections. Of course, the Impressionists he challenged are painters of the museum as well. With this book and museum survey, nearly one hundred and fifteen years after his death, and Cezanne already lionized as the father of modern painting, the question for me is: To what purpose is this new assessment set? A so-called artist's artist, Cezanne enjoyed some modest recognition in his lifetime. In his letters, he seemed humble and grateful for any public acknowledgment that his efforts were not completely in vain. With hindsight, Cezanne's status seems inevitable, but for any truly ambitious artist, critical affirmation in one's lifetime is the only assurance that counts.

And what about the durability Cezanne pursued? Is there still something vital for us in the pictures he made? Do they wear their age lightly? Pablo Picasso declared that for him, "there is no past or future in art. If a work cannot live always in the present, it must not be considered at all."[2] Artists who believe their work meets all the important criteria upheld by museums must internalize this in order to persevere. In 2022, however, we are well past the revolutionary phase of art, when the condition of painting as an essential mode of representation was vigorously contested. Today, every kind of image that gets made is presented as though it has an a priori claim to relevance. No one looks to nature or the self anymore as the source of revelation in art, as Cezanne did. These days, artists don't even learn to paint by copying other paintings. Examining pictures of paintings seems sufficient. Even so, the art of making paintings has, once again, taken on quasi-mystical overtones following a retreat from skill and renewed suspicion of authority.

Photography, having once liberated painters from faithful representations of the world around them, has reasserted its primacy in painting as the reference model of choice. Even Cezanne contradicted his worship of nature as the quintessential source by relying on a photograph for his famous painting of a male bather (cat. 99) now at the Museum of Modern Art, New York. We could ask: What sensations of vision, color, and light determined the arrangement of planes and strokes in this picture? Has rendering the irreconcilable discrepancies between seeing and painting become a formula readily applicable to any circumstance? Portraits and still lifes don't challenge a painter's powers of observation and selection the way painting landscapes out-of-doors does. The painter needed a series of long sessions—possibly extended over several years—to resolve *Madame Cezanne in a Yellow Chair*, which raises questions about its method of execution. What was Cezanne trying to get right after all that time? Every picture painted must be made to work. And all pictures work in accordance with a set of ideals and principles imagined beforehand.

Cezanne is not an outlier in this regard. Paul Gauguin, Claude Monet, George Seurat, Henri de Toulouse-Lautrec, and Vincent van Gogh. These painters all strove for singularity. They all produced radiant and captivating paintings. Of course, when I say "captivating," it is not the subject of the picture, per se, that draws me to it, even with the portraits. I am as indifferent to the identities and life stories of the sitters as most art historians who write about Cezanne claim he was. Figures are the means to a pictorial end. The best portraits by Jean-Auguste-Dominique Ingres, without parallel in the history of painting, were dismissed by Cezanne, who disparaged Ingres as "only a very little painter."[3] Rather, it is the integrated character of a picture, its color, the relationship of each part to the whole, that is beguiling. Do the people, whoever they might be, real or imagined, look good in the picture? Does it look right? This amalgamation, serene or dynamic, compels our attention and encourages closer examination.

For example: the picture *Madame Cezanne in a Yellow Chair* is singled out as a masterpiece in Rudolf Arnheim's book *Art and Visual Perception: A Psychology of the Creative Eye* (first published in 1954), even as he acknowledges "its simplicity," which museumgoers might not be inclined to spend a lot of time with. Arnheim performs a detailed analysis—which I mostly agree with—of the shapes and forces that give the painting its energy.[4]

This painting does not conform to the brick-by-brick pattern of colored planes generally agreed to reflect Cezanne's method but is rich with many of the formal idiosyncrasies we take for granted as being his today. Sections of the picture alternate between flatness and volume. Edges and contours are established, then disappear. Foreground objects and the background alternately overlap and merge. Continuous forms are misaligned from one side of a shape to the other. These are among the peculiar, yet deliberate, inconsistencies that give Cezanne's painting its vitality and contribute to an inexhaustible sense of fascination.

1. Paul Cezanne quoted in Richard W. Murphy, *The World of Cezanne: 1839–1906* (New York: Time-Life Library of Art, 1968), 70.
2. Pablo Picasso quoted in Robert Goldwater and Marco Treves, *Artists on Art: From the XIVth to the XXth Century* (New York: Pantheon Books, 1945), 418.
3. Paul Cezanne quoted in Goldwater and Treves, *Artists on Art,* 364.
4. Rudolf Arnheim, *Art and Visual Perception: A Psychology of the Creative Eye* (Berkeley: University of California Press, 1954), 27.

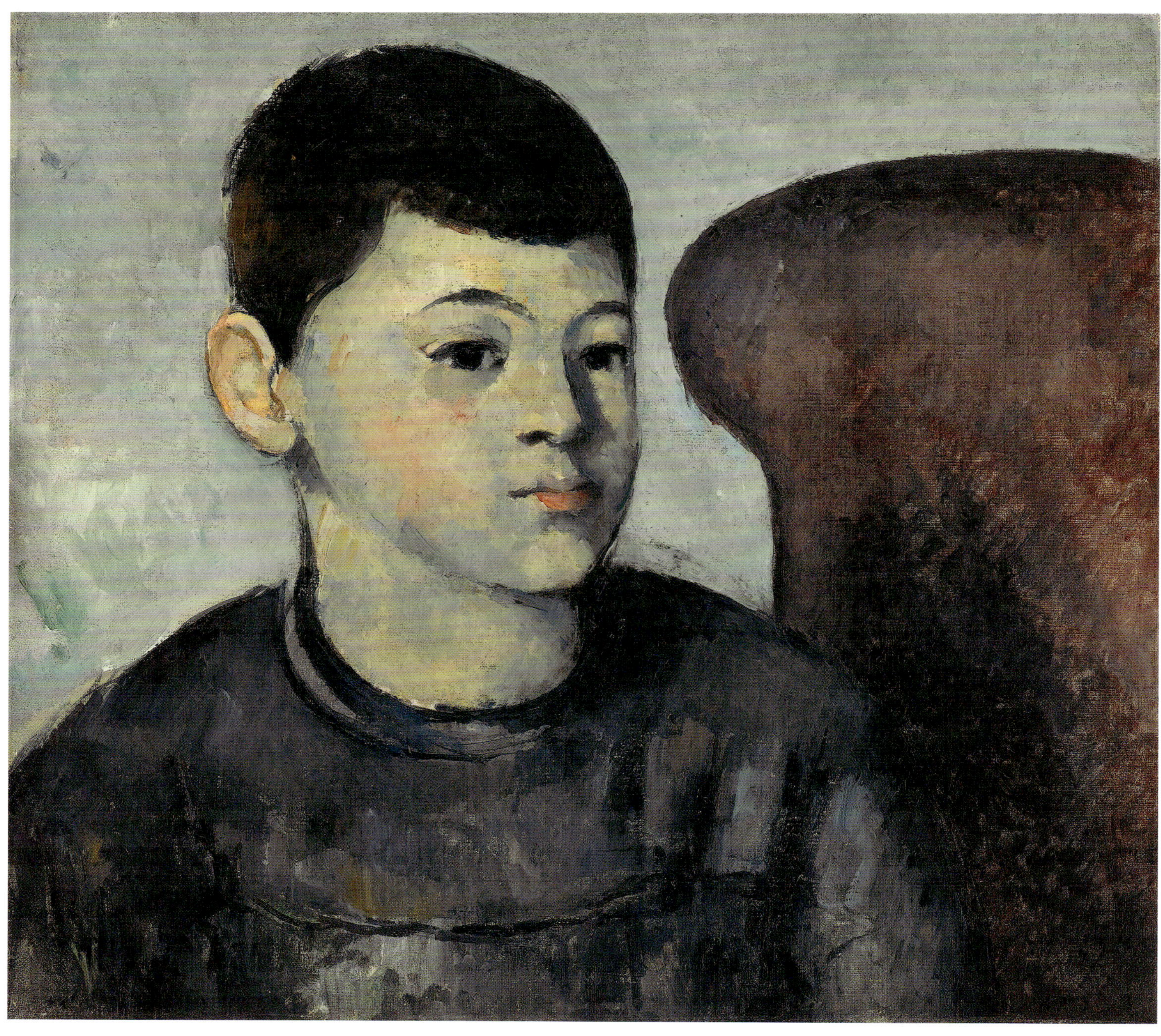

Cat. 37

Portrait of the Artist's Son
1880
Oil on canvas
35 × 38 cm (13 ¾ × 14 ¹⁵⁄₁₆ in.)
Musée de l'Orangerie, Paris, Jean Walter and
Paul Guillaume Collection, RF 1963 59
FWN 465

Cat. 38

Portrait of the Artist's Son
1881–82
Oil on canvas
28.6 × 32.5 cm (11 ¼ × 12 ¹³⁄₁₆ in.)
Private collection, Derbyshire, UK
FWN 459
London only

Cat. 39

Portrait of Madame Cezanne
c. 1883
Oil on canvas
20.3 × 14 cm (8 × 5 ½ in.)
Private collection
FWN 467
Chicago only

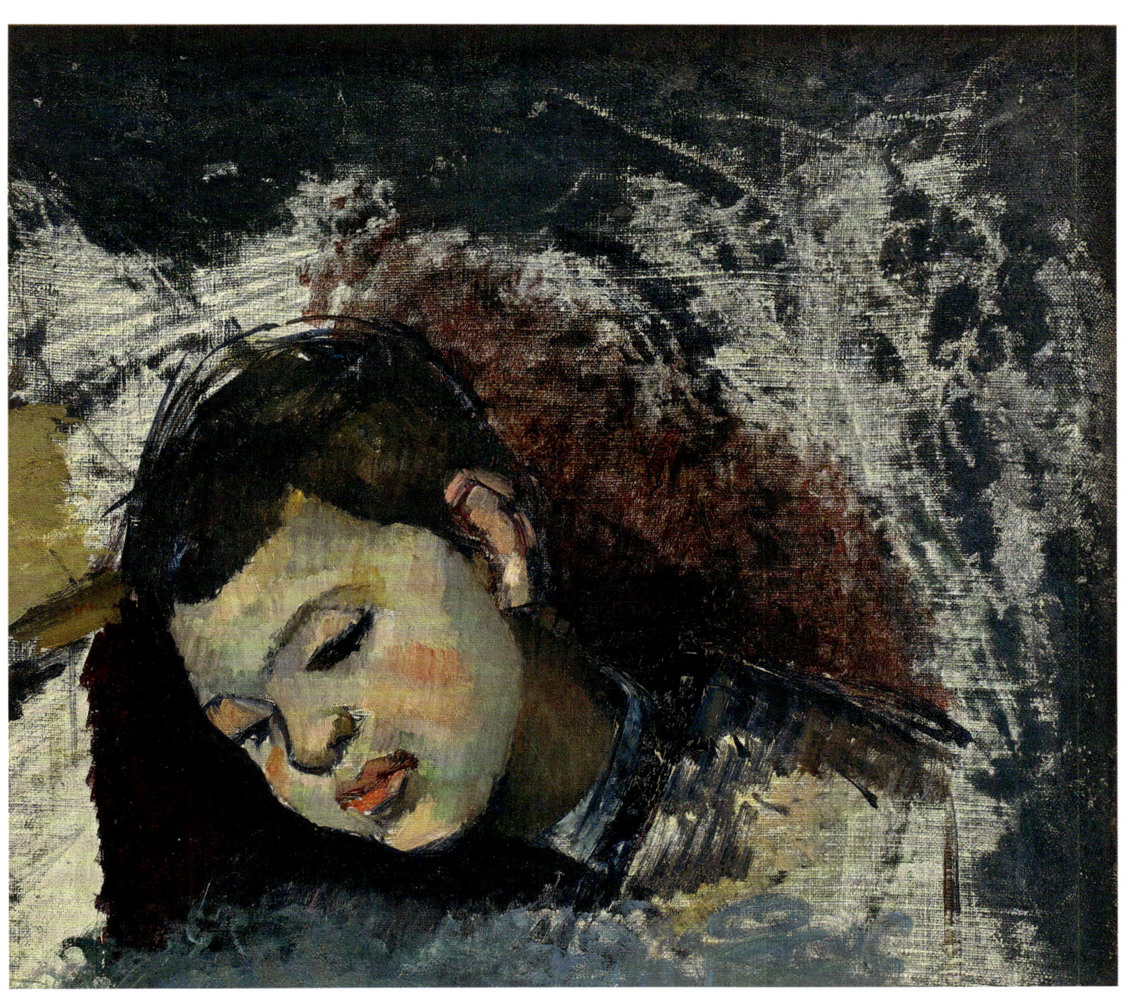

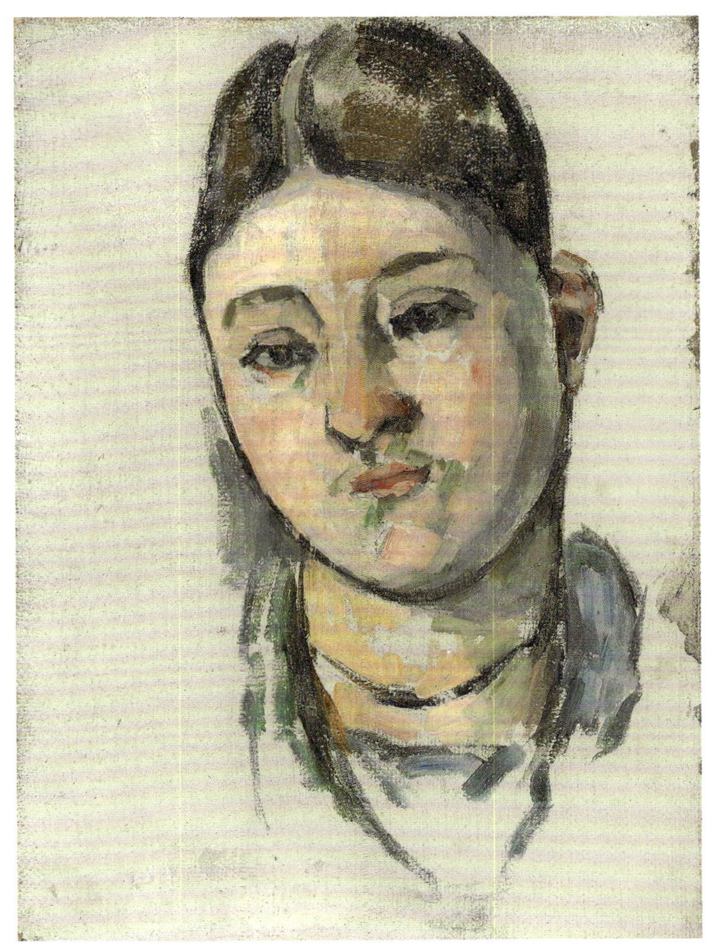

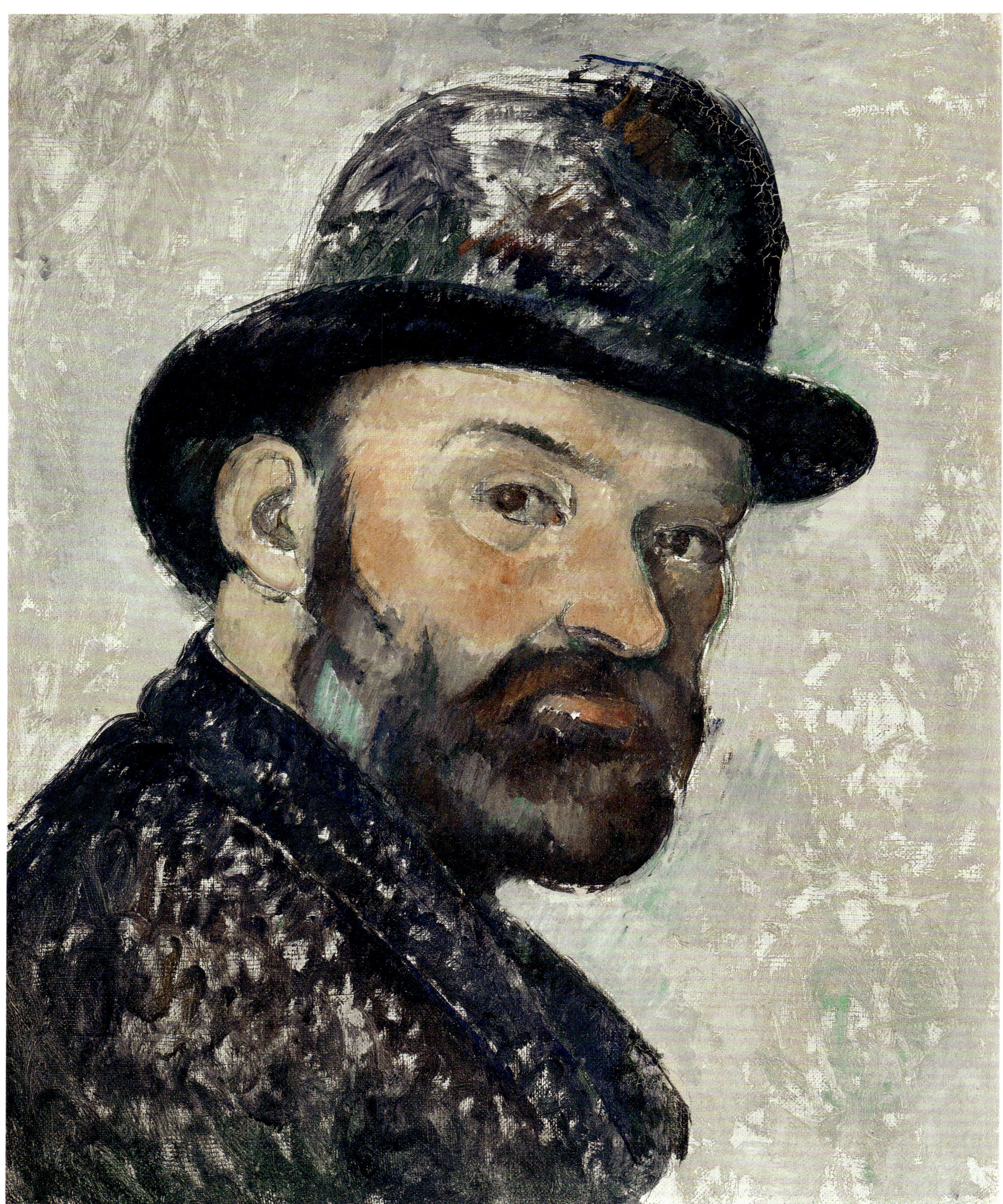

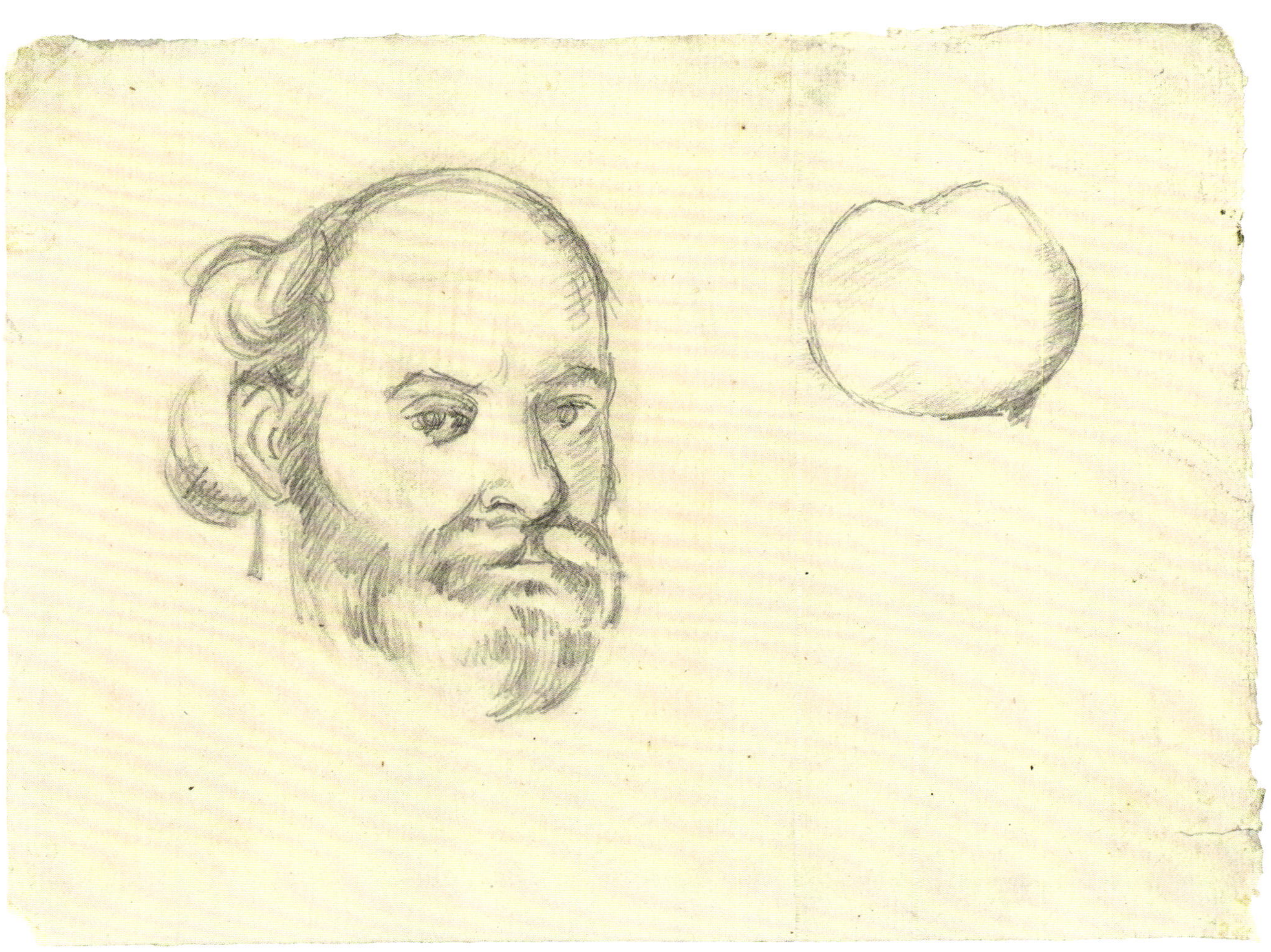

Cat. 40

Self-Portrait with Bowler Hat
1885–86
Oil on canvas
44.5 × 35.5 cm (17 ½ × 14 in.)
Ny Carlsberg Glyptotek, Copenhagen,
inv. nr. MIN 1892
FWN 478
Chicago only

Cat. 41

Self-Portrait and Apple
1882–83
Pencil on paper
17.3 × 23 cm (6 ¹³⁄₁₆ × 9 ¹⁄₁₆ in.)
Cincinnati Art Museum, Gift of Emily Poole, 1958.128
FWN 2306
Chicago only

Cat. 42

Sketchbook New York
c. 1875–85
Graphite, with watercolor on one sheet, on 48 sheets
of mixed white, blue, gray, beige, and brown wove
paper, bound in beige linen
Leaves (approx.): 12.6 × 21.6 cm (4 ¹⁵⁄₁₆ × 8 ½ in.)
Binding: 13.5 × 21.9 cm (5 ⁵⁄₁₆ × 8 ⁵⁄₈ in.)
The Morgan Library & Museum, New York, given in
honor of the 75th anniversary of the Morgan Library
and the 50th anniversary of the Association of Fellows,
1999.9
FWN 3009
Chicago only
(**a**) cover; (**b**) FWN 3009-00 and FWN 3009-01a;
(**c**) FWN 3009-10b and FWN 3009-11a; (**d**) FWN
3009-12b and FWN 3009-13a; (**e**) FWN 3009-43b
and FWN 3009-44a; (**f**) FWN 3009-48b and FWN
3009-49

a

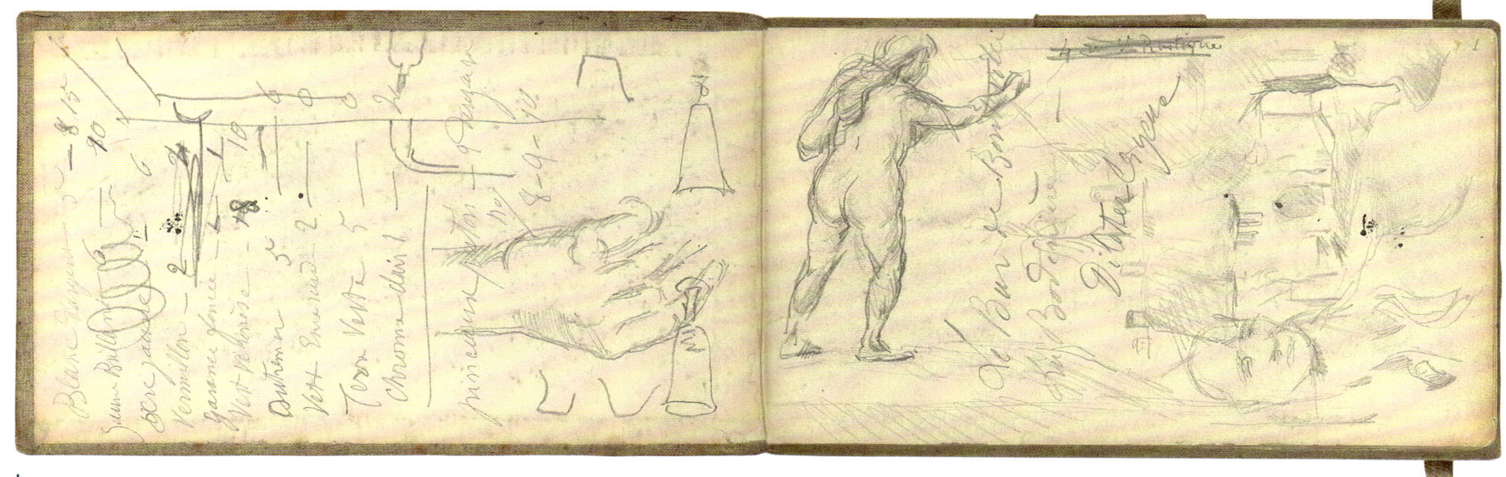

b

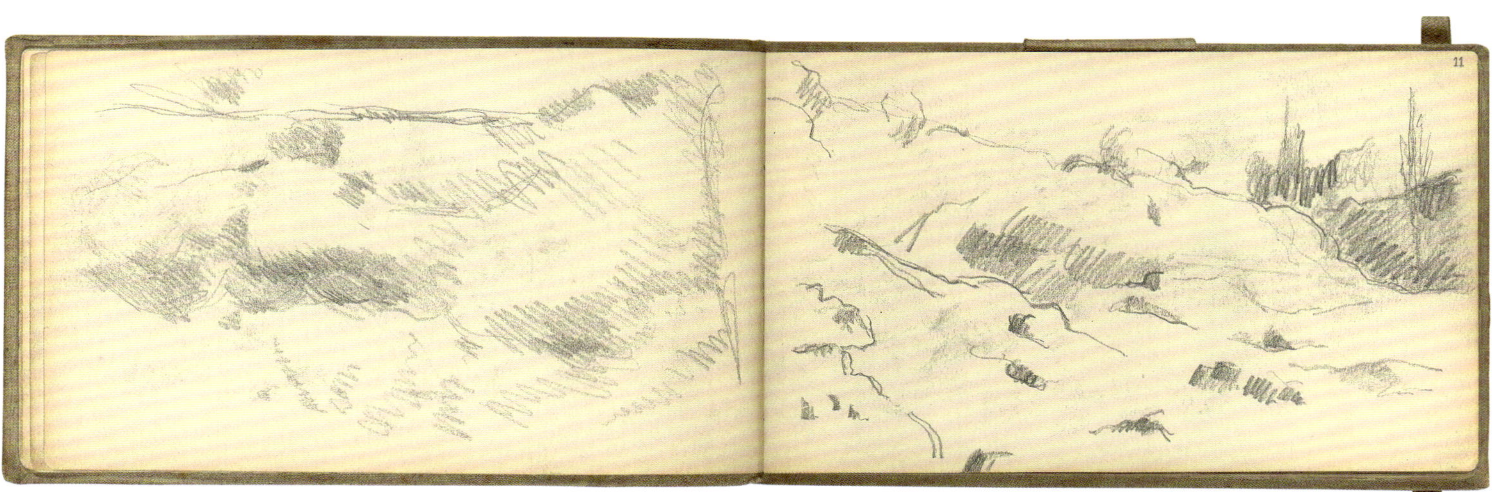

c

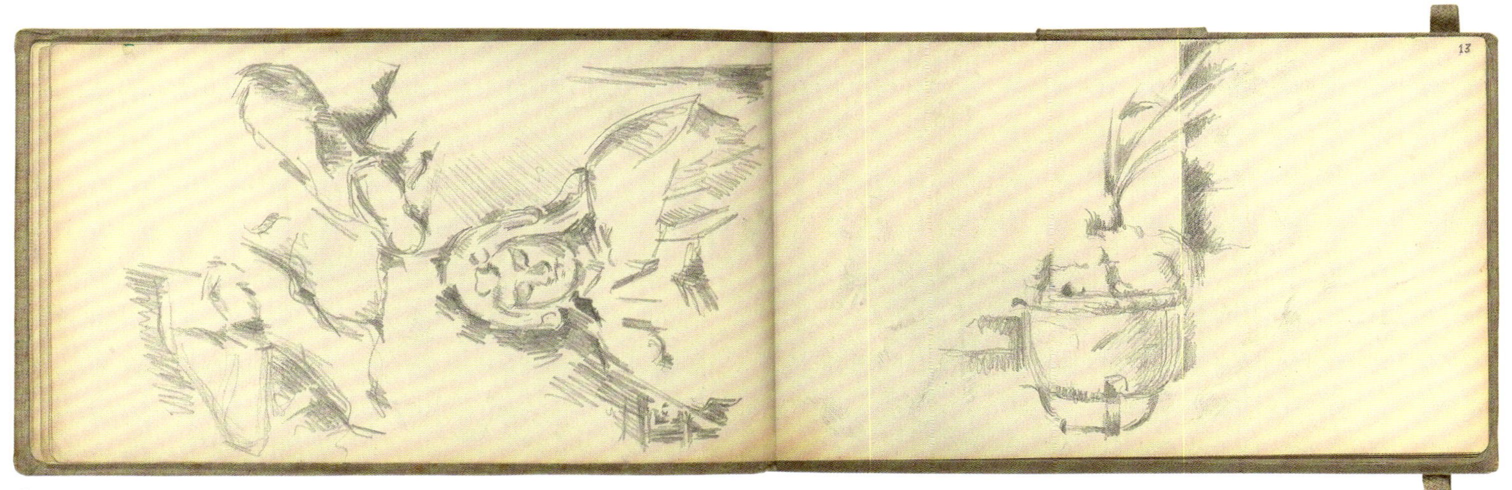

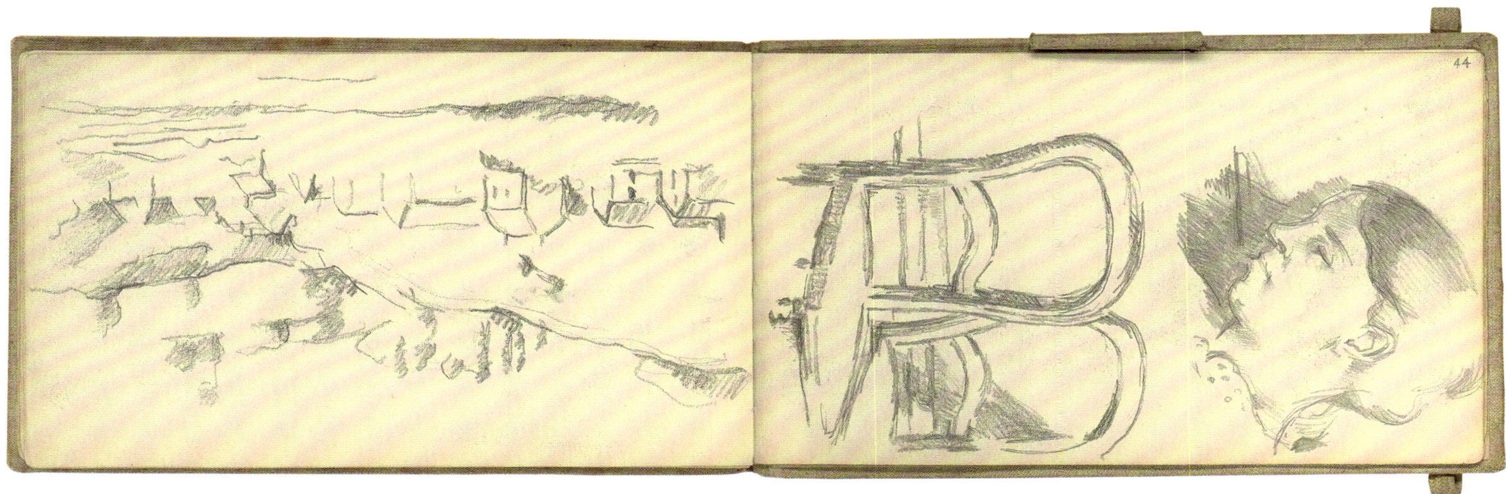

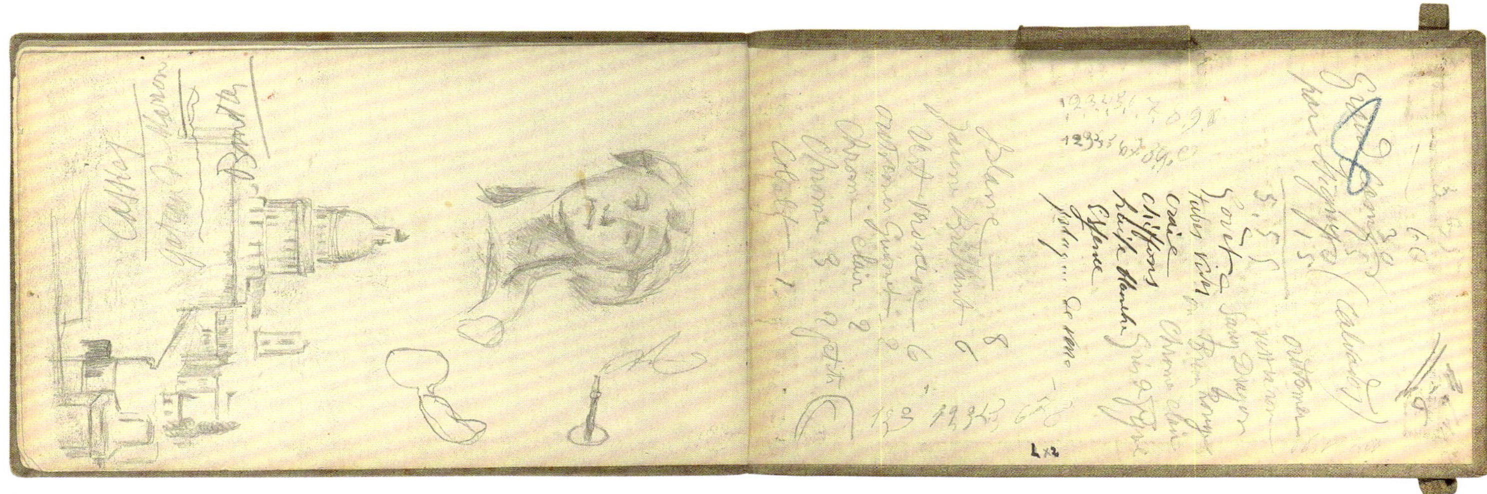

Cat. 43

Sketchbook Chicago
1875–86
Graphite and pen-and-ink drawings on paper, bound
into a book
Leaves: 12.4 × 21.7 cm (4 ⅞ × 8 ⁹⁄₁₆ in.)
Binding: 13 × 22 cm (5 ⅛ × 8 ¹¹⁄₁₆ in.)
The Art Institute of Chicago, Arthur Heun Purchase
Fund, 1951.1
FWN 3006
(**a**) cover; (**b**) FWN 3006-00 and FWN 3006-01a;
(**c**) FWN 3006-03b and FWN 3006-04a;
(**d**) FWN 3006-20b and FWN 3006-21a;
(**e**) FWN 3006-48b and FWN 3006-49a;
(**f**) FWN 3006-49b and Child's Drawing

a

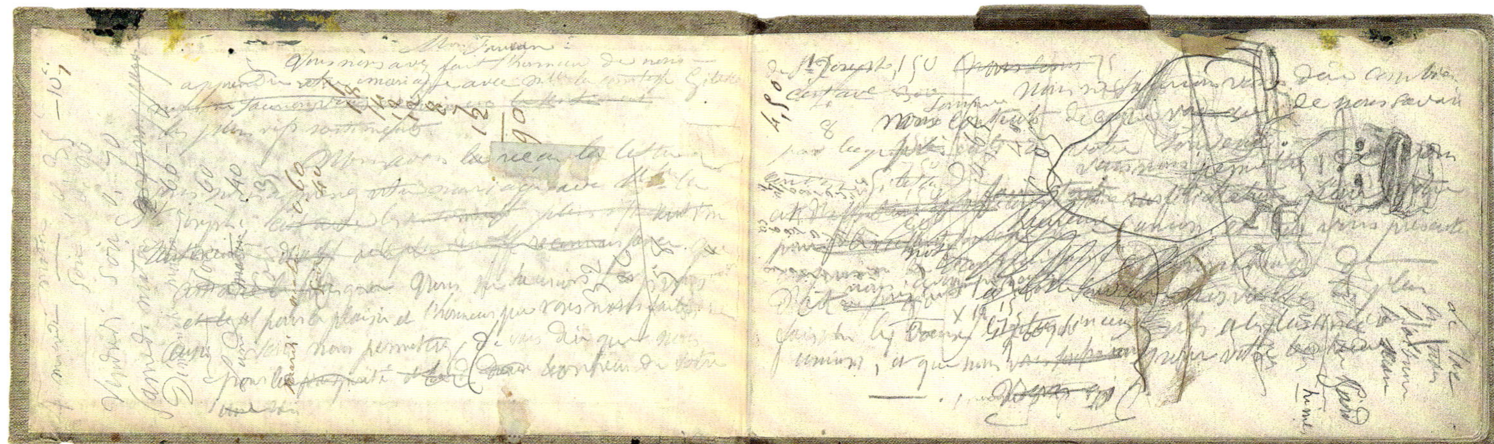

b

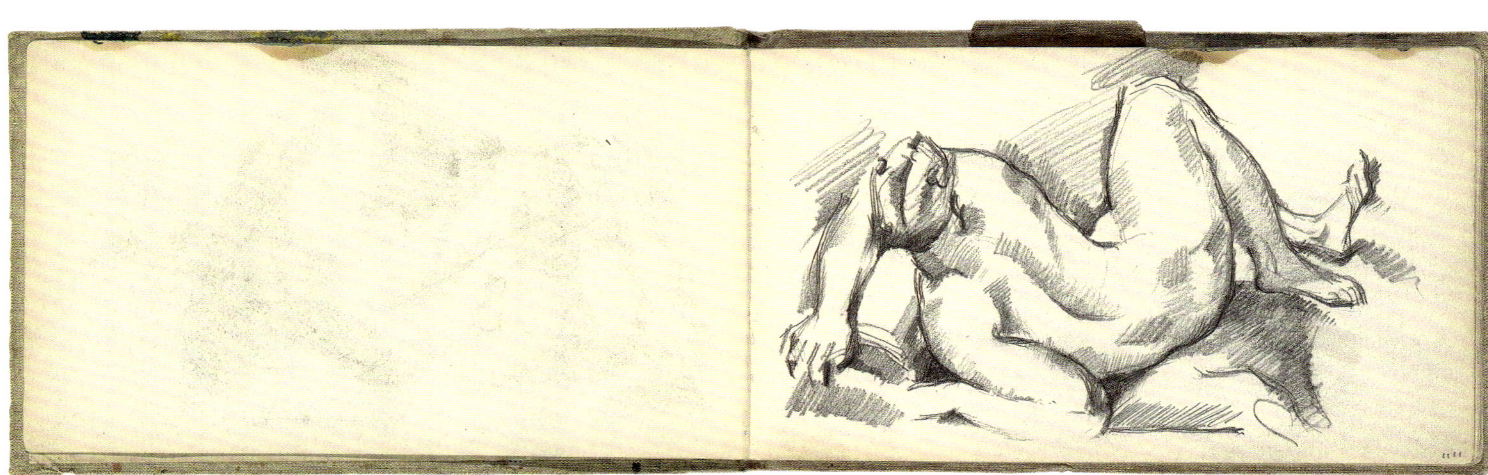

c

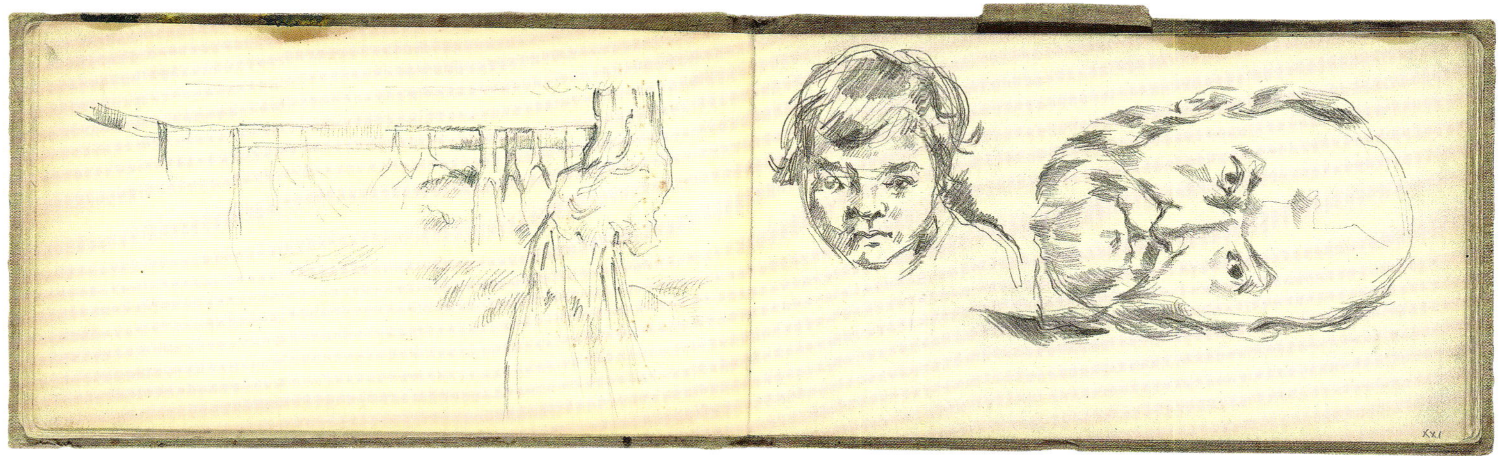

d

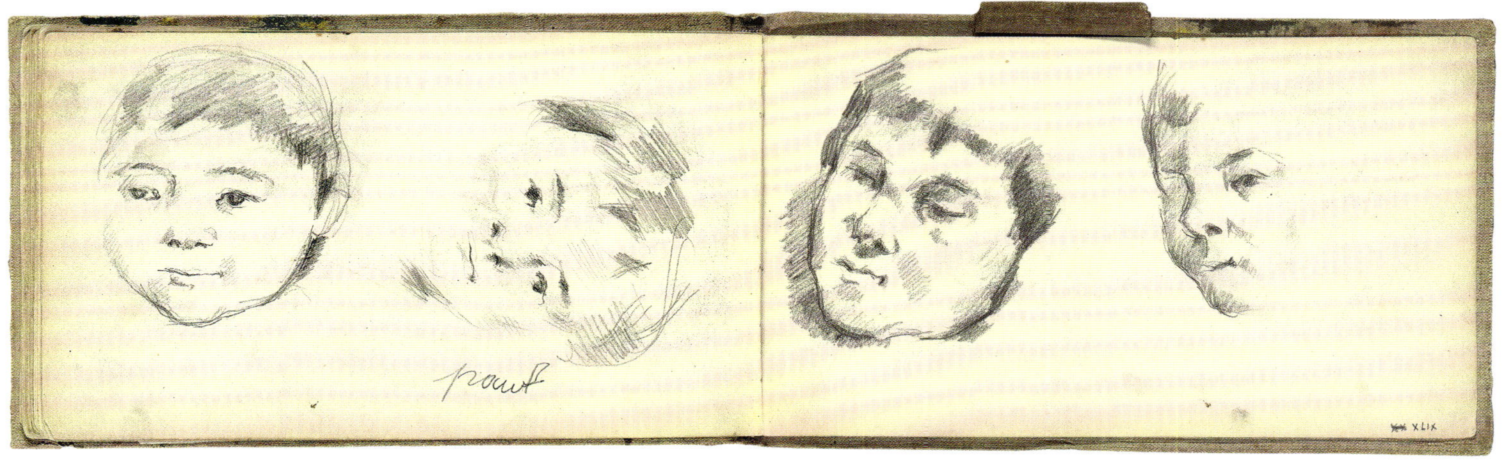

e

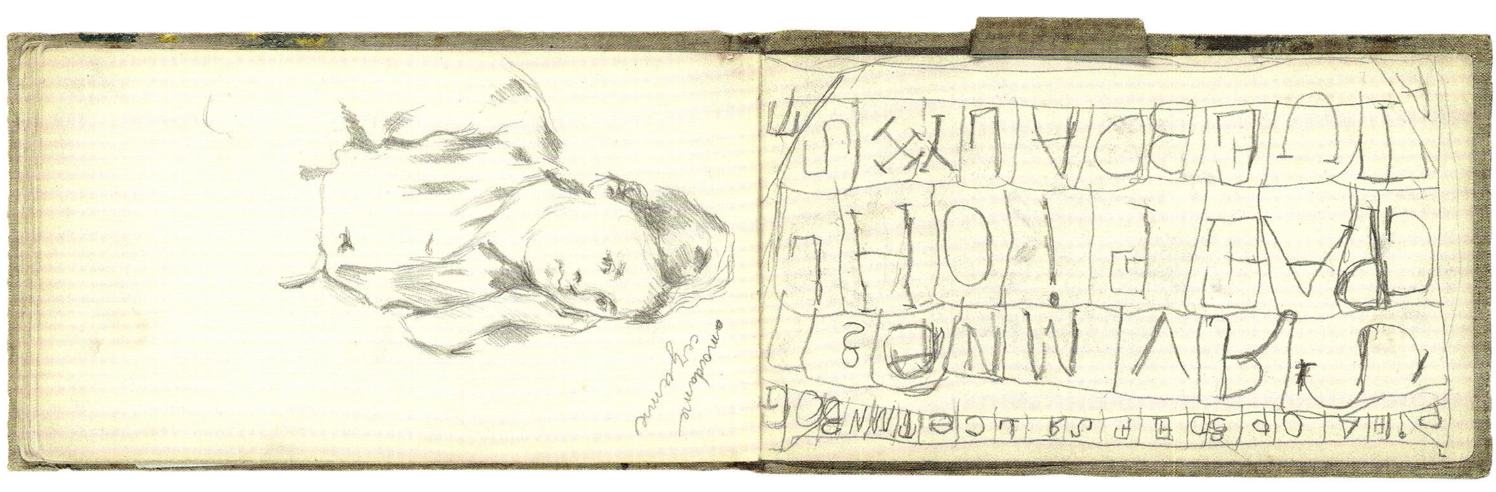

f

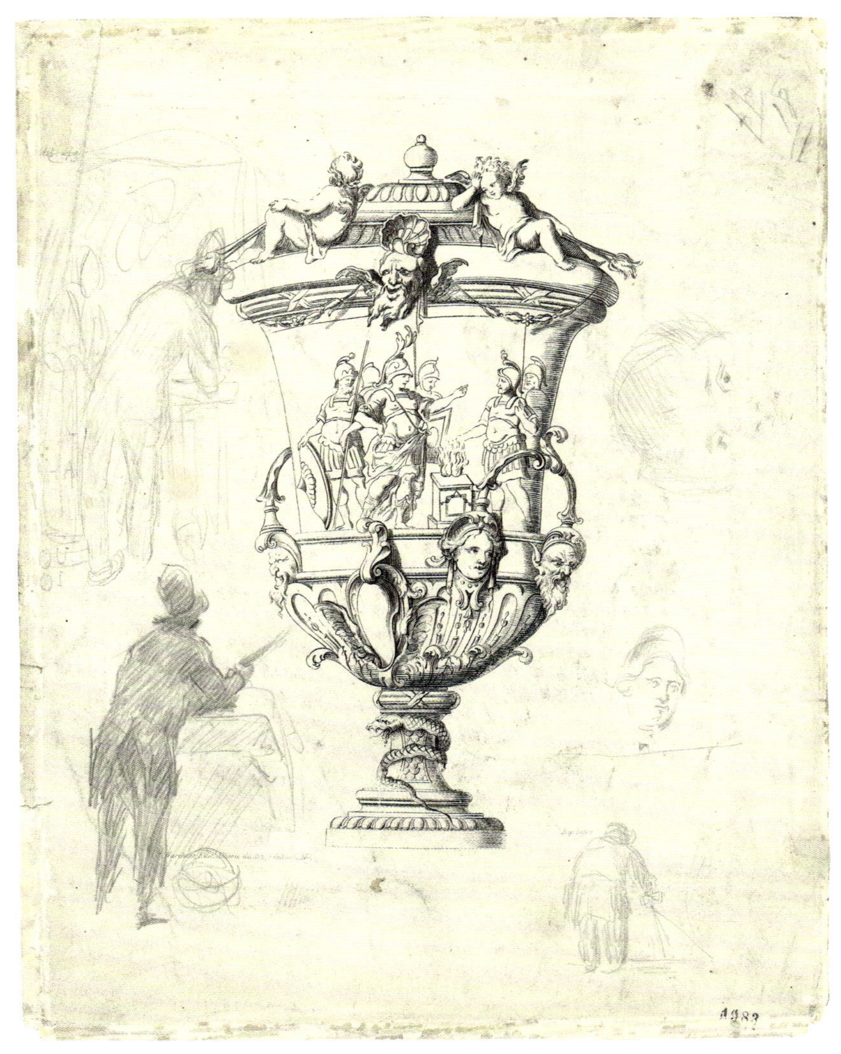

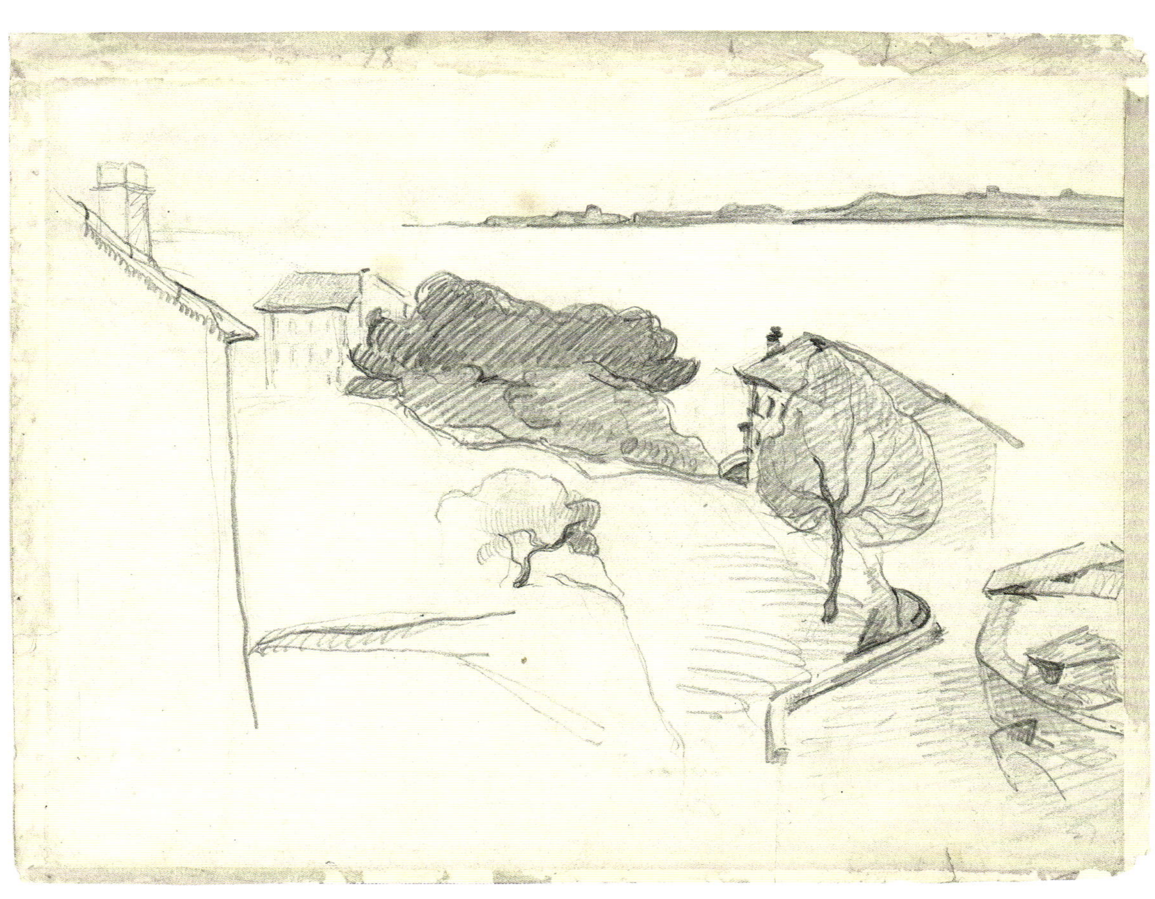

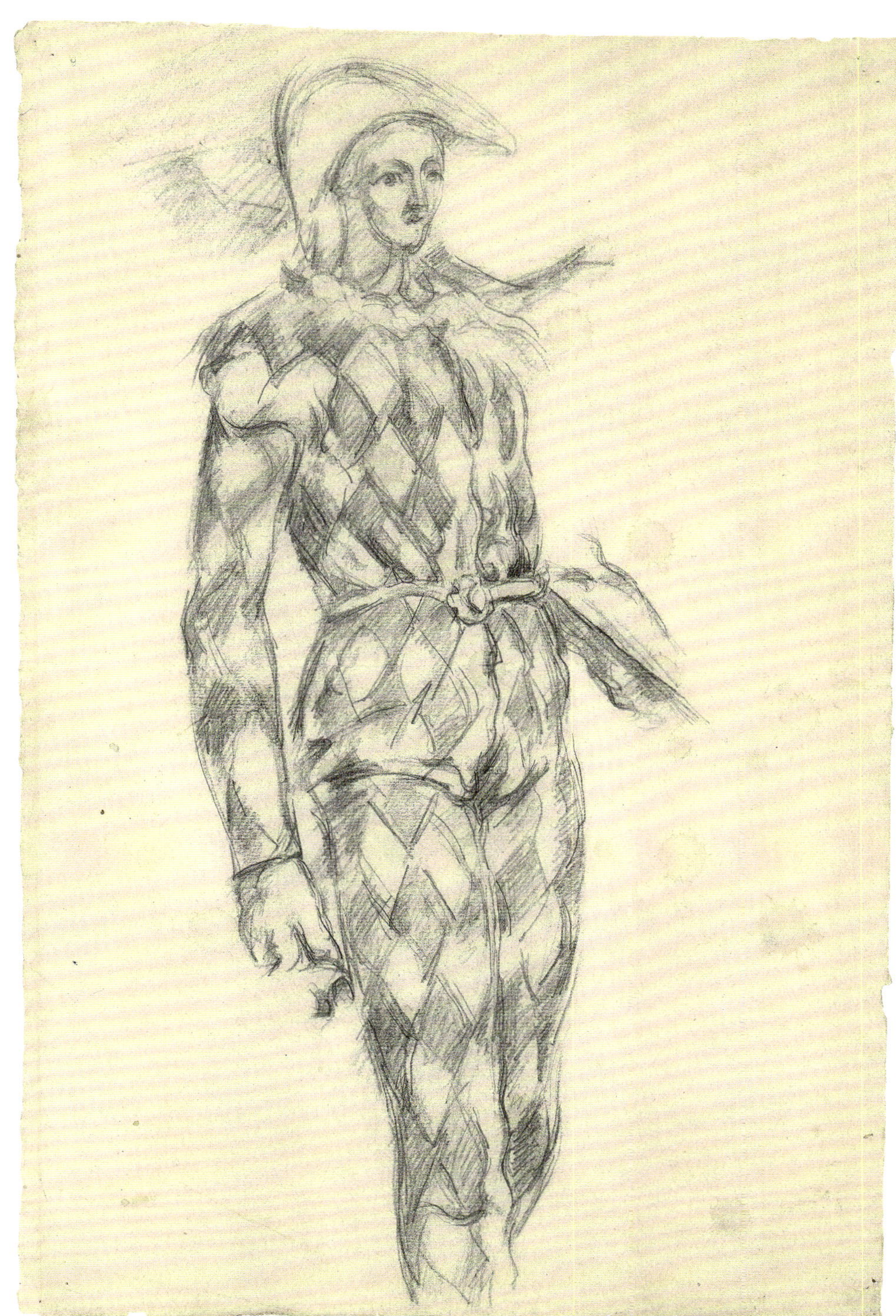

Cat. 44

**Figure Studies around an Engraving
of an Ornamental Vase**
1870–72
Graphite on ivory wove paper (verso)
31.6 × 24.3 cm (12 ⁷⁄₁₆ × 9 ⁹⁄₁₆ in.)
The Art Institute of Chicago, gift of Justin K.
Thannhauser, 1964.79v
FWN 2226
Chicago only

Cat. 45

L'Estaque
1870–72
Graphite on ivory wove paper (recto)
24.3 × 31.6 cm (9 ⁹⁄₁₆ × 12 ⁷⁄₁₆ in.)
The Art Institute of Chicago, gift of Justin K.
Thannhauser, 1964.79r
FWN 1022
Chicago only

Cat. 46

Study of a Harlequin
c. 1888
Graphite on ivory laid paper
47.8 × 31.7 cm (18 ¹³⁄₁₆ × 12 ½ in.)
The Art Institute of Chicago, Margaret Day Blake
Collection, 1944.577
FWN 1750
Chicago only

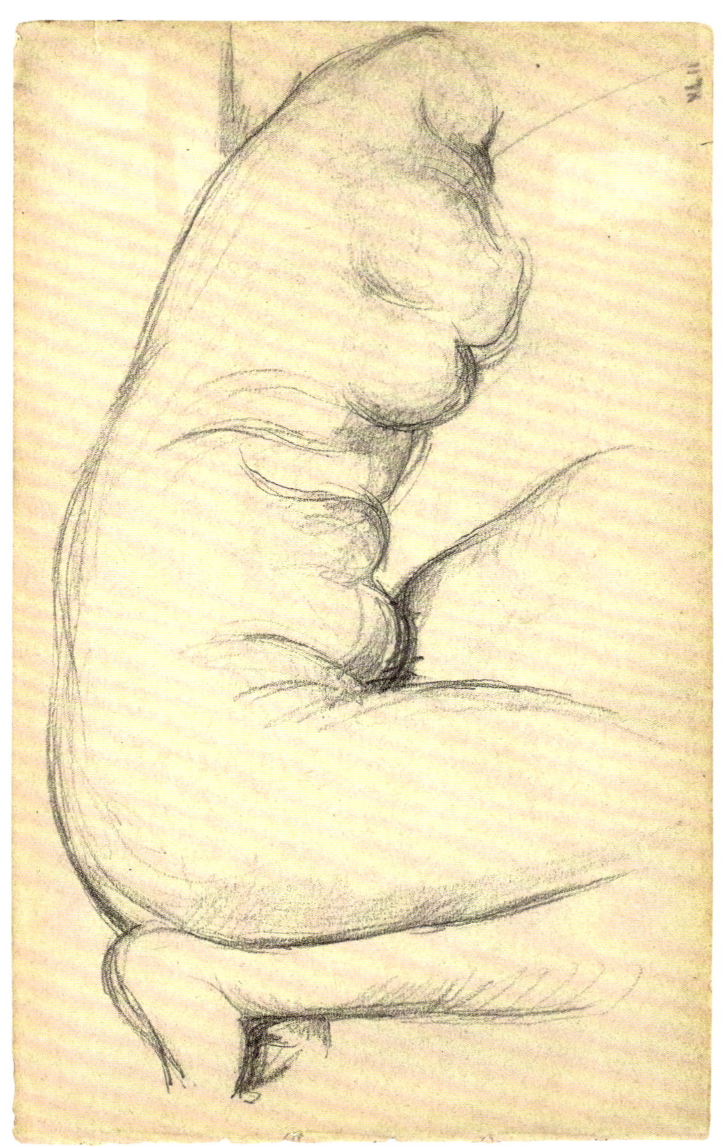

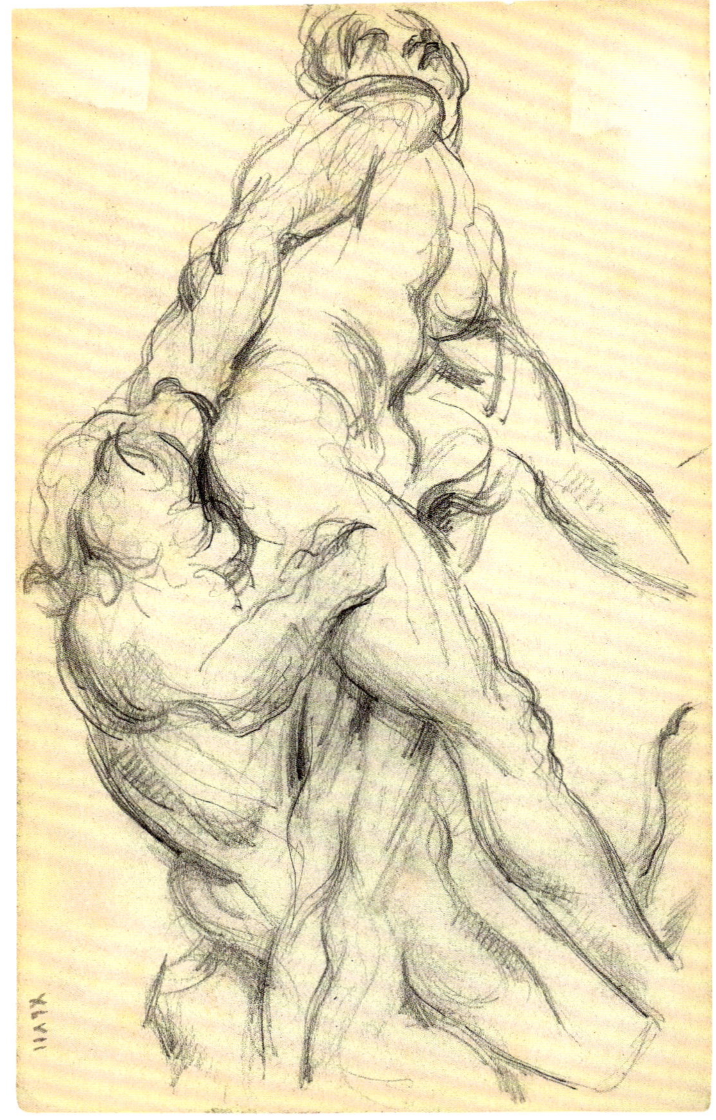

Cat. 47

After the Antique: Crouching Venus
c. 1894–97
Pencil on paper
19.6 × 12 cm (7 ¾ × 4 ¾ in.)
The Whitworth, The University of Manchester,
Karsten Schubert Gift, 2019, D.2020.4
FWN 3003-42a
London only

Cat. 48

After Pierre Puget (French, 1620–1694)
After Pierre Puget: Milo of Croton
c. 1882–85
Pencil on paper
19.6 × 11.9 cm (7 ¾ × 4 ¹¹⁄₁₆ in.)
The Whitworth, The University of Manchester,
Karsten Schubert Gift, 2019, D.2020.5
FWN 3003-47a
London only

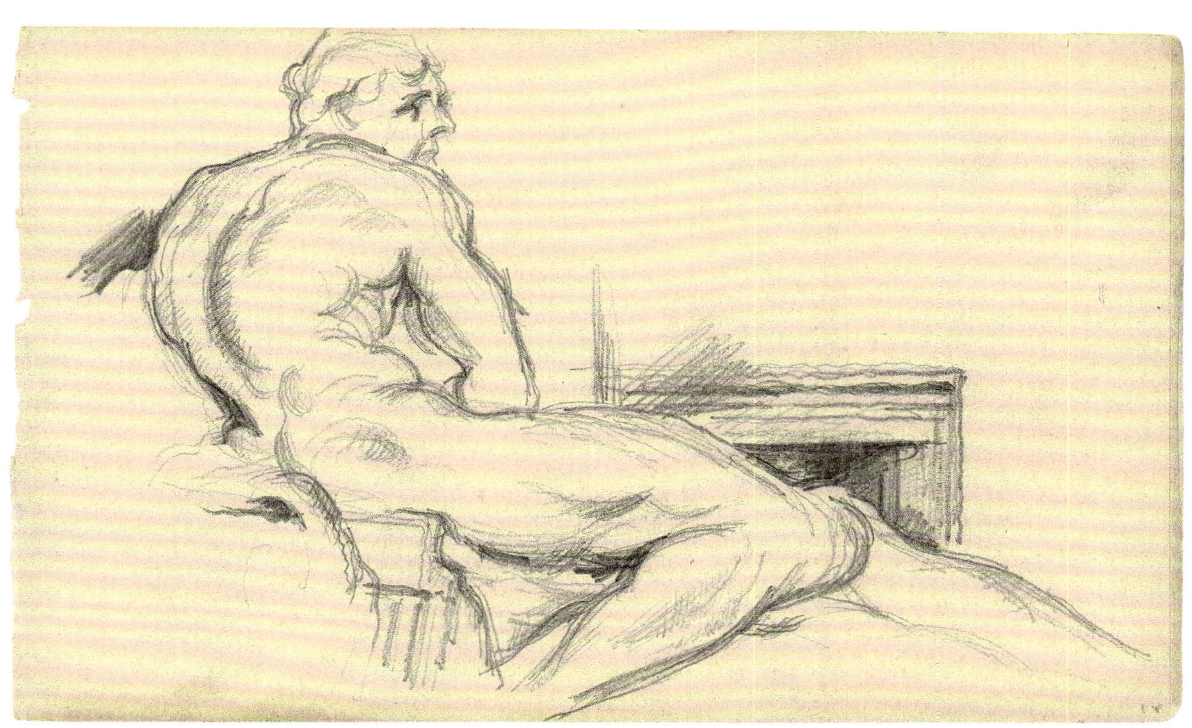

Cat. 49

After Pierre Puget (French, 1620–1694)
Hercules Resting
1897
Graphite on ivory wove paper (verso)
11.8 × 19.4 cm (4 ⁵⁄₈ × 7 ⁵⁄₈ in.)
The Art Institute of Chicago, gift of Dorothy Braude
Edinburg to the Harry B. and Bessie K. Braude
Memorial Collection, 1998.695v
FWN 3003-04a

Cat. 50

Milk Jug and Spirit Stove
1879–82
Graphite on ivory wove paper (recto)
19.4 × 11.8 cm (7 ⁵⁄₈ × 4 ⁵⁄₈ in.)
The Art Institute of Chicago, gift of Dorothy Braude
Edinburg to the Harry B. and Bessie K. Braude
Memorial Collection, 1998.695r
FWN 3003-04b
Chicago only

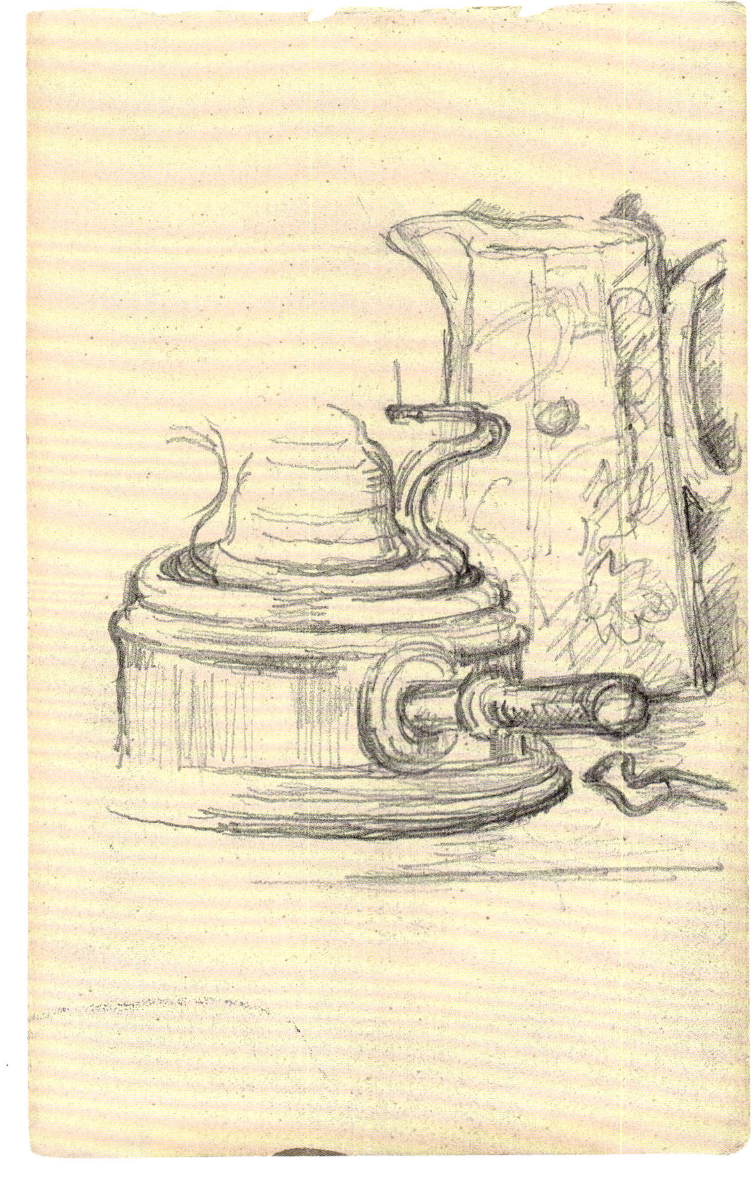

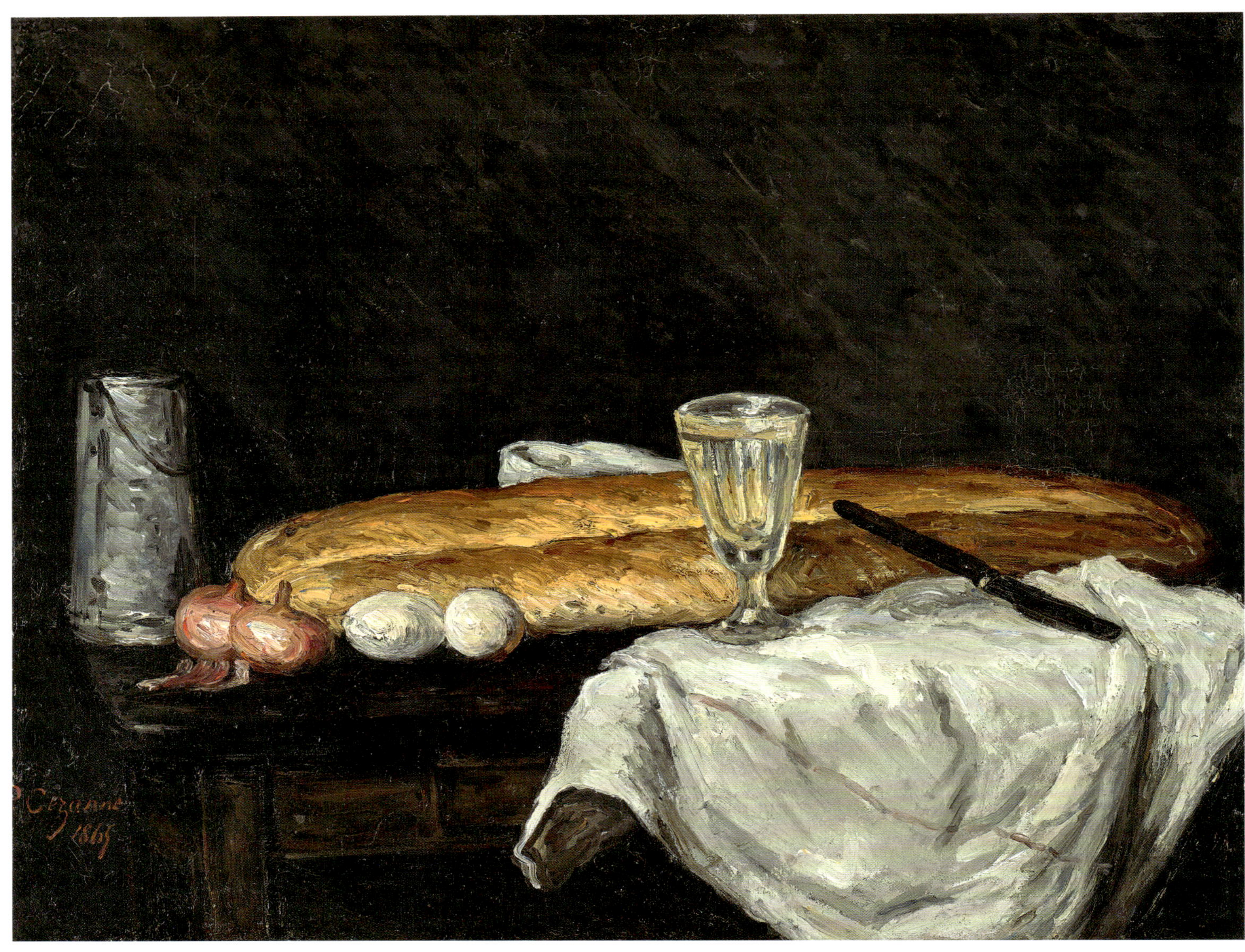

Cat. 51

Still Life with Bread and Eggs
1865
Oil on canvas
59.1 × 76.2 cm (23 ¼ × 30 in.)
Cincinnati Art Museum, Gift of Mary E. Johnston,
1955.73
FWN 704
Chicago only

Cat. 52

Le Buffet
1877–79
Oil on canvas
65 × 81 cm (25 ⅝ × 31 ⅞ in.)
Museum of Fine Arts, Budapest
(Gift of Baron Hatvany), inv. 371
FWN 746
Chicago only

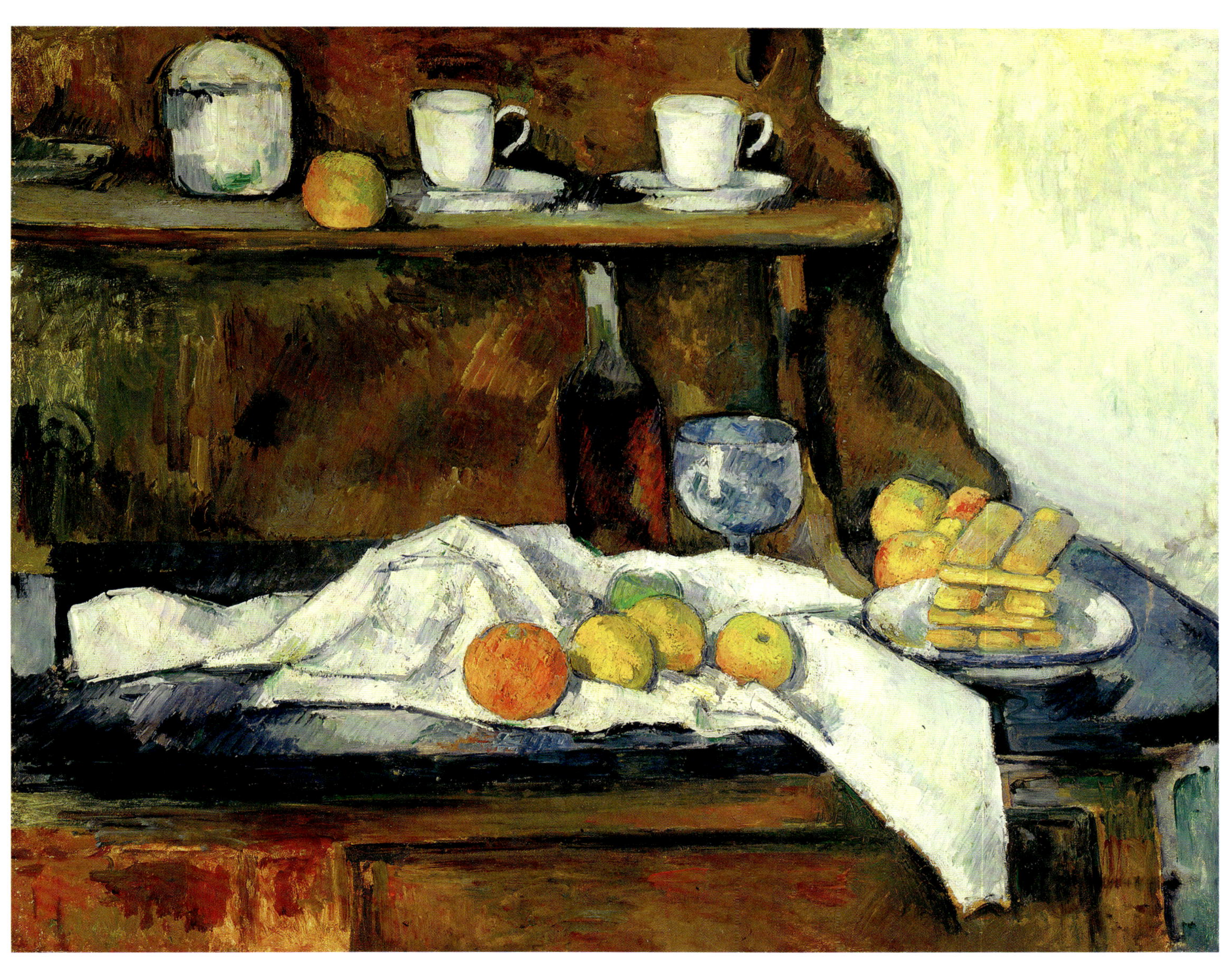

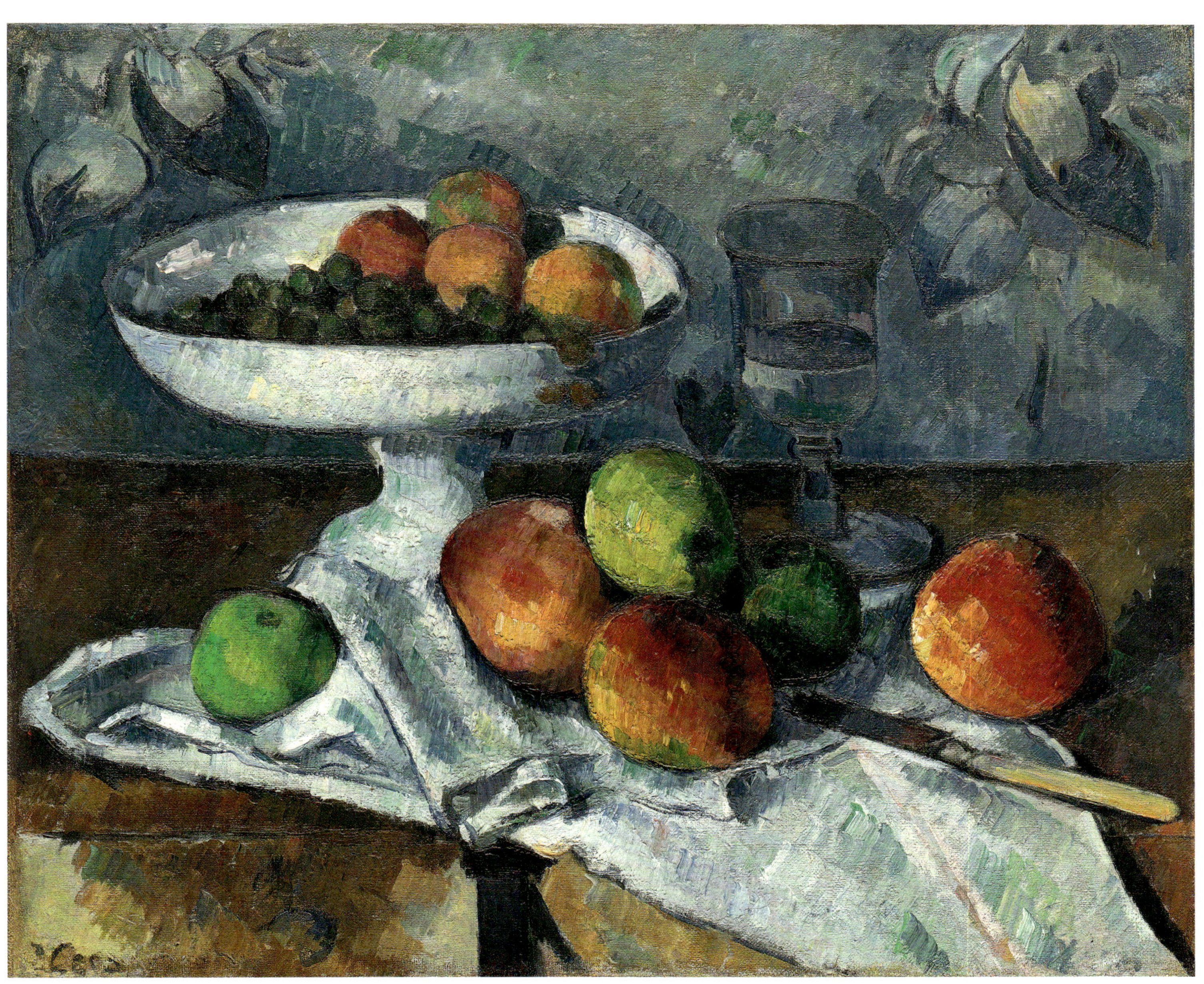

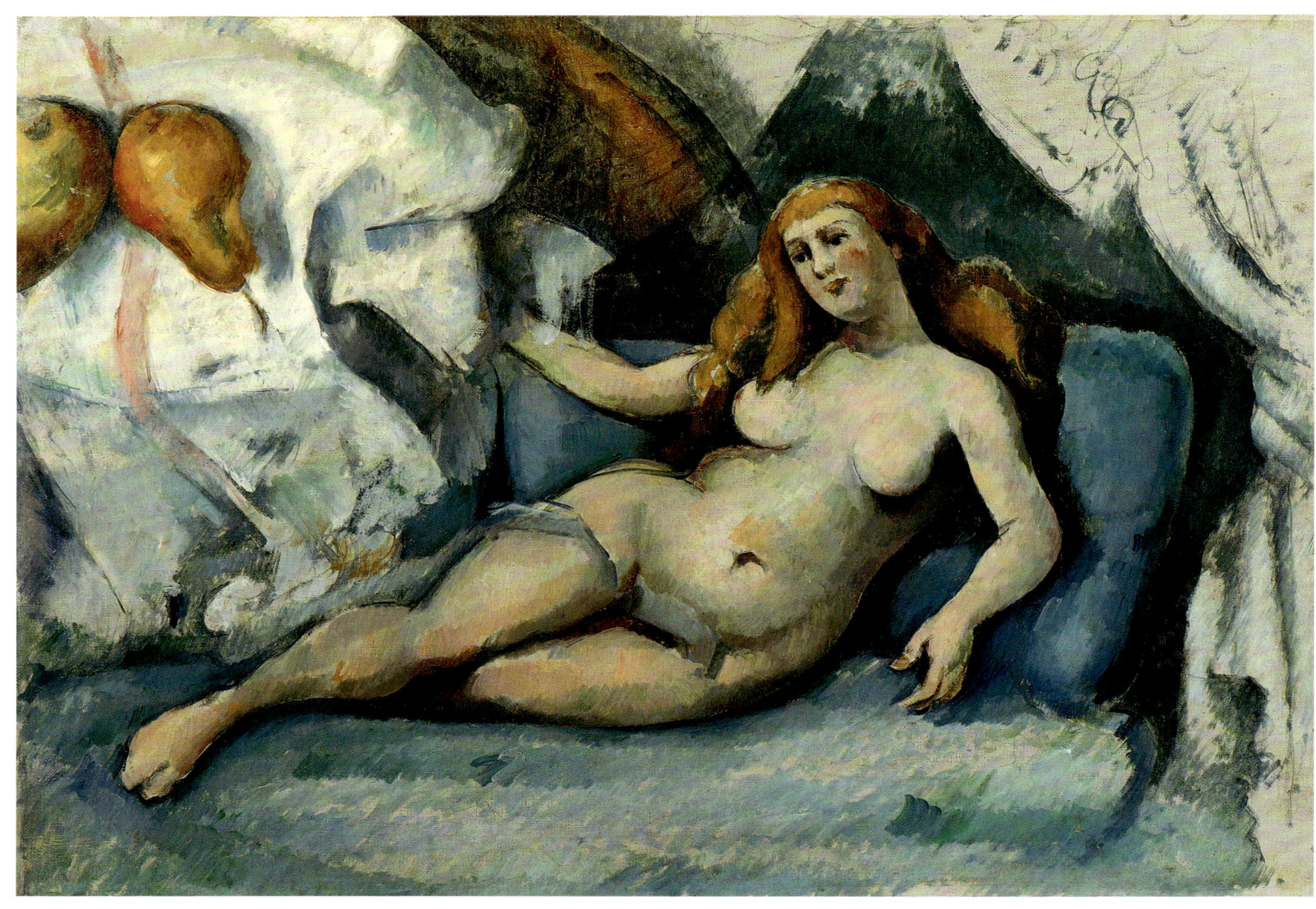

Cat. 54

Nude Woman (Leda?)
1885–87
Oil on canvas
44 × 62 cm (17 5/16 × 24 3/8 in.)
Von der Heydt Museum, Wuppertal, Germany,
Inv. Nr. G 1143
FWN 661

Cat. 55

Ginger Pot with Pomegranate and Pears
1893
Oil on canvas
46.4 × 55.6 cm (18 1/4 × 21 7/8 in.)
The Phillips Collection, Washington, DC,
Gift of Gifford Phillips in memory of his father,
James Laughlin Phillips, 1939, 0284
FWN 839
Chicago only

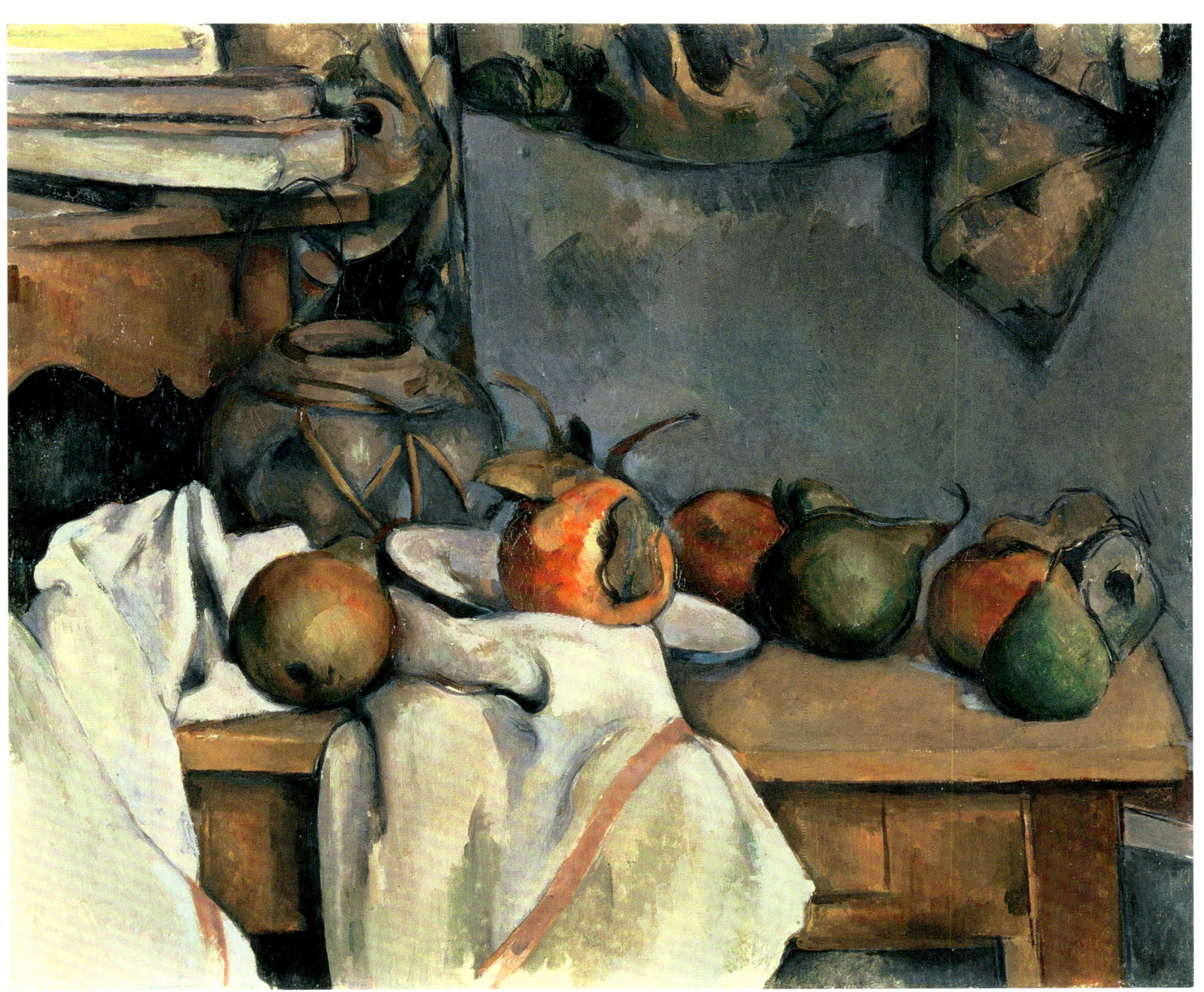

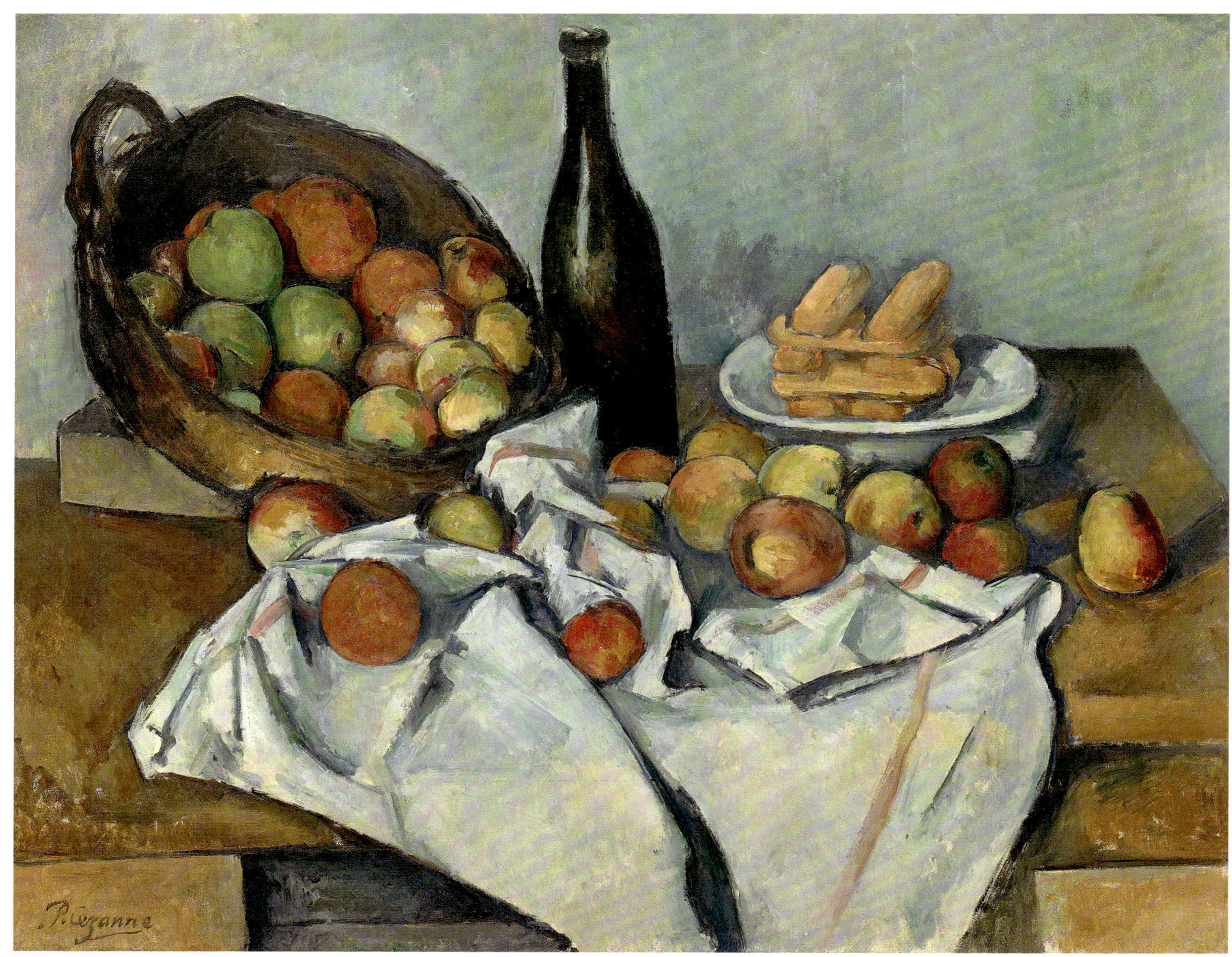

Cat. 56

The Basket of Apples
c. 1893
Oil on canvas
65 × 80 cm (25 7/16 × 31 1/2 in.)
The Art Institute of Chicago, Helen Birch Bartlett
Memorial Collection, 1926.252
FWN 860

Luc Tuymans

My first encounter with the works of Paul Cezanne was with reproductions of his paintings in books. The first physical, real-time experience was years later in the Kunstmuseum Bern. Looking at them, I immediately was struck with an utter sense of austerity and unease, as if something was superimposed over the image to suppress and contain it. The work portrayed a lugubrious, dull sense of euphoria pursuing perfection within a narrow range. In other words, the encounter was a violent one.

La Corbeille de pommes, c. 1893

The first overall visual impression is that of a distorted point of view seen from a slightly elevated position. One sees a cascade of apples onto a tabletop, falling out of the picture plane. In terms of perspective, the image dishabituates the idea of space or depth. Shadows are turned into a linear network that makes the composition directional, reducing it to an index. The shortened, nervous brushstrokes emphasize the idea of speed, transportation along multifaceted pathways allowing one to look at the painting in a rather subjective manner—as a glimpse of a particular, momentary shift in time. The colors are saturated; their temperature is indistinct and indifferent; heightened contrast separates the forms; and the light is reduced to a single highlight on the bottle. Strangely enough, through its rapid and deliberate execution the painting obtains a certain translucency or airiness that reminds me of stained glass; the painting works as if it is being pushed to its breaking point. Here fragility becomes dangerous and obstinate—a moment frozen in time, purposely trying to destroy the unified image in order to recreate it. The mark making is extremely intense and, in itself, knowledgeable about the sensuous idea of touch, something Cezanne was petrified of in real life. The painting functions as an echo chamber, incorporating the act of looking and separating the points of view of both eyes, combining the result into a single pictorial experience.

A still life is not a portrait nor is it a landscape, however it was and maybe still is perceived as the lowest denominator within painting as a discipline. Having lost most of its intrinsic iconographical signifiers—with the exception of the work of Jean Baptiste Siméon Chardin—by the time Cezanne revived it, its importance was next to nothing. I suspect that the neglect of still life made it attractive to Cezanne. It sort of opened up a free zone in which he could experiment in a fairly unhindered way. On the other hand, his choice might even have been an underhanded political statement against the more urban, worldly, and mundane themes in painting of the time, since the fruit was grown locally and the pottery made of clay from the surrounding landscape. All in all, I think Cezanne's quest was for the affirmation of his own eternity, driven by a monumental persistence.

The irony is that by using the most humble and unimportant subjects—such as an apple—Cezanne was able to crack depiction single-handedly.

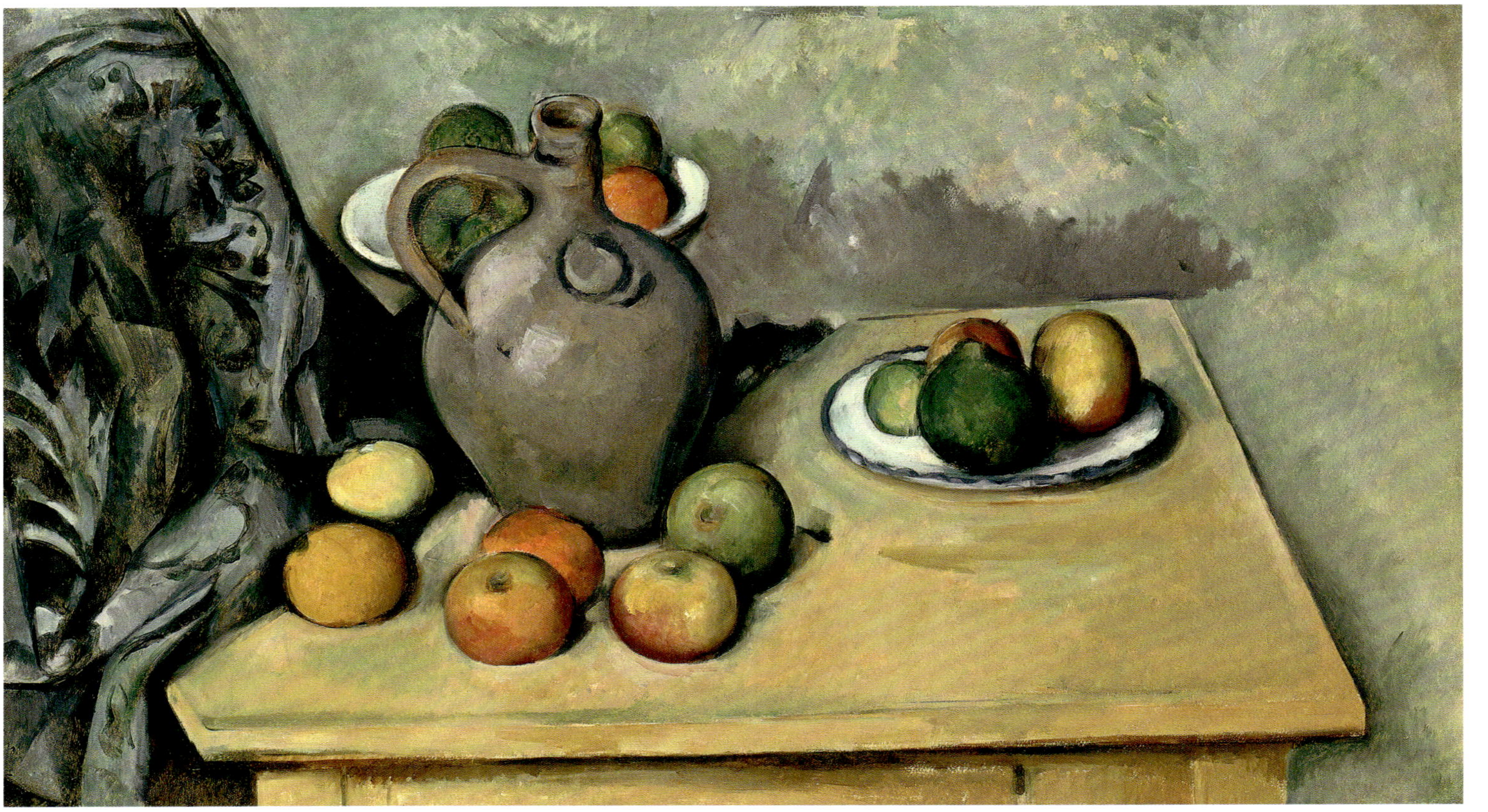

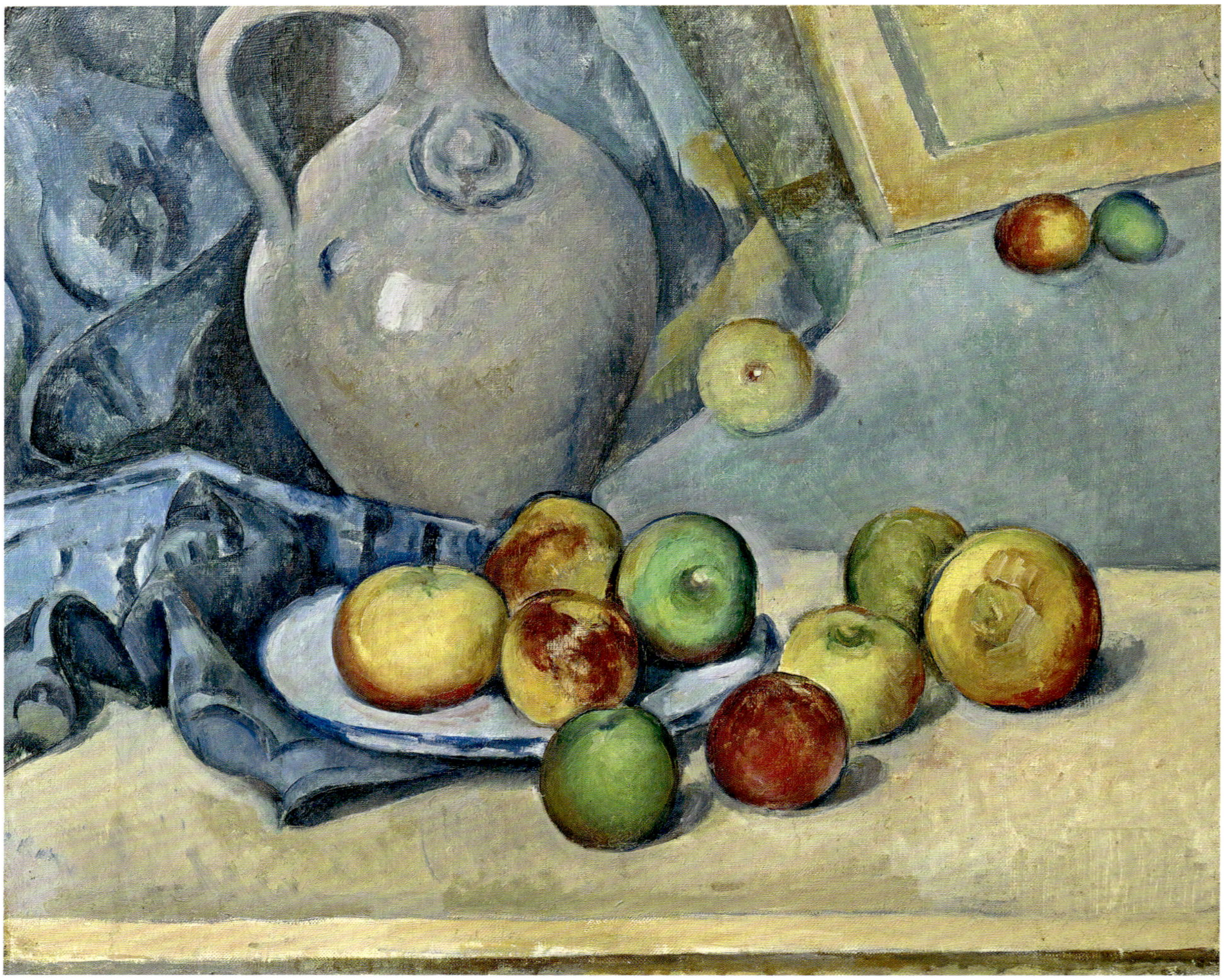

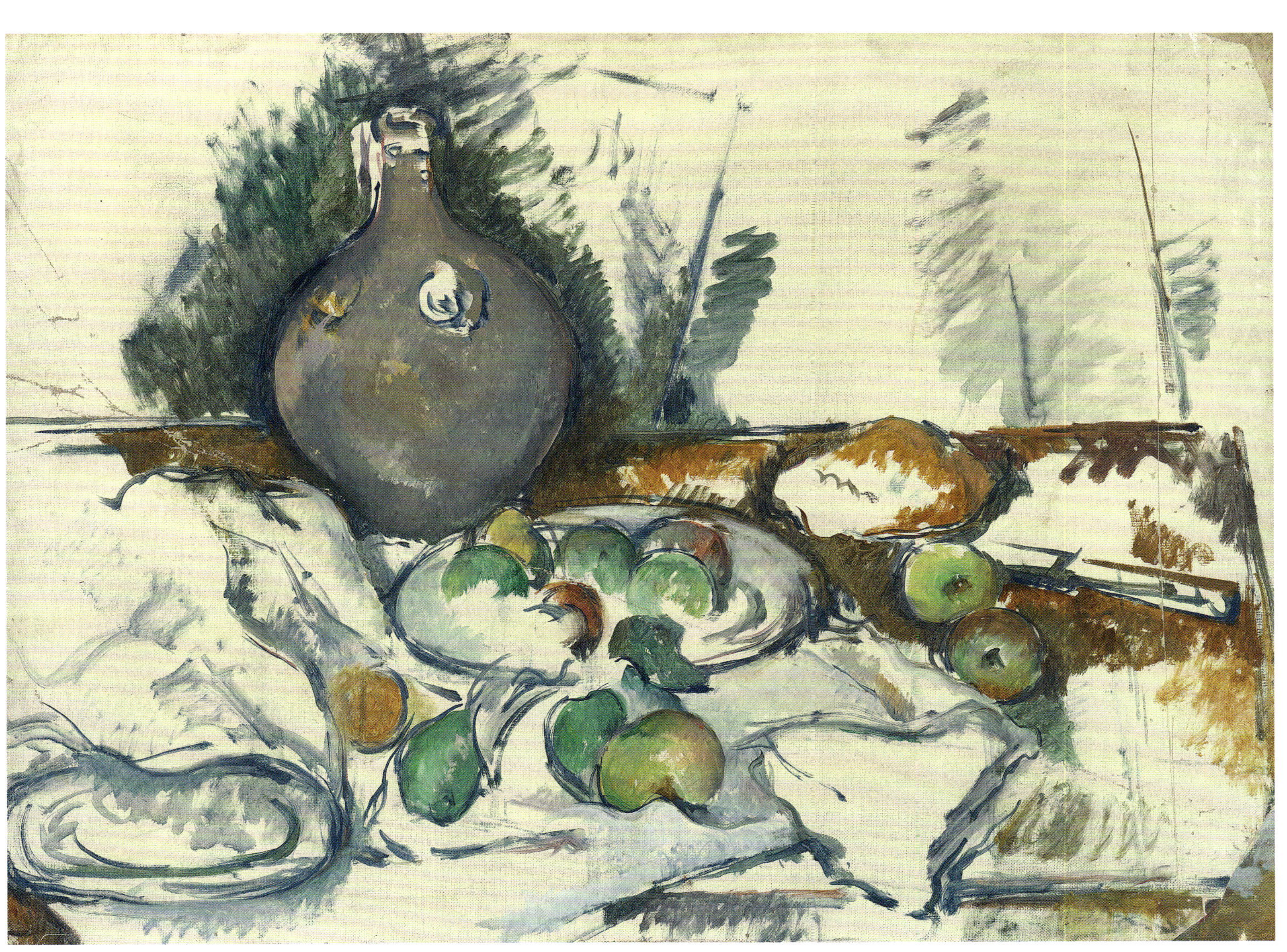

Cat. 57

Pitcher and Fruits on a Table
1893–94
Oil on paper mounted on board
42.5 × 72.4 cm (16 ¾ × 28 ½ in.)
Private collection
FWN 851

Cat. 58

Stoneware Pitcher
1893–94
Oil on canvas
38.2 × 46 cm (15 1/16 × 18 1/8 in.)
Fondation Beyeler, Riehen/Basel,
Sammlung Beyeler, inv. 99.7
FWN 853

Cat. 59

Still Life with Water Jug
c 1892–93
Oil on canvas
53 × 71.1 cm (20 7/8 × 28 in.)
Tate, London, Bequeathed by C. Frank Stoop 1933,
N04725
FWN 846

Cat. 60

Curtain, Pitcher, and a Fruit Bowl
1893–94
Oil on canvas
59.7 × 73 cm (23 ½ × 28 ¾ in.)
Private collection
FWN 854

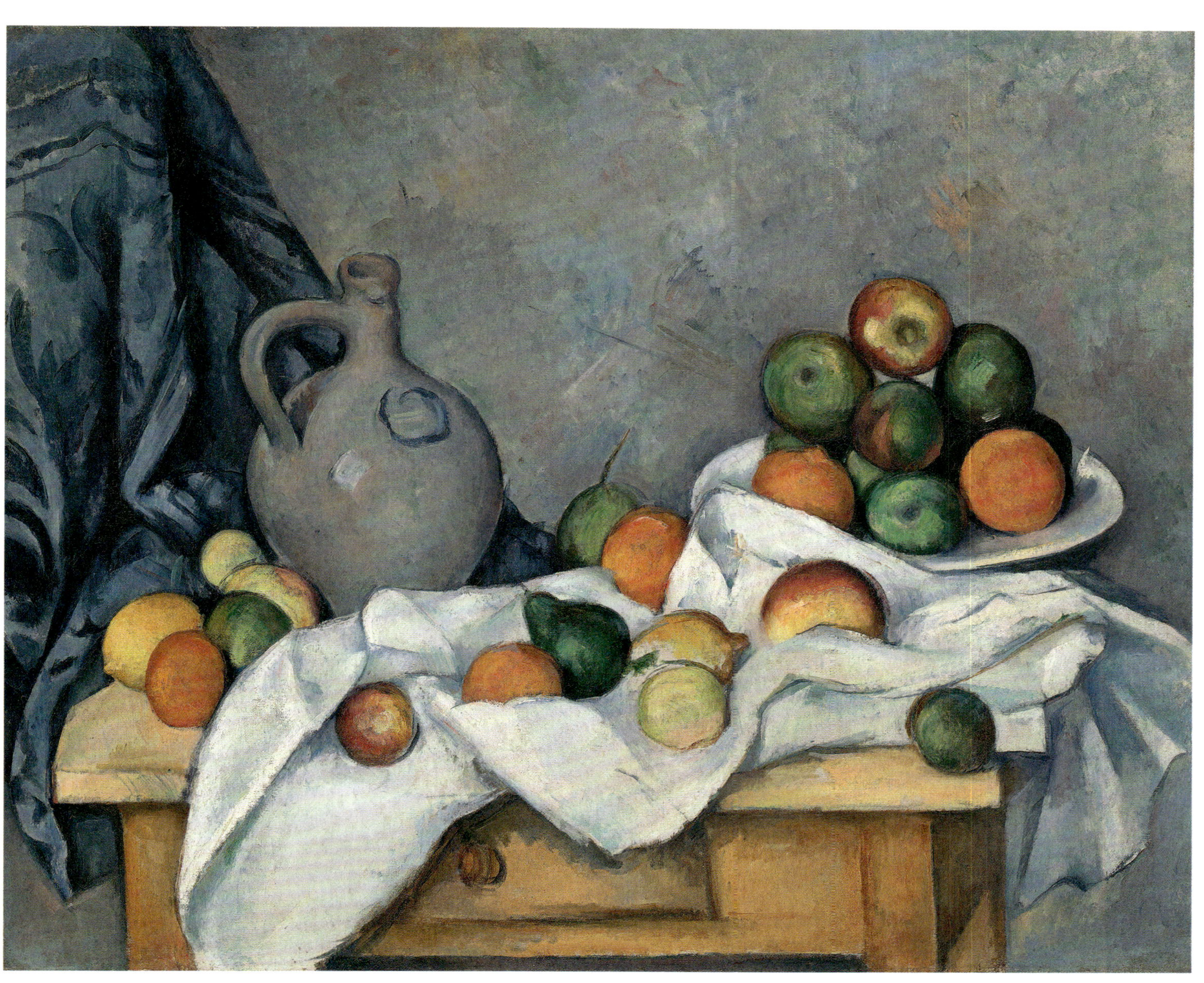

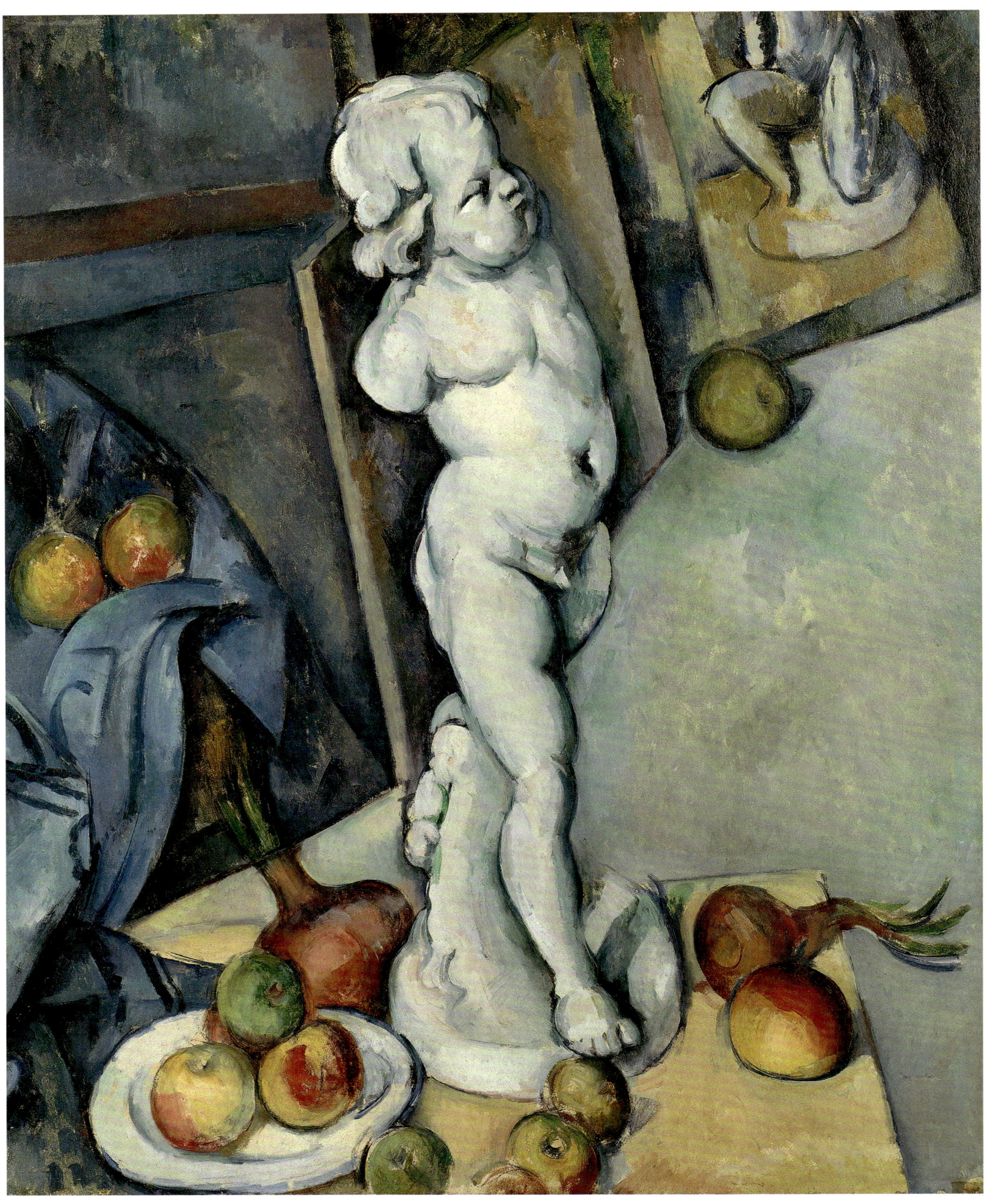

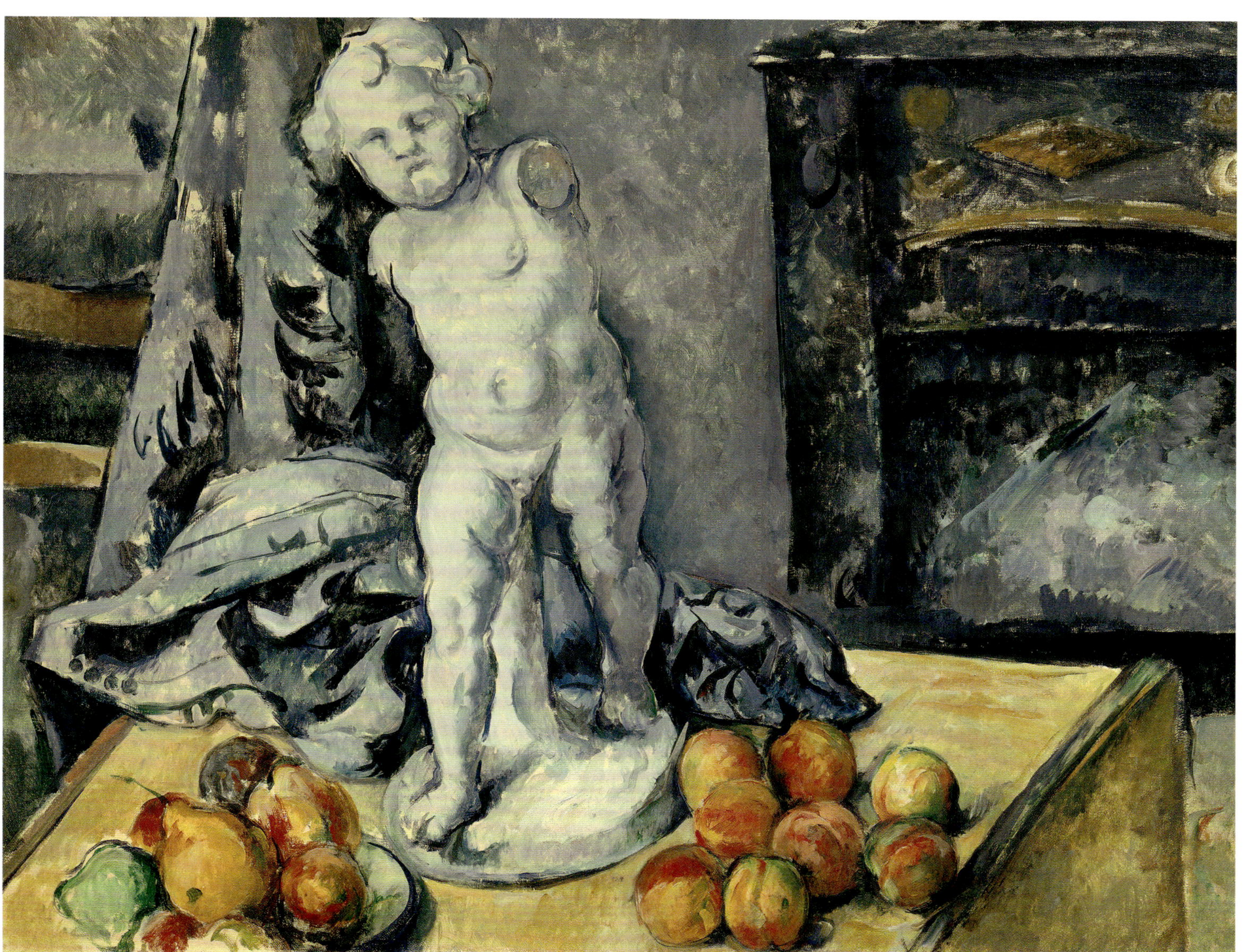

Cat. 61

Still Life with Plaster Cupid
c. 1894
Oil on paper on board
70.6 × 57.3 cm (27 ¹³⁄₁₆ × 22 ⁹⁄₁₆ in.)
The Courtauld Gallery, London (Samuel Courtauld
Trust), P.1948.SC.59
FWN 692
London only

Cat. 62

Still Life with Plaster Cupid
1894–95
Oil on canvas
63 × 81 cm (24 ¹³⁄₁₆ × 31 ⅞ in.)
Nationalmuseum, Stockholm, gift 1926
Nationalmusei Vänner, NM 2545
FWN 691

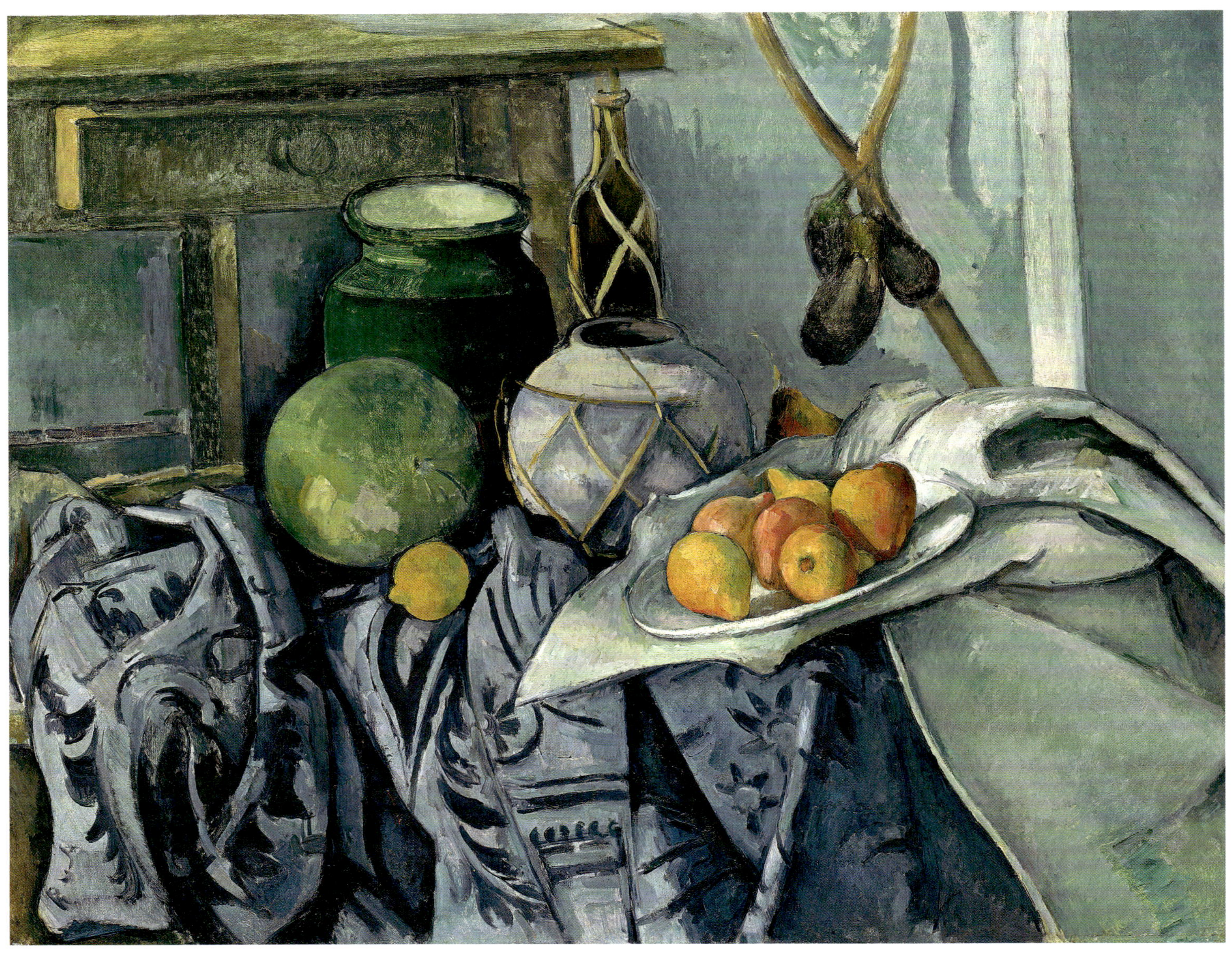

Cat. 63

Still Life with a Ginger Jar and Eggplants
1893–94
Oil on canvas
72.4 × 91.4 cm (28 ½ × 36 in.)
The Metropolitan Museum of Art, New York,
Bequest of Stephen C. Clark, 1960, 61.101.4
FWN 856

Cat. 64

Still Life with Apples
1893–94
Oil on canvas
65.4 × 81.6 cm (25 ¾ × 32 ⅛ in.)
The J. Paul Getty Museum, Los Angeles, 96.PA.8
FWN 855

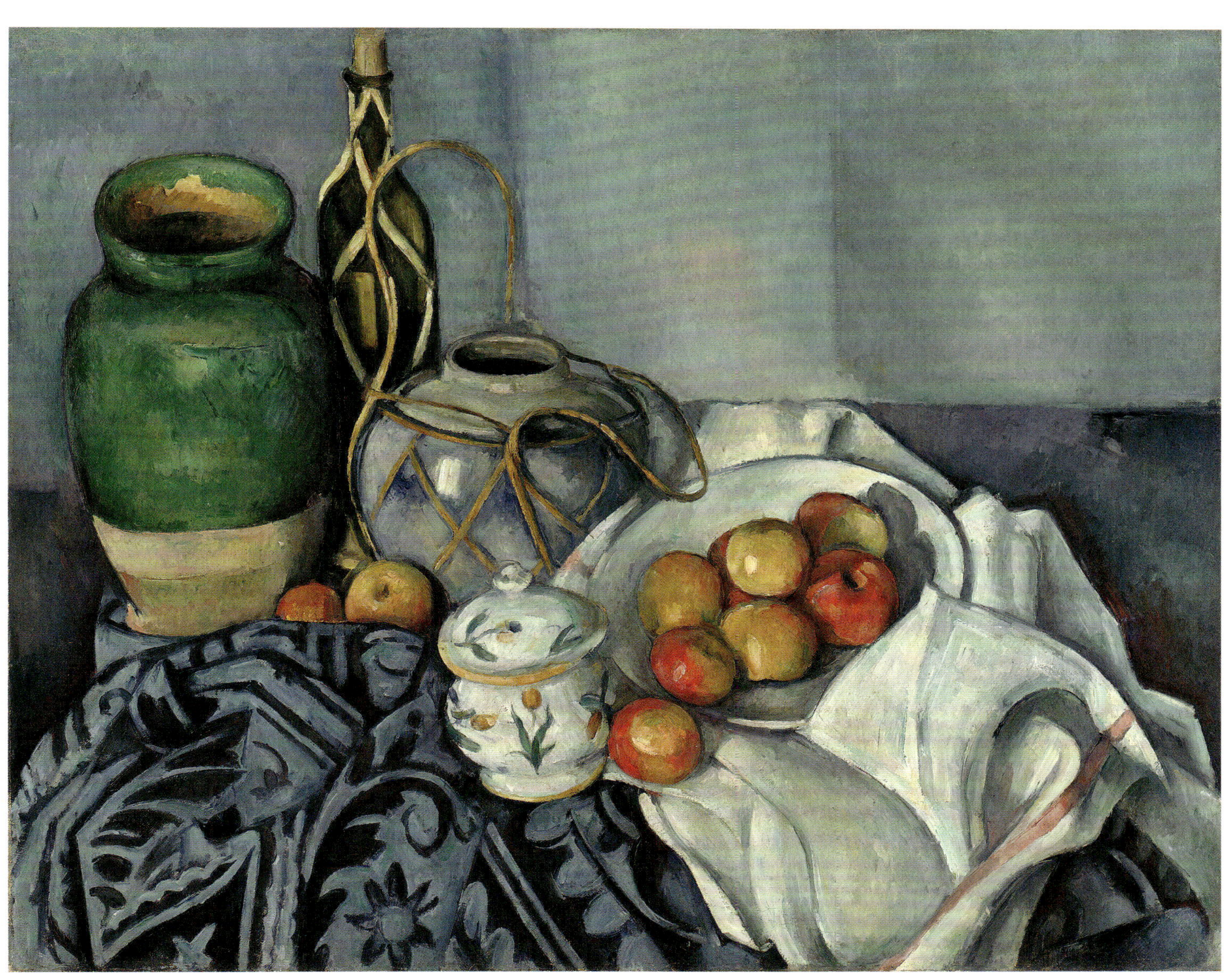

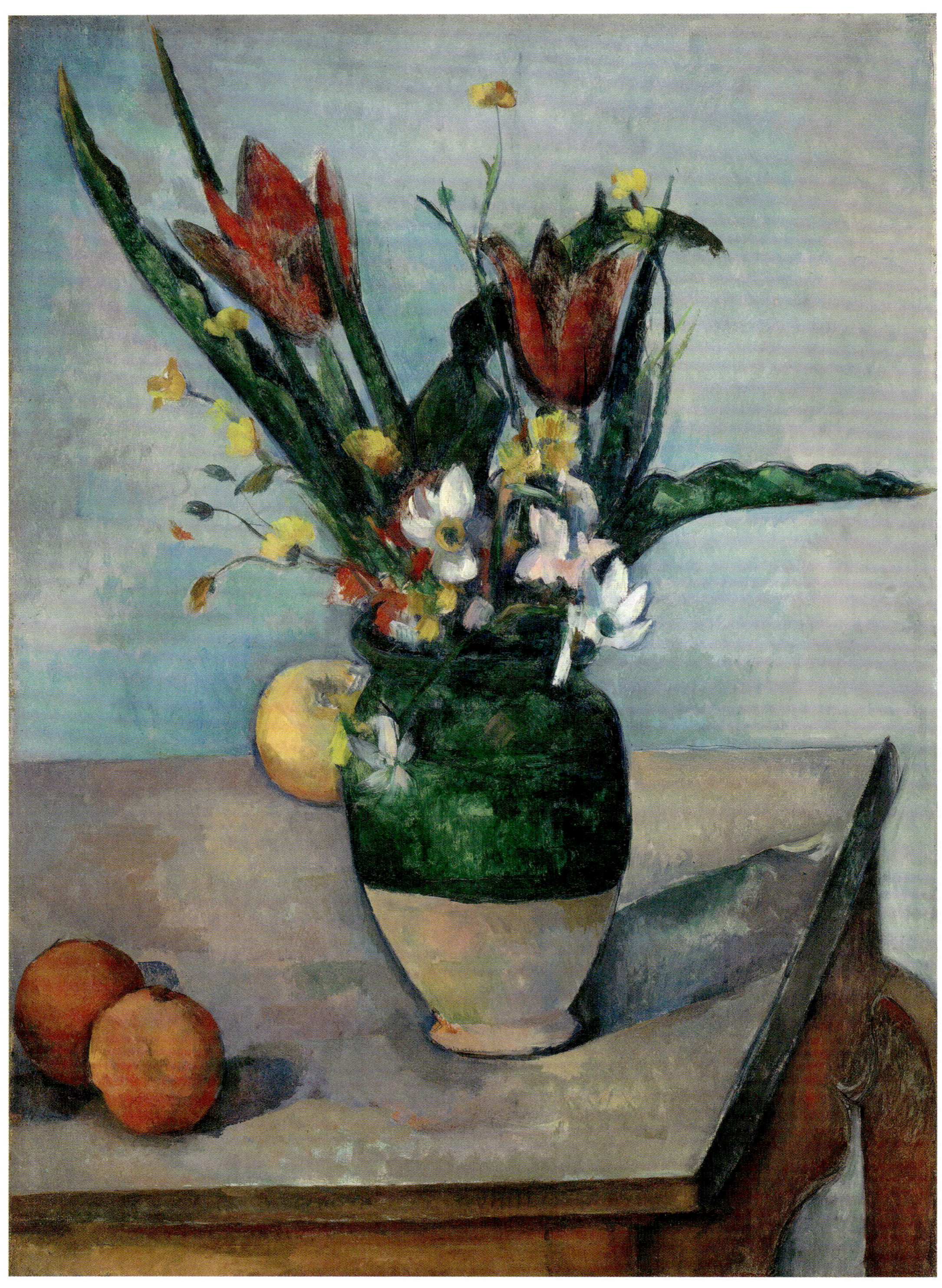

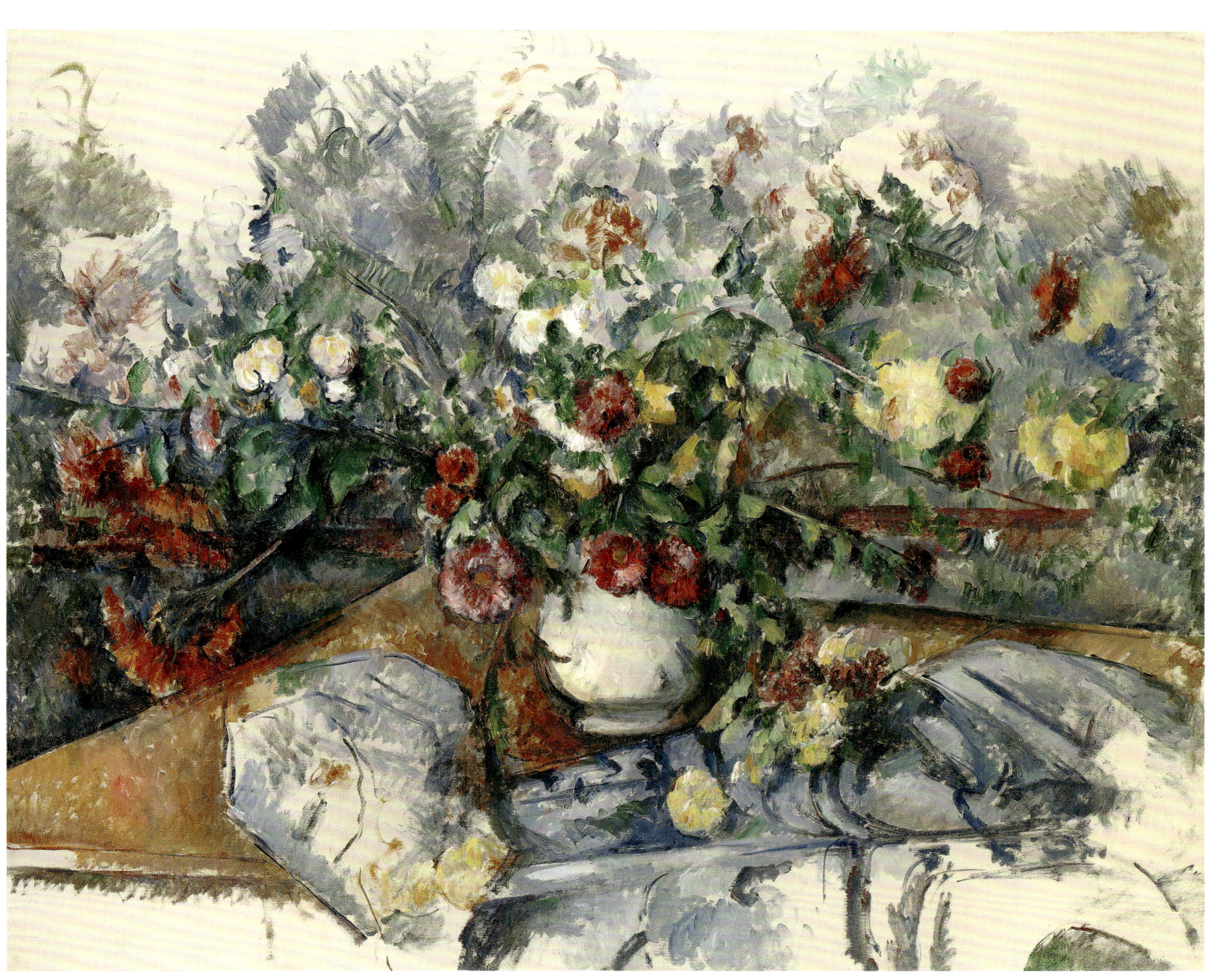

Cat. 65

The Vase of Tulips
c. 1890
Oil on canvas
59.6 × 42.3 cm (23 ½ × 16 ⅝ in.)
The Art Institute of Chicago, Mr. and Mrs. Lewis
Larned Coburn Memorial Collection, 1933.423
FWN 826
Chicago only

Cat. 66

Grand Bouquet of Flowers
c. 1892–95
Oil on canvas
81 × 100 cm (31 ⅞ × 39 ⅜ in.)
The National Museum of Modern Art, Tokyo,
O01245
FWN 859

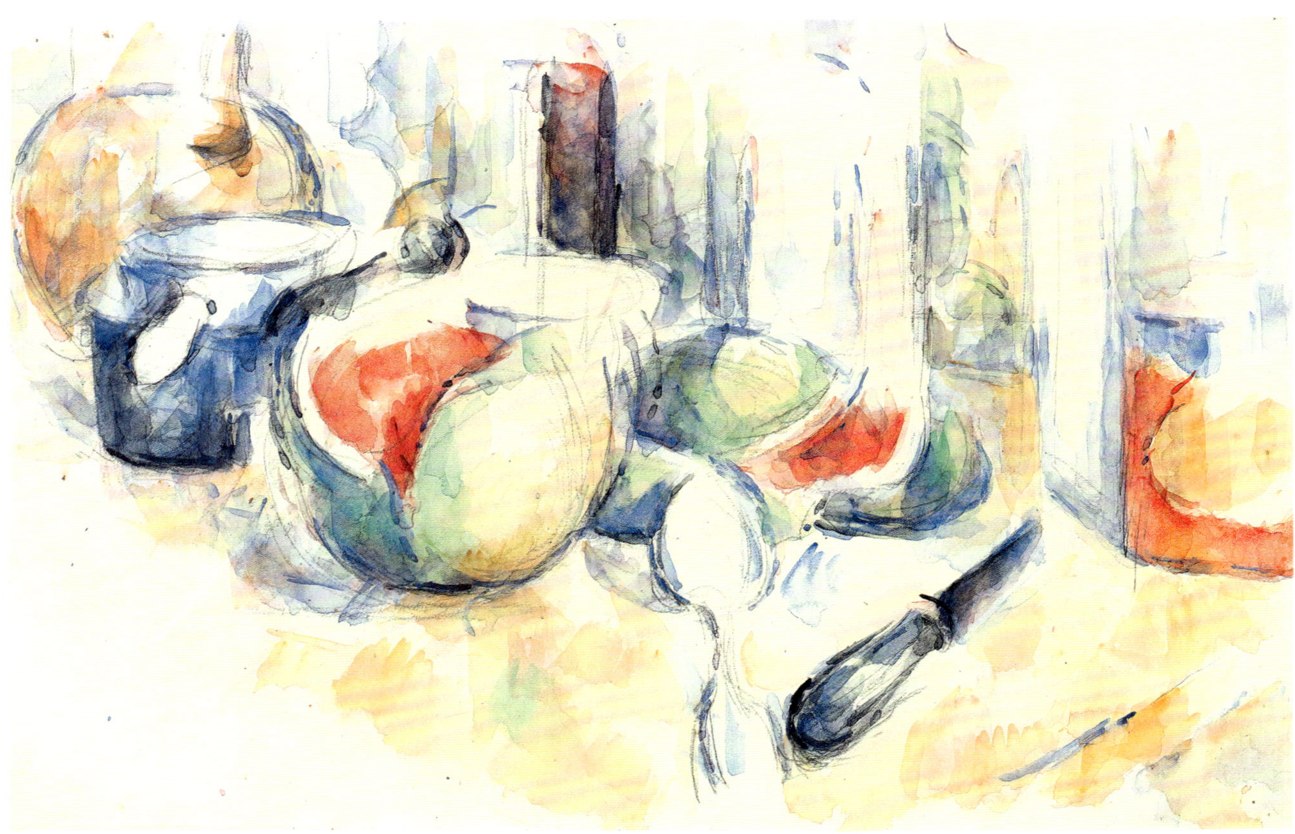

Cat. 67

Still Life with Sliced Watermelon
c. 1900
Watercolor and pencil on paper
31.5 × 47.5 cm (12 ⅜ × 18 ¹¹⁄₁₆ in.)
Fondation Beyeler, Riehen/Basel,
Sammlung Beyeler, inv. 78.1
FWN 1962

Cat. 68

The Dessert
c. 1900–1906
Graphite and watercolor on paper
47 × 61 cm (19 × 24 in.)
Private collection
FWN 1975
Chicago only

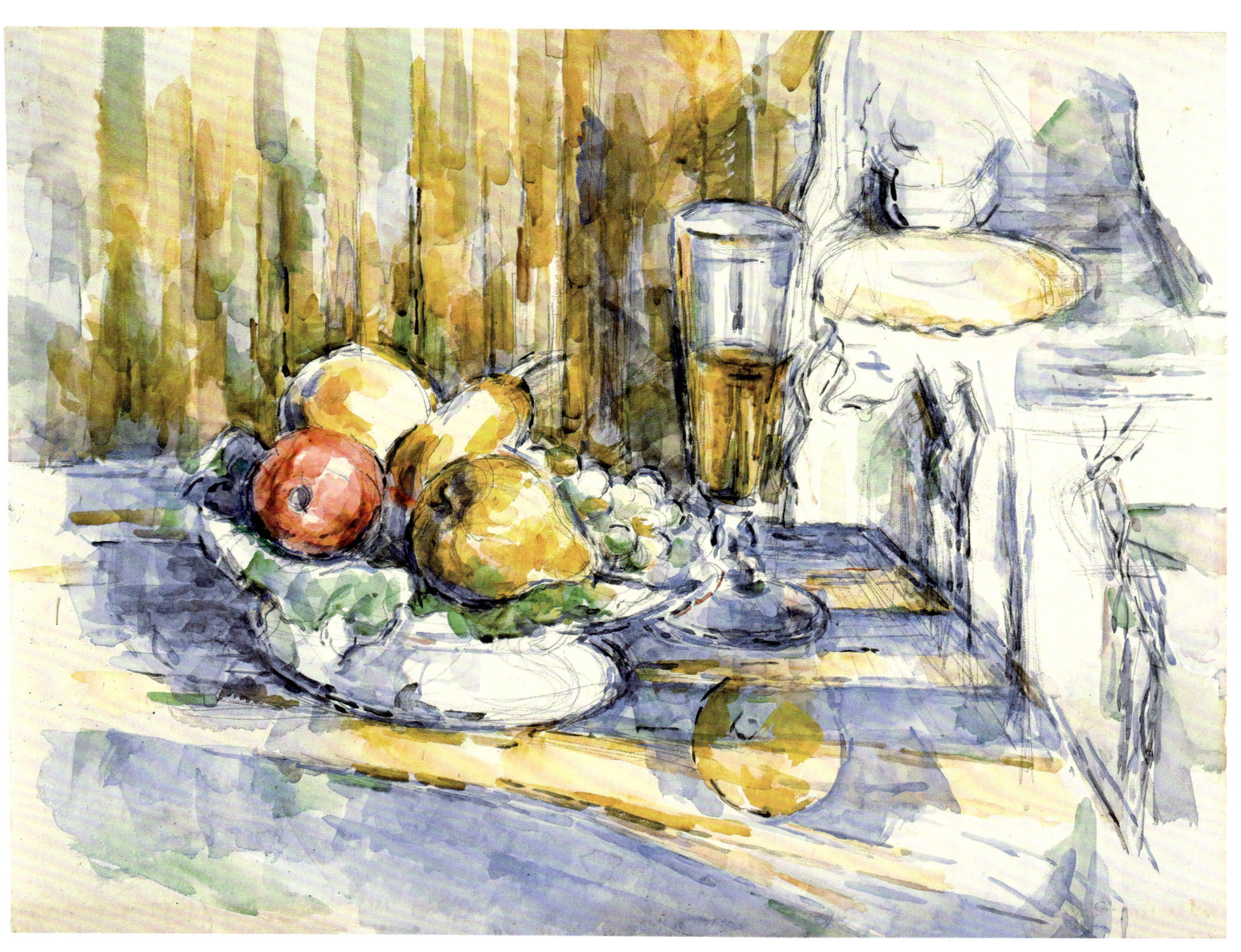

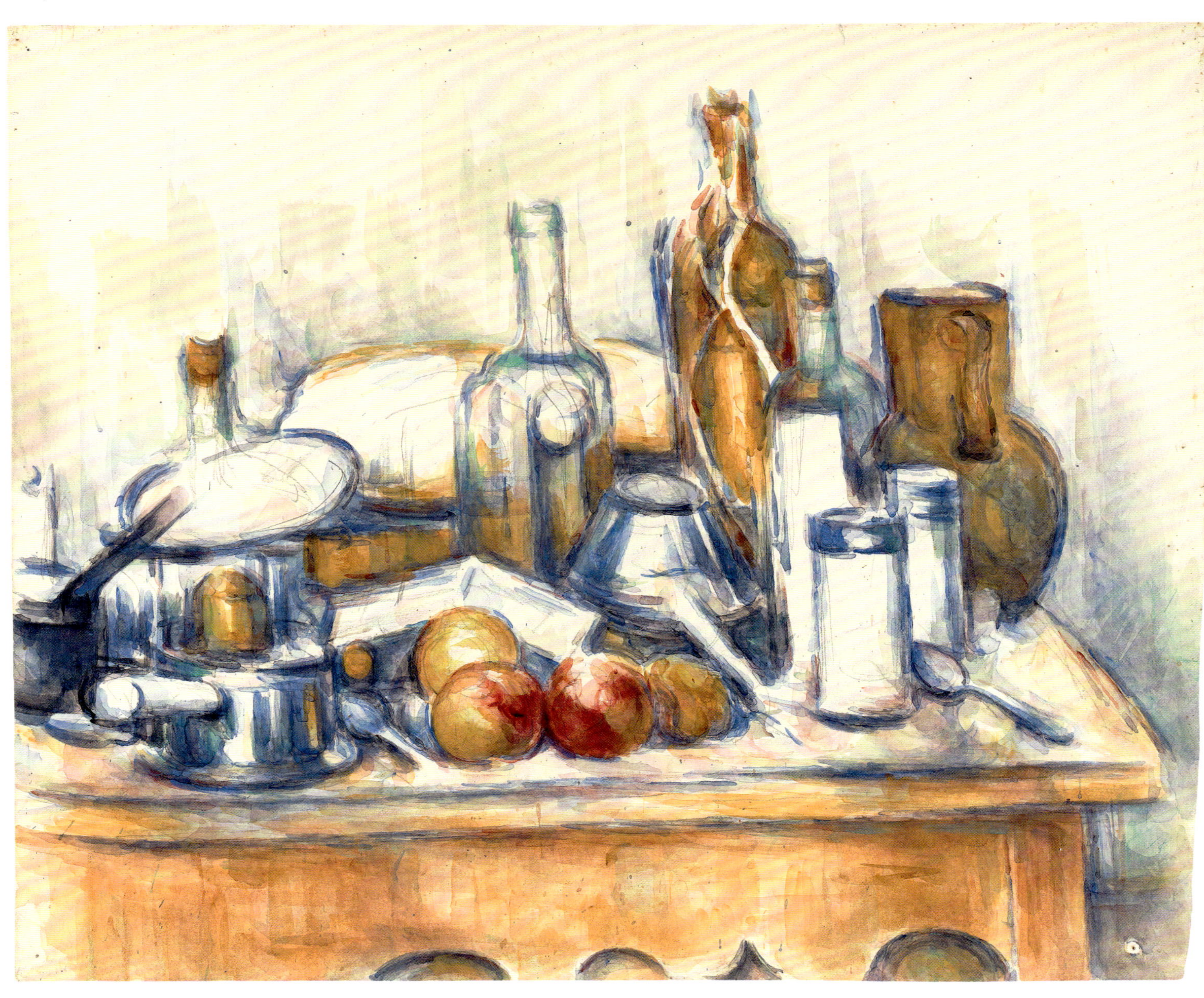

Cat. 69

Bottles, Pot, Alcohol Stove, and Apples
1900–1906
Graphite and watercolor on paper
47 × 56 cm (19 × 23 in.)
Private collection
FWN 1967
Chicago only

Cat. 70

Still Life with Apples on a Sideboard
1900–1906
Graphite and watercolor on paper
48.6 × 63.2 cm (19 $\frac{1}{8}$ × 24 $\frac{7}{8}$ in.)
Dallas Museum of Art, The Wendy and Emery
Reves Collection, 1985.R.12
FWN 1968
London only

Cat. 71

Bottle, Carafe, Jug, and Lemons
1902–6
Watercolor on paper
44.5 × 60 cm (17 $\frac{9}{16}$ × 23 $\frac{5}{8}$ in.)
Museo Nacional Thyssen-Bornemisza, Madrid,
inv. no. 489 (1979.18)
FWN 1976

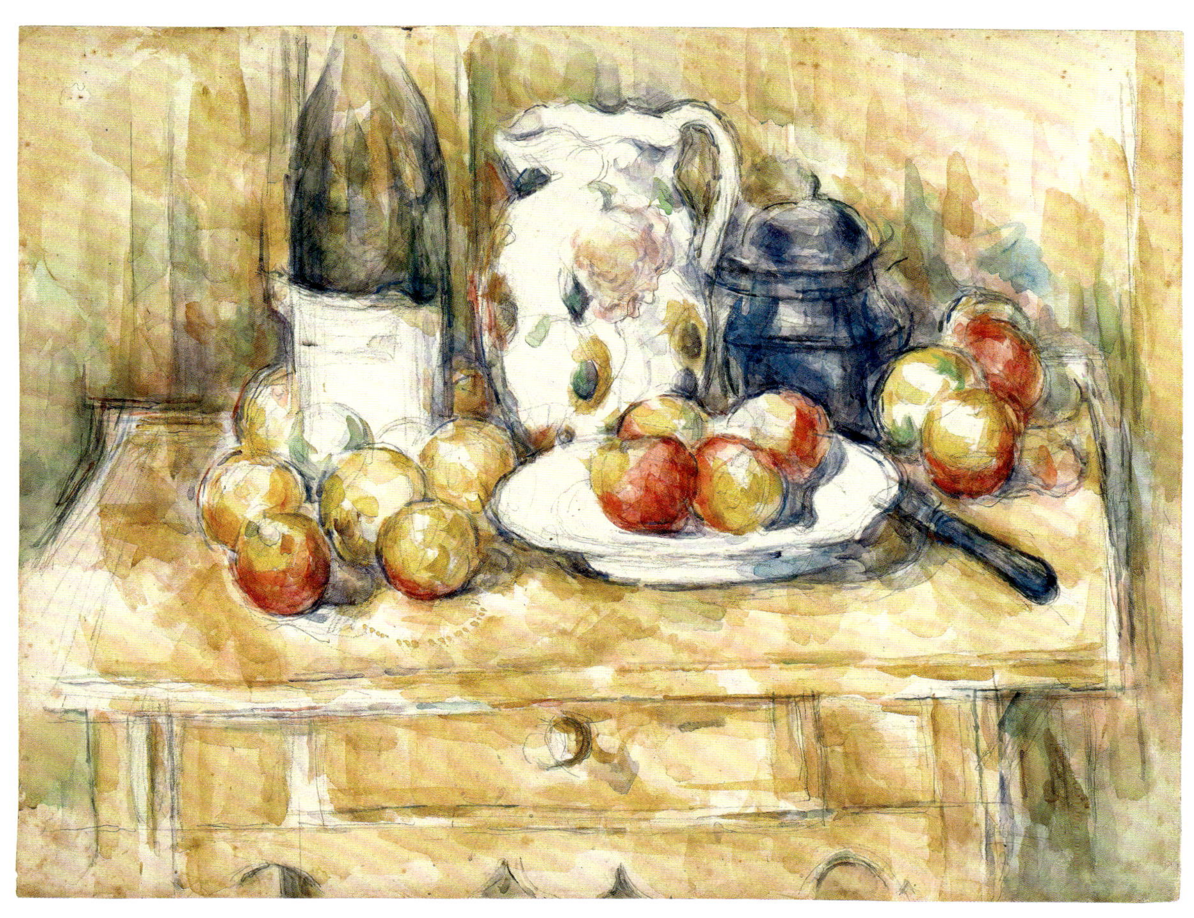

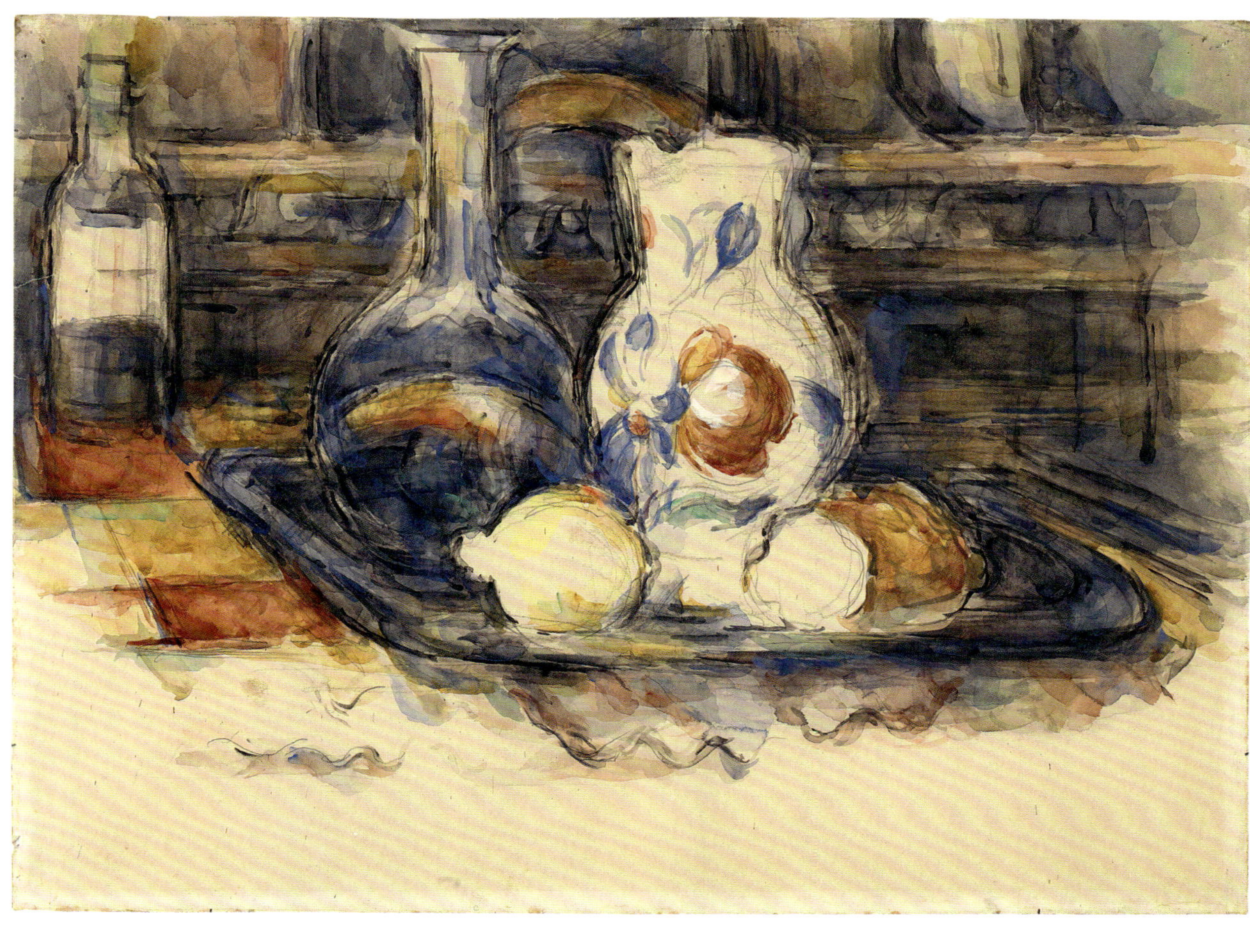

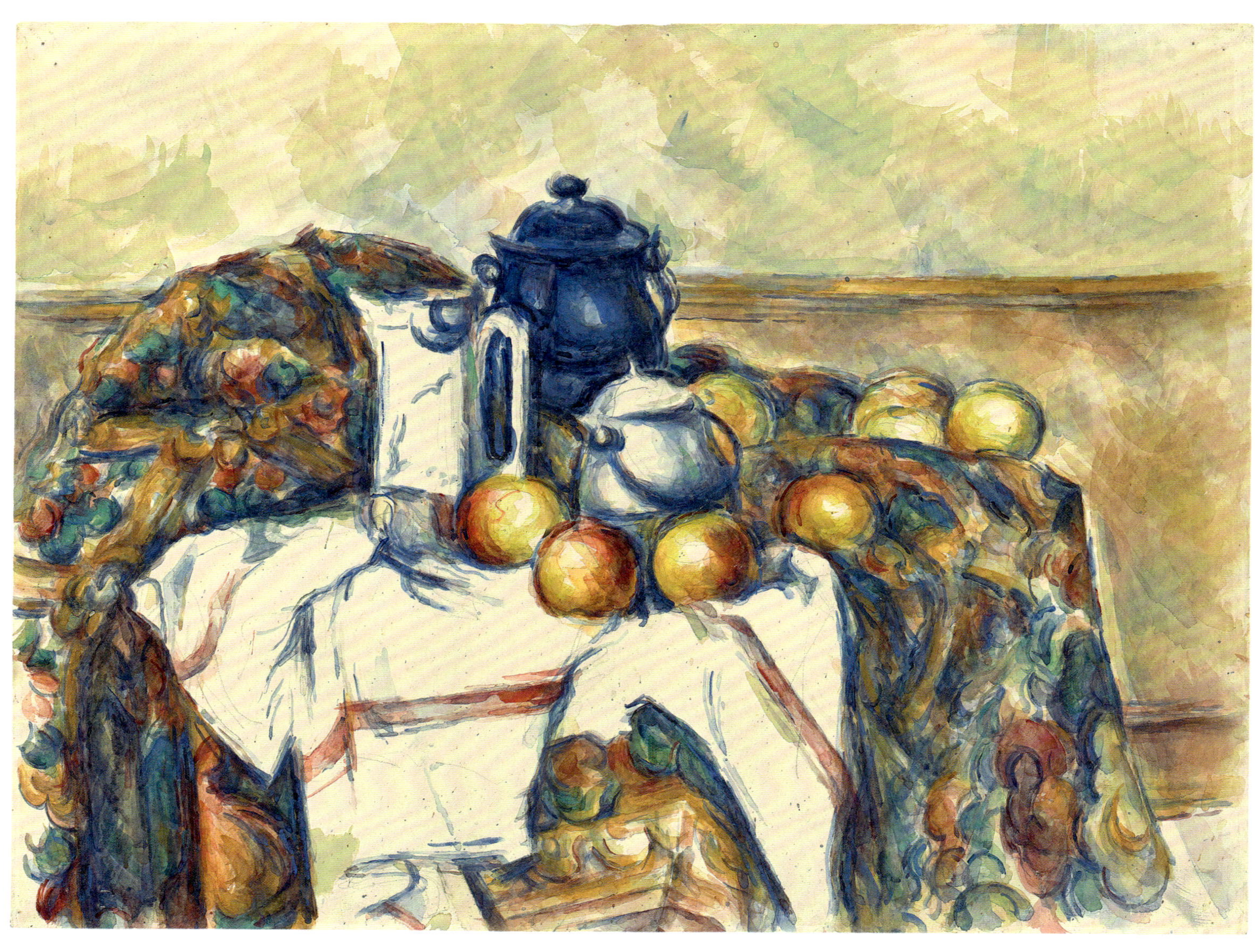

Cat. 72

Still Life with Blue Pot
c. 1900–1906
Watercolor on paper
48 × 63.2 cm (18 15/16 × 24 7/8 in.)
The J. Paul Getty Museum, Los Angeles, 83.GC.221
FWN 1970
Chicago only

Cat. 73

Still Life with Milk Pot, Melon, and Sugar Bowl
1900–1906
Graphite and watercolor on paper
48.2 × 62.2 cm (19 × 25 in.)
Private collection
FWN 1971

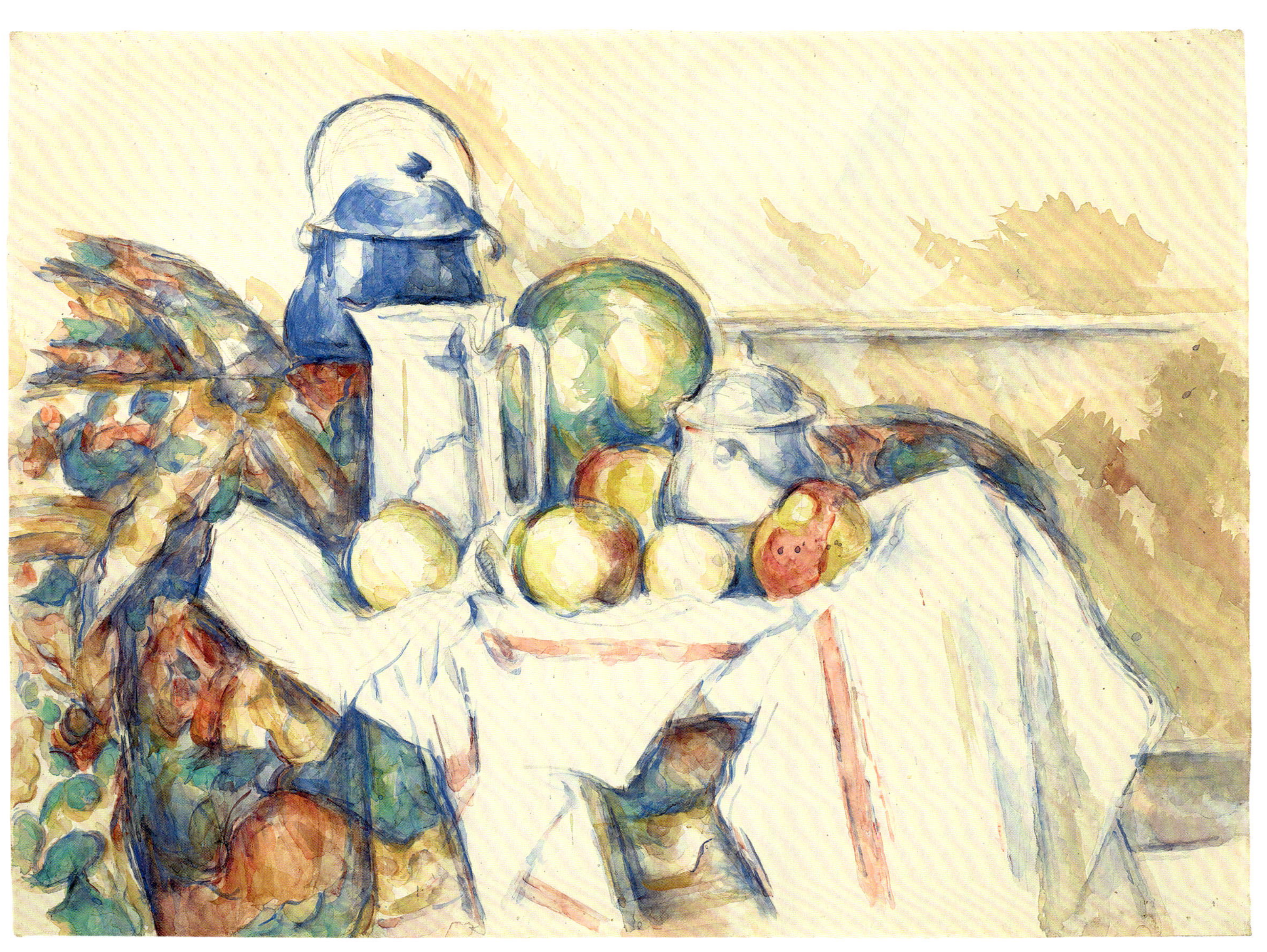

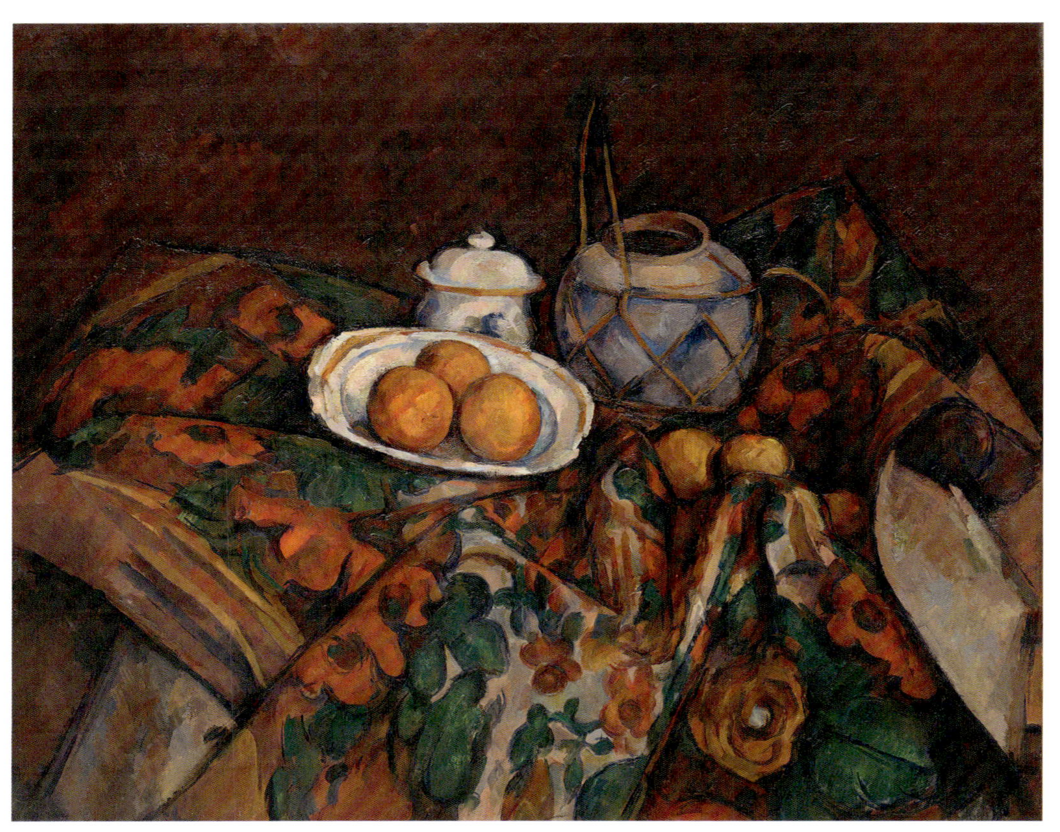

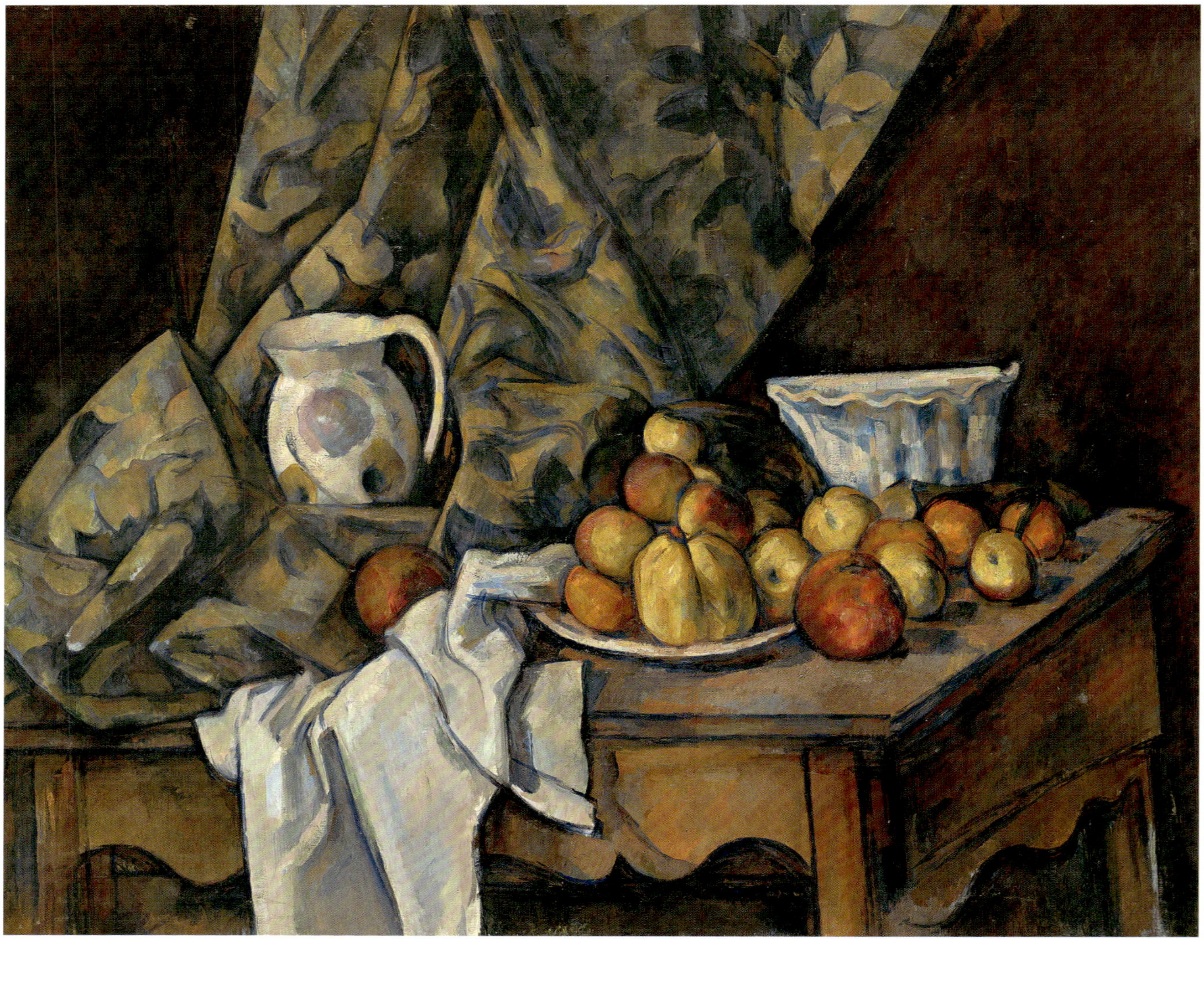

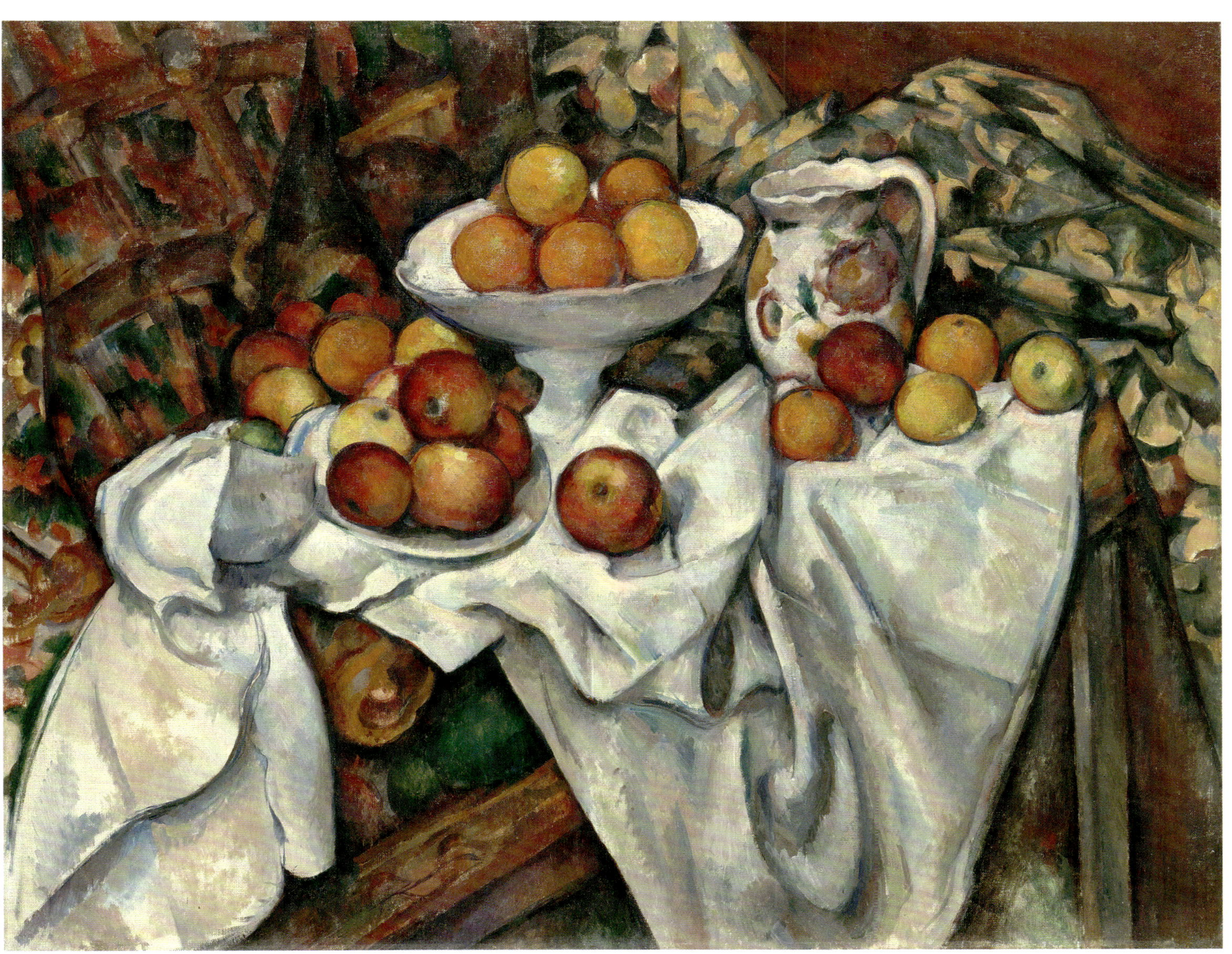

Cat. 74

Still Life with Ginger Jar, Sugar Bowl, and Oranges
1902–6
Oil on canvas
60.6 × 73.3 cm (23 ⅞ × 28 ⅞ in.)
The Museum of Modern Art, New York,
Lillie P. Bliss Collection, 18.1934
FWN 883

Cat. 75

Still Life with Apples and Peaches
c. 1905
Oil on canvas
81 × 100.5 cm (31 ⅞ × 39 ⁹⁄₁₆ in.)
National Gallery of Art, Washington, DC,
Gift of Eugene and Agnes E. Meyer, 1959.15.1
FWN 886

Cat. 76

Apples and Oranges
1899
Oil on canvas
74 × 93 cm (29 ⅛ × 36 ⅝ in.)
Musée d'Orsay, Paris, legs du comte
Isaac de Camondo, 1911, RF 1972
FWN 871
Chicago only

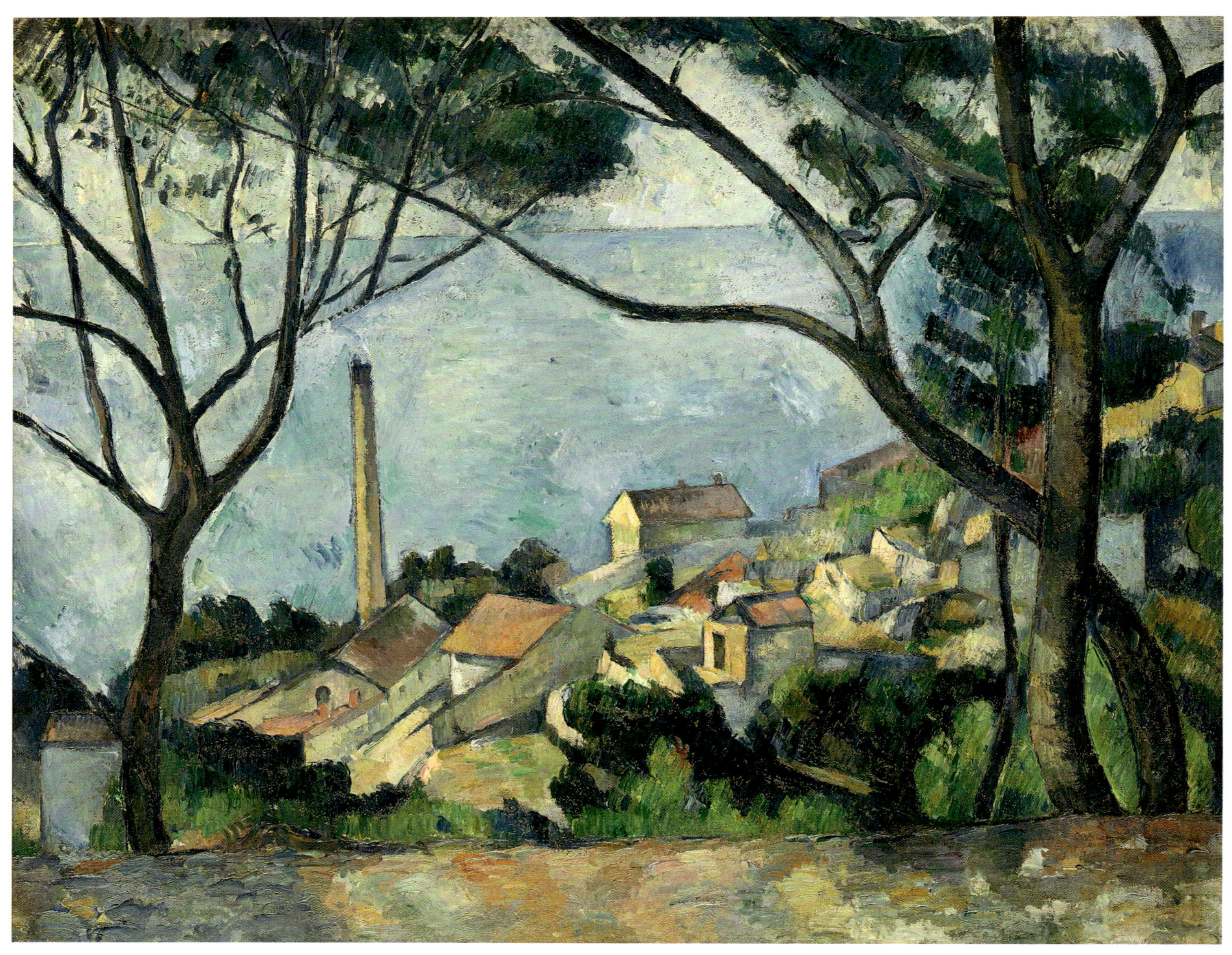

Cat. 77

The Sea at L'Estaque behind Trees
1878–79
Oil on canvas
73 × 92 cm (28 ¹¹⁄₁₆ × 36 ³⁄₁₆ in.)
Musée Picasso, Paris, MP2017-8
FWN 120

Je traîne seule

Laura Owens

Paul Cezanne wrote that, rather than disappoint again, he walked from Marseille to Aix on March 26, 1878. Earlier that month his father had learned that he had a six-year-old son that he had been hiding. "He's heard from various people that I have a child, and he's trying by every means possible to catch me out. He wants to rid me of it, he says."[1] Having misread the train timetable, he set off on foot, walking the nineteen miles from Marseille to Aix to have dinner with his parents.

April 9, 2021

I had planned to walk this same road but I had to come back to the US to see my kids in Los Angeles. I needed to return to France, only I didn't make it back in time. I missed many trains! I wanted to bump into his views and feel the ground connecting his family, past and future. A reason to wear myself out and not feel disappointed about how disappointing I am. Like Cezanne hiding fatherhood from his father.

It's the middle of the night in California. I am walking from Marseille to Aix. Humid clothes, the wrong socks are too heavy, and I hear cicadas. I smell the sea or the pine or the train.

I see a jumble of branches, dense and thick. I cross over the railroad keeping a pace, my French is not great, and equally I want to be lost and not lost. I walk the irregular ground patterns, like a folded piece of coarse linen, maybe a tablecloth with clouds that make a cartoony fieldstone wall. Tree bark shimmers like the eucalyptus in my yard, flaking lavender shapes on the ground.

I keep pain away with distractions. Fresh blowsy air and clearing branches; my headache lifts. I prune to make many soft blue triangles. Lessons I find for the future painter: No part of your picture is autonomous, or even a solid fact. Every plant and house you paint has a mirrorlike surface, a refracted symmetry, mini-tricornered and ovalish framed paintings hinged together. Two trees obstruct, contain, and surround both the water and the sky.

X marks imply the start of an open weave, an aborted grid. It is without regularity that the lines carve the sea, but each sideways cat's-eye, triangle, and brushstroke has a twin or cousin of varying size. Mirroring the left and right or top and bottom like an unfolded piece of origami, these flattened shapes remember space. Where air should penetrate, it resists. The volume behind the trees is equal to the space in front of the canvas, where cerulean paint bits flutter over a line-drawn trunk.

Air is solid, objects move.

Sevres-blue brush is never wiped completely clean, always loaded with three tinted colors, arranged on the palette close together. Gradients within each mark step sideways to make faceted shingles.

Walking outside is the air unframed. I am hoping to be there soon.

1. Paul Cezanne to Émile Zola, April 4, 1878, in *The Letters of Paul Cezanne*, edited and translated by Alex Danchev (Los Angeles: J. Paul Getty Museum, 2013), 170, letter 66.

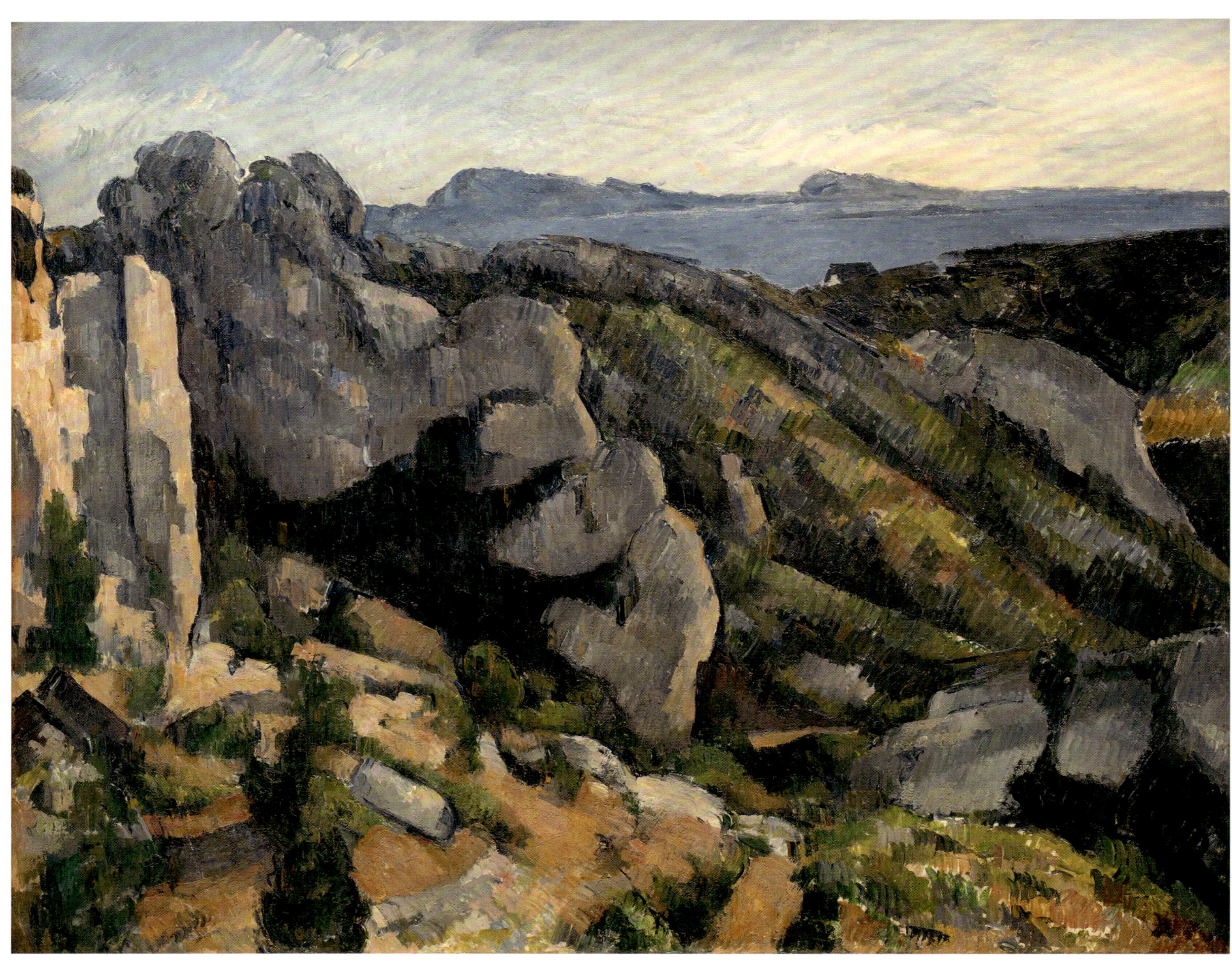

Cat. 78

Cliffs in L'Estaque
1882–85
Oil on canvas
73 × 92 cm (28 ¹¹⁄₁₆ × 36 ¼ in.)
Collection Museu de Arte de São Paulo Assis
Chateaubriand, Doação Edward Marvin, 1953,
MASP.00087
FWN 153

Cat. 79

The Bay of Marseille, Seen from L'Estaque
c. 1885
Oil on canvas
80.2 × 100.6 cm (31 ⅝ × 39 ⅝ in.)
The Art Institute of Chicago, Mr. and Mrs. Martin A.
Ryerson Collection, 1933.1116
FWN 196

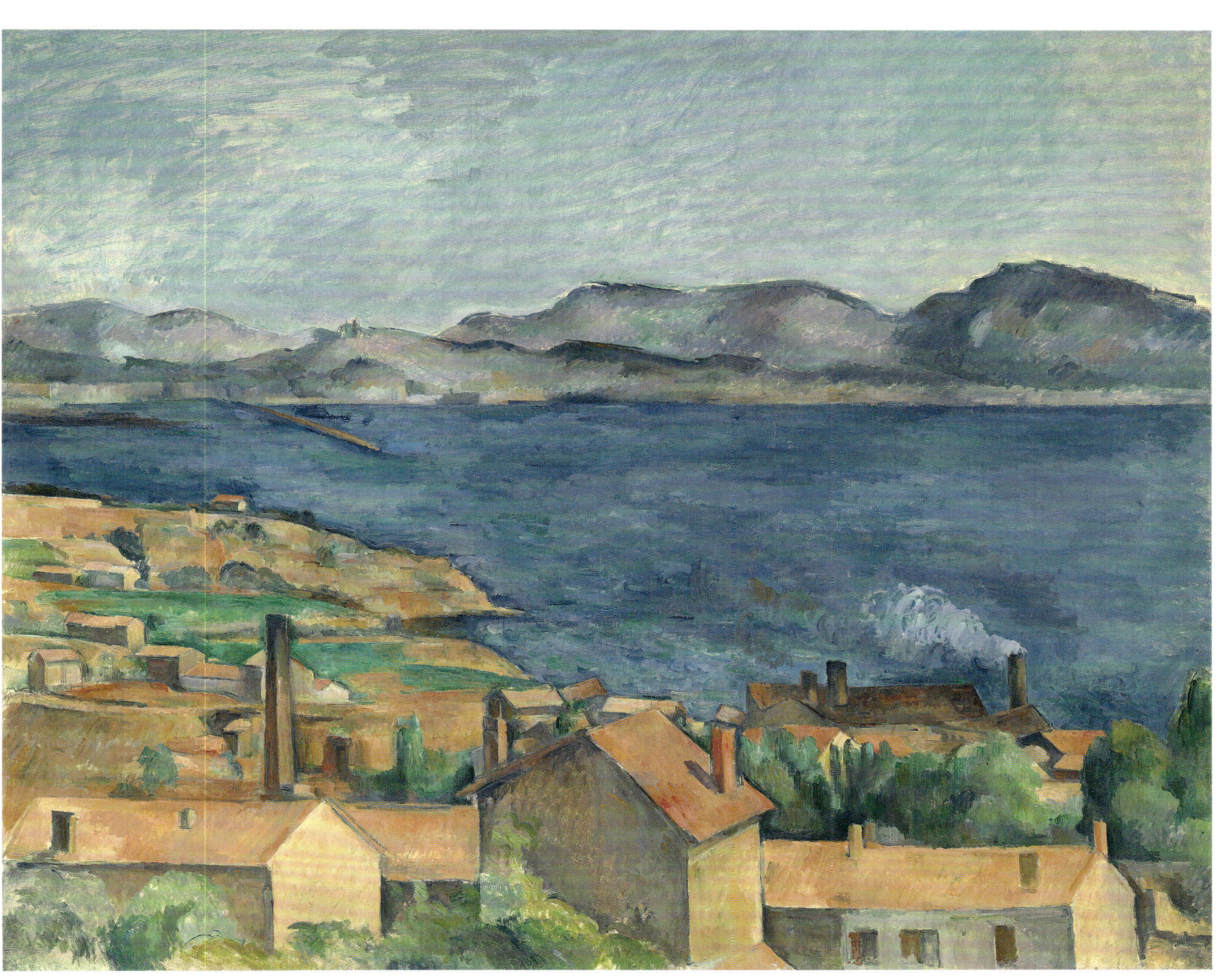

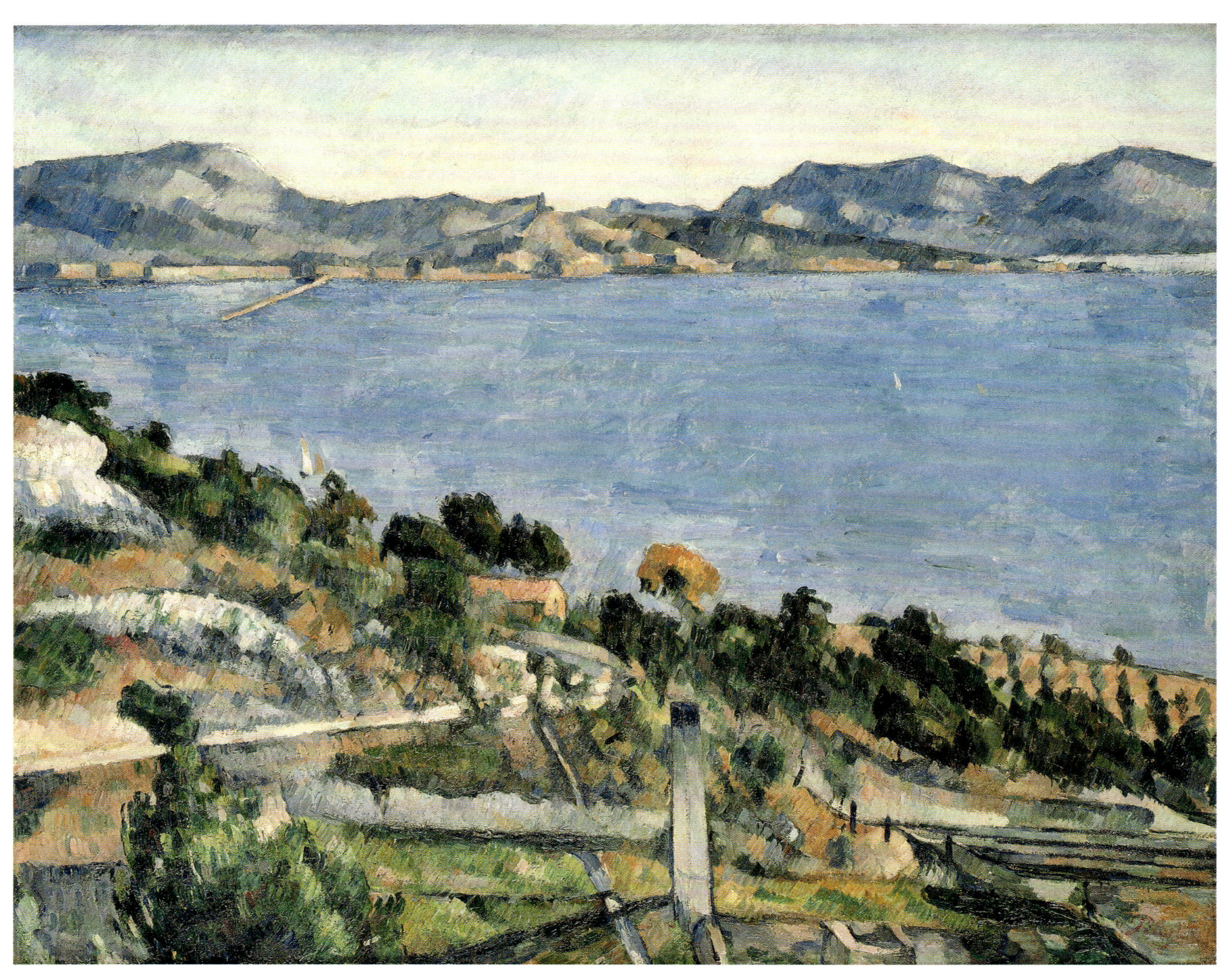

Cat. 80

The Gulf of Marseille Seen from L'Estaque
1878–79
Oil on canvas
59 × 73 cm (23 ¼ × 28 ¾ in.)
Musee d'Orsay, Paris, legs de Gustave Caillebotte,
1894, RF 2761
FWN 119

Cat. 81

**The Bay of Marseille, with a View
Overlooking the Saint-Jacut-Henri
Village, near L'Estaque**
1877–79
Oil on canvas
64.5 × 80.3 cm (25 ⅜ × 31 ⅝ in.)
Yoshino Gypsum Collection (Yoshino
Gypsum Co., Ltd.)
FWN 118

Cat. 82

The Bay at L'Estaque
1878–82
Pencil, watercolor, and gouache on
pale-yellow paper
29.1 × 45.5 cm (11 ⁷⁄₁₆ × 17 ¹⁵⁄₁₆ in.)
Kunsthaus Zürich, Grafische Sammlung,
1935, 2370
FWN 1056
Chicago only

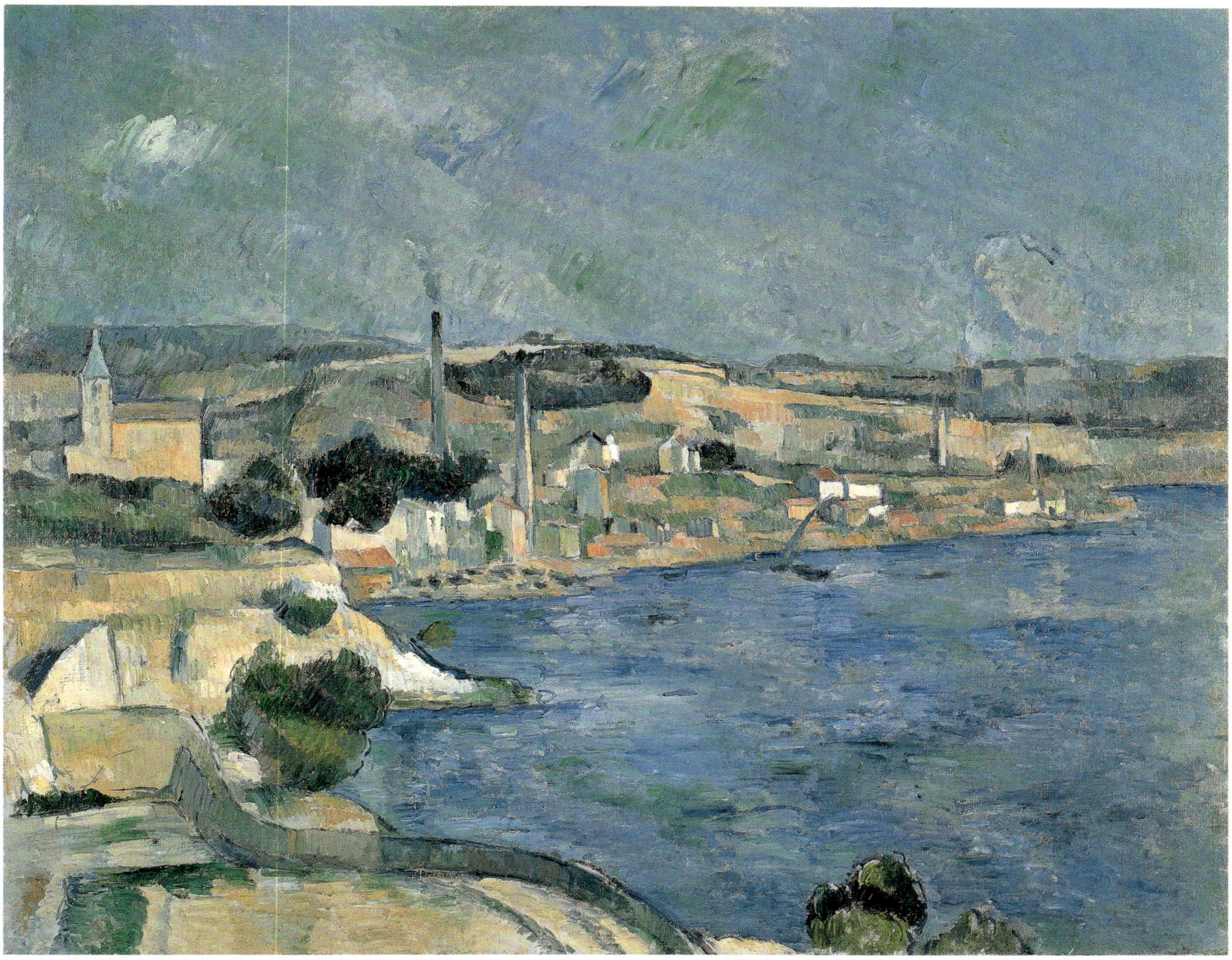

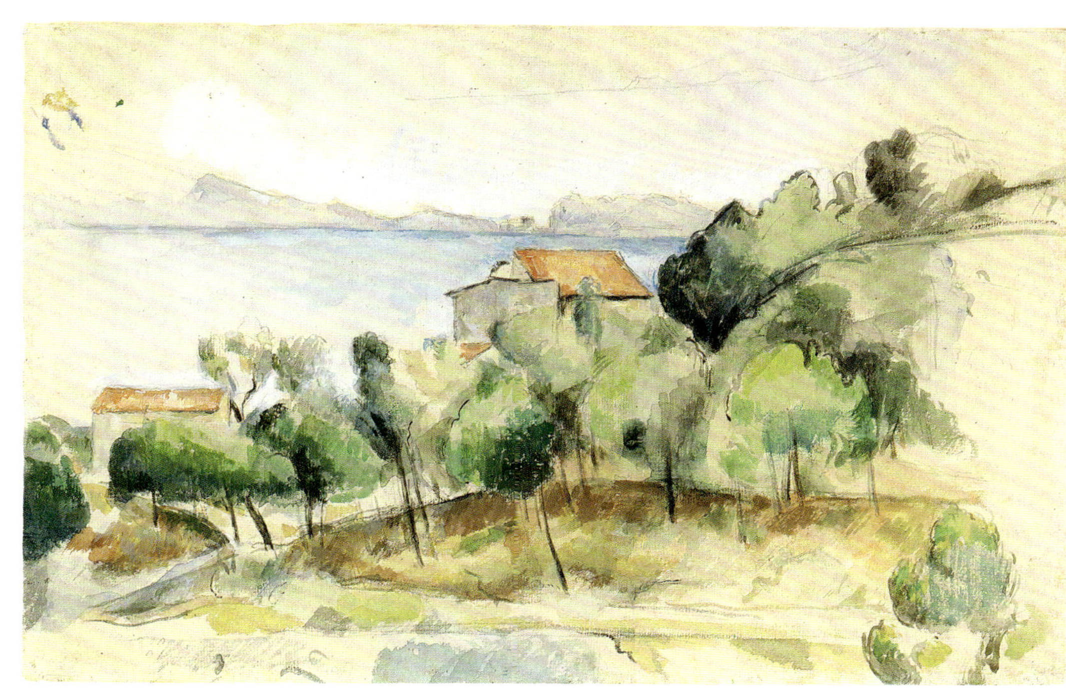

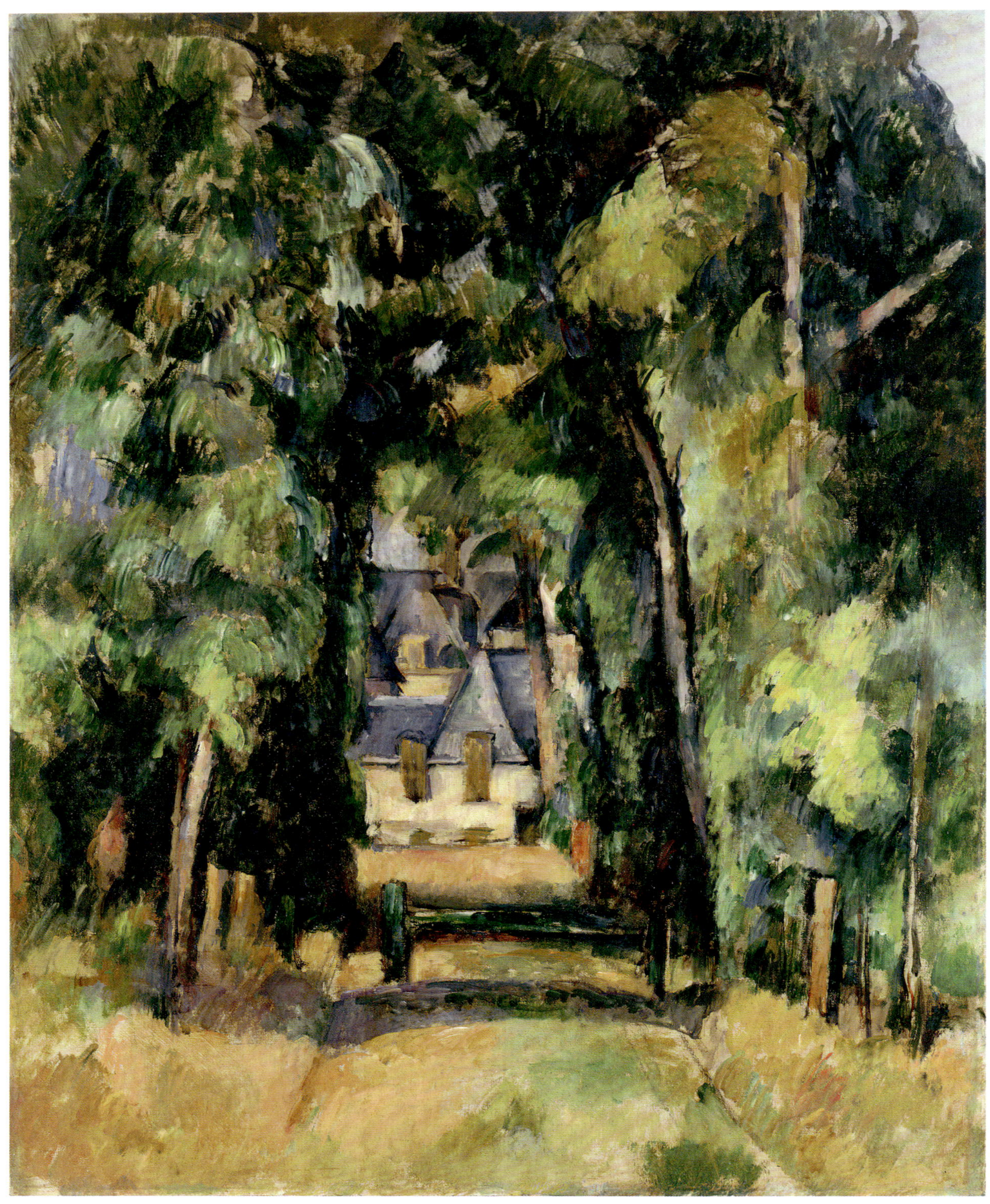

Cat. 83

Avenue at Chantilly
1888
Oil on canvas
81.3 × 64.8 cm (32 × 25 ½ in.)
Toledo Museum of Art, Gift of Mr. and Mrs. William E.
Levis, 1959.13
FWN 244
Chicago only

Cat. 84

Forest Interior
c. 1898–99
Oil on canvas
61 × 81.3 cm (24 × 32 in.)
Fine Arts Museum of San Francisco, museum
purchase, Mildred Anna Williams Collection, 1977.4
FWN 324
Chicago only

Cat. 85

Cistern in the Grounds of Château Noir
c. 1900
Oil on canvas
74.3 × 61 cm (29 ¼ × 24 in.)
The Henry and Rose Pearlman Foundation on
loan to the Princeton University Art Museum,
Princeton, New Jersey, L.1988.62.4
FWN 336
Chicago only

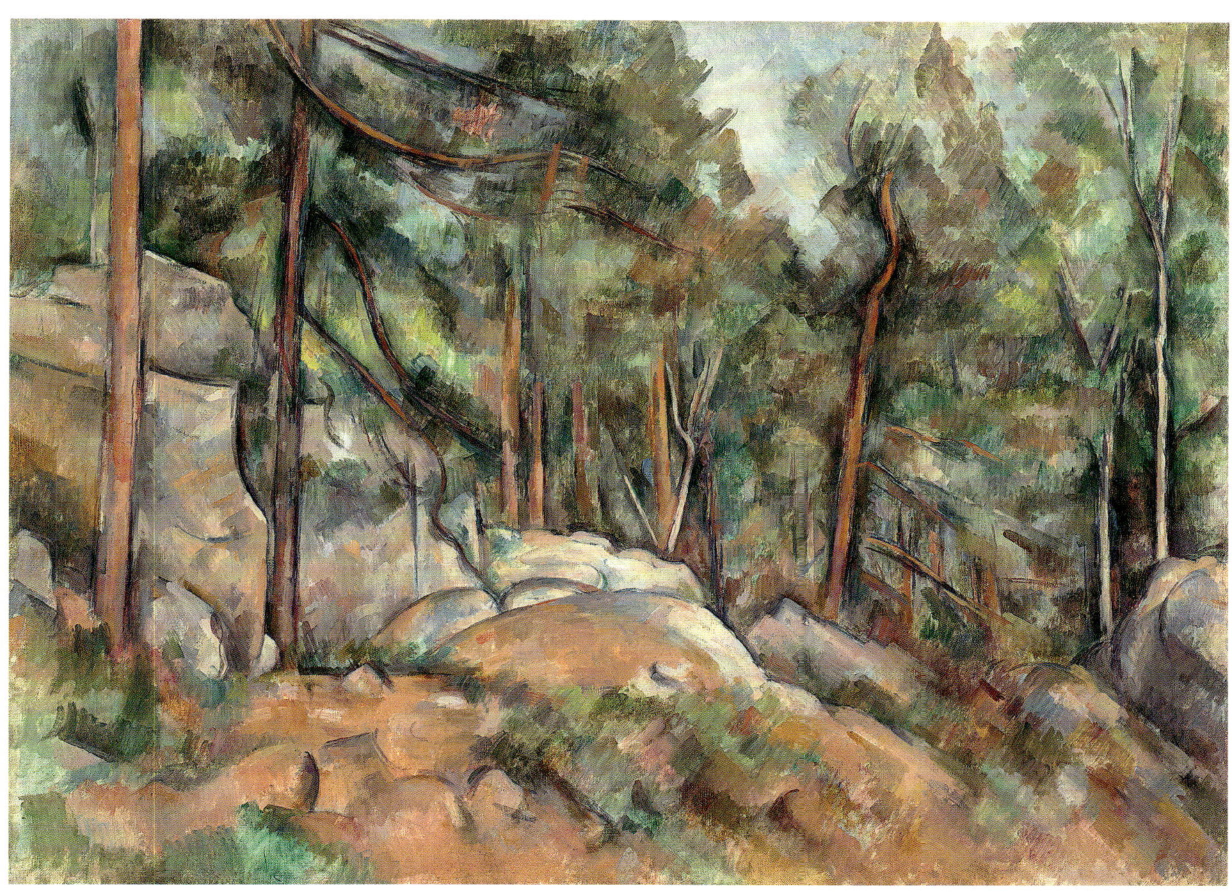

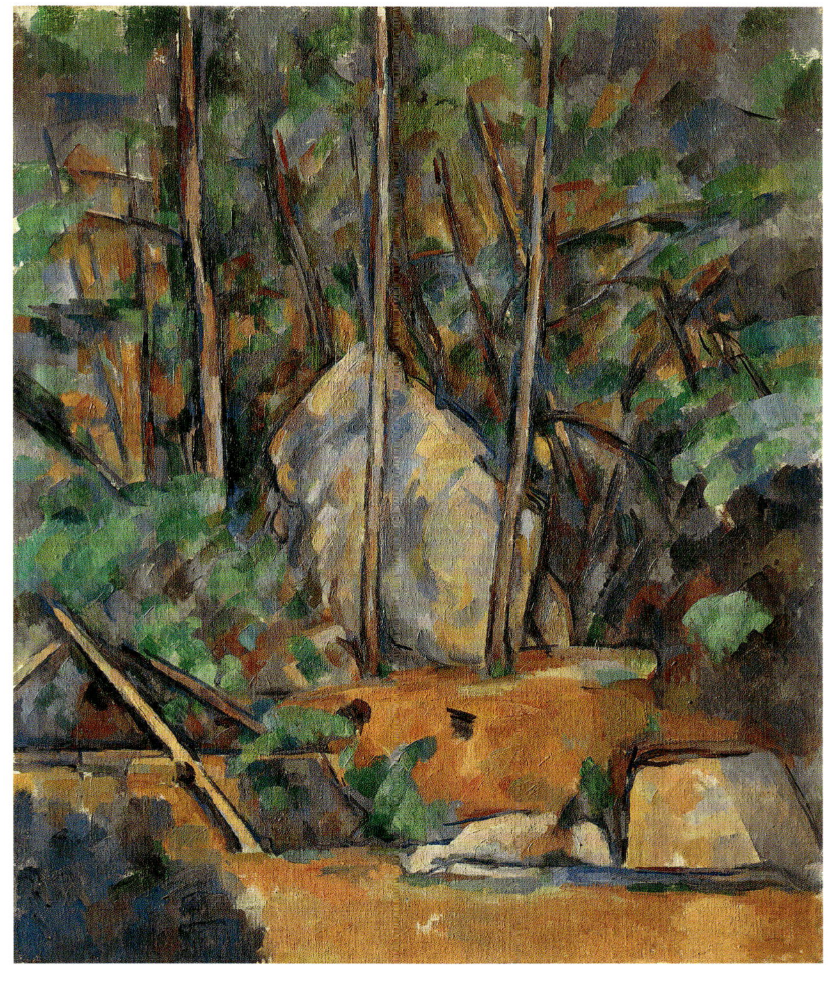

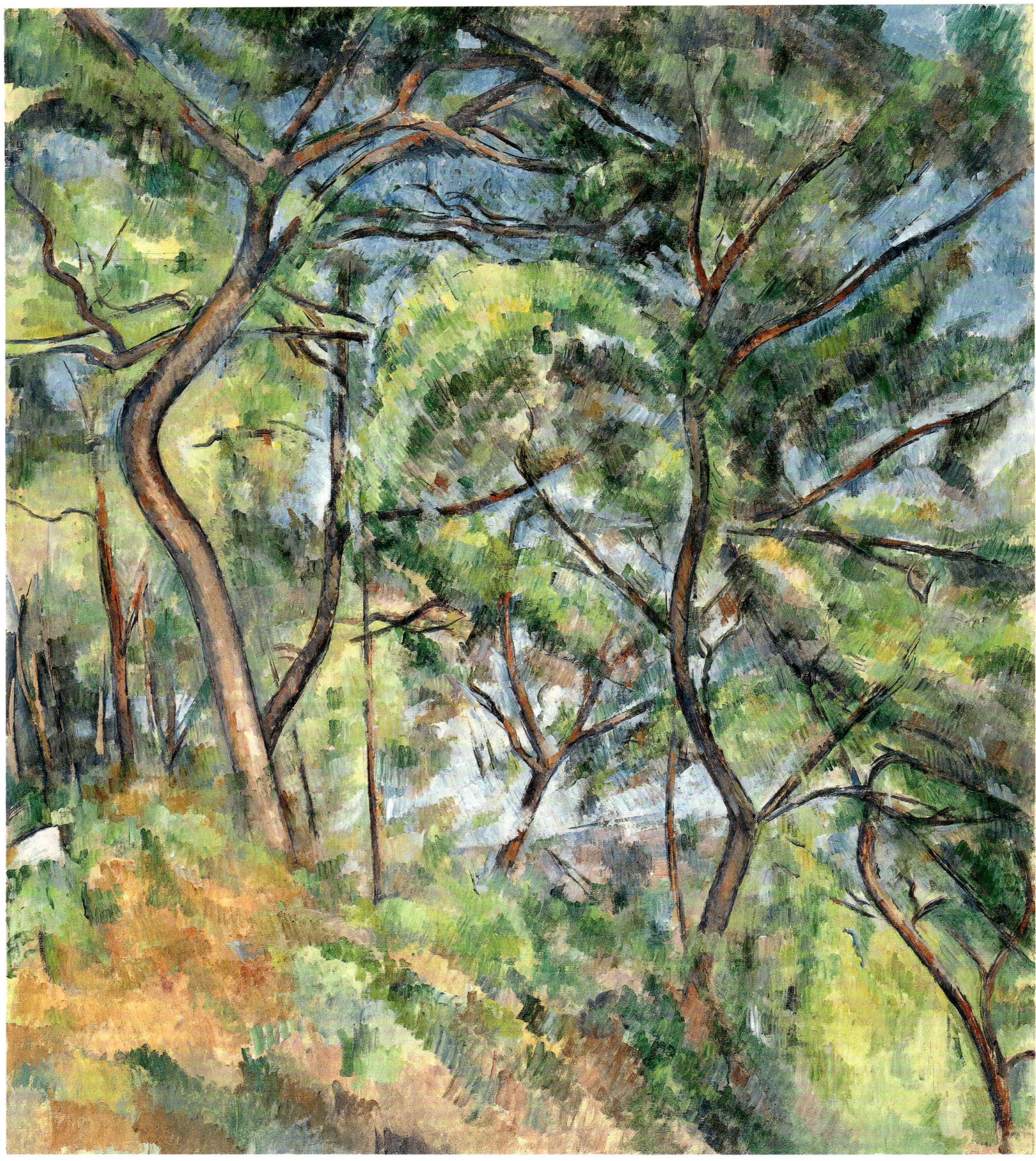

Cat. 86

Forest Floor (*Sous-Bois*)
c. 1894
Oil on canvas
116.2 × 81.3 cm (45 ¾ × 32 in.)
Los Angeles County Museum of Art, Wallis
Foundation Fund in memory of Hal B. Wallis,
AC1992.161.1
FWN 303

Rodney McMillian

I chose to look at and write about *Sous-Bois*. I liked its composition and I liked the title in relation to the image. One translation I found for "sous-bois" was "undergrowth." It is a painting in which the horizon line is really about the ground. I thought about what's underneath the ground. What histories are buried there? What about the larger, overarching histories being formed? The land is not inhabited and it appears to be untouched by people, so much so that there's a buildup of undergrowth. The reality of that place and moment was in sharp contrast to the lands being occupied and pillaged for France's and the French people's enrichment during the time this work was made.

I wonder what this landscape would have looked like to us without colonization? Would we care about Cezanne or his work? Better yet, would there even be a "Cezanne" without colonization? Would it matter that he broke up the picture plane? Would the idea of a picture plane even be an issue? How would we register the light between the branches? Would he have had an abundance of fruit, jars, and linen to paint? Could Cezanne even have afforded the pigment? I didn't ask many of these questions in 1998 while studying at the School of the Art Institute of Chicago, when I encountered a lot of his work up-close for the first time. I did, however, begin to pose similar questions about the institution and its collection and the volumes of work it housed and displayed. At that time I was simply trying to understand why he was important from a formal perspective, trying to discern the "greatness" of his work so I could one day be great too. I'd walk through the galleries studying different paintings, from different time periods, looking for specific things like different tones of gray or how to paint a shadow or an apple.

Could he have surveyed the land, creating a disintegrating picture plane, if he was unaware of the disintegration happening on his and his countrymen's

behalf in the likes of Algeria, the Congo, Vietnam, and the rest of France's colonies? I don't know if Cezanne had put two and two together. But how do you just see the formal properties of a painting or the scholarship or the invention his work evokes without foregrounding that history?

So, what do I see when I look at *Sous-Bois*? I see beautiful color and mark making, a forest. I see an illusion. I saw these qualities in Cezanne's work twenty years ago against the dense impasto, dark hues, stark white forms, and pathos of the Horace Pippin painting *Cabin in the Cotton* (fig. 1), which was hung seemingly miles away from the European wing. Like Michael Asher's project in 1979 (see fig. 2), in which he relocated Jean Antoine Houdin's eighteenth-century sculpture of George Washington from outside the museum to one of the European galleries. I knew the Pippin

painting, and the history of the people and the land he depicted belonged on prominent display even if it was not in a European gallery. Instead, if memory serves, it was hung in the back reaches of the museum near the American Decorative Arts section.

To enter the Art Institute of Chicago through its main doors, you walk up the stairs from Michigan Avenue between the two large patinated lions. Once inside, you walk up another set of stairs. And the gallery facing that entrance, the gallery that states what's most important to the institution, is the one for nineteenth-century European painting. So back to *Sous-Bois*—the airiness of his surface, the speed with which his gestures register, the deep philosophical musings that construct the disorientation and suggest the material experiences of his times. Experiences and histories folks today are, in some cases, quite literally dying to undo.

Fig. 1

Horace Pippin (American, 1888–1946). *Cabin in the Cotton*, c. 1931–37. Oil on cotton mounted on Masonite; 51 × 85 cm (20 × 33 ½ in.). The Art Institute of Chicago, restricted gift in memory of Frances W. Pick from her children Thomas F. Pick and Mary P. Hines, 1990.417.

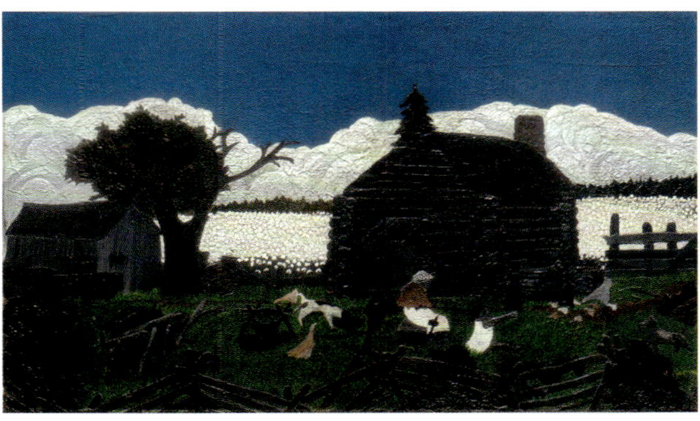

Fig. 2

Michael Asher (American, 1943–2012). Installation view of Gallery 219, with statue of George Washington by Jean Antoine Houdon after removal from Michigan Avenue entrance, Art Institute of Chicago, *73rd American Exhibition*, June 9–August 5, 1979.

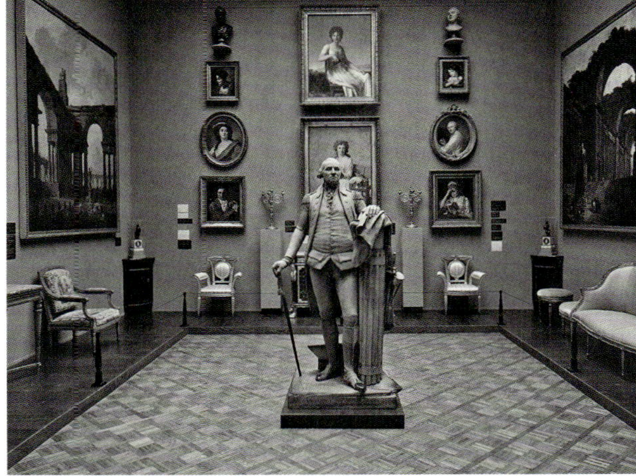

Cat. 87

The Big Trees
1902–4
Oil on canvas
81 × 65 cm (31⅞ × 25 ⁹⁄₁₆ in.)
National Gallery of Scotland, Presented by
Mrs. Anne F. Kessler 1958; received after her
death 1983, NG 2206
FWN 343
Chicago only

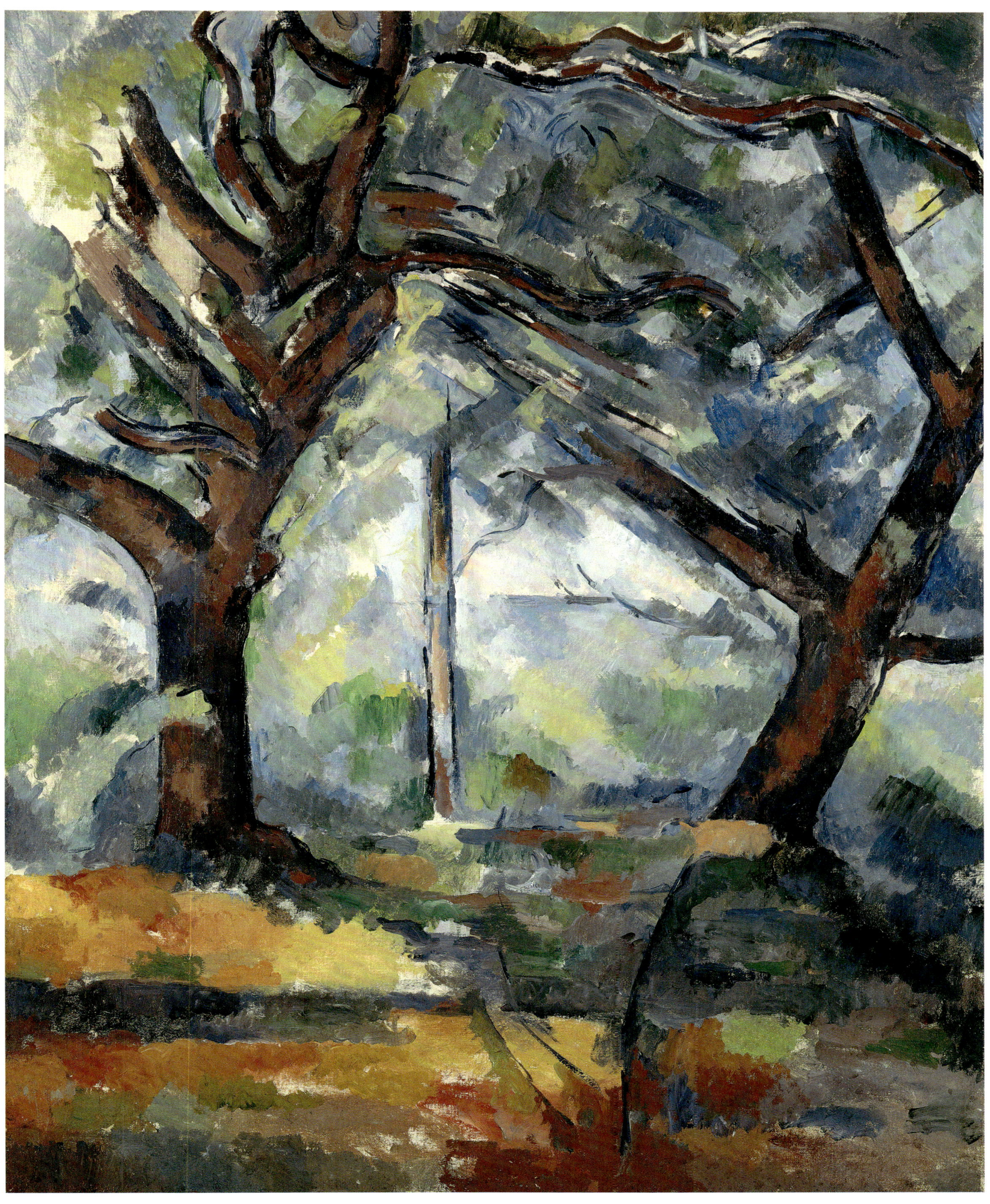

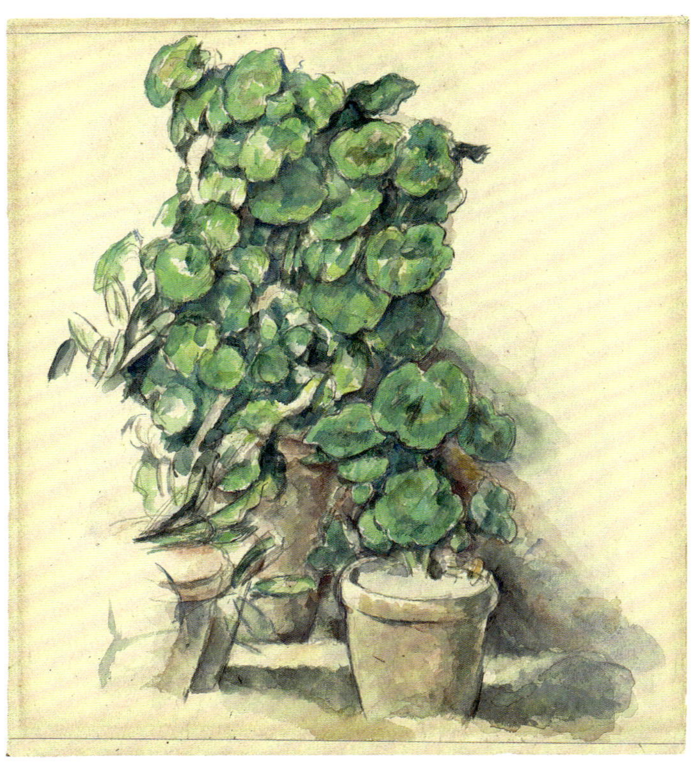

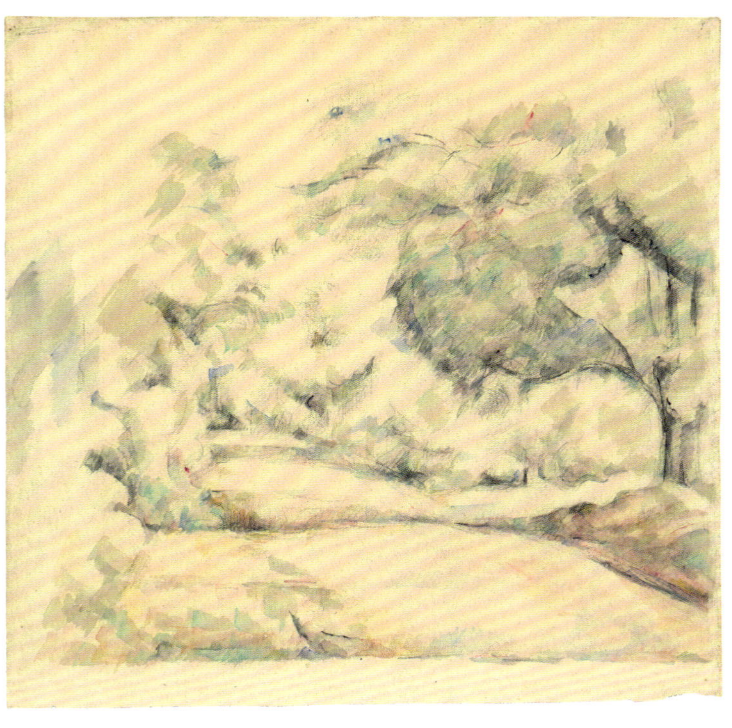

Cat. 88

Geraniums
1888–90
Watercolor over graphite on laid paper
30.5 × 28.5 cm (12 × 11¼ in.)
The National Gallery of Art, Washington, DC,
Collection of Mr. and Mrs. Paul Mellon, 1995.47.25
FWN 1920
Chicago only

Cat. 89

Road in Provence
c. 1885
Watercolor and graphite on tan wove paper
50.2 × 50.4 cm (19 ¾ × 19 ¹³⁄₁₆ in.)
The Art Institute of Chicago, Mr. and Mrs. Martin A.
Ryerson Collection, 1933.1221
FWN 1144
Chicago only

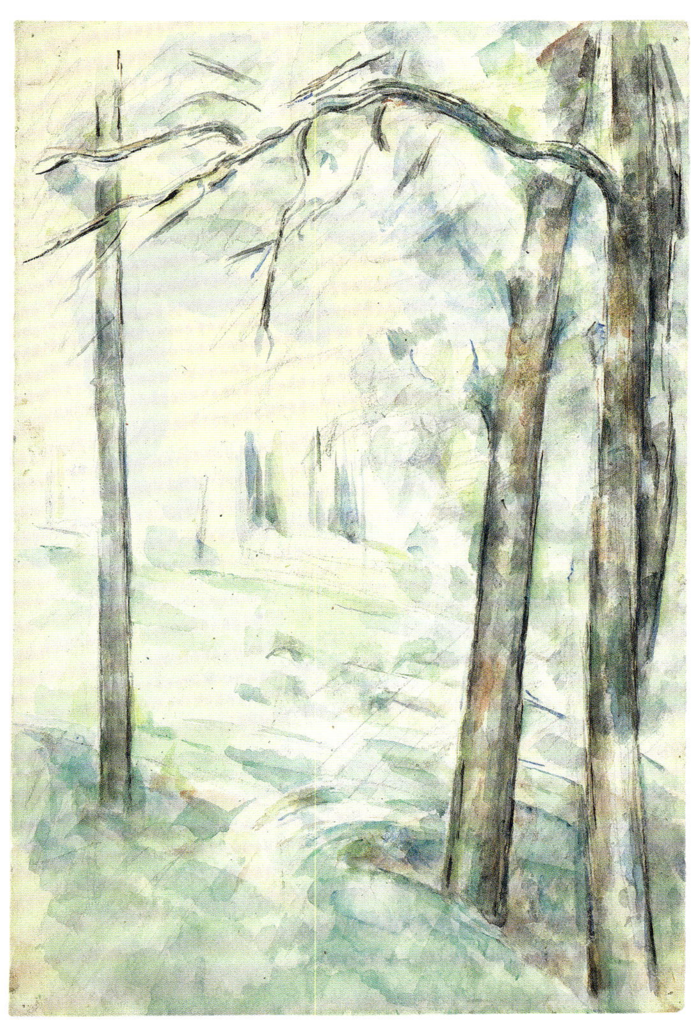

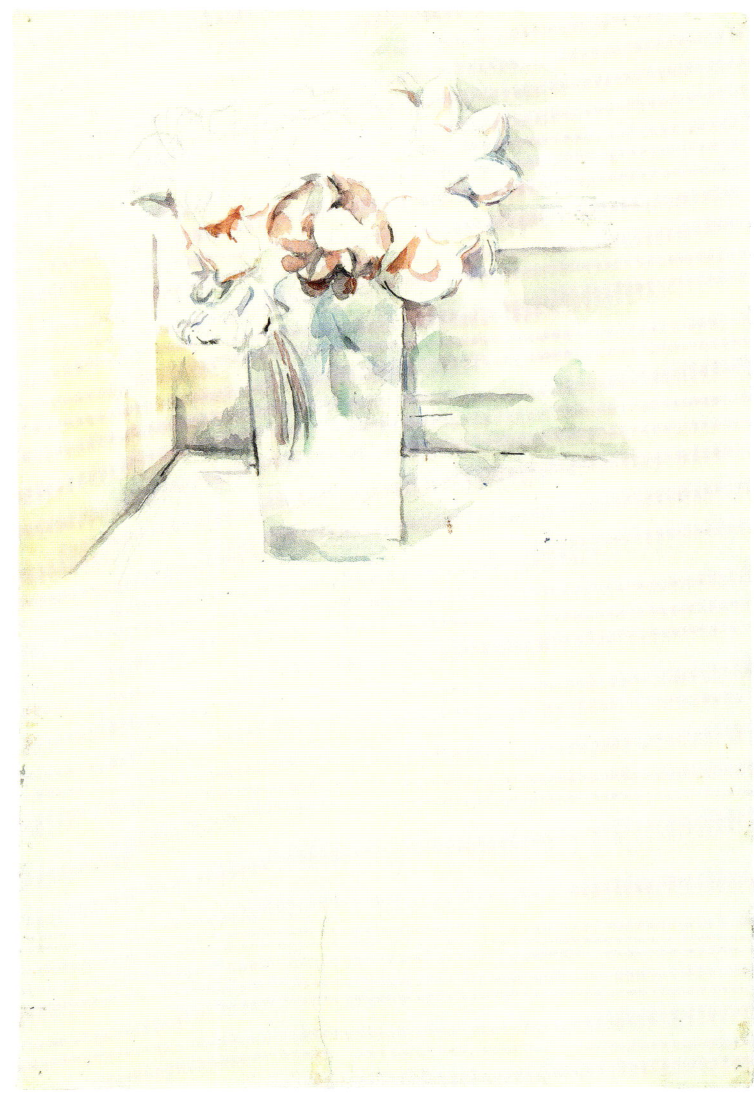

Cat. 90

Woods, Aix-en-Provence
1887–90
Graphite and watercolor on paper (verso)
46.6 × 30 cm (18 ⅜ × 11 ¹³/₁₆ in.)
The Syndics of the Fitzwilliam Museum,
University of Cambridge, UK, PD.6-1966
FWN 1225
Chicago only

Cat. 91

Vase of Flowers
c. 1885–88
Graphite and watercolor on paper (recto)
46.6 × 30 cm (18 ⅜ × 11 ¹³/₁₆ in.)
The Syndics of the Fitzwilliam Museum,
University of Cambridge, UK, PD.6-1966
FWN 1932
Chicago only

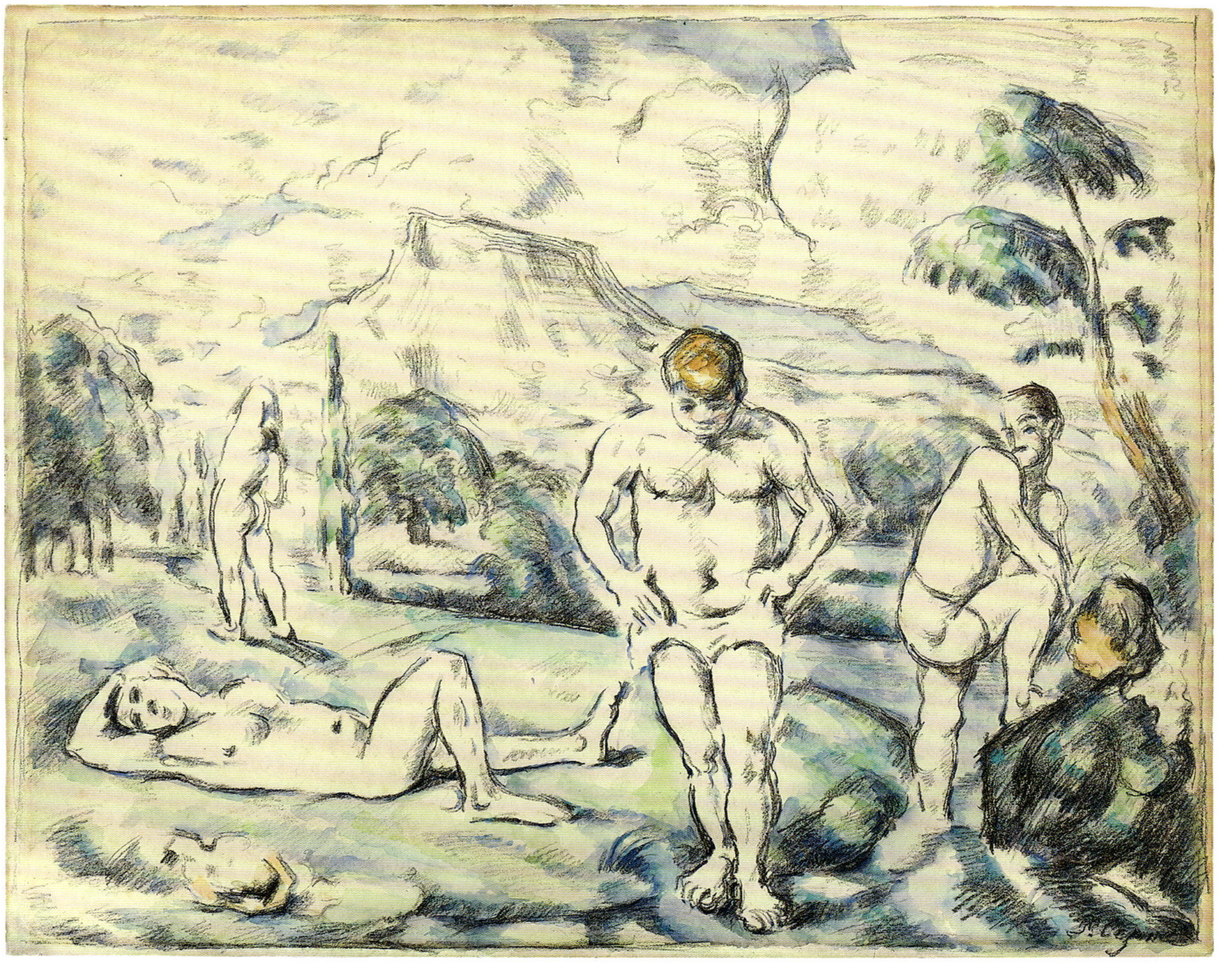

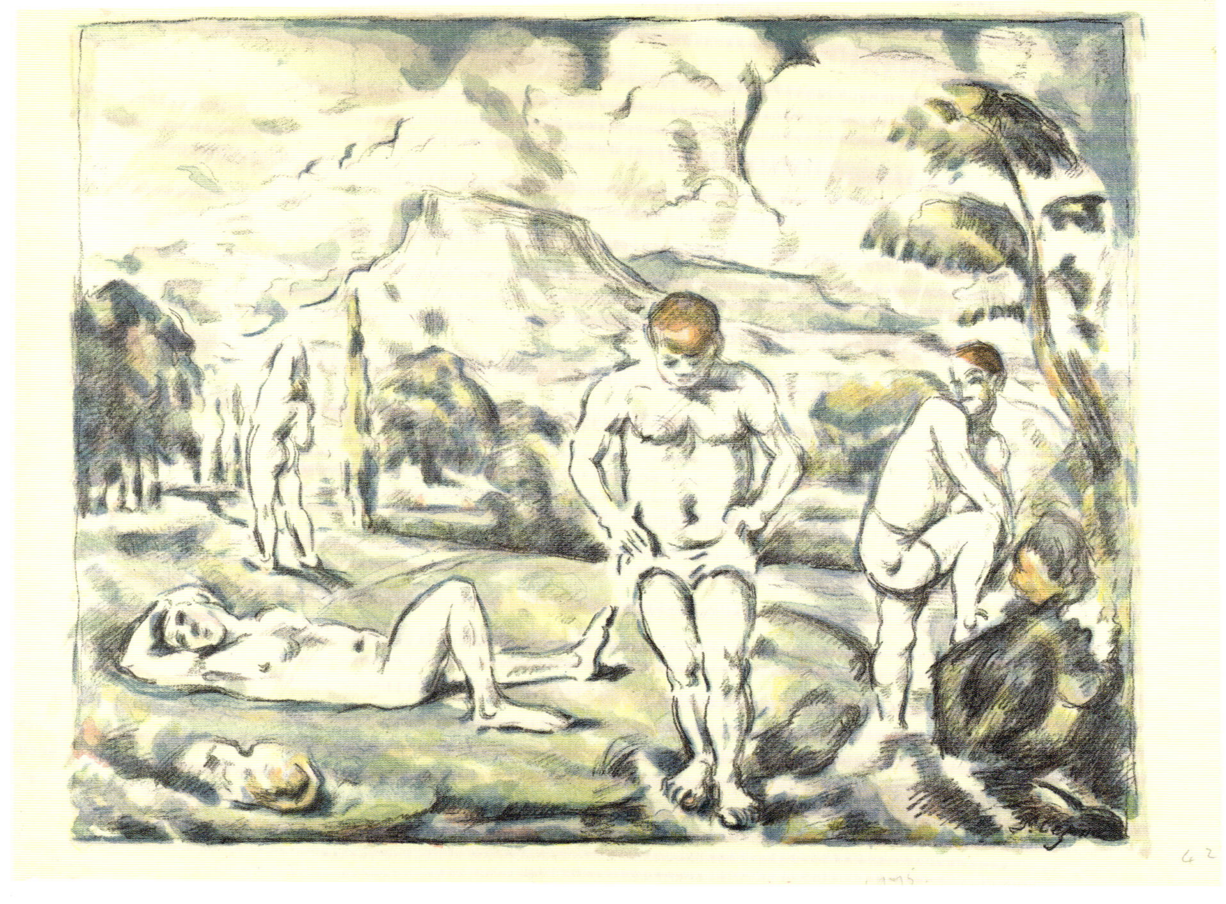

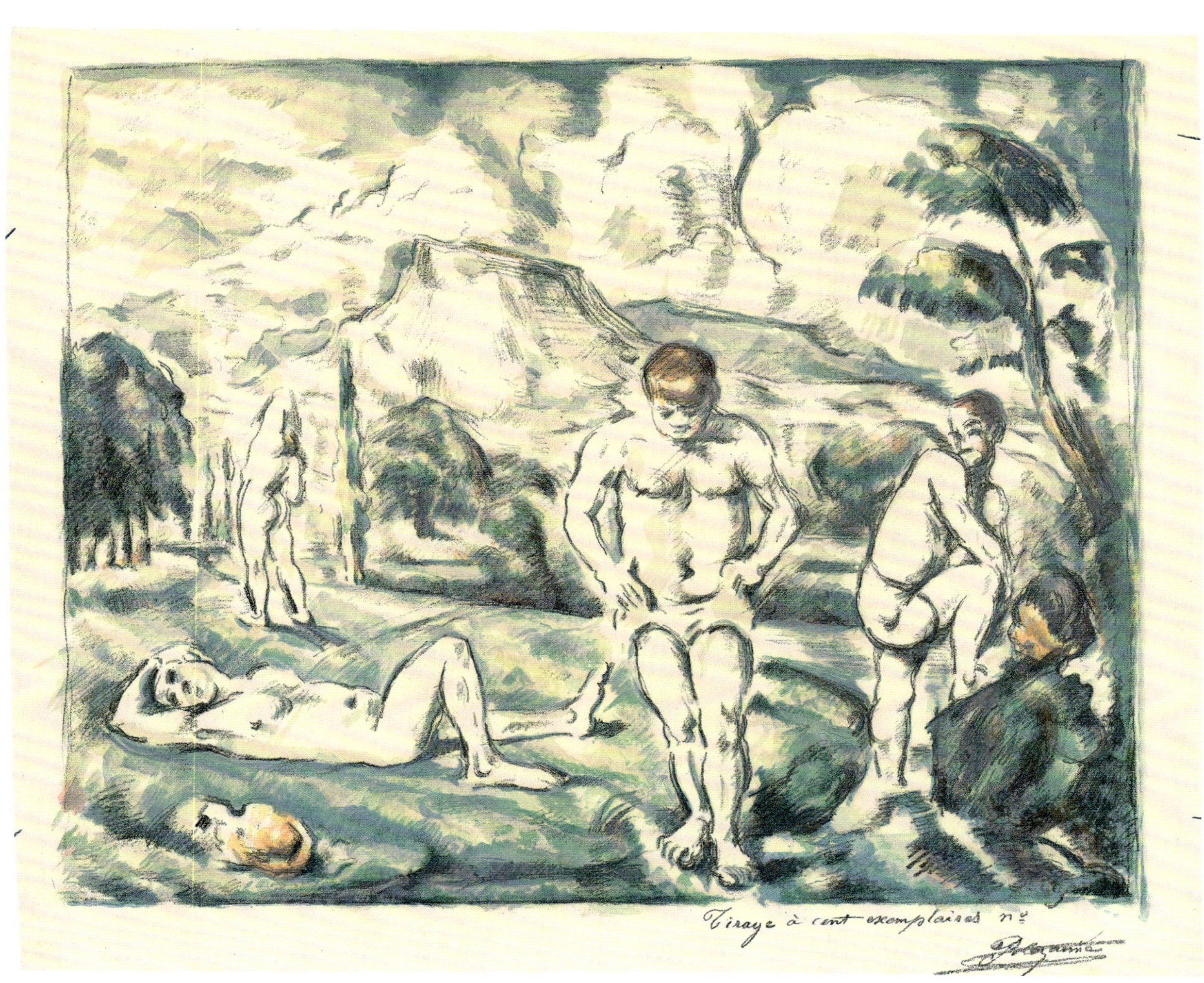

Cat. 92

Bathers
1896–97
Lithograph in black with watercolor on laid paper
42.6 × 51.5 cm (16 ¾ × 20 ¼ in.) (image);
48.3 × 63 cm (19 × 24 ¹³⁄₁₆ in) (sheet)
Private collection
Chicago only

Cat. 93

The Large Bather
c. 1898
Lithograph on paper
41 × 50.7 cm (16 ⅛ × 19 ¹⁵⁄₁₆ in.)
Tate, London, Presented by
Lord Duveen 1927, P01008
London only

Cat. 94

Bathers
1890–1900
Color lithograph on ivory laid paper
42.1 × 52.8 cm (16 ⁹⁄₁₆ × 20 ¹³⁄₁₆ in.) (image);
46.4 × 56.9 cm (18 ¼ × 22 ⅜ in.) (sheet)
The Art Institute of Chicago, William McCallin
McKee Memorial Endowment, 1932.1297
Chicago only

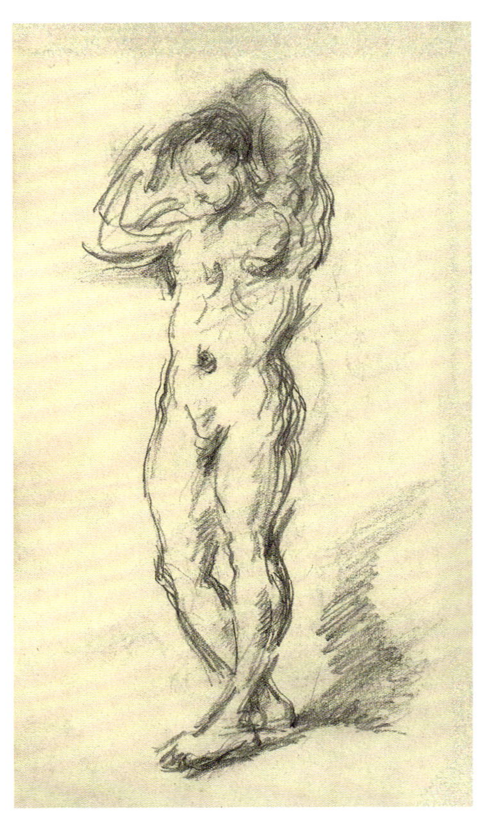

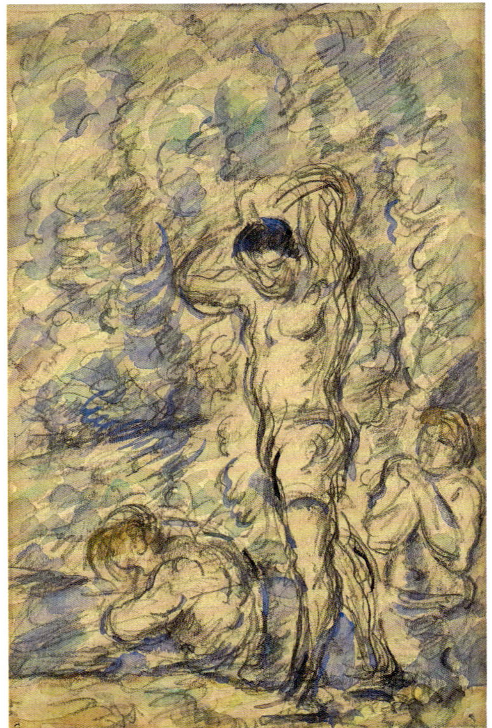

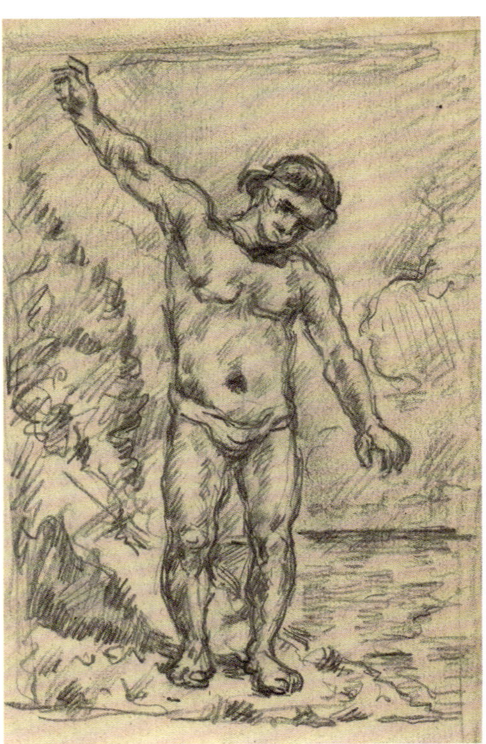

Cat. 95

Standing Bather
c. 1885
Graphite and watercolor on wove paper, p. XXXIII
verso removed from the EH II sketchbook
21 × 13 cm (8 ¼ × 5 ⅛ in.)
Collection of Jasper Johns
FWN 3010-33b

Cat. 96

Three Bathers
1882–85
Graphite and watercolor on wove paper, p. 46
removed from the EH I sketchbook
18 × 11 cm (7 ¹⁄₁₆ × 4 ⁵⁄₁₆ in.)
Collection of Jasper Johns
FWN 3002-46a

Cat. 97

Bather with Outstretched Arms
1874–77
Graphite on cream laid paper (pierced; recto)
17.9 × 11.1 cm (7 ¹⁄₁₆ × 4 ⅜ in.)
The Art Institute of Chicago, gift of Richard and
Mary L. Gray, 2019.840
FWN 2012

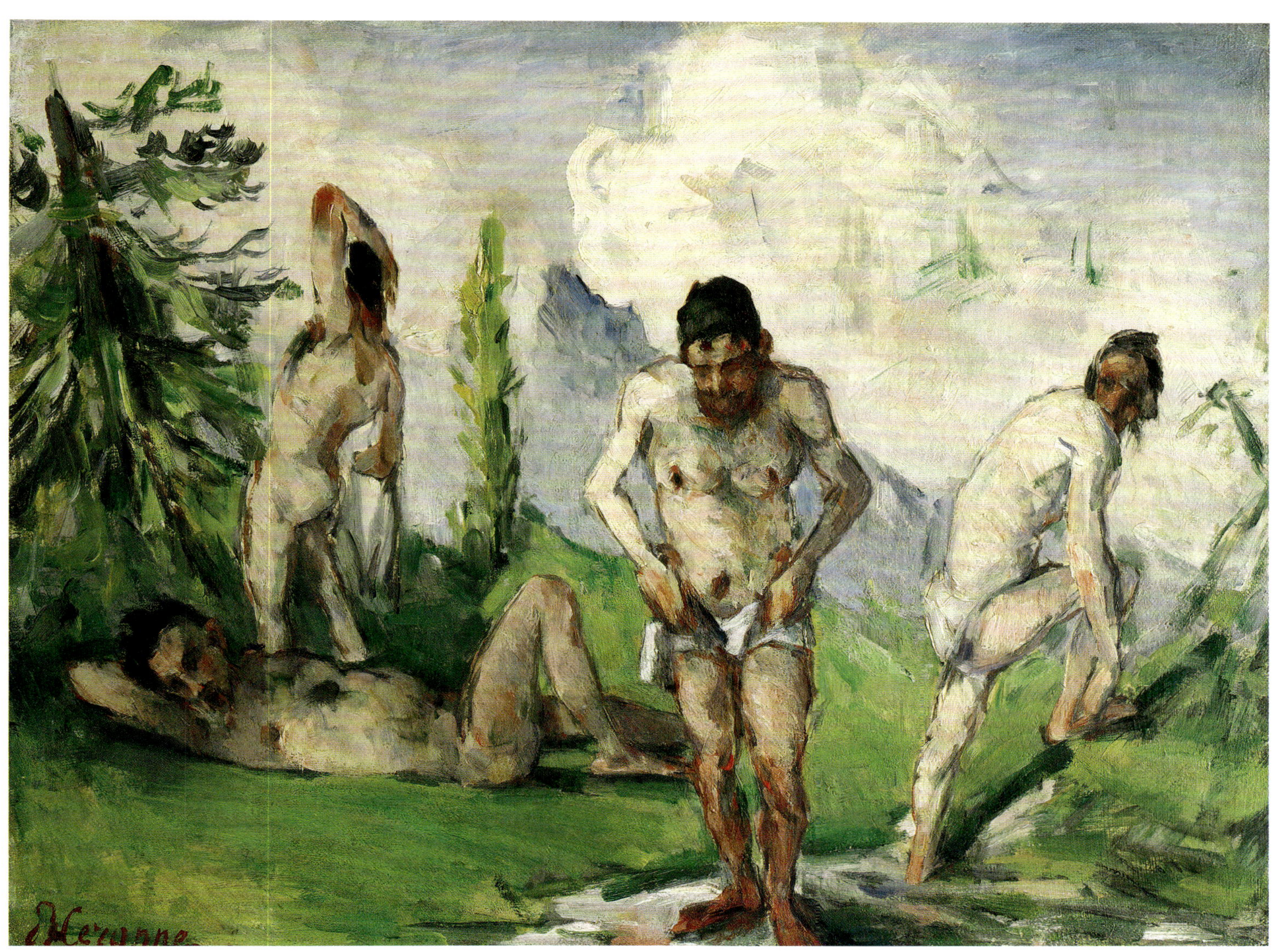

Cat. 98

Bathers at Rest
1875–76
Oil on canvas
35 × 45.5 cm (13 ¾ × 17 ¹⁵/₁₆ in.)
MAH Musée d'art et d'histoire, Geneva, Dépôt de la
Fondation Jean-Louis Prévost, Geneva, 1985,
1985-0017
FWN 924

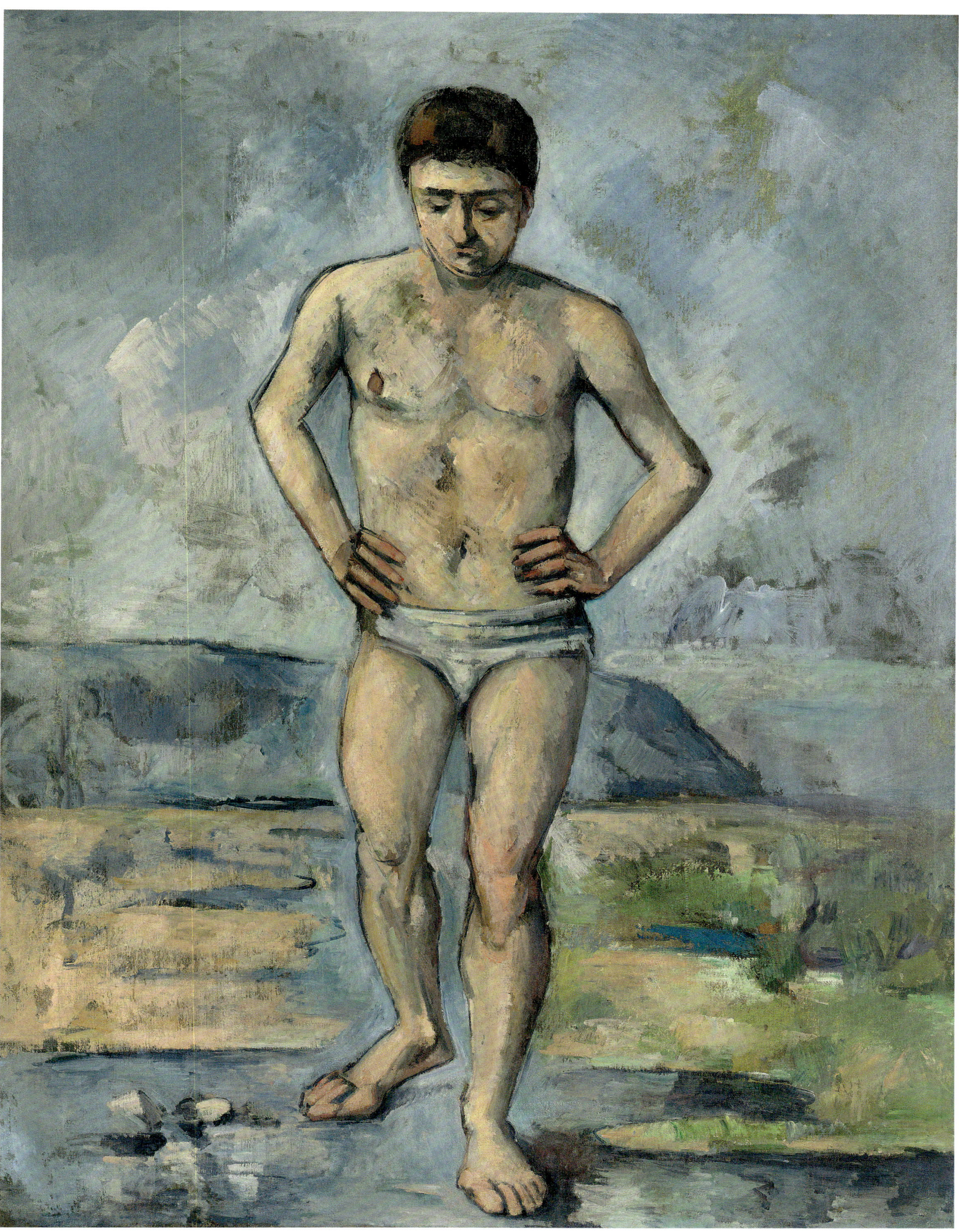

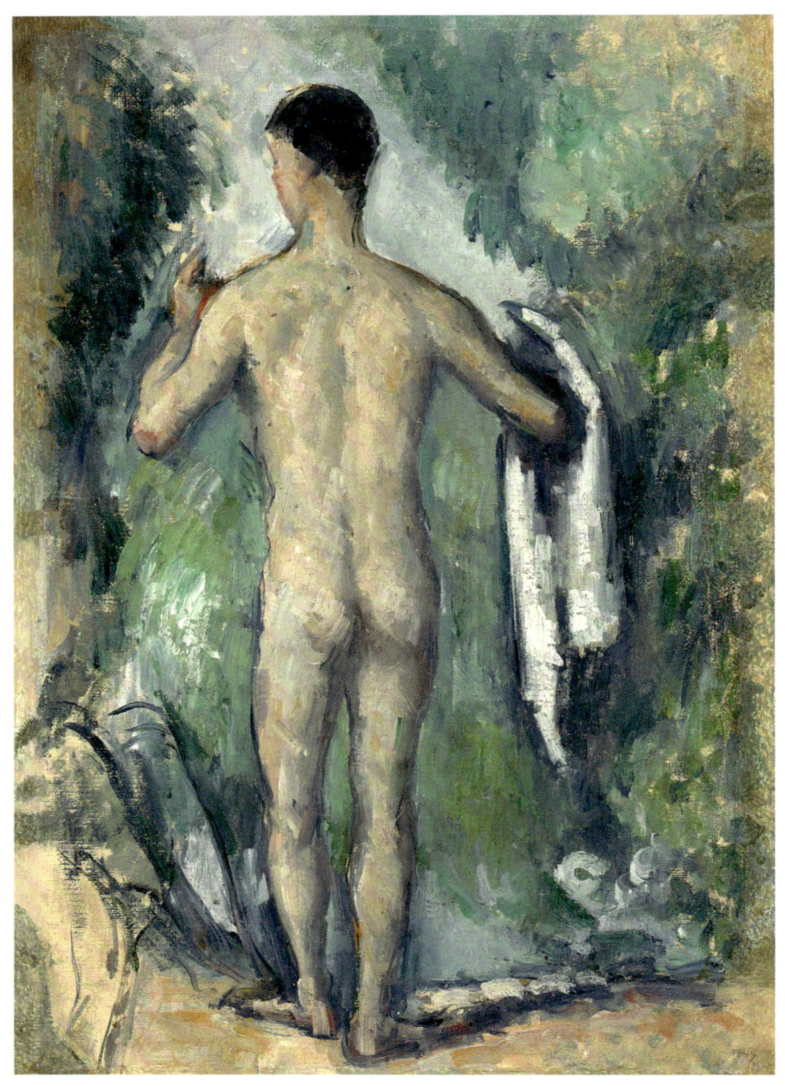

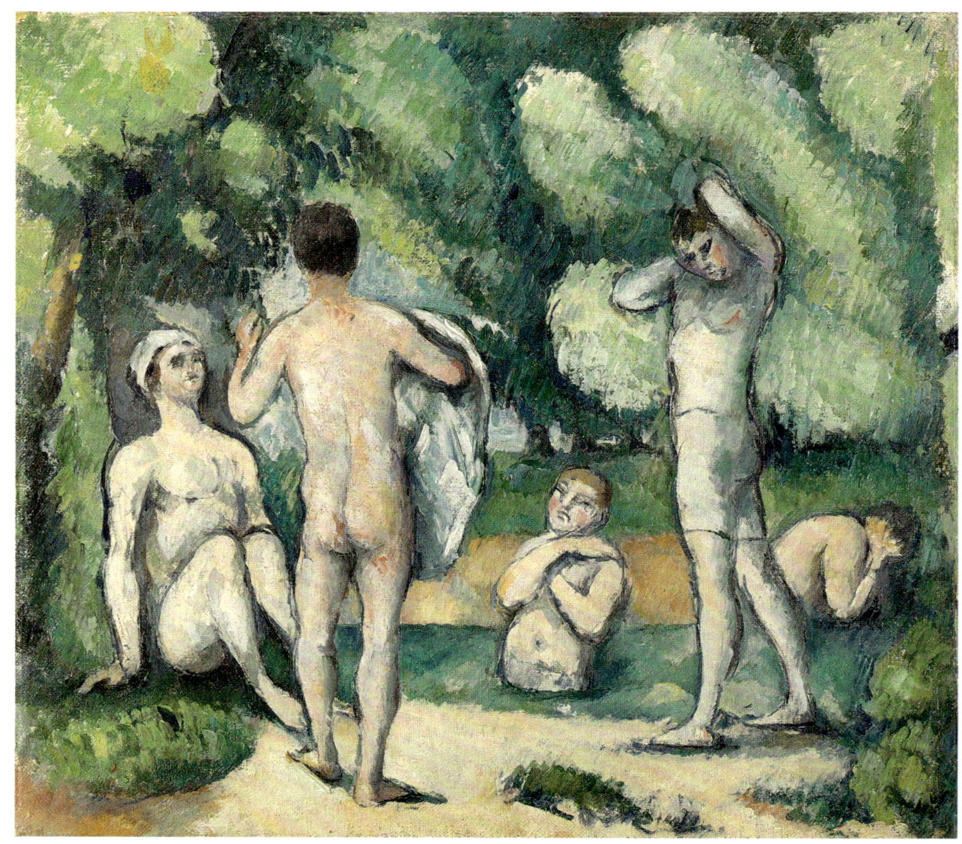

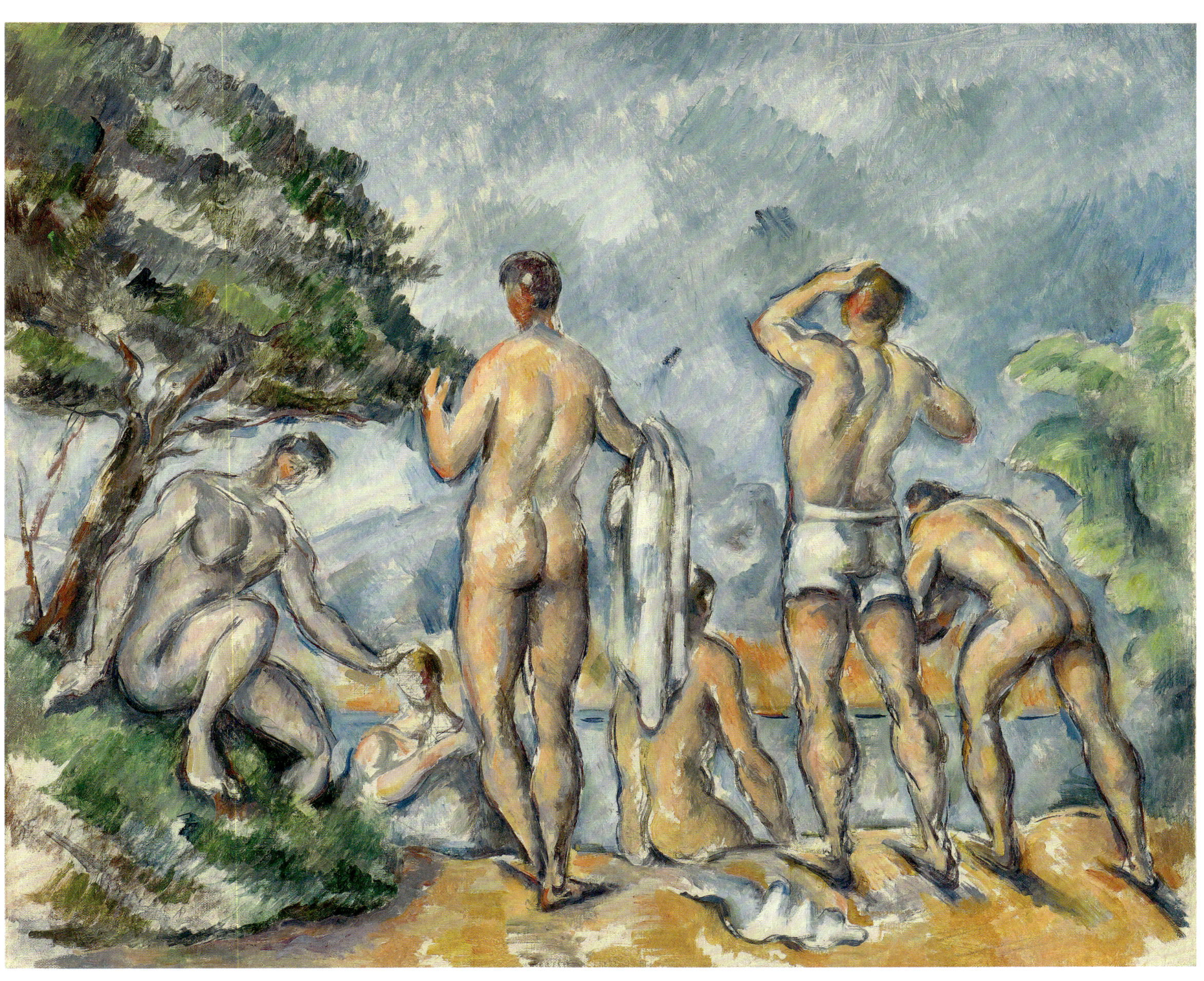

Cat. 100

Standing Bather, Seen from the Back
1879–82
Oil on canvas
31.7 × 21.6 cm (12 ½ × 8 ½ in.)
The Art Institute of Chicago, bequest of
Brooks McCormick, 2007.289
FWN 932
Chicago only

Cat. 101

Five Bathers
1879–80
Oil on canvas
34.6 × 38.1 cm (13 ⅝ × 15 in.)
Detroit Institute of Arts, Bequest of
Robert H. Tannahill, 70.162
FWN 935
Chicago only

Cat. 102

Bathers
1890–92
Oil on canvas
54.3 × 66 cm (21 ⅜ × 26 in.)
Saint Louis Art Museum, Funds given by
Mrs. Mark C. Steinberg, 2:1956
FWN 950

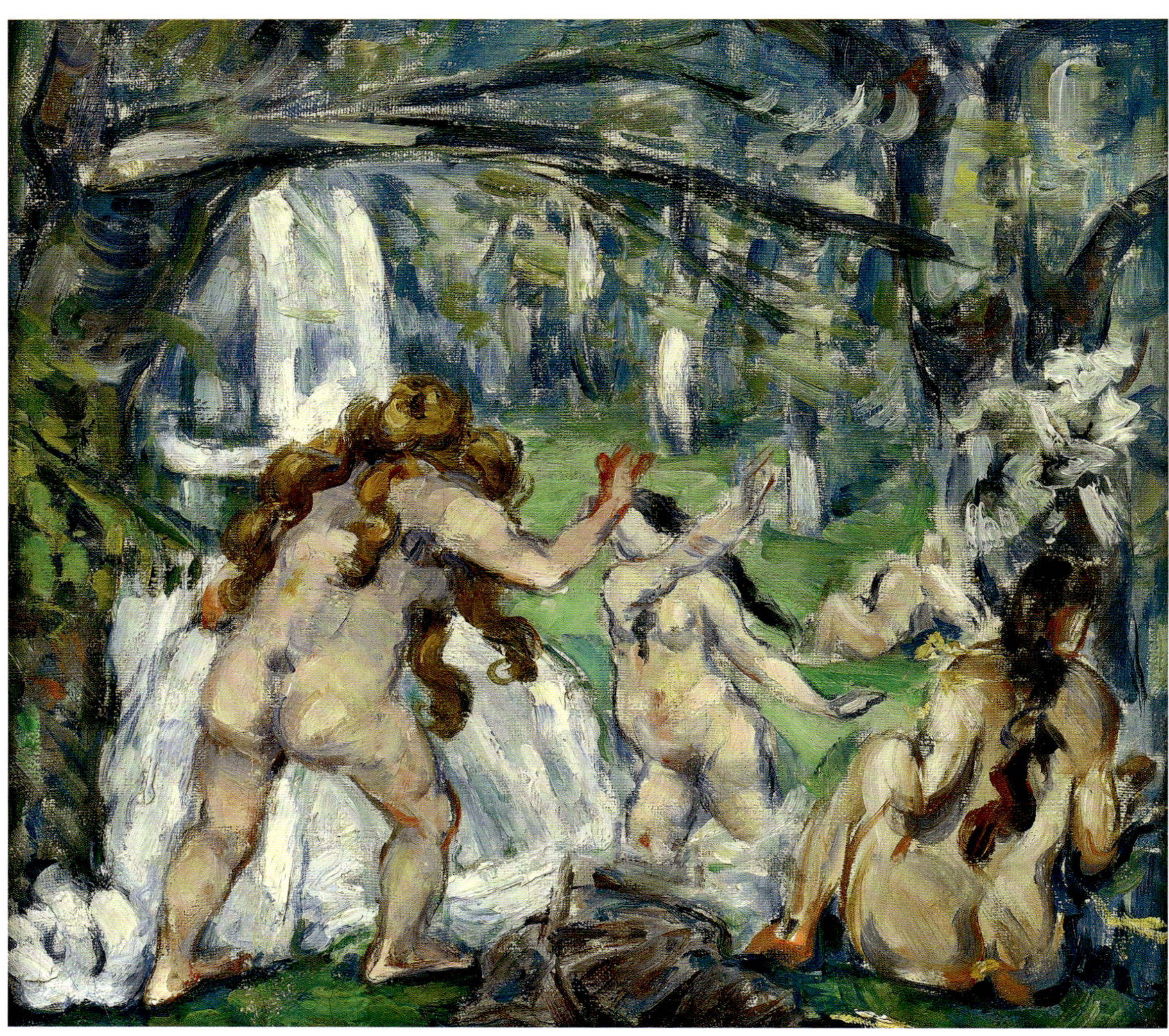

Cat. 103

Three Bathers
c. 1875
Oil on canvas
30.5 × 33 cm (12 × 13 in.)
Private collection; courtesy of Connery & Associates
FWN 920

Cat. 104

Three Bathers
1876–77
Oil on canvas
52 × 54.5 cm (20 ½ × 21 ⅜ in.)
Musée de la Ville de Paris, Petit Palais, Paris,
gift of Henri Matisse, PPP2099
FWN 923

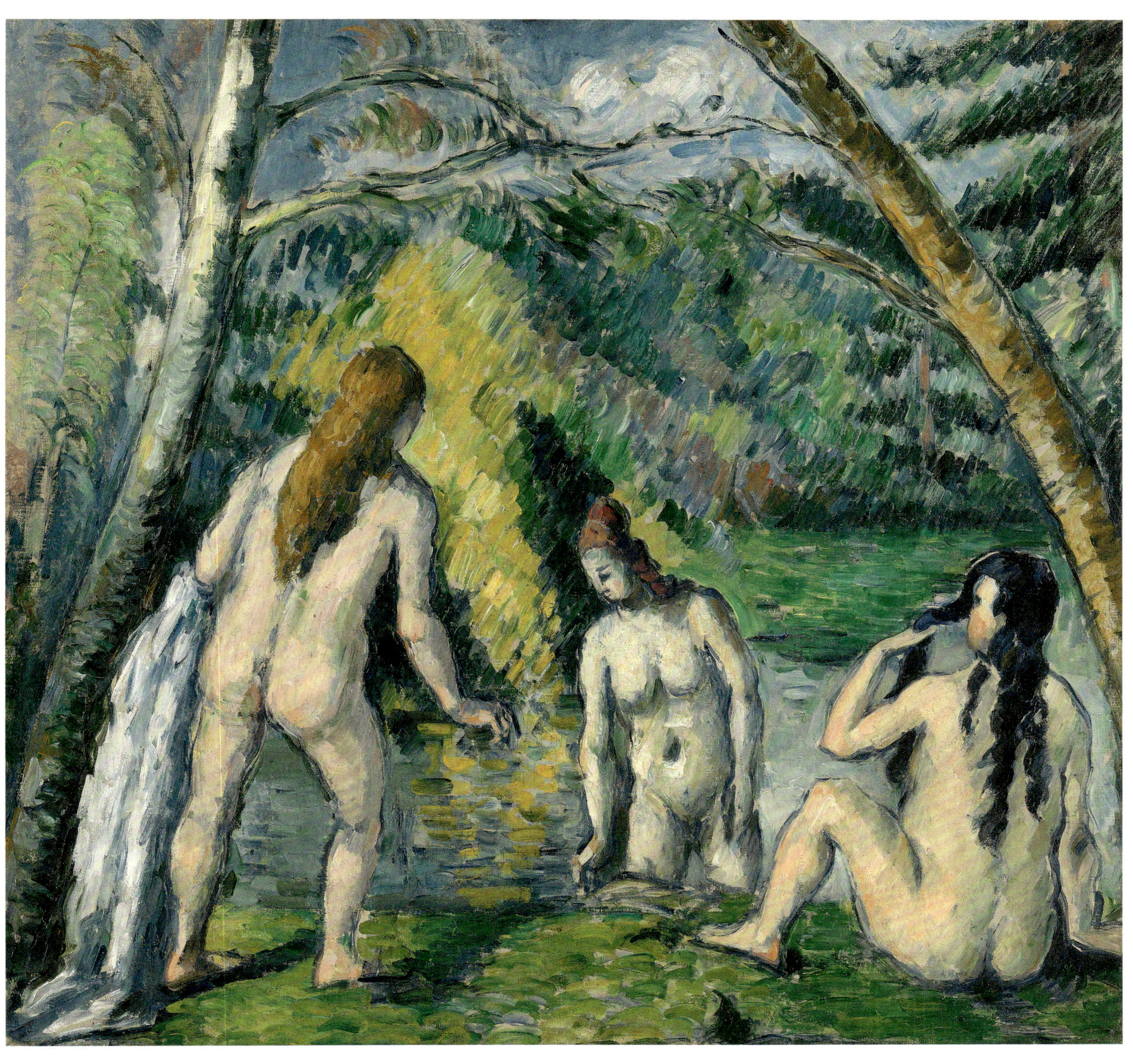

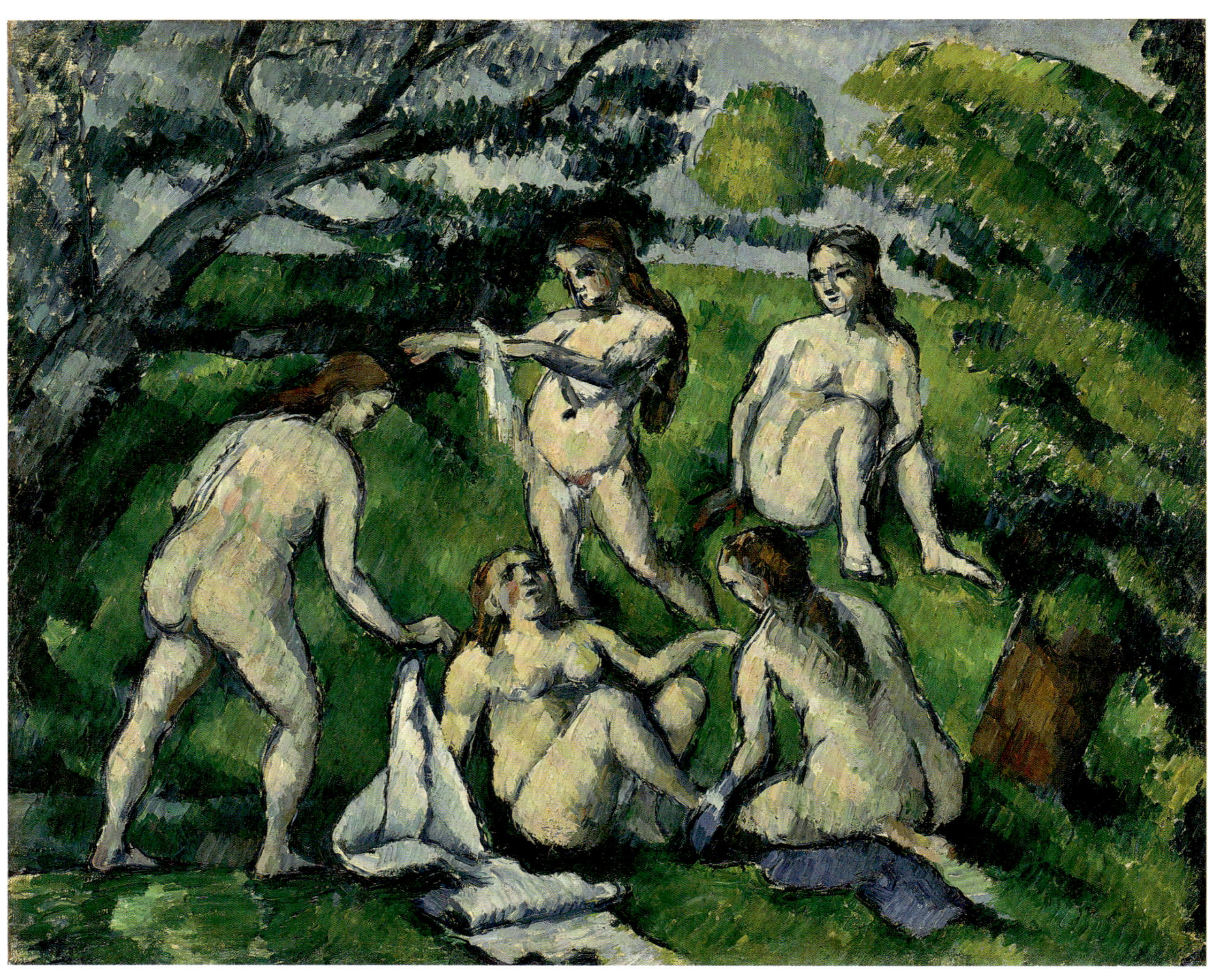

Cat. 105

Five Bathers
1877–78
Oil on canvas
45.5 × 55 cm (17 ⅞ × 21 ⅝ in.)
Musée Picasso, Paris, MP2017-10
FWN 940

Cat. 106

Five Bathers
1885–87
Oil on canvas
65.3 × 65.3 cm (25 ¹¹⁄₁₆ × 25 ¹¹⁄₁₆ in.)
Kunstmuseum Basel, mit Beiträgen der
Basler Regierung, der Max Geldner-Stiftung und
privater Kunstfreunde erworben 1960, inv. G 1960.1
FWN 945

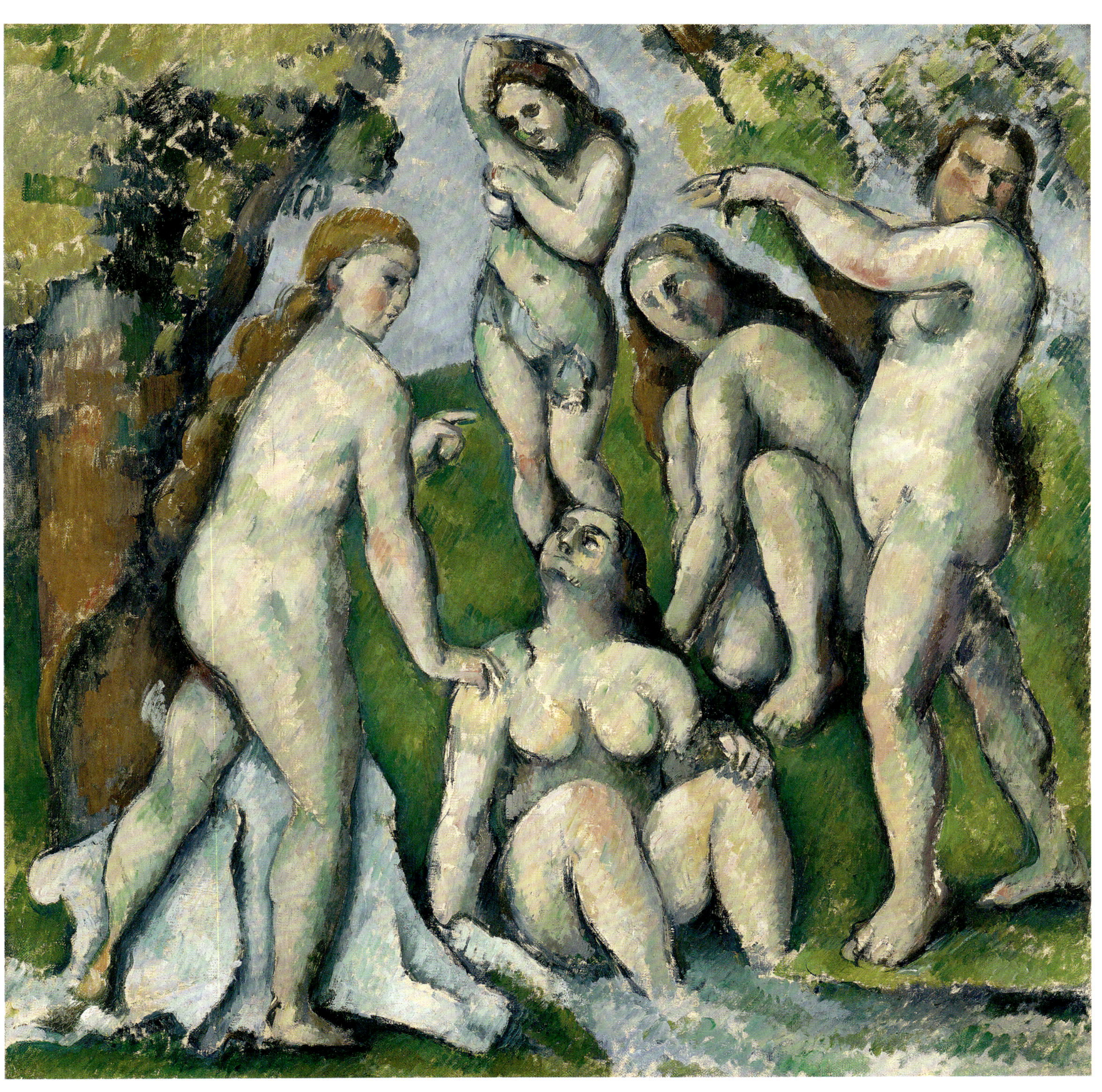

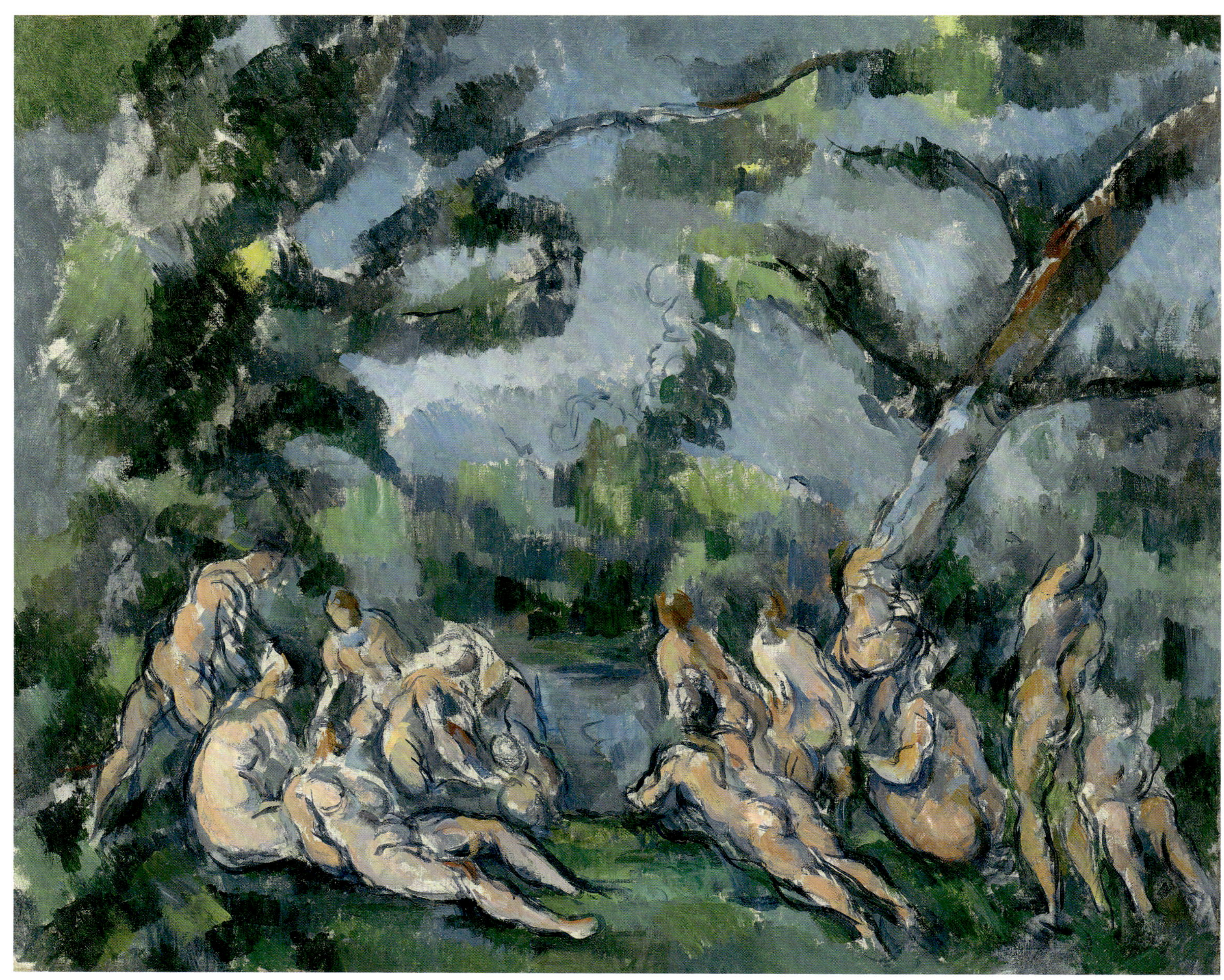

Cat. 107

The Bathers
1899–1904
Oil on canvas
51.3 × 61.7 cm (20 ³/₁₆ × 24 ¼ in.)
The Art Institute of Chicago, Amy McCormick
Memorial Collection, 1942.457
FWN 976

Between the Bathers and Us, the Living

Paul Chan

Cezanne's bathers look as if they are filled with more than what is supposed to be inside human forms, transfigured by a mysterious substance that subtly contorts and elongates their silhouettes. What's more, the trees, the river, the sky, even the dirt ground that frames the bathers are also visibly distorted, as if that same mysterious substance is exerting a field of influence that ripples through everything in the composition.

ἐνέργεια (energeia) is the term Aristotle used to describe a kind of substance living beings possess as a semblance of their "aliveness." It is energeia that empowers a being to think and move independently, or so Aristotle thought. What I like about this notion is that it binds movement with thought, which is something I intuitively understand as an artist. My interest in a work awakens when I recognize this sentiment within its composition. A genuine thought must be *moving* if it is a thought at all.

It is only very recently that I have looked to Cezanne for inspiration or solace. I was working on my own bathers and turned to him. I found his bathers full of movement, even at a standstill, and respected the economy with which he composed figures in ways that made me question whether it was the figure, the paint, or the inhabited movement that made the works memorable, even erotic.

But something entered the picture that wasn't part of the initial bargain. As I looked at Cezanne's paintings of bathers more, I noticed something obvious but noteworthy: none of them seem to be suffering, or filled with rage, or petrified with anxiety. I was looking at a group of works that portray a species of humanity I don't see much of—I mean people who are not mentally or physically afflicted with meaningless and arbitrary pain and misery from the overwhelming structural inequalities that so burden us, the living.

Cezanne's bathers seem at ease with themselves. They look pleased by simply being, enlivened by their surroundings and by each other, enjoying themselves without guilt, aggression, or fear. What I like most about looking at his bathers, especially this painting, is how they remind me of what it feels like to be renewed. Perhaps this feeling also reflects the notion that water represents a source of life, an instrument of cleansing, and a means of regeneration in virtually all cultures. Is this why I so strongly correlate the bathers motif with the notion of renewal?

It seems to me the best of pleasure renews us. And that works like this one act like reminders that pleasing and being pleased—without aggression or guilt—expands our capacity for fellow feeling. Genuine pleasure is rejuvenating, like that picture-perfect night of sleep. Pleasure can have a clarifying quality. This sense of being cleansed is stimulating and healing, insofar as it helps renew us to more ably face what the day demands.

Cat. 108

Bathers (*Les Grandes Baigneuses*)
c. 1894–1905
Oil on canvas
127.2 × 196.1 cm (50 1/16 × 77 3/16 in.)
The National Gallery, London, purchased with a
special grant and the aid of the Max Rayne Foundation,
1964, NG6359
FWN 979

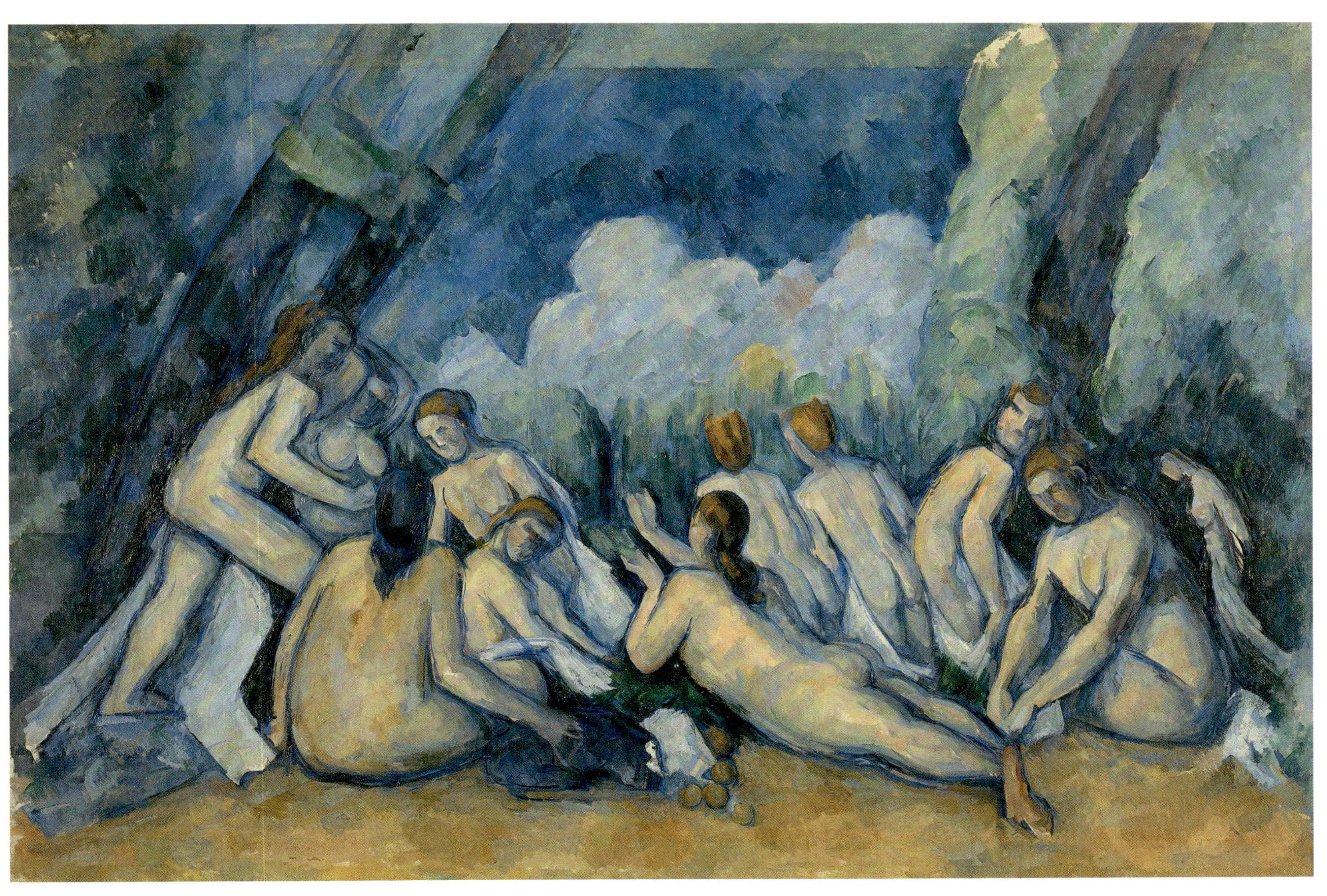

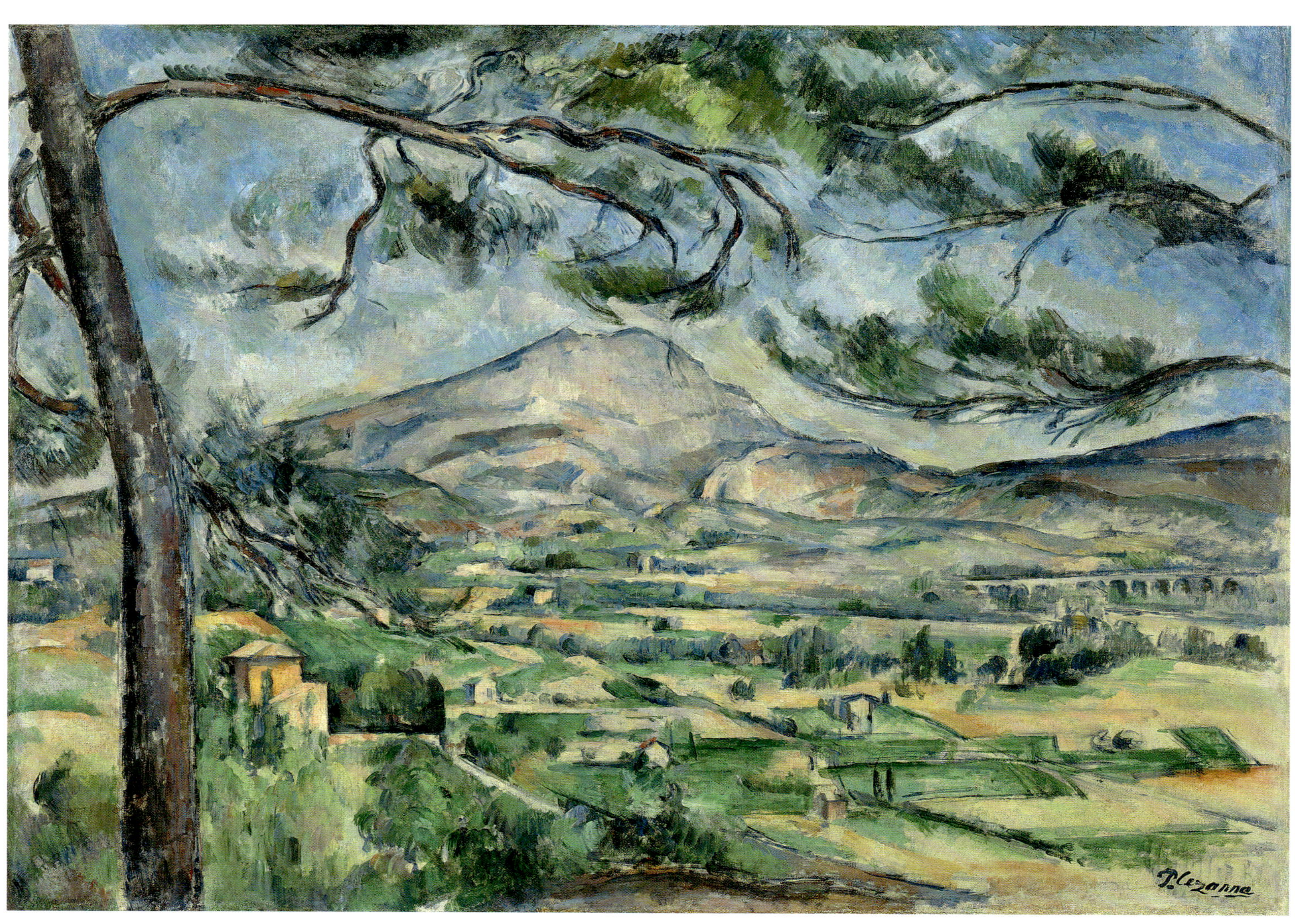

Cat. 109

Montagne Sainte-Victoire with Large Pine
c. 1887
Oil on canvas
66.8 × 92.3 cm (26 ⁵⁄₁₆ × 36 ⁵⁄₁₆ in.)
The Courtauld Gallery, London (Samuel Courtauld Trust), P.1934.SC.55
FWN 235
Chicago only

Cat. 110

Mont Sainte-Victoire
1886–87
Oil on canvas
59.7 × 72.4 cm (23 ½ × 28 ½ in.)
The Phillips Collection, Washington, DC, Acquired 1925, 0285
FWN 234

Cat. 111

Montagne Sainte-Victoire (The Arc Valley)
c. 1885
Watercolor, over graphite, heightened with white gouache, on buff wove paper
35.4 × 53.7 cm (13 ¹⁵⁄₁₆ × 21 ⅛ in.)
The Art Institute of Chicago, gift of Marshall Field, IV, 1964.199
FWN 1130
Chicago only

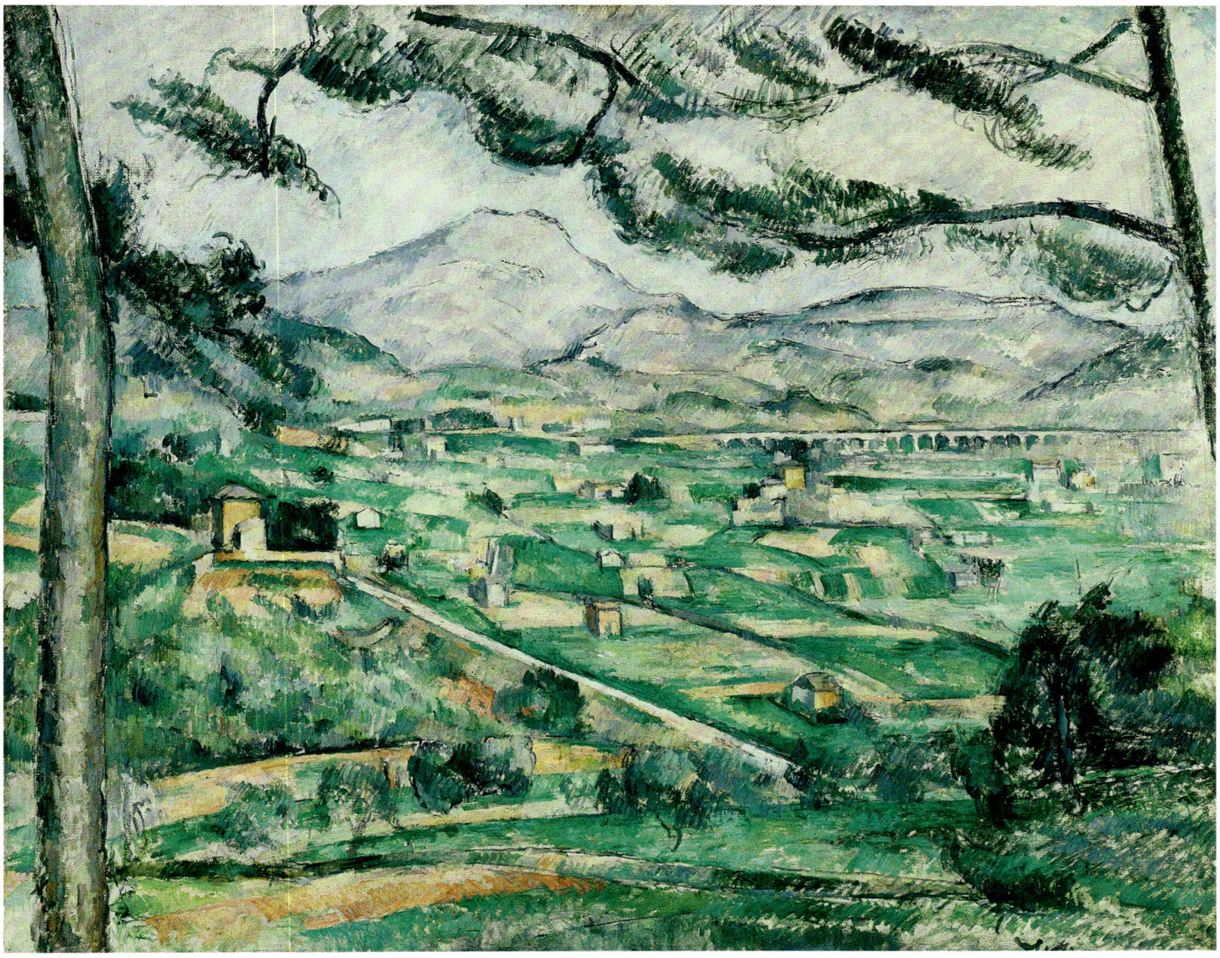

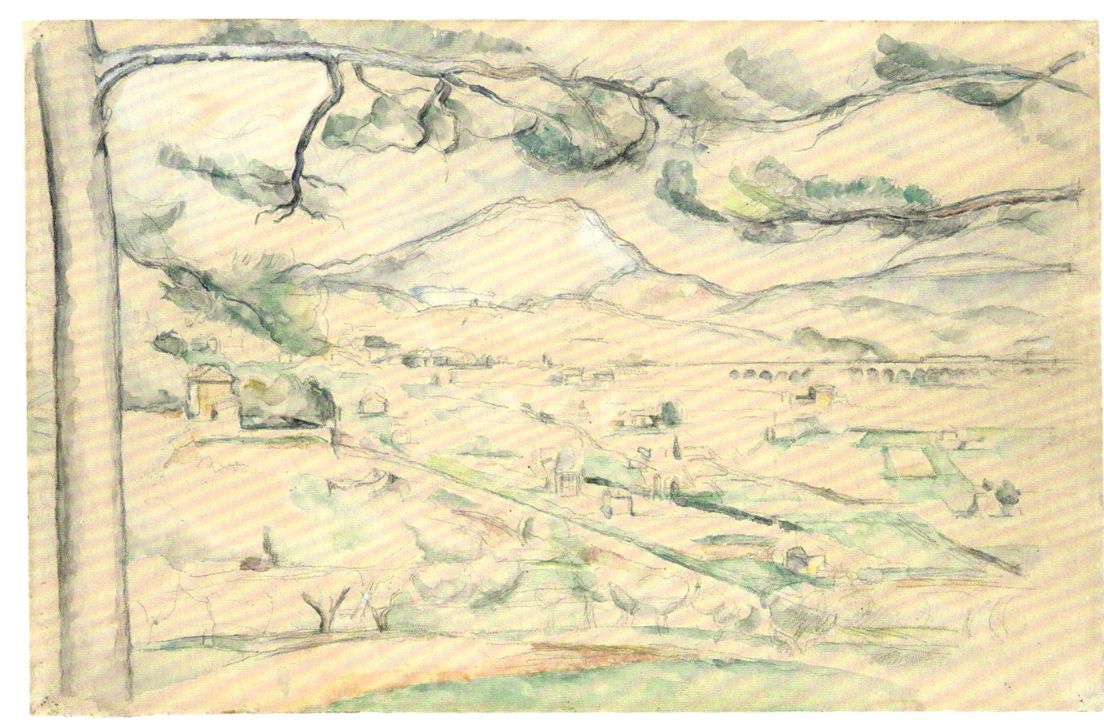

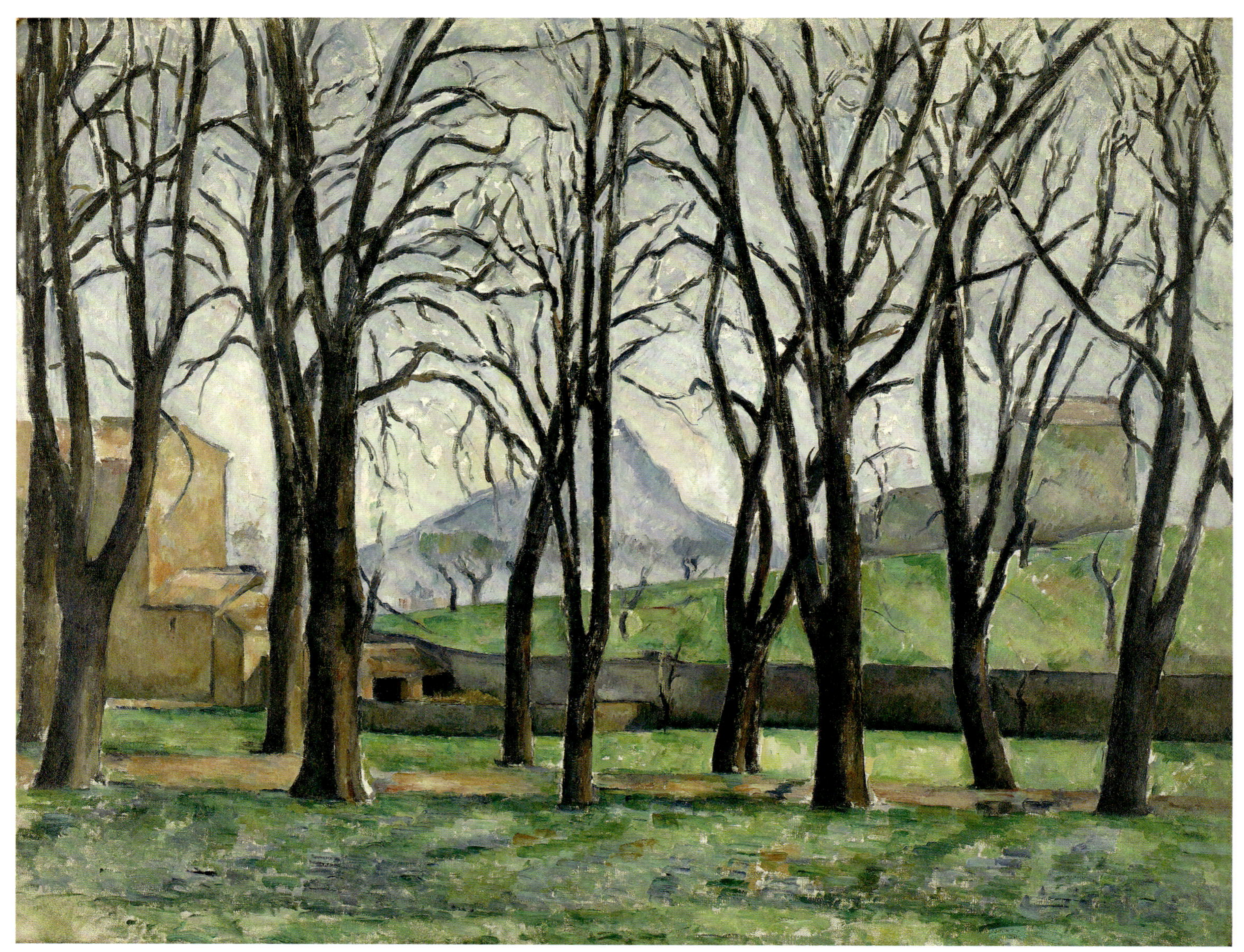

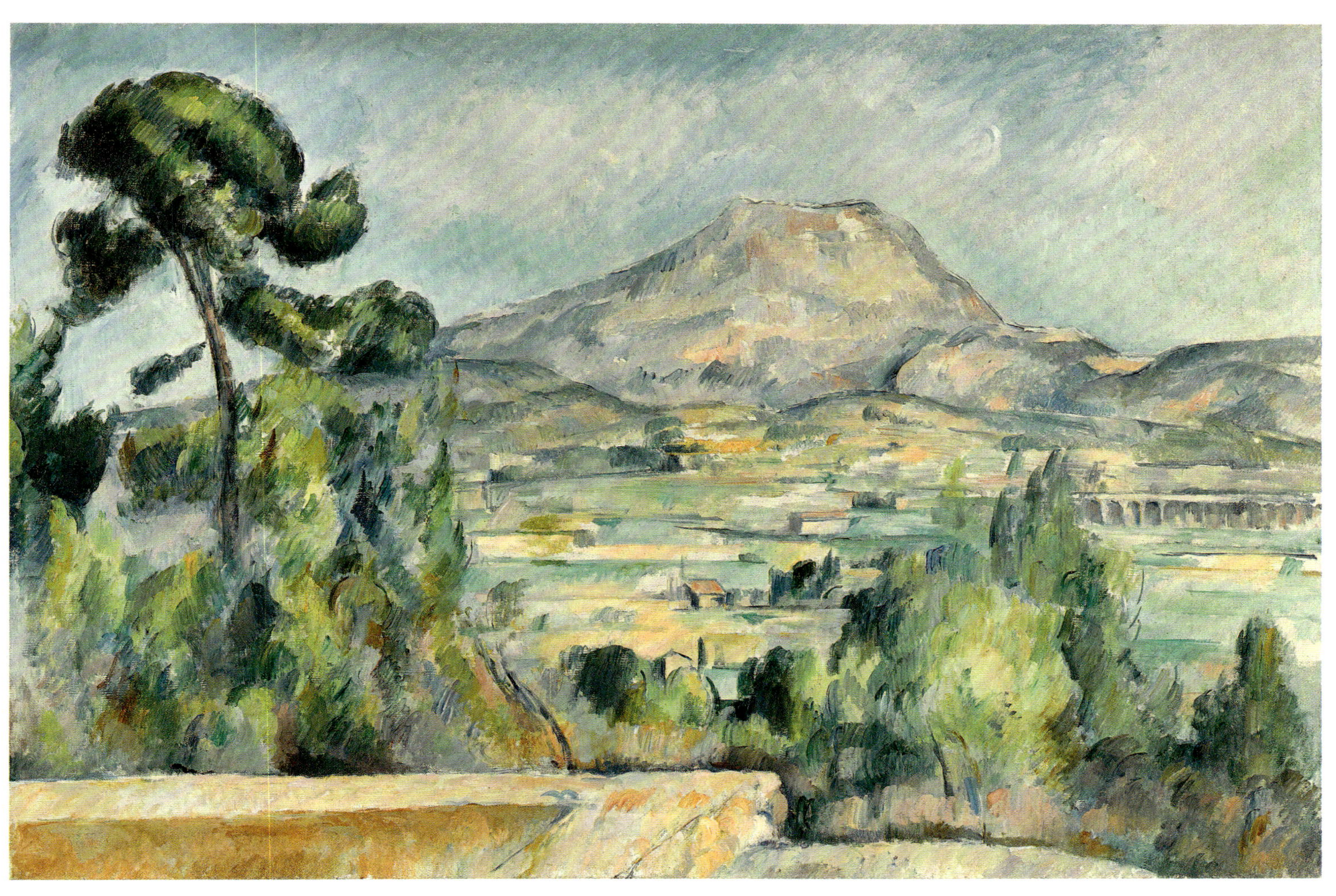

Cat. 112

Chestnut Trees at the Jas de Bouffan
c. 1885–86
Oil on canvas
71.1 × 90.2 cm (28 × 35 ½ in.)
Lent by the Minneapolis Institute of Art, The William
Hood Dunwoody Fund, 49.9
FWN 216

Cat. 113

Montagne Sainte-Victoire
c. 1890
Oil on canvas
65 × 92 cm (25 ⁹⁄₁₆ × 36 ¼ in.)
Musée d'Orsay, Paris, donation de la petite-fille
d'Auguste Pellerin, 1969, RF 1969 30
FWN 273

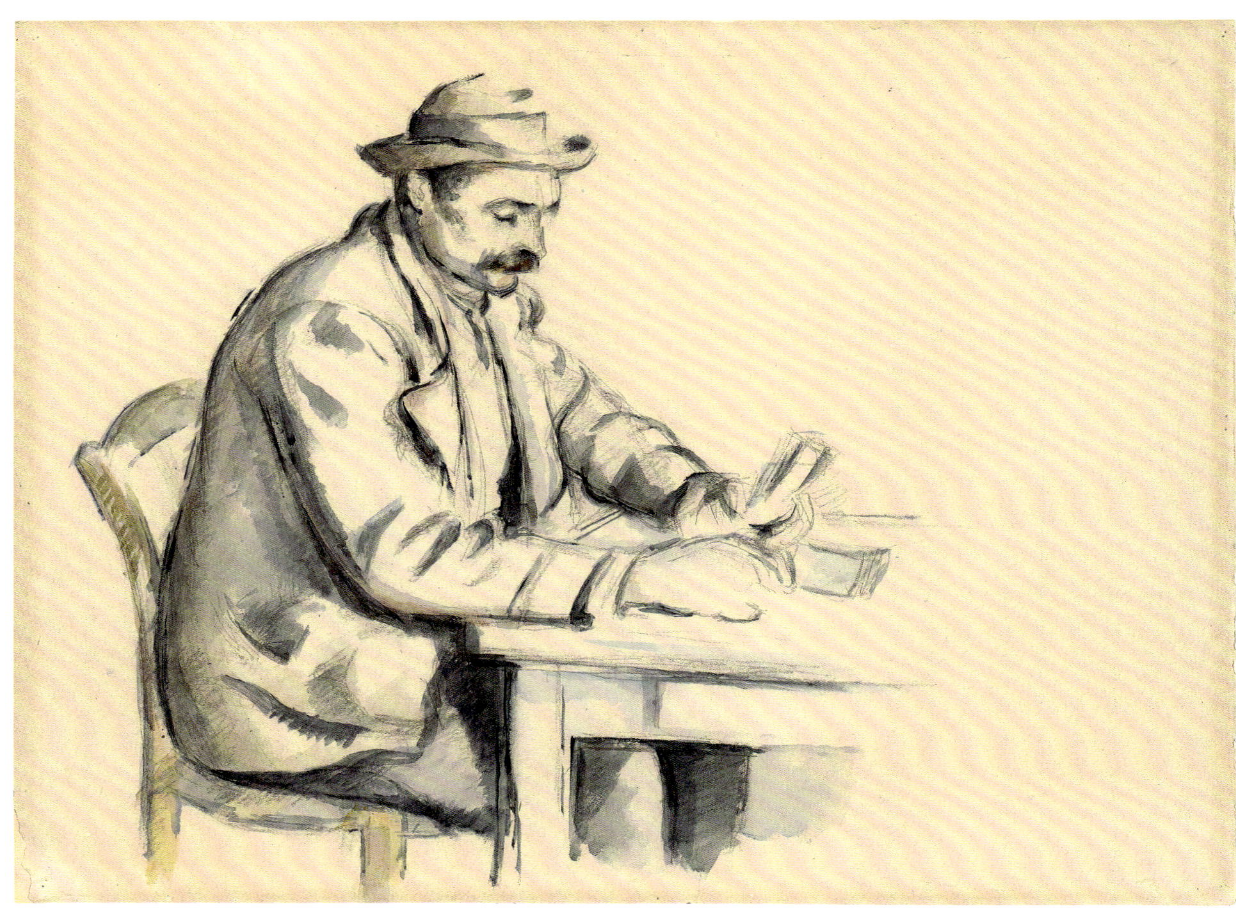

Cat. 114

A Study for the Card Players
1890–92
Watercolor on paper
36.2 × 48.5 cm (14 1/4 × 19 1/16 in.)
Anonymous loan
FWN 1760
Chicago only

Cat. 115

The Smoker
1890
Oil on canvas
92.5 × 73.5 cm (36 7/16 × 28 15/16 in.)
Kunsthalle Mannheim, Germany, acquired 1912,
inv. M303
FWN 505
Chicago only

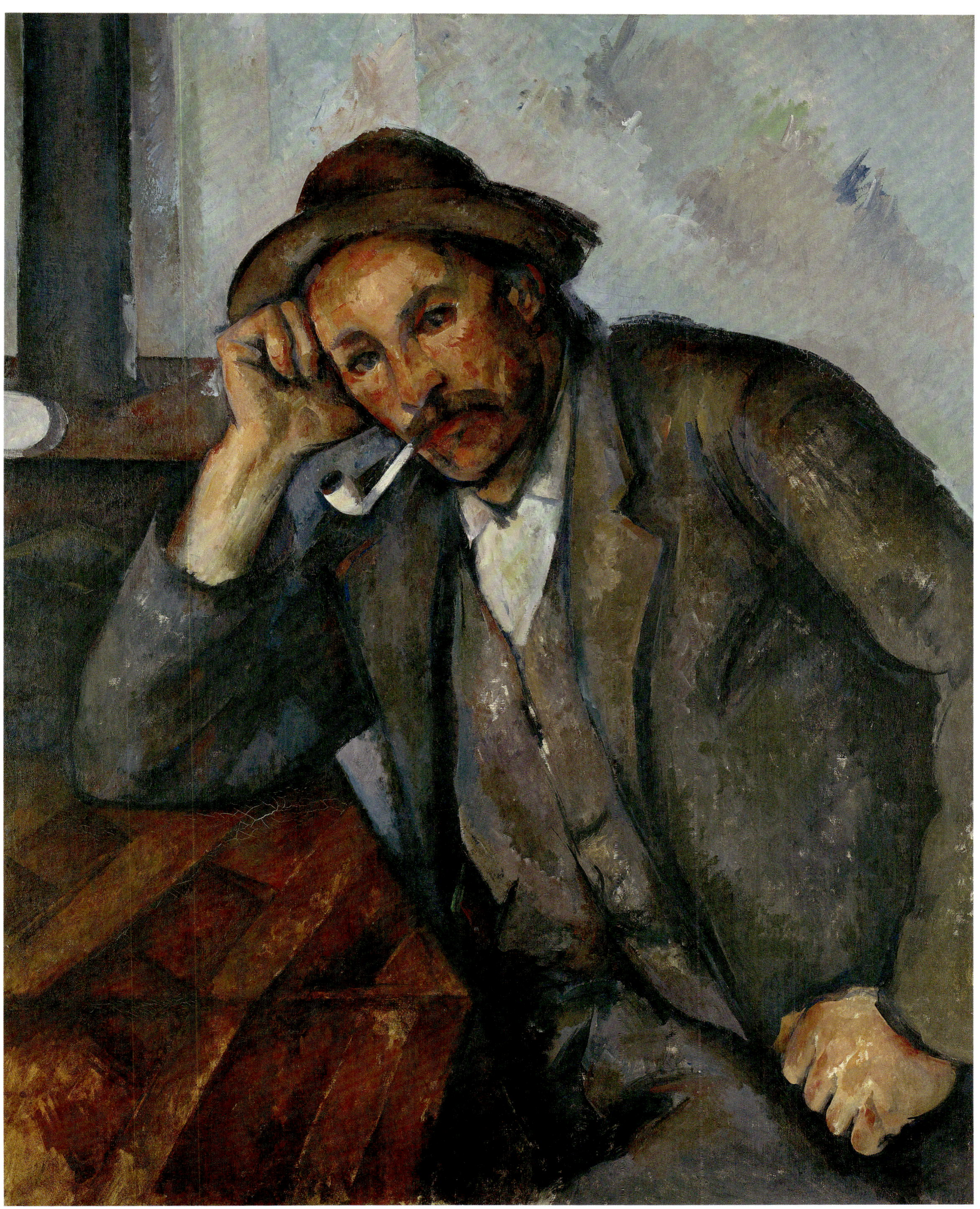

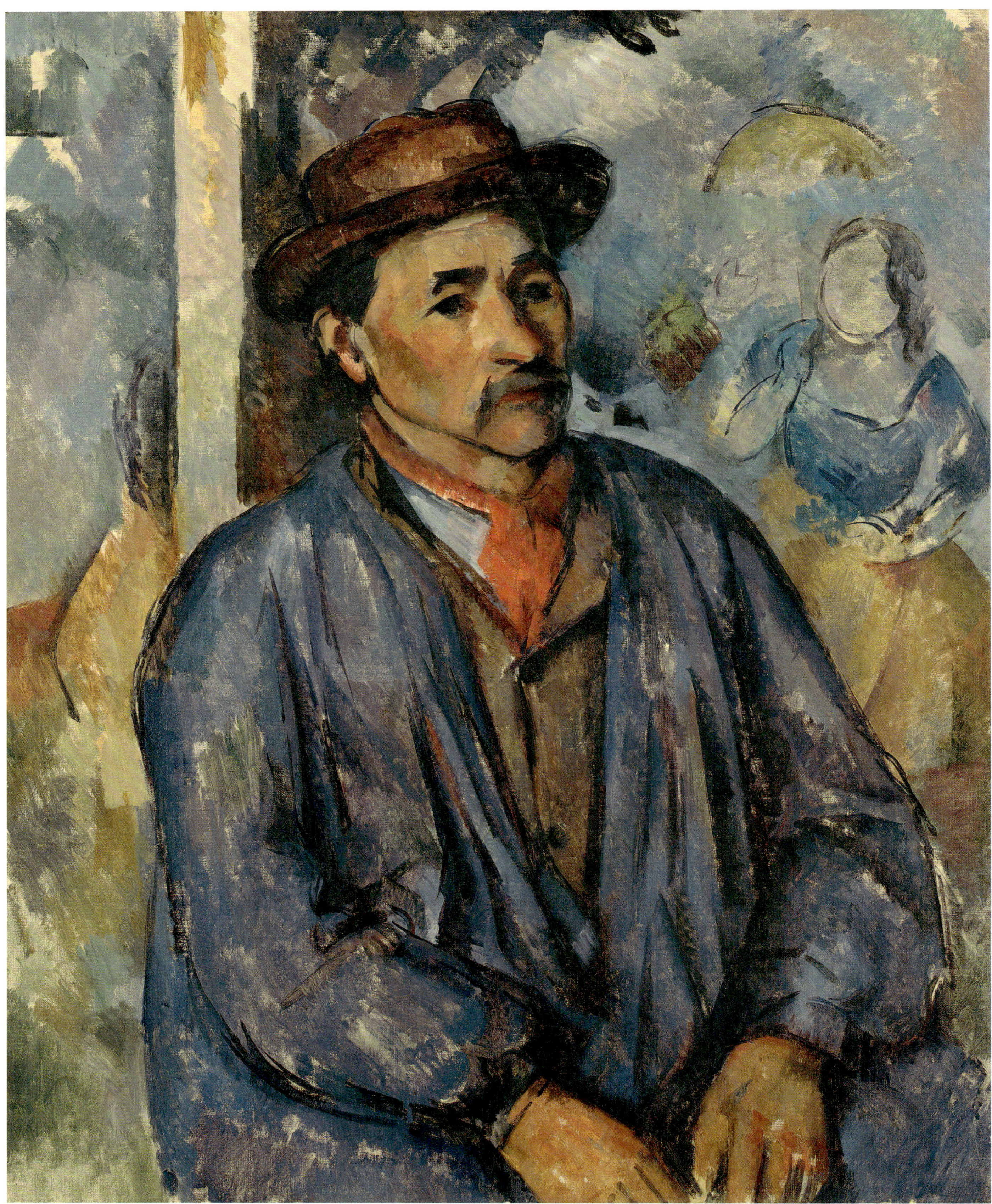

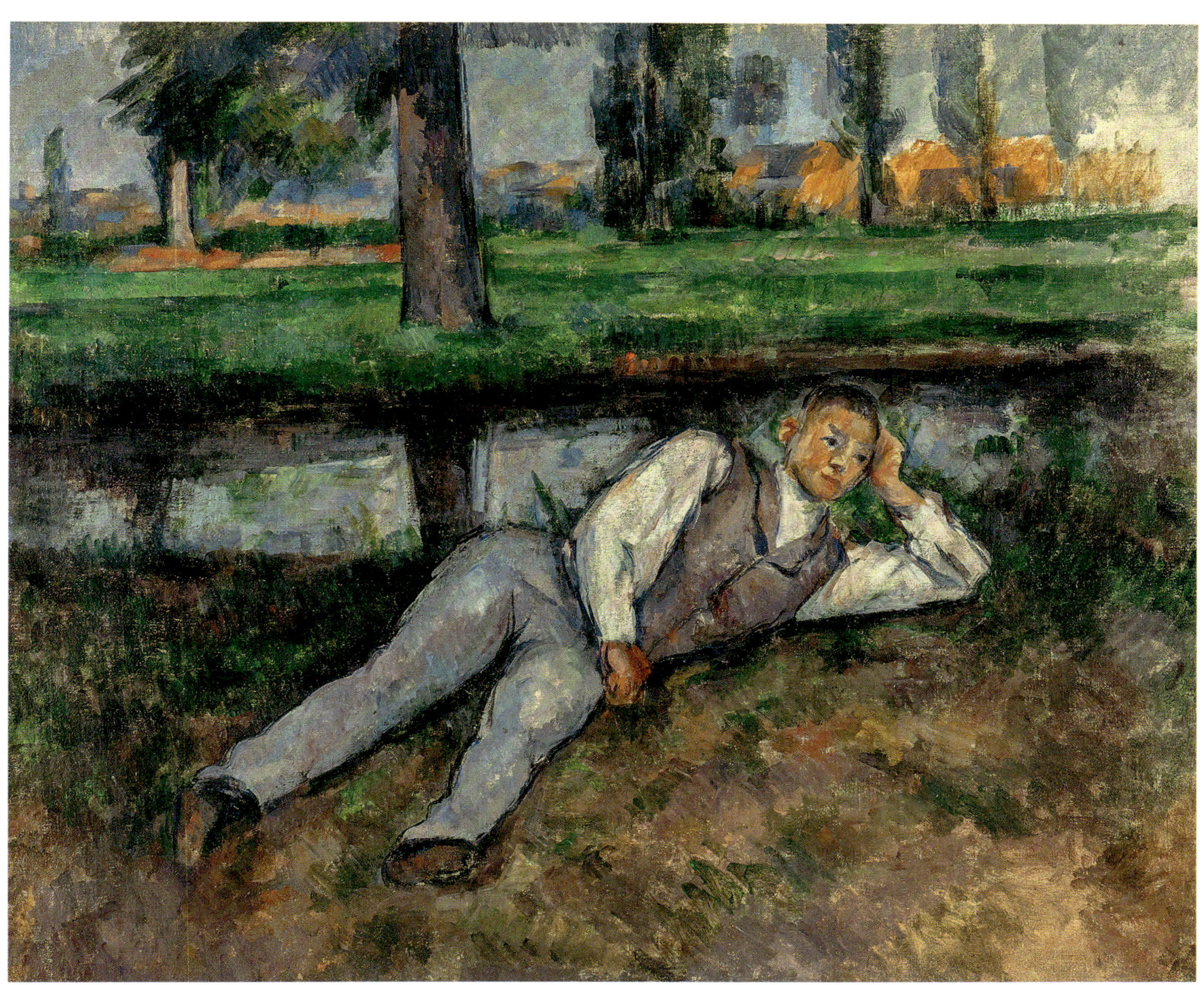

Cat. 116

Man in a Blue Smock
c. 1896–97
Oil on canvas
81.5 × 64.8 cm (32 1/16 × 25 1/2 in.)
Kimbell Art Museum, Fort Worth, Texas,
acquired in 1980 and dedicated to the memory
of Richard F. Brown, 1980.03
FWN 524

Cat. 117

Boy Resting
c. 1890
Oil on canvas
54 × 65.3 cm (21 1/4 × 25 13/16 in.)
Hammer Museum, Los Angeles, The Armand
Hammer Collection, Gift of the Armand Hammer
Foundation, AH.90.11
FWN 674

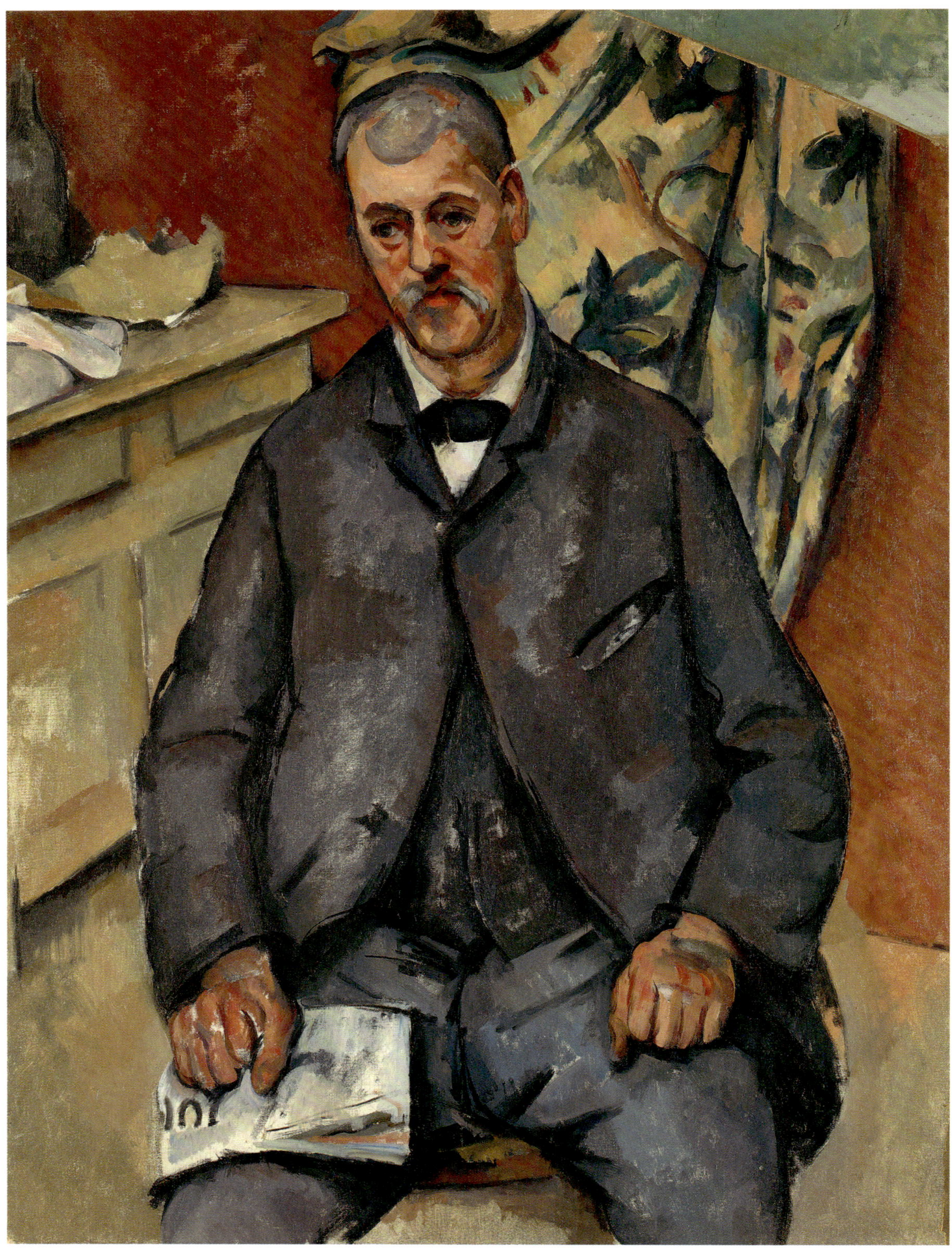

Cat. 118

Seated Man
c. 1889
Oil on canvas
102.5 × 76 cm (40 ⅜ × 29 ¹⁵⁄₁₆ in.)
The National Museum of Art, Architecture and Design,
Oslo, Gift from the Friends of the National Gallery
1918, NG.M.01287
FWN 530
Chicago only

Cat. 119

Man with Crossed Arms
c. 1899
Oil on canvas
92 × 72.7 cm (36 ¼ × 28 ⅝ in.)
Solomon R. Guggenheim Museum, New York,
54.1387
FWN 528
Chicago only

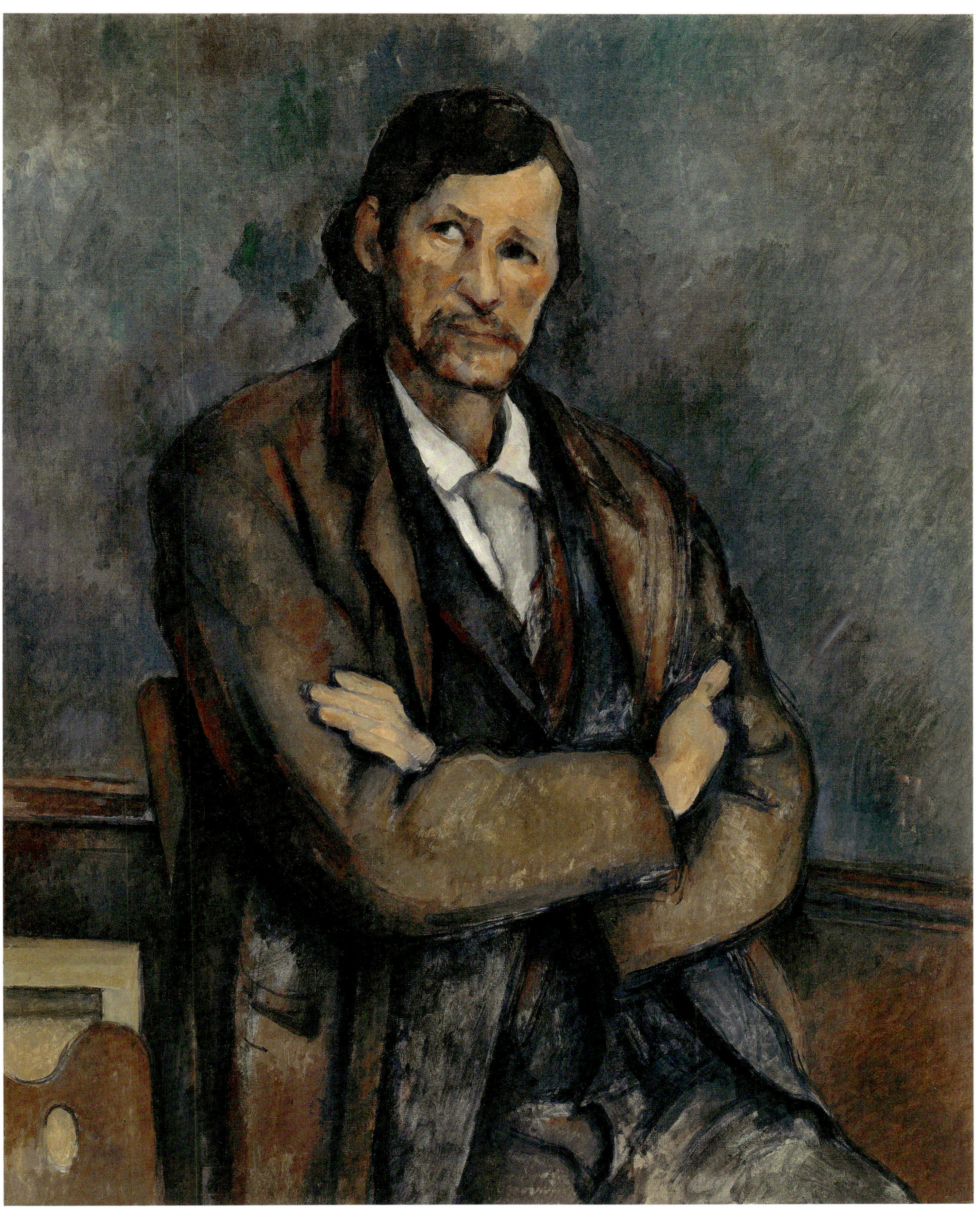

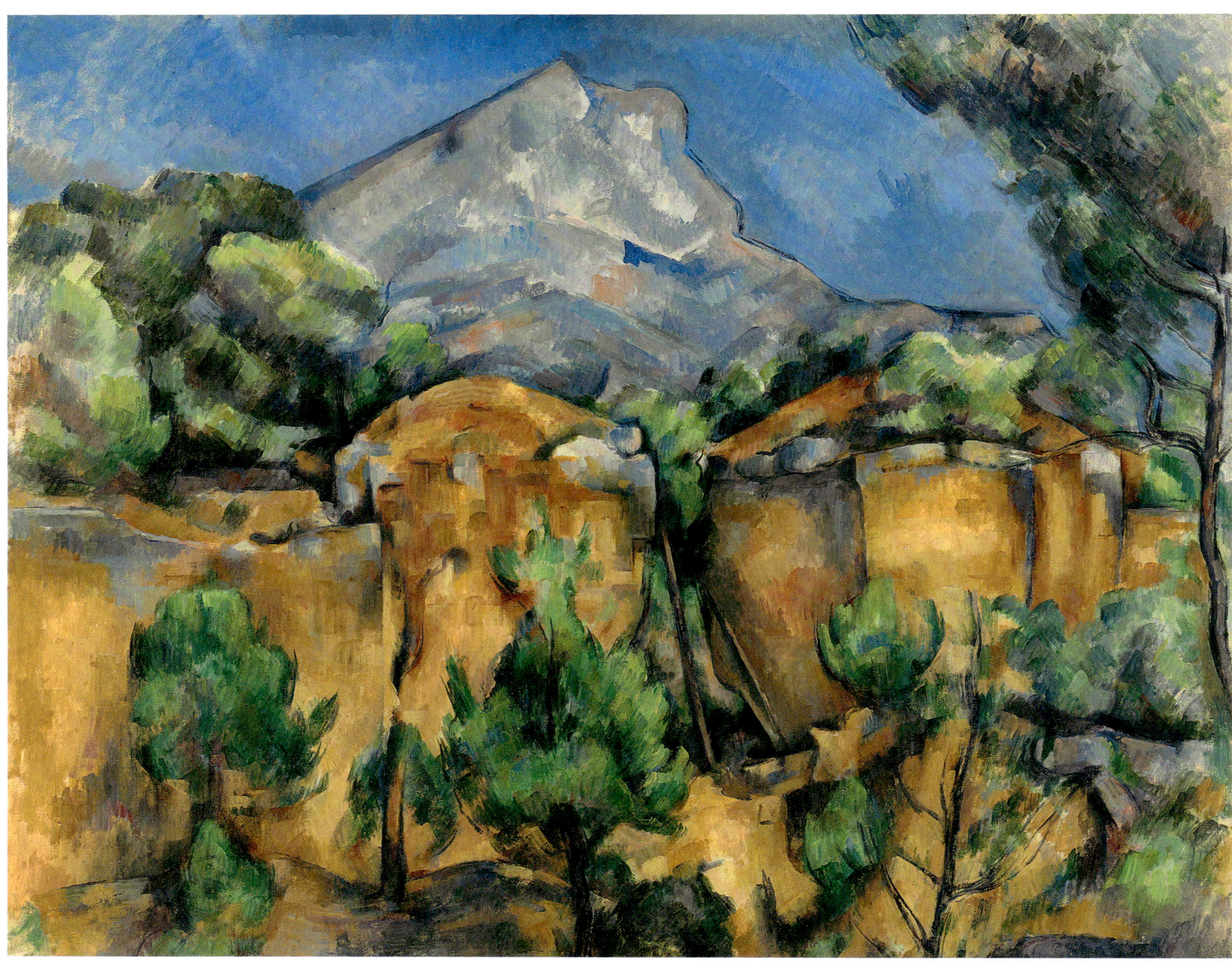

Cat. 120

**Mont Sainte-Victoire Seen from the
Bibémus Quarry**
c. 1895–99
Oil on canvas
65.1 × 81.3 cm (25 ⅝ × 32 in.)
The Baltimore Museum of Art: The Cone Collection,
formed by Dr. Claribel Cone and Miss Etta Cone of
Baltimore, Maryland, BMA 1950.196
FWN 315

Cat. 121

Mont Sainte-Victoire
c. 1904
Oil on fabric
72.2 × 92.4 cm (28 ⁷⁄₁₆ × 36 ⅜ in.)
The Cleveland Museum of Art, Bequest of Leonard C.
Hanna, Jr., 1958.21
FWN 350

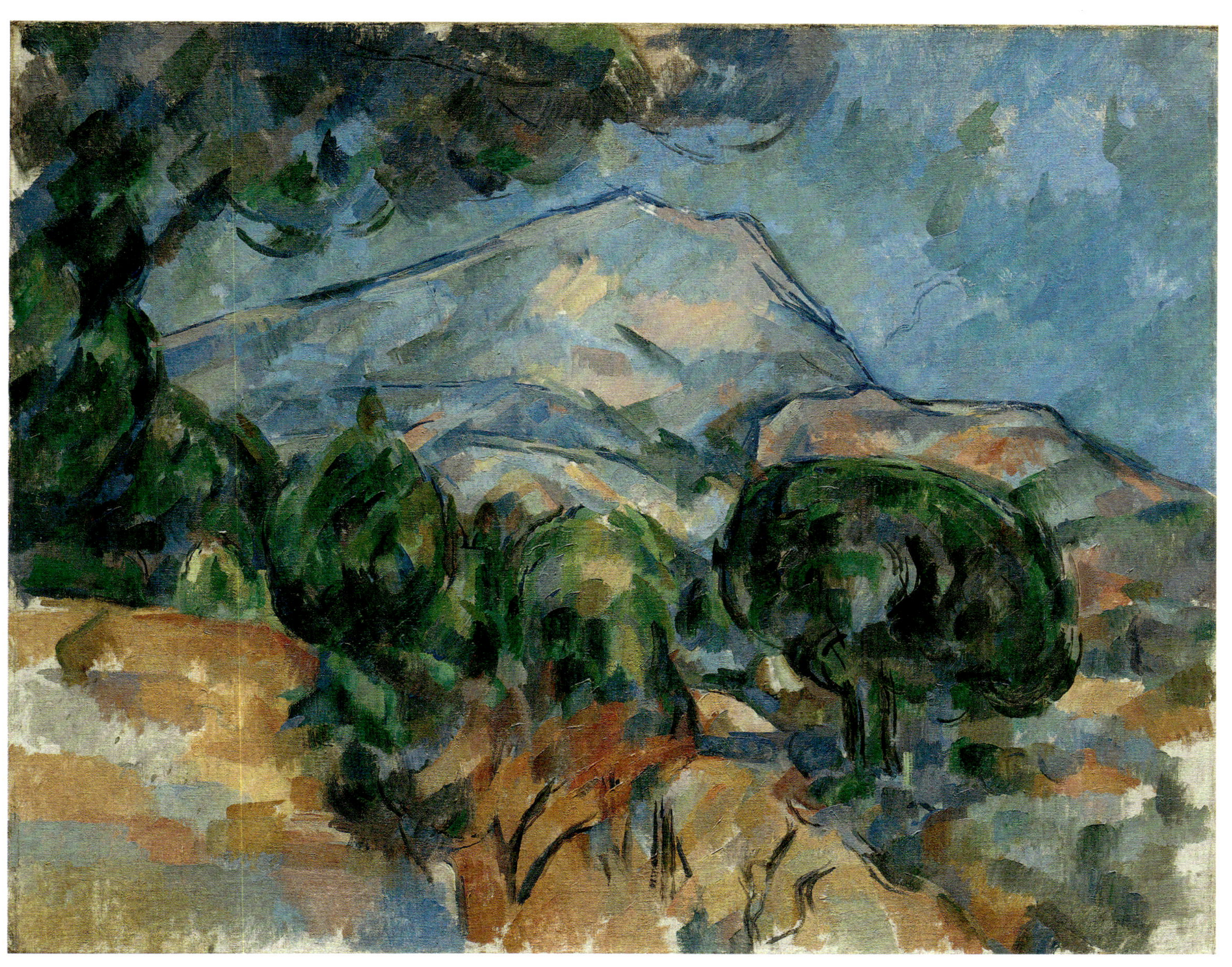

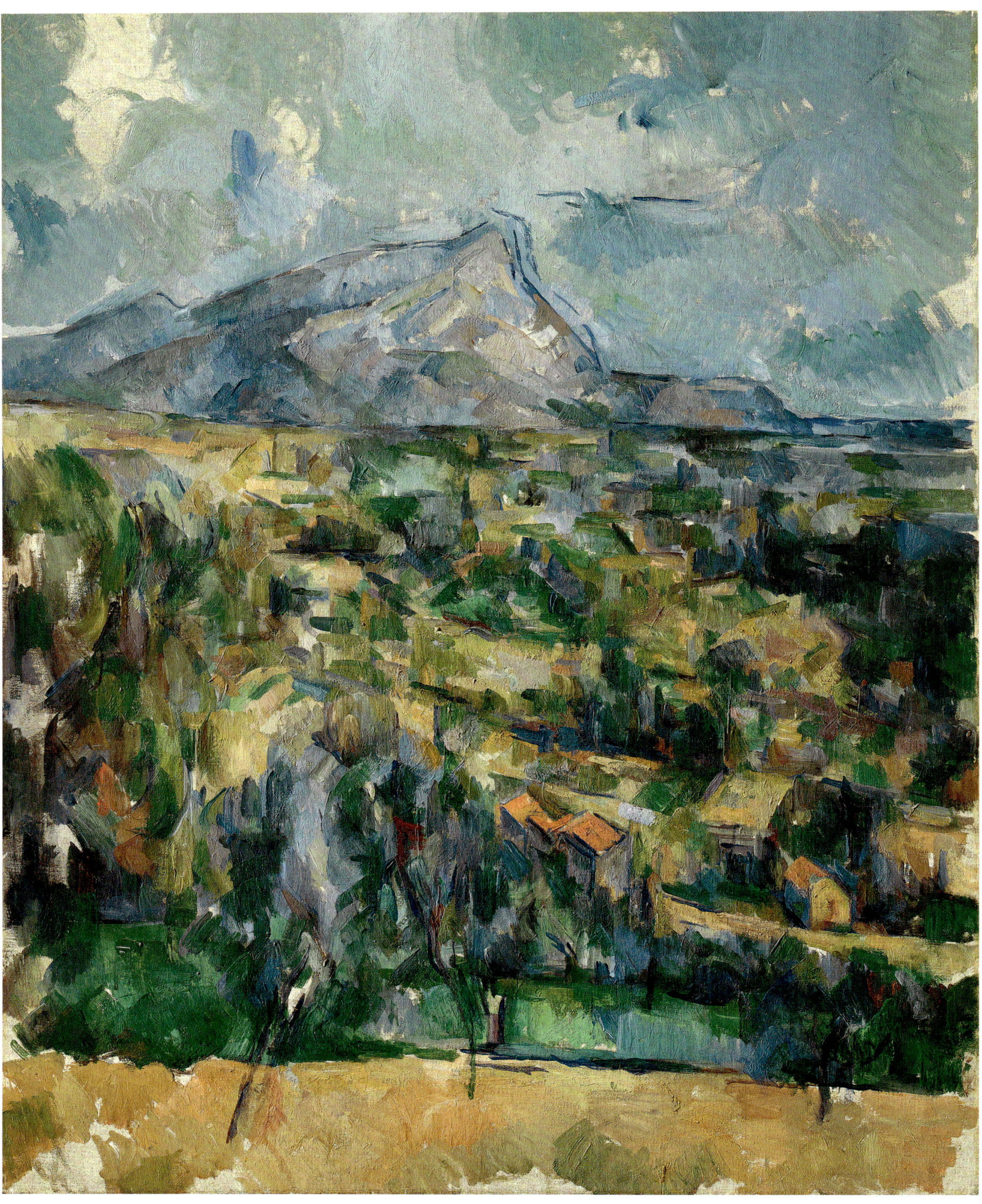

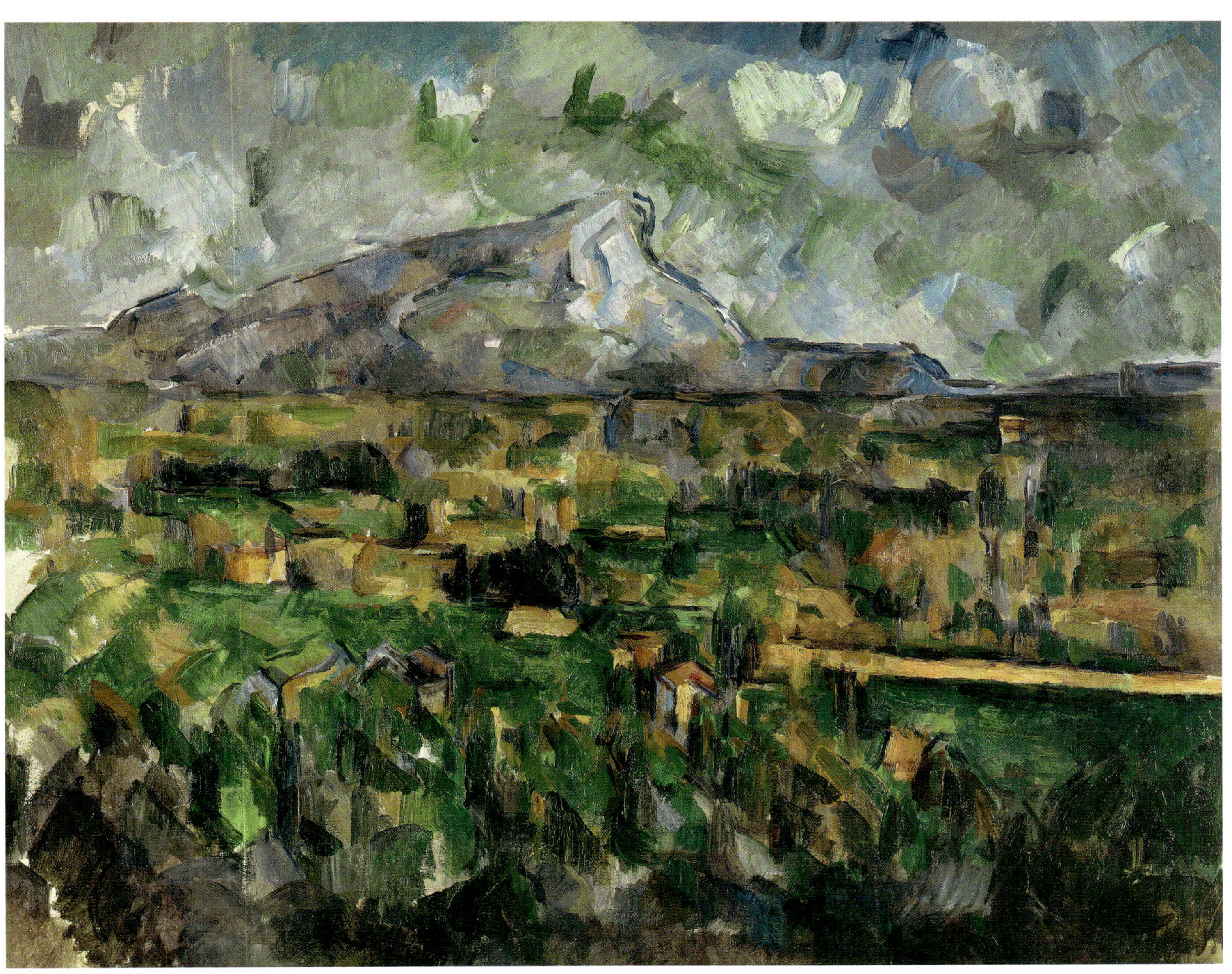

Cat. 122

Mont Sainte-Victoire
c. 1904–6
Oil on canvas
83.8 × 65 cm (33 × 25 ⅝ in.)
The Henry and Rose Pearlman Foundation on loan
to the Princeton University Art Museum, Princeton,
New Jersey, L.1988.62.5
FWN 355
Chicago only

Cat. 123

Mont Sainte-Victoire
1902–6
Oil on canvas
64.8 × 81.3 cm (25 ½ × 32 in.)
Philadelphia Museum of Art, Gift of Helen Tyson
Madeira, 1977, 1977-288-1
FWN 352

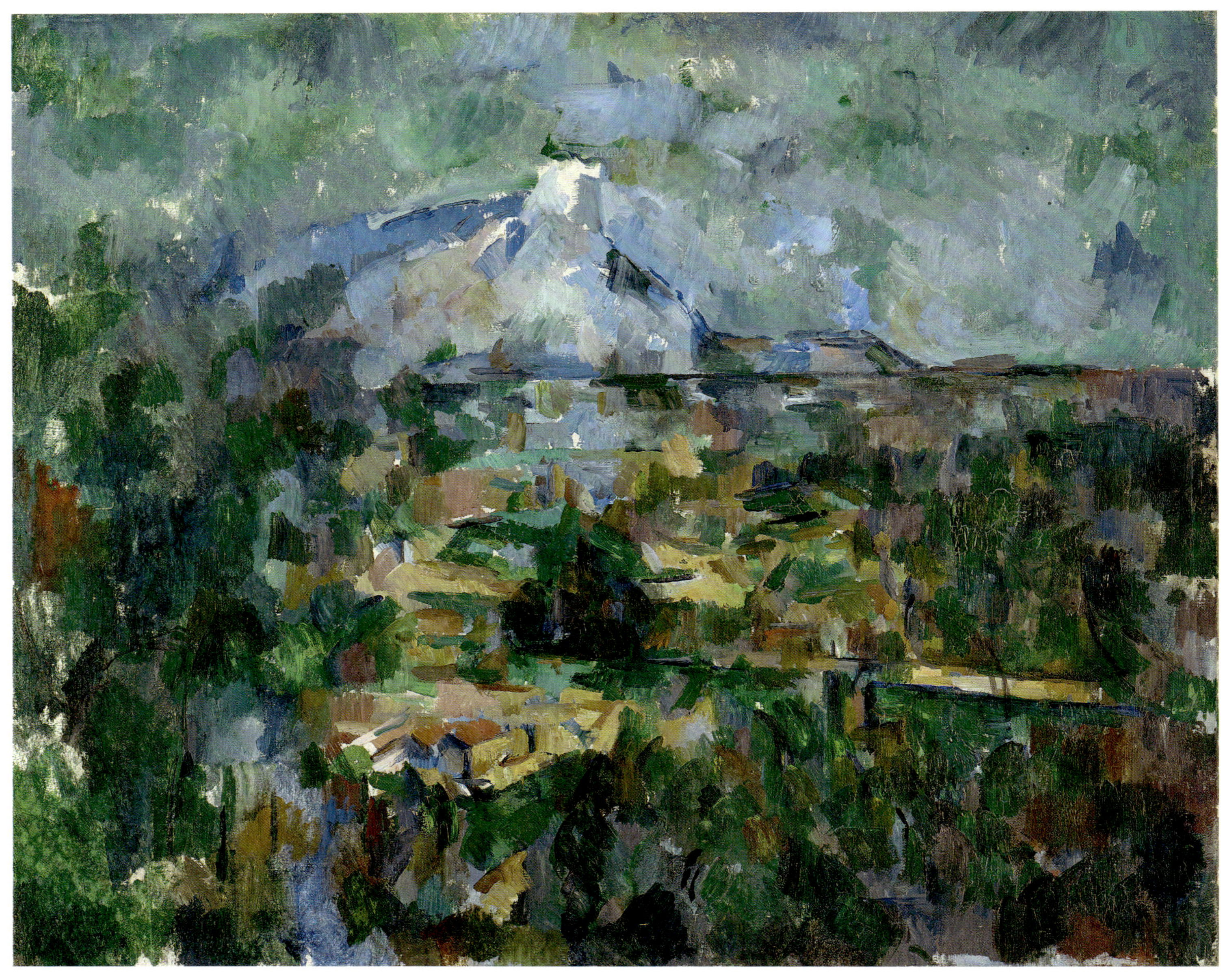

Cat. 124

Mont Sainte-Victoire Seen from Les Lauves
1904–6
Oil on canvas
59.9 × 72.2 cm (23 9/16 × 28 7/16 in.)
Kunstmuseum Basel, mit Beiträgen der Regierung des
Kantons Basel-Stadt, des Erziehungsdepartements
Basel-Stadt, der Firma CIBA AG, der Firma J. R. Geigy
AG, der Firma Sandoz AG und aus dem Meisterwerk-
Fonds erworben, 1955, inv. G 1955.12
FWN 367

Cat. 125

Mont Sainte-Victoire
1904–6
Oil on canvas
55.6 × 46 cm (21 7/8 × 18 1/8 in.)
Detroit Institute of Arts, Bequest of Robert H. Tannahill,
70.151
FWN 363

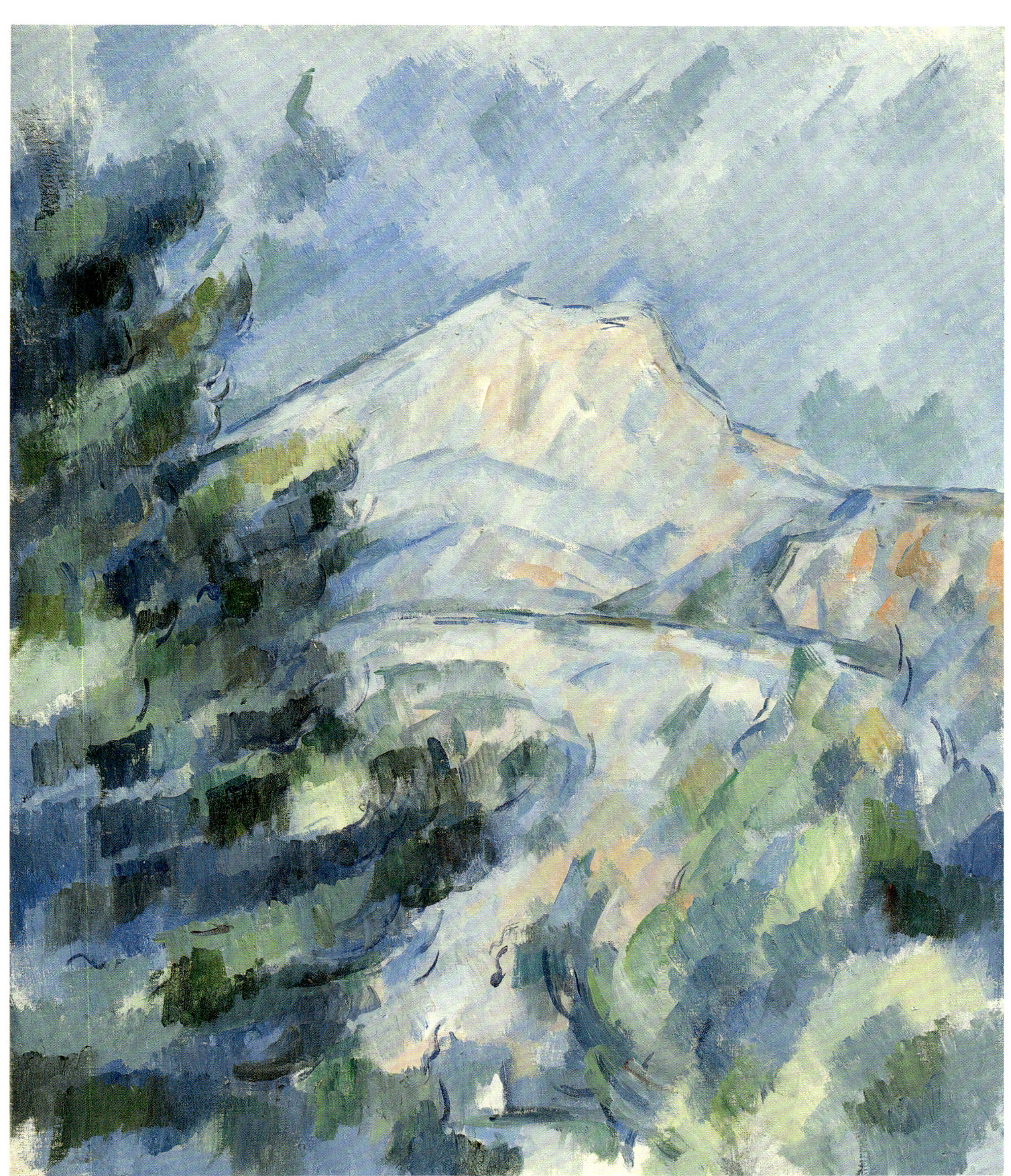

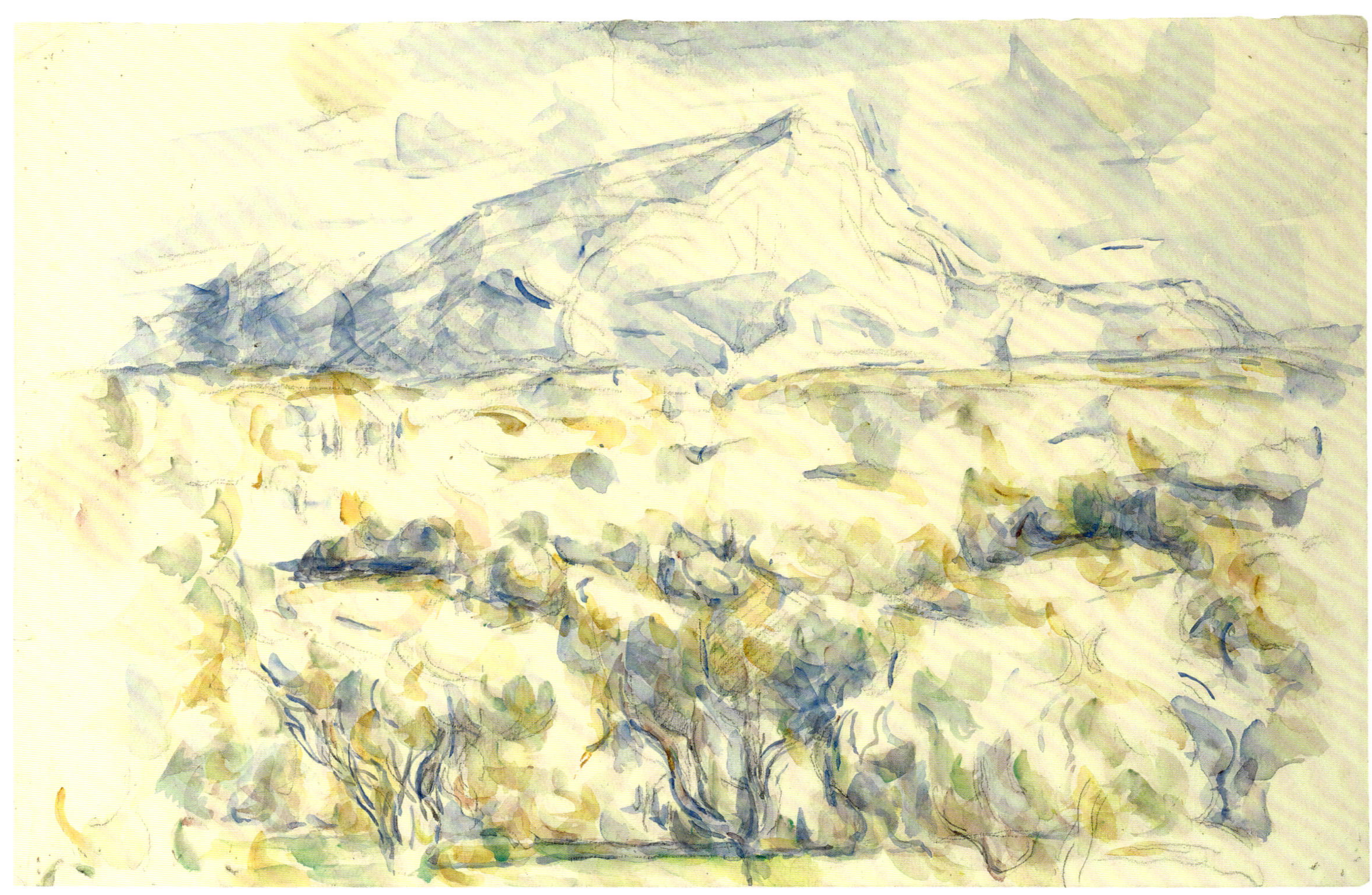

Cat. 126

Montagne Sainte-Victoire
1905-6
Watercolor on paper
36.2 × 54.9 cm (14 1/4 × 21 5/8 in.)
Tate, London, Bequeathed by Sir Hugh Walpole 1941,
N05303
FWN 1496

Then and Now

Phyllida Barlow

Then

"How old are you?"
"I'm five."
"Why do you still put the sky along the
    top of the paper?"
"Because it's up there above us."
"But look out of the window."
"You see those houses over there?"
"Yes."
"Well, can you see the sky comes right
    down to the roofs and all around
    those houses?"
"I'm painting a picture about being under
    the sky, not over there."
"But your sun isn't fitting into your strip
    of blue sky,
nor is the airplane, or the bird.
You're having to squeeze them into the
    strip of blue when you don't have to
because the sky comes down to the
    ground and everything can fit into it."
"No, it doesn't come down to the ground,
it's above us. I can make my sky a bit
    wider so the things can fit into it.
I don't want it to come down to the
    ground."
"Well now, what's between the yellow
    sand and green grass
at the bottom of your picture and the
    strip of blue sky at the top?
"That's air. The paper is air."

Now

This is not what I wanted—
looking at a screen,
looking at *Montagne Sainte-Victoire*,
    1905–6, on a screen,
or is it through a screen?
the reality of the object itself, removed,
shielded by the toxic backlight of a
    laptop screen,
glamorizing what doesn't have to be
    glamorized,
removing the materiality and physicality
    of paper, pencil, and watercolor;

but this is COVID time:
multiple realities and multiple virtual
    imposters have become fused;
have the real and the unreal become one
    and the same?
just as suspension of belief and suspen-
    sion of disbelief
can be one and the same.

Then

I recall my first experience
of looking at Cezanne's *Montagne
    Sainte-Victoire*,
when I was a student at Chelsea School
    of Art:

it was 1961 and at the Tate Gallery, now
    Tate Britain,
following a tutorial from Michael
    Andrews:
"line is a human invention—there are no
    lines in nature, or anywhere;
go and look at Cezanne's watercolor at
    the Tate, *Montagne Sainte-Victoire*,
and look at how little there is—the
    economy of color, line, space,
and where an empty space is in fact full."
and I have been back to look at
    Montagne Sainte-Victoire,
each time a shock,
comparable to listening to Beethoven's
    Opus 133,
or being caught in extreme weather—
    wind, rain, snow, things that
    disappear,
where remembering fails
the sentience of the experience.

Now

What is it that I am looking at?
and whilst I have to make do with this
    screen image,
it is essential to recall being there;

now I read the image as a script,
left to right,
and I do not see a landscape;
I am watching a sequence of translucent
    blues,
under and over yellows and greens, and
    faint pencil marks,
the lightest of touches,
tracing themselves across a surface
that rhythmically exposes itself
as the raw, buff color, unadorned,
    untouched paper;

what reality is this?
is this reveal of the paper just
    that—paper?
because that is not how it functions;
nor is it pretense—

an exposure of a surface to be something
    else,
maybe to masquerade as mist, cloud,
    snow—
to be a simile for something nameable;

no, this exposure of the intervals of the
    bare flesh of the paper,
which the sparse traces of exact and
    precise
actions of paint cancel out,
are a reality in their own right,
reciprocating the reality of the painterly
    gestures
and, eventually, the image;

how to account for these two realities:
paper and paint?
each one offers the substance that it is
but also what they become: an emerging
    presence of a place;
shouldn't these irrefutable realities of
    bare paper and translucent paint
challenge this becoming,
threatening this record of a place, a time,
    a mood,
and the irrefutable sense of being there
by the realities of their substance?

and it is the bare paper that asks the
    questions:
are these bare paper intervals
    transformed?
if so, what are they transformed into?
or are they experienced as unfinished?

which reality does the exposed paper
    claim?
is it to jolt the reality of the image
back to the reality of the materiality and
    physicality of paint and paper—
to momentarily suspend this sublime
    vision of a landscape?

and how to mentally and visually
    traverse
the potential conflicts between
painted and unpainted surfaces,
seamlessly unified as one totality;
and where the unpainted surfaces are
    anything but unpainted—
offering rich forms in perfect harmony

with the simple translucent strokes of
    blues, yellows, and greens
that encompass them;

the exposed paper intervals are voids to
    be absorbed into,
bottomless chasms and dynamic pauses,
contained vacuums and loud silences
that traverse the painterly score
as potently and as necessarily as the rest
    bars in music;
places where the acts of looking and
    seeing
are slowed down and paused;

tangible, desirous, dangerous,
calm, timeless, still,
the exposed paper refuses definition and
    rebukes language
but embraces the ambiguities of antici-
    pation and namelessness;

I might ask, "what is there?"
but there is no reply.

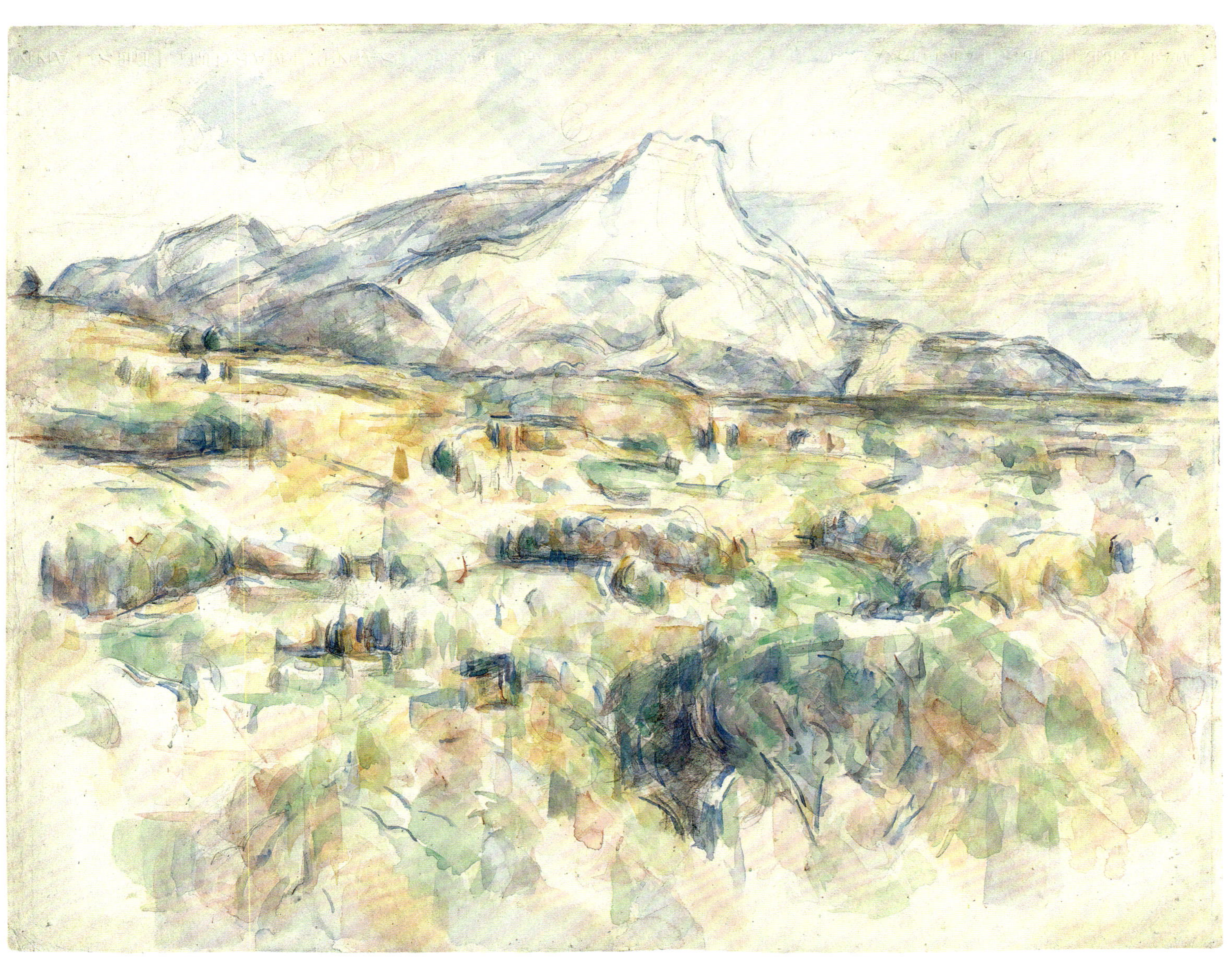

Cat. 127

Mont Sainte-Victoire
1902–6
Watercolor and pencil on paper
42.5 × 54.2 cm (16 ¾ × 21 ⅜ in.)
The Museum of Modern Art, New York, Gift of Mr. and
Mrs. David Rockefeller, 114.1962
FWN 1504
Chicago only

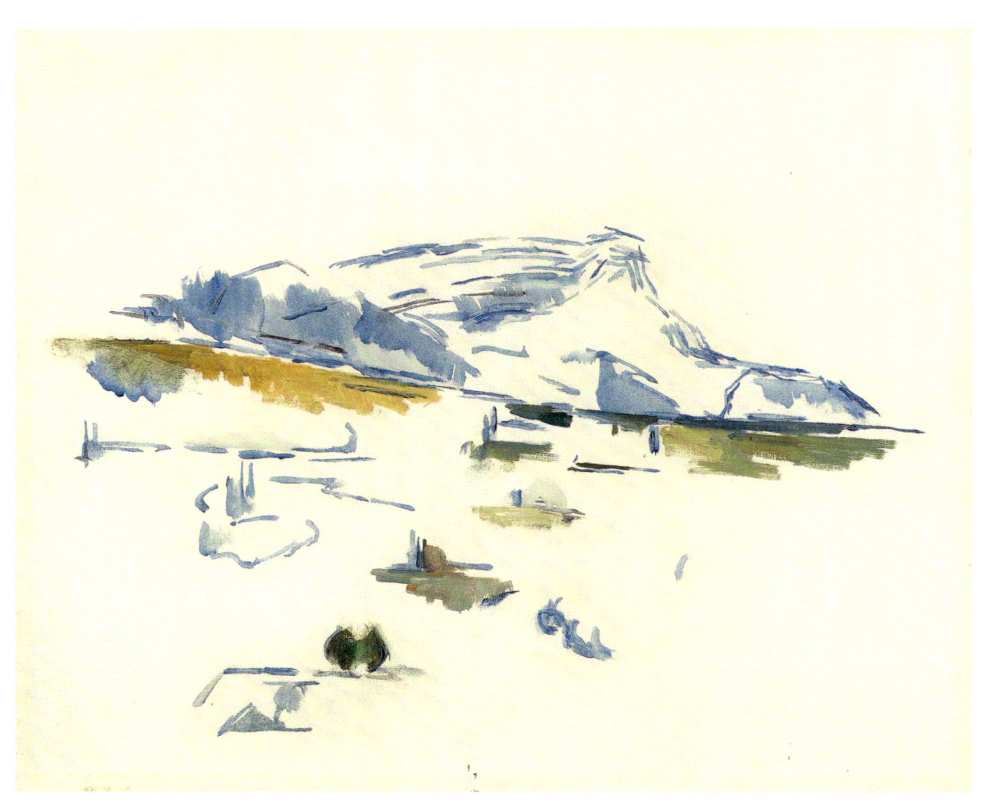

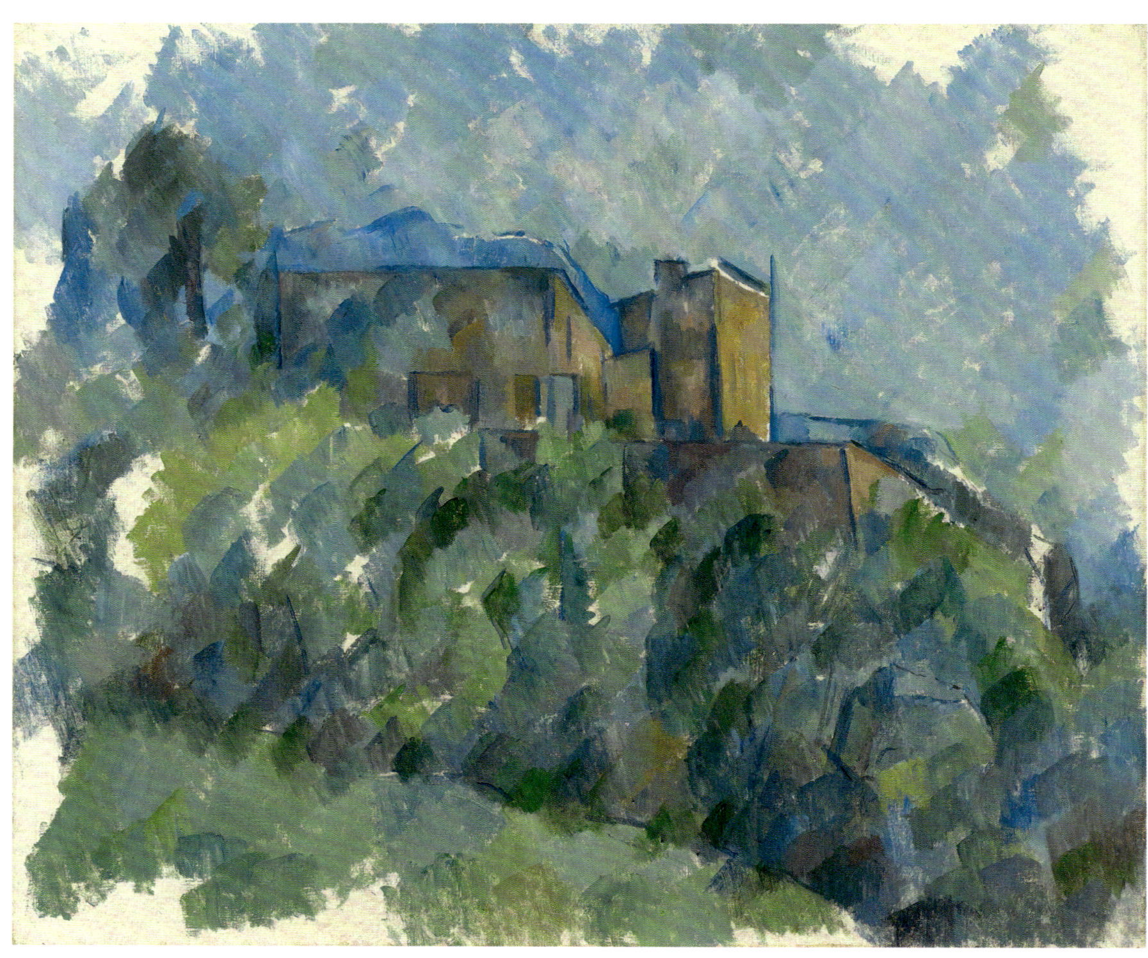

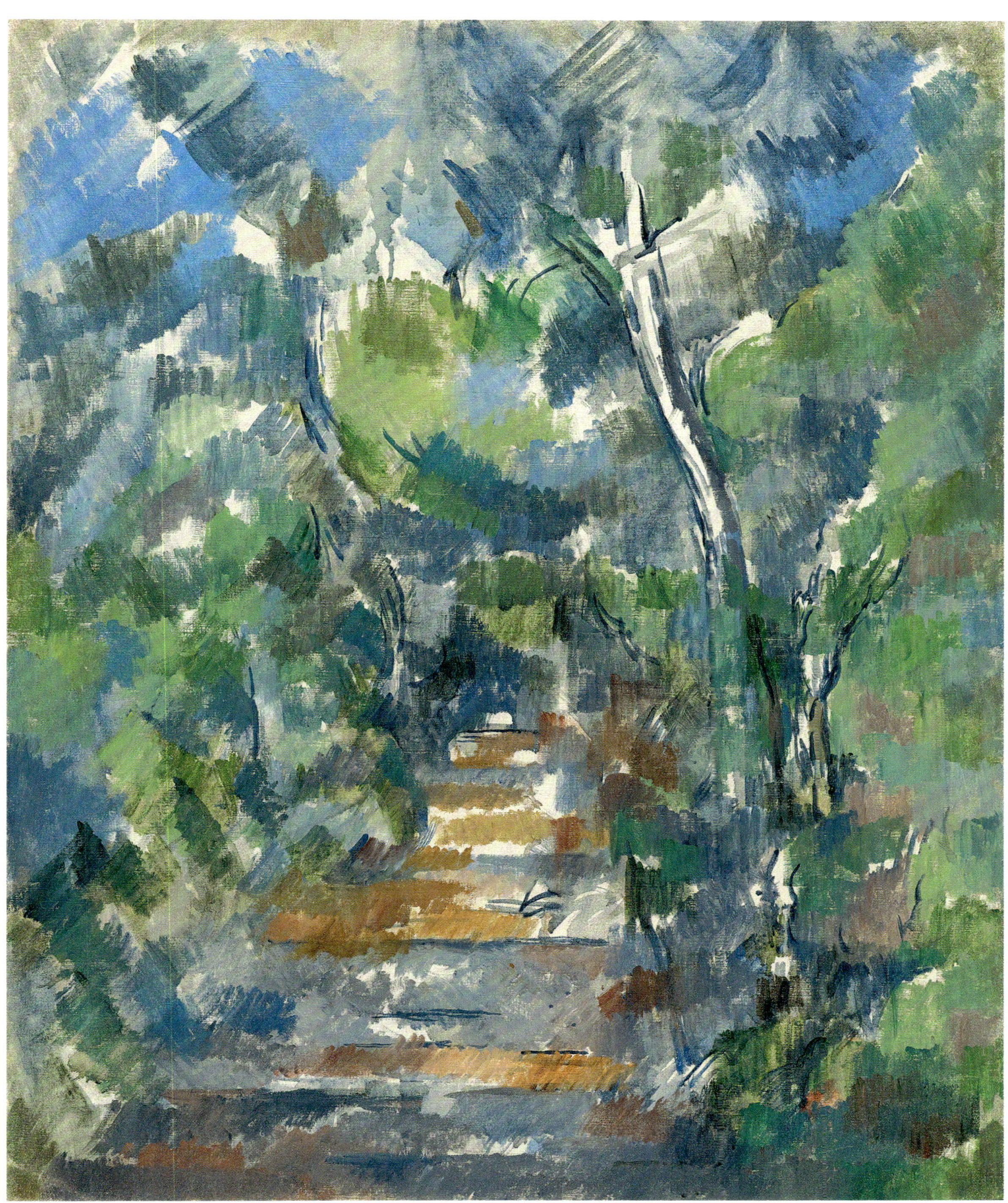

Cat. 128

Mont Sainte-Victoire Seen from Les Lauves
c. 1904
Oil on canvas
54 × 65 cm (21¼ × 25 9/16 in.)
Private collection, Derbyshire, UK
FWN 366
London only

Cat. 129

Château Noir
c. 1904
Oil on canvas
70 × 80 cm (27 5/8 × 31½ in.)
Private collection
FWN 358
Chicago only

Cat. 130

Undergrowth, Path of Mas Jolie at Château Noir
1900–1902
Oil on canvas
79.8 × 64.6 cm (31 7/16 × 25 7/16 in.)
Fondation Beyeler, Riehen/Basel, Sammlung Beyeler, inv. 67.1
FWN 339

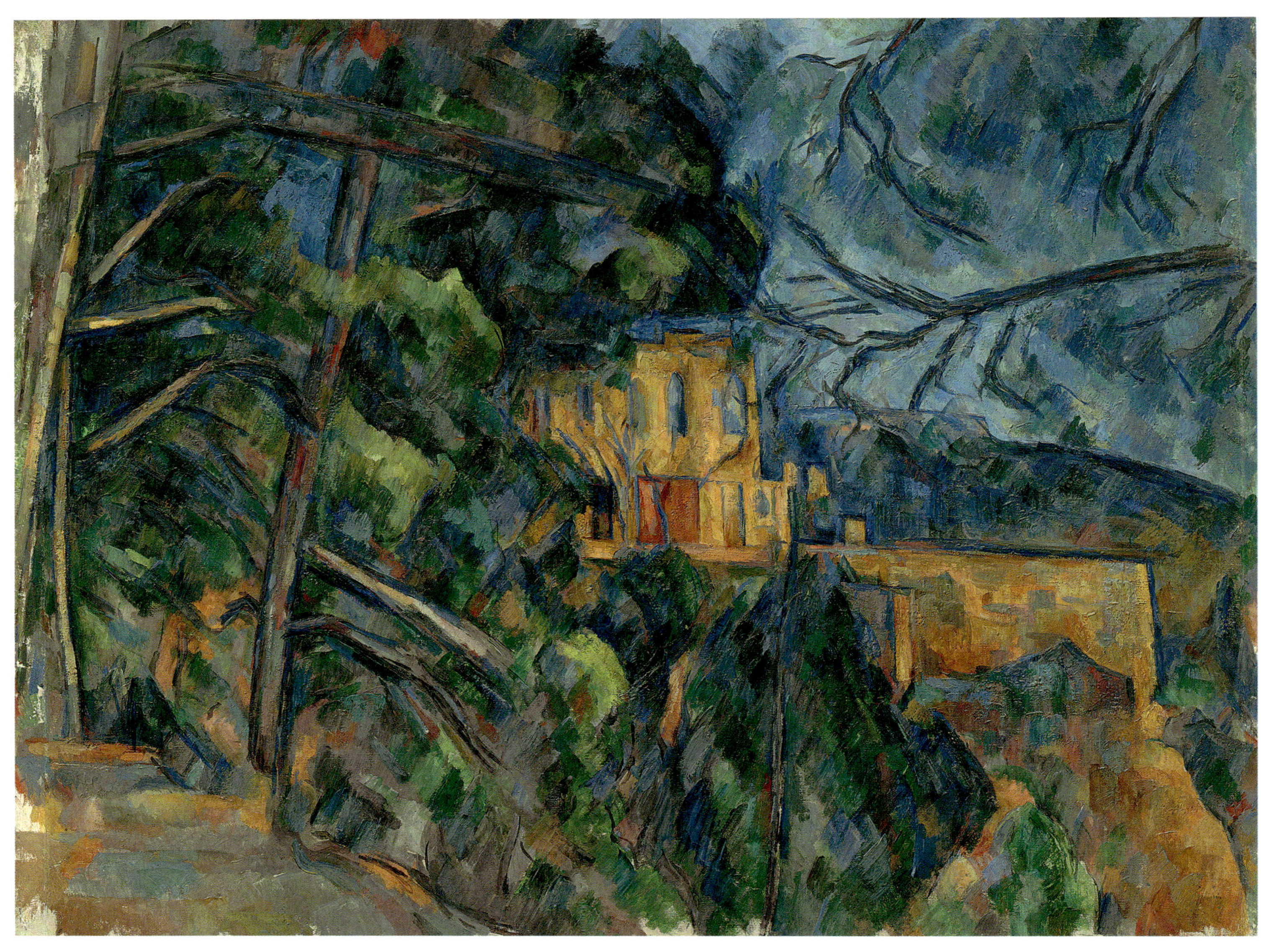

Cat. 131

Château Noir
1900–1904
Oil on canvas
73.7 × 96.6 cm (29 × 38 1/16 in.)
The National Gallery of Art, Washington, DC,
Gift of Eugene and Agnes E. Meyer, 1958.10.1
FWN 359

Cat. 132

Pistachio Tree at Château Noir
c. 1900
Watercolor with graphite on cream wove paper, laid
down on tan wove paper
54.2 × 43.3 cm (21 5/16 × 17 1/16 in.)
The Art Institute of Chicago, Mr. and Mrs. Martin A.
Ryeson Collection, 1937.1030
FWN 1450

Cat. 133

Château Noir
c. 1904
Graphite and watercolor on paper
41.9 × 55.2 cm (17 × 21 3/4 in.)
Private collection, Chicago
FWN 1508
Chicago only

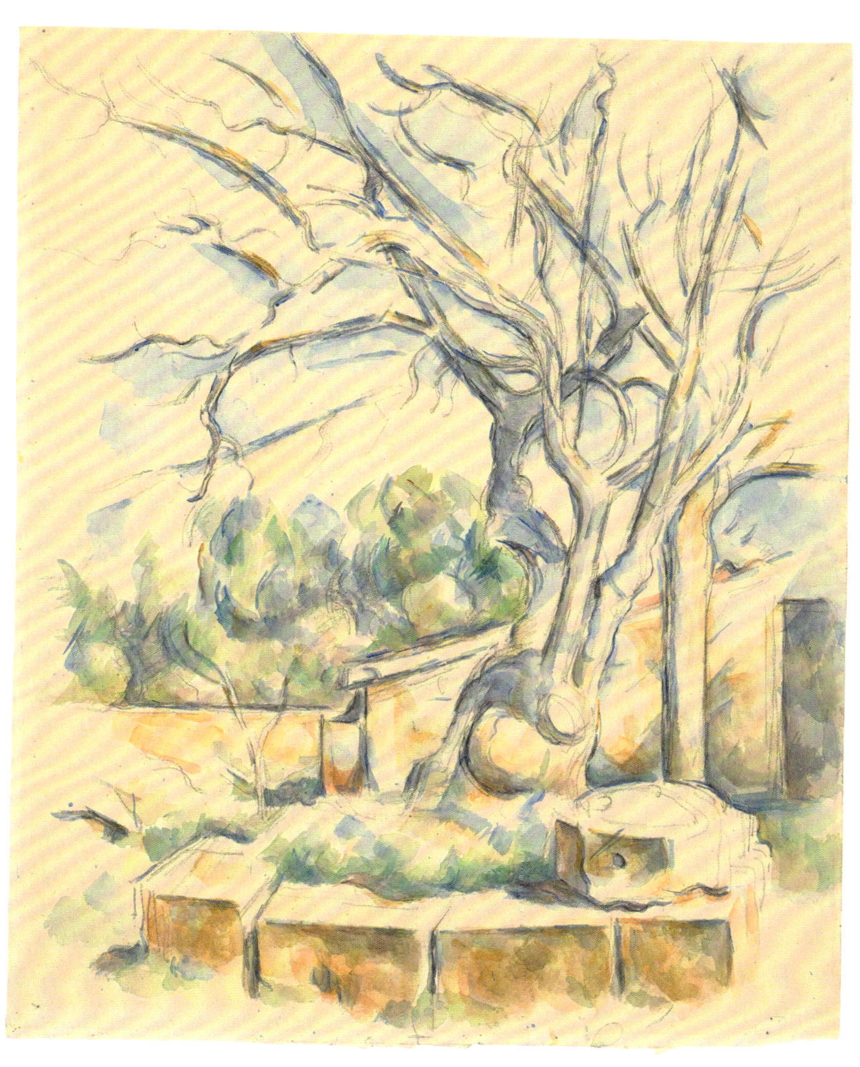

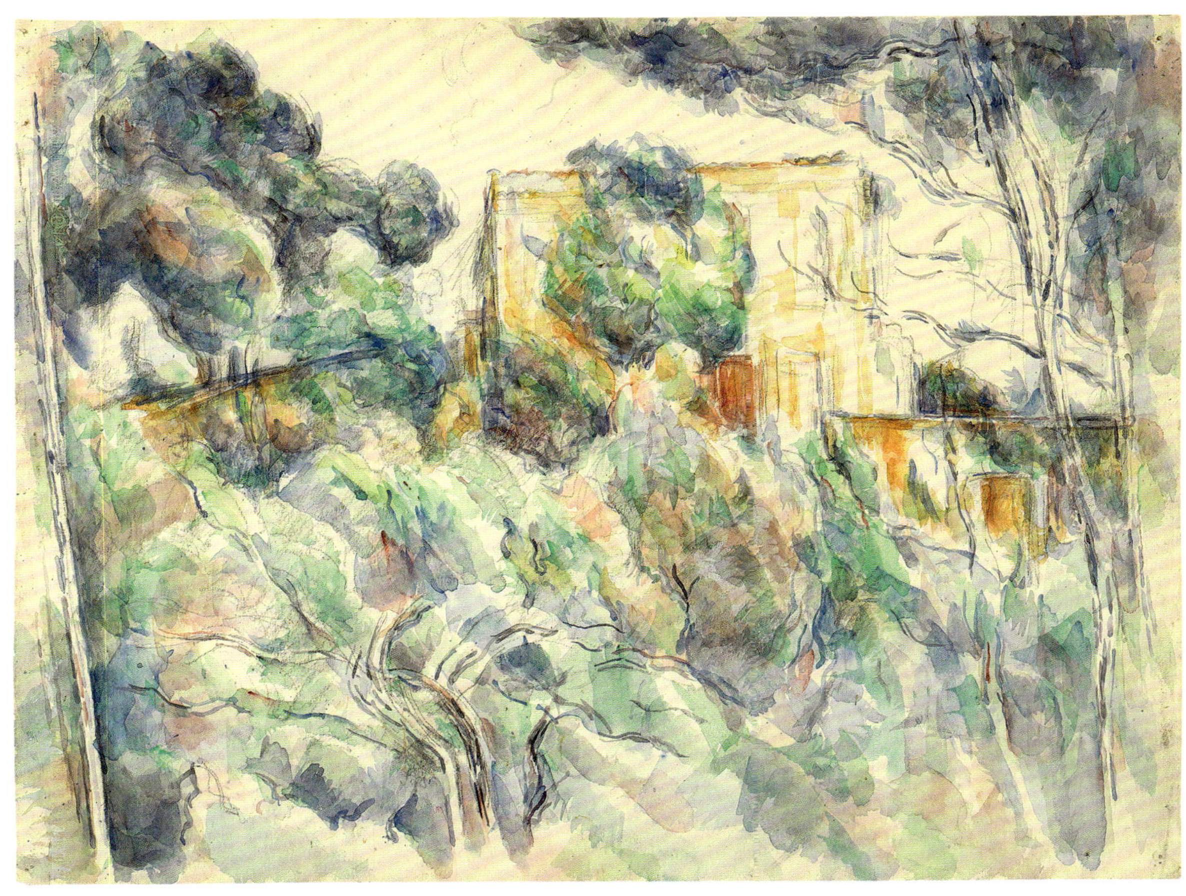

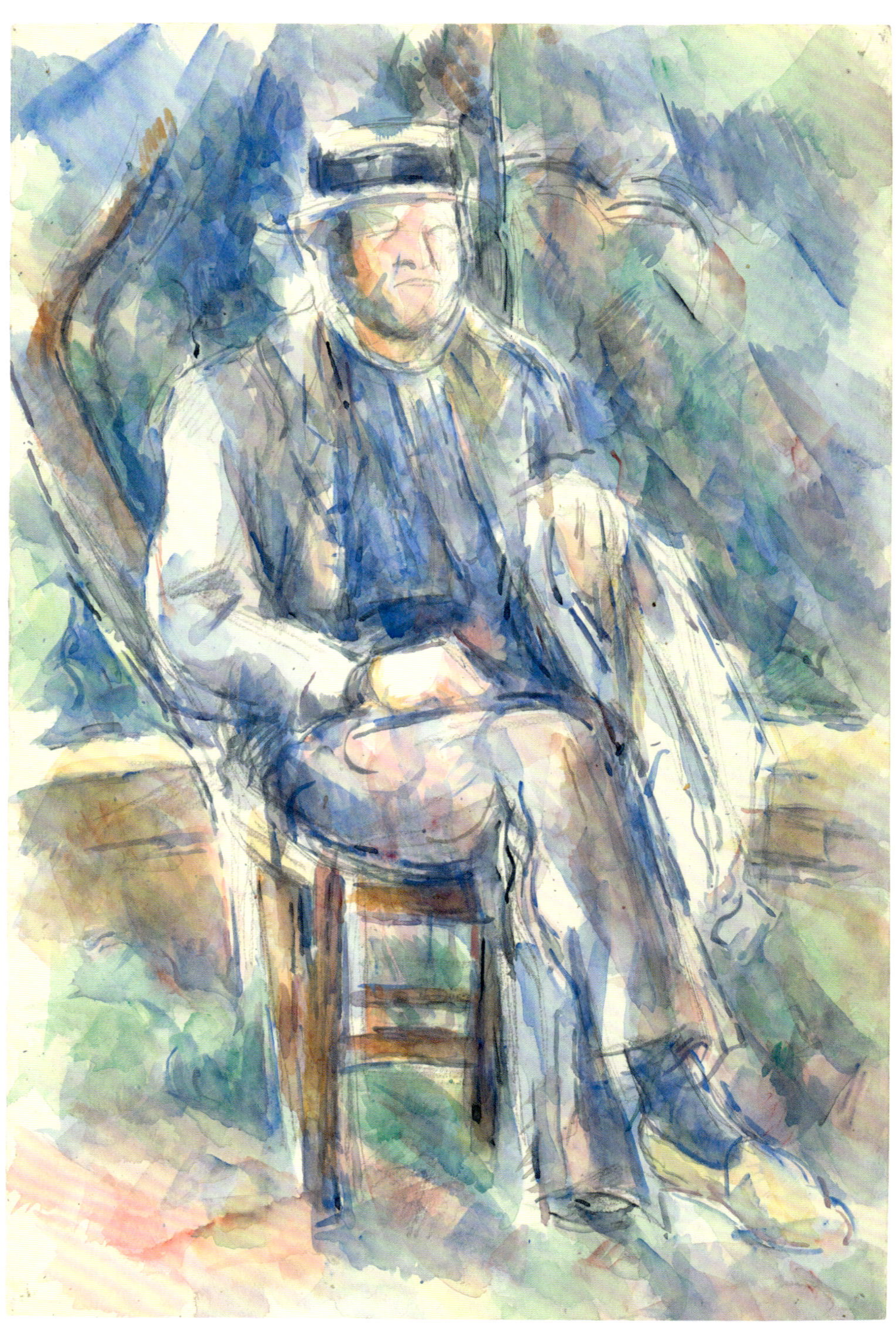

Cat. 134

Man Wearing a Straw Hat
1905–6
Watercolor over graphite on white wove paper
47.9 × 31.5 cm (18 ⅞ × 12 ⅜ in.)
The Art Institute of Chicago, gift of Janis H. Palmer in
memory of Pauline K. Palmer, 1983.1498
FWN 1779

Cat. 135

Seated Man
1905–6
Oil on canvas
64.8 × 54.6 cm (25 ½ × 21 ½ in.)
Museo Nacional Thyssen-Bornemisza, Madrid,
488 (1976.68)
FWN 546

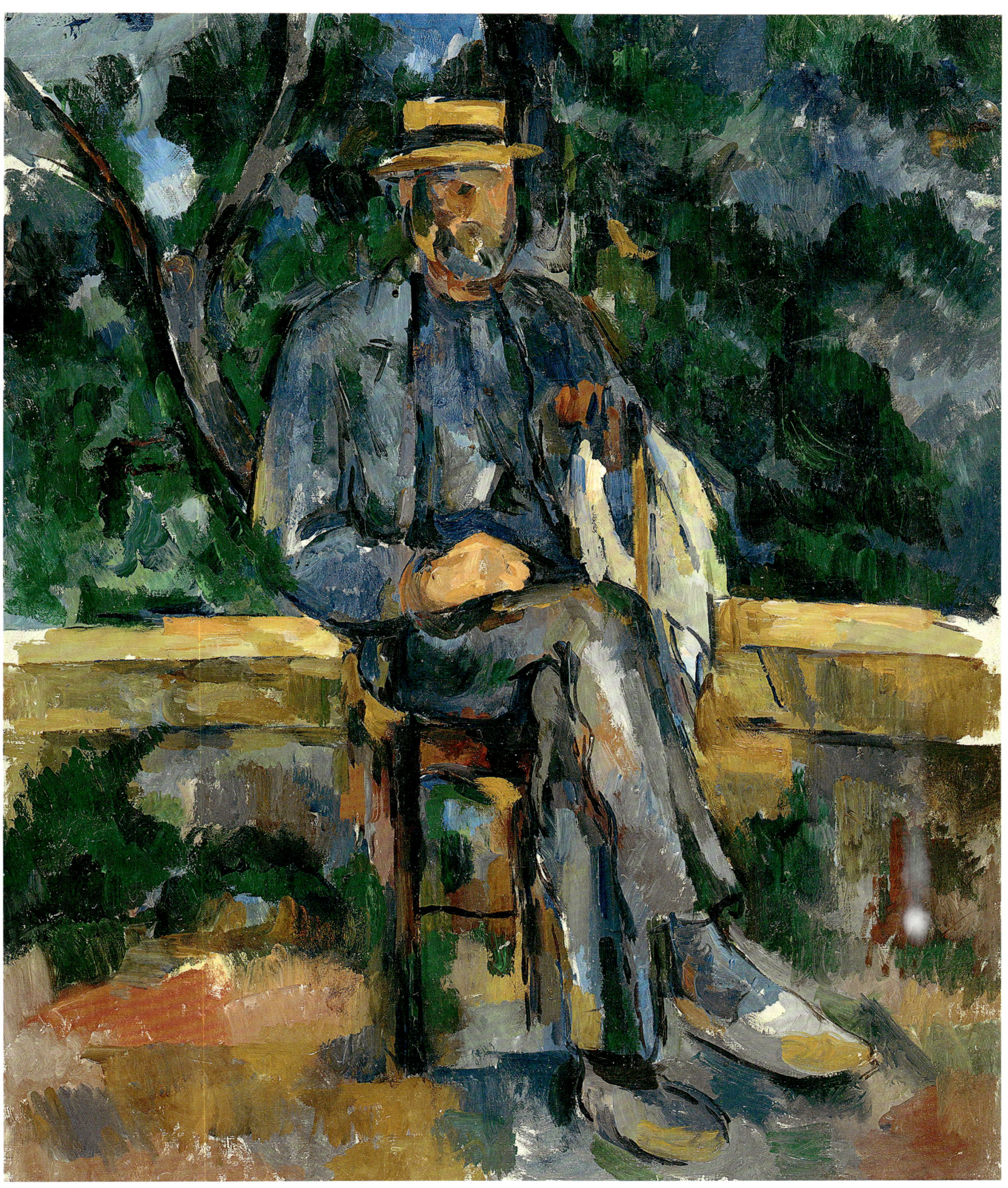

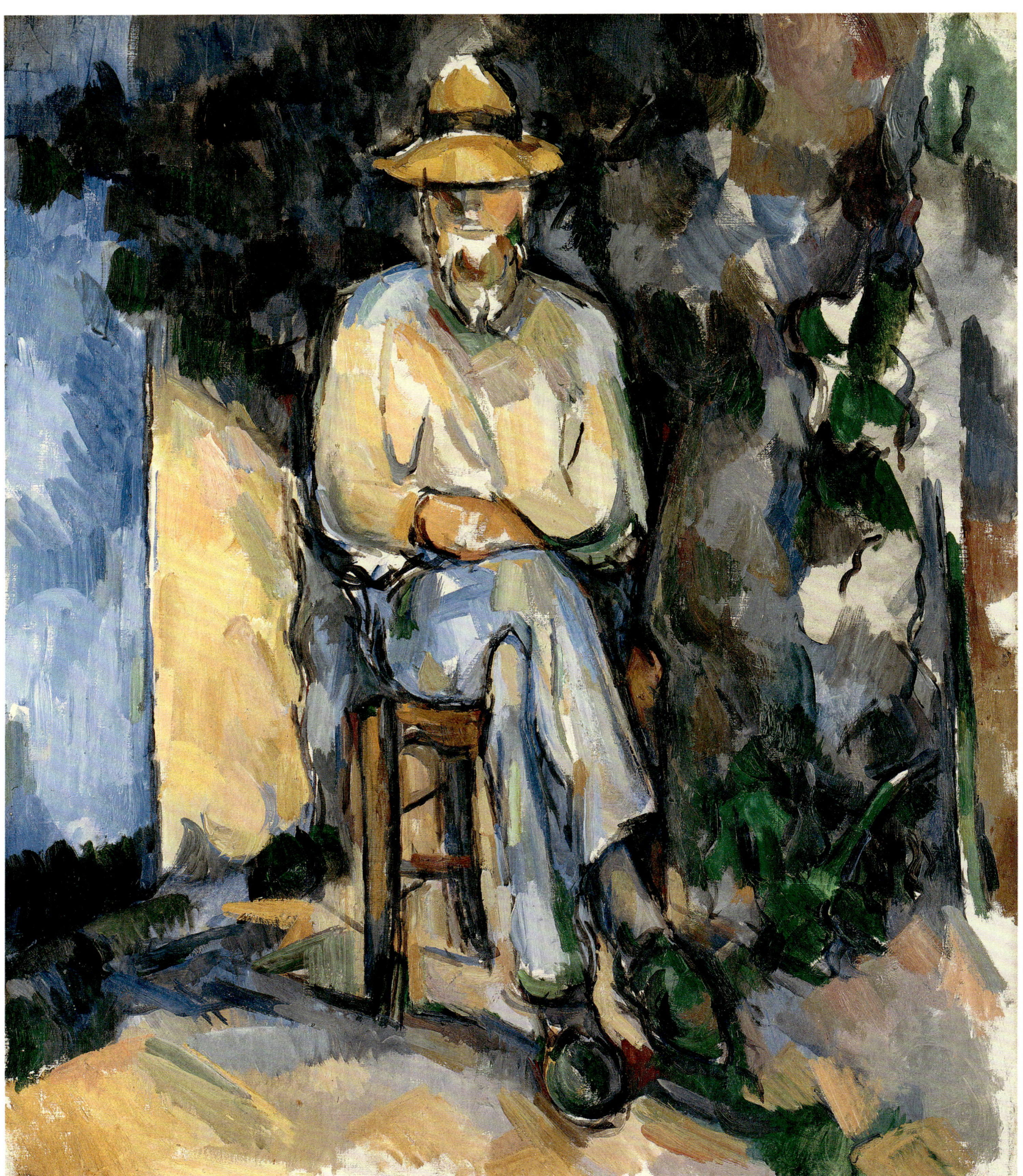

Immaterial Statements of Matter

Etel Adnan

Letter from Aix-en-Provence, July 23, 1990[1]

I'm in the countryside of Aix, . . . a dry country with an unforgiving light. That's why, I think, Cezanne stayed here. Because the light would allow him to go all the way. . . .

Cezanne is ravaged by his instinct for observation. His gaze eaten by the sun, his eagle eyes fix Madame Cezanne on paintings in which she seems to be dozing with boredom, knowing that she would never be the Sainte-Victoire. Two women dominate Cezanne's life: Madame Cezanne, and the mountain whose name is a woman's. . . .

In the penumbra of my thought a question arises: why does the feminine dominate the world of Cezanne, and of Pablo Picasso?

For Cezanne, nothing is less evident. I've just seen in his workshop some of the ordinary objects, placed one next to the other, which he used in his paintings: a kitchen table, pots and pans, ceramic ware, morose things that his genius, on the canvas, transfigured. I'm thinking about the flower vases, the apples, and his mountain. . . . I tell myself: art is the search for the feminine, and in turn, art feminizes the world. Hence its indispensable value to society and its powers of subversion.

Email, December 8, 2020

Last night, thinking of Cezanne, it became clear to me that a painting by him is mainly an organized chaos. Look at his tablecloths: they are verticals put on his tables; his apples on a table, though intensely lit, lack shadows and stare at us; in real life, his little ceramics would roll down on the floor and break, but the organization ends up making sense. And, going on, I looked at his watercolors, in my memory, and realized that his touches, his strokes of color, have a strangeness due to the fact that they are not three-dimensional but are pure vibrations, immaterial statements of matter making, aggregating in ghostlike mountains, the whole endeavor a pursuit of that immateriality which led the nineteenth century to the disintegration of matter through the atom bomb.

Email, June 19, 2020

Of all my experiences of Cezanne's works, the most haunting have been his portraits of the gardener Vallier. Of course, the Mont Sainte-Victoire paintings and watercolors have occupied my mind for years. But the epiphany came with the gardener's portraits. This is a simple man, maybe the closest to Cezanne. He is sitting on a small wall, or on a chair. He has a thin face and penetrating eyes, and is sunk in a meditation, probably in a lifetime of meditations. And the nobility it entails. It could be a self-portrait of Cezanne, unwillingly emerging from the paintings. The whole body is guessed. In a photograph of his I noticed his long legs with angular bones, the type of legs that I suppose Arthur Rimbaud had too, in the same end-of-a-century time when the poet in his restlessness used to walk on foot from northern France to Germany, while Cezanne was hurrying to the spot from which he would, again and again, try to catch the fluidity of the mountain's image. The gardener Vallier's portrait is Cezanne's ultimate "mountain," his *Ecce homo*, his real testament. The gardener is sitting cross-legged, looking from his bench at the master's studio, lost in his thoughts. And Cezanne, watching him, is overwhelmed. No philosopher's portrait has ever reached the evocative power of this one.

1. From *Of Cities and Women (Letters to Fawwaz)* (Sausalito, CA: The Post-Apollo Press, 1993), 17 and 22–23.

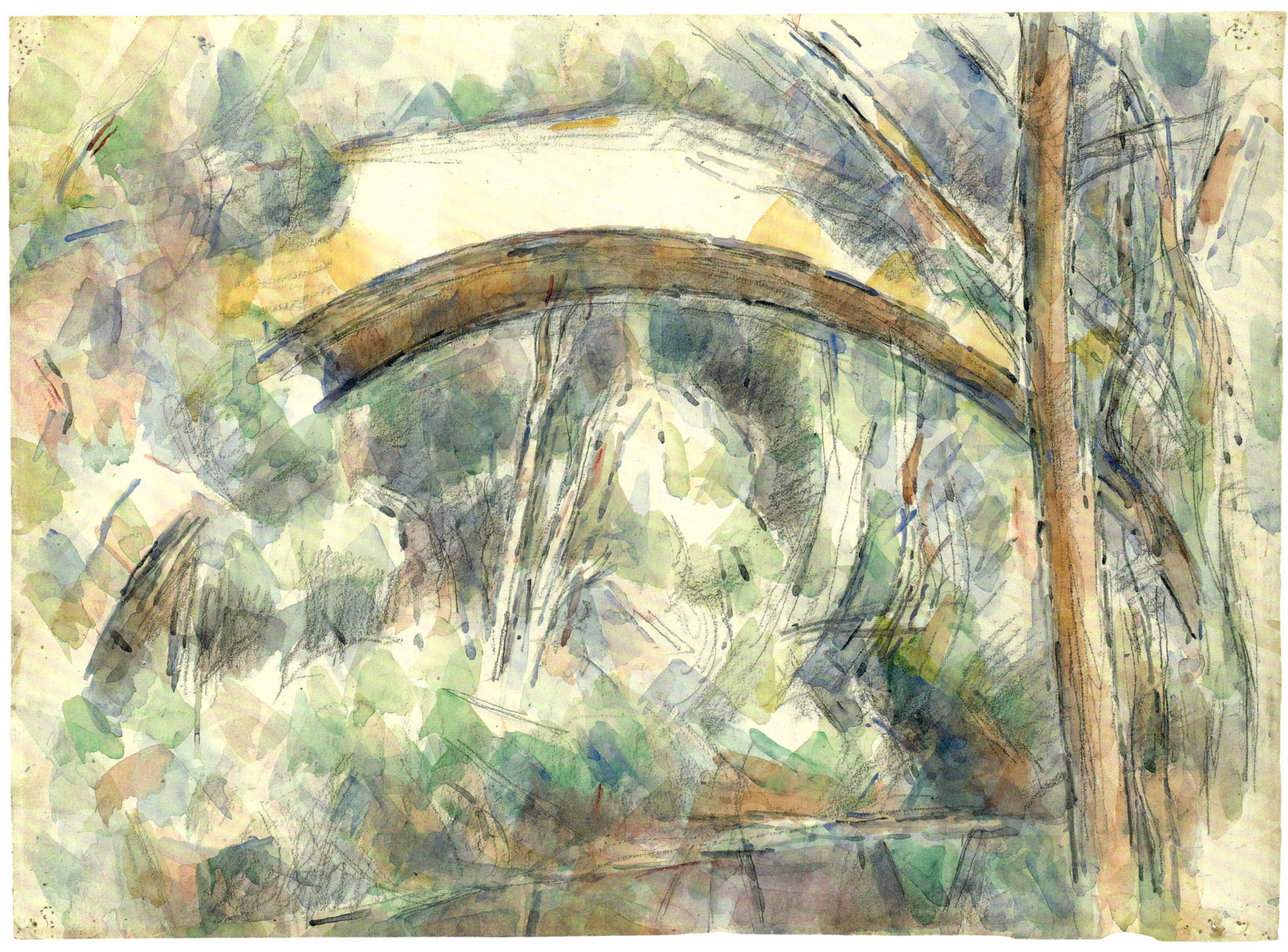

Cat. 137

The Bridge of Trois-Sautets
c. 1906
Watercolor and pencil on paper
40.8 × 54.3 cm (17 × 21⅜ in.)
Cincinnati Art Museum, Gift of John J. Emery,
1951.298
FWN 1519
Chicago only

Cat. 138

**The Garden at Les Lauves: View of Aix and
the Cathedral of Saint-Sauveur**
1902–6
Graphite and watercolor on wove paper
40 × 54 cm (15¾ × 22 in.)
Private collection
FWN 1486
Chicago only

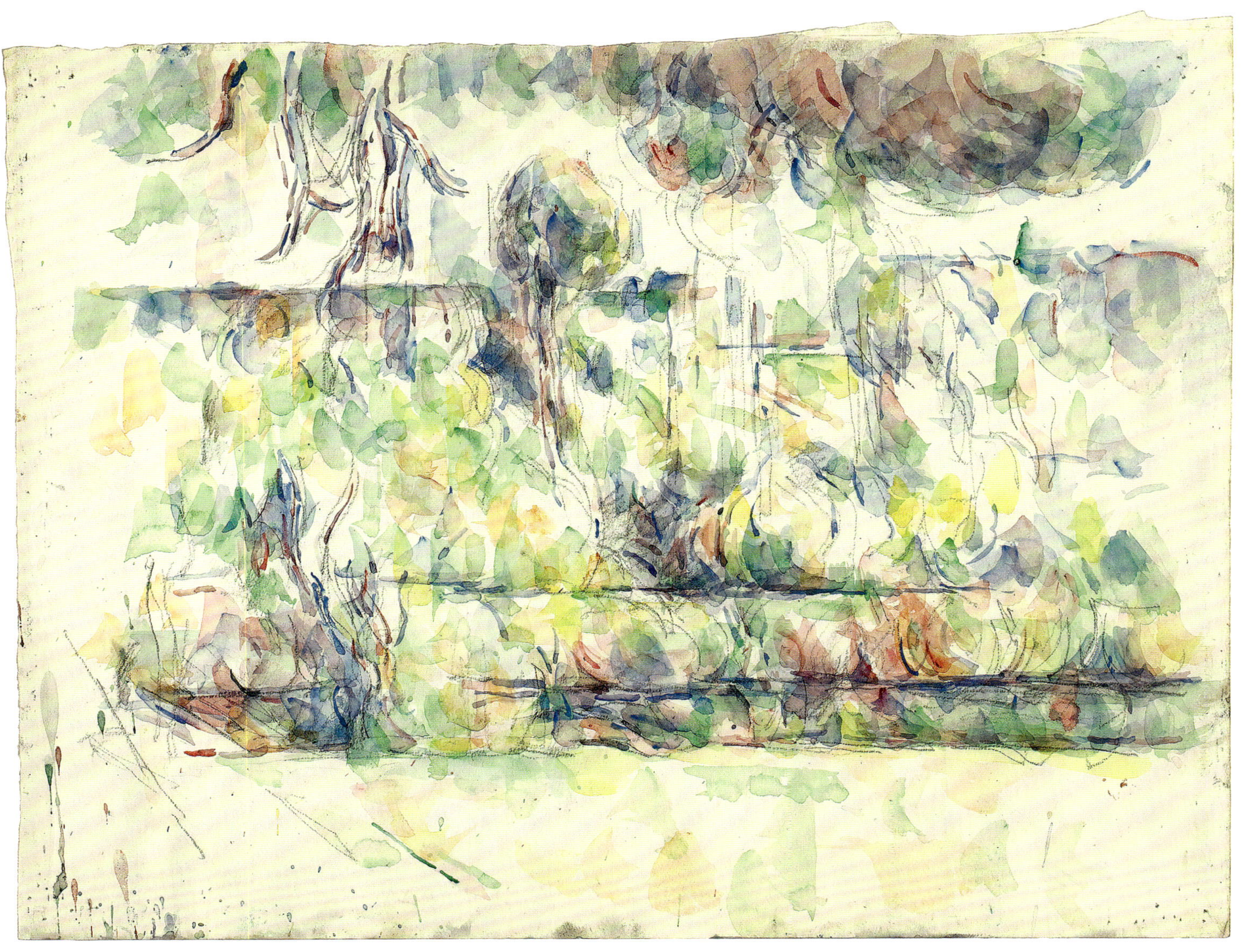

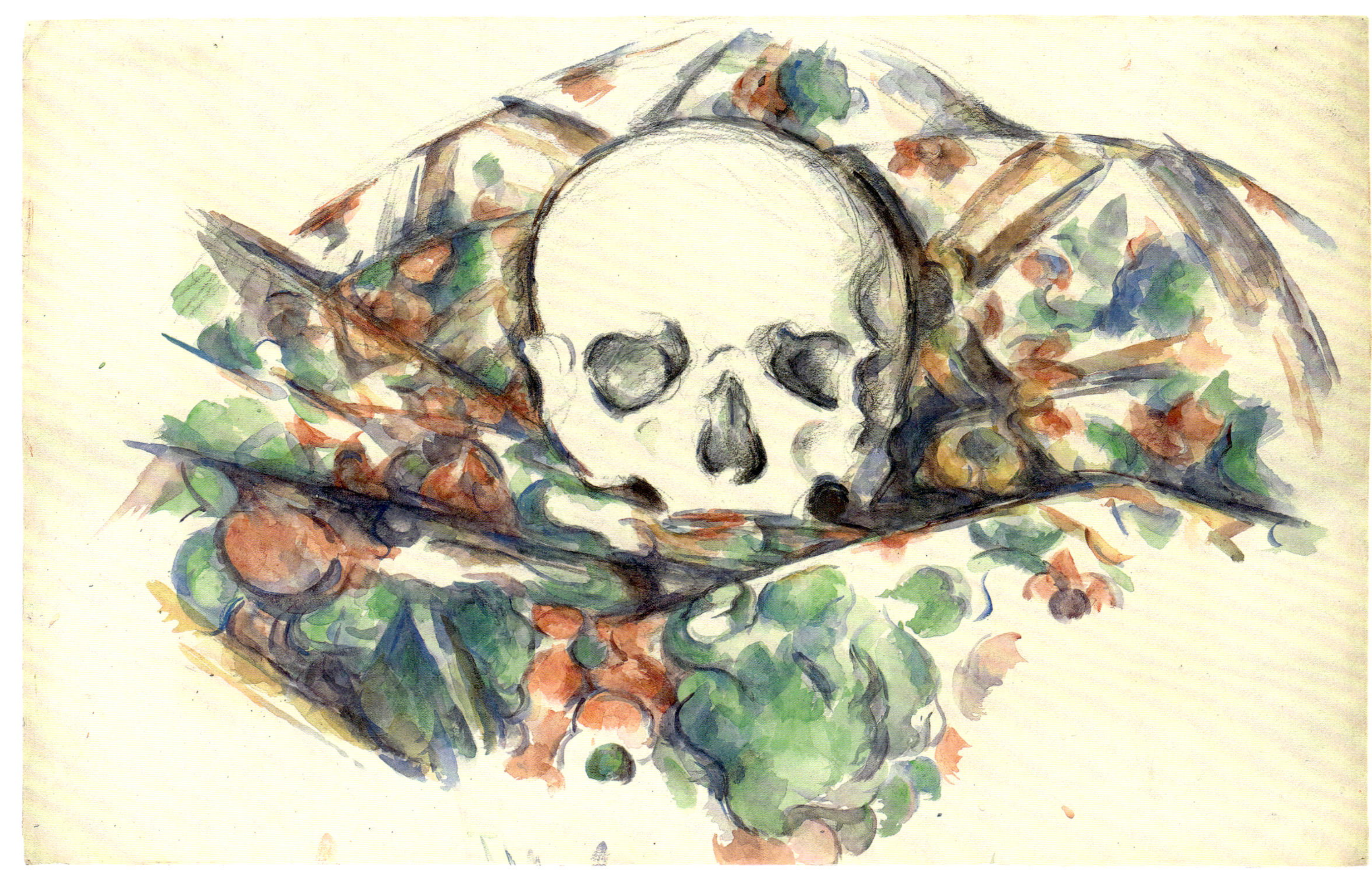

Cat. 139

The Skull
1902–6
Graphite, gouache, and watercolor on wove paper
31.7 × 47.6 cm (13 × 18 ¾ in.)
Private collection
FWN 1986
Chicago only

Cat. 140

Three Skulls on a Patterned Carpet
1904
Oil on canvas
54.5 × 65 cm (21 ⅜ × 25 ⅝ in.)
Kunstmuseum Solothurn (Dübi-Müller-Stiftung),
Switzerland, C 80.2
FWN 875

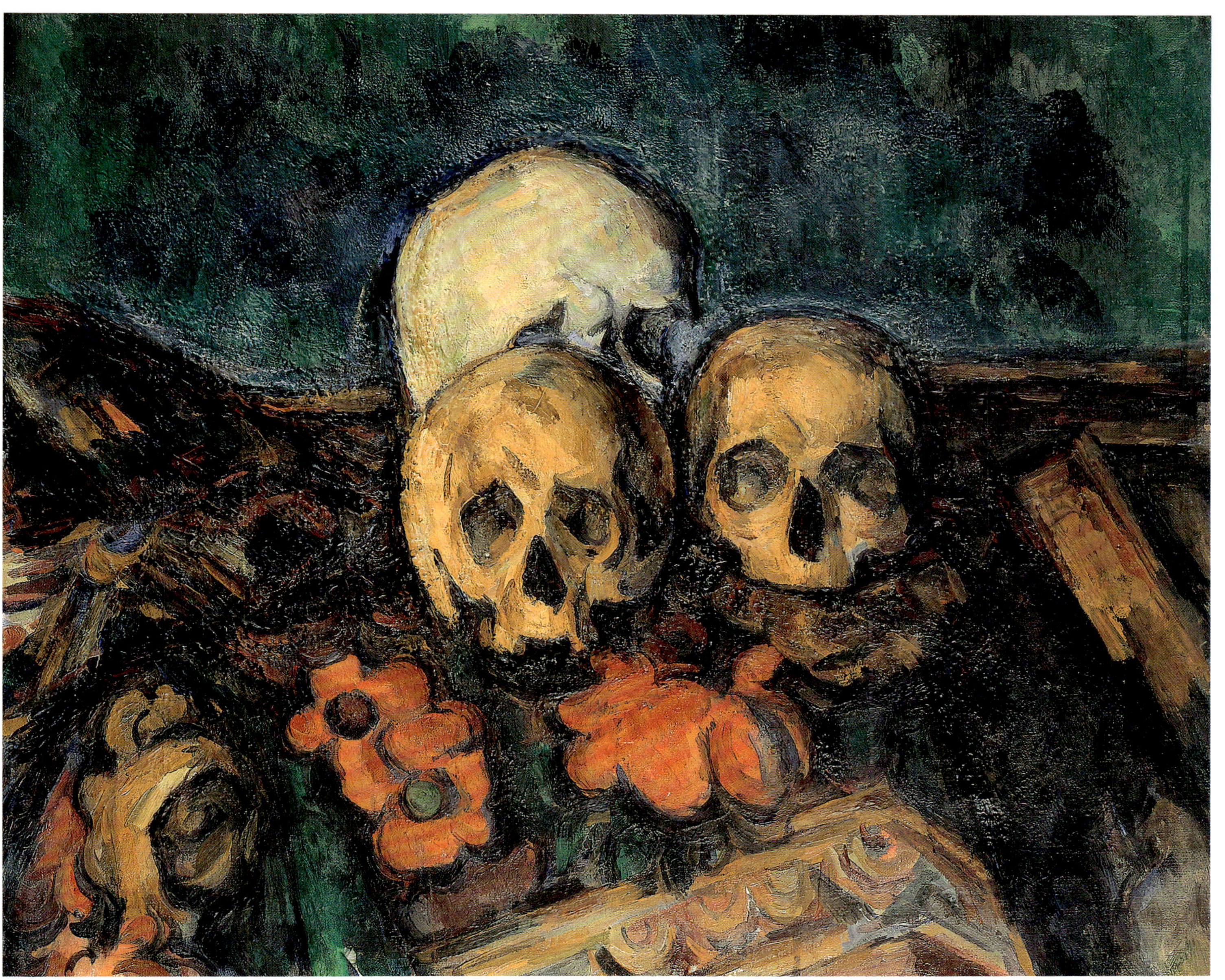

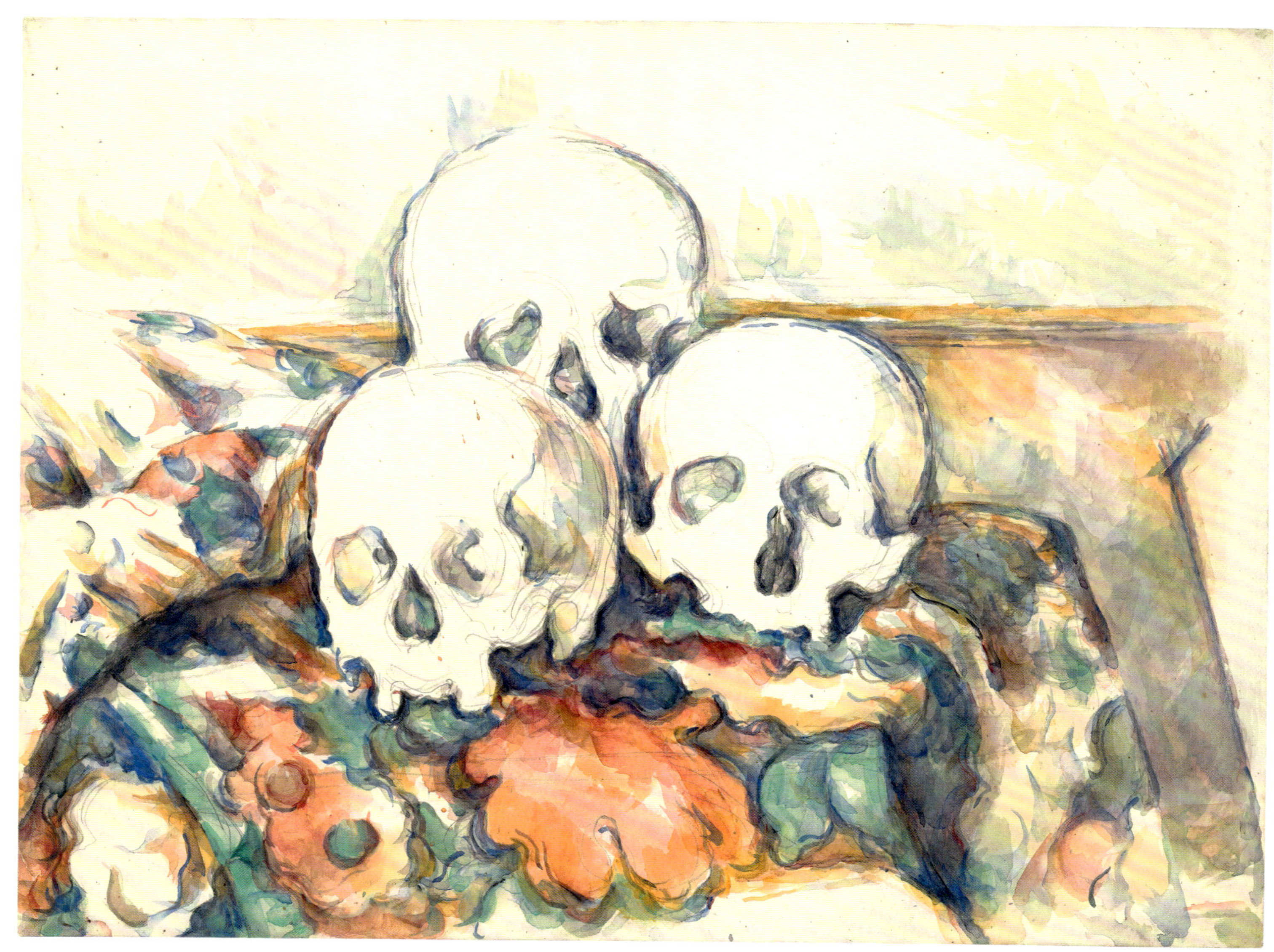

Cat. 141

The Three Skulls
1902–6
Watercolor with graphite and touches of gouache on
ivory wove paper
48 × 62.8 cm (18 ⅞ × 24 ¾ in.)
The Art Institute of Chicago, Olivia Shaler Swan
Memorial Collection, 1954.183
FWN 1987

Trio

Julia Fish

Dear Mr. Cezanne,

 Some months back, I received a
kind invitation on your behalf: would
I take a look at your *Three Skulls
(Trois Crânes)*—the watercolor'd
one—to note some thoughts and then,
prospectively, to further shape my
"seeing" for intended publication?
My "yes" confirmed: it would be an
honor and a privilege.

 Accordingly, I have carried the
"pictured" image and its given title—
back-of-mind, front-of-mind—brave
allies to my waking consciousness,
yet rattled by the force of facts and
of convergences that haunt us:
pandemic illness, death, and other
forms of loss—a year of seasons
from that first, invited moment.

 I've been fortunate to see *Trois
Crânes* twice over and with expert
guidance, in the calibrated light
of the Art Institute's conservation
lab. This study has now taken such
an inward turn that I am moved to
address my account to you directly:
to send these few abbreviated notes
and queries, as if reporting back
—or forward, to the yet-unknown.

 What follows is surely incomplete,
as you well understand: how pictures
wait, impatient for another view?
But this I know and must confirm:
your solemn trio illuminates a shared
and challenged present-tense, yet
also signals, prescient: that silent pact
we each must make with our own life,
that *will have been.*
 Yours and truly,
  JF / Chicago

March 29, 2021

from a viewing and a second look

Freed from its frame
displayed recumbent:
a palpable weight.
I offer to assist:
we lift the work with cautious care
—*Three Skulls* now steadied—
inclining at the table-easel.

It seems a faint-tint wash prepared
the sheet from edge to edge
in partnership
with fleeting graphite clues:
what's underlaid
retains a luminescent glow—
proof enough to name the color:
skull.

Although unsettled, settled-in:

one:
a furrowed-brow betrays the
centered elder—wisdom wedged
between the younger pair.

two:
at left advancing, fearless
    ! the carmine droplets
at right accepting fate ?
    or numb to it.

three:
snugged-up—*as if a selfie*
wincing, over-run by angled light.

ensemble'd:
incisors sunken, caught
in scalloped-bone-edged mutterance
[dismayed by absent tongues
and mandibles gone missing]
—yet dignified
in tablescape'd embrace:
a sympathetic garden.

Occurs to me
to test the title-words another way:
the three of skulls. . .
to face the image as if dealt—
or having drawn—the card, in turn.

Now, as noted in proximity:
see where the brush-point arcs those
lines shared by skull and air—
or air and wall —or skull when edged
with verdant tapestry.

Each searched-for, flourished mark:
an agitated wavering
deliberate or hesitant
disclosed by unforgiving paper.

Each absent place an eye should be
drinks-in
the spectrum of its circumstance:

thin'd red with blue
marks one
against a yellow'd pool

the other five make what they will
from annotated variants:
sparks or faded notes of green
gray'd-blues
indigos with cobalt-bits
water'd-sepias
blotched-pinks from red
ochre'd-mauves and violets.

Each absent nose inhales
an ever-shaded-palette-scent.

Each brush-marked gap
proposes "inside-ness"—
invokes a dome we cannot see:
where thought and recollection
once prevailed.

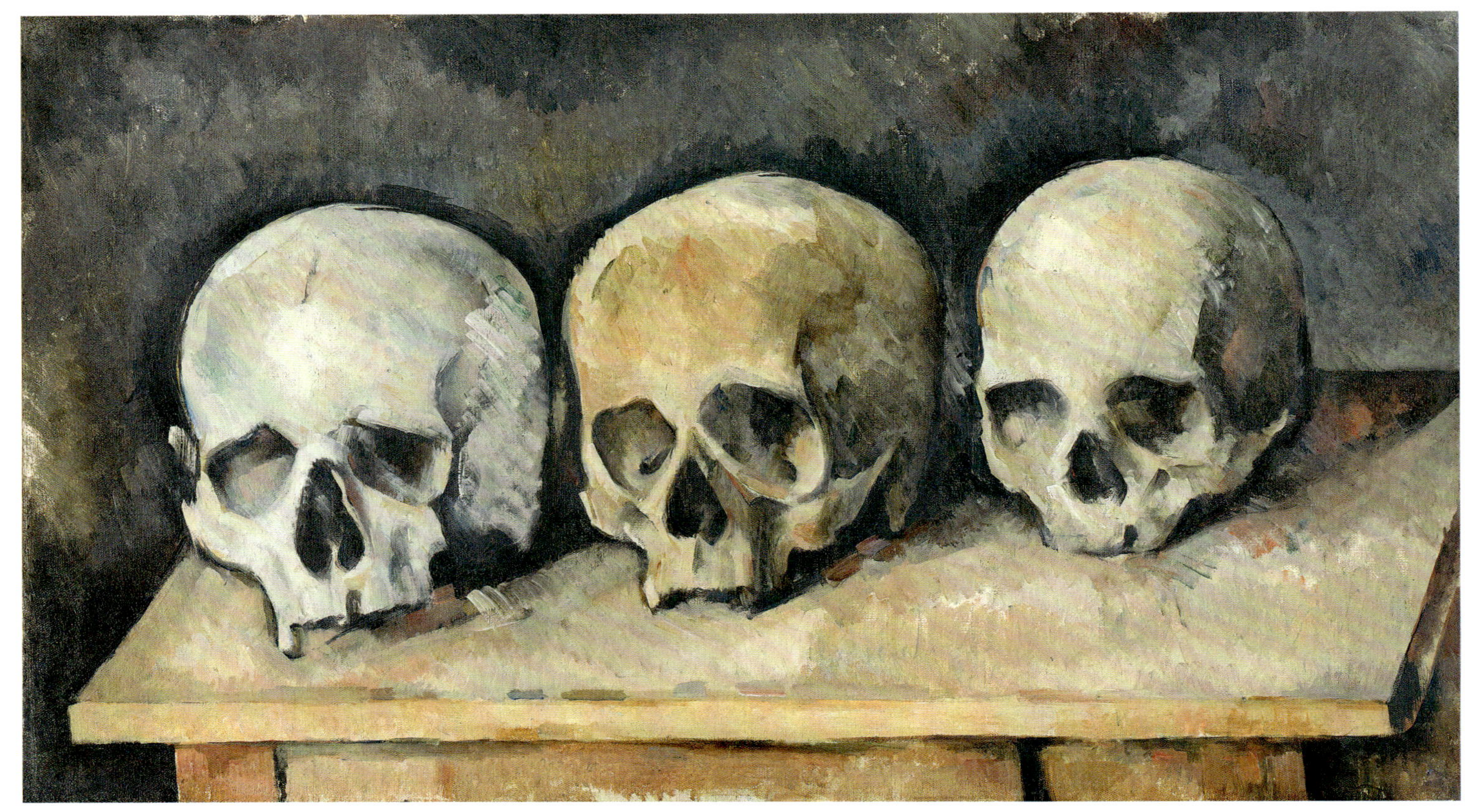

Cat. 142

The Three Skulls
c. 1898
Oil on canvas
34.9 × 61 cm (13 ¾ × 24 in.)
Detroit Institute of Arts, Bequest of Robert H.
Tannahill, 70.163
FWN 873
Chicago only

Mapping Cezanne

Kathryn Kremnitzer

The following series of maps represents Paul Cezanne's documented travel throughout the course of his career. He is often described as an artist who trod a well-worn path between Paris and Provence, but a closer look reveals much more mobility, especially as access to modern transportation increased during his lifetime. This approximation of his whereabouts was assembled using published letters, biographical information, and the catalogue raisonné (FWN), and reflects the limitations of those materials and the historical record. References to Parisian arrondissements accord with present-day locations. Readers are advised to consult the following for more granular accounts of particular journeys and periods:

Isabelle Cahn, "Chronology," in Françoise Cachin, Isabelle Cahn, Walter Feilchenfeldt, Henri Loyrette, and Joseph J. Rishel, *Cézanne*, 527–69. Exh. cat. Philadelphia: Philadelphia Museum of Art, 1996.

Alex Danchev, *Cézanne: A Life.* New York: Pantheon Books, 2012.

Alex Danchev, ed. and trans. *The Letters of Paul Cézanne.* Los Angeles: J. Paul Getty Museum, 2013.

Michael Doran, ed. *Conversations with Cézanne.* Trans. Julie Lawrence Cochran. Berkeley: University of California Press, 2001.

Société Paul Cezanne, "L'homme: biographie et chronologies," https://societe-cezanne.fr/lhomme.

Jayne Warman, "Chronology," in *Cézanne in the Barnes Foundation,* edited by André Dombrowski, Nancy Ireson, and Sylvie Patry, 57–65. New York: Rizzoli Electa, 2021.

1860s

1861

In April Paul Cezanne leaves Aix for Paris. Writer and childhood friend Émile Zola helps him organize his time, activities, and budget while there, encouraging him to visit museums and study the Old Masters. Cezanne enrolls at the Académie Suisse, where he meets fellow Aixois painters Achille Empéraire and Antoine Guillemet, as well as Camille Pissarro. He lives at 39, rue d'Enfer (today rue Bleue in the 9th arrondissement). Having failed to qualify for the École des Beaux-Arts, he returns to Aix in September and works at his father's bank.

1862

Cezanne spends summer and fall in Aix and comes back to Paris in early November.

1863

On November 20, Cezanne registers as a copyist at the Louvre and lists his address as 7, rue des Feuillantines (the 5th arondissement of Paris).

1864

He returns to Aix in July, visits L'Estaque in August for the first time, and remains in the South of France until January.

1865

From January to September, Cezanne lives in Paris at 22, rue Beautreillis (4th arrondissement). His first submission to the Salon, a still life (probably FWN 704), is rejected and he proceeds to Aix.

1866

Cezanne works in Paris from mid-February to mid-August and attends Thursday-evening gatherings organized by Zola, which are also frequented by fellow Aixois friends Jean-Baptiste Baille and Numa Coste. His submission to the Salon (FWN 399) is rejected. Throughout the spring and summer, Cezanne makes several trips to Bennecourt before coming back to Aix in mid-August.

1867

Cezanne is in Paris in February but returns to Aix by early June, where he stays for the rest of the year.

1868

From January to May, Cezanne is in Paris; on February 13 he registers as a copyist in the Louvre. His Salon submission (probably FWN 590) is rejected. He spends the rest of the year in Aix, arriving by mid-May. Throughout the summer he takes excursions to Saint-Antonin, a small village at the foot of Mont Sainte-Victoire.

1869

Back in Paris by the beginning of the year, Cezanne meets Hortense Fiquet, with whom he would have a son and later marry. Cezanne is in L'Estaque in April but travels to Paris to deliver his Salon submissions, which are again rejected. He summers in the Île-de-France, probably in Bennecourt and Gloton, where Zola is renting a house on the banks of the Seine. September finds him in Aix, where he remains until March 1870.

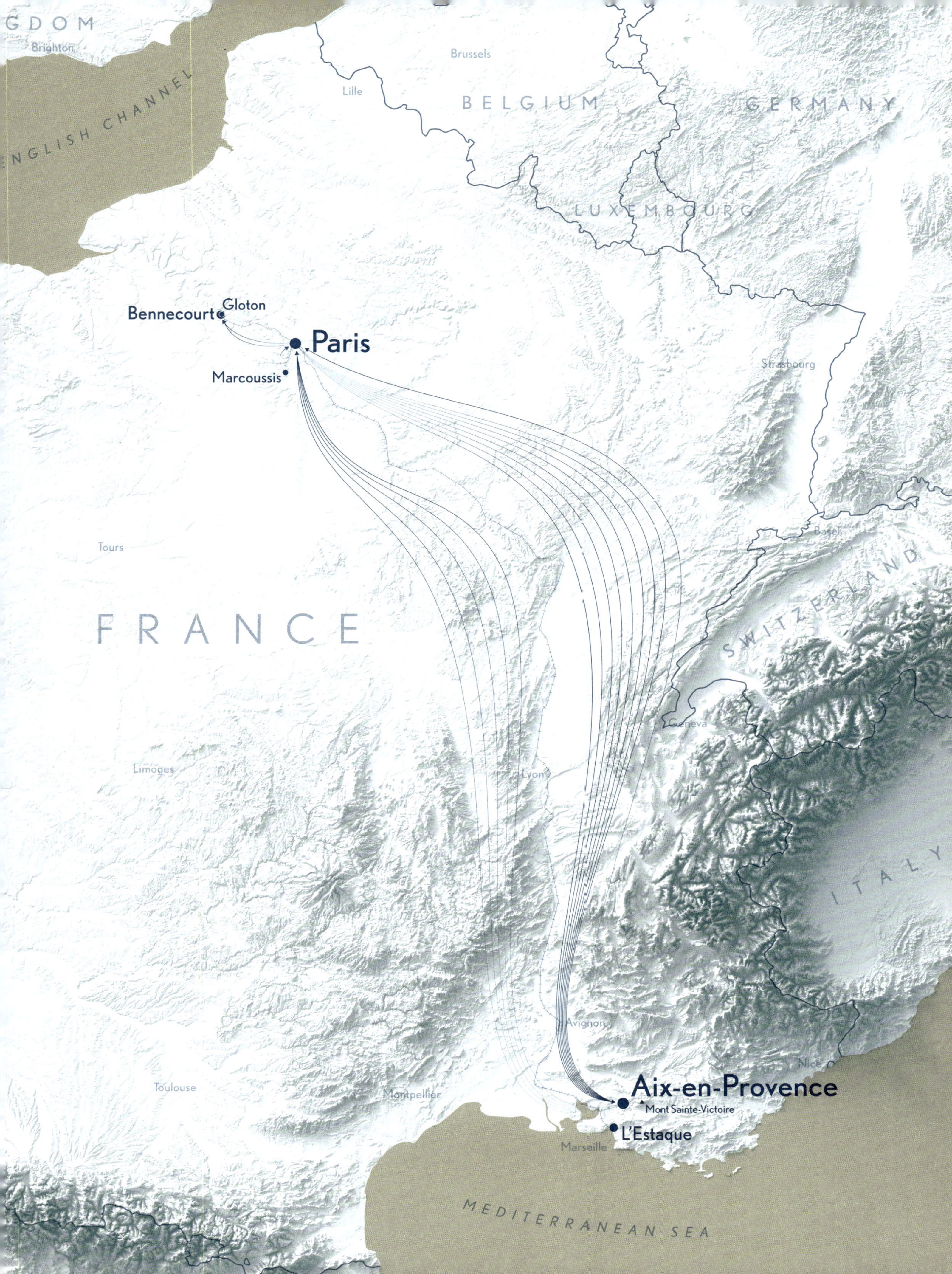

GDOM
Brighton
ENGLISH CHANNEL
Brussels
Lille
BELGIUM
GERMANY
LUXEMBOURG
Strasbourg
Bennecourt
Gloton
Paris
Marcoussis
Basel
Tours
SWITZERLAND
FRANCE
Geneva
Limoges
Lyon
ITALY
Toulouse
Avignon
Nice
Montpellier
Aix-en-Provence
Mont Sainte-Victoire
L'Estaque
Marseille
MEDITERRANEAN SEA

1870s

1870

In March he takes up residence in Paris at 53, rue Notre-Dame-des-Champs (9th arrondissement). His two Salon submissions (FWN 423; FWN 595) are rejected. France declares war on Prussia on July 19; by the end of the month, Cezanne flees to L'Estaque with Hortense, staying in a house on the place de l'Église. Cezanne shuttles between L'Estaque and Aix, where his family is at the Jas de Bouffan.

1871

In the Midi for much of the year, Cezanne returns to Paris with Hortense in July, living at 55, rue de Chevreuse (6th arrondissement) through November.

1872

Cezanne and Hortense occupy 45, rue de Jussieu, in the Latin Quarter, where they welcome their only child, a son, Paul, born on January 4. The family of three spends several weekends in Saint-Ouen l'Aumône, northwest of Paris, and later in the year they settle in Auvers-sur-Oise at 66, rue Remy. Between August and December Cezanne frequently walks or takes the train 3 kilometers (almost 2 miles) to join Pissarro in Pontoise.

1873

Cezanne resides in Auvers with Hortense and their young son for the entire year. He often walks to Pontoise to work alongside Pissarro. In Paris, he meets Julien-François "Père" Tanguy, who shows several of the artist's paintings in the storefront of his paint-supply shop on the rue Clauzel.

1874

In March Cezanne, Hortense, and young Paul are back in Paris, at 120, rue de Vaugirard (6th arrondissement). The artist participates in the First Impressionist Exhibition (April 15–May 15 at Studio Nadar, 35, boulevard des Capucines) with three paintings (FWN 77; FWN 81; FWN 628). In late May he goes to Aix and remains in the South through September before traveling to Paris.

1875

The family settles at 67, rue de l'Ouest (14th arrondissement) in mid-April, renting there until early 1880. During the summer Cezanne travels to Pontoise to paint alongside Pissarro.

1876

In February Cezanne visits fellow artist Claude Monet in Argenteuil. He is in Aix and L'Estaque from April until the end of August; he is then in Paris until March 1878. In the fall Cezanne works at Issy-les-Moulineaux, outside the city, with Armand Guillaumin.

1877

In Paris, Cezanne frequents the Café de la Nouvelle-Athènes and attends soirées organized by Nina de Villard. He participates in the Third Impressionist Exhibition (April 4–30), showing fifteen paintings and two watercolors (see FWN "Exhibition: 1877 Paris").

1878

From March through July Cezanne moves throughout the Midi, traveling between Aix, L'Estaque, and Marseille, where his wife and son are living. Hortense goes to Paris from early November to December 15 while Cezanne remains in L'Estaque with Paul *fils*.

1879

Cezanne leaves L'Estaque for Paris by way of Aix in February and by early April settles in Melun, at 2, place de la Préfecture, making regular trips to the capital. In June, he visits Zola at Médan, where he stays for twelve days before returning to Melun. He spends fall in Paris and on October 6 attends a performance of Zola's play *L'Assommoir*.

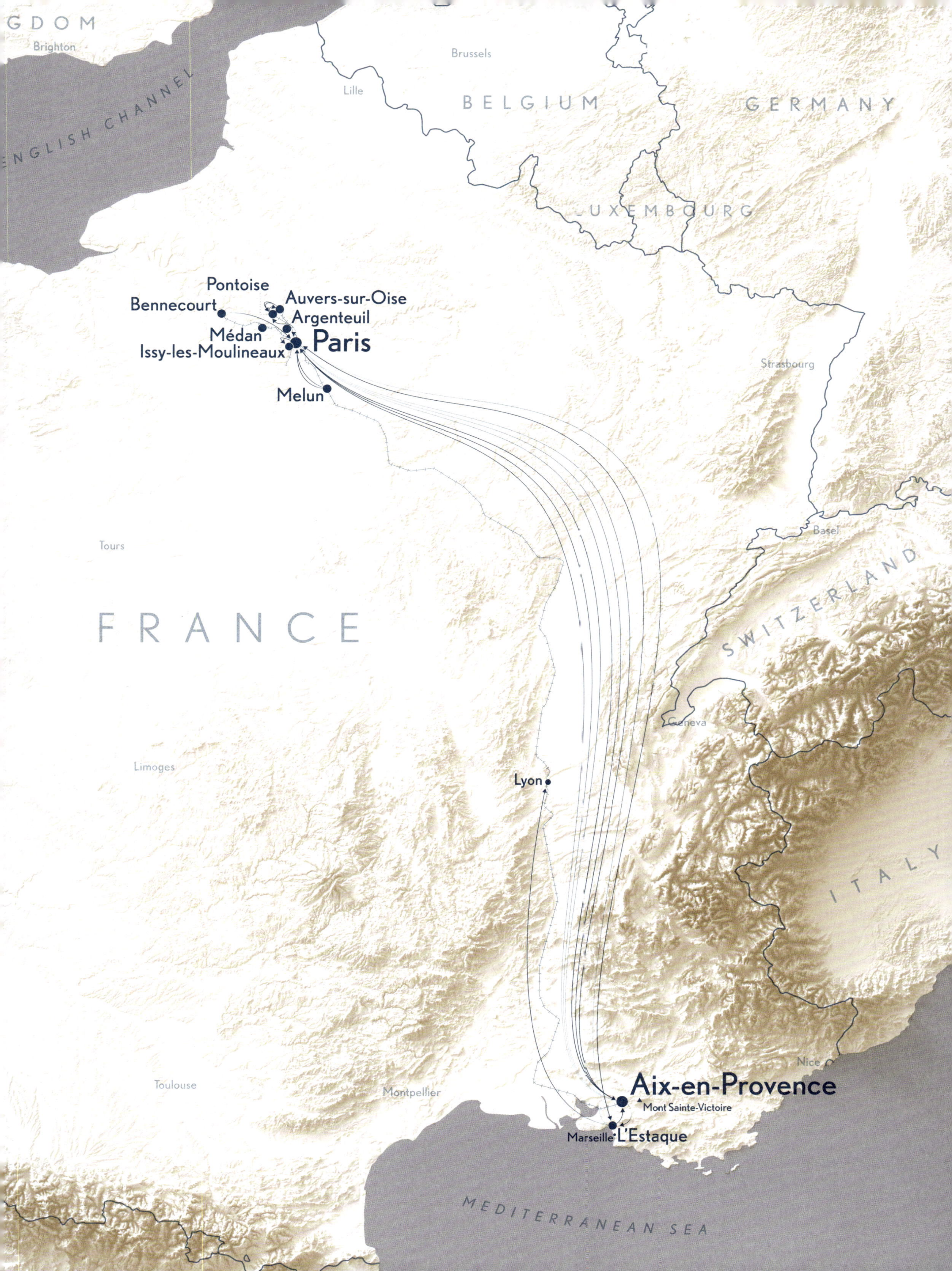

GDOM
Brighton
ENGLISH CHANNEL
Brussels
Lille
BELGIUM
GERMANY
LUXEMBOURG
Strasbourg
Pontoise
Bennecourt
Auvers-sur-Oise
Argenteuil
Médan
Issy-les-Moulineaux
Paris
Melun
Basel
Tours
FRANCE
SWITZERLAND
Limoges
Geneva
Lyon
ITALY
Toulouse
Montpellier
Aix-en-Provence
Mont Sainte-Victoire
Marseille
L'Estaque
Nice
MEDITERRANEAN SEA

1880s

1880

Cezanne leaves Melun in April and moves to Paris with Hortense and their son, residing at 32, rue de l'Ouest, until August 1885. In August, he visits Zola at Médan.

1881

In February Cezanne attends his sister Rose's wedding in Aix. He settles in Pontoise, at 31, quai du Pothuis (now quai Eugène-Turpin), with Hortense and Paul *fils* by May 5 and often sees Pissarro. He frequently walks from Pontoise to Médan, a distance of 14.5 kilometers (9 miles), to see Zola. In late May he spends several days in Paris with his sisters—accompanying them to Versailles—and afterward proceeds to Auvers until October. Cezanne stays with Zola at Médan for a week in late October before leaving for Aix.

1882

In late January Cezanne is visited by Auguste Renoir at L'Estaque, where he remains until early March. He then returns to Paris, still residing at 32, rue de l'Ouest. Cezanne and his family pass the summer in Hattenville, Normandy. They visit Pissarro in Pontoise and in September, Cezanne is with Zola at Médan for several weeks before going to Aix in early October. By November 14, Cezanne is at the Jas and that month drafts his will, leaving his income and property to his mother and son.

1883

From March until May, Cezanne divides his time between L'Estaque and Aix. He is in L'Estaque from November until February 1884 and in late December, Monet and Renoir visit him.

1884

Cezanne is primarily in L'Estaque and Aix while Hortense lives in Paris.

1885

Having spent the first half of the year mostly in the South, he settles in La Roche-Guyon (outside Paris) in mid-June and visits Villennes-sur-Seine and Vernon, close to Médan, the following month. Then the family parts: Hortense and young Paul go to Paris and Cezanne to Aix. By late August, the artist is working in Gardanne and its environs. His wife and son join him in November and they remain until October of the following year.

1886

In March Zola publishes his novel *L'Oeuvre* (The Masterpiece), the story of a talented but troubled artist, loosely based on Cezanne and several of his contemporaries. Cezanne and Hortense marry in Aix on April 28: he lives at the Jas de Bouffan while she and Paul *fils* are in Aix at 10bis, Cours Sextius, until the beginning of 1888. In December his father, Louis-Auguste, dies, leaving the artist an inheritance that affords him unprecedented financial stability.

1887

Early in the year, Cezanne rents a room at the Château Noir (outside Aix) to store supplies; he keeps it for fifteen years, until 1902.

1888

Cezanne is in Aix in January and hosts Renoir at the Jas. The Cezannes move back to Paris, living at 15, quai d'Anjou on the Île Saint-Louis, where the artist begins a series of portraits of Hortense in a red dress (including FWN 490–93; see cats. 35 and 36). He also rents a studio on the rue du Val de Grace (5th arrondissement). From July to November, Cezanne stays in Chantilly, north of Paris.

1889

For long periods, Cezanne lives in Aix while Hortense remains in Paris with their son. The family spends the month of June together in Hattenville.

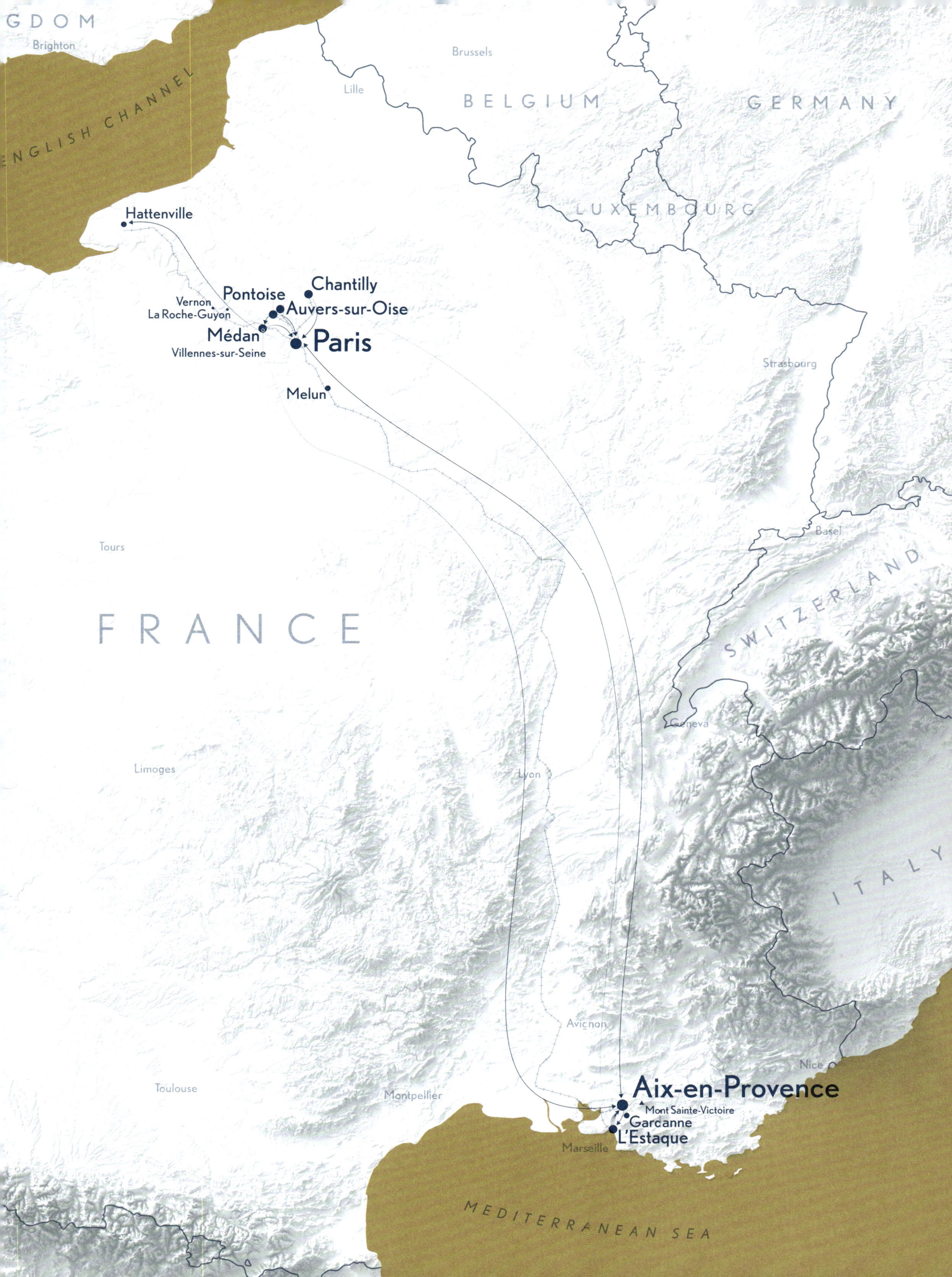

GDOM
Brighton
ENGLISH CHANNEL
Brussels
Lille
BELGIUM
GERMANY
LUXEMBOURG
Strasbourg
Hattenville
Chantilly
Pontoise
Auvers-sur-Oise
Vernon
La Roche-Guyon
Médan
Paris
Villennes-sur-Seine
Melun
Tours
Basel
FRANCE
SWITZERLAND
Limoges
Geneva
Lyon
ITALY
Avignon
Nice
Toulouse
Aix-en-Provence
Montpellier
Mont Sainte-Victoire
Gardanne
L'Estaque
Marseille
MEDITERRANEAN SEA

1890s

1890

Mostly in Paris for the winter, Cezanne spends mid-May to mid-November in Émagny with Hortense, who is a native of the Jura Mountains region, and their son. From there, they take a trip to Switzerland, visiting Neuchâtel, Bern, Fribourg, Lausanne, Vevey, and Geneva. By November, Hortense returns to Paris and Cezanne to the Jas de Bouffan, where he stays until the end of summer of the following year.

1891

For much of the year Cezanne is in Aix at the Jas de Bouffan while Hortense and young Paul reside in Paris at 9, rue de la Monnaie (2nd arrondissement). In the fall the family moves to 2, rue des Lions-Saint-Paul (4th arrondissement), where they live until March 1896.

1892–1893

Cezanne works in Île-de-France—Paris, Alfortville, Avon, Bourron-Marlotte, Fontainebleau, and Melun—and in Aix.

1894

Cezanne spends November 7–30 with Monet in Giverny; he leaves abruptly, without informing his host. At the end of November, Cezanne rents a studio in rue Bonaparte in Paris (6th arrondissement) until January 1896.

1895

Cezanne moves between Paris and Aix in the first half of the year, but in June he settles in the South, where he remains until mid-1896. Hortense and Paul *fils* pass fall and winter with the artist in Aix. He rents a small cabin at Bibémus, to store his painting materials, from November to 1899. He declines to travel to Paris for the exhibition of his work at Vollard's gallery from November 15 to December 15.

1896

Having spent spring in Aix, in June Cezanne takes a room at the Hôtel Molière in Vichy. In July, at the request of his wife and son, Cezanne goes to Talloires on the shore of Lake Annecy, which he paints (see p. 64, fig. 4). On his way he passes through Saint-Laurent-du-Pont, Chambéry, and Annecy, and returns to Aix through Lyon and Rognac. In late August Cezanne goes back to Paris, where he rents an apartment in the Batignolles quarter at 58, rue des Dames. Cezanne moves between Paris and Aix for the rest of the year.

1897

The family settles at 73, rue Saint-Lazare (near the train station of that name), at the beginning of the year. In June, Cezanne visits his mother in Aix; she dies on October 25.

1898

In January Cezanne is back in Paris, where he rents a studio in the Villa des Arts at 15, rue Hégésippe Moreau in the Montmartre neighborhood, for a year. In summer, he paints in Bourron-Marlotte and Montigny-sur-Loing while based in Fontainebleau (FWN 1515) at 11, rue Saint-Louis. He later paints landscapes in Montgeroult and Marines, both in the Val-d'Ois, not far from Paris. He spends winter with his wife and son at 31, rue Ballu in Paris (9th arrondissement), where they live until the beginning of 1904.

1899

Cezanne is in Paris for several months and travels to the Midi in late June. In September, Cezanne returns to the Jas de Bouffan to remove his personal belongings and painting materials; the property is sold on November 21. He settles into the second floor of a house at 23, rue Boulegon, where he has a studio built. By the end of October he is back in Paris.

100 KILOMETERS

Known journey

Approximate train route

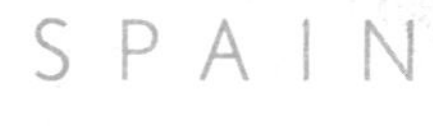

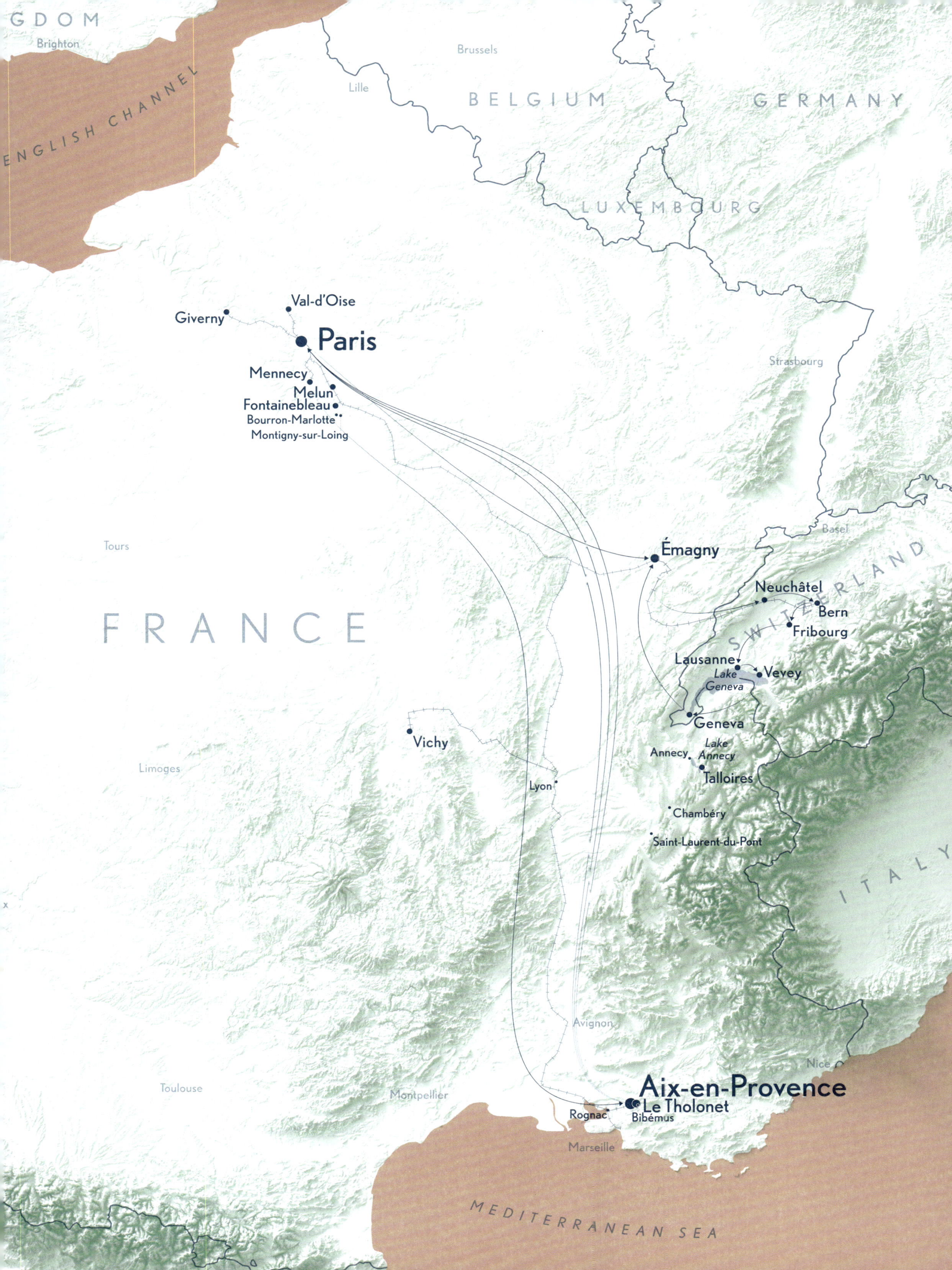

ENGLISH CHANNEL
GDOM
Brighton
BELGIUM
GERMANY
Brussels
Lille
LUXEMBOURG
FRANCE
Giverny
Val-d'Oise
Paris
Mennecy
Melun
Fontainebleau
Bourron-Marlotte
Montigny-sur-Loing
Strasbourg
Tours
Émagny
Basel
Neuchâtel
Bern
Fribourg
SWITZERLAND
Lausanne
Vevey
Lake Geneva
Geneva
Annecy
Lake Annecy
Talloires
Vichy
Limoges
Lyon
Chambéry
Saint-Laurent-du-Pont
ITALY
Toulouse
Montpellier
Avignon
Nice
Aix-en-Provence
Le Tholonet
Rognac
Bibémus
Marseille
MEDITERRANEAN SEA

1900

1900

Cezanne is in Aix, where he will remain for most of the rest of his life.

1901

In November he acquires a small property on the Lauves hill overlooking Aix and begins construction on a freestanding two-floor studio completed the following year.

1902

In September construction ends on the Les Lauves studio—the last of Cezanne's career—and he slowly settles in (FWN 366; FWN 367; FWN 1486).

1904

An entire room is devoted to Cezanne's work—thirty-one paintings and two drawings—at the second Salon d'Automne exhibition in Paris, held October 15–November 15, which the artist does not attend in person.

1905

During the summer Cezanne works in Fontainebleau, returning to Aix by October.

1906

Caught in a storm while working outdoors in Aix, Cezanne collapses in a field and is taken home by a passing driver. He develops pneumonia and dies a few days later, on October 22, at the age of sixty-seven, and is buried at the Saint-Pierre Cemetery in his hometown.

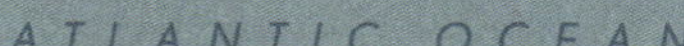

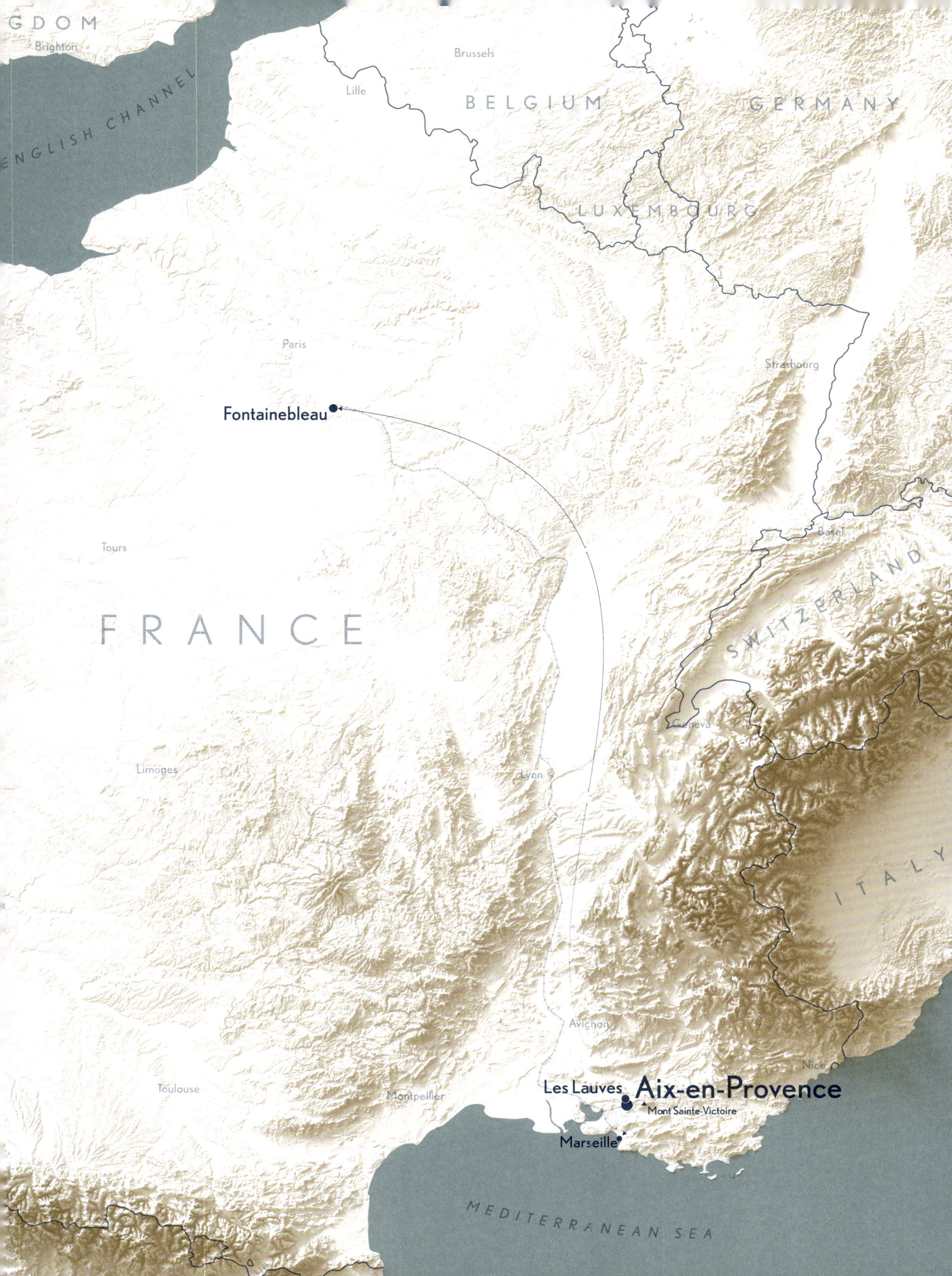
GDOM
Brighton
ENGLISH CHANNEL
BELGIUM
GERMANY
LUXEMBOURG
Brussels
Lille
Paris
Strasbourg
Fontainebleau
Tours
Basel
FRANCE
SWITZERLAND
Limoges
Geneva
Lyon
ITALY
Toulouse
Avignon
Nice
Montpellier
Les Lauves
Aix-en-Provence
Mont Sainte-Victoire
Marseille
MEDITERRANEAN SEA

Contextualizing Cezanne

Compiled by Michael Raymond

January 19, 1839
Paul Cezanne is born.

1848
Liberal uprisings spread across Europe in protest of authoritarian (monarchist) regimes. In France, King Louis Philippe is overthrown and a conservative-led Second Republic is established. When protests continue, the National Guard—comprised mainly of peasants from the provinces—quashes the liberal movement and Louis-Napoléon Bonaparte is elected President of the Republic.

Slavery is abolished by France for the second time.

1850
The French state implements new policies aimed at the "Francization" of French ethnic minorities. School education is increasingly used to teach the language and values of the urban middle class at the expense of provincial languages and customs.

1851
A coup results in the overthrow of the Second Republic and Louis-Napoléon Bonaparte is crowned Emperor Napoleon III, marking the start of the Second French Empire.

The Fête-Dieu (Feast of Corpus Christi) pageant is revived in Aix by a nascent regionalist movement. ◆ Cezanne and his friend Émile Zola take part as members of a brass band.[1]

1853
Georges Haussmann is appointed Prefect of the Seine and begins to modernize the medieval center of Paris by constructing new housing and infrastructure. Slums and industry are cleared from central Paris to make way for middle-class apartments and amenities.

1854
The Félibrige association is co-founded by writer Frédéric Mistral with the aim of promoting Provençal language and culture. ◆ Many of Cezanne's friends become involved in this movement.

1855
Paris's first Exposition Universelle is held.

1856
The railway is extended to Aix and the final section between Marseille and Paris is complete. ◆ The Cezanne family invests heavily in railway stocks and shares that Paul inherits upon his father's death in 1886.

1860
Around this date the Château Noir is built on the outskirts of Aix (see cats. 129–33) in a neo-Gothic style traditionally more common in northern France.

1861
The US Civil War halts cotton exports to Europe (see also p. 93), resulting in a shortage that affects 1.5 million French citizens.[2] While Republicans largely identify with the Union cause, Napoleon III favors the Confederacy and is supported by protesting cotton workers in Paris who demand that the government make cotton available.

The population of Paris reaches 1,696,141, up from 935,261 just twenty years earlier.[3] ◆ Cezanne moves to Paris for the first time.

1863
The first Salon des Refusés is held, displaying artworks rejected from the annual state-sponsored Salon. The exhibition emboldens avant-garde artists such as Gustave Courbet, Édouard Manet, and the Impressionist group.

1867
After an invasion in 1861, France's six-year war in Mexico comes to an end following US opposition and a costly guerrilla war. The French-backed puppet emperor Maximilian is executed, as later depicted by Manet.

The second Exposition Universelle is held in Paris, displaying Japanese art in the city for the first time.

1869
The Suez Canal opens in Egypt. Due to faster shipping and railways introduced a decade earlier, the port city of Marseille experiences an economic boom that impacts the surrounding region, including L'Estaque (see cats. 77–82).

1870
France declares war on Prussia, which results in a humiliating defeat for France and the fall of Napoleon III and the Second Empire. ◆ Cezanne hides with his family in L'Estaque to avoid being drafted into the military.

1871
The working classes of Paris rebel against the new elected conservative government and establish a rival regime known as the Paris Commune. The ensuing battle sees much of Paris reduced to ruins. Approximately 10,000 Communards are killed in the battle or executed afterwards and another 40,000 are imprisoned. ◆ Zola witnesses the destruction and writes to Cezanne in the aftermath, "Paris is reborn. As I've often told you, our reign has begun!"[4]

1872
Jules Verne's *Around the World in 80 Days* is first published. Print culture booms during this decade to capitalize on rising literacy rates.

1873
After completing a prison sentence, Courbet flees France in exile to avoid paying crippling reparations for his role in the Paris Commune, where he oversaw the destruction of the Vendôme Column. ◆ Camille Pissarro includes an image of Courbet in an 1874 portrait of Cezanne (National Gallery, London).

1874
The First Impressionist Exhibition is held April–May in a gallery in Paris on boulevard des Capucines. ◆ Cezanne shows three paintings (FWN 77; FWN 81; FWN 628).

1875
The Wallon Amendment passes by a single vote, cementing the establishment of the French Third Republic.

1876

The "State of Siege" enabling military rule, imposed on Paris since 1871, is lifted.

1877

A railway branch line linking Aix to Marseille is completed. ◆ Cezanne would later paint this line's viaduct over the Arc River (see cats. 109–11 and 113).

Zola publishes *L'Assommoir* to great success. The novel focuses on the Parisian working classes and argues that Haussmann's transformative building works in Paris had merely displaced poverty. To escape from the ensuing attention, Zola spends four months in L'Estaque.

The Third Impressionist Exhibition is held in Paris. ◆ Cezanne participates for the second and final time.

1878

Paris hosts its third Exposition Universelle, organized to celebrate France's recovery from the Franco-Prussian war and Paris Commune. As part of the exhibition electric lights are installed in the streets of Paris for the first time.

Marius Roux's novel *The Substance and the Shadow* is published (see also p. 32n10). The plot describes an art market moving away from the Salon and toward dealers capitalizing on bourgeois tastes.[5]

1879

Jules Grévy becomes the first Republican president of the Third Republic, ushering in a period that supports bourgeois values, colonial expansion, and patriotism.

Severiano de Heredia is elected president of the municipal council of Paris, in effect becoming the first person of African descent to act as mayor of a Western world capital.

1880

Zola publishes his novel *Nana*, about the life of a high-class prostitute in Paris, to great acclaim. ◆ Cezanne would later copy the label image of "Champagne Nana," launched to capitalize on the book's popularity (see cat. 54).

1881

Increased urbanization means that more than a third of France's population lives in a town or city for the first time in history.[6]

1884

A cholera outbreak in Marseille kills 1,777 people.

1885

The last *indienne* cloth-printing workshop closes in Aix.[7] ◆ Cezanne depicted indienne cloths, a Provençal specialty, in a number of his works (see cats. 57–64).

1889

The Eiffel Tower is constructed for Paris's fourth Exposition Universelle. ◆ Cezanne's *House of the Hanged Man* (c. 1873; FWN 81) is displayed at the exhibition.

After being outlawed for a century, Aix's carnival is revived. ◆ Cezanne makes several works depicting figures from the festivities (see cat. 46).

1892

Members of the French Government are discovered to have taken bribes to cover up a failed attempt to build a canal across Panama. Several Jewish bankers are at the heart of the affair, fueling anti-Semitism in France.

1894

Alfred Dreyfus, Jewish and a captain in the French army, is wrongly convicted of treason for allegedly passing military secrets to the Germans. The Dreyfus affair divides public opinion and embitters French politics for a generation.

1895

The French Empire expands to cover 9.5 million square kilometers, almost ten times its extent in 1880.[8]

1898

Zola publishes *J'Accuse…!*, denouncing the French president, government, and military leadership for covering up the truth of the Dreyfus affair. It results in Zola's prosecution for libel and he flees France for exile in England.

1900

The fifth Universelle Exposition is held and the first line of the Paris Metro is constructed.

1902

Gas and electric lighting continues to be rolled out across Marseille and L'Estaque. ◆ Cezanne complains about "hideous streets with gas lamps and—even worse—electric light" in L'Estaque.[9]

1903

Writer, former politician, and ardent anti-Dreyfusard Henri Rochefort publishes a widely circulated, blistering attack on Zola and Cezanne, conflating Impressionism with a pro-Dreyfus stance. ◆ Copies of the article are distributed across Aix, much to Cezanne's dismay.

1904

Mistral is awarded the Nobel Prize in Literature for his work promoting and preserving Provençal culture and heritage.

1906

Dreyfus is exonerated by France's supreme court and readmitted to the military, bringing legal closure to the affair.

October 22, 1906

Paul Cezanne dies, survived by his wife, Hortense, and their only son, Paul.

Notes

1. Nina Maria Athanassoglou-Kallmyer, *Cézanne and Provence: The Painter in His Culture* (Chicago: University of Chicago Press, 2003), 64–65.

2. Samuel Bernstein, "The Opposition of French Labor to American Slavery," *Science and Society* 17, no. 2 (Spring 1953): 138.

3. These numbers reflect census data; see discussions in, e.g., Tyler Stovall, *The Rise of the Paris Red Belt* (Berkeley: University of California Press, 1990).

4. Émile Zola to Paul Cezanne, July 4, 1871, in *The Letters of Paul Cézanne*, edited and translated by Alex Danchev (Los Angeles: J. Paul Getty Museum, 2013), 143, letter 46.

5. Paul Smith, "Introduction," in Marius Roux, *The Substance and the Shadow* (University Park, PA: Penn State University Press, 2007), xxiv–xxviii.

6. Peter McPhee, *A Social History of France, 1780–1880* (London and New York: Routledge, 1992), 188–89.

7. Jean Arrouye, ed., *Cezanne: Paris-Provence* (Paris: Textuel, 1995), 55.

8. Martin Evans, "Preface," in *Empire and Culture: The French Experience, 1830–1940*, edited by Martin Evans (Basingstoke, Hampshire, UK: Palgrave Macmillan, 2005), vii.

9. Paul Cezanne to Paule Conil in Danchev, *Letters*, 323, letter 220.

Cezanne in the Collections of the Impressionist Circle

Compiled by Kathryn Kremnitzer

Object information has been drawn primarily from Walter Feilchenfeldt, Jayne Warman, and David Nash, eds., *The Paintings, Watercolors and Drawings of Paul Cezanne: An Online Catalogue Raisonné* (2018–present), http://cezannecatalogue.com. The abbreviation *FWN* prefaces identification numbers used within that catalogue raisonné.

KEY

○ Exhibited at the Third Impressionist Exhibition in 1877
□ Exhibited at the gallery of Ambroise Vollard, Cezanne's first dealer, in 1895
△ Exhibited at the 1905 Salon d'Automne
★ Gift from Cezanne
☆ Purchased from Cezanne
◇ Purchased from Vollard
◆ Purchased from Julien-François "Père" Tanguy, a popular seller of art supplies who often accepted artworks as payment
* Acquired before 1895 and the Vollard exhibition

Gustave Caillebotte

The Rococo Vase, 1875–77
Oil on canvas; 73 × 60 cm
(28 ¹¹⁄₁₆ × 23 ⅝ in.)
FWN 722 ○ ★ □ △ *
The National Gallery of Art, Washington, DC

Bathers at Rest, c. 1876–77
Oil on canvas; 82.2 × 101.2 cm
(32 ⅜ × 39 ¹³⁄₁₆ in.)
FWN 926 □ * (purchased from Ernest Cabaner)
Barnes Foundation, Philadelphia
P. 26, fig. 3

The Pond, 1876–77
Oil on canvas; 44.5 × 53.5 cm
(17 ½ × 21 ¹⁄₁₆ in.)
FWN 637 □ △ ◆ *
Museum of Fine Arts, Boston

The Gulf of Marseille, Seen from L'Estaque, c. 1878–79
Oil on canvas; 58 × 72 cm (22 ¹³⁄₁₆ × 28 ⅜ in.)
FWN 119 ★ *
Musée d'Orsay, Paris
Cat. 80

Courtyard of the Farm, c. 1879
Oil on canvas; 63 × 52 cm
(24 ¹³⁄₁₆ × 20 ½ in.)
FWN 129 ★ *
Musée d'Orsay, Paris

Mary Cassatt

Apples and Linen, 1879–80
Oil on canvas; 25 × 44 cm
(9 ¹³⁄₁₆ × 17 ⁵⁄₁₆ in.)
FWN 763 □ ◇
Private collection, Japan

Edgar Degas

Portrait of Victor Chocquet, c. 1877
Oil on canvas; 35.2 × 27.3 cm
(13 ¹³⁄₁₆ × 10 ¹¹⁄₁₆ in.)
FWN 438 □ ◇
Virginia Museum of Fine Arts, Richmond

Bather with Outstretched Arms, 1877–78
Oil on canvas; 33 × 24 cm (13 × 9 ⅜ in.)
FWN 913 □ ◇
Collection of Jasper Johns

Still Life with Apples, c. 1878
Oil on canvas; 19 × 27 cm (7 ½ × 10 ⅝ in.)
FWN 760 □ ◇
Fitzwilliam Museum, Cambridge, UK
Cat. 3

Venus and Love, c. 1878
Oil on canvas; 21 × 21 cm (8 ⁵⁄₁₆ × 8 ⁵⁄₁₆ in.)
FWN 652 ◇
Private collection, Japan

Glass and Apples, 1879–80
Oil on canvas; 31.5 × 40 cm
(12 ⅜ × 15 ¹¹⁄₁₆ in.)
FWN 779 □
Rudolf Staechelin, Basel, Switzerland
P. 39, fig. 4

Portrait of the Artist, 1879–80
Oil on canvas; 33.5 × 24.5 cm
(13 ³⁄₁₆ × 9 ⅝ in.)
FWN 450 ◇
Sammlung Oskar Reinhart, "Am Römerholz," Winterthur, Switzerland

Two Fruits, c. 1887
Oil on canvas; 19 × 23.2 cm
(7 ½ × 9 ⅛ in.)
FWN 797 □ ◇
Private collection, Japan

Three Pears, 1888–90
Graphite and watercolor on laid paper; 24.2 × 31 cm (9 ½ × 12 ³⁄₁₆ in.)
FWN 1944 □ ◇
Henry and Rose Pearlman Foundation, New York (on loan to Princeton University Art Museum since 1976)

Assigned to Edgar Degas

Head of a Woman Asleep, 1876–79
Graphite on paper; 18 × 28 cm
(7 ¹⁄₁₆ × 11 in.)
FWN 2128
Private collection, Switzerland

After Puget: Miion de Crotone, c. 1879–82
Graphite on paper; 37 × 26.5 cm
(14 ⁹⁄₁₆ × 10 ⅞ in.)
FWN 2142
Nationalmuseum, Stockholm

After L'Ecorché, 1893–96
Graphite on paper; 18 × 28 cm
(7 ¹⁄₁₆ × 11 in.)
FWN 2175 (verso of 2128)
Private collection, Switzerland

After the Antique: Sleeping Hermaphrodite, 1895–96
Graphite on laid paper; 26.5 × 37 cm
(10 ⅞ × 14 ⁹⁄₁₆ in.)
FWN 2178
Nationalmuseum, Stockholm

Paul Gauguin

Nude, before 1870
FWN 595 ◆
Location unknown (probably destroyed by the artist)

The Reaper, c. 1877
Oil on canvas; 45.7 × 55.2 cm
(18 × 21 ¹¹⁄₁₆ in.)
FWN 651 △ ◆
Private collection, Japan

The François Zola Dam, c. 1879
Oil on canvas; 53.5 × 72.4 cm
(21 ¹⁄₁₆ × 28 ½ in.)
FWN 124 ◆ *
National Museum Cardiff, Amgueddfa Cymru – National Museum Wales
Cat. 26

Still Life with Fruit Dish, 1879–80
Oil on canvas; 46.4 × 54.6 cm
(18 ¼ × 21 ½ in.)
FWN 780 ★ *
The Museum of Modern Art, New York
Cat. 53

Émile Zola's Country-House, c. 1880
Oil on canvas; 59 × 72 cm
(23 ³⁄₁₆ × 28 ⁵⁄₁₆ in.)
FWN 149 ☆
Glasgow City Art Gallery, Burrell Collection

Avenue, c. 1880–82
Oil on canvas; 73.5 × 60.5 cm
(28 ⅞ × 23 ¹³⁄₁₆ in.)
FWN 130 ◆ *
Göteborg Konstmuseum, Sweden
Cat. 18

Édouard Manet

Sheet of Studies, 1879–82
Graphite on laid paper; 37.9 × 31.3 cm
(14 ¹⁵⁄₁₆ × 12 ⁵⁄₁₆ in.)
FWN 2301 ★
Albertina Museum, Vienna

Claude Monet

Portrait of a Man, 1866–67
Oil on canvas; 81.5 × 66 cm (32 ¹⁄₁₆ × 26 in.)
FWN 413 ◇
Sammlung Oskar Reinhart, "Am Römerholz," Winterthur, Switzerland

Scipio, 1866–68
Oil on canvas; 107 × 86 cm (42 ⅛ × 33 ⅞ in.)
FWN 422 □ ◇
Museu de Arte de São Paulo
Cat. 25

Picnic on a Riverbank, 1873–74
Oil on canvas; 26.5 × 34 cm
(10 ⅜ × 13 ⅜ in.)
FWN 626 *
Yale University Art Gallery, New Haven, Connecticut

The Beach at L'Estaque, 1877–78
Oil on canvas; 53.5 × 64.5 cm
(21 ¹⁄₁₆ × 25 ⅜ in.)
FWN 111 ◇
Private collection, Texas

Melting Snow at Fontainebleau, 1879–80
Oil on canvas; 73.6 × 100.6 cm
(29 × 39 ⅝ in.)
FWN 145
The Museum of Modern Art, New York

L'Estaque, 1879–83
Oil on canvas; 80 × 99.3 cm
(31 ½ × 39 ¹⁄₁₆ in.)
FWN 154 □ ◇
The Museum of Modern Art, New York

Turn in the Road, c. 1881
Oil on canvas; 60.6 × 73.3 cm
(23 ⅞ × 28 ⅞ in.)
FWN 163 ◇ (acquired 1907)
Museum of Fine Arts, Boston
Cat. 29

Boy in the Red Vest, 1888–90
Oil on canvas; 81.2 × 65 cm
(31 ¹⁵⁄₁₆ × 25 ⅝ in.)
FWN 495 □ ◇
The Museum of Modern Art, New York

Boy in the Red Vest, 1889–90
Watercolor on laid paper; 46 × 31 cm
(18 ⅛ × 12 ³⁄₁₆ in.)
FWN 1755 ◇
Private collection, Paris

Apples and Primroses, c. 1890
Oil on canvas; 72 × 92.4 cm
(28 ¾ × 36 ⅜ in.)
FWN 824 *
The Metropolitan Museum of Art, New York

Bathers, 1890–92
Oil on canvas; 54.3 × 66 cm
(21 3/8 × 26 in.)
FWN 950 ◇
Saint Louis Art Museum
Cat. 102

Ginger Pot with Pomegranate and Pears,
1893
Oil on canvas; 46.4 × 55.6 cm
(18 1/4 × 21 7/8 in.)
FWN 839 ◇
The Phillips Collection, Washington, DC
Cat. 55

Still Life, Apples, and Jug, c. 1900
Oil on canvas; 45.8 × 54.9 cm
(18 1/16 × 21 5/8 in.)
FWN 878 ◇
The National Gallery of Art, Washington,
DC

Vase in the Garden, 1900–1904
Oil on canvas; 65 × 54 cm
(25 5/8 × 21 1/4 in.)
FWN 880 ◇
Private collection, Japan

Château Noir, 1903–4
Oil on canvas; 73.6 × 93.2 cm
(29 × 36 11/16 in.)
FWN 360 ◇
The Museum of Modern Art, New York

Camille Pissarro

Group of Men Seated at a Table, n.d.
Graphite on paper; 11.5 × 19 cm
(4 1/2 × 7 1/2 in.)
FWN 1822 ★
Private collection

Seated Young Woman, 1865–68
Black crayon on paper; 21 × 13 cm
(8 1/4 × 5 1/8 in.)
FWN 1700 ★
Location unknown

Cabin, 1865–70
Oil on canvas; 22.5 × 35 cm
(8 7/8 × 13 3/4 in.)
FWN 1012
Private collection, New York

Toilette, c. 1867
Oil on canvas; 22.5 × 33 cm
(8 13/16 × 13 in.)
FWN 593 ★
Private collection

Woman Pulling on Her Stocking, 1867–69
Black crayon on blue wove paper
(fragment); 16 × 23 cm (6 5/16 × 9 1/16 in.)
FWN 2105 ★
Private collection

Studies, 1867–69
Black crayon on blue wove paper
(fragment); 17 × 25.1 cm (6 11/16 × 9 7/8 in.)
FWN 2107 ★
Private collection, New York

Woman Doing Her Hair, 1867–69
Black crayon on blue wove paper;
16.3 × 25.2 cm (6 7/16 × 9 15/16 in.)
FWN 2108 ★
Israel Museum, Jerusalem

The Fisherman, 1868–70
Oil on canvas; 27 × 36 cm
(10 5/8 × 14 3/16 in.)
FWN 604 □ ◇ *
Location unknown

Standing Bather, Wiping Her Hair, c. 1869
Oil on canvas; 29 × 13 cm (11 3/8 × 5 1/8 in.)
FWN 901 ◇
Private collection

*Woman Bathing, and Copies after
Delacroix*, 1869–72
Graphite on paper; 21 × 26 cm
(8 1/4 × 10 1/4 in.)
FWN 2231 ★
Location unknown

The Basin of the Jas de Bouffan, c. 1870
Oil on canvas; 11.5 × 19 cm (4 1/2 × 7 1/2 in.)
FWN 1017 ★
Private collection

Portrait of a Painter, 1871–74
Graphite on paper; measurements
unknown
FWN 1709 ★
Location unknown

Paris: Quai de Bercy—The Wine Market,
1872
Oil on canvas; 73 × 92 cm
(28 11/16 × 36 3/16 in.)
FWN 62 ★
Portland Art Museum, Oregon

Road in a Forest, c. 1872
Oil on canvas; 55.2 × 45.7 cm
(21 11/16 × 18 in.)
FWN 73 ★
Solomon R. Guggenheim Museum,
New York

Landscape around Auvers-sur-Oise,
1872–73
Graphite, watercolor, and gouache on
laid paper; 23 × 28 cm (9 1/16 × 11 in.)
FWN 1025 ★
Private collection

Portrait of Pissarro, c. 1873
Graphite on laid paper; 13.3 × 10.3 cm
(5 1/4 × 4 1/16 in.)
FWN 1712 ★
Musée d'Orsay, held in the Musée du
Louvre, Paris

*Entrance to the Farm, rue Rémy, at
Auvers-sur-Oise*, 1873
Oil on canvas; 60 × 49 cm
(23 5/8 × 19 5/16 in.)
FWN 76 ★
Private collection

Camille Pissarro, Seen from the Back,
1874–77
Graphite on paper; 12.7 × 15.3 cm
(5 1/2 × 6 in.)
FWN 1713 ★
Kunstmuseum Basel, Switzerland

Swimming, c. 1875–77
Oil on canvas; 19 × 27 cm (7 1/2 × 10 5/8 in.)
FWN 908 ◇ *
Private collection, New York

Flowers, c. 1877
Oil on canvas; 56 × 46.3 cm
(22 1/16 × 18 1/4 in.)
FWN 730 △
Private collection, New York

The Peasant Woman, c. 1877
Oil on canvas; 48 × 40 cm
(18 7/8 × 15 11/16 in.)
FWN 440 ★
Location unknown

Self-Portrait, c. 1877
Oil on canvas; 26 × 15 cm
(10 3/16 × 5 7/8 in.)
FWN 444 □ ◇
Musée d'Orsay, Paris

*The Etang des Soeurs [Nuns' Pond] at
Osny, near Pontoise*, 1877
Oil on canvas; 60 × 73.5 cm
(23 5/8 × 28 7/8 in.)
FWN 106 ★
The Courtauld, London

*Landscape of Pontoise, View of the
Hermitage*, 1877
Oil on canvas; 50 × 61 cm (19 11/16 × 24 in.)
FWN 109 ★
Private collection, Texas

Still Life with Soup Tureen, 1877
Oil on canvas; 65 × 83 cm
(25 5/8 × 32 11/16 in.)
FWN 726 ★
Musée d'Orsay, Paris

Sancho Pança, c. 1878
Oil on canvas; 47 × 55 cm
(18 1/2 × 21 5/8 in.)
FWN 653 ★
Private collection, Mexico

The Battle of Love, 1879–80
Oil on canvas; 42 × 55 cm
(16 1/2 × 21 5/8 in.)
FWN 656 ★
Private collection
Cat. 15

Fortifications at the Glacière, c. 1881
Oil on canvas; 54 × 65 cm
(21 1/4 × 25 5/8 in.)
FWN 171 ★
Location unknown

The Hermitage at Pontoise, 1881
Oil on canvas; 46.5 × 56 cm
(18 5/16 × 22 in.)
FWN 159
Von der Heydt Museum, Wuppertal,
Germany

Self-Portrait, c. 1881–82
Oil on canvas; 57 × 47 cm
(22 7/16 × 18 1/2 in.)
FWN 461 ★
Private collection (presently at The State
Hermitage Museum, St. Petersburg)

Portrait of Jules Peyron, 1885–87
Oil on canvas; 25.5 × 20 cm
(10 1/16 × 7 7/8 in.)
FWN 473 ★
Location unknown

Pierre-Auguste Renoir

The Hanged Man's House, 1872–73
Oil on canvas; 72.3 × 59.3 cm
(28 1/2 × 23 3/8 in.)
FWN 66 ★
Pola Museum of Art, Hakone, Japan

Carafe and Bowl, 1878–80
Oil on canvas; 17.5 × 11.2 cm
(6 7/8 × 4 7/16 in.)
FWN 1902 ★
Private collection, Switzerland

The Battle of Love, c. 1880
Oil on canvas; 38 × 46 cm
(14 15/16 × 18 1/8 in.)
FWN 657 □ ◇
The National Gallery of Art, Washington,
DC

Landscape, c. 1881
Oil on canvas; 80 × 63.5 cm
(31 1/2 × 25 in.)
FWN 167 ★
Private collection

The Road that Turns, 1885
Oil on canvas; 62.2 × 75.5 cm
(24 1/2 × 29 11/16 in.)
FWN 204 ★
Smith College Museum of Art,
Northampton, Massachusetts

*Page XLV from Basel Sketchbook III:
Landscape* (verso), n.d.; *Bathers* (recto),
c. 1888
Graphite and watercolor on wove paper;
12.6 × 20.8 cm (4 15/16 × 8 3/16 in.)
FWN 3007-45a/b ★
The Metropolitan Museum of Art,
New York

Cezanne's Materials

Contemporary accounts tell us a great deal about Paul Cezanne's theory and practice but many questions about his material preferences and processes could not be addressed until recently. The preparations for *Cezanne* allowed staff in the department of Conservation and Science at the Art Institute of Chicago to undertake analysis of the pigments and media in the painter's watercolor boxes. These boxes and an oil palette, all in the collection of the Musée Granet, were included in the display, providing us with a unique opportunity to further elucidate Cezanne's approach to making art. Each residual brushstroke is a tangible trace of the mechanics by which he recorded his "sensations."

Palettes like these examples are highly portable for indoor or outdoor use and may even come equipped with an ergonomic thumbhole. Historic images show Cezanne painting *en plein air* with similar equipment. Our scientific investigations of the watercolor boxes revealed the presence of pigments such as zinc white, bone black, vermillion, organic dyes of animal and plant origin, cobalt, Prussian and ultramarine blues, emerald green, viridian, chrome yellow, cadmium yellow, and earth pigments. These types of watercolor palettes were listed in trade catalogues of 1896, 1904, and 1912 produced by Gustave Sennelier, a French manufacturer of art materials who was famous for the vibrancy of his pigments and the quality of his paint formulations. Cezanne purchased supplies from Sennelier's shop, as did other artists including Pierre Bonnard, Paul Gauguin, Vasily Kandinsky, Claude Monet, Pablo Picasso, and Chaim Soutine. Surviving receipts and correspondence between Cezanne and paint manufacturers and merchants—including Sennelier as well as Julien-François "Père" Tanguy—testify to the artist's detailed attention to every stage of his creative process, including the sources of his choice of pigments. —Maria Kokkori

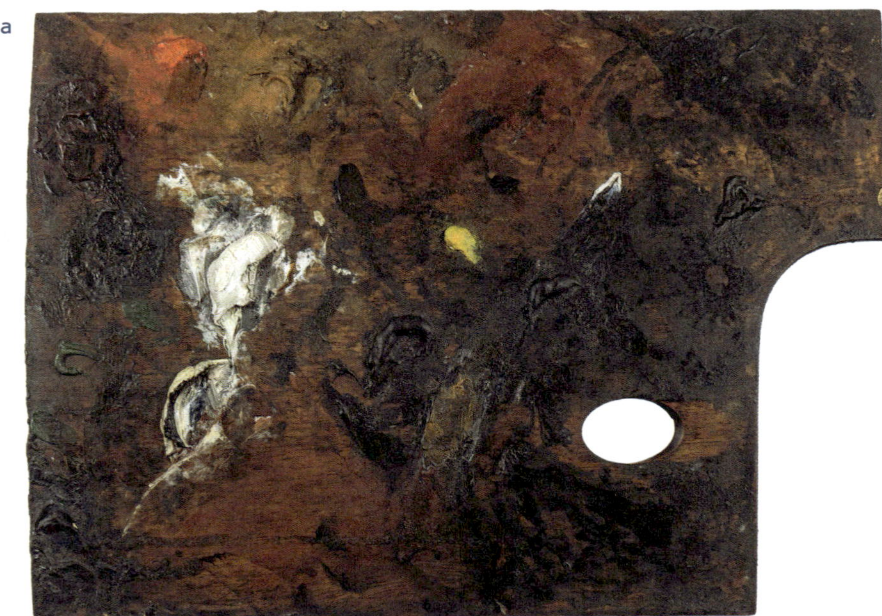

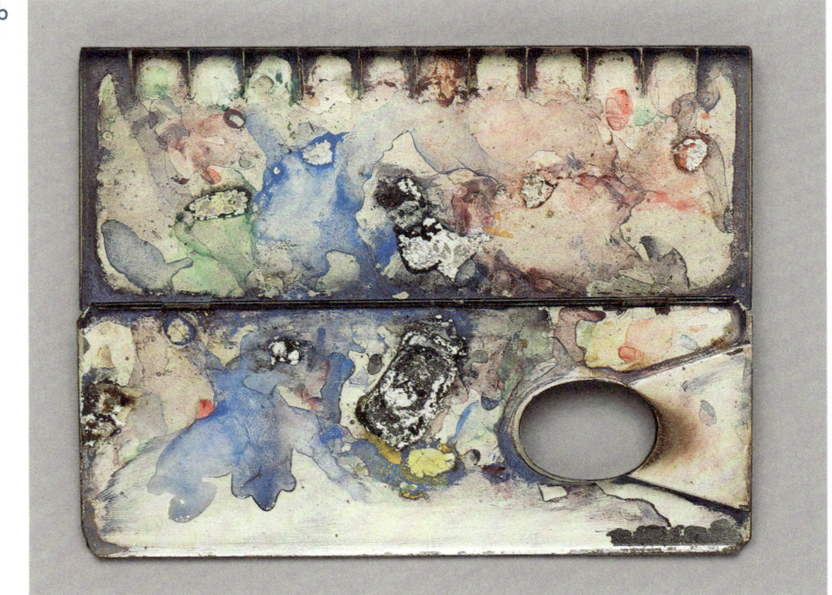

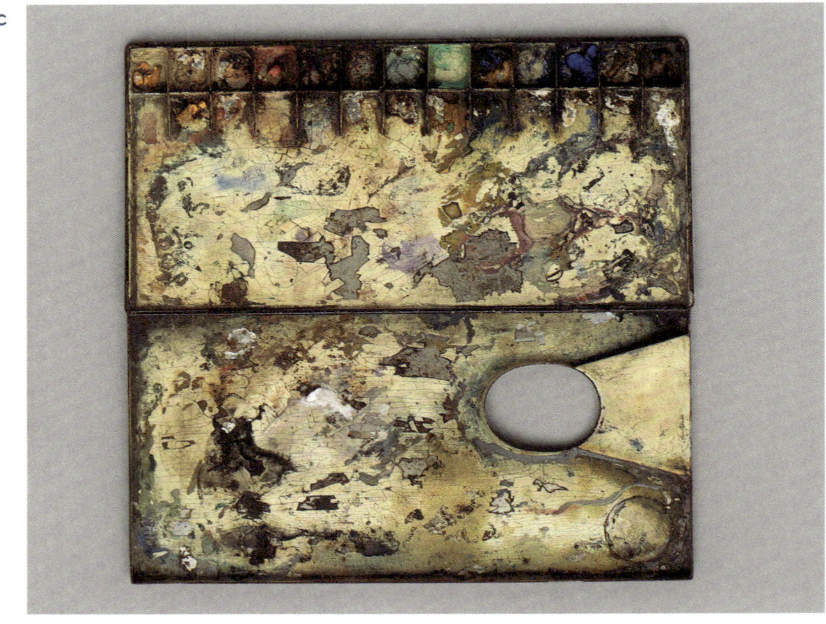

(a) Wooden palette
32.5 × 43 cm (12 ¹³⁄₁₆ × 16 ¹⁵⁄₁₆ in.)
Musée Granet, Aix-en-Provence

(b) Watercolor box (with hole for thumb)
22.1 × 9 × 0.7 cm (8 ¹¹⁄₁₆ × 3 ⁹⁄₁₆ × ¼ in.)
Musée Granet, Aix-en-Provence

(c) Watercolor box (with hole for thumb)
20.8 × 11 × 1 cm (8 ³⁄₁₆ × 4 ⁵⁄₁₆ × ⅜ in.)
Musée Granet, Aix-en-Provence

(d) Watercolor box (empty)
24.2 × 8.7 × 0.9 cm (9 ½ × 3 ⁷⁄₁₆ × ⅜ in.)
Musée Granet, Aix-en-Provence

(e) Watercolor box (with colors)
19 × 8.6 × 1.7 cm (7 ½ × 3 ⅜ × ¹¹⁄₁₆ in.)
Musée Granet, Aix-en-Provence

d

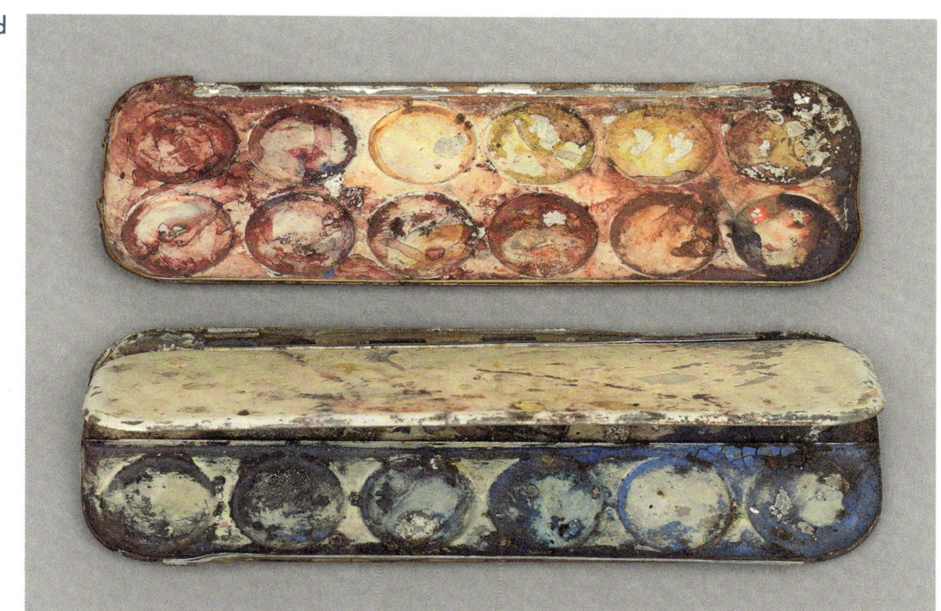

e

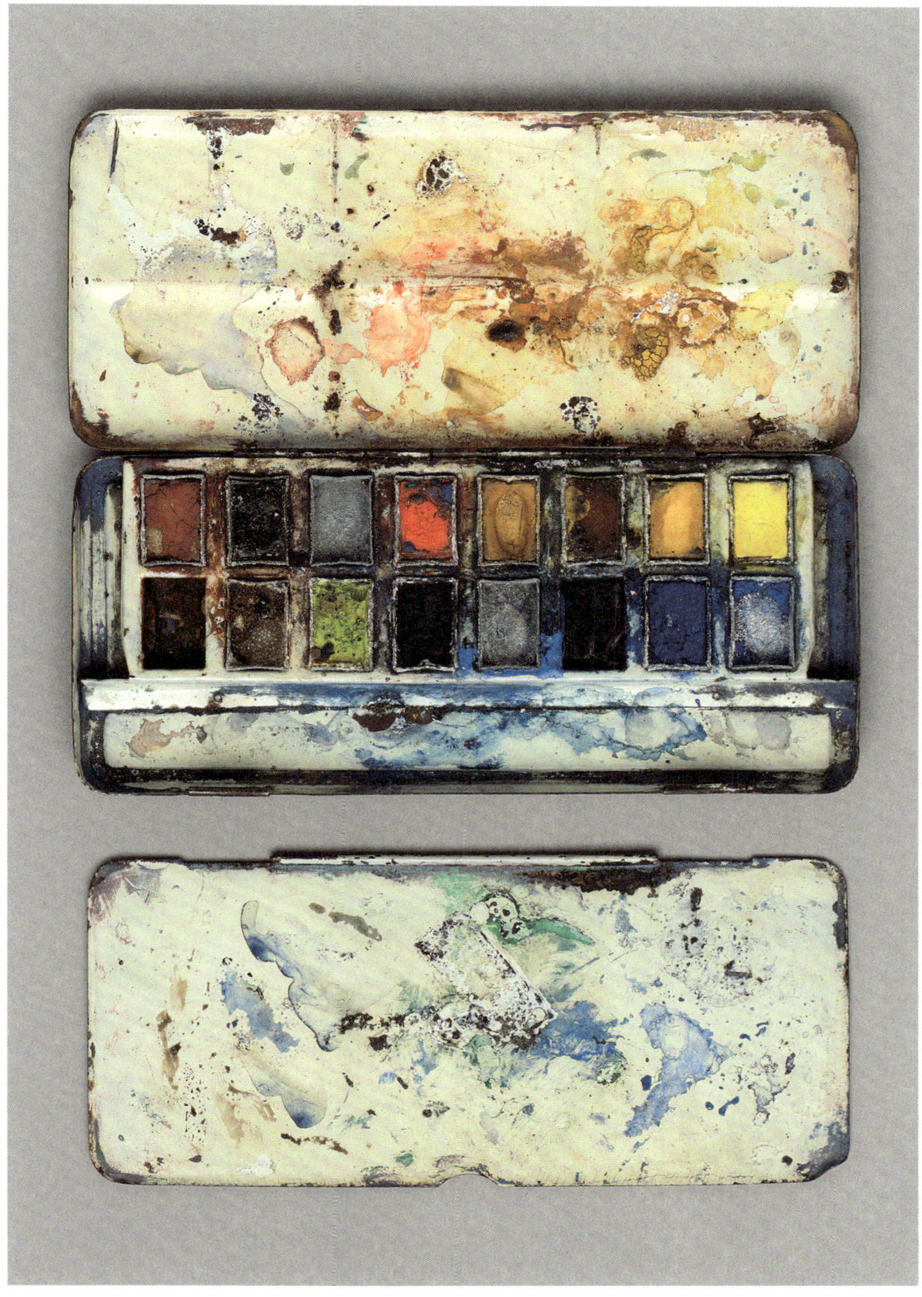

WORKS CITED

Adnan, Etel. *Of Cities and Women (Letters to Fawwaz)*. Sausalito, CA: Post-Apollo Press, 1993.

Aebi, Kiko. "From Study Sheet to Composite Canvas." In *Cézanne Drawing*, edited by Jodi Hauptman and Samantha Friedman, 182–83. Exh. cat. New York: Museum of Modern Art, 2021.

Aldrovandi, A., E. Buzzegoli, A. Keller, and D. Kunzelman. "Investigation of Painted Surfaces with a Reflected UV False Color Technique." In *Proceedings of Art '05: 8th International Conference on Non-Destructive Investigations and Microanalysis for the Diagnostics and Conservation of the Cultural and Environmental Heritage, 15–19 May, Lecce, Italy, 2005*, edited by C. Parisi, G. Buzzanca, and A. Paradisi, n.p. Lecce, Italy: Italian Society of Non-Destructive Testing Monitoring Diagnostics, 2005.

Alexis, Paul. *Émile Zola: Notes d'un ami*. Paris: G. Charpentier, 1882.

———. *Madame Meuriot: moeurs parisiens*. Paris: G. Charpentier, 1890.

Amory, Dita, Philippe Cézanne, Anne Dumas, Charlotte Hale, Kathryn Kremnitzer, Marjorie Shelley, and Hilary Spurling. *Madame Cézanne*. Exh. cat. New York: Metropolitan Museum of Art, 2014.

Andersen, Wayne. *Cézanne and the Eternal Feminine*. Cambridge, UK: Cambridge University Press, 2005.

Armstrong, Carol. *Cézanne in the Studio: Still Life in Watercolor*. Los Angeles: J. Paul Getty Trust, 2004.

Arnheim, Rudolf. *Art and Visual Perception: A Psychology of the Creative Eye*. Berkeley: University of California Press, 1954.

Arrouye, Jean, ed. *Cézanne, Paris-Provence*. Paris: Textuel, 1995.

Athanassoglou-Kallmyer, Nina Maria. *Cézanne and Provence: The Painter in His Culture*. Chicago: University of Chicago Press, 2003.

Bail, Murray. "A Painters' Painter: Introduction." In *Classic Cézanne*, edited by Terence Maloon, 165–67. Exh. cat. Sydney: Art Gallery of New South Wales, 1998.

Bailey, Colin. *Renoir's Portraits: Impressions of an Age*. New Haven, CT: Yale University Press, 1998.

Bailly-Herzberg, Janine, ed. *Correspondance de Camille Pissarro: Tome 1, 1865–1885*. Paris: Presses universitaires de France, 1980.

Baldassari, Anne, ed. *Icons of Modern Art: The Shchukin Collection*. Exh. cat. Paris: Fondation Louis Vuitton and Gallimard, 2016.

Barskaya, Anna, and Yevgenia Georgievskaya. *Paul Cézanne 1839–1906*. New York: Parkstone International, 2004.

Baumann, Felix, Evelyn Benesch, Walter Feilchenfeldt, and Klaus Albrecht Schröder, eds. *Cézanne: Finished – Unfinished*. Exh. cat. Ostfildern Ruit, Germany: Hatje Cantz, 2000.

Benesch, Evelyn. "From the Incomplete to the Unfinished: *Réalisation* in the Work of Paul Cézanne." In *Cézanne: Finished – Unfinished*, edited by Felix Baumann, Evelyn Benesch, Walter Feilchenfeldt, and Klaus Albrecht Schröder, 41–61. Exh. cat. Ostfildern Ruit, Germany: Hatje Cantz, 2000.

Bernard, Émile. "Memories of Paul Cézanne." In *Conversations with Cézanne*, edited by Michael Doran and translated by Julie Lawrence Cochran, 50–79. Berkeley: University of California Press, 2001.

———. "Paul Cézanne." *L'Occident* (July 1904): 17–30.

Bernstein, Samuel. "The Opposition of French Labor to American Slavery." *Science and Society* 17, no. 2 (Spring 1953): 136–54.

Bishop, Janet C., Cécile Debray, and Rebecca A. Rabinow. *The Steins Collect: Matisse, Picasso, and the Parisian Avant-Garde*. Exh. cat. New Haven, CT: San Francisco Museum of Modern Art with Yale University Press, 2011.

Blanc, Charles. "Salon de 1866." *Gazette des beaux-arts* 21 (July 1866): 38.

Bodelsen, Merete. "Early Impressionist Sales 1874–94 in the Light of Some Unpublished 'Procès-Verbaux'." *The Burlington Magazine* 110, no. 783 (June 1968): 330–49.

———. "Gauguin, the Collector." *The Burlington Magazine* 112, no. 810 (Sept. 1970): 590–616.

———. "Gauguin's Cézannes." *The Burlington Magazine* 104, no. 710 (May 1962): 204, 206–9, and 211.

Bois, Yve-Alain. "Cézanne: Words and Deeds." Translated by Rosalind Krauss. *October* 84 (Spring 1998): 31–43.

Boisvert, Marie. "La bohème au salon: les représentations du salon de Nina de Villard." In *Bohème sans frontière*, edited by Pascal Brissette and Anthony Glinoer, 173–83. Rennes, France: Presses universitaires, 2010.

Brassaï. *Conversations with Picasso*. Translated by Jane Marie Todd. Chicago: University of Chicago Press, 1999. Originally published as *Conversations avec Picasso*. Paris: Éditions Gallimard, 1964.

Brettell, Richard, and Anne-Birgitte Fonsmark. *Gauguin and Impressionism*. Exh. cat. New Haven, CT: Yale University Press, 2005.

Buck, Stephanie, John House, Ernst Vegelin van Claerbergen, and Barnaby Wright. *The Courtauld Cézannes*. Exh. cat. London: Courtauld Gallery in association with Paul Holberton, 2008.

Buckley, Barbara, Anya Shutova, and Jennifer Mass. "A Technical Study of *The Large Bathers*." In *Cézanne in the Barnes Foundation*, edited by André Dombrowski, Nancy Ireson, and Sylvie Patry. New York: Rizzoli Electa, 2021.

Butler, Marigene H. "An Investigation of the Materials and Technique Used by Paul Cézanne." In *AIC Preprints, American Institute for Conservation 12th Annual Meeting, Los Angeles, 1984*, 20–33. Washington, DC: American Institute for Conservation, 1984.

Cachin, Françoise. "A Century of Cézanne Criticism: I. From 1865 to 1906." In Françoise Cachin, Isabelle Cahn, Walter Feilchenfeldt, Henri Loyrette, and Joseph J. Rishel, *Cézanne*, 24–43. Exh. cat. Philadelphia: Philadelphia Museum of Art, 1996.

Cachin, Françoise, Isabelle Cahn, Walter Feilchenfeldt, Henri Loyrette, and Joseph J. Rishel. *Cézanne*. Exh. cat. Philadelphia: Philadelphia Museum of Art, 1996.

Cahn, Isabelle. "Chronology." In Françoise Cachin, Isabelle Cahn, Walter Feilchenfeldt, Henri Loyrette, and Joseph J. Rishel, *Cézanne*, 527–69. Exh. cat. Philadelphia: Philadelphia Museum of Art, 1996.

Callen, Anthea. *The Work of Art: Plein-air Painting and Artistic Identity in Nineteenth-Century France*. London: Reaktion Books, 2015.

Castagnary, Jules-Antoine. "Exposition du boulevard des Capucines: Les Impressionnistes." *Le Siècle*. April 29, 1874, 1–10.

Catalogue de la 3e Exposition de peinture. Exh. cat. Paris: 1877.

Catalogue des ouvrages de Peinture, Sculpture, Dessin, Gravure, Architecture, et Art decorative. Paris: Compagnie Française des Papier-Monnaie, 1907.

Cezanne, Paul. *The Letters of Paul Cézanne.* Edited and translated by Alex Danchev. London: Thames and Hudson, 2013.

———. "My Confidences." In *Conversations with Cézanne,* edited by Michael Doran and translated by Julie Lawrence Cochran, 100–103. Berkeley: University of California Press, 2001.

———. *Paul Cézanne: Correspondance.* Edited by John Rewald. Paris: Bernard Grasset, 1978.

Chakrabarty, Dipesh. *Provincializing Europe: Postcolonial Thought and Historical Difference.* Princeton, NJ: Princeton University Press, 2000.

Champsaur, Félicien. *Masques modernes.* Paris: Dentu, 1889.

Chappuis, Adrien. *The Drawings of Paul Cézanne: A Catalogue Raisonné.* 2 vols. London: Thames and Hudson, 1973.

Charlesworth, Michael. *Landscape and Vision in Nineteenth-Century Britain and France.* Aldershot, England: Ashgate, 2008.

Clark, T. J. "Strange Apprentice." *London Review of Books* 42, no. 19 (Oct. 8, 2020). https://www.lrb.co.uk/the-paper/v42/n19/t.j.-clark/strange-apprentice.

Conisbee, Philip, and Denis Coutagne, eds. *Cézanne in Provence.* Exh. cat. Washington, DC: National Gallery of Art; New Haven, CT: Yale University Press, 2006.

Courtauld Institute Galleries. *Impressionist and Post-Impressionist Masterpieces: The Courtauld Collection.* New Haven, CT: Yale University Press, 1987.

Coutagne, Denis. *Cezanne and Paris.* Paris: Musée du Luxembourg, 2011.

———. *Le Musée Granet, Aix-en-Provence.* Paris: Réunion des musées nationaux in association with Fondation BNP Paribas; Aix-en-Provence: Musée Granet, 2007.

Coutagne, Denis, and François Chédeville. *Cézanne, Jas De Bouffan: Art et Histoire.* Lyon, France: Fage Éditions, 2019.

Coutagne, Denis, and Bruno Ely. *Sainte-Victoire: Cézanne, 1990.* Exh. cat. Aix-en-Provence, France: Musée Granet; Paris: Reunion des musées nationaux, 1990.

Danchev, Alex. *Cézanne: A Life.* New York: Pantheon Books, 2012.

Danchev, Alex, ed. and trans. *The Letters of Paul Cézanne.* Los Angeles: J. Paul Getty Museum, 2013.

Denis, Maurice. "L'impressionnisme et la France" (1917). In *Nouvelles théories: Sur l'art modern, sur l'art sacré,* 59–70. Paris: Rouart et Watelin, 1922.

———. *Théories.* Paris: L. Rouart, 1920.

Dombrowski, André, Nancy Ireson, and Sylvie Patry, eds. *Cézanne in the Barnes Foundation.* New York: Rizzoli Electa, 2021.

Doran, Michael, ed. *Conversations with Cézanne.* Translated by Julie Lawrence Cochran. Berkeley: University of California Press, 2001.

Druick, Douglas. "Vollard and Gauguin: Fictions and Facts." In *From Cézanne to Picasso: Ambroise Vollard and the Avant-Garde,* edited by Rebecca A. Rabinow, 60–81. Exh. cat. New York: Metropolitan Museum of Art, 2008.

Duranty, Edmond. "Le Peintre Louis Martin." In Edmond Duranty, *Le Pays des arts,* 313–50. Paris: G. Charpentier, 1881.

Duret, Théodore. *Histoire des peintres impressionnistes: Pissarro, Claude Monet, Sisley, Renoir, Berthe Morisot, Cézanne, Guillamin.* Paris: H. Floury, 1906.

Eiling, Alexander, ed. *Cézanne: Metamorphoses.* Exh. cat. New York: Prestel, 2017.

Elder, Marc. *À Giverny, chez Claude Monet.* Giverny, France: Bernheim-Jeune, 1924.

Elderfield, John. *Cézanne: Portraits.* Princeton, NJ: Princeton University Press, 2017.

———. *Cézanne: The Rock and Quarry Paintings.* Exh. cat. Princeton, NJ: Princeton University Art Museum, 2020.

Evans, Martin, ed. *Empire and Culture: The French Experience, 1830–1940.* Basingstoke, Hampshire, UK: Palgrave Macmillan, 2005.

Feilchenfeldt, Walter. "Introductory Remarks on the Cézanne Research." In *Cézanne: Metamorphoses,* edited by Alexander Eiling, 12–13. Exh. cat. New York: Prestel, 2017.

Feilchenfeldt, Walter, Jayne Warman, and David Nash, eds. *The Paintings, Watercolors and Drawings of Paul Cezanne: An Online Catalogue Raisonné.* 2018–present. https://cezannecatalogue.com.

Friedman, Samantha. "Condensation: Cézanne's Study Sheets." In *Cézanne Drawing,* edited by Jodi Hauptman and Samantha Friedman, 20–45. Exh. cat. New York: Museum of Modern Art, 2021.

Fry, Roger. *Cezanne: A Study of His Development.* London: L. and V. Woolf, 1927.

Gasquet, Joachim. *Cézanne.* Giverny, France: Les Éditions Bernheim-Jeune, 1921.

Gauguin, Paul. *Avant et après.* Paris: Les Éditions G. Crès et Cie., 1923.

———. *Ramblings of a Wannabe Painter.* Edited and translated by Donatien Grau. New York: David Zwirner Gallery, 2016.

Geffroy, Gustave. *Claude Monet, sa vie, son temps, son œuvre.* Paris: Crès et Cie, 1922.

Georges-Michel, Michel. *Peintres et sculpteurs que j'ai connus: 1900–1942.* New York: Brentano, 1942.

Goldwater, Robert, and Marco Treves. *Artists on Art: From the XIVth to the XXth Century.* New York: Pantheon Books, 1945.

Grau, Donatien, ed. and trans. *Ramblings of a Wannabe Painter.* New York: David Zwirner Gallery, 2016.

Groom, Gloria. "Vollard, The Nabis, and Odilon Redon." In *From Cézanne to Picasso: Ambroise Vollard and the Avant-Garde,* edited by Rebecca A. Rabinow, 82–99. Exh. cat. New York: Metropolitan Museum of Art, 2008.

Gsell, Paul. "Interview d'Octave Mirbeau par Paul Gsell." In Octave Mirbeau, *Combats esthétiques,* edited by Pierre Michel and Jean-François Nivet, 2:419–20. Paris: Nouvelles Éditions Séguier, 1993.

Haas, Robert Bartlett. *Gertrude Stein: A Primer for the Gradual Understanding of Gertrude Stein.* Los Angeles: Black Sparrow, 1971.

Hale, Charlotte. "A Template for Experimentation: Cezanne's Process and the Paintings of Hortense Fiquet." In Dita Amory et al., *Madame Cézanne,* 45–71. Exh. cat. New York: Metropolitan Museum of Art, 2014.

Hauptman, Jodi. "Cézanne's Drawings: A Graphology." In *Cézanne Drawing,* edited by Jodi Hauptman and Samantha Friedman, 12–19. Exh. cat. New York: Museum of Modern Art, 2021.

Hauptman, Jodi, and Samantha Friedman, eds. *Cézanne Drawing.* Exh. cat. New York: Museum of Modern Art, 2021.

Hoffmann, Meike, and Nicola Kuhn. *Hitlers Kunsthändler: Hildebrand Gurlitt, 1895–1956: Die Biographie.* Munich: C. H. Beck, 2016.

Inaga, Shigemi. "Between Revolutionary and Oriental Sage: Paul Cézanne in Japan." *Japan Review*, no. 28 (2015): 133–72.

Jensen, Robert. "Vollard and Cézanne: An Anatomy of a Relationship." In *Cézanne to Picasso: Ambroise Vollard, Patron of the Avant-Garde*, edited by Rebecca A. Rabinow, 29–47. Exh. cat. New York: Metropolitan Museum of Art, 2008.

Kaufmann, Bettina, and Lothar Schirmer, eds. *Paul Cezanne: The Works of His 1907 Exhibition in Paris*. Munich: Schirmer/Mosel Verlag, 2018.

Kendall, Richard. "Degas and Cézanne: Savagery and Refinement." In *The Private Collection of Edgar Degas*, edited by Ann Dumas, 197–220. Exh. cat. New York: Metropolitan Museum of Art, 1997.

King, Ross. *Mad Enchantment: Claude Monet and the Painting of Water Lilies*. New York: Bloomsbury Press, 2016.

Larousse, Pierre. *Grand dictionnaire universel du XIXe siècle*. Paris: Larousse, 1866–77.

Lebensztejn, Jean-Claude. *Les couilles de Cézanne, suivi de Persistance de la mémoire*. Paris: Nouvelles Editions Séguier, 1995.

Madsen, Karl. "Kunst: Impressionisterne i Kunstforeningen, II." *Politiken*. Nov. 10, 1889.

Maloon, Terence, ed. *Classic Cézanne*. Exh. cat. Sydney: Art Gallery of New South Wales, 1998.

Manet, Julie. *Growing Up with the Impressionists: The Diary of Julie Manet*. London: Sotheby's Publications, 1987.

Marchesseau, Daniel, ed. *Paul Cezanne: Le Chant de la Terre*. Exh. cat. Martigny, Switzerland: Foundation Pierre Gianadda, 2017.

Mathieu, Marianne. *Monet the Collector*. Paris: Editions Hazan, 2017.

McPhee, Peter. *A Social History of France, 1780–1880*. London and New York: Routledge, 1992.

Meier-Graefe, Julius. *Modern Art: Being a Contribution to a New System of Aesthetics*. Translated by Florence Simmonds and George W. Chrystal. 2 vols. New York: G. P. Putnam's Sons, 1908.

Merleau-Ponty, Maurice. "Cezanne's Doubt." In *Sense and Non-Sense*, edited and translated by Hubert L. Dreyfus and Patricia Allen Dreyfus, 9–25. Evanston, IL: Northwestern University Press, 1964.

Merlhès, Victor, ed. *Correspondance de Paul Gauguin: Documents, Témoignages, 1873–1888*. Paris: Fondation Singer-Polignac, 1984.

Mirabeau, Octave. *Cézanne*. Paris: Bernheim-Jeune, 1914.

Modersohn-Becker, Paula. *Paula Modersohn-Becker: The Letters and Journals*. Edited by Günter Busch and Liselotte von Reinken; edited and translated by Arthur S. Wensinger and Carole Clew Hoy. Evanston, IL: Northwestern University Press, 1990.

Montifaud, Marc de. "Exposition du Boulevard des Capucines." *L'Artiste*. May 1, 1874, 307–313.

Morice, Charles. "Enquête [Part I]." *Mercure de France*. Aug. 1, 1905, 346–59.

———. "Enquête [Part II]." *Mercure de France*. Aug. 15, 1905 538–55.

———. "Enquête [Part III]." *Mercure de France*. Sept. 1, 1905, 61–85.

———. "Le Salon d'Automne." *Mercure de France*. Dec. 1, 1905, 376–93.

Murphy, Richard W. *The World of Cezanne: 1839–1906*. New York: Time-Life Library of Art, 1968.

Natanson, Thadée. "Paul Cézanne [exhibition review]." *La Revue Blanche* (Dec. 1895): 496–500.

Neufeld, Laura. "Belle Formule: Materials and Methods in Cézanne's Watercolors." In *Cézanne Drawing*, edited by Jodi Hauptman and Samantha Friedman, 200–205. Exh. cat. New York: Museum of Modern Art, 2021.

Nugent-Folan, Georgina. "Personal Apperception: Samuel Beckett, Gertrude Stein, and Paul Cézanne's 'La Montagne Sainte-Victoire.'" *Samuel Beckett Today / Aujourd'hui* 27 (2015): 87–101 and 202.

Olmsted, Galina. "Caillebotte: Making and Exhibiting Modernism: Gustave Caillebotte in Paris, New York, and Brussels." PhD diss. University of Delaware, 2019.

Pasco, Allan H. "Love *A La* Michelet in Zola's *La Faute de L'Abbé Mouret*." *Nineteenth-Century French Studies* 7, no. 3–4 (Spring–Summer 1979): 232–44.

Pissarro, Camille. *Pissarro: Letters to His Son Lucien*, edited by John Rewald. Mamaroneck, NY: P. P. Appel, 1972.

Platzman, Steven. *Cézanne: The Self-Portraits*. London: Thames and Hudson, 2001.

Pouyet, Emeline, Nicholas Barbi, Henry Chopp, Owen Healy, Aggelos Katsaggelos, Sophia Moak, Rick Mott, Marc Vermeulen, and Marc Walton. "Development of a Highly Mobile and Versatile Large MA-XRF Scanner for in Situ Analyses of Painted Work of Arts." *X-Ray Spectrometry* 50, no. 4 (July/Aug. 2021): 263–71. https://doi.org/10.1002/xrs.3173.

Reissner, Elisabeth. "Transparency of Means: 'Drawing' and Colour in Cézanne's Watercolours and Oil Paintings in The Courtauld Gallery." In *The Courtauld Cézannes*, edited by Stephanie Buck, John House, Ernst Vegelin van Claerbergen, and Barnaby Wright, 49–71. Exh. cat. London: Courtauld Gallery in association with Paul Holberton, 2008.

———. "Ways of Making: Practice and Innovation in Cezanne's Paintings in the National Gallery." *National Gallery Technical Bulletin* 29 (2008): 4–30.

Rewald, John. *The History of Impressionism*, 4th rev. ed. New York: Museum of Modern Art, 1973.

———. *The Paintings of Paul Cézanne: A Catalogue Raisonné*. New York: Abrams, 1996.

Rewald, John, ed. *Pissarro: Letters to His Son Lucien*. Mamaroneck, NY: P. P. Appel, 1972.

Richardson, John. *A Life of Picasso*. Vol. II: *1907–1917: The Painter of Modern Life*. London: Pimlico, 2009.

Rishel, Joseph J. "Cezanne and Hartley on Sacred Ground." In *Cézanne and Beyond*, edited by Joseph J. Rishel and Katherine Sachs, 159–83. Exh. cat. Philadelphia: Philadelphia Museum of Art, 2009.

Rivière, Georges. *Le Maître Paul Cézanne*. Paris: Librairie Floury, 1923.

Roux, Marius. *La Proie et l'ombre*. Paris: Dentu, 1878.

———. *The Substance and the Shadow*. Edited and with an introduction by Paul Smith. University Park, PA: Penn State University Press, 2007.

Ruppen, Fabienne. "Tackling Cezanne's Paper: On the Reconstruction of Loose Sheets." In Fabienne Ruppen, Walter Feilchenfeldt, and Yuval Etgar, *Reconstructing Cezanne: Sequence and Process in Paul Cezanne's Works on Paper*, 16–44. Exh. cat. London: Ridinghouse in collaboration with Luxembourg and Dayan, 2019.

Schwarz, Birgit. "Cat. 56: *Three Skulls on a Patterned Carpet*." In *Cézanne: Finished – Unfinished*, edited by Felix Baumann, Evelyn Benesch, Walter Feilchenfeldt, and Klaus Albrecht Schröder, 240. Exh. cat. Ostfildern Ruit, Germany: Hatje Cantz, 2000.

Shelley, Marjorie. "Cézanne as Draftsman. Sketchbooks and Graphite Drawings." In Dita Amory et al., *Madame Cézanne*, 107–45. Exh. cat. New York: Metropolitan Museum of Art, 2014.

Shiff, Richard. *Cézanne and the End of Impressionism.* Chicago: University of Chicago, 1984.

——. "Cézanne Photographic." *Nonsite*, no. 26 (Nov. 11, 2018). https://nonsite.org/cezanne -photographic.

——. "Cezanne's Physicality: The Politics of Touch." In *The Language of Art History*, edited by Salim Kemal and Ivan Gaskell, 129–80. Cambridge, UK: Cambridge University Press, 1991.

——. "Introduction." In *Conversations with Cézanne*, edited by Michael Doran and translated by Julie Lawrence Cochran, xix–xxxiv. Berkeley: University of California Press, 2001.

——. "Mark, Motif, Materiality: The Cezanne Effect in the 20th Century." In *Cézanne: Finished – Unfinished*, edited by Felix Baumann, Evelyn Benesch, Walter Feilchenfeldt, and Klaus Albrecht Schröder, 99–123. Exh. cat. Ostfildern Ruit, Germany: Hatje Cantz, 2000.

——. "Risible Cezanne." In *The Repeating Image*, edited by Eik Kahng. Baltimore: Walters Museum, 2007.

——. "Sensation, Movement, Cézanne." In *Classic Cézanne*, edited by Terence Maloon, 13–27. Exh cat. Sydney: Art Gallery of New South Wales, 1998.

Shutova, Anya, and Barbara Buckley. "Materials and Techniques: A Study of Cézanne's Paintings in The Barnes Foundation." In *Cézanne in the Barnes Foundation*, edited by André Dombrowski, Nancy Ireson, and Sylvie Patry, 31–57. New York: Rizzoli Electa, 2021.

Simms, Matthew. "Painting on Drawing: Cézanne's Watercolors." In *Cézanne in Focus: Watercolors from The Henry and Rose Pearlman Collection*, edited by Laura M. Giles and Carol Armstrong, 12–25. Exh. cat. Princeton, NJ: Princeton University Art Museum, 2002.

Smith, Paul. "Cézanne's Colour Lab: (not-so-) still life." In *The World Is an Apple: The Still Lifes of Paul Cézanne*, edited by Benedict Leca, 92–144. Exh. cat. Hamilton, Ontario: Art Gallery of Hamilton in association with D Giles Limited, 2014.

——. "Cézanne's Late Landscapes, or the Prospect of Death." In *Cézanne in Provence*, edited by Philip Conisbee and Denis Coutagne, 59–74. Exh. cat. Washington, DC: National Gallery of Art; New Haven, CT: Yale University Press, 2006.

——. "Cezanne's 'Primitive' Perspective or the 'View from Everywhere.'" *Art Bulletin* 95, no. 1 (March 2013): 102–19.

——. "Cézanne's Primitive Self and Related Fictions." In *The Life and the Work: Art and Biography*, edited by Charles G. Salas, 45–75. Los Angeles: Getty Publications, 2007.

——. "Introduction." In Marius Roux, *The Substance and the Shadow*, edited and with an introduction by Paul Smith, xi–xlv. University Park, PA: Penn State University Press, 2007.

Société Paul Cezanne. "L'homme: biographie et chronologies." https://societe-cezanne.fr /lhomme.

Sontag, Susan. *On Photography.* London: Penguin, 1977.

——. *Regarding the Pain of Others*. London: Penguin, 2003.

Stein, Gertrude. "Pictures." In *Poets and Painters: Essays on the Art of Painting by Twentieth-Century Poets*, edited by J. D. McClatchy, 81–106. Berkeley: University of California Press, 1988.

——. *Portraits and Prayers.* New York: Random House, 1934.

Stock, Henri-Charles. "Le Salon par Stock." *Stock-Album*, no. 2 (1870).

Stovall, Tyler. *The Rise of the Paris Red Belt.* Berkeley: University of California Press, 1990.

Sullivan, Edward. *From San Juan to Paris and Back: Francisco Oller and Caribbean Art in the Era of Impressionism.* New Haven, CT: Yale University Press, 2014.

Tabarant, Adolphe. *Manet et ses oeuvres.* 3rd. ed. Paris: Gallimard, 1947.

"A Typical Negro." *Harper's Weekly,* July 4, 1863.

Vauxcelles, Louis. "La vie artistique." *Gil Blas* (Sept. 28, 1905): 1.

Vermeulen, Marc, Kate Smith, Katherine Eremin, Georgina Rayner, and Marc Walton. "Application of Uniform Manifold Approximation and Projection (UMAP) in Spectral Imaging of Artworks." *Spectrochimica Acta. Part A: Molecular and Biomolecular Spectroscopy* 252 (2021): 119547. https://doi .org/10.1016/j.saa.2021.119547.

Verri, Giovanni, and David Saunders. "Xenon Flash for Reflectance and Luminescence (Multispectral) Imaging in Cultural Heritage Applications." *The British Museum Technical Bulletin* 8 (2014): 83–92.

Vollard, Ambroise. *Paul Cézanne.* Paris: Galerie A. Vollard, 1919.

——. *Paul Cézanne: Huit phototypies d'après Cézanne.* Paris: G. Crés et Cie, 1924.

Warman, Jayne. "Chronology." In *Cézanne in the Barnes Foundation*, edited by André Dombrowski, Nancy Ireson, and Sylvie Patry, 357–65. New York: Rizzoli Electa, 2021.

Wollheim, Richard. *Painting as an Art.* Princeton, NJ: Princeton University Press, 1987.

Zieske, Faith. "Paul Cézanne's Watercolors: His Choice of Pigments and Papers." In *The Broad Spectrum*, edited by Harriet Stratis and Brit Salvesen, 89–101. London: Archetype, 2002.

Zola, Émile. *Correspondance: Les lettres et les arts.* 2 vols. Paris: Bibliothèque-Charpentier, 1908.

——. *La Confession de Claude.* Paris: A. Lacroix, Verboeckhoven and Cie, 1866.

——. *Mon Salon.* Paris: Librairie Centrale, 1866.

CONTRIBUTORS

Etel Adnan

Poet, short-story writer, essayist, and artist Etel Adnan was born in Beirut in 1925 to a Syrian Muslim father and a Greek Christian mother. She lived in Lebanon, Syria, France, and the United States, and published many books in English and French. In her paintings Adnan sought to represent only the physical beauty of the universe and the intense bond she had with it.

Phyllida Barlow

For more than 50 years, British artist Phyllida Barlow has taken inspiration from her surroundings to create imposing installations that can be at once menacing and playful. She creates anti-monumental sculptures from inexpensive, low-grade materials such as cardboard, fabric, plywood, polystyrene, scrim, and cement, often painted in industrial or vibrant colors, the seams of their construction left at times visible, revealing the means of their making.

Achim Borchardt-Hume

Achim Borchardt-Hume was Director of Exhibitions at Tate Modern and Chair of the Steering Group for Hyundai Tate Research Centre: Transnational. His recent projects there included *The EY Exhibition: Picasso 1932—Love, Fame, Tragedy* (2018); *Robert Rauschenberg* (2016); and the first major Kasimir Malevich retrospective in the United Kingdom (2014). He also served on the advisory boards of Generali Foundation, Vienna, and Saradar Collection, Beirut.

Paul Chan

Born in Hong Kong, Paul Chan is an American artist, writer, and publisher. He is known for varied practices that range from animated video projections to drawings, public performances, and haunting pneumatic sculptures—and for founding the publishing house Badlands Unlimited in 2010.

Kristi Dahm

Kristi Dahm is an independent paper conservator and technical research consultant. From 2002 to 2020 she worked as a paper conservator at the Art Institute of Chicago, where she co-authored (with Martha Tedeschi) two exhibition catalogues detailing the materials and techniques of American watercolor painters: *John Marin's Watercolors: A Medium for Modernism* (2011) and *Watercolors by Winslow Homer: The Color of Light* (2007).

Julia Fish

Julia Fish's practice engages both site and context, in temporary public installations as well as the sustained sequence of paintings and works on paper developed in reference to the architecture of her home and studio. Fish's paintings were presented in 2010, the Whitney Biennial, and her more than two dozen solo exhibitions include DePaul Art Museum's recent ten-year survey. The recipient of numerous grants and awards, Fish is professor emerita, University of Illinois at Chicago.

Ellen Gallagher

Born in Providence, Rhode Island, in 1965, Ellen Gallagher lives and works between Rotterdam, Netherlands, and New York. She builds intricate, multilayered works that pivot between the natural world, mythology, and history. Over the course of a highly multifaceted career, her process has involved undoing and reforming trains of thought, often over long periods of time and across linked bodies of works.

Clara Granzotto

Clara Granzotto is the Andrew W. Mellon Assistant Conservation Scientist at the Art Institute of Chicago. She received her PhD in chemical sciences from the University of Venice and the University of Lille. Granzotto specializes in the analysis of traditional binding media in works of art by mass spectrometry, with a focus on polysaccharides and proteins, in order to understand artists' techniques and artworks' appearance and condition.

Gloria Groom

Gloria Groom is Chair of European Painting and Sculpture and the David and Mary Winton Green Curator at the Art Institute of Chicago. She is an internationally acclaimed and widely published scholar of nineteenth-century French painting. Since joining the Art Institute in 1984, she has been involved in numerous major exhibitions and catalogues and has led the museum's initiative for monographic digital scholarly collection catalogues on the Impressionist collection.

Caitlin Haskell

Caitlin Haskell is the Gary C. and Frances Comer Curator of Modern and Contemporary Art at the Art Institute of Chicago, where she has worked since 2018. A scholar of twentieth-century painting and sculpture, her research and writing address the production, critical reception, and legacies of the art of the historical avant-gardes in the Americas and Europe.

Lubaina Himid

Lubaina Himid is a British painter who has dedicated her career to uncovering marginalized and silenced histories, figures, and cultural expressions. She is also a professor of contemporary art at the University of Central Lancashire. She won the Turner Prize in 2017, and her work has been shown in significant solo exhibitions as well as acquired by major collections throughout the world.

Maria Kokkori

Maria Kokkori is associate conservation scientist at the Art Institute of Chicago and visiting professor at the University of Chicago. She received her PhD from the Courtauld Institute of Art, London, and completed postdoctoral fellowships at the Courtauld Institute and Museum of Modern Art, New York. Her research and teaching focus on modern and contemporary art and have been supported by the Courtauld Institute, Getty Research Institute, and the Malevich Society, New York, among others.

Kathryn Kremnitzer

Since 2018 Kathryn Kremnitzer has been a research associate in the department of Painting and Sculpture of Europe at the Art Institute of Chicago, where she worked on *Manet and Modern Beauty* (2019), *Monet and Chicago* (2020), and the present exhibition. In 2020 she earned her PhD at Columbia University with a dissertation that explored how Édouard Manet worked across media in the 1860s.

Kerry James Marshall

Born in 1955 in Birmingham, Alabama, Kerry James Marshall has exhibited widely throughout Europe and the United States since the late 1970s and early 1980s. His work in many media questions the social constructs of beauty and taste, history and power, and has been the focus of numerous solo exhibitions both domestic and international. His many honors include a 1997 grant from the MacArthur Foundation and the 2019 W. E. B. Du Bois Medal from Harvard University.

Rodney McMillian
A native of Columbia, South Carolina, Rodney McMillian is a Los Angeles-based artist who works with sculpture, installation, painting, video, and performance. He has had solo exhibitions at numerous museums and galleries in both the United States and in Europe, and his works are part of the permanent collections of the UCLA Hammer Museum and the Museum of Contemporary Art, Los Angeles, as well as the Studio Museum and the Museum of Modern Art, New York, among others.

Kimberley Muir
Kimberley Muir is Research Conservator for Paintings at the Art Institute of Chicago. She has a master's degree in art conservation and a PhD in art history from Queen's University, Canada. She has co-authored multiple digital scholarly catalogues for the Art Institute as part of her extensive published research on the working methods of artists including Édouard Manet, Claude Monet, Pablo Picasso, and James McNeill Whistler.

Laura Owens
In her experimental, often large-scale works, Laura Owens deploys a variety of materials, techniques and imagery ranging from the avant-garde to the vernacular, continually pushing the boundaries of what painting is, or can be. Her work has been shown internationally since the mid-1990s and can be found in numerous public collections in the United States as well as abroad. Born in Euclid, Ohio, she now lives and works in Los Angeles.

Michael Raymond
Since 2019 Michael Raymond has been Assistant Curator, International Art, at Tate Modern, where he helped realize the touring exhibition *Nam June Paik* (2019) and curated the installation of *Beuys' Acorns* by Ackroyd & Harvey. After studying history at the University of Sheffield, he worked at the British Museum on exhibitions including *Hokusai* (2017), *Rodin and the Art of Ancient Greece* (2018), and *Manga* (2019), and coordinated the Asahi Shimbun Displays.

Natalia Sidlina
Natalia Sidlina has worked at Tate Modern as Curator, International Art, since 2016. A specialist in modernist émigré art, her research and curatorial practice address transcultural histories, connections, and global exchange of ideas of the early avant-garde in Eastern and Western Europe. Her recent exhibitions include *Erik Bulatov* in Ekaterinburg, Russia (2018), *Naum Gabo – Constructions for Real Life* at Tate St. Ives (2020), and at Tate Modern, *Natalia Goncharova* (2019) and *Sophie Taeuber-Arp* (2021).

Luc Tuymans
Since emerging in the 1980s, Belgian artist Luc Tuymans has been known for a distinctive style of painting that demonstrates images' power to simultaneously communicate and withhold. Based on preexisting imagery culled from a variety of sources, his works are rendered in a muted palette that suggests blurry recollection or a fading memory. They have been shown in both group and solo exhibitions and acquired by public and private collections throughout the world.

Giovanni Verri
Since 2019, Giovanni Verri has been a conservation scientist at the Art Institute of Chicago. He holds a PhD in physics from the University of Ferrara, Italy, and an MA in conservation of wall paintings from the Courtauld Institute of Art, London. His research interests include the development and application of investigative techniques for analyzing color from antiquity to the present day.

INDEX

Unless otherwise noted, photographs of artworks in the collection of the Art Institute of Chicago are copyrighted by the Art Institute of Chicago.

Every effort has been made to identify, contact, and acknowledge copyright holders for all reproductions; additional rights holders are encouraged to contact the Art Institute of Chicago. The following credits apply to all images in this book for which separate acknowledgment is due.

Pp. 2–3 (detail): © Robert Bayer. P. 16 (detail); p. 135, cat. 62: Photo © Photo Josse / Bridgeman Images. P. 18, fig. 1: Photo: Christopher Campbell. P. 18, fig. 2; p. 101, cat. 31: Wildenstein & Co. Inc. P. 19, fig. 3: Musée Granet, Ville d'Aix-en-Provence / © Claude Almodovar. P. 24, fig. 1: Bibliotheque Nationale de France. P. 25, fig. 2: © RMN-Grand Palais / Art Resource, NY / Photo: Stéphane Maréchalle. P. 27, fig. 4: Alamy Stock Photo. P. 27, fig. 5; p. 147, cat. 76; p. 181, cat. 113: © RMN-Grand Palais / Art Resource, NY / Photo: Hervé Lewandowski. P. 30, fig. 7; p. 99, cat. 29; p. 107, cat. 35: Photo © 2022 Museum of Fine Arts, Boston. P. 30, fig. 8; p. 34 (detail); p. 103, cat. 32: © RMN-Grand Palais / Art Resource, NY / Photo: Adrien Didierjean. P. 36, fig. 1; p. 78, cat. 8; p. 191, cat. 123: The Philadelphia Museum of Art / Art Resource, NY. P. 37, fig. 2; p. 114, cat. 42a–f: The Morgan Library & Museum, New York. P. 39, fig. 3; p. 126, cat. 54: Von der Heydt-Museum Wuppertal / Photo: Antje Zeis-Loi, Medienzentrum Wuppertal. P. 40, fig. 5: Boston Public Library. P. 41, figs. 6–7: Bridgeman Images. Pp. 2–3 (detail); p. 42, fig. 8; p. 140, cat. 67: Photo © Peter Schibli. P. 22 (detail); p. 43, fig. 11; p. 125, cat. 53; p. 146, cat. 74; p. 167, cat. 99; p. 197, cat. 127: Digital Image © The Museum of Modern Art / Licensed by SCALA / Art Resource, NY. P. 63, fig. 2: Artizon Museum, Ishibashi Foundation, Tokyo. P. 46 (detail); p. 64, fig. 4; p. 134, cat. 61; p. 178, cat. 109: © Courtauld Gallery / Bridgeman Images. P. 70, cat. 1: © RMN-Grand Palais / Art Resource, NY / Photo: Daniel Arnaudet. P. 39, fig. 4; p. 72, cat. 3: Photo © The Provost and Fellows of King's College, Cambridge, UK. P. 75, cat. 6; p. 139, cat. 66: Photo © Christie's Images / Bridgeman Images. P. 79, cat. 9: Photo: John Riddy. P. 80, cat. 10; p. 82, cat. 12; p. 164, cats. 95–96: Jerry L. Thompson. P. 84, cat. 14: Image copyright © The Metropolitan Museum of Art / Art Resource, NY / Photo: Malcolm Varon. P. 86, cat. 16: CC BY-SA 4.0 Städel Museum, Frankfurt am Main P. 86, cat. 17;. 131, cat. 59; p. 162, cat. 93; . 194, cat. 126; p. 204, cat. 136; back cover

(detail): Photo: Tate. P. 87, cat. 18; p. 90, cat. 23: Erich Lessing / Art Resource, NY. P. 87, cat. 19: © Art Gallery of Ontario. P. 89, cat. 22: Image courtesy of Pyms Gallery, London. P. 92, cat. 25: Photo: João Musa. P. 93, fig. 1: Library of Congress Prints and Photographs Division, Washington, DC. P. 95, cat. 26: HIP / Art Resource, NY. P. 98, cat. 28: Todora Photography. P. 100, cat. 30: © Finnish National Gallery / Bridgeman Images. P. 105, cat. 34; p. 187, cat. 119: The Solomon R. Guggenheim Foundation / Art Resource, NY. P. 110, cat. 37: © RMN-Grand Palais / Art Resource, NY / Photo: Franck Raux. P. 111, cat. 38: Stephen White & Co. P. 111, cat. 39: Jamie Stukenberg, Prographics Inc. P. 112, cat. 40: Photo: Ny Carlsberg Glyptotek, Copenhagen. P. 114, cat. 41; p. 122, cat. 51; p. 206, cat. 137: © Cincinnati Art Museum / Bridgeman Images. P. 120, cats. 47–48: Image © The Whitworth, The University of Manchester / Photo: Michael Pollard. P. 123, cat. 52: © The Museum of Fine Arts Budapest / Scala / Art Resource, NY. P. 127, cat. 55; p. 179, cat. 110: The Phillips Collection, Washington, DC. P. 130, cat. 57: Private collection, courtesy of Sotheby's. P. 130, cat. 58; p. 199, cat. 130: Photo © Robert Bayer. P. 136, cat. 63: Image copyright © The Metropolitan Museum of Art / Art Resource, NY. P. 143, cat. 70: Image courtesy of Dallas Museum of Art. P. 145, cat. 73; p. 198, cat. 128: © 2020 Christie's Images Limited. P. 148, cat. 77; p. 172, cat. 105: © RMN-Grand Palais / Art Resource, NY / Photo: Mathieu Rabeau. P. 150, cat. 78: Photo: Eduardo Ortega. P. 152, cat. 80: © RMN-Grand Palais / Art Resource, NY / Photo: Thierry Le Mage. P. 155, cat. 84: Courtesy of Fine Arts Museums of San Francisco / Photo: Randy Dodson. P. 155, cat. 85; p. 190, cat. 122: Princeton University Art Museum / Art Resource, NY / Photo: Bruce M. White. P. 156, cat. 86: Digital Image © 2022 Museum Associates / LACMA / Art Resource, NY. P. 157, fig. 2: Photo: Rusty Culp, FAAR. © Michael Asher Foundation. P. 161, cats. 90–91: Photo © Fitzwilliam Museum, Cambridge, UK. P. 162, cat. 92: Michael David Rose. P. 165, cat. 98: © Musée d'art et d'histoire, Ville de Genève / Photo: Bettina Jacot-Descombes. P. 177, cat. 108: © The National Gallery, London. P. 180, cat. 112: © Minneapolis Institute of Art / The William Hood Dunwoody Fund / Bridgeman Image. P. 183, cat. 115: bpk Bildagentur / Kunsthalle Mannheim / Cem Yücetas / Art Resource, NY. P. 184, cat. 116: Kimbell Art Museum, Fort Worth, Texas / Art Resource, NY. P. 185, cat. 117: Photo: Charles White. P. 199, cat. 120: Photo: Mitro Hood. P. 201, cat. 133: Jamie Stukenberg.

Details, all by Paul Cezanne (French, 1839–1906)

Front cover: *The Basket of Apples*, c. 1893 (cat. 56)

Pp. 2–3: *Still Life with Sliced Watermelon*, c. 1900 (cat. 67)

P. 16: *Still Life with Plaster Cupid*, 1894–95 (cat. 62)

P. 22: *Still Life with Fruit Dish*, 1879–80 (cat. 53)

P. 34: *Portrait of the Artist with Pink Background*, c. 1875 (cat. 32)

P. 46: *Montagne Sainte-Victoire with Large Pine*, c. 1887 (cat. 109)

P. 60: *Château Noir*, 1900–1904 (cat. 131)

P. 69: *Still Life with Apples*, 1893–94 (cat. 64)

Back cover: *Montagne Sainte-Victoire*, 1905–6 (cat. 126)

This book was made using paper and materials certified by the Forest Stewardship Council, which ensures responsible forest management.

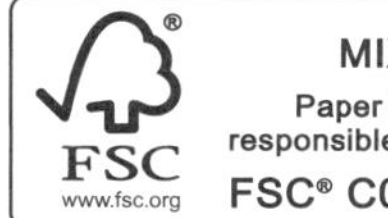

Published in conjunction with an exhibition
organised by Tate Modern and the Art Institute
of Chicago.

Cezanne
The Art Institute of Chicago
15 May–5 September 2022

The EY Exhibition: Cezanne
Presented in the Eyal Ofer Galleries
Tate Modern, London
6 October 2022–12 March 2023

The EY Exhibition: Cezanne is part of
The EY Tate Arts Partnership

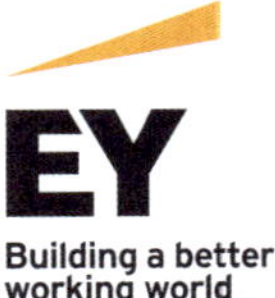

Supported by

the
HUO FAMILY
FOUNDATION

With additional support from

The Cezanne Exhibition Supporters Circle:
Eykyn Maclean

Tate Patrons and Tate Members